LANGUEDOC
ROUSSILLON
TARN GORGES

A. Thuillier/MICHELIN

Executive Editorial Director David Brabis

Chief Editor Cynthia Clayton Ochterbeck

THE GREEN GUIDE LANGUEDOC ROUSSILLON TARN GORGES

Editor Gwen Cannon

Principal Writers Jane Schofield, Anne Marie Scott

Production Coordinator Allison Michelle Simpson

Cartography Alain Baldet, Michèle Cana, Peter Wrenn

Photo Editor Brigitta L. House

Proofreader Nicole D. Jordan

Layout Allison Michelle Simpson, Nicole D. Jordan, Susan Young

Cover Design Laurent Muller

Interior Design Agence Rampazzo

Production Pierre Ballochard, Renaud Leblanc

Contact Us :
The Green Guide
Michelin Travel Publications
One Parkway South
Greenville, SC 29615
USA
☎ 1-800-423-0485
www.michelintravel.com
michelin.guides@us.michelin.com

Hannay House, 39 Clarendon Road
Watford, Herts WD17 1JA, UK
☎ 01923 205 240 - Fax 01923 205 241
www.ViaMichelin.com
TheGreenGuide-uk@uk.michelin.com

Special Sales :
For information regarding bulk sales, customized edit
and premium sales, please contact our Customer
Service Departments:
USA	1-800-423-0485
UK	(01923) 205 240
Canada	1-800-361-8236

One Team...
A Commitment to Quality

There's just one reason our team is dedicated to producing quality travel publications—you, our reader. We want you to get the maximum benefit from your trip—and from your money. In today's multiple-choice world of travel, the options are many, perhaps overwhelming.

In our guidebooks, we try to minimize the guesswork involved with travel. We scout out the attractions, prioritize them with star ratings, and describe what you'll discover when you visit them.

To help you orient yourself, we provide colorful and detailed, but easy-to-follow maps. Floor plans of some of the major museums help you plan your tour.

Throughout the guides, we offer practical information, touring tips and suggestions for finding the best views, good places for a break and interesting shops.

Lodging and dining are always a big part of travel, so we compile a selection of hotels and restaurants that we think convey the feel of the destination, and organize them by geographic area and price. We also highlight shopping, recreational and entertainment venues, especially the popular spots.

If you're short on time, driving itineraries are included so you can hit the highlights and quickly absorb the best of the place.

For those who love to experience a destination on foot, we add walking tours, often with a map. And we list other companies who offer boat, bus or guided walking tours, some with culinary, historical or other themes.

In short, we test and retest, check and recheck to make sure that our guidebooks are truly just that: a personalized guide to help you make the most of your visit. After all, we want you to enjoy traveling as much as we do.

The Michelin Green Guide Team
michelin.guides@us.michelin.com

PLANNING YOUR TRIP

INTRODUCTION TO THE REGION

SYMBOLS

ⓐ	**Tips to help improve your experience**
ⓐ	**Details to consider**
🕶	**Entry fees**
🔹	**Walking tours**
o━	**Closed to the public**
⏰	**Hours of operation**
⏱	**Periods of closure**
⏩	**See also, time permitting**

CONTENTS

DISCOVERING THE REGION

How to Use this Guide

Orientation

To help you grasp the "lay of the land" quickly and easily, so you'll feel confident and comfortable finding your way around, we offer the following tools in this guide:

- Detailed table of contents for an overview of what'll you find in the guide, and how it is organized.
- Map of Principal Sights showing the starred places of interest at a glance.
- Detailed maps of city centres, regions and towns.
- Floor and site plans of museums and cathedrals.
- Principal Sights ordered alphabetically for easy reference.

Practicalities

At the front of the guide, you'll see a section called "Planning Your Trip" that contains information about planning your trip, the best time to go, getting there and getting around, basic facts, tips for making the most of your visit, and more. It includes suggested driving tours, and a calendar of popular annual events in the region. Information on shopping, sightseeing, kids' activities, and sports and recreational opportunities is included as well.

LODGINGS

We've made a selection of hotels and arranged them within the cities and towns, categorized by price to fit all budgets *(see the Legend at the back of the guide for an explanation of price ranges)*. For the most part, we selected accommodations based on their unique regional character. So, unless the individual hotel embodies local ambience, it's rare that we include chain properties, which typically have their own imprint. If you want a more comprehensive selection of lodgings in the region, see the red-cover *Michelin Guide France*.

RESTAURANTS

We thought you'd like to know the quintessential eating spots in the cities and towns described in this guide. So we selected restaurants that capture the flavour of the area. Many of them feature regional specialties, though we're not rating the quality of the food per se. As we did with the hotels, we organized the restaurants within the Principal Sights and then categorized them by price to appeal to all wallets *(see the Legend at the back of the guide for an explanation of price ranges)*. If you want a more comprehensive selection of eateries in the region, see the red-cover *Michelin Guide France*.

Attractions

Contact information, admission charges and hours of operation are given for the majority of attractions. Unless otherwise noted, admission prices shown are for a single adult only. Discounts for seniors, students, military personnel, etc. may be available; be sure to ask. If no admission charge is shown, entrance to the attraction is free.

Within each Principal Sight, attractions within a town or city are described first, sometimes in the form of a walking tour. Then come outlying sights and Excursions. If you are pressed for time, we recommend you visit the three- and two-star sights first—the stars are your guide.

STAR RATINGS

Michelin has used stars as a rating tool for more than 100 years:

★★★	Highly recommended
★★	Recommended
★	Interesting

SYMBOLS IN THE TEXT

Besides the stars, other symbols in the text indicate tourist information 🚹; wheelchair access ♿; camping facilities ⚠; on-site parking 🅿; sights of interest to children 🄺𝗂𝖽𝗌; and hiking trails 🔆.

See the box appearing on the Contents page for other symbols used in the text.

See Maps explanation below for symbols appearing on the maps.

Throughout the guide you will find peach-colored text boxes or sidebars containing anecdotal or background information. Green-colored boxes contain information to help you save time or money.

Maps

All maps in this guide are oriented north, unless otherwise indicated by a directional arrow.

See the map legend at the back of the guide for an explanation of other map symbols.

A complete list of the maps found in the guide appears at the back of this book.

Addresses, phone numbers, opening hours and prices published in this guide are accurate at press time. We welcome corrections and suggestions that may assist us in preparing the next edition. Please send your comments to:

Michelin Travel Publications
Editorial Department
P.O. Box 19001
Greenville, SC 29602-9001
Email: michelin.guides@us.michelin.com
Web site: www.michelintravel.com

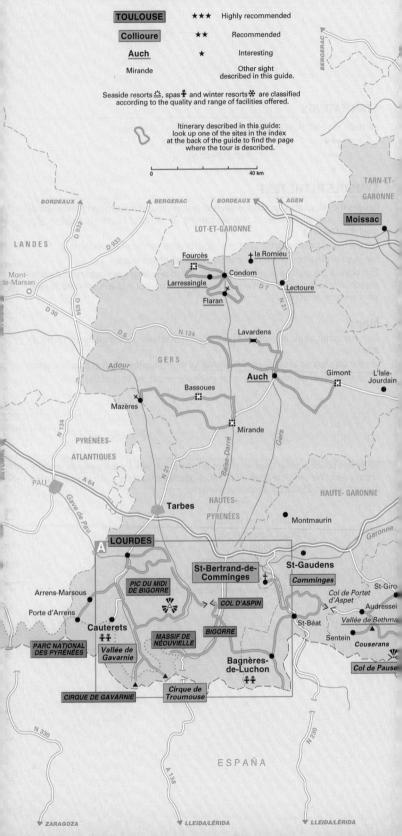

Principal sights

TOULOUSE	★★★	Highly recommended
Collioure	★★	Recommended
<u>Auch</u>	★	Interesting
Mirande		Other sight described in this guide.

Seaside resorts ⚓, spas ♨ and winter resorts ❄ are classified according to the quality and range of facilities offered.

Itinerary described in this guide: look up one of the sites in the index at the back of the guide to find the page where the tour is described.

0 ————— 40 km

�🏛 Roman ruins	🚢 Boat trips
⛪ Religious building	★ Outstanding site
🏰 Château, castle or historic house	🏘 Old town
▲ Outstanding natural feature	🍇 Vineyards
🏰 Fortifications	🏘 Picturesque village
∩ Cave	Ⓜ Museum, art gallery
✗ Historic site	© Regional specialities
🛶 Sports and recreation area	⛪ Pilgrimage site
🔻 Panorama	🍐 Arts and crafts
🐾 Wildlife park, zoo	

Glossary

Abîme . . . . Chasm

Aven . . . . Swallow-hole, chasm

Bambouseraie . . . .
. . . . Bamboo plantation

Bassin . . . . Lagoon, lake

Belvédère . . . . Viewpoint

Cap . . . . Cape

Cascade . . . . Waterfall, falls

Causse . . . . Limestone plateau

Chaos . . . .
   Group of scattered rocks or rock
   formations

Château, Chau . . . . Castle, château

Cirque . . . . Cirque, corrie

Col . . . . Pass

Corniche . . . . Ledge, overhang

Côte . . . . Coast

Défilé . . . . Narrow gorge, defile

Écluse . . . . Lock (canal)

Étang . . . . Lake, pool

Forêt . . . . Forest

Gorge, Gge . . . . Gorge

Gouffre . . . . Swallow-hole, chasm

Grotte . . . . Cave

Haute, Hte . . . . Upper

Lac . . . . Lake

Mas . . . . Farmhouse (south France)

Massif . . . Massif, mountain range

Mont, Mt, Montagne . . . .
. . . . Mount, mountain

Musée . . . . Museum

Parc . . . . Park

Pays . . . . Country, region

Pic . . . . Peak, summit

Plage . . . . Beach

Plateau, Plau . . . . Plateau

Port . . . . Harbour, port

Puy . . . .
. . . . Hill formed by a volcanic cone

Ravin . . . . Ravine, gully

Rivière souterraine . . . .
. . . . Underground river

Route, Rte . . . . Road

Site . . . . Site (archaeological)

Sommet . . . . Peak, summit

Terrasses . . . . Terraces, banks

Tour . . . . Tower

Vallée, Vée . . . . Valley

Viaduc . . . . Viaduct

Balme, baume . . . . . . cave, natural
   shelter

Buron . . . small stone hut used by
   cowherds on pasture land

Can . . . . small causse

Cazelle, chazelle . . . . drystone hut

Clède . . . . small
   drystone construction in which
   chestnuts used to be left to dry

Cros . small valley or glen, hollow

Devèze . . . . land grazed by flocks

Draille . . . . track once used for
   moving herds of animals from
   one pasture to another, often
   along mountain ridges

Gour . . . .
   small subterranean lake formed
   when calcite deposits build up
   into a dam

Grau . . . channel through which a
   river or lagoon runs into the sea

Lauze . . . .
   flat schist or limestone slab used
                   as roofing material

Lavogne . man-made water-hole

Masse (dimin. mazet) . . . . country
   house or farmstead

Ombrée . . slope shaded from the
   sun (in the Pyrenees)

Planèze . basalt plateau bordered
   by converging valleys

Puech . . . . hilltop, knoll

Ségalas . . . . ryefields

Serre . . . .
   long, narrow ridge stretching
   between two deep valleys

Soulane . . . .
   slope exposed to the sun (in the
   Pyrenees)

Summer pastures in the Pyrenees

PLANNING YOUR TRIP

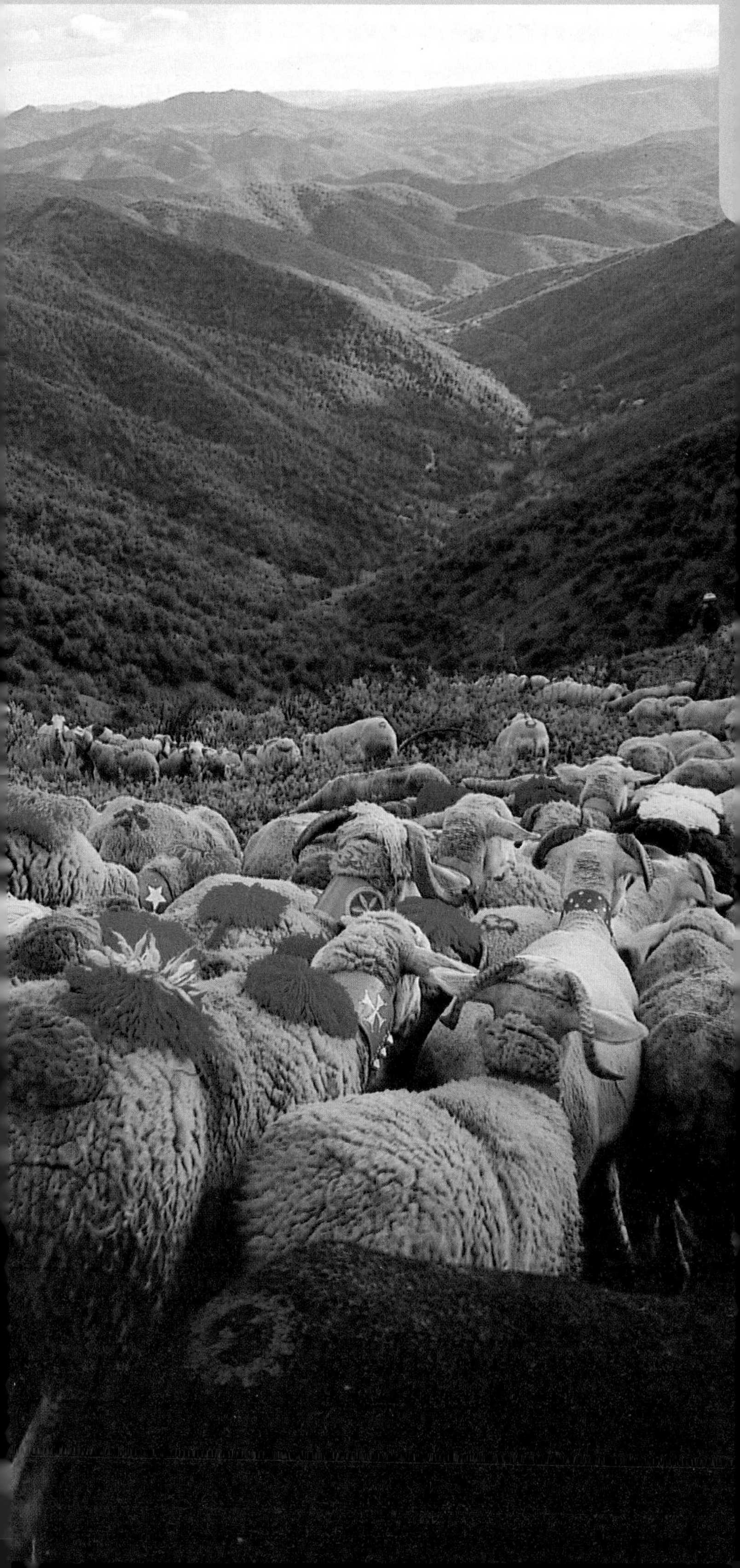

WHEN AND WHERE TO GO

Driving Tours

The following is a brief description of each of the driving tours shown on the map on page 12.

① BASTIDES AND STRONGHOLDS OF ARMAGNAC COUNTRY

225km/140mi starting from Auch

Gourmets rejoice! This may be called Armagnac country but it might as well be called foie gras country for this itinerary is lined with local producers who offer tourists ample opportunity to taste and buy this world-famous delicacy between visits to the bastides and strongholds which abound in the region: **Mirande, Montesquiou,** and **Bassoues** and its medieval keep. On the way to yet another castle at **Termes-d'Armagnac,** don't miss the Jazz Museum in **Marciac.** The picturesque village of **Sabazan** is close to **Aignan** where Armagnac tasting is a must. Beyond **Eauze** and its treasure is the Gallo-Roman villa of **Séviac** near Montréal-du-Gers. Two more *bastides* await you farther north, a round one at **Fourcès** and the smallest fortified town in France at **Larressingle.** **Condom** offers boat trips on the Baïse and La Romieu presents the musician angels of its collegiate church. Stop by **Lectoure's** Gallo-Roman museum and the **Abbaye de Flaran** before returning to Auch.

② PYRENEAN MINERAL SPRINGS

250km/155mi starting from Tarbes

The beneficial potential of Pyrenean thermal springs was already known to the Romans, but it was only in the 18C and above all in the 19C that taking the waters became fashionable. This fashion was at the origin of the advent of tourism in this mountainous region. Leave **Tarbes** south-east towards **Lourdes,** a world-famous place of pilgrimage. The Pyrenean summits and resorts (with attractive ski areas) are quite close: **Pic de Pibeste, Argelès-Gazost, Luz-St-Sauveur** and **Barèges;** they are the ideal starting points of hikes to the impressive **Col du Tourmalet** and **Pic du Midi**

de Bigorre. Beyond **Col d'Aspin** is **Arreau,** a quiet little town at the confluence of two rivers. Farther on, along the Route de Peyresourde, take time to admire the churches of the Louron Valley (particularly at **Mont**), with frescoes decorating their wooden vaulting. Continue to **Bagnères-de-Luchon** and turn north towards **Valcabrère** Basilica and **St-Bertrand-de-Comminges**. Farther north is the prehistoric **Grotte de Gargas** near Montréjeau and the last part of the itinerary includes **Bagnères-de-Bigorre** and its numerous hot springs.

③ TALES AND LEGENDS OF FOIX COUNTRY

280km/174mi starting from Foix

The Foix region is wrapped in mystery. This is no doubt due to the mist shrouding its narrow valleys and creating an uneasy impression or simply to the tales that have grown into legends. Follow in the footsteps of the Cathars from **Foix** to **Roquefixade** and **Montségur,** where they suffered their martyrdom. Close by, nature joins in with the intermittent **Fontestorbes** spring. On your way you will come to the splendid **Mirepoix** *bastide,* once devastated by the waters of Lake Puivert; in **Vals** you will see an amazing rock church, in **Pamiers** a lovely Gothic bell-tower and in **Mas-d'Azil** a prehistoric cave. To the south-west, the tiny episcopal city of St-Lizier boasts a prestigious past. Then when you cross the Ariège mountains, you will be won over by the beauty of the landscapes as you drive along valleys such as the **Bethmale** Valley where legend thrives. Farther on, past the Romanesque churches of **Vic** and **Massat** and the breathtaking panorama of **Port de Lers,** you will reach one of the main prehistoric areas in the Pyrenees: the **Grotte de Niaux** and its cave paintings, **Tarascon** and its **Parc pyrénéen d'Art préhistorique** and the **Grotte de Lombrives,** all within a short distance of one another. Having admired the Romanesque church in **Unac,** you will reach the French-chalk quarry at **Trimouns**.

④ PEAKS AND VALLEYS OF THE PYRENEES

270km/168mi starting from Font-Romeu

This drive takes you to the heart of the Pyrenees. From **Font-Romeu,** whose Hermitage is a place of pilgrimage, head for **Mont-Louis,** a stronghold built by Vauban, which now boasts a solar furnace seen from afar. The **Lac des Bouillouses** surrounded by a pine wood is nearby. At **Les Angles** you can have a go at skiing and meet bears and lizards in the zoological park. The **Grotte de Fontrabiouse** is the ideal refuge when it gets too hot outside. As for **Ax-les-Thermes,** you will love it for its skiing, rambling and mineral springs. And why not cross the border into Andorra via **Pas de la Casa** (winter sports resort offering duty free shopping). Drive down to **Andorra la Vella,** the capital of this tiny country. Back in France, go through the **Puymorens tunnel** to reach the **Chaos de Targasonne** and make a detour to the charming village of Llo before returning to Font-Romeu.

⑤ CATALAN ROMANESQUE AND BAROQUE ARCHITECTURE

290km/180mi starting from Perpignan

The discovery of Catalan art begins quite logically in **Perpignan,** which was the capital of the counts of Catalonia and later of the kings of Majorca. Nearby, **Cabestany** gave its name to the fine artist who carved the tympanum of its Romanesque church. The cathedral cloisters in **Elne** are a jewel of Romanesque and Gothic sculpture. Farther south, **Collioure** boasts a masterpiece of Catalan Baroque art, the monumental altarpiece of the Église Notre-Dame-des-Anges. The churches of **St-André** and **St-Génis-des-Fontaines** to the west have splendid carved Romanesque lintels, whereas the doorway of the Romanesque church in **Le Boulou** was carved by the Master of Cabestany. Nearby you can see the Romanesque frescoes decorating the chapel of **St-Martin-de-Fénollar,** including superb representations of the Three Wise Men. Continue westwards to **Arles-sur-Tech** to see the holy sepulchre, then on to **Coustouges** to admire the splendid wrought-iron railing separating the chancel from the nave. Between the Tech and Têt valleys stand the **Chapelle de la Trinité** and the

Prieuré de Serrabone both worth a visit for their Romanesque treasures, whereas the churches in **Vinca** and **Espira-de-Conflent** contain fine Baroque altarpieces. Near **Prades,** the abbeys of **St-Michel-de-Cuxa** and **St-Martin-du-Canigou** are a must. Drive on eastwards to **Ille-sur-Têt** and its wealth of Baroque ornamentation. As you leave Ille, do not miss the **Orgues,** where nature competes favourably with the splendours of human art. The tour ends in **Baixas** and the monumental Baroque altarpiece of its church.

⑥ THE VIA DOMITIA

300km/186mi from Lunel to Le Perthus or Port-Vendres

Twenty-one centuries ago, a Roman citizen named Domitius Ahenobarbus founded the first Roman colony outside Italy, Narbonne, and linked it to Rome by way of what we would now call a motorway, the Via Domitia, sections of which are still visible today. This journey starts from the **Oppidum d'Ambrussum,** near Lunel. Driving south-east, you first reach **Lattes** which has an interesting archaeological museum. Admire the fine mosaics of the Gallo-Roman villa of **Loupian,** standing on the shores of the Étang de Thau, then take an hour's walk between Montbazin and **Pinet** to go on to the Via Domitia. **Cap d'Agde** Museum contains the magnificent Éphèbe d'Agde, a bronze statue of a young Greek man found in the Hérault in 1964. Take a short break in **Béziers** and stroll along the narrow streets to the Musée du Biterrois and its Gallo-Roman collection. Return to the Via Domitia and the **Oppidum d'Ensérune.** Farther west, in Sallèdes-d'Aude, archaeological excavations have revealed a huge pottery workshop with numerous amphorae (Musée **Amphoralis**). The road then reaches **Narbonne,** which boasts an excellent archaeological museum (fine Roman painting collection), a *horreum* (Roman warehouse) and a section of Roman road running right across the central place de l'Hôtel-de-Ville. Head south along N 9 to the **Lapalme** crossroads to see the Via Domitia exhibition. From **Perpignan,** you can either follow the Roman road along the coast or through the Pyrenees, the very route followed by Hannibal and his elephants. The coastal route goes through **Elne** (archaeological museum) to reach **Port-Vendres,** "Venus' port". The mountain route leads to **Les Cluses** (beautiful panorama) then on to the **Fort de Bellegarde** and the **Site archéologique de Panissars,** close to the Spanish border.

7 CATHAR COUNTRY

300km/186mi starting from Carcassonne

The medieval atmosphere of the city of **Carcassonne** sets the scene. From there, drive south-west to **Limoux** where you can taste the famous sparkling *Blanquette* and see the Catharama audio-visual presentation before going on to visit several Cathar castles. Heading south through **Alet** and its Romanesque abbey, you soon reach the **Donjon d'Arques** then **Rennes-le-Château** and its legendary treasure. **Puivert** was one of the castles besieged during the Albigensian Crusade. To the south-east (via the **Défilé de Pierre-Lys**) stands another Cathar castle, **Puilaurens.** Farther east are the castles of **Peyrepertuse** and **Queribus** towering above the surrounding landscape, almost out of reach, it seems. From the nearby **Grau de Maury** pass, there is a view of the Canigou in the distance. The itinerary then takes in the ruins of **Padern, Aguill lar** and **Durban-Corbières** castles. On your way back to Carcassonne, take time to visit the **Château de Villerouge-Termenès,** where you can enjoy medieval cooking in the former stables, then on to the **Château des Termes** and **Lagrasse Abbey** to complete the tour.

8 THE MONTAGNE NOIRE

170km/106mi starting from Caunes-Minervois

After admiring the handsome 16C mansions of **Caunes-Minervois,** head for the heights of the Montagne Noire, stopping on the way to visit the **Gouffre de Cabrespine** and **Grotte de Limousis**. Halfway up the slopes, the four **Lastours** castles bear witness to the fighting that took place during the Albigensian Crusade. Other half-ruined castles overlook **Saissac** and **Mas-Cabardès,** adding to the charm of these villages. **Revel,** on the other hand, is a peaceful little town with a picturesque arcaded square where you can see some interesting inlaid furniture. The Montagne Noire is also the area where the 17C engineer who built the Canal du Midi created a vast complex of lakes and reservoirs from **St- Ferréol** to the **Seuil de Naurouze** in order to supply it with water. Having reached the plain through which the canal meanders, take a break in **Castelnaudary** to indulge in a cassoulet, the town's renowned gastronomic speciality. Drive south-east to **Fanjeaux** then turn east to **Carcassonne,** still surrounded by its ramparts, before returning to **Caunes-Minervois**.

9 LAND OF MILK AND HONEY

230km/143mi starting from Toulouse

This is a land of plenty indeed, which has prospered for centuries on a series of wealth-producing activities beginning with dyer's woad in the 14C and culminating with the aerospace industry based in **Toulouse,** the starting point of this drive. Before leaving, don't miss the Bemberg Collection housed in the Hôtel d'Assézat, a fine Renaissance mansion built for a rich merchant, and the Airbus industrial complex as well as the Cité de l'Espace on the outskirts of town. Drive south-east to **Port-Lauragais** along the **Canal du Midi,** a wonderful piece of engineering dating from the 17C and visit the Ovalie, a museum devoted to rugby, South-West France's national sport. Turn north-east through the Lauragais hills via **St-Félix** and **Revel** to the **Bassin de Saint-Ferréol,** ideal for the practice of water sports, but in fact created to supply the Canal du Midi. The road wends its way through **Arfons** to **Mazamet,** with its long-standing tawing tradition, and **Castres,** where you can take a trip on the River Agout aboard a picturesque passenger barge *(coche d'eau),* then on to **Lautrec** and its pink garlic, **Graulhet** and its leather, **Lavaur** and its old town. On the way back to Toulouse, D 130 between **Magrin** and **Loubens-Lauragais** will take you through the heart of dyer's woad country, otherwise known as the land of milk and honey.

10 RUGGED LIMESTONE PLATEAUX

290km/180mi starting from Millau

Millau is at the heart of the four main limestone plateaux which this tour explores. Driving eastwards, you soon come across the impressive rock formation known as the **Chaos de**

Montpellier-le-Vieux. The **Grotte de Dargilan** with its pink concretions is located a few miles farther on. On the border of the Causse Noir and Causse Méjean stands the picturesque village of **Meyrueis** with its weathered stone houses. The road runs through the barren yet fascinating Causse Méjean before reaching the **Aven Armand,** one of the most attractive underground caves in France. **Ste-Énimie,** towering above the Tarn is another picturesque village, well worth exploring. The road then crosses the Causse de Sauveterre towards **La Canourgue,** a peaceful village crisscrossed by a network of charming canals. Take a break and visit the medieval castle of **Séverac-le-Château** then continue on your journey along D 995 towards the **Tarn Gorges;** canoeing down the river at its narrowest, rambling or driving along its course…the choice is yours! Whichever, the end of this spectacular section is **Le Rozier;** from there, head south to Millau then on to **Roquefort-sur-Soulzon** and its extensive galleries hewn out of the rock, where the famous cheese is left to mature. Flocks of sheep are a familiar sight on the Causse de Larzac which has retained medieval fortifications built by the Knights Templars and Knights Hospitallers; some of the most remarkable can be seen in La **Couvertoirade** before returning to Millau.

11 CAVES, CIRQUES AND ROCK FORMATIONS

425km/264mi starting from Ganges

This tour leads in turn to all the natural wonders which the area has to offer. The impressive **Grotte des Demoiselles** is located a few miles from **Ganges**. Farther east, near Anduze, is the **Grotte de Trabuc,** lined with tiny soldiers! You next enter the **Cévennes** mountain area and follow the famous **Corniche** north to Florac. The road then skirts the southern border of the Causse Méjean to reach a stunning rock formation known as the **Chaos de Nîmes-le-Vieux.** Across the River Jonte towers **Mont Aigoual,** offering a breathtaking panorama from its summit. To the west is the **Abîme de Bramabiau,** where you can see the resurgence of the River Bonheur. Not far from there are three more natural wonders, the **Aven Armand,** the **Grotte de Dargilan** and

the **Chaos de Montpellier-le-Vieux.** Turning south along the **canyon of the River Dourbie,** the road leads to the vast and barren **Cirque de Navacelles**. Continuing south past the **Lac du Salagou,** you reach the rock-strewn **Cirque de Mourèze** and visit one last cave, the **Grotte de Clamouse** before returning to Ganges.

Themed Tours

Travel itineraries on specific themes have been mapped out to help you discover the regional architectural heritage and the traditions which make up the cultural heritage of the region. You will find brochures in tourist offices, and the routes are generally well marked and easy to follow (⊛ *signs posted along the roads*).

HISTORY

Some of these itineraries are managed by the **Fédération Nationale des Routes Historiques** *(www.routes-historiques.com)*. Apply to local tourist offices for leaflets with mapped itineraries. The list below includes a local contact when appropriate:

Route historique du pastel en pays de cocagne (dyer's woad country between Toulouse and Albi; contact M. Rufino, Château-Musée du Pastel, 81220 Magrin, ☎ 05 63 70 63 82).

Route historique en Languedoc-Roussillon (Château de Flaugergues, 1744 avenue Albert-Einstein, 34000 Montpellier, ☎ 04 99 52 66 46).

Route historique en Terre Catalane: de l'Homme de Tautavel à Picasso (Réseau culturel Terre catalane, 16 avenue des Palmiers, BP 60244, 66002 Perpignan Cedex, ☎ 04 68 51 52 90).

Other thematic itineraries (🔋 *information available from local tourist offices*) include:

Route des Cadets de Gascogne

Maison Départementale du Tourisme, 3 boulevard Roquelaure, BP 106, 32002 Auch Cedex ☎ 05 62 05 95 95 www.gers-gascogne.com

Route des Comtes de Toulouse

north-east of Toulouse as far as the Gorges de l'Aveyron. contact M. Lyonnel de Lastic Saint Jal, 43 rue du Parc-de-Clagny, 78000 Versailles ☎ 01 39 54 79 85

Via Domitia

along the old Roman road running from Beaucaire in Provence, via Béziers and Narbonne to Spain across Panissars pass.
Association Via Domitia, CRT, 20 rue de la République, 34000 Montpellier, ☎ 04 67 22 81 00 www.viadomitia.org

Route de la Catalogne Romane

Romanesque art in Catalonia and Roussillon; tourist office, Perpignan.

TRADITIONS AND NATURE

- **Sur les pas de St-Jacques-de-Compostelle** (on the way to Santiago de Compostela), 137km/85mi from Toulouse to St-Bertrand-de-Comminges.

- **Sur la route des vins** (wine tour of the area between the River Garonne and River Tarn).

- **Route des grottes en Ariège** (tour of natural and prehistoric caves of the Ariège region).

- **Chemin de la soie** (itinerary focusing on traditional silk production in the region: museums, silk worm breeding establishments, spinning mills; 95 Grand'Rue, 30270 St-Jean-du-Gard, ☎ 04 66 85 10 48).

When to Go

CLIMATE

Although this region is predominantly Mediterranean (Bas-Languedoc and Roussillon) in climate, it is open to oceanic influences from the Atlantic and, in its northern part (Aubrac, Margeride, Cévennes, limestone plateaux), to the harsher climatic conditions of the Massif Central. As for the Pyrenees mountain range, its valleys are under the influence of several weather systems determined by the altitude and the direction the slopes are facing.

Late **winter** and **early spring** offer plenty of snow for cross-country skiing in the Aubrac, and Alpine skiing in the Pyrenees.

Spring is the ideal season for hiking and riding tours and for discovering the region in general.

Summer is dry and hot with luminous skies, particularly along the Mediterranean (Perpignan boasts the highest average summer temperature in France, 22.3°C/ 72.1°F), but also in the Toulouse, Albi and Gers areas. Sudden, violent storms bring relief from the scorching heat from time to time but the sun rarely admits defeat for more than a few hours.

In **autumn**, rainfall is often abundant particularly in the Toulouse and Albi areas, while warm south-west winds blowing over the whole region bring alternating periods of dry and wet weather.

⏱ *See also The Climate in the Introduction.*

WHAT TO PACK

As little as possible! Cleaning and laundry services are available everywhere. Most personal items can be replaced at reasonable cost. Try to pack everything into one suitcase and a carry-on bag. Porter help may be in short supply, and new purchases will add to the original weight. Take an extra bag for packing new purchases, shopping at the open-air market, carrying a picnic etc. Be sure luggage is clearly labelled and old travel tags removed. Do not pack medication in checked luggage, but keep it with you.

WEATHER FORECAST

Météo-France offers recorded information at national, regional and local level. This information is updated three times a day and is valid for five days.

National forecast: ☎ 08 36 68 00 00.
Regional forecast: ☎ 08 36 68 01 01.

Local forecast: ☎ 08 36 68 02 followed by the number of the *département* (Ariège: 09; Aude: 11; Aveyron: 12; Gard: 30; Gers: 32; Haute-Garonne: 31; Hautes-Pyrénées: 65; Hérault: 34; Lozère: 48; Pyrénées-Orientales: 66; Tarn: 81; Tarn-et-Garonne: 82).

Seaside weather forecast: ☎ 08 92 68 08 followed by the number of the coastal *département*; for information about the weather at sea, ☎ 08 92 68 08 77.

Mountain weather forecast: ☎ 08 92 68 04 04; for information about snow cover and avalanche risk, ☎ 08 92 68 10 20.

KNOW BEFORE YOU GO

Useful Web Sites

CYBERSPACE

www.info.france-usa.org

The **French Embassy**'s Web site provides basic information (geography, demographics, history), a news digest and business-related information. It offers special pages for children, and pages devoted to culture, language study and travel, and you can reach other selected French sites (regions, cities, ministries) with a hypertext link.

www.franceguide.com

The **French Government Tourist Office/Maison de la France** site is packed with practical information and tips for those travelling to France. The home page has a number of links to more specific guidance, for American or Canadian travellers for example, or to the FGTO's London pages.

www.fr-holidaystore.co.uk

The **Travel Centre in London** has gone on-line with this service, providing information on all of the regions of France, including updated special travel offers and details on available accommodation.

www.FranceKeys.com

This site has plenty of practical information for visiting France. It covers all the regions, with links to tourist offices and related sites. Very useful for planning the details of your tour in France!

www.franceway.com

This is an on-line magazine which focuses on culture and heritage. For each region, there are also suggestions for activities and practical information on where to stay and how to get there.

www.visiteurope.com

The **European Travel Commission** provides useful information on travelling to and around 27 European countries, and includes links to some commercial booking services (ie vehicle hire), rail schedules, weather reports and more.

www.pyrenees-online.fr

This regional site has a mine of information about accommodation, ski resorts and activities in the Pyrenees mountains.

www.randonnees-ariege.com

This site focuses on walking and hiking in the Ariège, offering some 50 different itineraries in the area.

Tourist Offices

For information, brochures, maps and assistance in planning a trip to France travellers should apply to the official French Tourist Office or Maison de France in their own country:

Australia – New Zealand

Sydney

BNP Building, 12 Castlereagh Street, Sydney, New South Wales 2000, ☎ (02) 9 231 52 44 Fax: (02) 9 221 86 82.

Canada

Toronto

30 St Patrick's Street, Suite 700, Toronto, ONT M5T 3A3 ☎ (416) 979 7587.

Montreal

1981 McGill College Avenue, Suite 490, Montreal PQ H3A 2W9 ☎ (514) 288-4264 Fax: (514) 845 48 68.

Ireland

Dublin

10 Suffolk St, Dublin 2 ☎ (1) 679 0813, Fax: (1) 679 0814

United Kingdom

London

178 Piccadilly, London WI ☎ (09068) 244 123 Fax: (020) 793 6594

United States

East Coast

New York – 444 Madison Avenue, NY 10022, ☎ 212-838-7800 Fax: (212) 838 7855.

West Coast

Los Angeles – 9454 Wilshire Boulevard, Suite 715, Beverly Hills, CA 90212, ☎ (310) 271 6665 Fax: (310) 276 2835.

LOCAL TOURIST OFFICES

Visitors may also contact local tourist offices for more precise information, and to receive brochures and maps. The addresses and telephone numbers of tourist offices in the larger towns are listed after the symbol 🛈. Below, the addresses are given for local tourist offices of the *départements* and *régions* covered in this guide.

For each département within the region, address inquiries to the Comité départemental de tourisme (C.D.T.):

Ariège
31 bis av. du Gén.-de-Gaulle,
BP 143 09004 Foix Cedex
☏ 05 61 02 30 70
www.ariegepyrenees.com

Aude
Conseil général, 11855
Carcassonne Cedex 9
☏ 04 68 11 66 00
www.audetourisme.com

Aveyron
17 rue Aristide-Briand, BP 831
12008 Rodez, ☏ 05 65 75 55 75
www.tourisme-aveyron.com

Gard
3 place des Arènes, BP 122
30010 Nîmes Cedex 04
☏ 04 66 36 96 30
www.tourismegard.com

Gers
3 boulevard Roquelaure, BP 106
32002 Auch Cedex
☏ 05 62 05 95 95
www.gers-gascogne.com

Haute-Garonne
14 rue Bayard, BP 845
31015 Toulouse Cedex 6
☏ 05 61 99 44 00
www.tourisme-haute-garonne.com

Hautes-Pyrénées
Htes-Pyrénées Tourisme
Environnement
11 rue Gaston-Manent, BP 9502
65950 Tarbes Cedex 9
☏ 05 62 56 70 65, www.cg.fr

Hérault
avenue des Moulins
34034 Montpellier Cedex 4
☏ 04 67 67 71 71
www.tourisme-herault.com

Lozère
14 boulevard Henri-Bourillon, BP 4
48001 Mende Cedex
☏ 04 66 65 60 00
www.france48.com

Pyrénées-Orientales
16 avenue des Palmiers, BP 540
66005 Perpignan Cedex
☏ 04 68 51 52 53, www.cg66.fr

Tarn
41 rue Porta, BP 225
81006 Albi Cedex
☏ 05 63 77 32 10
www.tourisme-tarn.com

Tarn-et-Garonne
7 boulevard Midi-Pyrénées, BP 534
82005 Montauban Cedex
☏ 05 63 21 79 09
www.tourisme82.com

Two regional tourist offices are concerned with the area covered by this guide; address inquiries to the *Comité régional de tourisme (C.R.T.):*

Midi-Pyrénées:
54 boulevard de l'Embouchure, BP 2166, 31022 Toulouse Cedex 2,
☏ 05 61 13 55 55;
www.tourisme-midi-pyrenees.com

Languedoc-Roussillon:
417 rue Samuel-Morse, CS 79507, 34960 Montpellier,
☏ 04 67 22 81 00;
www.sunfrance.com

In addition there are interesting **Maisons de Pays** (regional promotion centres) in Paris and other major towns; they include:

Maison de l'Aveyron
46 rue Berger, 75001 Paris,
☏ 01 42 36 84 63;
www.maison-aveyron.com

Maison de la Lozère
4 rue Hautefeuille, 75006 Paris,
☏ 01 43 54 26 64; 27 rue de l'Aiguillerie, 34000 Montpellier,
☏ 04 67 66 36 10

Maison des Pyrénées
15 rue St-Augustin, 75002 Paris,
☏ 01 42 86 51 86;
6 rue Vital-Carles, 33000 Bordeaux,
☏ 05 56 44 05 65;
7 rue Paré, 44000 Nantes,
☏ 02 40 20 36 36;

Espace Tarn
111 rue Réaumur, 75002 Paris,
☏ 01 40 13 81 81 (🕐 *Mon-Fri 11am-7pm*).

🔖 See the Principal Sights in the *Discovering the Region* section for the addresses and telephone numbers of the local tourist offices *(Syndicats d'Initiative)*; they provide information on craft courses and itineraries with special themes – wine tours, history tours, artistic tours.

Eight towns and areas, labelled **Villes et Pays d'Art et d'Histoire** by the Ministry of Culture, are mentioned in this guide (Lectoure, Mende, Montauban, Narbonne, Perpignan, Pézenas, Toulouse and the Têt Valley). They are particularly active in promoting their architectural and cultural heritage and offer guided tours by highly qualified guides as well as activities for 6 to 12-year-olds. More information is available from local tourist offices and from *www.vpah. culture.fr*.

International Visitors

EMBASSIES AND CONSULATES

Australia   **Embassy**
4 rue Jean-Rey, 75015 Paris
☎ 01 40 59 33 00
Fax: 01 40 59 33 10

Canada   **Embassy**
35 avenue Montaigne, 75008 Paris
☎ 01 44 43 29 00
Fax: 01 44 43 29 99

Ireland   **Embassy**
4 rue Rude, 75016 Paris
☎ 01 44 17 67 00
Fax: 01 44 17 67 60

New Zealand   **Embassy**
7 ter rue Léonard-de-Vinci, 75016 Paris
☎ 01 45 01 43 43
Fax: 01 45 01 43 44

UK   **Embassy**
35 rue du Faubourg St-Honoré, 75008 Paris
☎ 01 44 51 31 00
Fax: 01 44 51 31 27

UK   **Consulate**
16 rue d'Anjou, 75008 Paris
☎ 01 44 51 31 01 (visas)

USA   **Embassy**
2 avenue Gabriel, 75008 Paris
☎ 01 43 12 22 22
Fax: 01 42 66 97 83

USA   **Consulate**
2 rue St-Florentin, 75001 Paris
☎ 01 42 96 14 88.

DOCUMENTS

Passport – Nationals of countries within the European Union entering France need only a national identity card. Nationals of other countries must be in possession of a valid national **passport**. In case of loss or theft, report to your embassy or consulate and the local police.

Visa – No **entry visa** is required for Canadian, US or Australian citizens travelling as tourists and staying less than 90 days, except for students planning to study in France. If you think you may need a visa, apply to your local French Consulate. US citizens should obtain the booklet *Safe Trip Abroad* (US$1), which provides useful information

on visa requirements, customs regulations, medical care etc for international travellers. Published by the **Government Printing Office**, it can be ordered by phone – ☎ *(202) 512-1800* – or consulted on-line *(www. access.gpo.gov)*. General passport information is available by phone toll-free from the **Federal Information Center** (item 5 on the automated menu), ☎ 800-688-9889. US passport application forms can be downloaded from *http://travel.state.gov*.

CUSTOMS

Apply to the Customs Office (UK) for a leaflet on customs regulations and the full range of duty-free allowances; available from **HM Customs and Excise**, *Thomas Paine House, Angel Square, Torrens Street, London EC1V 1TA,* ☎ *08450 109 000*. The **US Customs Service** offers a publication *Know Before You Go* for US citizens: for the office nearest you, consult the phone book, Federal Government, US Treasury *(www.customs.ustreas.gov)*. There are no customs formalities for holidaymakers bringing their caravans into France for a stay of less than six months. No customs document is necessary for pleasure boats and outboard motors for a stay of less than six months but the registration certificate should be kept on board. Americans can take home, tax-free, up to US$ 400 worth of goods (limited quantities of alcohol and tobacco products); Canadians up to CND$ 300; Australians up to AUS$ 400 and New Zealanders up to NZ$ 700.
Residents from a member state of the European Union are not restricted with regard to purchasing goods for private use, but the recommended allowances for alcoholic beverages and tobacco are as follows:

Duty-Free Allowances	
Spirits (whisky, gin, vodka etc)	10 litres
Fortified wines (vermouth, port etc)	20 litres
Wine (not more than 60 sparkling)	90 litres
Beer	110 litres
Cigarettes	800
Cigarillos	400
Cigars	200
Smoking tobacco	1 kg

HEALTH

First aid, medical advice and chemists' night service rotas are available from chemists drugstores *(pharmacie)* identified by the green cross sign. All prescription drugs should be clearly labelled; it is recommended that you carry a copy of the prescription. It is advisable to take out comprehensive insurance coverage as the recipient of medical treatment in French hospitals or clinics must pay the bill. **Nationals of non-EU countries** should check with their insurance companies about policy limitations. Reimbursement can then be negotiated with the insurance company according to the policy held.

British and Irish citizens should apply to the Department of Health and Social Security **before travelling** for Form E 111, which entitles the holder to urgent treatment for accident or unexpected illness in EU countries. A refund of part of the costs of treatment can be obtained on application in person or by post to the local Social Security Offices *(Caisse Primaire d'Assurance Maladie).*

Americans concerned about travel and health can contact the International Association for Medical Assistance to Travelers, which can also provide details of English-speaking doctors in different parts of France: ☎ (716) 754-4883.

✚ **The American Hospital of Paris** is open 24hr for emergencies as well as consultations, with English-speaking staff, at 63 boulevard Victor-Hugo, 92200 Neuilly-sur-Seine, ☎ 01 46 41 25 25. Accredited by major insurance companies.

✚ **The British Hospital** is just outside Paris in Levallois-Perret, 3 rue Barbès, ☎ 01 46 39 22 22.

Accessibility

The sights described in this guide which are easily accessible to the disabled and another people of reduced mobility are indicated in the Admission times and charges by the symbol ♿.
On TGV and Corail trains operated by the national railway (SNCF), there are special wheelchair slots in 1st class carriages available to holders of 2nd-class tickets. On Eurostar and Thalys, special rates are available for accompanying adults. All airports are equipped to receive physically disabled passengers.

Web-surfers can find information for slow walkers, mature travellers and others with special needs at *www. access-able.com.* For information on museum access for the disabled contact La Direction, *Les Musées de France, Service Accueil des Publics Spécifiques,* 6 rue des Pyramides, 75041 Paris Cedex 1, ☎ 01 40 15 80 72. The **Michelin Guide France** and the **Michelin Camping France** indicate hotels and camp sites with facilities suitable for physically handicapped people.

GETTING THERE

By Air

The various international and other independent airlines operate services to **Paris** (Roissy-Charles de Gaulle and Orly airports), **Montpellier** and **Toulouse**. Check with your travel agent, however, before booking direct flights, as it is sometimes cheaper to travel via Paris. Air France (☎ *0820 820 820; www.airfrance.fr)*, the national airline, links Paris to Montpellier, Béziers-Agde and Toulouse several times a day.

Other airlines offering flights to several towns in the region include British Airways, British European, Easy Jet and Ryanair.

Contact airline companies and travel agents for details of package tour flights with a rail or coach link-up as well as fly-drive schemes.

By Sea

There are numerous **cross-Channel services** (passenger and car ferries, hovercraft) from the United Kingdom and Ireland, as well as the rail Shuttle through the Channel Tunnel (**Le Shuttle-Eurotunnel**, ☎ 0990 353-535). For details apply to travel agencies or to:

P & O Stena Line Ferries
  Channel House, Channel View Road, Dover CT17 9JT,
  ☎ 0990 980 980 or 01304 863 000 (Switchboard), www.pogroup.com

Hoverspeed
  International Hoverport, Marine Parade, Dover, Kent CT17 9TG,
  ☎ 0990 240 241,
  Fax 01304 240088,
  www.hoverspeed.co.uk

Brittany Ferries
  Millbay Docks, Plymouth, Devon. PL1 3EW, ☎ 0990 360 360,
  www.brittany-ferries.com

Portsmouth Commercial Port (and ferry information)
  George Byng Way, Portsmouth, Hampshire PO2 8SP,
  ☎ 01705 297391,
  Fax 01705 861165,
  www.portsmouth-port.co.uk

Irish Ferries
  50 West Norland Street, Dublin 2,
  ☎ (353) 16 610 511,
  www.irishferries.com

Seafrance
  Eastern Docks, Dover, Kent, CT16 1JA,
  ☎ 01304 212696,
  Fax 01304 240033,
  www.seafrance.fr

By Rail

Eurostar runs via the Channel Tunnel between **London** (Waterloo) and **Paris** (Gare du Nord) in less than 3hr (bookings and information ☎ 0345 303 030 in the UK; ☎ 1-888-EUROSTAR in the US). In Paris it links to the high-speed rail network (TGV). **TGV** departures for Toulouse are from the Gare Montparnasse, departures for Montpellier are from the Gare de Lyon and departures for Perpignan are from the Gares d'Austerlitz, Lyon or Montparnasse.

Eurailpass, Flexipass, Eurailpass Youth, EurailDrive Pass and **Saverpass** are some of the travel passes which may be purchased by residents of countries outside the European Union. In the US, contact your travel agent or **Rail Europe** 2100 Central Ave. Boulder, CO, 80301 ☎ 1-800-4-EURAIL or **Europrail International** ☎ 1 888 667 9731. If you are a European resident, you can buy an individual country pass, if you are not a resident of the country where you plan to use it. In the UK, contact **Europrail** at 179 Piccadilly, London W1V OBA, ☎ 0990 848 848. Information on schedules can be obtained on Web sites for these agencies and the **SNCF**, respectively: *www.raileurop.com.us, www.eurail.on.ca, www.sncf.fr*. At the SNCF site, you can book ahead, pay with a credit card, and receive your ticket in the mail at home.

There are numerous discounts available when you purchase your tickets in France, from 25-50% below the regular rate. These include **discounts** for using senior cards and youth cards (the cards with the holder's name and a photograph must be purchased – 44 and 41 euros, respectively), and lower rates for 2-9 people travelling together (no card required, advance purchase necessary). There are a limited number of discount seats available during peak travel times, and the best discounts are available for travel during off-peak periods. To benefit from these discounts you are advised to book well in advance.

Tickets must be validated *(composter)* by using the orange automatic date-stamping machines at the platform entrance (🖚 *failure to do so may result in a fine)*.

The French railway company SNCF operates a telephone information, reservation and prepayment service in English from 7am to 10pm (French time). In France call ☎ 08 36 35 35 39 (when calling from outside France, drop the initial 0).

By Bus

Eurolines (London), 4 Cardiff Road, Luton, Bedfordshire, LU1 1PP, ☎ 0990 08705 143219, Fax 01582 400694, on-line welcome@eurolinesuk.com.

Eurolines (Paris), 22 rue Malmaison, 93177 Bagnolet, ☎ 01 49 72 57 80, Fax 01 49 72 57 99.

www.eurolines.com is the international Web site with information about travelling all over Europe by coach (bus).

Driving in France

ROUTE PLANNING

The area covered in this guide is easily reached by main motorways and national routes. **Michelin map 726** indicates the main itineraries as well as alternate routes for avoiding heavy traffic during busy holiday periods, and gives estimated travel times. **Michelin map 723** is a detailed atlas of French motorways, indicating tolls, rest areas and services along the route; it includes a table for calculating distances and times. The latest Michelin route-planning service is available on Internet, **www.ViaMichelin.com**. Travellers can calculate a precise route using such options as shortest route, route avoiding toll roads, Michelin-recommended route and gain access to tourist information (hotels, restaurants, attractions). The service is available on a pay-per-route basis or by subscription. The roads are very busy during the holiday period (particularly weekends in July and August) and, to avoid traffic congestion it is advisable to follow the recommended secondary routes (signposted as *Bison Futé – itinéraires bis).* The motorway network includes rest areas *(aires de repos)* and gasoline stations *(stations-service)*, usually with restaurant and shopping complexes attached, about every 40km/25mi, so that long-distance drivers have no excuse not to stop for a rest every now and then.

DOCUMENTS

Travellers from other European Union countries and North America can drive in France with a valid national or home-state **driving licence.** An **international driving licence** is useful because the information on it appears in nine languages (keep in mind that traffic officers are empowered to fine motorists). A permit is available (US$10) from the **National Automobile Club**, 1151 East Hillsdale Blvd., Foster City, CA 94404, ☎ 650-294-7000 or nationalautoclub.com; or contact your local branch of the **American Automobile Association**. For the vehicle, it is necessary to have the registration papers (logbook) and a nationality plate of the approved size.

INSURANCE

Certain motoring organisations (AAA, AA, RAC) offer accident **insurance** and breakdown service schemes for members. Check with your current insurance company in regard to coverage while abroad. If you plan to hire a car using your credit card, check with the company, which may provide liability insurance automatically (and thus save you having to pay the cost for optimum coverage).

ROAD REGULATIONS

The minimum driving age is 18. Traffic drives on the right. All passengers must wear **seat belts**. Children under the age of 10 must ride in the back seat. Headlights must be switched on in poor visibility and at night; use side-lights only when the vehicle is stationary.

In the case of a **breakdown**, a red warning triangle or hazard warning lights are obligatory. In the absence of stop signs at intersections, cars must **yield to the right**. Traffic on main roads outside built-up areas (priority indicated by a yellow diamond sign) has the right of way. There are many **roundabouts** (traffic circles) located just on the edge of towns; they are designed to reduce the speed of the traffic entering the built-up area and you must slow down when you approach one and yield to the cars in the circle. Vehicles must stop when the lights turn red at road junctions and may filter to the right only when indicated by an amber arrow.

- The regulations on **drinking and driving** (limited to 0.50g/l) and **speeding** are strictly enforced – usually by an on-the-spot fine and/or confiscation of the vehicle.

Speed limits – Although liable to modification, these are as follows:

- toll motorways *(autoroutes)* 130kph/ 80mph (110kph/68mph when raining);

- dual carriageways and motorways without tolls 110kph/68mph (100kph/62mph when raining);

- other roads 90kph/56mph (80kph/50mph when raining) and in towns 50kph/31mph;

- outside lane on motorways during daylight, on level ground and with good visibility – minimum speed limit of 80kph/50mph.

Parking Regulations – In town there are zones where parking is either restricted or subject to a fee; tickets should be obtained from the ticket machines *(horodateurs – small change necessary)* and displayed inside the windscreen on the driver's side; failure to display may result in a fine, or towing and impoundment. Other parking areas in town may require you to take a ticket when passing through a barrier. To exit, you must pay the parking fee (usually there is a machine located by the exit – *sortie)* and insert the paid-up card in another machine which will lift the exit gate.

Tolls – In France, most motorway sections are subject to a toll *(péage)*. You can pay in cash or with a credit card (Visa, Mastercard).

CAR RENTAL

There are car rental agencies at airports, railway stations and in all large towns throughout France. European cars have manual transmission; automatic cars are available in larger cities only if an advance reservation is made. Drivers must be over 21; between ages 21-25, drivers are required to pay an extra daily fee; some companies allow drivers under 23 only if the reservation has been made through a travel agent. It is relatively expensive to hire a car in France; Americans in particular will notice the difference and should make arrangements before leaving, take advantage of **fly-drive offers**

when you buy your ticket, or seek advice from a travel agent, specifying requirements. There are many on-line services that will look for the best prices on car rental around the globe. **Nova** can be contacted at *www.rentacar-worldwide.com* or ☎ 0800 018 6682 *(freephone UK)* or ☎ 44 28 4272 8189 *(calling from outside the UK)*. All of the firms listed below have internet sites for reservations and information. In France, you can call the following numbers:

Rental Cars – Central Reservation in France	
Avis:	☎ 08 20 05 05 05
Europcar:	☎ 08 25 82 54 57
Budget France:	☎ 08 25 00 35 64
Hertz France:	☎ 01 47 03 49 12
SIXT-Eurorent	☎ 08 20 00 74 98
National-CITER	☎ 01 45 22 77 91

A Baron's Limousine ☎ 01 45 30 21 21 provides cars and drivers (English-speaking drivers available).

MOTORHOME RENTAL

Worldwide Motorhome Rentals

Offers fully equipped camper vans for rent. You can view them on the company's web page.

☎ 888- 519-8969 *US toll-free*
☎ 530-389-8316 *outside the US*
Fax 530-389-8316.
www.mhrww.com

Overseas Motorhome Tours Inc.

Organises escorted tours and individual rental of recreational vehicles.

☎ 800-322-2127 *US*
☎ 1-310-543-2590 *outside the US*
www.omtinc.com.

PETROL/GASOLINE

French service stations dispense:

- *sans plomb 98* (super unleaded 98)

- *sans plomb 95* (super unleaded 95)

- *diesel/gazole* (diesel)

- *GPL* (LPG).

Gasoline, is considerably more expensive in France than in the USA. Prices are listed on signboards on the motorways; it is usually cheaper to fill up after leaving the motorway; check the large hypermarkets on the outskirts of town.

WHERE TO STAY AND EAT

Hotel & Restaurant listings fall within the Address Books within the Discovering the Region section of the guide.

Finding a Hotel

The Green Guide is pleased to offer descriptions of selected lodgings for this region. The Address Books in the *Discovering the Region* section of the guide give descriptions and prices *(based on double ocupancy)* of typical places to stay with local flair. The Legend at the back of the guide explains the symbols and abbreviations used in the Address Books. We have reported the prices and conditions as we observed them, but of course changes in management and other factors may mean that you will find some discrepancies. Please feel free to keep us informed of any major differences you encounter.

Use the **map of Places to Stay** that follows to identify recommended places for overnight stops. For an even greater selection, use the **Michelin Guide France**, with its famously reliable star-rating system and hundreds of establishments all over France. Book ahead to ensure that you get the accommodation you want, not only in tourist season, but year round, as many towns fill up during trade fairs, arts festivals etc. Some places require an advance deposit or a reconfirmation. Reconfirming is especially important if you plan to arrive after 6pm.

For further assistance, **Loisirs Accueil** is a booking service that has offices in some French *départements* – contact the tourist offices listed above for further information.

A guide to good-value, family-run hotels, **Logis et Auberges de France**, is available from the French Tourist Office, as are lists of other kinds of accommodation such as hotel-châteaux, bed-and-breakfasts, etc.

Relais et châteaux provides information on booking in luxury hotels with character: 15 rue Galvani, 75017 Paris, ☎ 01 45 72 90 00.

Economy Chain Hotels – If you need a place to stop en route, these can be useful, as they are inexpensive (30-45€ for a double room) and generally located near the main road. While breakfast is available, there may not be a restaurant; rooms are small, with a television and bathroom. Central reservation numbers:

- 🛏 **Akena** ☎ 01 69 84 85 17
- 🛏 **B&B** ☎ 0 803 00 29 29 (in France); 33 02 98 33 75 00 (when calling from outside France)
- 🛏 **Mister Bed** ☎ 01 46 14 38 00
- 🛏 **Villages Hôtel** ☎ 03 80 60 92 70

The hotels listed below are slightly more expensive (from 45€), and offer a few more amenities and services. Central reservation numbers:

- 🛏 **Campanile, Climat de France, Kyriad** ☎ 01 64 62 46 46

Many chains have online reservations: *www.etaphotel.com www.ibishotel.com.*

RENTING A COTTAGE, BED AND BREAKFAST

The **Maison des Gîtes de France** is an information service on self-catering accommodation throughout France. Gîtes usually take the form of a cottage or apartment decorated in the local style where visitors can make themselves at home, or bed and breakfast accommodation *(chambres d'hôtes)* which consists of a room and breakfast at a reasonable price.

Contact the **Gîtes de France** office in Paris: 59 rue St-Lazare, 75439 Paris Cedex 09, ☎ 01 49 70 75 75, or their representative in the UK, **Brittany Ferries** *(address above)*. The Internet site, **www.gites-de-france.fr**, has a good English version. From the site, you can order catalogues for different regions illustrated with photographs of the properties, as well as specialised catalogues (bed and breakfasts, farm stays etc.) You can also contact the local tourist offices which may have lists of available properties and local bed and breakfast establishments.

The **Fédération nationale Clévacances,** 54 boulevard de l'Embouchure, BP 2166, 31022 Toulouse Cedex 09, ☎ 05 61 13 55 66, www.clevacances.com, offers a wide choice of accommodation (rooms, flats, chalets and villas) throughout France. It publishes a brochure for each *départment.*

The **Fédération des Stations vertes de vacances et Villages de neige** (6 rue Ranfer-de-Bretenières, BP 71698, 21016 Dijon Cedex, ☎ 03 80 54 10 50; www.stationsvertes.com) is an association which promotes 865 rural localities throughout France, selected for their natural appeal as well as for the quality of their environment, of their accommodation and of the leisure activities available.

FARM HOLIDAYS

The guide *Bienvenue à la ferme,* lists the addresses of farms providing guest facilities, which have been vetted for quality and for meeting official standards. For more information, apply to local tourist offices *(addresses above)* or to Service Agriculture et tourisme, 9 avenue George-V, 75008 Paris, ☎ 01 53 57 11 44; www.bienvenue-a-la-ferme.com.

HOSTELS, CAMPING

To obtain an **International Youth Hostel Federation** card (there is no age requirement, and there is a senior card available too) you should contact the IYHF in your own country for information and membership applications (US ☎ 202 783 6161; UK ☎ 01727 855215; Canada ☎ 613-273 7884; Australia ☎ 61-2-9565-1669). There is a new booking service on Internet *(iyhf.org)*, which you may use to reserve rooms as far as six months in advance.

The main youth hostel association *(auberges de jeunesse)* in France is the **Ligue Française pour les Auberges de la Jeunesse**, 67 rue Vergniaud, 75013 Paris, ☎ 01 44 16 78 78; www.auberges-de-jeunesse.com.

There are numerous officially graded **camp sites** with varying standards of facilities throughout the Languedoc-Roussillon region. The **Michelin Camping France** guide lists a selection of camp sites. The area is very popular with campers in the summer months, so it is wise to reserve in advance.

HIKERS

Hikers and those who enjoy bike touring, canoeing, etc., will find the guide *Gîtes d'étapes,* refuges by A and S Mouraret most useful. It is published by **Rando-Éditions**, BP 24, 65421 Ibos,

☎ 05 62 90 09 90; www.gites-refuges. com (order the catalogue on-line, consult the list of properties, or pay to consult the entire catalogue and book).

Finding a Restaurant

The Green Guide is pleased to offer a selection of restaurants for this region. The Address Books in the *Discovering the Region* section of the guide give descriptions and prices of typical places to eat with local flair. The Legend at the back of the guide explains the symbols and abbreviations used in the Address Books. Use The **Michelin Guide France**, with its famously reliable star-rating system and descriptions of hundreds of establishments all over France, for an even greater choice. If you would like to experience a meal in a highly rated restaurant from The Michelin Guide, be sure to book ahead! In the countryside, restaurants usually serve lunch between noon and 2pm and the evening meal between 7.30 and 10pm. It is not always easy to find something in-between those two meal times, as the "non-stop" restaurant is still a rarity in small towns in the provinces. However, a hungry traveller can usually get a sandwich in a café, and ordinary hot dishes may be available in a brasserie.

For information on local specialities, see the Introduction.

In French restaurants and cafés, a service charge is included. Tipping is not necessary, but French people often leave the small change from their bill on their table, or about 5% for the waiter in a nice restaurant.

For assistance in ordering a meal in France, see the Menu Reader on p 34.

Gourmet guide – The Languedoc region boasts some spots which appeal to the gourmet tourist interested in discovering local specialities. Among the places which have been awarded the *Site remarquable du goût* (for "remarkable taste sensations") distinction are the Aubrac area for its Laguiole and Fourme cheeses, the Rocher de Combalou for its Roquefort cheese, the Étangs de Thau for their production of oysters, and mussels, Banyuls for its sweet wine, Limoux for its Blanquette de Limoux, a sparkling white wine and Collioure for its anchovies.

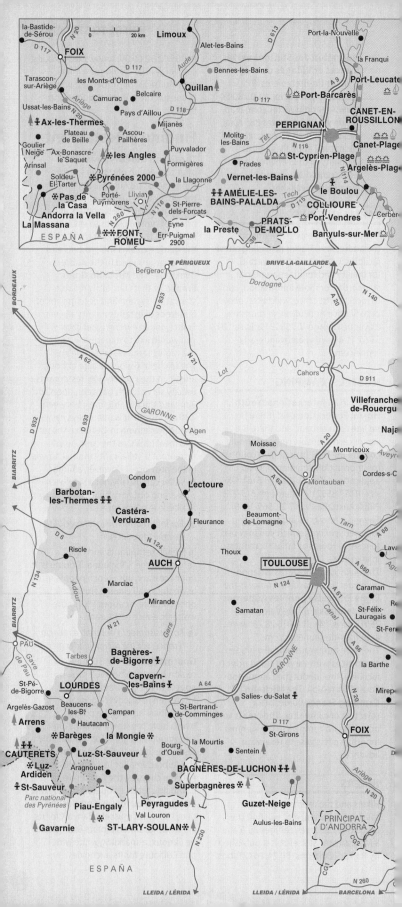

MENU READER

La Carte..The Menu

ENTRÉES .... STARTERS

Crudités ....Raw vegetable salad

Terrine de lapin ....Rabbit terrine (pâté)

Frisée aux lardons ....Curly lettuce with bacon bits

Escargots ....Snails

Cuisses de grenouille .... Frog's legs

Salade au crottin ....Goat cheese on a bed of lettuce

PLATS (VIANDES) ....MAIN COURSES (MEAT)

Bavette à l'échalote.................................Sirloin with shallots

Faux filet au poivre ....Sirloin with pepper sauce

Côtes d'agneau..Lamb chops

Filet mignon de porc .... Pork fillet

Blanquette de veau..................................Veal in cream sauce

Nos viandes sont garnies...... Our meat dishes are served with vegetables

PLATS (POISSONS, VOILAILLE) .... MAIN COURSES (FISH, FOWL)

Filets de sole ....Sole fillets

Dorade aux herbes .... Sea bream with herbs

Saumon grillé .... Grilled salmon

Coq au vin .... Chicken in red wine sauce

Poulet de Bresse rôti............Free-range roast chicken from the Bresse

Omelette aux morilles .... Wild-mushroom omelette

PLATEAU DE FROMAGES.................... SELECTION OF CHEESES

DESSERTS ....DESSERTS

Tarte aux pommes.. Apple pie

Crème caramel .... Cooled baked custard with caramel sauce

Sorbet: trois parfums ....Sherbet: choose 3 flavours

BOISSONS.. BEVERAGES

Bière.. Beer

Eau minérale (gazeuse) ....(Sparkling) mineral water

Une carafe d'eau ....Tap water (no charge)

Vin rouge, vin blanc, rosé ....Red wine, white wine, rosé

Jus de fruit ....Fruit juice

MENU ENFANT.................................CHILDREN'S MENU

Jambon..Ham

Steak haché .... Ground beef

Frites ....French fried potatoes

Well-done, medium, rare, raw = *bien cuit, à point, saignant, cru*

WHAT TO DO AND SEE

Sightseeing

TOURIST TRAINS

These are a pleasant and original way of exploring the region and seeing countryside which one might otherwise not reach by car or on foot. In the Cévennes, a little steam train runs between Anduze and St-Jean-du-Gard, via Prafrance bamboo plantation and following the courses of the Gardon rivers.

The **Autorail touristique du Minervois** takes passengers from Narbonne to Bize-Minervois, where the olive-growers cooperative can be visited; the train stops in Sallèdes-d'Aude on the way allowing passengers to visit Amphoralis (*see NARBONNE*).

The **Petit train des Lagunes** links Narbonne and Perpignan via Île Ste-Lucie and the lagoons lining the coastline.

The **Petit train jaune** (in service since 1895) offers a picturesque journey through the Cerdagne and Conflent regions; it runs between Latour-de-Carol and Villefranche-de-Conflent, once a day each way.

FROM ABOVE

For a bird's-eye-view of the region either as passenger or pilot, apply to flying clubs usually located within the perimeter of airports:

Fédération française de planeur ultra-léger motorisé, 96 bis rue Marc-Sangnier, BP 341, 94709 Maisons-Alfort Cedex, ☎ 01 49 81 74 50.

COOKING COURSES

If your favourite recreation takes place with pots and pans for equipment, why not spend 2 or 3 days in a French kitchen for a holiday? In the Gers, the season for preparing *foie gras* is generally from October to mid-December and from mid-January to April. A number of farmhouse-inns offer sessions which include lessons on preparing *foie gras, confits, cou farci* and other delights, as well as lodging and board. For information, contact:

Loisirs-Accueil du Gers, Maison de l'agriculture, route de Tarbes, BP 178, 32003 Auch Cedex, ☎ 05 62 61 79 00, Fax 05 62 61 79 09.

WINE-TASTING

Information on visiting wine-growing establishments and local wine cooperatives, many of which offer the opportunity to taste their products (in moderation of course), can be obtained from the following addresses:

Vins de pays d'Oc, Addresses of wine-growers and cooperatives are available from the Syndicat des Producteurs de Vin de Pays d'Oc, Domaine de Manse, avenue Paysagère, Maurin, 34970 Lattes, ☎ 04 67 13 84 20.

Wine tasting and guided tours of vineyards are organised by the:

Maison des Vins, 1 avenue de la Promenade, 34360 St-Chinian, ☎ 04 67 38 11 69; www.saint-chinian.com *(tasting of St-Chinian wine year-round daily 9am-noon and 2-6.30pm; St-Chinian wine festival on third Sunday in July).*

Maison des pays d'Agde, route de St-Thibéry, 34550 Bessan, ☎ 04 67 77 41 12; www.agde-vins.com *(tasting of AOC Picpoul-de-Pinet wine).*

Minervois – Syndicat du cru Minervois, Château de Siran, avenue du Château, 34210 Siran, ☎ 04 68 27 80 00.

Vins de l'Aveyron – Cave des vignerons des gorges du Tarn, 12520 Aguessac, ☎ 05 65 59 48 11 *(tasting of VDQS Côtes-de-Millau).*

A reserve of vintage wines at Banyuls

L. Campion/MICHELIN

Syndicat des vins VDQS Estaing, l'Escalière, 12190 Estaing, ☎ 05 65 44 75 38.

Syndicat des vins VDQS Entraygues-Le-Fel, Les Buis, 12140 Entraygues-sur-Truyère, ☎ 05 64 44 50 45.

Vins du Roussillon – Conseil Interprofessionnel des Vins du Roussillon, 19 avenue de Grande-Bretagne, 66000 Perpignan, ☎ 04 68 51 21 22, www.vins-du-roussillon.com.

Blanquette de Limoux – Contact the Syndicat des vins AOC de Limoux, 20 avenue du Pont-de-France, ☎ 04 68 31 12 83, or the tourist office at Limoux.

Vins des Corbières – Maison des Terroirs en Corbières, Le Château, 11200 Boutenac, ☎ 04 68 27 73 00; www.aoc-corbieres.com *(June to September daily, October to May weekdays only)*.

Cru Fitou – Maison des vignerons du Fitou, RN 9, aire de la Via Domitia, 11480 La Palme, ☎ 04 68 40 42 77; www.cru-fitou.com.

Gaillac – Comission Interprofessionnelle des Vins de Gaillac, Maison des Vins, Abbaye St-Michel, 81600 Gaillac, ☎ 05 63 57 70 60; www.vins-gaillac.com.

Madiran and Pacherenc du Vic-Bilh Maison des vins de Madiran et Pacherenc du Vic-Bilh, Le Prieuré, place de l'Église, 65700 Madiran, ☎ 05 62 31 90 67, Fax 05 62 31 90 79.

Armagnac and Floc de Gascogne Bureau national interprofessionnel de l'Armagnac AOC, 11 place de la Liberté, BP 3, 32800 Eauze, ☎ 05 62 08 11 00, Fax 05 62 68 11 01. Maison du Floc de Gascogne, rue des Vignerons, 32800 Eauze, ☎ 05 62 09 85 41.

Activities for Children

This region of France has a lot to offer children from swimming and playing in the sand along the sunny Mediterranean coast to having fun in amusement parks (Cap d'Agde, St-Cyprien-Plage, Narbonne-Plage, Port-Leucate and La Grande-Motte), or visiting zoos, safari parks, aquariums, museums and sights of special interest. See also Tourist trains above. Throughout the *Sights* section of the guide, your attention is drawn to activities particularly suited to children by the symbol [Kids].

Eco-Tourism

RIVER AND CANAL CRUISING

Rivers, canals and lakes offer numerous possibilities to enjoy pleasant boat trips (sometimes aboard craft of a bygone age), thus slowing down the pace and alleviating the stress of a busy touring holiday.

House-boats – House-boats with a capacity for 6 to 8 people enable visitors to get a different perspective on the region from the Canal du Midi, the Canal de la Robine or the Rhône-Sète canal. For boats with a horsepower of less than 10 it is not necessary to have a permit. Nautical maps and plan-guides are available from:

Éditions Grafocarte-Navicarte, 125 rue Jean-Jacques Rousseau, BP 40, 92132 Issy-les-Moulineaux Cedex, ☎ 01 41 09 19 00. Order the guide "Canaux du Midi" in English (internet orders: www.guide-fluvial.com).

Éditions du Plaisancier, 43 porte du Grand-Lyon, Neyron 01707 Miribel Cedex, ☎ 04 72 01 58 68; e-mail jacquartth@wanadoo.fr.

Companies from which houseboats can be hired (or contact local tourist offices for information):

Amica Tours, La Maison du Canal, Port Neuf, 8 rue des Péniches, 34500 Béziers, ☎ 04 67 62 18 18; www.adnavis.com.

Camargue Plaisance, Base fluviale de Carnon, 34280 Carnon, ☎ 04 67 50 77 00; www.camargueplaisance.com.

Caminav, Base fluviale, CD 62, 34280 Carnon, ☎ 04 67 68 01 90.

Connoisseur: Port de plaisance, 11800 Trèbes, ☎ 04 68 78 73 75, or 7 quai d'Alsace, 11100 Narbonne, ☎ 04 68 65 14 55, reservations ☎ 03 84 6 4 95 20.

Crown Blue Line, Port Cassafières, 34420 Portiragnes, ☎ 04 67 90 91 70, or Le grand bassin, BP 1201, 11492 Castelnaudry, ☎ 04 68 94 52 72; www.crown-blueline.com.

Gascogne Navigation, Capitainerie de Condom, quai de la Bouquerie, 32100 Condom, ☎ 05 62 28 46 46.

Locaboat Plaisance, Port Occitanie, 11120 Argens-Minervois, ☎ 04 68 27 03 33, reservations ☎ 03 86 91 72 72; www.locaboat.com.

Luc Lines: Quai des Tonneliers, BP 2, 11200 Homps, ☎ 04 68 91 33 00.

Nicols: Port du Somail, allée de la Glacière, 11120 Le Somail, b 04 68 46 00 97, reservations ☎ 02 41 56 46 56; www.nicols.com.

Rives de France, Port de plaisance, 34440 Colombiers, ☎ 04 67 37 14 60, reservations ☎ 0 810 80 80 80; www.rivedefrance.com.

Boat trips – Take a boat trip (sometimes aboard a traditional craft) of a few hours or more, without the responsibility of the helm, on the lakes of the Narbonne region, down the River Tarn, along the Canal du Midi or along the coast from Sète.

Trips aboard a passenger barge, & see CASTRES and ALBI.

Trips on the Garonne and Canal du Midi, Péniche Baladine and Le Capitole, & see TOULOUSE.

Trips on the Canal du Midi, Bateau Lucie, & see Canal du MIDI.

Trips on the River Baïse, Gascogne-Navigation, & see CONDOM.

Trips down the River Tarn, & see Gorges du TARN.

Sea trips, & see SÈTE.

NATIONAL AND REGIONAL NATURE PARKS

The reception and information centre for the **Parc national des Cévennes** is located in the Château de Florac, 6 bis place du Palais, 48400 Florac, ☎ 04 66 49 53 01. To view the latest information on park activities on Internet, go to *www.bsi.fr* and click on the Parc national des Cévennes link. Useful information on the park includes the Institut Géographique National (IGN) maps at a scale of 1:100 000 or 1:25 000, "Topo-guides" of the long-distance footpaths which cross the region and the tourist guide "Parc national des Cévennes" *(description and map,* & *see Le PONT-DE-MONTVERT in the Sights section).*
For information on the **Parc national des Pyrénées,** apply to 59 route de Pau, 65000 Tarbes, ☎ 05 62 44 36 60; www.parc-pyrenees.com. Several *Maisons du Parc* throughout the park provide information on the park's flora and fauna and on rambling opportunities in this mountainous area *(*& *description and map, see Parc national des PYRÉNÉES in the Sights section).*
The information centre of the **Parc naturel régional du Haut-Languedoc** is located at Maison du tourisme du Parc, place fu Foirail, 34220 St-Pons-de-Thomières, ☎ 04 67 97 06 65 *(description and map,* & *see SAINT-PONS-DE-THOMIÈRES in the Sights section).*
The **Parc naturel régional des Grands Causses** has its main office in Millau, at 71 avenue de l'Ayrolle, BP 126, 12101 Millau Cedex, ☎ 05 65 61 35 50 *(description and map,* & *see MILLAU in the Sights section).*

Outdoor Fun

WATER SPORTS

Swimming, water-skiing, sailing

Beaches – Since the project to clean up and develop the Languedoc coast, vast sandy beaches now stretch invitingly for miles, often sandwiched between the sea and lagoons. The

L. Campion/MICHELIN

The beach at Frontignan

best are to be found between La Grande-Motte and Palavas-les-Flots, from Sète to Cap-d'Agde, and around Cap-d'Agde and Valras.

Bathing conditions are indicated by flags on beaches which are surveyed by lifeguards (no flags means no lifeguards): green indicates it is safe to bathe and lifeguards are on duty; yellow warns that conditions are not that good, but lifeguards are still in attendance; red means bathing is forbidden as conditions are too dangerous.

Quality control tests take place regularly from June onwards. Well-equipped beaches offer facilities such as swimming pools, water-skiing, diving, jet skiing, landsailing, kite-flying, rowing etc. Information is available from local tourist offices.

Lakes and reservoirs – The main lakes and reservoirs with facilities for swimming and various water sports, including sailing and windsurfing, and where it is possible to go for walks or picnic on the lake shore, include: Bages, Sigean, Leucate, Ganguise, Jouarre (in the **Aude**); Pareloup, Pont-de-Salars, Villefranche-de-Panat (in the **Aveyron**); Les Camboux (in the Gard); La Ravière, Thau, Salagou (in the **Hérault**); Naussac, Villefort (in the **Lozère**), Matemale (in the **Pyrénées-Orientales**).

Useful addresses

Fédération française de Voile, 55 avenue Kléber, 75784 Paris Cedex 16, ☎ 01 44 05 81 00; www.ffvoile.org.

Ligue de voile du Languedoc-Roussillon, Maison départementale des Sports, 200 avenue du Père-Soulas, 34094 Montpellier Cedex 05, ☎ 04 67 41 78 35.

France Station Voile – Nautisme et Tourisme, 17 rue Boissière, 75116 Paris, ☎ 01 44 05 96 55; www.france-nautisme.com.

Fédération française de ski nautique, 27 rue d'Athènes, 75009 Paris, ☎ 01 53 20 19 19.

Marinas – The numerous marinas dotted along the coast offer pleasure craft over 100 000 moorings. They are shown on the map of *Places to Stay* at the beginning of the guide. Information is available from the various harbour master's offices or from the **Association des ports de plaisance du Languedoc-Roussillon**, Hôtel de Ville, 34250 Palavas-les-Flots, ☎ 04 67 07 73 50.

CANOEING, KAYAKING AND RAFTING

Canoeing is a popular family pastime on the peaceful waters of the region. **Kayaking** is practised on the lakes and, for more experienced paddlers, rapid sections of the rivers. The upper and middle valley of the Tarn, and the valleys of the Dourbie, the Orb, the Hérault and the Garonne among others are wonderful places to explore by canoe, with their beautiful scenery, stretches of rapids and tiny beaches ideal as picnic spots. Centres for canoeing have been set up in the Parc régional du Haut-Languedoc.

Various canoeing guides (to different stretches of river etc) and a map, *France canoe-kayak et sports d'eau*, are on sale from the **Fédération française de canoë-kayak**, 87 quai de la Marne, BP 58, 94344 Joinville-le-Pont, ☎ 01 45 11 08 50; www.ffcanoe. asso.fr.

Other useful addresses

Comité départemental de canoe-kayak de l'Ariège, Complexe sportif de l'Ayroule, 09000 Foix, ☎ 05 61 65 20 65.

L'Échappée Verte, 7 avenue Charles-Flahault, 34090 Montpellier, ☎ 04 67 41 20 24 (canoe and kayak trips throughout the region).

Rafting is the easiest of these freshwater sports, since it involves going down rivers in inflatable craft steered by an instructor; special equipment is provided.

Information from: **AN Tour**, 144 rue de Rivoli, 75001 Paris, ☎ 01 42 96 63 63; www.an-tours.com.

Canoeing in the Gorges de l'Ardèche at Pont d'Arc

J. Damase/MICHELIN

CANYONING, HYDROSPEED AND DIVING

Canyoning is a technique for body-surfing down narrow gorges and over falls, as though on a giant water slide, whereas **hydrospeed** involves swimming down rapids with a kickboard and flippers. These sports require protection: wear a wet suit and a helmet.

Information: 👂 see **AN Tour** *listing in Rafting*.

The list of **diving** clubs in the region is available from the **Fédération française d'études et de sports sous-marins**, 24 quai de Rive-Neuve, 13284 Marseille Cedex 07, ☎ 04 91 33 99 31; www.ffessm.fr.

FISHING

Freshwater fishing

A brochure called *Pêche en France* is available from the **Conseil Supérieur de la Pêche,** 134 avenue de Malakoff, 75116 Paris, ☎ 01 45 02 20 20. This can also be obtained from local branches of the **Fédérations départementales de Pêche et de Pisciculture** (at Albi, Carcassonne, Mende, Montpellier, Nîmes, Perpignan, Rodez, Tarbes and Toulouse).

Mountain lakes and streams of the Pyrenees region are ideal for trout fishing. Two-week holiday fishing permits are available in some areas – contact the local federation for details (or try local fishing tackle shops or tourist offices). For information on fishing regulations in the 20 or so lakes in the Bouillouses area, contact the tourist office in Font-Romeu.

SEA FISHING

Salt-water fishing can be practised on foot, from a boat or underwater with diving gear along the coast and in the lagoons where fish abound.

Information is available from the:

Fédération française des pêcheurs en mer, résidence Alliance, centre Jorlis, 64600 Anglet, ☎ 05 59 31 00 73

Fédération française Pêche Mer Languedoc-Roussillon, 12 rue Font-Martin, 34470 Pérols, ☎ 04 67 17 04 93.

HIKING

There is an extensive network of well-marked footpaths in France which make hiking or walking *(la randonnée)* easy. Several **Grande Randonnée (GR)** trails, recognisable by the red and white horizontal marks on trees, rocks and in town on walls, signposts etc go through the region, the most famous being, no doubt, the Santiago de Compostela trail from Moissac to St-Jean-Pied-de-Port (GR 65). Along with the GR trails are the **Petite Randonnée (PR)** paths, which are usually blazed with blue (2hr walk), yellow (2hr 15min – 3hr 45min) or green (4-6hr) marks. Of course, with appropriate maps, you can combine walks to suit your desires.

To use these trails, obtain the *"Topo-Guide"* for the area published by the **Fédération Française de la Randonnée Pédestre**, 14 rue Riquet, 75019 Paris, ☎ 01 44 89 93 90; www.ffrp.asso.fr. Some English-language editions are available as well as an annual guide (*"Rando Guide"*) which

---

Stepping Smart

Choosing the right equipment for a rambling expedition is essential: flexible hiking shoes with non-slip soles, a rain jacket or poncho, an extra sweater, sun protection (hat, glasses, lotion), drinking water (1-2l per person), high energy snacks (chocolate, cereal bars, bananas), and a first aid kit. Of course, you'll need a good map (and a compass if you plan to leave the main trails). Plan your itinerary well, keeping in mind that while the average walking speed for an adult is 4kph/2.5mph, you will need time to eat and rest, and children will not keep up the same pace. Leave your itinerary with someone before setting out (innkeeper or fellow camper).

Respect for nature is a cardinal rule and includes the following precautions: don't smoke or light fires in the forest, which are particularly susceptible in the dry summer months; always carry your rubbish out; leave wild flowers as they are; walk around, not through, farmers' fields; close gates behind you.

In the dry, rocky scrubland of the garrigues and the causses, walkers may come across the odd viper, so it is important to wear stout footwear, preferably with some protection around the ankle. Most of the time the snakes will make themselves scarce as soon as they hear someone coming, so make plenty of noise, and avoid lifting up rocks so as not to disturb any serpents slumbering beneath them.

includes ideas for overnight itineraries and places to stay together with information on the difficulty and accessibility of trails.

Another source of maps and guides for excursions on foot is the **Institut National Géographique (IGN),** which has a boutique in Paris at 107 rue de la Boétie (off the Champs-Elysées); to order from abroad, visit the Web site *(www.ign.fr)* for addresses of wholesalers in your country. Among their publications, France 1M903 is a map showing all of the GR and PR in France (4.90€); the *"Série Bleue"* and "Top 25" maps, at a scale of 1:25 000 (1cm=250m), show all paths, whether waymarked or not, as well as refuges, camp sites, beaches etc (7-9€). In the region, you can find many of the publications cited above in bookstores, at sports centres or equipment shops, and in some of the country inns and hotels which cater to the sporting crowd. The **Globe Corner Bookstore** (Cambridge, MA ☎ 617 497 6277) has a wide selection of books and maps for travellers on offer via internet: *www. globecorner.com.*

Suggestions and useful addresses

The **Parc National des Pyrénées** is a paradise for hikers, whether your expedition is planned for half a day or includes overnight stops. July through September, mountain refuges under park surveillance are open to accommodate 30-40 people a night; there are also smaller, year-round refuges which are not guarded. In the summer, it is imperative to reserve in advance. One or two-night stays are generally the rule; some refuges may provide meals prepared by the guardian (◖ *see Parc National des PYRÉNÉES).*

La Balaguère, 65400 Arrens-Marsous, ☎ 05 62 97 20 21; www.balaguere. com, organises hiking trips in the Pyrenees, sometimes round a theme (history, flora, fauna…).

Chamina Sylva, BP 5, 48300 Langogne, ☎ 04 66 69 00 44, organises hikes with or without guide in the southern part of the Massif Central and in the Pyrenees.

It is also possible to follow **herds** on their way to summer pastures in the Aubrac region (apply to the tourist office in St-Chély-d'Aubrac, ☎ 05 65 44 21 15) or to take a **donkey** with you to carry your gear if you plan a long walking tour (contact the **Fédération**

Hiking on Mont Lozère

nationale ânes et randonnées, Le Pré du Meinge, 26560 Eourres, ☎ 04 92 65 09 07; www.ane-et-rando.com, for a list of organisers).

The **Association "Sur le chemin de R.L. Stevenson",** 48220 Le Pont-de-Montvert, ☎/Fax 04 66 45 86 31; www.chemin-stevenson.org, provides a list of B&B, hotels, restaurants, places where donkeys can be hired and tourist offices along the itinerary followed by Stevenson in 1878 and described in his *Travels With a Donkey in the Cévennes.*

CYCLING AND MOUNTAIN BIKING

Many GR and GRP footpaths are accessible to mountain bikers. However, in areas particularly suitable for cycling, there are special trails waymarked by the **Fédération française de cyclisme** (5 rue de Rome, 93561 Rosny-sous-Bois Cedex, ☎ 01 49 35 69 24; www.ffc.fr); these are graded in difficulty *(green is easy; blue is fairly easy; red is difficult; black is very difficult);* ask for the *"Guide des centres VTT",* which supply itineraries and brochures as well as information on where to stay and where to call for urgent repairs.

The **Office national des Forêts** publishes some 20 mountain-biking guides under the general heading *VTT Évasion,* focusing on the discovery of the Languedoc-Roussillon forests. These guides are available from the Comité régional du tourisme Languedoc-Roussillon (◖ *see Planning your trip, Local tourist offices).*

For additional information about cycling clubs, rental etc, contact the **Fédération française de cyclotourisme** (12 rue Louis-Bertrand, 94200 Ivry-sur-Seine, ☎ 01 56 20 88 88; www.ffct.org), the **Ligue** régionale de cyclotourisme du Languedoc-Roussillon (M. Morand Guy, 4 rue Ernest-Vieu, 11000 Narbonne, ☎ 04 68 32 52 62) as well as local tourist offices.

RIDING TOURS

There are numerous itineraries suitable for riding tours through forested areas, across the causses and along the main river valleys.

The **Comité national du tourisme équestre** (9 boulevard MacDonald, 75019 Paris, ☎ 01 53 26 15 50; www. eii.fr) publishes a brochure updated yearly, *Cheval Nature, l'Officiel du Tourisme Équestre en France,* listing horse-riding leisure activities throughout France. In addition, this organisation will give you the address of the nearest Comité départemental du tourisme équestre (CDTE) who can provide maps and brochures and lists of riding centres in your area.

It is also possible to contact regional associations directly:

Association régionale pour le tourisme équestre et l'équitation de loisirs en Languedoc-Roussillon (ATECREL), 14 rue des Logis, 34140 Loupian, ☎ 04 67 43 82 50.

Ligue Midi-Pyrénées Tourisme Équestre (ARTEMIP) 31 chemin des Lanalets, 31400 Toulouse, ☎ 05 61 14 04 58; www.artemip.com.

EXPLORING CAVES

Some of the numerous caves and chasms in the region, such as the avens (swallow-holes) of the limestone plateaux, are among the most famous in France. Exploring caves can be a dangerous pastime; it is therefore essential to have the right equipment and be accompanied by a qualified guide – many local clubs can provide both. For more information contact:

Fédération française de Spéléologie, 130 rue St-Maur, 75011 Paris, ☎ 01 43 57 56 54.

École française de Spéléologie, 28 rue Delondine, 69002 Lyon, ☎ 04 72 56 35 76.

Comité régional de Spéléologie Midi-Pyrénées, 7 rue André-Citroën, 31130 Balma, ☎ 05 61 11 71 60.

GOLF

The Michelin map Golf, les parcours français (French golf courses) will help you locate golf courses in the region covered by this guide.

For further information, contact the **Fédération française de golf**, 68 rue Anatole-France, 92309 Levallois-Perret Cedex, ☎ 01 41 49 77 00; www.ffg.org.

The **Comité régional de tourisme Languedoc-Roussillon** (& *see Planning your trip, Local tourist offices*) proposes a golf pass (150€) for five days' green fees, which can be used on 20 different courses during 21 consecutive days, allowing holders to play on the same course on two consecutive days. The golf courses in the scheme in the region covered by this guide are Carcassonne, Montpellier-Massane, Montpellier-Fontcaude, Béziers, Le Cap-d'Agde, La Grande Motte, La Canourgue, Langogne, La Garde-Guérin, Font-Romeu, St-Cyprien and St-Laurens-de-Cerdans. Reservations can be made at the golf course of your choice 48hr in advance.

MOUNTAIN SPORTS

Safety first is the rule for beginners and old hands when it comes to exploring the mountains as a climber, skier or hiker. The risk associated with avalanches, mud slides, falling rocks, bad weather, fog, glacially cold waters, the dangers of becoming lost or miscalculating distances, should not be underestimated.

Avalanches occur naturally when the upper layer of snow is unstable, in particular after heavy snowfalls, and may be set off by the passage of numerous skiers or hikers over a precise spot. A scale of risk, from 1 to 5, has been developed and is posted daily at resorts and bases for hiking trails. It is important to consult this *Bulletin Neige et Avalanche* (BNA) before setting off on any expeditions cross-country or off-piste. You can also call toll free ☎ 08 92 68 10 20 *(in French)*.

Lightning storms are often preceded by sudden gusts of wind, and put climbers and hikers in danger. In the event, avoid high ground, and do not move along a ridge top; do not seek shelter under overhanging rocks, isolated trees in otherwise open areas, at the entrance to caves or other openings in the rocks, or in the proximity of metal fences or gates

For general information on mountain sports in the Pyrenees, apply to:

Centre d'information Montagne et Sentiers (CIMES-Pyrénées), 1 rue Maye-Lane, 65420 Ibos, ☎ 05 62 90 09 92; www.cimes-pyrenees.net. Mountain guides suggest a choice of guided activities from cross-country skiing and snowshoeing to climbing, rafting and mountain biking.

Bureau des guides de Luchon,
18 allée d'Étigny, 31110 Luchon, ☎ 05 61 79 69 38

Bureau des guides de St-Savin,
1 place du Trey, 65400 St-Savin, ☎ 05 62 97 91 09

Bureau des guides de la vallée de Cauterets,
2 place Georges-Clemenceau, 65110 Cauterets, ☎ 05 62 92 62 02

Bureau des guides de la vallée de Luz, 1 pl du 8-Mai, 65120 Luz-St-Sauveur, ☎ 05 62 92 87 28

Bureau des guides de la vallée d'Aure, 65170 St-Lary-Soulan, ☎ 05 62 40 02 58

Bureau des guides des vallées d'Ax,
11 rue du Gén.-de-Gaulle, 09110 Ax-les-Thermes, ☎ 05 61 64 31 51

CLIMBING

The Pyrenees, the Cévennes and even the deep Tarn Gorges provide excellent conditions for climbing with the assistance of local guides (see above). Beginners should take advantage of the numerous courses available to learn a few basic techniques. For additional information, contact:

Fédération française de la Montagne et de l'Escalade, 8-10 quai de la Marne, 75019 Paris, ☎ 01 40 18 75 50; www.ffme.fr.

The *Guide des sites naturels d'escalade en France* by D Taupin (published by Cosiroc/FFME) provides the location of all the rock-climbing sites in France.

SKIING

Southern part of the Massif Central – The wide expanses of the Aubrac, Mont Lozère and around the Aigoual summit lend themselves perfectly to cross-country skiing in the winter. *Consult the Map of places to stay pp 32-33.*

Further details can be obtained from local tourist offices or:

Comité Régional de Ski Cévennes-Languedoc, Espace République, 20 rue de la République, 34000 Montpellier, ☎ 04 67 22 94 92.

Comité départemental de ski en Lozère, Maison départementale des sports, rue du Faubourg-Montbel, 48000 Mende, ☎ 04 66 49 12 12.

Office de tourisme, place du Foirail, 12210 Laguiole, ☎ 05 65 44 35 94.

Pyrenees – In the central Pyrenees, there are **valley resorts**, with high curving slopes and plateaux (Cauterets, St-Lary, Superbagnères) and **mountaintop resorts** which, with the exception of Barèges, the cradle of Pyrenean skiing, are entirely contemporary communities (Arette-Pierre-St-Martin, Gourette, La Mongie, Plau-Engaly). Some of the resorts in the Pyrenees are comparable, in facilities and slopes, to their Alpine counterparts.

The snowy slopes of the Ariège and the Catalan Pyrenees are well equipped with facilities for all sorts of snow sports, including some of the more recent activities such as para-skiing or snow motorbikes. To compensate for uneven snowfall, most ski resorts have snow cannon. Cross-country skiing has been practised as a sport in the Pyrenees since 1910, and it is made all the more enjoyable beneath the Mediterranean sunshine of the Capcir and Cerdagne regions. The Capcir in particular is covered by a network of cross-country ski tracks linking all the villages.

Andorra – www.skiandorra.com

Useful tips – Always bear ski-slope etiquette in mind when out on the piste: never set off without checking that the way uphill and downhill is clear; skiers coming from farther up the slope must give way to skiers downhill from them; never ignore signposts; beware of the danger of avalanches on loosely packed snow (especially skiing off-piste). If in any doubt, check the rules at the ski resort before setting off.

HANG-GLIDING, PARAGLIDING AND KITE-FLYING

If you are up for a faster-paced, wider view of the landscape, head for the wild blue yonder. On **hang-gliders** *(deltaplanes)*, fliers suspend themselves from what is little more

SKI RESORTS	SKI LIFTS	CROSS-COUNTRY TRACKS (KM)	N° OF DOWNHILL SLOPES
Les Angles	25	102	32
Ascou-Pailhères	–	5	15
Ax-Bonascre-Le Saquet	–	60	25
Bourg-d'Oueil	–	14	3
Espace Cambre d'Aze	17	8	25
Camurac	7	15	16
Cauterets	15	36	25
Chioula	-	60	-
Err-Puigmal 2600	8	10	18
Font-Romeu	33	80	40
Formiguères	8	53	18
Gavarnie-Gèdre	11	7	21
Guzet-Neige	20	4	28
Hautacam-Ski	11	15	18
Luchon-Superbagnères	14	4	24
Luz-Ardiden	19	5	32
Mijanès-Donezan	5	36	9
Les Monts d'Olmes	13	-	23
Le Mourtis	-	11	20
Ordino (Andorra)	14	3	25
Pal-Arinsal (Andorra)	31	23	41
Pas de la Casa (Andorra)	31	12	55
Peyragudes	17	15	38
Piau	21	-	38
Plateau de Beille	-	65	1
Porté-Puymorens	12	21	16
Puyvalador	7	5	16
Pyrénées 2000	32	90	40
St-Lary-Soulan	48	10	48
Soldeu-El-Tarter (Andorra)	29	3	52
Tourmalet: Barèges and La Mongie	57	2.5	64

than a rudimentary, kite-like wing and work the updraughts along cliffs and bluffs; this requires skill and practice. Almost anyone with the willpower to jump off a cliff can give **paragliding** *(parapente)* a try (with the assistance of trained professionals, of course). Warm and cold air currents carry you, strapped in a harness attached to a sort of rectangular parachute, across the valley and down.

A number of centres offer instruction and rent materials, particularly in the following areas: around Millau, in the Grands Causses, around Marvejols and Mende and in the Pyrenees (Barèges, Campan, Peyragudes, Superbagnères, Moulis near St-Girons, Prat d'Albi near Foix).

Kite-flying is a popular activity in the region, particularly on the beaches of Languedoc-Roussillon. To obtain a good kite and learn how to fly it, it is advisable to join a club or an association (addresses are available from local tourist offices).

General information (hang-gliding, paragliding and kite-flying) is available from: **Fédération Française de Vol Libre**, 4 rue de Suisse, 06000 Nice, ☎ 04 97 03 82 82; www.ffvl.fr.

SPECTATOR SPORT – RUGBY

Rugby is big in the South-West. An early form of the game was practised in France and Great Britain in the Middle Ages, and folks have been playing rugby as we know it since 1900. This popular sport has its own periodical *(Midi Olympique)*. Although two types of rugby (teams of 13 or 15) are played throughout the Midi, Rugby Union (15 players) is the more common. Every town and village has its team, and passions run high as enthusiastic supporters follow their team's progress in the weekly Sunday matches which take place from October to May.

Women's teams mostly play "touch" rugby, without tackling each other to the ground (*Les Lionnes* in Auch).

More information is available from the **Fédération française de rugby,** 9 rue de Liège, 75431 Paris Cedex 09, ☎ 01 53 21 15 39; www. ffr.fr and www. xvfrance.com.

Spas and Sea-Water Therapy

SPAS

🕭 *The spa resorts in this region are shown on the map of Places to Stay.*

The Pyrenees are home to numerous mineral and thermal springs, which have brought fame to the area for their health restoring qualities since Antiquity. The differing properties of the springs mean that a wide range of therapeutic remedies can be offered. The earlier fashion for taking the waters has continued as modern visitors flock to spa resorts to treat a variety of afflictions, mostly respiratory or rheumatic. Pyrenean spas fall into two categories: sulphurated or salt water springs.

Sulphurated springs – These are situated mainly in the central Pyrenees, stretching towards the Mediterranean, from Ax-les-Thermes to Balaruc-les-Bains. Their waters can reach temperatures up to 80°C/176°F. Sulphur, highly valued by the Greeks for its medical properties, is present in the form of chloro-sulphates or sodium sulphates. Sulphurated spa waters are used (baths, showers and inhalations) to treat a number of illnesses of the ears, nose, throat and respiratory tract, rheumatism or bone disorders, renal infections and female complaints. The main spa resorts in this category are **Cauterets, Bagnères-de-Luchon, Saint-Sauveur, Ax-les-Thermes, Amélie-les-Bains, Bagnols-les-Bains and Balaruc-les-Bains.**

Salt water springs – These are to be found along the line of the primary massif. They differ in mineralogical composition from sulphated, or solutions of chalky bicarbonate of soda, known as "sedative" waters, to sodium chlorinated waters. The first type (found at **Ussat-les-Bains, Alet-les-Bains, Le Boulou, Lamalou-les-Bains** etc) are used in the treatment of diseases of the nervous system, liver and kidneys. The second type (Ussat-les-Bains), used as baths or showers, can be helpful for gynaecological complaints, skin complaints or infants' diseases. Finally, the complex mineralogical composition of the water in **Avène-les-Bains** makes it particularly suitable for the treatment of skin diseases.

The Michelin Guide France indicates the official dates of the beginning and end of the spa season.

Useful addresses

Chaîne thermale du Soleil/Maison du Thermalisme, 32 avenue de l'Opéra, 75002 Paris, ☎ 01 44 71 37 00; www.sante-eau.com.

Union Nationale des Établissements Thermaux, 1 rue Cels, 75014 Paris, ☎ 01 53 91 05 75; www.france-thermale.org.

SEA-WATER THERAPY

Known as *thalassothérapie* in French, this kind of cure has increased in popularity in recent years, despite the fact that it is not considered a proper "medical" cure (and so is not reimbursed under the French social security system). Sea water has certain properties which make it useful in beauty treatments and cures for stress, back problems, expectant mothers etc. The main centres in Languedoc-Roussillon are at **La Grande-Motte, Cap-d'Agde, Port-Barcarès** and **Banyuls-sur-Mer,** which cater for cures lasting anything from a day to several weeks, with or without accommodation included.

Useful addresses

Fédération Mer et Santé, 8 rue de l'Isly, 75008 Paris, ☎ 01 44 70 07 57; www.mer-et-sante.asso.fr.

Maison de la Thalassothérapie, 5 rue Denis-Poisson, 75017 Paris, ☎ 08 25 07 97 07.

Calendar of Events

The list below is a selection of the many events which take place in the regions described in this guide. Visitors are advised to contact local tourist offices for fuller details of musical events, *son et lumière* shows, arts and crafts fairs, etc, especially during July and August.

Traditional festivities, fairs and historical pageants

SATURDAYS AND SUNDAYS FROM JANUARY TO MARCH

Limoux

Traditional carnival with 3 parades at 11am, 5pm and 9pm; Sunday before Palm Sunday, at midnight, judgment is passed on the Carnival King followed by an all-night *"Blanquette"* party. ☎ 04 68 31 11 82.

FEBRUARY

Prats-de-Mollo, Arles-sur-Tech, St-Laurent-de-Cerdans

Traditinal carnival and *"Fête de l'Ours"* (bear festival).

Albi

Carnival (2nd week of the month)

Toulouse

"Fête de la Violette" (violet festival)

GOOD FRIDAY

Arles-sur-Tech

Evening procession by the Pénitents noirs. ☎ 04 68 39 11 99.

Collioure

Procession by the Penitents' brotherhoods (9pm). www.collioure.com.

Perpignan

Procession by the Pénitents de la Sanch. ☎ 04 68 66 30 30. www.perpignantourisme.com.

PALM SUNDAY, EASTER DAY AND EASTER MONDAY

St-Félix-Lauragais

"Fête historique de la Cocagne" (concerts, circus, jugglers, historical pageant). ☎ 05 62 18 96 99.

SUNDAY NEAR 25 MAY

Aubrac

"Fête de la transhumance": livestock taken up to summer pastures.

JUNE

Perpignan

Saint-Jean Festa Major (with midsummer bonfires around 21 June).

Nasbinals

Handicraft and antique fair (3rd Sunday).

JULY

Sète

Festival of St Peter (1st weekend).

Céret

"Céret de Toros": various events involving bulls (fighting, racing etc), sardana dancing (2nd weekend). ☎ 04 68 87 00 53.

Carcassonne

Medieval Cité is "set alight" by an evening firework display (14 July).

Cordes

"Fête médiévale du Grand Fauconnier" (historical pageant and various other "medieval" entertainments, mid-July). ☎ 05 63056 03 76.

Frontignan

Muscat festival. ☎ 04 67 18 50 04.

Bize Minervoi

"Fête de l'olivier" (olive tree festival; 3rd weekend).

Cap d'Agde

"Fête de la Mer" (sea festival; last weekend).

JULY - AUGUST

Foix

Son et lumière show, "Il était une Foix... l'Ariège" (scenes from local history). ☎ 05 61 02 88 26.

Lastours

Son et lumière show. ☎ 04 68 77 04 95.

Agde

"Joutes nautiques" (sea jousting). ☎ 04 67 94 44 73.

AUGUST

Lautrec
Garlic festival (1st Friday).

Bread festival (15 August)

Gaillac
Wine festival (1st weekend).

Vic-Fezensac
Feria (1st week).

Mirepoix
Pottery fair (2nd Tuesday and Wednesday).

Medieval festival (3rd weekend). ☎ 05 61 68 83 76.

Carcassonne
Medieval pageants and tournaments including jousting and falconry demonstrations. ☎ 04 68 10 24 30.

Béziers
"Féria" (around 15 August). ☎ 04 67 36 76 76.

Palavas-les-Flots
Jousting by night on the canal (14 and 15 August).

Sète
Festival of St Louis: *"joutes nautiques"*, fireworks displays, swimming across Sète (3rd or 4th week in the month). www.ville-sete.fr.

Osséja
International sheep-dog trials (2nd Sunday in the month). ☎ 04 68 04 53 86.

Bagnères-de-Luchon
Flower festival (last Sunday).

Bouzigues
Oyster fair (1st weekend in the month). ☎ 04 67 78 3 2 93.

Tarascon-sur-Ariège
European archery championships (using prehistoric weapons).

SEPTEMBER

Mialet
French Protestant gathering at Mas Soubeyran (1st Sunday in the month). ☎ 04 66 85 02 72.

Méritxell
National festival of Andorra. ☎ (376) 82 02 14 (8 September).

OCTOBER

Béziers
Festival of new wine (dancing, blessing of new wine etc).

Montpellier
International fair. ☎ 04 67 17 67 17. www.foire-montpellier.com.

NOVEMBER

Nasbinals
Horse fair (7 November).

Festivals

APRIL TO OCTOBER

Parc national des Cévennes
Nature festival: themed hikes, exhibitions, lectures, shows, fairs and markets. www.cevennes-parcnational.fr.

LATE JUNE

Toulouse
Garonne le Festival: rock, jazz, pop, tango dancing, visual arts. ☎ 05 61 25 96 93.

LAST WEEK IN JUNE AND 1ST WEEK IN JULY

Montpellier
"Montpellier-Danse" (traditional music and dance festival). ☎ 04 67 60 83 60.

JULY

Carcassonne
"Festival de la Cité" (concerts, theatre, opera, dance etc). ☎ 04 68 11 59 15.

Luz-St-Sauveur
"Jazz à Luz" (early July). ☎ 05 62 92 38 38.

St-Guilhem-le-Désert
Musical season at the abbey (1st fortnight). ☎ 04 67 57 44 33.

La Grande-Motte
Jazz festival (2nd fortnight). ☎ 04 67 56 40 50.

Montpellier
"Festival de Radio-France et de Montpellier Languedoc-Roussillon" (opera, symphonies, chamber music, jazz; 2nd fortnight). ☎ 04 67 02 02 01.

Perpignan
"Estivales" (theatre festival).

Albi
"L'Été de musique en Albigeois" (2nd fortnight). ☎ 05 63 49 48 80.

Castres
Extravadanses: dance festival (2nd fortnight). ☎ 05 63 71 56 58.

Montauban

Jazz festival (2nd fortnight). ☎ 05 63 20 46 72.

Céret

International Sardana festival (400 dancers in costume; 2nd fortnight). ☎ 04 68 87 00 53.

Cordes-sur-Ciel

"Musiques sur Ciel" music festival (late July-early August). ☎ 05 63 56 00 75.

JULY – AUGUST

Toulouse

Summer music festival (classical, jazz, folk). ☎ 05 61 11 02 33.

Conques

Music festival (mid-July to end of August). ☎ 05 65 71 24 00.

Moissac

Musical evenings. ☎ 05 63 04 0 6 81.

St-Michel-de-Cuxa-Prades

Pablo Casals festival (concerts in the abbey, mid-July to mid-August). ☎ 04 68 96 33 07.

St-Bertrand-de-Comminges, St-Just-de-Valcabrère, St-Girons

"Festival du Comminges", mid-July to end of August). ☎ 05 61 88 32 00.

Le Vigan

Classical music festival (mid-July to end of August). ☎ 0 1 47 01 05 57.

Abbaye de Sylvanès

International festival of sacred music. ☎ 05 65 98 20 20. www.sylvanes.com.

AUGUST

Mirepoix

Puppet festival (1st weekend). ☎ 05 61 68 83 76.

Amélie-les-Bains

International folklore festival (2nd week). ☎ 04 68 39 01 98.

Sète

Festival Latino: Mediterranean music (early August). ☎ 04 67 46 05 06.

Pont-de-Salars

International folklore festival (2nd week). ☎ 05 65 46 80 67. www.festival-rouergue.com.

Banyuls-sur-Mer

Sardana festival (2nd weekend). ☎ 04 68 88 31 50.

SEPTEMBER

Toulouse

Piano recitals at Les Jacobins. ☎ 05 61 22 40 05.

OCTOBER

Perpignan

Jazz festival; ☎ 04 68 66 30 30.

Shopping

BUSINESS HOURS

Most of the larger shops are open Mondays to Saturdays from 9am to 6.30 or 7.30pm. Smaller, individual shops may close during the lunch hour. Food shops – grocers, wine merchants and bakeries – are generally open from 7am to 6.30 or 7.30pm; some open on Sunday mornings. Many food shops close between noon and 2pm and on Mondays. Bakery and pastry shops sometimes close on Wednesdays. Hypermarkets usually stay open non-stop from 9am until 9pm or later.

People travelling to the USA cannot import plant products or fresh food, including fruit, cheeses and nuts. It is acceptable to carry tinned products or preserves.

VALUE ADDED TAX

In France a sales tax (TVA or Value Added Tax ranging from 5.5% to 19.6%) is added to almost all retail goods – it can be worth your while to recover it. VAT refunds are available to visitors from outside the EU only if purchases exceed US$200 per store, but repeat visits to a store can be combined. The system works in large stores which cater to tourists, in luxury stores and other shops advertising "Duty Free". Show your passport, and

Handcrafted espadrilles

J. Aalburet/MICHELIN

the store will complete a form which is to be stamped (at the airport) by a European customs agent. The sum due can be collected at the airport or by mailing the forms from home.

MARKETS AND LOCAL SPECIALITIES

Traditional markets known as *marchés au gras* were previously held in winter months only for the sale of ducks and geese, prepared and raw livers. The most picturesque of these markets are now held in Samatan *(Gers)* on Mondays year-round and in Mirande *(Gers)* on Mondays from November through March.

LOCAL SPECIALITIES

Gastronomy – Apart from foie gras and confit (duck or goose preserved in its own fat), the region is rich in gastronomic products: cassoulet from the Toulouse region (tinned), thrush pâté from Le Vigan, honey from the Cévennes, nougat from Limoux, cured ham and varied charcuterie from the mountainous areas, not forgetting mouth-watering cheeses such as Roquefort (made from ewe's milk) and Fourme de Laguiole. The region also offers a choice of red, rosé and white wines, natural sweet wines and stronger beverages such as Armagnac enjoyed after a copious meal.

Handicraft – Glazed pottery adds a touch of colour to most local markets in the Cévennes and Languedoc regions, whereas the Cerdagne specialises in rope-soled shoes ideal for summer wear. The acquisition of a Laguiole knife is a must for anyone visiting the region…and you don't need to go to Laguiole for it, although a visit to the authentic workshops situated in the village is an interesting experience. The Pyrenees are famous for the softness of their woollen blankets and pullovers, which can be bought directly from the manufacturers.

BASIC INFORMATION

Electricity

The electric current is 220 volts. Circular two-pin plugs are the rule. Adapters and converters (for hairdryers, for example) should be bought before you leave home; they are on sale in most airports. If you have a rechargeable device (video camera, portable computer, battery recharge), read the instructions carefully or contact the manufacturer or shop. Sometimes these items only require a plug adapter; in other cases you must use a voltage converter as well or risk ruining your device.

Public Holidays

Public services, museums and other monuments may be closed or may vary their hours of admission on the following public holidays:

1 January	New Year's Day (Jour de l'An)
	Easter Day and Easter Monday (Pâques)
1 May	May Day (Fête du Travail)
8 May	VE Day (Fête de la Libération)
Thurs 40 days after Easter	Ascension Day (Ascension)
7th Sun-Mon after Easter	Whit Sunday and Monday (Pentecôte)
14 July	France's National Day (Fête de la Bastille)
15 August	Assumption (Assomption)
1 November	All Saint's Day (Toussaint)
11 November	Armistice Day (Fête de la Victoire)
25 December	Christmas Day (Noël)

National museums and art galleries are closed on Tuesdays; municipal museums are generally closed on Mondays. In addition to the usual school holidays at Christmas and in the spring and summer, there are long mid-term breaks (10 days to a fortnight) in February and early November.

Mail/Post

Post offices open Mondays to Fridays, 8am to 7pm, Saturdays, 8am to noon. Smaller branch post offices often close at lunchtime between noon and 2pm and in the afternoon at 4pm.

Postage via air mail to

UK:
> ✉ letter (20g) 0.50€

North America:
> ✉ letter (20g) 0.90€

Australia and NZ:
> ✉ letter (20g) 0.90€

Stamps are also available from newsagents and tobacconists.
Stamp collectors should ask for *timbres de collection* in any post office.
Poste Restante (General Delivery) mail should be addressed as follows: Name, Poste Restante, Poste Centrale, post code of the *département* followed by town name, France. **The Michelin Guide France** gives local post codes.

Discounts

Significant discounts are available for senior citizens, students, young people under the age of 25, teachers, and groups for public transportation, museums and monuments and for some leisure activities such as the cinema (at certain times of day). Bring student or senior cards with you, and bring along some extra passport-size photos for discount travel cards.

The **International Student Travel Confederation** (www.isic.org), global administrator of the International Student and Teacher Identity Cards, is an association of student travel organisations around the world. ISTC members collectively negotiate benefits with airlines, governments, and providers of other goods and services for the student and teacher community, both in their own country and around the world. The non-profit association sells international ID cards for students, under 25-year-olds and teachers (who may get discounts on museum entrances, for example). The ISTC is also active in a network of international education and work exchange programmes. The corporate headquarters address is Herengracht 479, 1017 BS Amsterdam, The Netherlands ☎ 31 20 421 28 00; Fax 31 20 421 28 10.

Carte Intersites Terre Catalane
– This "passport" is available at many sites in the area where the Catalonia culture and traditions are still strongly felt. Visitors pay the full price at the first site they tour, and thereafter the

Conversion Tables

Weights and measures

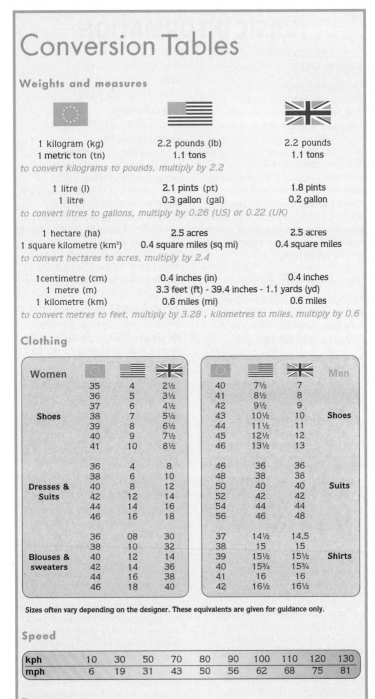

| 1 kilogram (kg) | 2.2 pounds (lb) | 2.2 pounds |
| 1 metric ton (tn) | 1.1 tons | 1.1 tons |

to convert kilograms to pounds, multiply by 2.2

| 1 litre (l) | 2.1 pints (pt) | 1.8 pints |
| 1 litre | 0.3 gallon (gal) | 0.2 gallon |

to convert litres to gallons, multiply by 0.26 (US) or 0.22 (UK)

| 1 hectare (ha) | 2.5 acres | 2.5 acres |
| 1 square kilometre (km²) | 0.4 square miles (sq mi) | 0.4 square miles |

to convert hectares to acres, multiply by 2.4

1 centimetre (cm)	0.4 inches (in)	0.4 inches
1 metre (m)	3.3 feet (ft) - 39.4 inches - 1.1 yards (yd)	
1 kilometre (km)	0.6 miles (mi)	0.6 miles

to convert metres to feet, multiply by 3.28 . kilometres to miles, multiply by 0.6

Clothing

Women / Men

Women							Men
	35	4	2½	40	7½	7	
	36	5	3½	41	8½	8	
	37	6	4½	42	9½	9	
Shoes	38	7	5½	43	10½	10	**Shoes**
	39	8	6½	44	11½	11	
	40	9	7½	45	12½	12	
	41	10	8½	46	13½	13	
	36	4	8	46	36	36	
	38	6	10	48	38	38	
Dresses &	40	8	12	50	40	40	**Suits**
Suits	42	12	14	52	42	42	
	44	14	16	54	44	44	
	46	16	18	56	46	48	
	36	08	30	37	14½	14,5	
	38	10	32	38	15	15	
Blouses &	40	12	14	39	15½	15½	**Shirts**
sweaters	42	14	36	40	15¾	15¾	
	44	16	38	41	16	16	
	46	18	40	42	16½	16½	

Sizes often vary depending on the designer. These equivalents are given for guidance only.

Speed

kph	10	30	50	70	80	90	100	110	120	130
mph	6	19	31	43	50	56	62	68	75	81

Temperature

Celsius (°C)	0°	5°	10°	15°	20°	25°	30°	40°	60°	80°	100°
Fahrenheit (°F)	32°	41°	50°	59°	68°	77°	86°	104°	140°	176°	212°

To convert Celsius into Fahrenheit, multiply °C by 9, divide by 5, and add 32.
To convert Fahrenheit into Celsius, subtract 32 from °F, multiply by 5, and divide by 9.

passport entitles them to reductions of up to 60% at the other sites. Each site is associated with a walking tour or hike (1 to 3hr, not climbing more than 400m/1 300yd from the starting point). The sites are: Ste-Léocadie, Eyne, Villefranche-de-Conflent, St-Michel-de-Cuixa, Prades, Serrabone, Bélesta, Ille-sur-Têt, Castelnou, Tautavel, Salses, Perpignan, Elne, Saint-Génis-des-Fontaines, Saint-Martin-du-Canigou, Arles-sur-Tech, Prats-de-Mollo, Céret, Coullioure, Marcevol, Mont-Louis, Le Pertus, Corneilla-de-Conflent, St-Martin-de-Fenollar *(www. paisos-catalans.com)*.

Carte Intersites Pays Cathare – This is a similar offer covering 16 sites of Cathar heritage: the châteaux of Lastours, Arques, Quéribus, Puilaurens, Termes, Villerouge-Termenès, Saissac, Peyrepertuse, Usson, the château Comtal de Carcassonne, the abbeys of Caunes-Minervois, Saint-Papoul, Saint-Hilaire, Lagrasse, Fontfroide and the Musée du Quercorb in Puivert. It also gives free admission for one child. It is on sale at all the sites at a price of 4€.

Metric System

France operates on the metric system. Some equivalents:
 See the Conversion Tables opposite.

1 gram = 0.04 ounces	
1 meter = 1.09 yards	
1 kilogram = 2.20 pounds	
1 kilometer = 0.62 miles	
1 litre = 0.53 pints	

Money

CURRENCY

There are no restrictions on the amount of currency visitors can take into France. Visitors carrying a lot of cash are advised to complete a currency declaration form on arrival, because there are restrictions on currency export.

NOTES AND COINS

 See the illustrations on the following page of this section. Since 17 February 2002, the **euro** has been the only currency accepted as a means of payment in France, as in the 11 other European countries participating in the monetary union. It is divided into 100 cents or centimes. Old notes in French francs can be exchanged only at the Banque de France until 2012.

BANKS

Although business hours vary from branch to branch, banks are usually open from 9am to noon and 2pm to 5pm and are closed either on Mondays or Saturdays. Banks close early on the day before a bank holiday. A passport is necessary as identification when cashing travellers cheques in banks. Commission charges vary and hotels usually charge more than banks for cashing cheques.

One of the most economical ways to use your money in France is by using **ATM machines** to get cash directly from your bank account (with a debit card) or to use your credit card to get a cash advance. Be sure to remember your PIN number, you will need it to use cash dispensers and to pay with your card in shops, restaurants etc. Code pads are numeric; use a telephone pad to translate a letter code into numbers. Pin numbers have 4 digits in France; inquire with the issuing company or bank if the code you usually use is longer. Visa is the most widely accepted credit card, followed by Mastercard; other cards, credit and debit (Diners Club, Plus, Cirrus etc) are also accepted in some cash machines. American Express is more often accepted in premium establishments. Most places post signs indicating which card they accept; if you don't see such a sign and want to pay with a card, ask before ordering or making a selection. Cards are widely accepted in shops, hypermarkets, hotels and restaurants, at tollbooths and in petrol stations.

Before you leave home, **check with the bank that issued your card for emergency replacement procedures.** Carry your card number and emergency phone numbers separate from your wallet and handbag; leave a copy of this information with someone you can easily reach. You must report any loss or theft of credit cards or travellers cheques to the French police who will issue you with a certificate (useful proof to show the issuing company). **24-hour hotline numbers** are posted at most ATM machines.

Notes and coins

The euro banknotes were designed by Robert Kalinan, an Austrian artist. His designs were inspired by the theme "Ages and styles of European Architecture". Windows and gateways feature on the front of the banknotes, bridges feature on the reverse, symbolising the European spirit of openness and co-operation.
The images are stylised representations of the typical architectural style of each period, rather than specific structures.

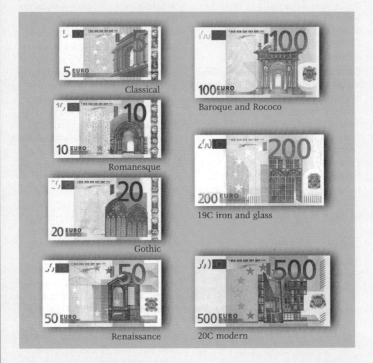

Classical

Baroque and Rococo

Romanesque

19C iron and glass

Gothic

Renaissance

20C modern

Euro coins have one face common to all 12 countries in the European single currency area or "Eurozone" (currently Austria, Belgium, Finland, France, Germany, Greece, Ireland, Italy, Luxembourg, The Netherlands, Portugal and Spain) and a reverse side specific to each country, created by their own national artists.

Euro banknotes look the same throughout the Eurozone. All Euro banknotes and coins can be used anywhere in this area.

PRICES AND TIPS

Since a service charge is automatically included in the prices of meals and accommodation in France, it is not necessary to tip in restaurants and hotels. However, if the service in a restaurant is especially good or if you have enjoyed a fine meal, an extra tip (this is the pourboire, rather than the service) will be appreciated. Usually 1.5 to 3.5 euros is enough, but if the bill is big (a large party or a luxury restaurant), it is not uncommon to leave 7 to 8 euros or more.

As a rule, the cost of staying in a hotel and eating in restaurants is significantly higher in Paris than in the French regions. However, by reserving a hotel room well in advance and taking advantage of the wide choice of restaurants, you can enjoy your trip without breaking the bank. Restaurants usually charge for meals in two ways: a *menu* that is a fixed-price menu with 2 or 3 courses, sometimes a small pitcher of wine, all for a stated price, or à la carte, the more expensive way, with each course ordered separately.

Cafés have very different prices, depending on where they are located. The price of a drink or a coffee is cheaper if you stand at the counter *(comptoir)* than if you sit down *(salle)* and sometimes it is even more expensive if you sit outdoors *(terrasse)*.

Telephone

Most public phones in France use prepaid phone cards *(télécartes),* rather than coins. Some telephone booths accept credit cards (Visa, Mastercard/ Eurocard). *Télécartes* (50 or 120 units) can be bought in post offices, branches of France Télécom, *bureaux de tabac* (cafés that sell cigarettes) and newsagents and can be used to make calls in France and abroad. Calls can be received at phone boxes where the blue bell sign is shown; the phone will not ring, so keep your eye on the little message screen.

Emergency numbers	
Police:	17
SAMU (Paramedics):	15
Fire (Pompiers):	18

NATIONAL CALLS

French telephone numbers have 10 digits. Paris and Paris region numbers begin with 01; 02 in north-west France; 03 in north-east France; 04 in south-east France and Corsica; 05 in south-west France.

To use your personal calling card	
AT&T	☎ 0-800 99 00 11
Sprint	☎ 0-800 99 00 87
MCI	☎ 0-800 99 00 19
Canada Direct	☎ 0-800 99 00 16

INTERNATIONAL CALLS

To call France from abroad, dial the country code (33) + 9-digit number (omit the initial 0). When calling abroad from France dial 00, then dial the country code followed by the area code and number of your correspondent.

International Dialling Codes (00 + code)			
Australia	☎ 61	New Zealand	☎ 64
Canada	☎ 1	United Kingdom	☎ 44
Eire	☎ 353	United States	☎ 1

International information:
  US and Canada: 00 33 12 11
International operator:
  00 33 12 + country code

MICHELIN

Local directory assistance: 12

Minitel – France Télécom operates a system offering directory enquiries (free of charge up to 3min), travel and entertainment reservations, and other services (cost per minute varies). These small computer-like terminals can be found in some post offices, hotels and France Télécom agencies and in many French homes. 3614 PAGES E is the code for **directory assistance in English:** turn on the unit, dial 3614, hit the connexion button when you get the tone, type in "PAGES E", and follow the instructions on the screen.

CELLULAR PHONES

In France these have numbers which begin with 06. Two-watt (lighter, shorter reach) and eight-watt models are on the market, using the Orange (France Télécom) or SFR networks. *Mobicartes* are prepaid phone cards that fit into mobile units. Cell phone rentals (delivery or airport pick-up provided):

- **Rent a Cell Express**
  ☏ 01 53 93 78 00
  Fax 01 53 93 78 09

- **A.L.T. Rent a Phone**
  ☏ 01 48 00 06 60
  E-mail altloc@jve.fr

- **Ellinas Phone Rental**
  ☏ 01 47 20 70 00

TIME

France is 1hr ahead of Greenwich Mean Time (GMT). France goes on daylight-saving time from the last Sunday in March to the last Sunday in October.

When it is **noon in France**, it is	
3am	in Los Angeles
6am	in New York
11am	in Dublin
11am	in London
7pm	in Perth
9pm	in Sydney
11pm	in Auckland

In France "am" and "pm" are not used but the 24-hour clock is widely applied.

USEFUL WORDS AND PHRASES

ARCHITECTURAL TERMS

♫ *See the ABC of Architecture in the Introduction*

SIGHTS

abbaye	abbey
beffroi	belfry
chapelle	chapel
château	castle
cimetière	cemetery
cloître	cloisters
cour	courtyard
couvent	convent
écluse	lock (canal)
église	church
fontaine	fountain
halle	covered market
jardin	garden
mairie	town hall
maison	house
marché	market
monastère	monastery
moulin	windmill
musée	museum
parc	park
place	square
pont	bridge
port	port/harbour
porte	gate/gateway
quai	quay
remparts	ramparts
rue	street
statue	statue
tour	tower

NATURAL SITES

abîme	chasm
aven	swallow-hole
barrage	dam
belvédère	viewpoint
cascade	waterfall
col	pass
corniche	ledge
côte	coast, hillside
forêt	forest
grotte	cave
lac	lake
plage	beach
rivière	river
ruisseau	stream

signal	beacon
source	spring
vallée	valley

ON THE ROAD

car park	parking
driving licence	permis de conduire
east	Est
garage (for repairs)	garage
left	gauche
motorway/highway	autoroute
north	Nord
parking meter	horodateur
petrol/gas	essence
petrol/gas station	station essence
right	droite
south	Sud
toll	péage
traffic lights	feu tricolore
tyre	pneu
west	Ouest
wheel clamp	sabot
zebra crossing	passage clouté

TIME

today	aujourd'hui
tomorrow	demain
yesterday	hier
winter	hiver
spring	printemps
summer	été
autumn/fall	automne
week	semaine
Monday	lundi
Tuesday	mardi
Wednesday	mercredi
Thursday	jeudi
Friday	vendredi
Saturday	samedi
Sunday	dimanche

NUMBERS

0	zéro
1	un
2	deux
3	trois
4	quatre
5	cinq
6	six
7	sept

8	huit
9	neuf
10	dix
11	onze
12	douze
13	treize
14	quatorze
15	quinze
16	seize
17	dix-sept
18	dix-huit
19	dix-neuf
20	vingt
30	trente
40	quarante
50	cinquante
60	soixante
70	soixante-dix
80	quatre-vingt
90	quatre-vingt-dix
100	cent
1000	mille

SHOPPING

bank	banque
baker's	boulangerie
big	grand
butcher's	boucherie
chemist's	pharmacie
closed	fermé
cough mixture	sirop pour la toux
cough sweets	cachets pour la gorge
entrance	entrée
exit	sortie
fishmonger's	poissonnerie
grocer's	épicerie
newsagent, bookshop	librairie
open	ouvert
post office	poste
push	pousser
pull	tirer
shop	magasin
small	petit
stamps	timbres

FOOD AND DRINK

beef	bœuf
beer	bière
butter	beurre
bread	pain
breakfast	petit-déjeuner
cheese	fromage
chicken	poulet
dessert	dessert
dinner	dîner
fish	poisson
fork	fourchette
fruit	fruits
sugar	sucre
glass	verre
ice cream	glace
ice cubes	glaçons
ham	jambon
knife	couteau
lamb	agneau
lunch	déjeuner
lettuce salad	salade
meat	viande
mineral water	eau minérale
mixed salad	salade composée
orange juice	jus d'orange
plate	assiette
pork	porc
restaurant	restaurant
red wine	vin rouge
salt	sel
spoon	cuillère
vegetables	légumes
water	de l'eau
white wine	vin blanc
yoghurt	yaourt

PERSONAL DOCUMENTS AND TRAVEL

airport	aéroport
credit card	carte de crédit
customs	douane
passport	passeport
platform	voie
railway station	gare
shuttle	navette
suitcase	valise
train/plane ticket	billet de train/d'avion
wallet	portefeuille

CLOTHING

coat	manteau
jumper	pull
raincoat	imperméable
shirt	chemise
shoes	chaussures
socks	chaussettes
stockings	bas
suit	costume
tights	collants
trousers	pantalons

USEFUL PHRASES

goodbye	au revoir
hello/good morning	bonjour
how	comment
excuse me	excusez-moi
thank you	merci
yes/no	oui/non
I am sorry	pardon
why	pourquoi
when	quand
please	s'il vous plaît

Do you speak English?
Parlez-vous anglais?

I don't understand
Je ne comprends pas

Talk slowly
Parlez lentement

Where's...?
Où est...?

When does the ... leave?
À quelle heure part...?

When does the ... arrive?
À quelle heure arrive...?

When does the museum open?
À quelle heure ouvre le musée?

When is the show?
À quelle heure est la représentation?

When is breakfast served?
À quelle heure sert-on le petit-déjeuner?

What does it cost?
Combien cela coûte-t-il?

Where can I buy a newspaper in English?
Où puis-je acheter un journal en anglais?

Where is the nearest petrol/gas station?
Où se trouve la station essence la plus proche?

Where can I change travellers' cheques?
Où puis-je échanger des travellers' cheques?

Where are the toilets?
Où sont les toilettes?

Do you accept credit cards?
Acceptez-vous les cartes de crédit?

Abbaye St-Martin-du-Canigou

NATURE

Landscapes

The regions described in this guide encompass a wealth of incomparable natural features. To the north-east lie the rounded hills of the Auvergne. The empty rolling green expanses of the Aubrac are essentially given over to pasture. The region really comes to life during the cattle fairs of Laissac and Nasbinals. In the winter, a covering of snow intensifies the region's prevailing sense of isolation, broken only by cross-country skiers in search of silence and pure fresh air. Farther east lie the undulating plateaux of the Margeride, chequered with pastureland and forests which provide vital resources for the local economy.

As we approach the River Lot to the south, the countryside changes dramatically. Vast limestone plateaux, delineated by sheer cliffs, stretch away, separated by deeply incised river gorges. These limestone plateaux, with their often arid, rocky surfaces devoid of water, are known as the **Causses**. The spectacular river gorges cutting between them, at the bottom of which a seemingly innocuous thread of water is capable at any time of becoming a raging torrent, are known as canyons.

To the east of this breathtaking landscape of causses and river gorges rise the **Cévennes**, rugged mountains characterised by a complicated network of ridges and gullies, with numerous, tortuous ramifications. For centuries, this region was impenetrable, and even now it retains something of an air of mystery, offering those who do decide to explore it the increasingly rare sense that they are treading where no one has trodden before.

The somewhat harsh landscape of the Grands Causses gives way, to the west, to the ségalas (literally "rye fields"), where fertile valleys rub shoulders with gentle hills.

The Causses and the Cévennes do not lead directly into the wine-growing plains of the Bas Languedoc. The transition is made by the **Garrigues**, limestone hills scorched by the sun, bristling with white rocks and isolated clumps of holm-oak, broom or aromatic plants (wild thyme or rosemary, for example). These, with the types of vegetation predominantly cultivated here (olive trees, mulberry bushes, vines), form a truly Mediterranean landscape.

Between the garrigues and the long straight Languedoc coast, lined with a glittering string of lagoons, vineyards stretch as far as the eye can see over the plains and hillsides. This slightly monotonous landscape is enlivened in the summer months by noisy, colourful crowds of holidaymakers who flock to the **Languedoc Coast** and, at the start of autumn, by the cheerful bustle of the grape harvest.

Moving farther south, we come to the Pyrenees, forming a natural frontier between France and Spain which is not easily crossed. The steep slopes on the French side drop quite sharply down into France. They are scored by a series of valleys, separated by high ridges, which link the Pyrenees to the inland plains and the coast. From the Montcalm summit (3 078m/10 098ft) to the Albères massif (1 256m/4 120ft at the Neulos peak), the Pyrenean range drops gradually until it finally sinks into the Mediterranean.

The formation of the Pyrenees began at the end of the Secondary Era and continued during the Tertiary Era, when massive folding motions in the earth's crust disturbed the old Hercynian layers. Erosion then played its part, levelling the mountain range to reveal primary sedimentary rock formations and even, along the axial crests, the granite core itself.

THE CAUSSES, THE CÉVENNES AND THE TARN GORGES

The Aubrac and the Margeride

The **Aubrac** mountains run from north-west to south-east, between the Truyère and Lot valleys. They are made up of formidable streams of solidified basalt, several hundred metres thick, the product of volcanic activity in the Tertiary Era, which cover a granite core. The asymmetric mountain range slopes gently down to the Truyère in the north-east, never going lower than about 1 000m/3 280ft above sea level. The steeper slopes to the south-west are scored by ravines.

Above 850m/2 788ft, the Aubrac is one vast pasture, with, however, a wide variety of flora. Daffodils and narcissi flourish in the spring. Beech woods, moorland and the occasional lake are to be found

Landscape in the Aubrac region

in the west. Hardly any crops are grown, for they would not thrive, in this, one of the most sparsely populated regions in France (14 inhabitants per km², compared to an average in France of 96 per km²). Winters are long and arduous; the plateau is buried beneath snow for several months every year.

Stock rearing is the principal livelihood of those who live here. Traditionally, huge flocks of sheep from the Bas Languedoc would spend the summer in the Aubrac; nowadays, it is cattle that graze on all the pastures. At the end of May, following tradition, cows that have wintered at the foot of the mountain slopes move up to the meadows, where they remain until mid-October, without returning to the cowsheds. One or two local cheesemakers still produce *fourme de Laguiole* in their drystone huts. The livestock fairs of Laissac and Nasbinals, especially those in spring and autumn, are major events rich in local colour. All over the Aubrac massif, you will come across drailles, a kind of track running between low drystone walls, along which herds are moved from one pasture to the other.

The **Margeride**, a granite massif running parallel to the volcanic mountains of the Velay to the north, stretches between the Allier, to the east, and the high volcanic plateaux of the Aubrac, to the west. It reaches its highest point at the Randon beacon (signal), 1 551m/5 088ft above sea level.

The high-lying ground, known as the **Montagne**, has an average altitude of 1 400m/4 593ft. It consists of undulating plateaux covered by vast stretches of pastureland, the monotony of which

is broken by forests of pine, fir and birch. North of Mende, the plateaux (Palais du Roi, La Boulaine) are littered with granite rocks eroded into columns, obelisks or rounded blocks, here and there poised somewhat precariously on top of one another.

Below the Montagne lie rolling plains (the **Plaines**) scattered with numerous rocky outcrops. More people live down here, in large farmhouses which are either isolated or grouped in little hamlets. The main sources of income in the Margeride are timber, livestock and uranium.

West of the mountain range lies the **Gévaudan**, a lower-lying plateau (alt 1 000-1 200m/3 280-3 937ft) and kind of corridor lying in the shadow of the Aubrac.

For more details on the northern part of the Margeride, consult the *The Green Guide Auvergne Rhône Valley*.

The Causses

The vast limestone plateaux of the Causses, south of the Massif Central, constitute one of the most unusual natural regions in France. They are bordered by the Cévennes to the east, by the Lot Valley to the north and by the plains of the Hérault and Bas Languedoc to the south. To the west they stretch as far as the Lévézou and Ségala plateaux, and beyond to the *causses* of Quercy which form the eastern limit of the Aquitaine basin.

The limestone rock gives rise to a landscape rich in contrasts: the arid tablelands of the causses, the colossal depths of the river gorges, and the natural wells formed by swallow-holes. Villages and hamlets consist of white drystone dwellings which accentuate the rugged atmosphere of their surroundings. Since 1995, the causses have been incorporated in part into the Parc naturel régional des Grands Causses for the conservation of the natural, architectural and cultural heritage of this unique region.

In contrast to the deep, but generally fresh and green ravines, the causses stretch away as a seemingly endless expanse of grey, rocky semi-desert. The austere grandeur of these vast plateaux, with barely a dip to break their flat surface and no sign of water, is nevertheless impressive. The dryness of the ground is due to the limestone rock of which it is formed which soaks up rainwater like a sponge; beneath this surface aridity, however, lies a hive of subterranean aquatic activity. The plateaux, at around 1 000m/3 280ft above sea level, have a harsh climate, with dry, scorching summers and long, cold winters when deep snow covers the ground and violent gales sweep unobstructed across the countryside.

To the west, at the edge of the cliffs, beside new plantations of black Austrian pine, grow groves of beech, oak and Scots pine, all that remain of the ancient forest cover which, already sparse, was denuded during the Middle Ages by flocks of grazing animals. To the east, on the moorland, rocky outcrops are dotted with thistles or tufts of lavender which form soft blue splashes of colour. Here and there grow clumps of juniper, either as stunted bushes or small trees up to almost 10m/33ft high. These plants require a lot of light, but are also resistant to frost. They have sharp, spiny leaves and produce small blueish-black berries as fruit, which add a unique flavour to many local dishes (especially game).

Traditionally, the causses have always been the preserve of sheep, whose meagre needs are satisfied by the sparse local vegetation. For many years, flocks of sheep were kept for their wool which supplied the textile industries in the towns (serge and caddis) and for their droppings which were used to fertilise the soil. Nowadays, sheep – about 500 000 head in the Roquefort area – are reared for their ewe's milk (lait des brebis) which is transformed into the famous cheese and matured underground in caves. Lambskin is processed in Millau, the capital of the Causses, situated at the confluence of the Tarn and the Dourbie. *Bleu des Causses*, a blue cheese, is manufactured from cows' milk not far from Millau.

Limestone relief landscapes (known also to geographers as karst relief, from Karst, a limestone region in northern Slovenia) have a vocabulary all of their own.

Lavognes – This the local name for special ponds used as watering holes by the flocks. They are a feature unique to the causses (they are particularly numerous around Roquefort), and generally take the form of an oval or teardrop-shaped pool in which water is prevented from soaking into the limestone by an underlying layer of clay or stone paving.

Eroded rock formations – Here and there, in a vast dip in the causses or outlined against the sky on the edge of an escarpment, strange landscapes of bizarrely shaped rocks can be seen. The size and arrangement of the rock strata, with protruding ledges and sheer sides, combine to resemble abandoned cities complete with streets, monumental doorways, ramparts and strongholds all falling into ruin.

These fantastic natural phenomena are due to the presence of a rock known as **dolomite** (named after Dolomieu, the geologist who discovered it) comprising carbonate of lime, which is soluble, and carbonate of magnesium, which is far less so. The chemical action of water streaming down the rocks, causing erosion, has chiselled them in part into these "ruins" with rounded crests, often as high as 10m/33ft, forming pillars, arcades, towers, animal shapes and weird cliffs for which imagination, given its head, can invariably find a name.

The clay residues formed by the erosion of the rock have helped to sustain a vegetation that enhances the scenic beauty of these areas. Particularly interesting examples of this are to be found at Montpellier-le-Vieux, Nîmes-le-Vieux, Mourèze, Les Arcs de St-Pierre, Roquesaltes and Le Rajol.

The river gorges

Known also as *canyons*, from the Spanish *cañon*, these are river valleys sunk amid massive, limestone outcrops either on the crest of slopes, or in the depths of hollows in the causses. The Tarn gorges between Les Vignes and Le Rozier, and the Jonte and Dourbie gorges are magnificent examples of *canyons*.

Suddenly, at a bend in the road, the ground seems to fall away; the sweeping horizons of the causses are replaced by a vertiginous landscape of vertical cliff faces. A deep gorge, sometimes dropping 500m/1 640ft or more, opens up, as if someone had gashed the plateau with an enormous saw. The valley sides are crowned with magnificent jagged cliffs, up to 100m/328ft tall, in shades of colour ranging from black to rust.

The cliff walls are peppered with caves formed by the erosive action of draining water. The large number of these caves (or baumes, from the local word balma used even before the arrival of the Romans) is reflected in the name of many a local village or hamlet: Cirque des Baumes and Les Baumes-Hautes in the Tarn gorges; Baume-Oriol on the Causse du Larzac; St-Jean-de-Balmes on the Causse Noir; and so on.

Caves and chasms

The caves *(grottes)* and chasms *(avens)* on the surface of the causses or in the hollow of a valley reveal a strange subterranean world, in which flowing water contrasts with the aridity of the plateaux.

Water infiltration – Instead of simply flowing across the limestone plateaux of the Causses, rainwater infiltrates them. The carbonic acid with which it is charged dissolves the carbonate of lime in the limestone to form small depressions, known as **cloups**, or larger ones, known as **sotchs**. Where rainwater percolates down the numerous fissures in the plateau, the hollowing out and dissolution of the limestone layer produces wells or natural chasms which are called **avens** or **igues**.

Gradually, these swallow-holes increase in size, extending into underground tunnels which branch out, link up with each other and widen into caves.

Underground rivers and resurgent springs – The disappearance of a water course into a chasm in the causses, or the accumulation of infiltrated water reaching non-porous strata (marl or clay) creates a network of underground rivers, sometimes covering several hundred miles. These then drain, following the line of the strata, and join up into larger rivers which bore tunnels, widening their course and often gushing along as cascades. When the impermeable rock strata break through onto the side of a hill, the water emerges once more above ground, with a varying degree of force, as a resurgent spring. Where the underground rivers flow slowly, they form little lakes above natural dams, known as **gours**. These low natural walls are built up gradually by deposits of lime carbonate on the edge of the pools of water, which are saturated with it, and subsequently impede the river's flow. There are good examples of gours in the Grotte de Dargilan.

Tarn Gorge

A. Thuillier/MICHELIN

Although underground rivers are not easily accessible (entrance is either via the resurgent spring or the chasm), they are thought to be quite numerous. Some have been located by speleologists: on the Causse du Larzac, the underground river Sorgues was discovered through the **Aven du Mas Raynal**; on the Causse du Comtal north of Rodez, the Salles-la-Source stream can be visited via the **Gouffre du Tindoul de la Vayssière**. Similarly, the Bonheur, which gushes into the open air at the Bramabiau "Alcôve", is a further example of an underground river.

In some cases the dissolution of the limestone crust continues above these subterranean streams; blocks of stone fall from the roof, leaving domes curving upwards towards ground level. When the roof of the dome wears thin it may suddenly cave in, revealing the cavity and forming a chasm.

Speleology – The first speleologists probably date from the Paleolithic Age (the age of flint knapping). They may have been looking, some 50 000 years ago, for the entrance of caves and shelters beneath the rocks in order to inhabit them. Later, in the Neolithic Age (the age of polished stone), humans used the caves as burial places.

During Antiquity, one or two bolder types braved the dangers of this underworld in the hope of finding precious metals, whereas in the Middle Ages the caves were thought to be inhabited by demons and therefore studiously avoided.

In the 18C, systematic explorations were undertaken. However, it was not until 1890 and Édouard-Alfred Martel that speleology won acclaim and recognition as a science. Knowledge of this subterranean world is still incomplete, and numerous chasms remain to be discovered.

Édouard-Alfred Martel (1859-1938) – The name of this famous speleologist is linked with the history of the exploration of the *causses*. An attorney at the Paris courts (Tribunal de Commerce), Martel had been keenly interested in geography since adolescence and turned to geology and travel as a relaxation from his legal career. An intrepid explorer and mountaineer, he toured Italy, Germany, Austria, the United Kingdom and Spain, visiting famous caves, discovering new ones and giving his name to numerous caves and tunnels hitherto undiscovered.

However, it was in France that he concentrated his efforts. In 1883, he undertook a methodical study of the Causses, about which nothing was known at the time. A series of underground explorations, at some risk to his own life, brought to light hundreds of amazing natural features – hidden marvels beyond people's wildest dreams.

Martel was also fascinated by the Pyrenees, the Vercors and the Dévoluy. His daring expedition along the Grand Canyon of the River Verdon opened the way for the general public to be able to explore in their turn what is undoubtedly one of the most breathtaking natural features in France *(see The Green Guide Alpes du Sud in French)*.

Martel was also a scientist at heart. Having made a wealth of observations, he devoted himself to the study of the laws of erosion in limestone soils and founded a new branch of scientific study, underground geography or **speleology**. His numerous publications made him world-famous.

In his writings, he summarised the work he had done, which provided an invaluable resource for those explorers who came after him. His style successfully imbues the reader with his enthusiasm.

Martel's work was also of great benefit to the inhabitants of the Causses. Perhaps his most important contribution was that his studies of the network of underground rivers in the region directly influenced the creation of a more hygienic public water supply, which up until then had been prone to all sorts of life-threatening contamination. Furthermore, his discoveries and the publicity surrounding them attracted tourists to this otherwise impoverished area, giving the local economy a much needed boost.

Journey into the realm of shadows – A speleologist must first find a way of getting underground. In winter, the misty vapour caused by warm air rising from underground caverns can be a useful indication of their whereabouts. The presence of animals that frequent caves, such as bats or jackdaws, can also often point the way. Some explorers prefer to look out for resurgent springs.

Once this preliminary fieldwork has been carried out, the expedition can begin. Speleologists should be equipped with a helmet with a lamp attached to shield them from falling stones, a set of waterproofs and boots for crossing rivers and as a protection against waterfalls which might drench them at any moment. At times they will be making their way along tunnels so narrow that they have to crawl along on their belly like a snake to make any progress. Other obstacles they may have to contend with include sumps, for which diving suits may be needed, lakes with indistinct edges, or rocks made slippery with wet clay. Then there are sudden underground floods, due to storms, or the natural dams formed by underground lakes or **gours**. To combat the fatigue of particularly long expeditions, there have been successful attempts at underground camping. In most caves, the carbon dioxide content in the air is no higher than that at ground level; apart from the psychological unease unleashed by staying underground, the main problem is caused by the humidity in the air.

Speleology is both a sport and a discipline, leaving no room, for reasons of facilities and safety, for individual exploits. Numerous sciences have benefited from its discoveries: prehistory, archaeology, geology, biology, physics, chemistry, and, more recently, psychology.

In 1962, Michel Siffre spent two months in the Scarasson chasm, west of Tende pass, where he completely lost all track of time.

Fauna – Since the Upper Paleolithic Age, "cave bears" have disappeared. Nowadays, a badger, stone marten or polecat might occasionally get lost underground, or fish might be swept along by rivers in spate, but they are only there by chance. However, caves are pretty much without exception the permanent residence of bats. These interesting and very useful animals leave the cave at night to go hunting and return at dawn.

They can cover the entire roof of a cave, making deep scratches in the domed ceiling with their claws. Armed with their

> And still it was perhaps the wildest view of all my journey. Peak upon peak, chain upon chain of hills ran surging southward, channelled and sculptured by the winter streams, feathered from head to foot with chestnuts, and here and there breaking out into a coronal of cliffs. The sun, which was still far from setting, sent a drift of misty gold across the hilltops, but the valleys were already plunged into a profound and quiet shadow.
>
> **Robert Louis Stevenson:** *Travels With a Donkey in the Cévennes*

own inbuilt radar system, they have no problems moving around in the dark. Their excrement, guano, can build up into gigantic cones on the cave floor – a speleologist's nightmare. Besides bats, caves are inhabited by a huge variety of invertebrates, such as beetles, millipedes etc. The underground laboratory of Moulis in Ariège *(○━ not open to the public)* is devoted to the study of these cave dwelling animals.

The Cévennes

Lying to the south-east of the Massif Central, the Cévennes cannot really be called a mountain range in the true sense of the term. These schist and granite peaks stretching from the Tarnague to the Aigoual appear as a succession of almost flat, rather dreary plateaux, clad in peat bogs – the *Aigoual Pelouse* (or "lawn") and the Mont Lozère Plat ("dish").

There is a sharp contrast between the very steep Mediterranean side, and that towards the Atlantic, which slopes more gently on either side of a watershed at the eastern end of Mont Lozère, at the Col de Jacreste *(pass on N 106, east of Florac)* and at the Col du Minier.

The crests – The crests of the Cévennes are not very high; Mont Lozère, with its long granite ridges, has an altitude of 1 699m/5 574ft. Similarly, Mont Aigoual,

from which there is a wonderful panorama on a clear day, does not exceed 1 567m/5 141ft.

The crests are covered by meagre pastureland, only suitable for sheep. Pastoral hamlets, with houses made from granite blocks, built very low to resist the wind, are scattered here and there. Lower down, there are holm-oaks, heather and *châtaigneraies* (chestnut groves) together with little villages.

The upper valleys – Numerous streams flow along deep ravines with steep though by no means sheer sides, created by erosion of a rock which bears no relation to the limestone of the *causses*; this is real granite and schist relief, with its impermeable ground.

Some of these ravines, with their surging streams full of trout and grassy slopes studded with apple trees, are reminiscent of the Alps.

The lower valleys – These all face south and they mark the transition between the Cévennes and Mediterranean country. As the sun is already quite strong, green meadows rub shoulders with sheltered slopes given over to terraced cultivation: vines, olive trees, mulberry bushes. Throughout the region, lavender is distilled. As a reminder of the once flourishing intensive silkworm breeding,

Cévennes landscape seen from Mont Aigoual

A. Cassaigne/MICHELIN

numerous old silkworm farms *(magnaneries)*, large usually three-storey buildings easily recognisable by their narrow windows, and spinning mills can still be seen.

The Cévennes landscape – The population of the upper valleys of the Cévennes has become increasingly sparse, with only meagre crops to support it. Alongside small streams, meadows planted with apple trees are interspersed with fields. The predominant tree, however, is the sweet chestnut, which occupies most of the slopes, leaving only a little room for vines trained to grow on trees, vegetable gardens and fruit trees scattered at the bottom of the valleys and near water sources.

In certain villages, on the periphery of Mont Lozère and in the Margeride, owners of sheep who have agreed to group their sheep together gather them into a communal flock which is led by a single shepherd to graze by day on the mountain. By night, they return to enclosures where they fertilize the soil.

The Ségalas and the Lévézou

The Grands Causses are separated from the Quercy Causses by the Lévézou massif and by a group of plateaus named the Ségalas because for a long time they were devoted to the cultivation of rye *(seigle)*.

The Lévézou – This is a large rugged massif of crystalline rock, situated between Millau and Rodez, rising to 1 155m/3 789ft at the Puech del Pal, its highest point. The uplands around Vezins are much bleaker than the lowlands, featuring clumps of undergrowth and moorland mainly inhabited by flocks of sheep. The lowlands are more hospitable with patchworks of woodland and meadows dotted with large lakes. Since it is some distance away from the main railway lines, the Lévézou has not enjoyed the same revival as the Ségalas. Its rivers, which have been developed for the production of hydroelectric power and tourism (the lakes of Pont-de-Salars, Bage, Pareloup and Villefranche-de-Panat), nonetheless encourage new economic activity.

The Ségalas – During the 19C, the Ségalas, traditionally poor in comparison to Fromental, the wheat-producing region of Aquitaine, began to prosper. At that time, it was decided to take advantage of the proximity of the Carmaux coal basin and the Aquitaine limestone rocks to produce lime. The development of railway lines (Carmaux-Rodez, Capdenac-Rodez) made it possible to transport this precious soil conditioner. Thus, moorland and rye fields were replaced by the cultivation of clover, wheat, maize and barley. Stock rearing also developed: cattle and pigs in the west, and sheep in the east and in the south-east, particularly around Roquefort. Nowadays the gently undulating landscape of the Ségalas is covered with green pastures, copses and meadows hedged with hawthorn. There are often chapels on the hilltops *(puechs)*.

Anyone exploring the Ségalas will be struck by the rich red colour of the local soil, particularly in the Camarès or Marcillac regions, caused by the high percentage of iron oxide in the sediments. This extremely fertile soil is ideal for growing fruit.

The main town in the Ségalas is Rodez, followed by Villefranche-de-Rouergue on the boundary of the Ségalas and the Quercy Causses.

Forests

The Causses and the Cévennes were once thickly covered by forests, in which wild beasts roamed. In the 18C, the *"Bête du Gévaudan"* terrorised the region for three years, devouring more than 50 people (seeming to show a preference for young girls and children) and successfully evading all attempts to hunt it down. Superstitious speculation abounded, with the general consensus being that the "beast" was some kind of Divine scourge. Finally, a huntsman shot what was most probably a wolf, and the "beast" passed into local folklore, particularly effective as a means of subduing uncooperative offspring.

The dangers of deforestation – The majority of the beech forests were destroyed by glass-makers, who used them to manufacture the charcoal they required for their trade. The consequences of deforestation have been particularly severe in the Cévennes, a region prone to violent storms (98cm/38in of rainfall in 48 hours in Valleraugue in September 1900, that is about 40cm/15in more than the average annual rainfall in Paris). The water, which cannot be contained by the remaining plant cover, streams downhill and gushes into the valleys, causing flood waves up to 18-20m/59-65ft high. These inundations destroy everything in their path.

The Bête du Gévaudan

S. Sauvignier/MICHELIN

Sheep: an enemy of the forest – All along the **drailles** (tracks) taken by flocks moving to and from mountain pastures, and on the ridges and plateaux where they grazed, sheep feeding on young leaves and shoots also contributed to the destruction of the forest. Towards the mid-19C, only tiny areas remained of the immense forests which once covered the countryside. At this point Georges Fabre, the forest's benefactor, undertook to reafforest the massif.

Reafforestation – Afforestation by sowing seed directly on the ground is a method hardly ever used nowadays. Much more common is the method of afforestation by planting out seedlings. This involves transporting seedlings, raised in nurseries for a year, in the case of cedar, or three or four years, in the case of most other species, to the designated area where they are then planted out. Nowadays, the area between the valleys, home to beech trees, a good fire break, is planted with pine, firs and spruce. About 14 000ha/34 594 acres have been reafforested by Fabre and his successors. The French National Forestry Commission is justly proud of this achievement.

However, much still remains to be done; other areas which have become denuded of trees need to be replanted, and areas in which the forest cover consists largely of pine trees need to be replanted with hardier species of tree less susceptible to fire and better adapted to the conditions of the environment.

The chestnut – Even if the chestnut no longer features as part of the staple diet for the inhabitants of the Cévennes, chestnut trees nonetheless continue to adorn this region. They can be seen growing at an altitude of 600m/1 968ft, sometimes even as high up as 950m/3 116ft on well-exposed slopes. In order to flourish, the chestnut needs to anchor its powerful roots into schist, granite, sandstone or sand; however it does not thrive in limestone soils. From May, leaves cover the tree; it flowers in June and towards the middle of September produces the first chestnuts, grouped in threes and enclosed in a shell bristling with spines.

Unfortunately, chestnuts are a threatened species. After any felling, new shoots require considerable care and attention. Pruning, trimming and grafting are necessary to combat the damage caused by grazing flocks of animals. The havoc wrought by cryptogamic diseases such as canker makes the preservation of chestnut groves very difficult.

Chestnut tree

M. Janvier/MICHELIN

F. Gégot/MICHELIN

Lagoon near Maguelone

Languedoc

BAS LANGUEDOC

Languedoc is the region stretching from the Rhône to the Garonne, with Toulouse as the capital of Haut Languedoc and Montpellier as the capital of Bas (Mediterranean) Languedoc. Bas Languedoc is a strip, about 40km/25mi wide, along the Mediterranean coast. South of the Cévennes, the Garrigues stand about 200-400m/600-1 400ft above sea level. Below the Garrigues stretches a sandy plain, covered with vineyards, with a necklace of lagoons dotted along the coast. The line of the plain is broken only by the odd limestone outcrop (La Gardiole mountain at Montpellier, Mont St-Clair at Sète, La Clape mountain at Narbonne) and the mountains of Agde (Pic St-Loup), a prolongation of the solidified lava flow of Escandorgue. Bas Languedoc lies sandwiched between mountains which are part of the outlying primary deposits of the Massif Central, from the Cévennes, the Espinouse, Minervois and Lacaune mountain ranges as far as the Montagne Noire, and the first limestone foothills of the Pyrenees, the Corbières.

The Languedoc vineyards, which for centuries concentrated on the production of table wine, are now putting the emphasis on quality, not quantity, and efforts including detailed studies of the soil and climate and a judicious selection of grape varieties are paying off with the region's wines being ranked among the fine wines of France.

The Garrigues – This is the name given to a region of limestone plateaux and mountain ranges, through which flow the Hérault, the Vidourle and the Gard. The mountains of St-Loup and Hortus are rare outcrops in an otherwise flat landscape. Formed, like the causses, by marine deposits from the Secondary Era, the Garrigues (this name is derived from the Occitan garric: kermes oak) are covered by stunted, fragrant scrubland vegetation: dwarf kermes oak shrubs, tufts of thyme and lavender, rockroses and pasture land scorched by the sun.

In spring, this arid countryside, much frequented by hunters, is scattered with brilliantly coloured flowers. The *garrigues* remain the preserve of sheep.

The coast – The Mediterranean coast in the Languedoc is lined with lagoons. The sand bars separating these lagoons from the sea were created by the waves and currents. Gravel and sand carried by the Rhône to the sea were washed towards the Languedoc coast, eventually forming barriers of sand at the mouths of the bays. The sand bars, as they gradually increased in size, transformed each bay into a shallow lagoon isolated from the open sea. These salt water lagoons are filled with eels, grey mullet, sea perch, sea bream and clams. The Aude and the Orb did not form such lagoons, however, nor did they succeed in creating deltas, because the coastal currents constantly swept away their alluvial deposits.

The invasive sand left the old ports of Maguelone and Agde stranded inland. Only the Thau lagoon, virtually an inland sea, is navigable; it is noted for its oyster and mussel farms. Two little fishing ports, Marseillan and Mèze, have adapted to modern demands by developing marinas.

Sète, built in the 17C, has continued to expand since then, but only by a ceaseless struggle against silting up has it been able to maintain its position as the second largest French port on the Mediterranean.

THE GARONNE CORRIDOR

The Garonne is a capricious river, with an irregular rate of flow and frequent spates. Together with its tributaries, it cuts a vast corridor linking Aquitaine and Languedoc.

On either side stand ranges of hills moulded from the thick **molassic** substratum typical of the Toulouse region. Molasse, a product of the accumulation of layers of debris churned up from the Pyrenees in the middle of the Tertiary Era (sand, marl, clay, easily eroded limestone), is a soft assortment of material in which a network of rivers had no trouble becoming established.

At the edges of the corridor, the relief becomes undulating: to the south, tiny beaches at the foot of the Pyrenees are shored up by gravel; to the north, the ancient plateau and the sedimentary hills intermingle (Tarn region).

The geographical area around Albi encompasses some of the plateaux situated south-east of the Aquitaine basin. The landscape alternates between molassic hills (soft yellow sandstone broken by intermittent strata of limestone and marl) and small limestone plateaux (Cordes, Blaye) or rocky outcrops (puechs) often with a village perched on top.

HAUT LANGUEDOC, BETWEEN THE AUDE AND THE GARONNE

Agricultural regions – Traditional mixed cultivation (wheat, maize, vines) was perfectly suited to the capacity of small-scale concerns. These, pressurized by the need for technical innovation and increased specialisation, are now expanding. The land under cultivation is divided between the **terreforts**, heavy fertile clay soils on which cereals are grown, and the **boulbènes**, lighter, poor quality terrain consisting of sand, clay, silt and pebbles.

The Toulouse and Lauragais regions are considered to be the "granary" of the south of France, with a prospering agricultural industry, despite a massive rural exodus. On the other hand, the alluvial plains of the Garonne and the Tarn are the region's orchard (apples, pears, peaches, strawberries). Market gardening also plays an important part in agricultural life, and it is easily combined with poultry farming. Apart from the Gaillac slopes to the west, vineyards are mainly found in the areas around Carcassonne and Limoux.

The appearance of rural houses changes with the landscape. In the Lauragais and Toulouse regions, low brick houses are built, in which the various parts of the building (living quarters, stable, barn, cart shed) are covered by the same gently sloping roof. In contrast, houses in Bas Languedoc are taller: the stable and cellar (cave) are on the ground floor, the living quarters (which once consisted of a single room) on the first floor, and the hay loft above.

D. Pazery/MICHELIN

Canal du Midi

Industrial modernity – A number of small enterprises have grown up around the aerospace industries of Toulouse. Chemical, electrometallurgical, textile, leather, farm-produce and granite industries further contribute to the economic growth of the area. In the Carmausin, coal-mining at the Découverte Ste-Marie pit is restricted to open-cast only.

The Canal du Midi in itself does not play a particularly vital role in the local economy; however, it is becoming increasingly important as a tourist attraction.

The conurbation of Toulouse (with about 600 000 inhabitants) is the focal point of the Midi-Pyrénées region. With its considerable resources for research, its state-of-the-art industries and its public facilities, Toulouse exerts an influence far beyond regional boundaries.

The Pyrenees and Roussillon

THE CENTRAL PYRENEES

The structure of the Pyrenean range is characterised by the juxtaposition of large geological formations running longitudinally.

The Pre-Pyrenees – The "Petites Pyrénées" and the Plantaurel ridge were caused by Jurassic folding movements which created this landscape of rows of limestone ridges, intersected by transverse valleys (ravines of Boussens on the Garonne, and of Labarre on the Ariège) cutting a path through to the plain for the rivers.

The foothills – These consist of strata dating from the Secondary Era, Cretaceous or Jurassic, which were folded more violently. The deeply grooved limestone or sandstone ridges give way, around Foix, to crystalline massifs of dark rock detached from the axial zone, such as the St-Barthélemy massif.

The axial zone – This section constitutes the very backbone of the Pyrenees. From among the primary sediments rise towering crags of the granite core, recognisable by the outline of their crests, which are jagged from glacial erosion. The granite massifs are home to the greatest number of mountain lakes in the Pyrenees.

Peaks and valleys – The absence of a valley running the length of the chain, downhill from and parallel to the line of the axial ridge, which would thus have linked the transverse valleys, has remained an obstacle to communications within the chain. These are dependent on mountain passes which are impassable in winter. For years the transverse valleys have been affected by this enforced segregation, which has encouraged the survival of various local ways of life, as if each valley were a miniature country in itself.

The massive, fortress-like mountains of **Andorra** and the **upper Ariège valley**, carved out of hard gneiss, seem to stand guard over a bleak and rugged landscape (rocks and scree). Gorges gouged out by glaciers during the Quaternary Era, which frequently end in a mountain lake, stand out dramatically amid the surrounding landscape. These isolated regions link the Central and Mediterranean Pyrenees.

THE MEDITERRANEAN PYRENEES

The Mediterranean Pyrenees, perhaps the section of the chain most open to the outside world, rub shoulders to the north with the Corbières massif. This stretches as far as the Montagne Noire, the furthest southern outpost of the Massif Central, and separates the Aquitaine basin from the plains of Mediterranean Languedoc.

The mountains – Between the Corbières and the axial ridge of the Pyrenees lie limestone foothills, which differ in various aspects of their relief and landscape from the northern sedimentary surface of the Central Pyrenees. **The Plateau de Sault,** a sort of causse covered with forests, gives way to rows of crests whose jagged silhouettes tower above the deep furrow of the **Fenouillèdes.** The River Aude, which rises in the axial zone, cuts through this crust in a series of breathtaking gorges.

The eastern Pyrenees, which were pushed the furthest upwards by the ancient folding movements of the earth's crust, have nonetheless been reduced to a lower altitude than that of the Central Pyrenees. The first peaks to emerge, they were exposed to wear and tear by erosion for a longer period. They underwent only a relatively short period of glaciation, centred around the Carlit summit, which briefly boasted a thick ice cap.

The **Cerdagne** and the **Capcir**, high-altitude valleys (1 200m/3 937ft and 1 600m/5 249ft above sea level) formed by erosion in the flanks of the Pyrenees, are filled with an assorted debris of clay, marl and gravel accumulated towards the end of the Tertiary Era. The valleys are home to villages and cultivated land.

East of the Canigou (alt 2 784m/9 133ft), the Pyrenean range drops into the trench occupied by the Mediterranean. The **Albères**, the chain's final set of peaks, formed of crystalline rock, cut between two sections of subsided ground: the Roussillon, to the north, and the Ampurdan, to the south (in Spain).

The Roussillon – The parallel valleys of the Têt and the Tech enhance the majestic Canigou peak, by allowing Mediterranean influences to penetrate to the heart of the mountain range. Resorts in these valleys are renowned for their exposure to sunlight, their dry climate and their vegetation (orange trees and pink oleander).

The mountain rivers are subject to dramatic variations in rate of flow. The floods in autumn 1940 were memorable: between 16 and 19 October, rainfall recorded in Amélie was as great (758mm/29in) as the usual annual average. It was estimated that during those three days, the Tech swept along, in the space of a few miles, one third more water than the total volume transported by the Rhône in one year.

The Roussillon plain, which stretches for 40km/24mi, was originally a gulf which was filled in (at the end of the Tertiary/beginning of the Quaternary Era) with debris from the mountain range. Arid rocky terraces (**Les Aspres**), pocked with wide valleys and dotted with hillocks, are cultivated with fruit trees and vines. An offshore sand bar separates the sea from the **salanques** marshes, where alluvial deposits from the Têt and the Agly have accumulated to a depth of several hundred metres.

TRADITION AND MODERNITY

Straddling two regions (Midi-Pyrénées and Languedoc-Roussillon), the Pyrénées-Roussillon-Albigeois area is characterised by contrasts where tradition rubs shoulders with modernity.

The Mountains

Traditional rural life – Mountain countryside can be divided into three zones: the lower slopes with cultivated fields and villages; an intermediate level where forests alternate with hay meadows; and high mountain pastures. Wheat, rye and maize are still grown in Haut Vallespir, Cerdagne and Conflent. The vines and olive trees which once grew in abundance in the Mediterranean valleys have now all but disappeared.

Hay meadows are grown exclusively on the wetter slopes. Groves of holm-oak, Scots pine and beech, on the outskirts of the villages, have been somewhat reduced by felling and have now given way to scrubland of broom or garrigues. These mountain valleys make a pretty sight with their groups of villages and chessboard fields separated by hedges and trees. Flocks are still transferred from winter to summer pastures, and large flocks of sheep can be seen grazing in the summer, making the upkeep of the pastures economically viable.

Traditional rural life no longer plays that important a role in the activities of modern mountain dwellers. The areas worst hit by rural depopulation are the little dead-end valleys, or isolated villages on the slopes of the mountain which are not exposed to the sun where cultivated land and meadows have been gradually left to go fallow or revert to heathland.

Castelnou

J. Malburet/MICHELIN

Renewed growth – The industrial potential of the Pyrenees depends on exploitation of its energy sources. The old Catalan forges were fuelled with charcoal. But from 1901, hydroelectric schemes were set up in the mountains, which are still being developed today (the Hospitalet plant dates from 1960).

Besides hydroelectricity, a great variety of industrial concerns (French chalk mines at Luzenac, cement works, textile manufacturing, aluminium works, various metallurgy and timber industries etc) boost the economic activity of the valleys. Nevertheless, industrialisation is somewhat limited here; it has not been sufficient to stem the rural exodus and, because of its age, it has great difficulty in adapting to modern conditions.

The liveliest valleys are crisscrossed by busy roads; they are densely populated, well developed, and place great emphasis on tourism as a means of supporting their economy. In spas and winter sports resorts, accommodation is steadily increasing. All this has brought about a new mix in the population. The departure of the local inhabitants has been offset by the arrival of French or foreign newcomers who have come to settle here.

The Roussillon Coast

The garden of Roussillon – With its orchards, market gardens and vineyards, Roussillon resembles an enormous allotment. A well-designed irrigation system and the use of greenhouses and plastic cloches and tunnels have helped improve vegetable production. Vegetables grown here are mainly tomatoes, new potatoes, winter lettuce and endive, while local fruit is principally peaches, nectarines and apricots. These plant varieties are now established in the Roussillon plain, but they can also be cultivated on the intermediate mountain slopes up to an altitude of 600m/1 968ft. Other crops include early cherries from the Céret orchards and apples from Vallespir and central Conflent.

In Roussillon, houses are mostly grouped in villages, but in some areas, the presence of the odd mas (isolated farmhouse) amid acres of cultivated land is evidence of farming on a larger scale. The towns of Perpignan, Elne and Ille-sur-Têt are geared to wholesale markets.

Vineyards – Vineyards cover the banks of the Agly, the rocky terrace of Les Aspres and the sweep of land along the Côte Vermeille, which is the most typical region of the Roussillon coast. The grape varieties cultivated have resulted in the production of a vast range of vins de coteaux, including young white wines, rosés and robust, heady reds. The **Côtes du Roussillon** covers the sun scorched marl and schist of the southern slope of the Corbières as well as the arid terraces of Les Aspres as far as the Albères range.

Most of the wine produced locally is still the vin doux naturel (dessert wine), such as Rivesaltes, Banyuls and Maury. The production of local table wines is giving way to the development of better quality vintage wines. The wine-growing industry has also branched out into new sidelines, such as apéritifs (Thuir), vermouths (Noilly Prat at Marseillan) and liqueurs.

Corbières vineyards

D. Pazery/MICHELIN

The Climate

The climate in the Languedoc region is basically Mediterranean, with summer temperatures soaring towards 30°C (over 80°F) in Perpignan – one of the hottest places in France in season. The region has its own version of the Provençal mistral in the shape of the **tramontane**, which periodically whistles through the Languedoc corridor from the north-west. July and August are hot and, as elsewhere in France, can tend to be crowded, especially towards the coast, although the Languedoc coast is nowhere near as busy as the Côte d'Azur at this time of year. Those seeking respite from the blistering heat of the coastal plain should head up to the mountains...or down into some of the numerous caves which pepper the region. June and September are generally good months to visit, as the weather is fine and warm (apart from the odd outbreak of rain).

Autumn on the Mediterranean coast remains relatively mild, making this a good time of year for a tour of the Corbières vineyards and neighbouring ruined Cathar strongholds. Rainfall in the Pyrenees and over Mont Aigoual is heavy, in particular in the autumn. However this is also the harvest season, which adds a splash of colour, amid the rain, to the Cévennes and the Montagne Noire.

The first snow falls from late October, and by Christmas the resorts are alive with keen skiers, both downhill and cross-country in the Pyrenees, Andorra, and the Capcir and Cerdagne mountain plateaux, and predominantly cross-country in the Aubrac, Mont Lozère and Aigoual massif.

The coming of milder spring weather brings a burst of colour to the Pyrenees, with the blossoming of mountain flora, and to the orchards of Roussillon in full bloom. Spring and summer are the best seasons to visit the Causses, as temperatures are rarely oppressively hot. It is the ideal time of year for exploring the gorges by canoe, or for pot-holing, rock-climbing and hiking.

Sea fishing – The fishing fleets in the harbours along the Côte Vermeille and coast of the Aude delta have diversified into four different areas.

Lamparo or lamplight fishing, mainly for sardines or anchovies, requires the installation of powerful lamps on an adjacent vessel. Powerful deep-sea fishing vessels are used for red tunny fishing. The fish are caught with a huge net which is wound mechanically. Trawling, mainly from Port-Vendres, Port-la-Nouvelle and St-Cyprien, uses huge pocket-shaped nets which are dragged along the sea bed. Small-scale fishing with mesh nets, trammel nets or floating lines is a method used at sea and in the coastal lagoons (for eels).

At the same time, oyster-farming on the Leucate lagoon and mussel-farming in the open sea near Gruissan and Fleury-d'Aude are on the increase.

Beaches – From the mouth of the Aude, the coast of the Golfe du Lion comprises 70km/43mi of flat shore terminating in the jagged rocky cliffs of the Côte Vermeille, towards the Spanish border. As a result of the development of the Languedoc-Roussillon coast, modern tourist seaside resorts have been built along the sandy shore, in contrast to the old fishing ports on the rocky coast, tucked in narrow bays and still reminiscent of their traditional role as tiny maritime cities.

HISTORY

Prehistory

During the Quaternary Era which began about two million years ago, glaciers developed, spreading over the highest mountains (Günz, Mindel, Riss and Würm Ice Ages). A much more significant event, however, was the advent of humans in Europe, and particularly in the Pyrenees.

Various phases of evolution, subdivisible into periods, can be classified thanks to archaeology and scientific methods of dating – Paleolithic (Old Stone Age), Mesolithic (Middle Stone Age), Neolithic (New Stone Age).

LOWER PALEOLITHIC

The Lower Paleolithic period is represented in the Pyrenees by **Tautavel man**, who came to light when the remains of a human skull were discovered in a layer of ancient sediment in the **Caune de l'Arago** by a team led by Professor H de Lumley in 1971 and 1979. Tautavel man belongs to the "Homo erectus" genus, which inhabited Roussillon 450 000 years ago. He was 20-25 years old, able to stand upright and about 1.65m/5ft 6in tall. He had a flat, receding forehead, prominent cheekbones, and rectangular eye sockets beneath a thick projecting brow. Since no trace of any hearth has been found, it is assumed that this intrepid hunter, who had not mastered the use of fire, ate his meat raw. He used caves for several purposes: as a look-out to keep track of the movements of animals, as a temporary place to set up camp and dismember prey, and as a workshop for manufacturing tools.

Palynology (the analysis of fossilised pollen grains) has helped to determine the specific characteristics of flora and fauna from different prehistoric periods. Although the alternation of climates produced changes (from grassy steppes to deciduous forests), Mediterranean plant species (pines, oaks, walnut trees, plane trees, wild vines etc) have always been present. Large herbivores to be found in the area included various types of deer and mountain goats, prairie rhinoceros, bison, musk ox and an ancient species of wild sheep. Carnivores (bears, wolves, dogs, polar foxes, cave lions, wild cats) were hunted for their fur. Small game comprised rodents (hares, voles, beavers, field mice) and birds still found nowadays (golden eagles, lammergeyer vultures, pigeons, rock partridges, red-billed choughs).

The tools found are in general quite small (scrapers, notched tools). The largest are stones, measuring on average 6-10cm/ 2-4in, made into choppers, or flat two- or more-sided implements of varying degrees of sharpness.

MIDDLE PALAEOLITHIC

The presence of numerous Mousterian deposits is evidence that Neanderthal man was present in the Pyrenees. Taller than "homo erectus," he had a well-developed skull (1 700cm^3/103in^3). He produced more sophisticated, specialised tools, fashioning numerous double-sided implements, stone knives with curved edges, chisels, scrapers, pointed tools and all kinds of notched implements. His evolution is also evident in the construction of vast dwelling and burial places.

UPPER PALEOLITHIC

With the advent of "homo sapiens," there was now a significant human presence in the Pyrenees. During the Aurignacian period, stone implements were supplemented with tools made of bone and horn, and technical evolution progressed still further during the Solutrean and Magdalenian periods. Towards the end of the last Würm Glacial Period (Würm IV), landscape and fauna were transformed, with boar and deer predominating from now on. Humans both hunted and fished. However, the most revolutionary change was the birth of art, reflected by sculpted human figures (the Aurignacian "Venuses") and cave paintings of exceptional interest.

MESOLITHIC AGE

At the end of the Ice Age, the historical landscape of the Pyrenees settled down. The Mesolithic Age is, in fact, an intermediary phase during which a multitude of civilisations appeared. During the Azilian culture (named after the **Mas d'Azil** cave), which began at the end of the Upper Paleolithic period, the harpoon became an increasingly important weapon. Art, however, was restricted to enigmatic pebbles with symbolic markings.

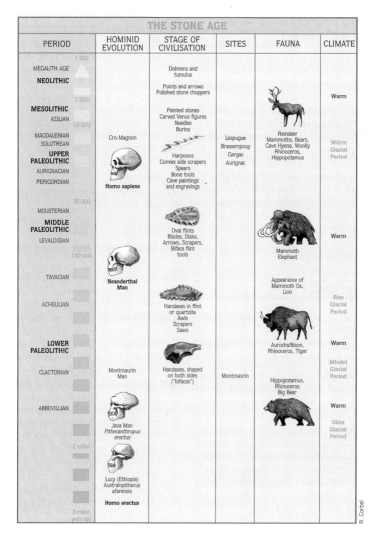

	THE STONE AGE				
PERIOD	HOMINID EVOLUTION	STAGE OF CIVILISATION	SITES	FAUNA	CLIMATE
MEGALITH AGE **NEOLITHIC** 1 500		Dolmens and tumulus Points and arrows Polished stone choppers			Warm
MESOLITHIC AZILIAN 7 500 10 000		Painted stones Carved Venus figures Needles Burins			
MAGDALENIAN SOLUTREAN **UPPER PALEOLITHIC** AURIGNACIAN PERIGORDIAN	Cro-Magnon **Homo sapiens**	Harpoons Convex side scrapers Spears Bone tools Cave paintings and engravings	Lespugue Brassempouy Gargas Aurignac	Reindeer Mammoths, Bears, Cave Hyena, Woolly Rhinoceros, Hippopotamus	Würm Glacial Period
35 000					
MOUSTERIAN **MIDDLE PALEOLITHIC** LEVALOISIAN 150 000		Oval flints Blades, Disks, Arrows, Scrapers, Biface flint tools		Mammoth Elephant	Warm
TAYACIAN	**Neanderthal Man**			Appearance of Mammoth Ox, Lion	Riss Glacial Period
ACHEULIAN		Handaxes in flint or quartzite Awls Scrapers Saws		Aurochs/Bison, Rhinoceros, Tiger	Warm
LOWER PALEOLITHIC		Handaxes, shaped on both sides ("bifaces")			Mindel Glacial Period
CLACTONIAN	Montmaurin Man		Montmaurin	Hippopotamus, Rhinoceros Big Bear	Warm
ABBEVILLIAN					Günz Glacial Period
2 million	Java Man *Pithecanthropus erectus*				
3 million years ago	Lucy (Ethiopia) *Australopithecus afarensis* **Homo erectus**				

R. Corbel

NEOLITHIC AGE

The Neolithic Age is characterised by polished (rather than chipped) stone tools and the use of earthenware. However, in the eastern Pyrenees and the Ariège, the local post-Paleolithic population continued to live in caves, and earthenware came into use only sometime later.

Farther north, valuable ethnological information was discovered in the Font-Juvénal shelter, between the River Aude and the Montagne Noire. As early as the fourth millennium, agriculture and cattle-rearing had become a means of subsistence, with wheat and barley being cultivated. At the same time, dwellings became more elaborate, illustrated by the discovery of flat hearths for cooking, air vents to raise the combustion temperature, supporting structures (posts and slabs) and silos for storage.

In the Narbonne region, rural communities with specialised activities, using complex implements started to barter and trade with each other. Megalithic constructions (dolmens and tumuli) were introduced to the Pyrenees from the western zone during the third millennium. The middle mountain slopes were the most densely populated. Activities included stock-rearing and, increasingly, the making of weapons (arrows, axes and knives). Jewellery (necklaces and bracelets) and earthenware (bowls and vases) became more widespread. In the Catalan region, the Megalithic culture lasted until the Bronze Age.

75

THE PYRENEAN DOLMENS (2500-1500 BC)

The majority of dolmens lie at altitudes ranging from 600-1 000m/1 968-3 280ft. They were originally covered by a tumulus of earth or a heap of stones, which might measure anything up to 20m/65ft, with perhaps a circle of stones around it. The largest dolmens, erected in areas with a stable population, contain the remains of hundreds of people. On the higher pastures, they are smaller and were later replaced by cists (stone chests), individual burial chests for shepherds who had died during the summer.

Time Line

ANTIQUITY

BC

1800-50 – Metal Age.

1800-700 – Bronze Age. End of Pyrenean Megalithic culture.

1000-600 – End of Bronze Age and first Iron Age. Penetration of external influences, first continental, then Mediterranean.

600-50 – Foundation of Massalia (Marseille) by the Phoceans. Development of metallurgy in ancient Catalonia (Catalan forges). The eastern Pyrenees are composed of numerous small clans.

6C – The Celts invade Gaul.

214 – Passage of Hannibal across the Pyrenees and into Roussillon.

2C – Roman Conquest. The Romans occupy the region later known as Bas Languedoc.

118 – Foundation of Narbonne, capital of Gallia Narbonensis, at the crossing of the Via Domitia and the road to Aquitaine.

58-52 – Conquest of Gaul by Caesar.

27 – Bas Languedoc becomes part of Gallia Narbonensis. This marks the start of a long period of prosperity.

AD

3C and 4C – Christianity arrives in the region. Decline of Narbonne and Toulouse.

313 – Edict of Milan. Emperor Constantine grants Christians freedom of worship.

356 – Council of Béziers, Arian heresy.

INVASIONS, THE MIDDLE AGES

3C-5C – Invasions of the Alemanni, the Vandals, then the Visigoths. Toulouse becomes the capital of the Visigothic kingdom.

507 – Battle of Vouillé: Clovis's defeat of the Visigoths, whose kingdom is now restricted to seven cities (Carcassonne, Narbonne, Béziers, Agde, Nîmes, Elne and Maguelone).

719 – Capture of Narbonne by the Saracens.

732 – Charles Martel defeats the Saracens at Poitiers.

737 – Charles Martel recaptures the seven cities from the Visigoths.

759 – Pépin the Short recaptures Narbonne.

801 – Charlemagne marches into Spain; Catalonia is integrated into his Empire, but remains autonomous.

843 – Under the Treaty of Verdun, Charlemagne's Empire is divided: the territories extending from the west of the Rhône to the Atlantic Ocean are given to Charles the Bald.

877 – On the death of Charles the Bald, most of the great princely houses that will rule the south of France until the 13C are established. The counts of Toulouse own the old kingdom of seven cities and the Rouergue; the Gévaudan belongs to the Auvergne family.

10C – Religious revival and pilgrimages to St James's shrine in Santiago de Compostela, Spain.

987 – Hugues Capet is crowned king of France.

11C – Renewed economic and demographic growth in the West. The counts of Toulouse assert their power. Wave of construction of ecclesiastical buildings. Tour of Languedoc by Pope Urban II.

1095 – First Crusade.

1112 – The count of Barcelona becomes viscount of Béziers, Agde, Gévaudan and Millau.

UNION WITH THE FRENCH CROWN

12C-13C – Flowering of the art of the troubadours. First appearance of bastides (fortified towns).

1140-1200 – Spread of the Cathar doctrine.

1152 – Marriage of Henry II Plantagenet with Eleanor of Aquitaine.

1204 – The king of Aragon gains sovereignty of Montpellier, Gévaudan and Millau.

1207 – Excommunication of Raymond VI, count of Toulouse.

1208 – Assassination of Pierre de Castelnau, legate to Pope Innocent III.

1209 – Albigensian Crusade *(further details in the section on The Cathars below)*. Capture of Béziers and Carcassonne by Simon de Montfort.

1213 – Battle of Muret.

1226 – A new crusade: Louis VIII seizes Languedoc.

1229 – The war against the Albigensians ends with the Treaty of Paris. St Louis annexes the whole of Bas Languedoc. Foundation of Toulouse University.

1250-1320 – The last strongholds of Catharism are quelled by the Inquisition.

1270 – Death of St Louis.

1276-1344 – Perpignan is capital of the kingdom of Majorca and the Balearic Islands founded by Jaime I of Aragon, which also includes the Cerdagne, Roussillon and Montpellier.

1290 – The counts of Foix inherit the Béarn.

1292 – Annexation of Pézenas, the Rouergue and the Gévaudan.

1312 – Dissolution of the Order of the Templars by Philip the Fair; the Templars' considerable estates in the Causses are handed over to the Knights Hospitallers of St John of Jerusalem (or of Malta).

1331-91 – Life of Gaston Fébus.

1337 – Beginning of the Hundred Years War (which lasts until 1453).

1348 – A third of the population of Languedoc perishes from the Black Death.

1349 – The king of Majorca sells the seigneury of Montpellier to Philip of Valois.

1350-1450 – The Pyrenees and Languedoc endure a lengthy period of war, unrest, epidemics and famine.

1360 – Treaty of Bretigny: end of the first part of the Hundred Years War. Saintonge, Poitou, Agenais, Quercy, Rouergue and Périgord are ceded to the king of England. Languedoc is then divided into three seneschalsies: Toulouse, Carcassonne and Beaucaire.

1361 – The countryside is plundered by outlaws

1420 – Charles VII enters Toulouse.

1462 – Intervention of Louis XI in Roussillon.

WARS OF RELIGION AND UNION WITH FRANCE

1484 – The princes of Albret, "kings of Navarre," gain ascendancy in the Gascon Pyrenees (Foix, Béarn, Bigorre).

1512 – Ferdinand, the Catholic monarch, divests the Albrets of their territory.

1539 – Under the edict of Villers-Cotteret, French is decreed the legal language.

1560-98 – Wars of Religion between the Protestants and the Roman Catholics.

1598 – Edict of Nantes. Protestants obtain freedom of worship and guaranteed strongholds (Puylaurens, Montauban).

1607 – Henri IV unites his own royal estate (Basse-Navarre and the fiefs of Foix and Béarn) to the French Crown.

1610 – Assassination of Henri IV and renewal of religious strife.

1629 – Treaty of Alès. The Protestants keep their freedom of worship, but lose their strongholds.

1643-1715 – Reign of Louis XIV.

1659 – Under the Treaty of the Pyrenees, Roussillon and the Cerdagne are united with the French Crown.

1666-80 – Construction of the Canal du Midi by Riquet.

1685 – Revocation of the Edict of Nantes. Numerous Protestants flee the country.

1702-04 – War of the Camisards.

FROM FIRST SPA RESORT TO MODERN TIMES

1746 – The thesis of De Bordeu on the mineral springs of Aquitaine plays an important role in the setting up of spa resorts and the rise in popularity of taking cures.

1787 – Ramond de Carbonnières, first enthusiast of the Pyrenees, stays in Barèges.

1790 – The Languedoc is divided into new administrative districts *(départements)*.

1804-15 – First Empire. Discovery of new thermal springs in the Pyrenees.

1852-1914 – Second Empire and Third Republic. Development of spa resorts, rock climbing and scientific study of the Pyrenees.

1875 – Destruction of the Languedoc vineyards by phylloxera.

1901 – First hydroelectric schemes set up.

1907 – Uprising of the wine-growers (*"Mouvement des gueux"*) in Bas Languedoc, in protest against overproduction, competition from imported Algerian wines and falling prices.

1920 – The Pyrenees convert to hydro-electric power.

1940-44 – The Pyrenees prove to be of vital importance to the French Résistance. The Massif de l'Aigoual is a major headquarters for the maquis.

1955 – Inauguration of the Compagnie Nationale d'Aménagement du Bas-Rhône-Languedoc, to develop an irrigation system in the region.

1963 – Plans for the development of the Languedoc-Roussillon coastline.

1969 – Maiden flight of "Concorde 001."

1970 – Designation of the Parc National des Cévennes. Founding of Airbus Industrie.

1973 – Designation of the Parc naturel régional du Haut Languedoc.

1992-97 – Opening in progressive sections of the new motorway (A 75) linking Clermont-Ferrand with Béziers.

1993 – Toulouse underground railway (*métro*) begins operation.

1994 – Puymorens tunnel is opened in the Pyrenees.

1995 – Designation of the Parc naturel régional des Grands Causses.

1996 – Opening of a high-speed rail link (TGV) between Paris and Perpignan (*journey time: 6hr*).
The Canal du Midi is included on the UNESCO World Heritage List.

1997 – The medieval city of Carcassonne and the Cirque de Gavarnie are included on the UNESCO World Heritage List.

1999 – Massive storms slam the south-west coast of France in December.

THE NEW MILLENNIUM

2001 – Explosion rocks the AZF chemical plant near Toulouse, killing 29 and wounding 2,400.

March 2005 - Aibus 380, a 555-seat superjumbo jet assmbled in Toulouse, makes its maiden flight. Scheduled to enter service in 2006.

The Way of St James

According to legend, St James travelled from Palestine to Spain in order to Christianize the country; however, he was beheaded and two of his disciples carrying his body were stranded on the coast of Galicia where they buried him. Around 813, a shower of stars falling over an earth mound drew a hermit's attention to the saint's grave and a chapel was erected on the spot which became known as *Campus stellae* (Compostela). Before long, St James had become the patron saint of all Christians and the symbol of the Spaniards' struggle to win their land back from the Moors. The first French pilgrimage took place in 951 and Compostela soon became as famous as Rome and Jerusalem, attracting millions of pilgrims from all over Europe.

During the Middle Ages, people could tell a pilgrim from any other traveller by the strong staff he held in his hand and the medal and scallop shell he wore as a badge.

In 1130, a French monk, Aymeri Picaud, wrote a tourist guide to help pilgrims on their way; known as the Codex Calixtinus, it included a layout of the routes leading to Santiago de Compostela. Three of these, crossing the region described in this guide towards St-Jean-Pied-de-Port at the foot of the Pyrenees, formed the *camino frances* (the French way): the **via Podiensis** (linking the Aubrac mountains and Condom), the **via Tolosane** (coming from Arles and going through Toulouse and Auch) and the **Caussade** (via Conques, Rodez, Foix and Lourdes).

Over the past 1 000 years, the pilgrimage tradition has considerably enhanced the region's cultural heritage, namely in Conques, Rocamadour, Saint-Sernin de Toulouse and St-Bertrand-de-Comminges; in addition, numerous small chapels, hospices, fountains, bridges… provide us with an invaluable insight into the way of life of pilgrims on their way to Santiago de Compostela.

The Cathars

The repression of the Cathar sect, in the 13C, profoundly affected the history of the Languedoc, which then became linked with that of the French kingdom.

THE CATHAR DOCTRINE

The origins of Cathar doctrine are lost in a labyrinth of complex and distant Eastern influences (including the powerful Bogomiles in Bulgaria), which were propagated in Europe during the 11C and 12C and became rooted in Languedoc towards 1160.

The basic tenet of Cathar doctrine is the dualistic separation of "Good" from "Evil"; God, who reigns over a spiritual world of beauty and light, is opposed by the material world governed by Satan, and man is no more than a spirit trapped in the material world by a Satanic ruse. The Cathars (from the Greek *kathari* or "pure ones") were obsessed with a fear of evil and so sought to free man from the material world, restoring him to divine purity. They interpreted biblical texts in the light of their doctrine and came into head-on confrontation with the orthodox Christian church, for example by denying the divinity of Christ, whom they nonetheless strove to emulate.

THE CATHAR CHURCH

This breakaway Church was headed by four bishops, from Albi (which earned the Cathar Church the name "Albigensian"), Toulouse, Carcassonne and Agen. A significant feature of the Cathar Church was its hierarchy of vocations, distinguishing between **Parfaits** ("Perfect ones") and **Croyants** ("Believers").

As a reaction against the obvious laxity of the Roman Catholic clergy, the Par-faits had to lead an austere life, following the ascetic ideals of poverty, chastity, patience and humility. They were considered men of God who had already seen the light and, as such, were venerated and cared for by the Croyants.

The Cathar Church administered only one sacrament, the **Consolamentum**, which varied according to the occasion, be it the ordination of a Parfait, or the blessing of a Croyant on the point of death as a means of admission into the world of light. The faithful gathered together for other liturgical events, such as prayer meetings, public confessions etc.

The beliefs, way of life and religious rituals of the Cathars conflicted with Roman Catholic thought. Their rejection of the traditional sacraments of baptism and marriage, and their tolerance of different customs and attitudes (particularly in financial and commercial matters) gave rise to violent disputes with the clerics.

A FAVOURABLE ENVIRONMENT

The Cathar heresy reached the towns, centres of culture and trade, and then spread into the lowlands of Languedoc. It has been pointed out that it may be no coincidence that the area where the Cathar Church flourished, between Carcassonne and Toulouse, Foix and Limoux, corresponded exactly with that dominated by the Languedoc cloth industry, which exported from Narbonne to the Levant. Indeed, the **"Bonshommes"** (Parfaits) were very often textile manufacturers or merchants. Powerful lords, such as Roger Trencavel, viscount of Béziers and Carcassonne, and Raymond, count of Foix, supported the heresy. Women, far from being excluded from the Cathar Church, founded their own communities of Parfaites.

From Military Stronghold to Religious Refuge

The castles now associated with the Cathars were originally built as defensive outposts. They were built c 1000 by local noblemen seeking to protect their lands from the armed forces of the King of Aragon. In this way, the fortresses at Aguilar, Termes, Quéribus, Puilaurens and Peyrepertuse were built to defend Carcassonne. At the beginning of the 13C, these bastions of Occitan independence transformed themselves quite naturally into entrenched camps for Cathar refugees, earning them the label "châteaux cathares" in French annals.

After the Albigensian Crusades, they were rebuilt and modified to participate in the defence of the new French territory, once more against attack from Aragonese troops. However, the Treaty of the Pyrenees in 1659 annexed Roussillon to France, depriving the citadels of their defensive function, now that the French border was pushed south to the Pyrenees. They were left to fall into ruins, until a regional programme of economic renewal set up in the 1980s converted the castles into a major tourist attraction. Nowadays, the Châteaux Cathares have a new defensive role to play, against rural impoverishment of the Aude region.

THE WAR AGAINST THE CATHARS

In 1150 St Bernard arrived in the Albigeois region on a mission to convert the Cathar heretics. In view of his minimal success, the Third Lateran Council (1179) drew up plans to enlist some secular muscle to further their cause. In 1204, Pope Innocent III sent three legates to preach against the Cathars and persuade the Count of Toulouse, **Raymond VI**, to withdraw his protection of them. This the count refused to do and was consequently excommunicated in 1207.

In January 1208, Pierre de Castlenau, one of the papal legates, was assassinated. Raymond VI was immediately accused of his murder. The incident sparked off the **First Albigensian Crusade**, preached by Pope Innocent III in March 1208. Knights from the Paris region, Normandy, Picardy, Flanders, Champagne and Burgundy, as well as noblemen from the Rhineland, Friesland, Bavaria and even Austria rallied forces under the command of Abbot Arnaud-Amaury of Cîteaux and then under **Simon de Montfort**. The "Holy War" was to last for more than 20 years. In 1209, 30 000 residents of Béziers were massacred. Carcassonne was besieged in 1209 and fell because of lack of water. Viscount Raymond-Roger de Trencavel was taken prisoner and his place taken by Simon de Montfort, who continued his crusade, capturing one Cathar fortress after another: Lastours, Minerve, Termes and Puivert (1210). By 1215, the whole of the Count of Toulouse's territory was in the hands of Montfort. Raymond VII avenged his father by waging a war of liberation which lasted eight years. Simon de Montfort died in 1218 but was succeeded by his son, Amaury.

Strongholds might fall, but the Cathar doctrine was not so easily quashed. In 1226, a **Second Albigensian Crusade** was preached, under the leadership this time of the King of France himself, Louis VIII. The Holy War very rapidly became a political struggle, however. In the Treaty of Meaux-Paris in 1229, Blanche de Castille effectively annexed a vast territory, to become the Languedoc a century later, to the French Royal estate. The battle against heresy was not over; this time the **Inquisition** intervened. Pope Gregory IX entrusted it to the Dominican Order in 1231. In 1240, the Crusaders captured Peyrepertuse. The governor of the main Cathar stronghold at Montségur, Pierre-Roger de Mirepoix, undertook an expedition to Avignonet in 1242, with the intention of killing off the members of an Inquisition tribunal. Six thousand Crusaders promptly installed themselves at the foot of his castle, where they remained for a siege which lasted ten months. At the end of it, in March 1244, the fortress capitulated and the besiegers built an enormous pyre on which they burned alive 215 unrepentant Cathars. Those still espousing the Cathar doctrine took refuge in the fortress at Puilaurens, where they were butchered shortly after the fall of Montségur. The war against the Cathars reached its final bloody conclusion in 1255 with the siege and fall of Quéribus, the last remaining Cathar stronghold.

ART AND CULTURE

ABC OF ARCHITECTURE

Religious architecture

CORNEILLA-DE-CONFLENT – Ground plan of the church of Ste-Marie (11-12C)

This church originally had a basilical ground plan with three aisles, a very common layout in Roussillon in the 11C. The transept was added in the 12C.

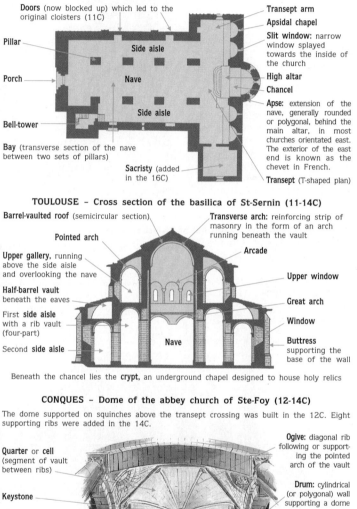

Doors (now blocked up) which led to the original cloisters (11C)

Pillar

Side aisle

Porch

Nave

Side aisle

Bell-tower

Bay (transverse section of the nave between two sets of pillars)

Sacristy (added in the 16C)

Transept arm

Apsidal chapel

Slit window: narrow window splayed towards the inside of the church

High altar

Chancel

Apse: extension of the nave, generally rounded or polygonal, behind the main altar, in most churches orientated east. The exterior of the east end is known as the chevet in French.

Transept (T-shaped plan)

TOULOUSE – Cross section of the basilica of St-Sernin (11-14C)

Barrel-vaulted roof (semicircular section)

Pointed arch

Upper gallery, running above the side aisle and overlooking the nave

Half-barrel vault beneath the eaves

First **side aisle** with a rib vault (four-part)

Second **side aisle**

Nave

Transverse arch: reinforcing strip of masonry in the form of an arch running beneath the vault

Arcade

Upper window

Great arch

Window

Buttress supporting the base of the wall

Beneath the chancel lies the **crypt,** an underground chapel designed to house holy relics

CONQUES – Dome of the abbey church of Ste-Foy (12-14C)

The dome supported on squinches above the transept crossing was built in the 12C. Eight supporting ribs were added in the 14C.

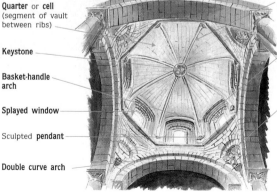

Quarter or **cell** (segment of vault between ribs)

Keystone

Basket-handle arch

Splayed window

Sculpted **pendant**

Double curve arch

Ogive: diagonal rib following or supporting the pointed arch of the vault

Drum: cylindrical (or polygonal) wall supporting a dome

Squinch: small series of corbelled arches bridging the gaps at the corners between a square plan structure, such as a tower, and a circular or polygonal superstructure (dome etc). In this case it is decorated by figures sculpted in **high relief.**

R. Corbel/MICHELIN

ST-MICHEL-DE-CUXA – Bell-tower of the abbey church (11C)

The Romanesque churches in Roussillon and Catalonia nearly all feature one or two Lombard bell-towers. This style was probably imported from Italy in the 11C, making its earliest appearance at St-Michel-de-Cuxa, and later became typical of the architecture of this region. The bell-tower at Cuxa stands at the far south end of the transept (originally, there was a matching tower at the far north end).

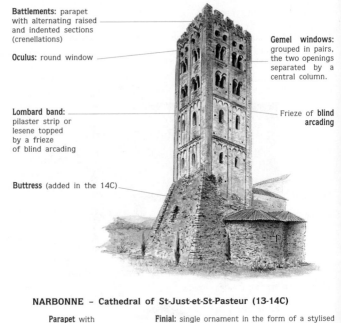

Battlements: parapet with alternating raised and indented sections (crenellations)

Oculus: round window

Lombard band: pilaster strip or lesene topped by a frieze of blind arcading

Buttress (added in the 14C)

Gemel windows: grouped in pairs, the two openings separated by a central column.

Frieze of **blind arcading**

NARBONNE – Cathedral of St-Just-et-St-Pasteur (13-14C)

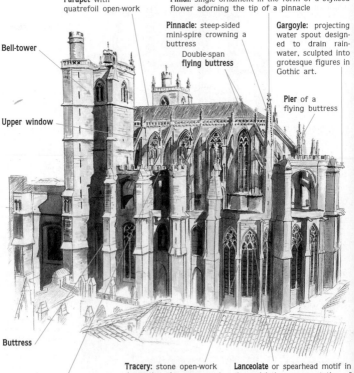

Parapet with quatrefoil open-work

Finial: single ornament in the form of a stylised flower adorning the tip of a pinnacle

Pinnacle: steep-sided mini-spire crowning a buttress

Double-span **flying buttress**

Gargoyle: projecting water spout designed to drain rainwater, sculpted into grotesque figures in Gothic art.

Bell-tower

Upper window

Pier of a flying buttress

Buttress

Watch-path with **battlements**

Tracery: stone open-work decorating the upper part of the windows

Lanceolate or spearhead motif in the undulating ornamentation of a Flamboyant Gothic window

ELNE – Cloisters of the cathedral of Ste-Eulalie-et-Ste-Julie (12-14C)

The cloisters are a set of four roofed galleries around a central quadrangle, enabling monks to walk under cover from the conventual buildings to the church.

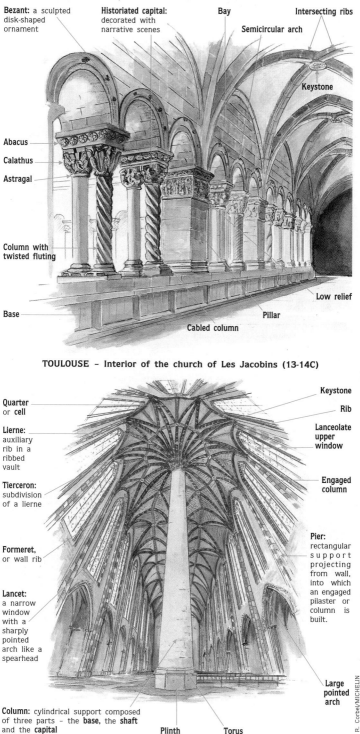

Bezant: a sculpted disk-shaped ornament

Historiated capital: decorated with narrative scenes

Bay

Intersecting ribs

Semicircular arch

Keystone

Abacus

Calathus

Astragal

Column with twisted fluting

Base

Cabled column

Pillar

Low relief

TOULOUSE – Interior of the church of Les Jacobins (13-14C)

Quarter or **cell**

Lierne: auxiliary rib in a ribbed vault

Tierceron: subdivision of a lierne

Formeret, or wall rib

Lancet: a narrow window with a sharply pointed arch like a spearhead

Keystone

Rib

Lanceolate upper window

Engaged column

Pier: rectangular support projecting from wall, into which an engaged pilaster or column is built.

Large pointed arch

Column: cylindrical support composed of three parts – the **base**, the **shaft** and the **capital**

Plinth

Torus

R. Corbel/MICHELIN

83

Military architecture

CARCASSONNE – East gateway of the Château Comtal (12C)

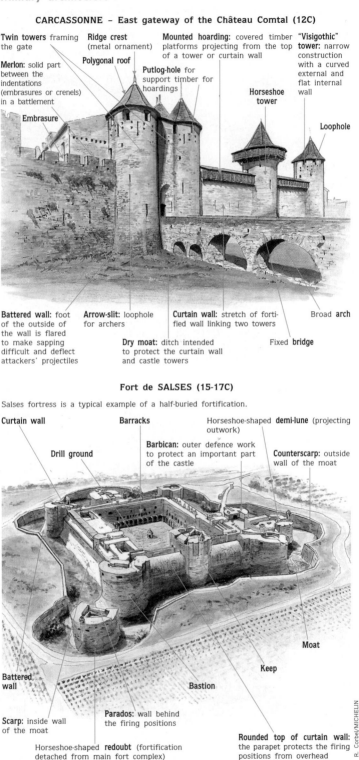

Twin towers framing the gate

Ridge crest (metal ornament)

Polygonal roof

Merlon: solid part between the indentations (embrasures or crenels) in a battlement

Embrasure

Putlog-hole for support timber for hoardings

Mounted hoarding: covered timber platforms projecting from the top of a tower or curtain wall

"Visigothic" tower: narrow construction with a curved external and flat internal wall

Horseshoe tower

Loophole

Battered wall: foot of the outside of the wall is flared to make sapping difficult and deflect attackers' projectiles

Arrow-slit: loophole for archers

Dry moat: ditch intended to protect the curtain wall and castle towers

Curtain wall: stretch of fortified wall linking two towers

Fixed **bridge**

Broad **arch**

Fort de SALSES (15-17C)

Salses fortress is a typical example of a half-buried fortification.

Curtain wall

Drill ground

Barracks

Barbican: outer defence work to protect an important part of the castle

Horseshoe-shaped **demi-lune** (projecting outwork)

Counterscarp: outside wall of the moat

Moat

Keep

Battered wall

Bastion

Scarp: inside wall of the moat

Parados: wall behind the firing positions

Horseshoe-shaped **redoubt** (fortification detached from main fort complex)

Rounded top of curtain wall: the parapet protects the firing positions from overhead

R. Corbel/MICHELIN

Secular architecture

TOULOUSE – Hôtel d'Assézat (16C)

The Hôtel d'Assézat, designed by Nicolas Bachelier, is the earliest example of Palladian style architecture in Toulouse, with its characteristic superposition of the Classical decorative orders – Doric, Ionic and Corinthian.

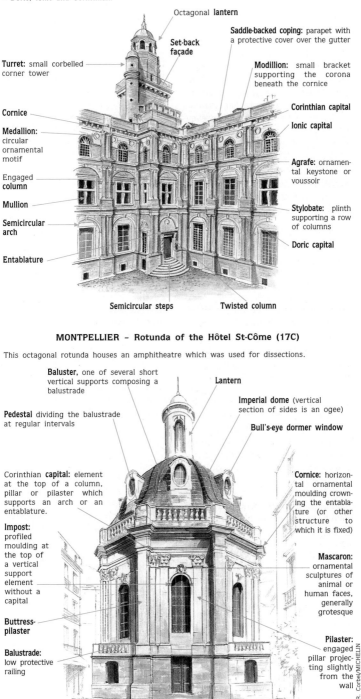

Octagonal **lantern**

Saddle-backed coping: parapet with a protective cover over the gutter

Set-back façade

Turret: small corbelled corner tower

Modillion: small bracket supporting the corona beneath the cornice

Corinthian capital

Ionic capital

Cornice

Medallion: circular ornamental motif

Agrafe: ornamental keystone or voussoir

Engaged column

Mullion

Stylobate: plinth supporting a row of columns

Semicircular arch

Doric capital

Entablature

Semicircular steps

Twisted column

MONTPELLIER – Rotunda of the Hôtel St-Côme (17C)

This octagonal rotunda houses an amphitheatre which was used for dissections.

Baluster, one of several short vertical supports composing a balustrade

Lantern

Imperial dome (vertical section of sides is an ogee)

Pedestal dividing the balustrade at regular intervals

Bull's-eye dormer window

Corinthian capital: element at the top of a column, pillar or pilaster which supports an arch or an entablature.

Cornice: horizontal ornamental moulding crowning the entablature (or other structure to which it is fixed)

Impost: profiled moulding at the top of a vertical support element without a capital

Mascaron: ornamental sculptures of animal or human faces, generally grotesque

Buttress-pilaster

Pilaster: engaged pillar projecting slightly from the wall

Balustrade: low protective railing

R. Corbe/MICHELIN

THE ARTISTIC HERITAGE OF PREHISTORY AND ANTIQUITY

The Causses and the Cévennes are rich in vestiges of the art of Neolithic civilisations.

Megaliths – These large (Greek: *mega*) stone (Greek: *lithas*) monuments comprise dolmens, menhirs, covered alleyways, alignments of menhirs and "cromlechs" (groups of menhirs serving as boundary markers). The Aveyron *département* has the greatest concentration of dolmens in France. Rare menhirs are found both in the Gard and the Aveyron. Scientists consider the first megaliths to date from slightly earlier than the Bronze Age (which began approximately 1 800 BC).

Menhirs – These colossal standing stones, deeply embedded in the ground, probably had some sort of symbolic significance. In the south of the Aveyron *département* numerous statue-menhirs, or menhirs carved to depict a human figure, have been found. Features include a face (with eyes and nose, although the mouth is always missing), arms, hands, short lower limbs and jewellery (necklaces or patterns tattooed on the face). It is not known whether these figures represent people or some sort of protective goddess.

Dolmens – Consisting of a horizontal slab supported by several vertical stones, these are thought to have been tombs. Originally some were buried beneath a tumulus, or mound of earth or stones.

The craftsmen behind these mysterious megalithic monuments may well have been a seafaring people who had come and taught the local inhabitants how to erect such massive blocks. Team work and innovative techniques would have been required (an inclined ramp, a plumb line, rollers capable of transporting stones weighing up to 350t), and the construction of roads presupposes quite advanced technical prowess. By way of comparison, the installation (in 1836) of the Luxor obelisk, which weighs "only" 220t, on place de la Concorde in Paris was considered a tremendous feat.

The Bronze and Iron Ages – The fine, elegantly shaped bowls and jewellery on display in the Musée Ignon-Fabre in Mende date from these periods.

The Gallo-Roman period – Ceramic ware from the Graufesenque pottery, near Millau, was renowned throughout the Roman Empire. At about the same time, Banassac was reputed for the high quality of its earthenware.

MILITARY ARCHITECTURE IN THE MIDDLE AGES

The intense military activity of the Middle Ages has left many traces throughout the Languedoc. The Albigensian Crusade, the bands of outlaws pillaging the country during the Hundred Years War, and the proximity of Guyenne, which remained under English rule until 1453, prompted feudal lords to have well-organised defences. They built their castles at the mouths of canyons or upon rocky pinnacles. The southern face of the Montagne Noire once bristled with fortresses; reduced to ruins, they lend a note of austere grandeur to the landscape.

The collapse of public power and the crumbling authority of the princes and counts in the 10C and 11C led to a significant rise in the number of fortified strongholds built. During the 12C and 13C, the castles were once again in the hands of the king and great feudal lords; they were a source of frequent rivalry in Languedoc, which was always seething with border disputes.

Castles – Cities could be defended by the consolidation and reinforcement of the Gallo-Roman city walls (as at Carcassonne). Outside the city limits, fortresses were built on high ground. Originally somewhat crude, the 10C **mounds** (natural or man-made hillocks), which were large enough for a simple shelter, multiplied rapidly on flat land. They were subject to constant improvement, eventually becoming impregnable citadels, like Cathar castles, which were purely military in purpose.

The end of the 11C marked the advent of stone **keeps** or donjons, either rectangular (Peyrepertuse) or rounded (Catalonia) in shape, with thick walls and narrow window slits. The interior was divided into several storeys: the dark and vaulted ground floor was a store room; the upper floors could be used as reception or living rooms. The only means of access was on the first floor, via a ladder or a retractable gangway.

Most of the keeps had limited facilities as residences. Many were merely defensive towers, which housed a garrison. The lords preferred to live in a larger building in the **lower courtyard**, either adjacent to or detached from the keep.

During the 13C and 14C, the main castle building was extended, making it more comfortable as a residence. The keep then became incorporated with the other buildings and acquired one or several enclosing walls, interrupted at intervals by towers. **Puilaurens Castle**, with its fortified wall and four corner towers, is a fine example of this new trend, whereas the keep at **Arques** is a remarkable specimen of 13C military construction.

Watchtowers – These are a common feature in the Corbières, Fenouillèdes, Vallespir and Albères. They transmitted signals, using fire by night and smoke by day, and employing a specific code to convey the nature or gravity of the danger. These visual communications links in the Catalan mountains sent information from the far reaches to **Castelnou Castle** in Les Aspres during the Catalan earldoms of the early Middle Ages and to Perpignan during the reign of the kings of Aragon.

Fortified churches – Towards the end of the 10C, the custom of fortifying churches became widespread in southern France. Traditionally a place of asylum – the areas of immunity, as defined in the Truce of God, extended as far as 30 paces all around the building – the church, with its robust architecture and its bell-tower ideally suited for keeping watch, provided a refuge for the local inhabitants in times of warfare.

Machicolations, either mounted on corbels or supported on arches between buttresses, as in Beaumont-de-Lomagne (ⓒ *see The Green Guide Atlantic Coast*), were first seen in France at the end of the 12C on Languedoc churches.

However, strict regulations on the fortification of churches were prescribed at the time of the Albigensian Crusade. The count of Toulouse and his vassals were accused of abusing their privilege in this regard. Thus the bishops regained a monopoly which had long evaded them.

The 13C, which for Languedoc marked the union with the French crown and the triumph of orthodoxy over heresy, was a time when large brick churches in the Gothic style of Toulouse were constructed, with a layout and height appropriate for the potential part of a system of fortifications.

In 1282, Bernard de Castanet, Bishop of Albi, laid the first stone of the cathedral of Ste-Cécile. The severity of its mighty walls, 40m/131ft high, give it the appearance of a massive fortress at the heart of the subjugated Cathar country.

Well preserved fortified churches and villages are still to be seen in the upper valleys of the Pyrenees; the church of Stes-Juste-et-Ruffine in Prats-de-Mollo is a curious blend of roofs and fortifications. One of the finest sights is Villefranche-de-Conflent with its ramparts refurbished by Vauban. Languedoc abounds with fine examples of fortified churches – the cathedral at Maguelone, the church of St-Étienne in Agde, the cathedral of Notre-Dame in Rodez and the cathedral of St-Nazaire in Béziers, to name but a few.

Bastides – In 1152, Eleanor of Aquitaine took as her second husband Henry Plantagenet, count of Anjou and lord of Maine, Touraine and Normandy. Their joint estates were as great as those of the King of France. Two years later, Henry Plantagenet inherited the throne of England, which he ruled as Henry II. The balance of power was destroyed and the Franco-English wars which broke out were to last for the next 300 years or more. *Bastides*, or fortified "new" towns, were built in the 13C by kings of France and England in the hope of consolidating their position and justifying their territorial claims.

The *bastides*, both French and English, were mostly built to an identical grid street layout – in so far as the local terrain allowed. Their straight streets intersect at right angles. At the centre of town is a square surrounded by covered arcades, called *couverts* (Mirepoix). Carcassonne's "Ville Basse," Montauban and Villefranche-de-Rouergue are particularly fine examples of these "new towns" (13C and 14C).

Siege warfare – When it was not possible to take a castle by surprise attack, lengthy sieges often ensued. Cathar fortresses undoubtedly presented the greatest challenge to any assailant. Perched on rocky outcrops, surrounded by steep, vertiginous rock faces, they confounded all the conventional techniques of siege warfare.

In 1210, it was thirst and sickness rather than any skill on the attackers' part which forced the fortress of **Termes** to succumb, and in 1255 the fall of **Quéribus**, last bastion of the Cathars, was only accomplished by treacherous means.

When laying a siege, the attackers first had to surround the stronghold. To this end they would build fortifications (trenches, stockades, towers, blockhouses etc) designed not only to prevent those under siege from making a possible sortie, but also to counter any attack by a relief army.

During lengthy sieges, which could go on for months if not years, an entire fortified town would be built round the besieged fortress.

To break through the stronghold's curtain wall, sappers would dig tunnels into the foot of it, shoring up the cavity with wooden props which were then set alight so that the tunnel and part of the curtain wall above collapsed. Slings, mobile siege towers and battering rams would be pressed into service. Military engineers supervised the construction of the various siege devices, for which the Crusades had provided the most recent testing ground.

The age of the cannon – Early methods of bombardment increased in effectiveness. Towards the mid-15C, under the inspiration of two talented gunners, the Bureau brothers, the French royal artillery became the most effective in the world. No feudal fortress could withstand French attacks. In one year, Charles VII recaptured from the English 60 positions which until then resisted sieges lasting four to six months.

Military architecture therefore underwent a complete transformation: towers were replaced by low, thick bastions, and curtain walls were built lower but much thicker (up to 12m/40ft thick). In the 17C, **Vauban** perfected these new defence systems.

The **Fort de Salses** is a perfect example of the changes brought about in the face of improved artillery. Half-buried, and well protected with the ingenious device of curtain walls with rounded tops, the fortress is shielded both from bullets and against the possibility of attackers scaling the walls.

RELIGIOUS ARCHITECTURE

Romanesque architecture

Languedoc, the crossroads of many civilisations, has been exposed to a variety of influences: from Auvergne, in the church of Ste-Foy in Conques; from Provence, in the abbey of St-Victor in Marseille, which had numerous dependent priories by the end of the 11C; from Aquitaine, in the basilica of St-Sernin in Toulouse and the church of St-Pierre in Moissac. Red or grey sandstone was employed in the Rouergue region in preference to schist, which is very difficult to carve, whereas, farther south, brick and stone were combined harmoniously.

Early Romanesque churches – At the beginning of the 11C, the prosperity of the Church stimulated a dramatic increase in the construction of ecclesiastical buildings. They are characterised by rustic masonry consisting of rough-hewn stones mixed with mortar. Around the outside of the apse, the walls are often adorned with Lombard bands, vertical pilasters projecting only slightly from the wall of the apse and linked at the top by a series of small arcades.

Inside, naves were roofed with barrel vaulting and ended in an oven-vaulted apse (quarter sphere). The ribbed vault, adopted some time later, is formed by the intersection of two barrel vaults; it was often used for crypts and side aisles.

The overall appearance of these churches is quite austere. They feature only a few, very narrow and deeply splayed windows. The heavy stone vaulting tended to put far too heavy a load on the supporting walls, so it was necessary to reduce windows to a minimum and to build the side aisles, designed to buttress the nave, up to the level from where the arch of the vaulting sprang. The abbey church at St-Guilhem-le-Désert is just one example from this period.

The Romanesque churches of Gévaudan in Haut Languedoc – The churches in this area encompass a wide range of layouts. Nonetheless, the single nave predominates and, at the end of the 11C, it was even made a feature of some of the larger churches (Maguelone Cathedral, St-Étienne in Agde).

On the exterior of such churches, massive, sturdy walls reinforced by arcades and a sober architectural style reflect Provençal influence. Inside, the ambulatories and radiating chapels characteristic of great pilgrimage churches, such as Ste-Foy in Conques or St-Sernin in Toulouse, are rarely seen in the less wealthy countryside churches. Further features inherited from neighbouring Provence were the polygonal apse and twin columns.

A magnificent example of the sculpted decoration of churches of this period can be seen at Ste-Foy in Conques, a jewel of 12C Romanesque sculpture.

Catalan architecture – An original architectural style combining Mozarabic and Carolingian influences appeared in the Catalan Pyrenees towards the mid-10C. The abbey church of **St-Michel-de-Cuxa**, in Conflent, exhibits a variety of features – a low, narrow transept, an elongated chancel with an apse, side aisles, barrel vaulting throughout – which lend it the complex appearance typical of Early Romanesque architec-

Detail on the tympanum of the Ste-Foy church doorway in Conques

ture. The simpler style of **St-Martin-du-Canigou** was widely copied during the 11C. Numerous local churches of this period have a vaulted nave supported by pillars, for example.

The next stage in architectural evolution was the construction of churches with barrel vaulting supported by transverse arches (Arles-sur-Tech, Elne) and the use of richer decorative motifs. Nor should one forget one of the most remarkable achievements of Catalan architecture, the introduction of domes on pendentives.

Mountain sanctuaries, often situated some way away from main communications routes and built somewhat crudely from roughly hewn rock, are most notable for their fine square towers, decorated with small arcades and with their otherwise forbidding appearance alleviated somewhat by Lombard bands, which were constructed down to the 13C.

Sculptural elements were frequently made of the grey or pink marble from the Conflent and Roussillon quarries. Capitals embellished with simple floral motifs and later with narrative scenes, and altar tables were produced in ever larger numbers by Pyrenean craftsmen. The 12C decoration of **Serrabone** priory, particularly the tribune used as a choir by the monks, is one of the finest examples of Romanesque art in Roussillon.

Painted mural decoration, usually a feature of smooth walls with only a few narrow window openings, is an important characteristic of the architecture of this period. Apses were decorated with the image of Christ in Majesty, or of the Apocalypse, or of the Last Judgement,

urging the faithful to work hard for their salvation, as on the doorways of Languedoc churches.

Moissac – A major stopping place on the road to Santiago de Compostela, Moissac Abbey exerted a considerable influence throughout Languedoc in the 11C and the 12C. Its doorway and cloisters are masterpieces of Romanesque art.

The **tympanum**, a rendering in stone of an illumination from a book, gave rise to a whole school of imitations. It represents Christ in Majesty surrounded by the symbols of the four Evangelists. The composition, and particularly the face of Christ, with its harsh and somewhat disturbing expression, suggests a latent Eastern influence which would have come via Spain. Similarly, the trefoil and polylobed arcades are reminiscent of Mozarabic art.

Rich decorative elements are also evident in the harmonious sculpture of the cloisters. The Apostles carved on the corner pillars (on white marble facings) are depicted standing with their body facing forwards and their head in profile. The capitals on the galleries display a great variety of geometrical and floral motifs, animals and narrative scenes. The decorative style at Moissac bears some relation to that of Toulouse, another cradle of medieval Romanesque sculpture.

Toulouse – Toulouse flourished as the centre of the Languedoc Romanesque School at the peak of its glory.

A major pilgrimage church, the basilica of **St-Sernin** – the largest Romanesque basilica in western Europe – was designed on a grandiose scale. A subtle blend of stone and brick, it is vaulted

S. Sauvignier/MICHELIN

Moissac cloisters

throughout and features a number of typical Romanesque techniques: semi-circular barrel vaulting on transverse arches in the main nave; half-barrel vaulting in the galleries; ribbed vaulting in the side aisles; and a dome over the transept crossing. The sculpted decoration was completed in less than 40 years (1080-1118) by Bernard Gilduin's workshop. The symbolism and logical ordering of the scenes depicted on the church doorways point to a deep and well-informed faith, drawing on imagery from the Old and New Testaments. The **Porte Miègeville**, leading into the south side aisle of the basilica, was completed in 1100; it reflects interesting Spanish influences from the workshops of Jaca and Compostela (the figure of King David depicted on the left on the lintel is identical to that on the Goldsmiths' Doorway in the cathedral at Santiago de Compostela, as is the figure of St James to the left of the tympanum).

The shape of the capitals is interesting, as it is obviously influenced by the classical Corinthian order, to which decorative motifs of animals or narrative scenes have been added. Unfortunately, the cloisters of St-Sernin Abbey, La Daurade Monastery and St-Étienne Cathedral were destroyed in the 19C (fragments of the capitals are exhibited in the Musée des Augustins).

Southern French Gothic architecture

The south of France did not adopt the principles of Gothic architecture used in the north of France, instead developing its own new architectural style closely linked with the Romanesque tradition.

The chancel of Narbonne Cathedral is virtually the only construction in the northern French Gothic style.

Languedoc Gothic – In the 13C, a specifically southern French Gothic style, known as Languedoc Gothic, developed. It is characterised by the use of brick, and by the presence of a belfry wall or a bell-tower decorated with mitre-shaped arched openings, as in the church of Notre-Dame-du-Taur or the upper storeys of the bell-tower of the basilica of St-Sernin, both in Toulouse. In the absence of flying buttresses, the load of the roof vault was supported by massive buttresses between which chapels were inserted.

Inside churches in this style, the single nave is relatively dark, stands almost as wide as it is high, and terminates in a polygonal apse. Its vast size was designed to accommodate the large congregations sought after by preachers in the wake of the Albigensian Crusade. The empty wall surfaces were adorned with painted decoration.

The light weight of brick made it possible to build vaulted roofs instead of the earlier timber roofing.

Albi Cathedral – The Ste-Cécile Cathedral at Albi is a magnificent example of southern French Gothic art at its best. The cathedral comprises a single nave, 100m/328ft long and 30m/98ft high, with 12 bays, supported by massive buttresses and lit through very narrow window openings. Despite the cathedral's strong resemblance to a fortress, it exhibits great purity of line. The absence of side aisles, transept or ambulatory resulted in a better structural balance.

The cathedral was begun in 1282, but not finished until two centuries later. In 1500, the Flamboyant Gothic style made its first appearance, in the shape of the choir screen and **rood screen**, and in the last three storeys of the bell-tower added to the square tower. In 1533, the addition of an ornate canopy porch completed the impressive appearance of the building.

The mendicant orders – The Dominican friars, known as "Jacobins" in France, built their first monastery in Toulouse, in 1216. It was occupied by the Franciscan Order, during the lifetime of their founder St Francis of Assisi, in 1222 (the church was destroyed by fire in 1871).

The vaulting of the church of **Les Jacobins** with its audacious "palm-tree" ribbing supported on a single pillar to overcome the problem of vaulting a semicircular space (the apse) and the restrained cloisters with their delicate twin colonnettes contribute to the overall grace of this marvellous architectural ensemble which radiates spirituality.

The bastide churches – The *bastides*, or "new towns," gave rise to numerous construction projects for churches on the edge of or close to the single central market place surrounded by covered arcades *(couverts)*. The southern French Gothic style was particularly suitable, since the churches had to be fitted into a confined space.

Although it has been modified a number of times over the centuries, the church of St-Jacques in Montauban is a good example of the Languedoc School, with its single nave and octagonal brick bell-tower. The church at Grenade was inspired by Les Jacobins in Toulouse.

Church in Narbonne

CATALAN BAROQUE

Catalan Baroque art, Spanish in origin and inspiration, developed at a time when Catalonia was embroiled in a critical territorial dispute (1640-60) which resulted in its being divided between Spain and France (Cerdanya, hitherto part of Catalonia, was annexed to Roussillon under the Treaty of the Pyrenees in 1659). Catalan Baroque art, primarily religious, was to become to some extent a manifestation of the unification in artistic expression achieved by a people otherwise torn asunder.

Altarpieces – By far the most significant work of art produced in the Catalan Baroque style is the altarpiece. From 1640, even the smallest parishes were commissioning their own. The necessary materials were right at hand: marble from Caune (Aude) and Villefranche-de-Conflent, pine from the forests of

Sculpted face and lion's head on Mirepoix's covered arcades

the Canigou and Spanish gold imported from America. The Catalan Baroque altarpiece might almost qualify as a work of architecture, so much do the two art forms have in common. It is in fact quite impressive to see how the altarpiece, built to increasingly huge dimensions and incorporating architectural elements such as the column, entablature, cornice, baldaquin or niche, ultimately becomes an architectural feature in its own right. The art of making these altarpieces evolved over the years. During the early decades of the 17C, they remained a sensible size with fairly restrained ornamentation. Between 1640 and 1675, altarpieces entirely covered in sculpture and gilding gained in popularity. They followed a strictly uniform design: two or three tiers embellished with increasing numbers of pinnacle turrets, broken pediments and canopies, accompanied by a wealth of ornamentation using geometric motifs, winged cherubs and fluted columns. From 1670 to 1730, the style became unreservedly Baroque. Architectural order was swamped by a profusion of decorative elements: pediments were invaded by crowds of angels; every available space was covered with floral motifs (bouquets, garlands, foliage); and the fluted column was replaced by the twisted one. The best example of a Catalan Baroque altarpiece at the height of the style's exuberance is that at Notre-Dame-des-Anges (1699) in Collioure.

Masters of Catalan Baroque – Numerous workshops flourished throughout Roussillon with the advent of Catalan Baroque. After 1640, several schools sprang up around **Lazare Tremullas**, a Catalan sculptor who introduced the carved altarpiece to France. It is to this artist that we owe the altarpiece in Notre-Dame-du-Rosaire (now on display in the church of St-Jacques in Perpignan). **Lluis Generès** was very productive during the second half of the 17C. His works include the high altar at Espira-de-Conflent *(18km/11mi E of Prades)* and the altarpieces at Prats-de-Mollo and Baixas *(13km/8mi NW of Perpignan)*. Much more everyday figures were introduced by Jean-Pierre Geralt, sculptor of the high altars at Pallalda and Trouillas and the altarpiece at Notre-Dame-du-Rosaire. However, the incontestable master of late-17C and early-18C Catalan Baroque extravagance was **Joseph Sunyer**, whose talent gave rise to the high altar of St-Pierre in Prades (1695), that of Notre-Dame-de-l'Assomption in Collioure and one of the altarpieces in Vinça. The decoration of the high altar and the camaril in the hermitage in Font-Romeu are also his works.

Sculpture – Catalan Baroque altarpieces make enormous recourse to sculpture. Lazare Tremullas introduced the use of sculpture to decorate altarpieces and this continued to evolve until the 18C. The Rosary altarpiece in the church in **Espira-de-Conflent** is a masterpiece of its kind. It was sculpted in 1702 by an anonymous artist, the "Master of Espira". The low-relief sculptures on this altarpiece in particular are characteristic: profusion and animated line of the figures; attention given to detail; rounded forms; and faces with smooth features. In the same church, there is a sculpture group of the Entombment by Sunyer with quintessentially Baroque theatricality. The sculpted figures, both those that are part of and those separate from the altarpiece, are of course painted and gilded. The treatment of the statues of the saints to whom the altarpieces are dedicated evolves in true Baroque fashion also: the dignified figures well tucked into their niches in the mid-17C literally seem to have taken flight by the end of the same century.

SECULAR ARCHITECTURE

In the "triangle" between Albi, Toulouse and Carcassonne, the centre of production of dyer's woad, wealthy merchants had beautiful Renaissance mansions built for themselves during the economic boom in the textiles and dyeing industries, from the mid-15C to the mid-16C. In the 17C and 18C, private mansions – or *hôtels particuliers* – inspired by the Italian Renaissance were built, particularly in Montpellier and Pézenas.

The façades overlooking the courtyard feature loggias and superimposed colonnades, crowned with balusters or pediments. Interior decoration is lavish, and monumental staircases abound.

At the end of the 17C, the architect **D'Aviler** revolutionised the appearance of such mansions; decoration was transferred to the exterior, particularly the porches. D'Aviler replaced lintels with heavily depressed arches, which came to be called davilerte arches. Above these was a triangular pediment with a certain amount of ornamentation. Magnificent openwork staircases with balusters were reminiscent of the preceding period. Towards the end of the century, pilasters and superimposed orders of columns were no longer a feature, and windows were built without any decorative frame.

However, façades were adorned with sculptures and wrought-iron balconies. The school of architecture in Montpellier is represented by D'Aviler, the Girals and Jacques Donnat. It also numbered in its ranks master craftsmen in wrought iron and carved wood. The school of painting includes such famous names as: Antoine Ranc, Hyacinthe Rigaud, Jean de Troy (17C), Jean Raoux and Joseph-Marie Vien (18C). Pretty fountains, and the Peyrou water tower (château d'eau) and aqueduct show another aspect of the artistic creativity of this fertile period.

TRADITIONAL RURAL ARCHITECTURE

Built primarily for practical, rather than aesthetic, purposes, rural houses can be particularly revealing about local rural industry. Their layout, construction and materials are often evidence of a traditional way of life deeply rooted in its region of origin. Thus in the Causses, the Cévennes and the Aubrac, where stock raising is the main livelihood, sheepfolds are a significant architectural feature, whereas in the plains of Bas Languedoc, the wine cellar (chai) is of primary importance.

Construction materials nearly always come from local sources, forging a further link between the house and its surrounding landscape. The following materials are used for roofing: volcanic lava, slate and schist slabs from the Cévennes, generally referred to as **lauzes**, as are the limestone slabs used in the Causses.

Nowadays, rural houses are adapting to new ways of life, showing the influence of new construction methods, and frequently suffering from the lack of craftsmen trained to rebuild or restore traditional constructions. Similarly, the evolution of agricultural techniques has had an impact on the appearance of the traditional rural cottage: there are fewer large lofts, now that grain is stored in silos.

Aubrac – A typical construction of this region is the **buron**, a solidly built hut of lava and granite with a single opening, found in the middle of pastureland generally standing on sloping ground near a spring. Burons are used as temporary living quarters by cowherds from May to October, while the cows are in their summer pastures. The huts are roofed in heavy stone lauzes, and inside they have a room used for both accommodation and cheesemaking, leading to a cellar, entirely hollowed out of the slope on which the buron stands, in which the cheese is left to mature. A few of these huts are still in use.

Causses – On the *causses*, houses are grouped in hamlets on the banks of rivers or else scattered singly to be as close as possible to land suitable for cultivation. They are robust buildings, with thick walls and an outside staircase leading to the upper floor. The cistern, near the kitchen, is always an important feature in these areas where water is scarce. Dry, white limestone is used for both the walls and the roof. The house and the sheepfold, usually a vast low-lying rectangular building of rough-hewn stone, are two distinct buildings, sometimes quite far removed from one another. The house comprises a cellar and a tool room on the ground floor and living quarters on the first floor. In these regions where wind and lack of rain result in there being no trees of any great height, the traditional timber frame roof is replaced with a stone vault.

Cévennes – Typical of this area are solid mountain houses, built halfway down the valley sides and designed to withstand the rigorous climate. The walls and roofs are built of unevenly shaped schist, and the walls feature small window openings.

Depending on the region, the lintels, window frames and corner stones are built of sand- or limestone; timberwork is made from the wood of the chestnut tree.

The first floor, where the living quarters are located, is reached up a flight of stone steps which can sometimes look more like a bridge, if the house stands on sloping ground. The stable and barn are on the ground floor. The second floor was sometimes reserved for silkworm breeding. On the roofs covered with rough schist slabs *(lauzes)*, the only decorative feature is the chimneys.

East of the Cévennes, towards the Vivarais mountains, houses are more Mediterranean in style, with roofs of half-cylindrical brick tiles, or pantiles, and the characteristically wavy edged cornices formed when such tiles are laid.

On the Lozère and Sidobre slopes, granite becomes a feature in walls and around window openings.

Espinouse range – Between the Lacaune mountain range and the Montagne Noire lie the Monts de l'Espinouse, cloaked in forests of beech, oak and chestnut, with intermittent patches of pastureland and broom-covered heath. The farmhouses typical of this region are protected by large slate tiles on the walls exposed to the prevailing, rainladen north-westerly winds. In Fraisse-sur-Agout, there are still one or two houses thatched with broom. The barn of the Prat d'Alaric farmstead is a large two-storey building (cowshed below, barn above), with walls built of granite and gneiss, a timber framework and a roof thatched with broom. Local barns typically feature gable walls with stepped edges. Each step is covered by a lauze laid so as to drain rainwater off to the sides.

Languedoc – Bas Languedoc is a land of vineyards, exposed to the Mediterranean climate. Houses here are inhabited by wine-growers and have tiny windows designed to keep the inside of the house cool. The walls are traditionally plastered with a sand-based material, usually in shades of pink or ochre. Haut Languedoc, with Toulouse as its capital, is a region of cereal crop farming. Its rich clay soils are reflected in the fact that buildings here are almost exclusively made of brick. A feature shared by all Languedoc houses is their gently sloping roof, covered by curved brick pantiles.

Bas Languedoc – The main façade of houses in this region often has a triangular pediment. The residential part of the building is separated from the stable and the barn. The rectangular wine cellar (chai), lit through semicircular dormer windows, occupies the whole of the ground floor. There are two doors in the façade: a large round-arched doorway leading into the wine cellar, and a smaller entrance opening onto the staircase which leads to the first-floor living quarters.

Haut Languedoc – In the Castres region, as in the region around Albi, walls are built entirely of brick, whereas in the eastern parts of Haut Languedoc brick is used only for framing doors and windows, and sometimes also decoratively arranged in horizontal bands beneath the cornice.

Many farms in Haut Languedoc boast a **dovecot**. Some are attached to the main farmhouse, but in most cases they are situated close by in some choice spot. In past centuries, pigeons were valued for their droppings, which were used to fertilise poor soils, and they were therefore a sign of special wealth or privilege.

Mediterranean Languedoc – Small drystone huts, known locally as **capitelles** or **cazelles**, can be seen dotted amid the garrigue and vineyards of this region. The walls, generally circular, are built of blocks of schist or limestone, with a break for the doorway. The roof is formed by laying lauzes to overlap like the scales of a fish, and shifting them gradually inwards to meet, forming a corbelled roof vault capped by a single flat slab. These huts were used as shelters by shepherds or as stores for farming implements.

Small, square-shaped, drystone constructions known as **mazets**, with two-sided or pyramidal roofs, are to be found in wine-growing areas, in the Hérault département. They are used as shelters by those tending the vineyards, at lunchtime, during storms and sometimes overnight.

Rouergue – The walls are built of schist or granite rubble masonry. On the roof, covered with schist or slate lauzes, are dormer windows which make the main façade look as if it has pediments, thereby adding interest to the line of the roof. The houses are again laid out on several floors: on the ground floor, are the wine cellar and tool room; on the first floor, the living quarters. The attic is used for drying chestnuts. The space beneath the outside staircase leading to the living quarters is sometimes converted into a pigsty. If the farmer is comfortably off, his house will comprise several buildings (living quarters, stable, barn and a turret serving as a dovecot) standing round a courtyard which is entered through a gateway with a sloping roof.

Dotted here and there in the fields, are isolated small, round drystone huts with conical roofs. These strange little buildings, which resemble the bories of Haute Provence, are used as shelters, barns or tool-sheds. Drystone huts such as these are a common architectural feature of Jurassic limestone regions in general (although they are known by a wide variety of local names), where it was necessary to clear the ground of blocks of limestone to be able to cultivate it. The rocks were then used to build low stone walls and temporary shelters from the elements.

In the Lot Valley, some of the barns feature roofs shaped like the keel of an upturned boat, thus increasing the amount of storage space available inside.

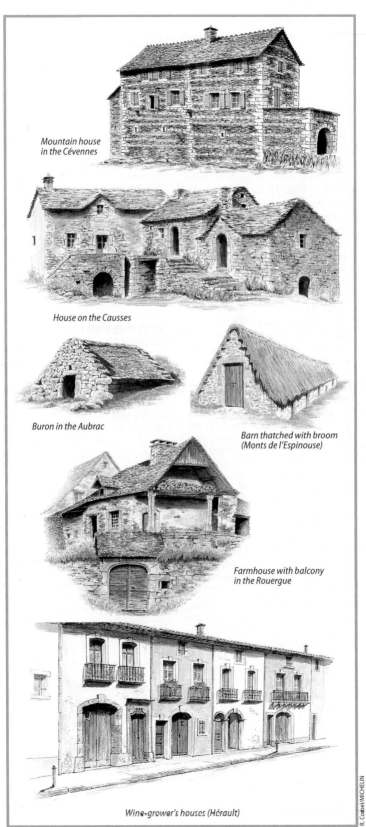

Mountain house
in the Cévennes

House on the Causses

Buron in the Aubrac

Barn thatched with broom
(Monts de l'Espinouse)

Farmhouse with balcony
in the Rouergue

Wine-grower's houses (Hérault)

R. Corbel/MICHELIN

Traditions

THE "LANGUE D'OC"

The fusion of Vulgar Latin with the old Gallic language gave rise to a group of "Romance" languages, including in France the "Langue d'Oïl" (in the north) and the "Langue d'Oc" (in the south), depending on how *oui* was pronounced in each region. The border between the two lay north of the Massif Central. **Occitan** thus comprises several major dialects: those spoken in Languedoc, Gascony, Limousin, Auvergne and Provence.

The language of the troubadours – The language of Oc is above all the language of the troubadours, who flourished during the 11C to 13C. These were poets who composed their own songs and, together with jugglers, travelled round the courts of southern France, entertaining the nobility with their plaintive songs of unrequited love.

This poetry of "courtly love" evolved from the earthy, even faintly erotic lyrics of the 12C into a purely spiritual celebration of love, often embellished with references to the Virgin Mary. Famous troubadours include Bernard de Ventadour from the Limousin, who sang at the court of Raymond V of Toulouse; Peire Vidal, a lyricist given to extravagant images whose reputation stretched from Provence to the Holy Land; Jaufré Rudel and Guiraut Riquier. The influence of the troubadours made itself felt as far away as Germany and Italy, where Dante is even said to have hesitated between Provençal and Tuscan when choosing in which language to write his *Divine Comedy*. At the same time, political satire, directed almost exclusively against Rome and the clergy, held a special place in Occitan literature.

Included in the tide of destruction unleashed by the Albigensian Crusade was the beginning of the decline of the Occitan tongue. There was an attempt to revive it in the early 14C, when a group of poets from Toulouse initiated the Jeux Floraux medieval poetry competition, but the Edict of Villers-Cotterêts in 1539, imposing Parisian French as the official language throughout France, dealt Occitan a heavy blow. The reforms introduced for Provençal by Frédéric Mistral and the Félibrige gave renewed impetus to the interest in reviving Occitan. Two organisations were founded in the early 20C (Escola Occitana in 1919 and the Institut d'Études Occitanes in Toulouse in 1945) with the aim of standardising as well as disseminating the language. A law was passed in 1951 allowing Occitan to be taught in schools and since 1969 it has been on the list of languages which it is possible to submit for examination at *baccalauréat* level.

Catalan – The Catalan language is very close to Occitan. It comes from the geographical area extending from Salses in Roussillon to Valencia in Spain, bounded to the west by Andorra and Capcir. Catalan was at its height during the 13C, a time when it became renowned through the writings of the poet and philosopher Ramon Llull. Like the language of Oc, it began to decline in the 16C, when the centralised monarchy of Philip II imposed Castilian Spanish, to the detriment of the other regional dialects. While Catalan is still spoken in everyday life, the literary renaissance begun in the 19C is contributing to the establishment of Roussillon's cultural identity.

FOLKLORE AND RELIGIOUS FESTIVALS

Local legends – There are numerous megalithic monuments to be found throughout the Languedoc region, many in the middle of nowhere. Their presence has often given rise to local superstitions reflected by the names they have been given: Planted Stone, Giant's Tomb, Fairies' Dwellings etc. The unusual shapes of many natural rock formations have also resulted in folk tales on their origins.

Most villages have tales of animals that have been mysteriously bewitched – cows which no longer give milk, dogs which apparently lose their sense of smell. To guard against malevolent spirits, local people have frequently developed practices such as wearing clothes back to front or throwing salt on the fire. Myths such as that of the Bête du Gévaudan abound in regions where wild beasts preyed on livestock and even occasionally people.

Wild animals particular to a region, such as the Pyrenean bears, have had festivals dedicated to them, in this case the Fête de l'Ours held in the Vallespir region (Arles-sur-Tech, Prats-de-Mollo and St-Laurent-de-Cerdans) in late February-early March and again during the summer for the benefit of tourists.

Carnival time – In the Aude, carnival time traditionally begins during winter with the slaughtering of the pig. Children with masked or blackened faces go from house to house to ask for food. During this season when the status quo is thrown to the wind, people dress back-to-front, or cross-dress, or dress up as babies or old people. A straw dummy is paraded round the village and made the scapegoat for all the misfortunes which have befallen the villagers, for which it is sentenced before a mock court held in the local *patois* before being hanged or burnt as punishment. The children dance around the fire.

One of the most famous carnivals in the region covered in this guide is that celebrated in Limoux. Every Sunday from January to March, as well as Shrove Tuesday and Ash Wednesday, people dressed as Pierrot figures dance slowly round place de la République, beating time with sticks decorated with ribbons. They are followed by revellers in various disguises all acting the clown. The festivities last until nightfall, when the square is lit by resin torches. The climax of the carnival is the Nuit de la Blanquette, during which the Carnival King is burned.

Sardana – This dance is one of the most colourful of Catalan traditions. It is set to the music of an accompanying **cobla**, a special orchestra with a dozen or so original instruments (brass, wind and percussion) capable of evoking a range of emotions, from the most gentle to the most passionate. The dance itself involves different sequences of long and short steps and some fairly complicated footwork. The sight of the whirling dancers flourishing garlands during festivals or local competitions is one to be remembered (the sardana festival at Céret is the most famous). The grand finale of any such event is traditionally the *sardane de la fraternité*, in which all the various teams join together to dance in circles.

Religious festivals – The most common religious festivals are those held in honour of the local patron saint or saints. For example, St Peter the patron saint of fishermen is honoured in Gruissan on 29 June. A bust of the saint is paraded around town behind a splendid float and the fishermen's standard. A Mass is celebrated with local fishermen at the parish church; then the procession continues to the harbour where a floral wreath is cast into the water in memory of those lost at sea.

In Perpignan, on Good Friday, a procession is held by the Pénitents de la Sanch, a religious brotherhood dedicated to the Holy Blood, founded in the 15C by Spanish Dominican friar St Vincent to accompany people about to be executed along the final stage of their journey. These rather bizarrely dressed penitents, in long black or red robes with pointed hoods covering their faces, walk in procession to the sound of hymns through the streets of Perpignan to the cathedral, carrying *misteris* – painted or sculpted images of Scenes of the Passion of Christ.

RUGBY

The game of rugby was born in England in 1823 during a game of football at Rugby College when William Webb Ellis broke the rules in a moment of heightened tension and grabbed the ball with both hands. Rugby was not introduced to France until the early 20C and only really caught on in the South-West, perhaps because it strikes a particular chord with the robust Occitan temperament. It is now both played and followed with equally huge enthusiasm throughout the Pyrenees, where the strong sense of solidarity needed to make a successful team is to be found in every town and village community, with the result that defending the local team colours has become a matter of pride and honour. Despite the rough physical nature of the game, which is played to the full in true Occitan "*jusqu'au bout*" spirit, rivalry between teams lasts for the length of the match only and is laid aside immediately afterwards during the "third half," or lavish meal that the players eat together to round off the event.

Rules of the game – Rugby is played between two teams of 15 players, using an oval-shaped ball which can be carried or kicked. The aim is to score as many points as possible during two 40min halves with a break of 5min at half-time. Each team consists of a full-back, four half-backs, a fly-half, a scrum-half and eight forwards. A try (5 points) is scored when a player succeeds in touching the ball down past the opposing team's goal line and a **goal** (3 points) is scored if a player kicks the ball over the crossbar (3m/10ft high) of the opposing team's goal. A try can be "converted" by scoring a goal from a free kick to earn an extra 2 points. Players must only pass the ball backward; if it is passed forward, the opposing forwards form a scrum, into which the scrum-half of the non-offending team throws the ball which the forwards then have to try to get into their team's possession by shoving and kicking. If the ball goes offside, there is a throw-in, when the players from both teams line up perpendicular to where the ball went off and have to try to catch the ball when it is thrown back into play.

RUGBY

The tackle – Perpignan vs Narbonne

The hand-off – Colomiers vs Villefranche-de-Lauragais

The throw-in – Montauban vs Graulhet

The scrum pass – Stade Toulousain

The try – Argelès-sur-Mer

The drop goal – Pamiers vs Albi

The penalty kick or conversion – Carcassonne

R. Corbel/MICHELIN

In the region centred around Carcassonne, **rugby league**, a variation of rugby with teams of 13 players (jeu à XIII), is played, earning itself the nicknames "heretic rugby" or "the Cathar sport".

Star teams – There is fierce competition for the French national rugby championships. Since they were first held in 1892, the **Championnats de France** have been won:

– 16 times by Toulouse (star player Jean-Pierre Rives)

– 11 times by Béziers

– 6 times by Perpignan

– 3 times by Castres

– twice by Narbonne (star players the Spanghero brothers)

– once each by Montauban, Carmaux and Quillan

The fact that rugby is much more popular and widespread a sport in the South-West than elsewhere in France is reflected in the French international rugby team (victor 10 times of the Five Nations Tournament and 4 times of the Grand Slam) which is made up almost entirely of players from South-West France. The most famous of these include Spanghero (Narbonne), Rives (Toulouse), Castaignède and Christian Califano (both from Toulouse).

Recognising the teams:

– Toulouse	red and black strip
– Béziers	red and blue strip
– Perpignan	red and gold strip
– Narbonne	orange and black strip

TRADITIONAL CRAFTS

The Cévennes, Rouergue, Causses and Languedoc, home to a host of tiny isolated villages in enchanting settings and quaint old town centres, in which traditional ways of life can still be upheld, have attracted numerous craftsmen who have set up their workshops here.

Revel has been famous for its fine furniture and marquetry ever since the cabinet-maker Alexandre Monoury came here from Versailles in 1889. It is also home to a variety of other craftsmen: weavers, gilders, lacquerers, sculptors on wood, bronze-smiths and blacksmiths. Wool-making and associated crafts have been centred around **Mazamet** since the mid-19C. From the late Middle Ages **Durfort** specialised in beating copper. Of the numerous hydraulic hammers set up along the River Sor, two dating from the 15C are still in operation. Traditionally the beaten copper is used to make pots and cauldrons. **Laguiole** is renowned for its elegant pocket knives, with curved handles made of horn or some other natural material. Fine kid gloves are made in and around **Millau**, whereas the **Cévennes** are the place to go for silk items since the revival of silk farming in the region. The wood of the nettle tree is also used to make various items, such as pitchforks at **Sauve** (Gard). Glazed vases produced in **Anduze**, which adorn many a garden, have been renowned since the 17C. The sheep bells which can be heard tinkling as the flock makes its way to the pastures in the mornings are more often than not the product of village workshops at Castanet-le-Bas or Hérépian in the Hérault Valley.

Craft workshops remain numerous heading south. From Albi to the Pyrenees, amid the diversity to be found as local natural resources change, the use of brick for both civil and religious architecture remains constant. Brickworks abound on the river plain of the Garonne, as well as along the Roussillon coast where there is a plentiful supply of red clay.

In the Albi region, **Graulhet** specialises in the production of leather for lining shoes, so there are a number of tanning workshops and other activities associated with the leather and shoemaking trades in the area. Dyer's woad (Isatis tinctoria) is still cultivated around **Magrin** and the resulting dye used to colour clothes and textiles in shades of blue. Stone has been cut and polished in the Ariège region since the end of the 19C and **Saurat** is home to the last operational sandstone quarry as well as the last producer of millstones in France. The **Bethmale Valley** is a centre of production for traditional wooden sabots, made out of locally grown beech or birch, marked with a heart shape linked with the somewhat macabre legend of a local shepherd betrayed by his fiancée who returned from a confrontation with her and her new lover, with their hearts nailed to his clogs. Horn combs are made in **Lavelanet**, near Foix, and the quality of their craftsmanship means that they retain their hold on the luxury end of the market against cheaper plastic competition.

In French **Catalonia**, typical crafts include the making of whips from the wood of the nettle tree at Sorède in the Lower Tech Valley, corks from the cork oak in Roussillon, notably at Céret and Le Boulou, espadrilles at St-Laurent-de-Cerdans, the brightly coloured (predominantly red and yellow) Catalan textiles in cheerful geometrical designs, and the cutting and setting of garnets at Perpignan.

THE REGION TODAY

Food and Drink

ON THE MOUNTAIN PLATEAUX

Far from the coast, the region stretching from the Aveyron *département* to the Cévennes has developed a rich and flavoursome local cuisine, based largely around the livestock bred on the *causses*. The region is particularly famous for its cheeses: Fourme de Laguiole, a type of Cantal, which is used to make the local dish *aligot*; Bleu de Causses, a blue cheese also made from cow's milk; Pérail, small and strong, and the well-known Roquefort, both from ewe's milk; and Cabécou or Cévennes *pélardons* from goat's milk. Lamb from the causses is a delicious, but pricey, option for the main course. On the whole, local recipes use mutton or pork, as is usual in traditional peasant cooking. Offal (variety meat), such as tripe, also features widely on local menus: *tripoux de Naucelles* (tripe stewed in white wine with ham and garlic); charcuterie from Entraygues; sausages from St-Affrique and Langogne; *trénels de Millau* (sheep's tripe stuffed with ham, garlic, parsley and egg); *alicuit* from Villefranche-en-Rouergue (stewed chicken livers). Visitors to the Tarn should be sure not to miss charcuterie from the Montagne Noire, *bougnettes* from Castres (small, flat pork sausages) and cured hams and sausages from Lacaune. Fresh fish is hard to come by, apart from river trout, but recipes featuring salted or dried fish are common, such as *estofinado* (stockfish stew). Chestnuts are another traditional local ingredient, used in soups and stews or roasted and eaten whole with a glass of cider. For those with a sweet tooth, there are a number of interesting local sweetmeats such as *soleils* from Rodez (round yellow cookies flavoured with almonds and orange blossom), fouaces from Najac (*brioches* flavoured with angelica), Cévennes *croquants* (hard almond cookies) and nènes (small aniseed biscuits) from St-Affrique.

LANGUEDOC

The cuisine of the Languedoc is typical of the Mediterranean, using herbs from the *garrigues* (rosemary, thyme, juniper, sage, fennel), garlic and olive oil, with fresh vegetables such as aubergines, tomatoes, courgettes and peppers. There is a local garlic soup called aigo boulido, made with garlic, olive oil and thyme. Sometimes dishes will include snails, delicious wild mushrooms (*cèpes, morilles*) or even – as a special treat – truffles, found growing at the foot of the holm-oaks on the slopes of the Hérault and the Gard.

Most commonly, meat dishes involve mutton or pork, occasionally veal. Local game, which has fed on fragrant wild herbs, juniper berries and thyme all its life, has a delicious flavour, as do the lambs and sheep raised on the causses. They can be served in pies or stews. Cheeses from this region are mainly from goat's milk, very tasty when heated and served on a bed of lettuce. Near the coast, menus reflect the variety of seafood at hand: oysters and mussels from Bouzigues, *bourride sétoise* (fish stew from Sète), gigot de mer de Palavas (fish baked with garlic and vegetables) and seafood pasties. In Montpellier, fish dishes are accompanied by beurre de Montpellier, a sauce of mixed herbs, watercress, spinach, anchovies, yolks of hard-boiled eggs, butter and spices. Sweets include *oreillettes* (orange biscuits fried in olive oil), eaten in Montpellier at Epiphany and on Shrove Tuesday, or grisettes (candy made from honey, wild herbs and liquorice).

FROM TOULOUSE TO THE PYRENEES

Farther west, towards Toulouse, and stretching from here south towards the Pyrenees, the rich local cuisine is that associated with the Périgord or South-West France in general. Goose and duck feature in many forms on local menus, either preserved as *confits*, or as foie

Cargolade

Aligot

This tasty cheese and potato dish comes from the regions of Rouergue and Aubrac.

- rub a casserole dish with garlic

- melt 150g/6oz of butter and 150g/6oz of cream over a high heat and gradually stir in 400g/14oz of Tomme or Cantal cheese cut into thin strips and 600g/1lb 4oz of mashed potato.

- Using a strong, long-handled wooden spoon keep stirring the mixture *(hard work, can take up to 45min),* always in the same direction so as not to break the strings of cheese.

- When the mixture is smooth and no longer sticks to the sides of the casserole, the aligot is ready to be eaten.

gras, or in stews. Assorted charcuterie includes the delicious *saucisson sec* (a sort of local salami). Meat dishes are usually stews which have been allowed to simmer gently for hours. Undoubtedly the most famous dish from this region is **cassoulet**, a thick stew of haricot beans, sausage, pork, mutton and preserved goose. Vegetables include sweetcorn, olives, asparagus from the Tarn Valley and the fragrant purple garlic from Lautrec. The Pyrenees produce a tasty ewe's milk cheese called brebis. Those with a sweet tooth should sample nougat from Limoux, *marrons glacés* (candied chestnuts) from Carcassonne or rosemary-scented honey from the Corbières.

Catalan cuisine – This is a typically Mediterranean cuisine, with its use of olive oil, and specialities such as garlic mayonnaise (*ail y oli in Catalan, aïoli* in French) and a paste made of anchovies, olive oil and garlic (el pa y all, or anchoïade). **Bouillinade**, the Catalan version of bouillabaisse (fish soup), and civet de langouste au Banyuls – spiny lobster stewed in Banyuls wine (dry Banyuls is very good for cooking, whereas the sweet variety goes well with creamy sweets and fruit salads) – make a delicious follow-up to a starter of Collioure anchovies. In Les Aspres, **escalade** is a fragrant soup made with thyme, garlic, oil and egg. Mushrooms fried in oil with an olive sauce are eaten with game (partridge and hare). Catalan charcuterie includes such delicacies as black pudding (boutifare or boudin), pig's liver sausage, and cured hams and salami from the Cerdagne mountain. **Cargolade**, snails from the garrigue grilled over burning vine cuttings, frequently feature in the open-air meals which follow prayer retreats at the hermitages.

Sweets include crème catalane (crème brûlée with caramel), bunyettes (orange-flavoured doughnuts), rousquilles from Amélie-les-Bains (small almond biscuits)

and the variety of fresh fruit from Roussillon's many orchards (peaches, pears, cherries and melons).

WINE

Coteaux du Languedoc – Wine-growers in the Languedoc vineyards, the main area for production of French table wine *(vins de table and vins de pays),* are nowadays concentrating on improving grape varieties and the way they are blended, efforts which have been rewarded with an increase in the number of designated AOCs (Appellations d'Origine Contrôlée) in the region. Prime advantages of the Languedoc as a wine-growing region are the variety of its soil types (layers of schist, pebble terraces and red clay) and its Mediterranean climate.

Promoted to AOC in 1985, the **Coteaux du Languedoc** appellation includes red, rosé and white wines produced in the Hérault, Gard and Aveyron *départements*. Besides Faugères and St-Chinian, whose heady, powerful wines have won these areas their own AOC designations, the AOC has been awarded to particular vintages; for red and rosé wines: Cabrières, La Clape, La Méjanelle, Montpeyroux, Pic-St-Loup, St-Christol, St-Drézéry, St-Georges-d'Orques, St-Saturnin and Vérargues; for white wines: Picpoul-de-Pinet, aged in oak casks. The main grape variety cultivated in the region is the Carignan grape.

The Cabrières region also produces **Clairette du Languedoc**, a dry white wine made from the Clairette grape which has won an AOC.

Local table wine is sold under the label "Vins de pays d'Oc" or "Vin de Pays" followed by the name of the département it comes from.

Notable vins doux naturels from the Coteaux du Languedoc include Muscat de Frontignan, Muscat de Mireval and Muscat de Lunel.

Minervois – The vineyards of the Minervois AOC are situated on terraces clinging to the flanks of the Montagne Noire as the mountain range gradually drops down into the Aude Valley. The Minervois region is reputed for its fine, fruity red wines which are robust and well balanced with a deep, rich red colour. The St-Jean-du-Minervois vineyard, which occupies the limestone *garrigues* on the uplands in the north-west, produces a fragrant muscat dessert wine.

The vineyards of the Aveyron – Once a source of great wealth to the region, thanks to the work put in by the monks from Conques, the Aveyron vineyards are characteristically located on steep slopes where they stand out from the surrounding mountain landscape. The red wines of **Marcillac** (AOC) are well balanced with a hint of raspberry and go well with the tripe dishes of the Rouergue region.

The red wines from **Entraygues** and **Fel**, classified as VDQS (*Vin Délimité de Qualité Supérieure* – one step down from AOC), have plenty of substance and a good fruity flavour; the whites from these designations are lighter with more finesse. In the Lot Valley, the **Estaing** VDQS vineyards are cultivated on the valley sides up to an altitude of 450m/1 476ft and produce subtle, fragrant red wines and pleasant dry whites.

The sheltered sides of the Tarn Valley between Peyreleau and Broquiès are home to the **Côtes de Millau** VDQS vineyards, which produce mainly red and rosé wine; **Cerno** is a local aperitif made from Côtes de Millau wine and herbal extracts.

Gaillac – The wines produced from the Gaillac vineyards, to the west of Albi, are officially classified as *Appellation d'Origine Contrôlée*. White wines are made using local grape varieties Mauzac, Len de Lel and Ondec which produce dry wines with a fragrant bouquet. There are three types of Gaillac white: sweet (moelleux), very slightly sparkling (perlé) and sparkling (mousseux). Gaillac red is made from traditional grapes such as Gamay, Syrah, Merlot and Cabernet, mixed with typically local varieties such as Braucol or Duras, for a robust wine, or Négrette. These wines are fruity and can be laid down.

Slightly farther west, just north of Toulouse, **Côtes du Frontonnais** wines are produced from a very old grape variety, the Négrette, mixed with Cabernet, Syrah, Fer Servadou and Cot to give supple, fruity wines, which are best drunk young. Around Carcassonne, there are two AOCs: Cabardès, well balanced with

The Knights Templars' cellars in Banyuls

J. Malburet/MICHELIN

plenty of body, and Malepère, a fruity red wine – both of which complement game and red meat perfectly.

Corbières and Roussillon wines – The **Fitou** *Appellation d'Origine Contrôlée* is reserved for a red wine from a certain area in the Corbières. Its alcohol content must be at least 12%, output is limited to 30hl per hectare/330gal per acre, and the wine must have been aged in a cellar for at least nine months. Fitou wines, produced from high quality grapes, are strong and full-bodied.

The **Corbières** *Appellation d'Origine Contrôlée* covers an area with a mixture of soil types, producing a varied range of wines. Besides red wines with a fine bouquet, production includes fruity rosés and some dry white wines.

The Roussillon vineyards are noted for their high quality vins doux naturels (dessert wines), the **Côtes du Roussillon** and **Côtes du Roussillon Village** wines classified as Appellation d'Origine Contrôlée, and their robust, earthy local wines. Just north of Agde, the tiny village of Pinet produces a dry white wine called Picpoul de Pinet (from the Picpoul grape) which makes the perfect accompaniment to a dozen or so oysters from the nearby Bassin de Thau.

The *vins doux naturels* produced in this region represent the majority of French production of wines of this type. The grape varieties – Grenache, Maccabeu, Carignan, Malvoisie, among others – add warmth and bouquet to these wines. The warm local climate and the vineyards well exposed to sunlight mean that these wines mature perfectly and have a high natural sugar content. The most famous examples are **Banyuls, Maury, Muscat de Rivesaltes and Rivesaltes**.

Blanquette de Limoux – This sparkling white wine is made from the Mauzac and Clairette grapes ripened on the slopes around Limoux, and is much in demand due to its fine quality.

Sète

L'ANCHOIS

Massif de l'AIGOUAL★★★

MICHELIN LOCAL MAP 339: G-4

The Aigoual mountain massif is crisscrossed by scenic roads that cut through the young forests cloaking the mountainside or running along ridges from which there are splendid views. An observation post on the summit permits a fine panorama, weather permitting. Breathtaking river gorges, such as those of the Dourbie, the Jonte and the Trévezel, carve their way across the slopes of the massif, part of which falls within the boundaries of the Parc national des Cévennes.

▶ **Orient Yourself:** The route, described below in two sections for travellers by car, covers the whole Aigoual massif and leads to the summit itself. We recommend following it from Meyrueis to Le Vigan, as the particularly spectacular stretch of road across the Minier Pass and down to the Arre Valley is best appreciated when travelling downhill.

🕐 **Organising Your Time:** Allow about 5hr total for the driving excursion below: 3hr for Meyrueis to Mont Aigoual and 1hr 30min for the stretch to Le Vigan.

A Bit of History

👍 *See the box below about Reafforestation.* From July 1944 onwards, the Aigoual massif played a role as the centre of the important "Aigoual-Cévennes" resistance movement, which had its headquarters at L'Espérou.

Geological Notes

A gigantic water tower – The Aigoual is one of the major water catchment areas in the Massif Central, as clouds rolling in from the chilly Atlantic converge with warm Mediterranean air currents right above the summit. The resulting rainfall has earned the mountain its name: "Aiqualis" or "the watery one." In an average year rainfall can measure up to 2.25m/over 7ft.

This rainwater drains off the mountain into two very different regions – the south face towards the Mediterranean is riddled with deep river gorges and jagged rocky ridges, whereas the gentler western slopes towards the Atlantic link the Aigoual massif with the vast limestone plateaux known as the Causses.

Excursion

🚗 *Driving: between November and May the roads may be blocked by snow.*

🥾 *Hiking: the GR 6 (Alps-Atlantic) and GR 7 (Vosges-Pyrenees) footpaths meet in the Aigoual massif and have interesting subsidiaries such as GR 66, for which a topoguide entitled Tour du mont Aigoual has been published. In addition, the Parc national des Cévennes organises 1hr guided walks around the Aigoual summit in summer.*

Reafforestation on the Aigoual

Only a century ago, the mountain massif was a sorry spectacle, bare of trees or any other vegetation. A reafforestation scheme was launched in 1875 by **Georges Fabre**, head warden of the French Rivers Authority and Forestry Commission. To add weight to his cause, he proved that much of the sand clogging up the port of Bordeaux had been washed down from the Aigoual. He obtained legal authorisation to purchase both communal and privately owned plots of land on which he planted large stands of trees to replace the existing straggly rows of trees along the river banks designed to prevent soil erosion. Despite the hostility of some towns and villages which refused to part with their pastureland, and the at times incendiary opposition of certain shepherds not averse to setting fire to the young trees, Fabre gradually managed to restore the Aigoual to its former forested glory.

Fabre did not content himself only with reafforestation; he also developed the network of mountain footpaths which now covers the Aigoual, restored foresters' lodges, set up arboretums (such as that at l'Hort-de-Dieu) for the study of growth patterns in trees and an observatory for meteorological research.

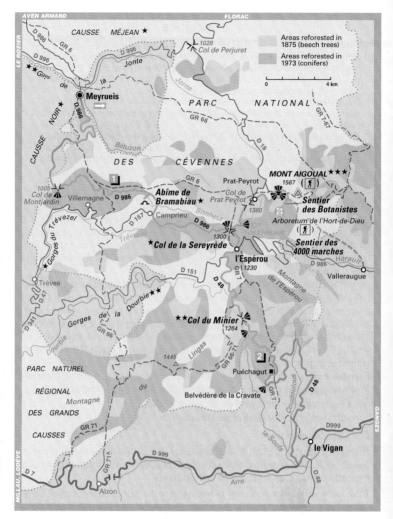

From Meyrueis to Mont Aigoual ①

32km/20mi – allow 3hr.

▶ Take D 986.

The road up to the Col de Montjardin initially runs through forest along the west bank of the Bétuzon before climbing along the edge of the Causse Noir. From the pass there is a good view of this plateau and that of Larzac and, shortly afterwards, of the Aigoual and Espérou peaks. The road then enters a forest, largely of larch trees, and follows a dizzying course cut into the rock face, offering delightful views of the old mines for silver-bearing lead ore in Villemagne. Farther along on the right is the curious rocky cirque known as "l'Alcôve" in which the Bramabiau tumbles down as a waterfall, having flowed across the Camprieu plateau underground.

Abîme de Bramabiau★

Temperature: 8°C/46°F ⚧ 2km there and back - ⏱ ⚹ Jul and Aug: guided tour (50min) 9am-7pm: Apr-Jun and Sep: 9am-6pm; mid-Oct to mid-Nov: 10am-5.30pm. 6.50€. ☎ 04 67 82 60 78.

The River Bonheur, which rises at the foot of Mont Aigoual at the Sereyrède Pass, used to flow across the small Causse de Camprieu, before cascading into its lower reaches. The Bonheur left its surface bed to bury itself in the causse. After a subterranean course of more than 700m/2 300ft, it emerges through a high, narrow cleft and bursts into a rocky cirque called the "Alcôve" as a glorious waterfall. When the river is in spate, the deafening noise of the waterfall is not unlike the bellowing of a bull – hence the name "Bramabiau" (*Brame-Biâou*: singing bull) given to the river from its resurgence until it flows into the Trévezel farther downstream.

Exploration

The river's underground course was first followed, with enormous difficulty, by E-A Martel and his companions on 27-28 June 1888 while water levels were low. As well as the 700m/2 300ft of the main river course, they discovered more than 1 000m/3 300ft of secondary galleries. From 1890 to 1892, and then again in 1924, 7km/4mi of new subterranean ramifications were explored.

This labyrinth, nearly 10km/6mi in length, consists of galleries 20-40m/65-130ft in diameter, at times up to 50m/165ft high, linked by extremely narrow passages and numerous cascades. E-A Martel declared Bramabiau to be a remarkable example of still active subterranean erosion. As the fast-flowing water gradually increases the size of the galleries, the cave roofs will fall in, transforming caverns into canyons, and, perhaps in thousands of years time, the Bonheur will once again find itself flowing in the open air, at the bottom of a deep gorge.

Visit

Visitors enter the underground world at the point where the river emerges from it. After crossing the Bramabiau between the first waterfall (in the open) and the second (underground), called the "Échelle" (ladder), the path leads along an impressively high gallery, with deep crevices caused by subterranean erosion, to the "Salle du Havre" (harbour chamber).

From this gallery, a recent modification gives access to the **"Grand Aven"** (swallowhole), where visitors can admire the work of cave painter Jean Truel. A path along a ledge more than 20m/65ft above the river, leads back up the Martel gallery, overlooking the "Pas de Diable" (devil's footprint), to a mineral seam. At this point some 200m/220yd of the cavern's length are dug out of a whitish barite seam, opening up into the "Petit Labyrinthe." A few steps lead to the **"Salle de l'Étoile"** (star chamber), with an unusual roof made up of rocks bound together with calcite.

From some steps leading out of the underground chasm, there is a magnificent view from a height of more than 50m/160ft against the light down onto the river.

▷ *A few hundred yards beyond the Abîme de Bramabiau is the junction with D 157, which leads off to the* **Gorges du Trévezel**★.

Col de la Sereyrède★

This pass is situated 1 300m/4 265ft above sea level, astride the Atlantic-Mediterranean watershed. Beneath the pass lies the Hérault Valley, which runs east towards the peaks of the Cévennes towering in the distance.

The road leading from the Col de la Sereyrède to the Aigoual summit offers some spectacular **views** over the Hérault Valley, along which runs the winding road to Valleraugue. Nearer the summit, the road re-enters the forest.

Sentier des Botanistes

1.5km/1mi below the summit, a signpost indicates the start of the trail. 20min walk.

🚶 This trail loops round the Trépaloup Peak for 1km/0.6mi and overlooks the **Hort-de-Dieu** (literally, "God's garden"), an arboretum created in order to study growth patterns in tropical trees. From the footpath there are some marvellous views of the south face of the Aigoual with its craggy ridges, the Cévennes peaks beyond, and the forest-covered east slopes of the Aigoual.

The Great "Draille du Languedoc"

The Col de la Sereyrède was once part of the great "draille du Languedoc," or wide sheep trail used for transferring flocks from summer to winter pastures, which until not so very long ago would be milling with sheep every June making their annual trip from the Languedoc garrigues up to summer pastures on the Aubrac plateau, or the slopes of Mont Lozère or La Margeride. *(The path of the old "draille" can be followed to the north along D 18 and to the south along the GR 7 as far as the town of L'Espérou, where the track turns off towards Valleraugue.)* Such sheep tracks, some of which are still in use, are much in evidence, recognisable by the deep channels they cut into the Cévennes ridges. Nowadays, the sheep are, for the most part, taken up to their summer pastures by lorry. Some herds are still driven up to L'Espérou on foot on the occasion of the Fête de la Transhumance every summer in mid-June.

Mont Aigoual★★★

The **meteorological observatory** built on the summit (alt 1 567m/5 141ft) in 1887 by the French Rivers Authority and Forestry Commission is currently occupied by the French meteorological office (Météo France). The site, overlooking the Gard, Hérault and Tarn valleys, is ideal. Increasingly sophisticated instruments enable researchers to record, among other things, the speed and direction of winds which herald either torrential Mediterranean downpours, flattening anything in their path, or the kinder Atlantic rainfall responsible for the region's lush green vegetation. A centre for testing all the equipment under extreme conditions is set up in the observatory.

For coin ranges, see the Legend at the back of the guide.

WHERE TO STAY

Auberge Cévenole – La Pénarié - 30570 Valleraugue - 4km/2.5mi W of Valleraugue towards Mont-Aigoual - ☎ 04 67 82 25 17 - auberge.cevenole@wanadoo.fr - closed Mon evening and Tues, except Jul-Aug. This modest inn on the banks of the Hérault has a number of attributes to recommend it: straightforwardness; mountain-chalet style restaurant with wooden tables; unpretentious local country cooking; and a small peaceful terrace. Six well renovated white rooms.

Inside the observatory is an interesting exhibition, **Exposition Météo-France** (May-Sep: 10am-7pm. No charge. ☎ 04 67 82 60 01), on weather forecasting past and present, with a section on the French Météotel system, which processes satellite images for weather reports.

From the viewing table at the top of the observatory tower, the **panorama**★★★ encompasses the Causses and the Cévennes and, in fine weather, the Cantal range, Mont Ventoux, the Alps, the Languedoc plain, the Mediterranean and the Pyrenees. In January, conditions are exceptional and it is possible to see Mont Blanc (Alps) and Maladetta (Pyrenees) simultaneously. In July and August, a heat haze often blurs the landscape and it is preferable to avoid reaching the summit during the hottest hours of the day. It is well worth climbing by night in order to reach the summit at daybreak, when visibility is excellent, particularly in September.

From Mont Aigoual to Le Vigan ②

39km/24mi – allow 1hr 30min.

▶ From the summit of Mont Aigoual, return to the Col de la Sereyrède.

Just before the pass, to the left of the road, the waterfall formed by the sprightly young Hérault can be seen in a ravine on the far side of the valley.

L'Espérou

This small, south-facing town lies amid wood and pastureland. Its picturesque mountain setting (alt 1 230m/4 035ft), well protected from northerly winds, and the ski slopes at **Prat-Peyrot** make it a popular holiday destination in both summer and winter.

Col du Minier★★

This pass is 1 264m/4 147ft above sea level. In fine weather, you can see as far as the Mediterranean. A memorial stone commemorates Général Huntziger (Commander of the French II Armée in Sedan) and his colleagues killed in an air crash in November 1941.

As the vertiginous cliff road begins its long, steep drop down the south face of the Aigoual, it overlooks the deep Souls ravine, giving a magnificent view of the Montdardier plateau and the Séranne range farther south. It then passes through a broken and chaotic granite rock formation.

The road passes the **Puéchagut** forester's lodge to the right, surrounded by another arboretum for the study of tropical forest species. Then the road curves sharply left, round the Belvédère de la Cravate, from which can be seen a panoramic view of the Arre Valley in the foreground, the Larzac plateau, the Séranne range, the St-Loup Peak and beyond towards the Mediterranean. Farther on, the road overlooks the Coudoulous Valley, its sides thick with chestnut trees, before crossing countryside more Mediterranean in character (vines, mulberry bushes, olive and cypress trees) to reach Le Vigan.

Le Vigan

This little town in the Cévennes lies on the southern slope of Mont Aigoual in the fertile Arre Valley. An old bridge dating from before the 13C spans the Arre. There is a good view of it from a platform on the river bank, upstream of the bridge.

Musée cévenol★– ◷ *Apr-Oct: daily except Tue 10am-noon, 2-6pm; Nov-Mar: Wed 10am-noon, 2-6pm.* ◷ *Closed 1 May. 4.50€.* ☏ *04 67 81 06 86.* – This museum, located in an 18C silk spinning mill, is almost entirely devoted to the popular crafts and traditions of the Cévennes.

The Salle des Métiers displays basket weaving, wickerwork, gold panning and tinsmithing. There are also reconstructions of craftsmen's workshops and a typical Cévennes interior. A room is devoted to André Chamson (1900-83), a writer from the Cévennes who set some of his novels in the foothills of the Aigoual. Note also the collection of silk costumes from the Cévennes.

Hiking Tour

Sentier des 4 000 marches (four-thousand-step path)
21km/13mi. Allow one day.

 *This hike, which starts from the Hort-de-Dieu arboretum, is suitable for experienced hikers. Follow the signposts showing a walking shoe or two footprints.*

This stony footpath (the steps appear only in the name!) wends its way through the Hort-de-Dieu arboretum and across wilder heathland dotted with broom. It then runs down the chestnut-covered slopes, offering fine views of Valleraugue and the upper Hérault Valley. From Valleraugue, return along the same path or follow a more varied but longer itinerary via Aire-de-Côte *(leave Valleraugue along D 10 to Berthézène).*

ALBI★★★

POPULATION 66 231

MICHELIN LOCAL MAP 338: E-7

Albi's enormous cathedral-with-fortress towers above the rooftops of the red-brick town, dwarfing all else. Albi "la rouge" lies on the banks of the Tarn, which flows at a sedate pace now that it has left the last foothills of the Massif Central. The city was at the height of its importance during the mid-15C to mid-16C, and the many beautiful Renaissance mansions in the old town are evidence of the economic and artistic boom created by the textile and dyeing industries. ▮ *Palais de la Berbie, pl. Ste-Cécile, 81000 Albi,* ☏ *05 63 49 48 80. www.mairie-albi.fr.*

▸ **Orient Yourself:** This charming, friendly town is at its most appealing when seen from the 11C **Pont Vieux**★, or when strolling around the old town, along narrow, winding streets lined with attractive old houses. The brick buildings of the **old mills** across the river have been successfully restored and now house a hotel, the local tourist board, private residences and a museum in honour of Lapérouse. From the terrace in Botany Bay square, there is a pretty **view**★ of the Tarn, the Pont Vieux and the part of town on the south bank, with the cathedral towering on the skyline.

⊚ **Don't Miss:** Cathédrale Ste-Cécile, Palais de la Berbie, Musée Toulouse-Lautrec.

A Bit of History

The "Albigensians" – This was the name given in the 12C to followers of Catharism – an academic term not used at the time – since Albi was the first place to offer them refuge. The name may also derive from an episode that took place in Albi, when the townspeople saved some of the heretics from the stake. A crusade, launched in 1209 under the leadership of **Simon de Montfort**, succeeded in placing the Languedoc region under the aegis of the French monarch. However, 20 years of bloody slaughter failed to stamp out the Albigensian heresy altogether; it took the Inquisition and the massacre at Montségur in 1244 to finish it off once and for all.

Powerful bishops – Meanwhile, the temporal power of the Roman Catholic bishops was dangerously growing; they became lords in all but name, constantly involved in legal or military wrangles. They did, however, find time to patronise the arts as well. **Bernard de Combret**, bishop from 1254 to 1271, began construction of an episcopal residence, the Palais de la Berbie, and **Bernard de Castanet** (1276-1308) undertook that of the cathedral of Ste-Cécile, at least until he was forced to retire to a monastery

Address Book

TOUR

Guided tour of the Old Town *(1hr) – organised by the Tourist Office, mid-Jul-late Aug: Mon-Sat except public holidays at 12.15pm. Book at the Tourist Office. 4€ (under 14: no charge).*

Walks – Three walks allow the visitor to discover Albi : the circuit Pourpre goes through the heart of old Albi and takes in the main historic sites, characters and monuments; the circuit Or focuses on the growth of Albi over two thousand years; the circuit Azur leads along the banks of the Tarn, taking in the Pont Vieux and the Pont Neuf, and provides some fine views of the town (routes marked by explanatory signposts in three languages). Depart from the Tourist Office.

For coin ranges, see the Legend at the back of the guide.

EATING OUT

Le Poisson d'Avril – *17 r. d'Engueysse -* ☎ *05 63 38 30 13 – closed Mon noon and Sun Oct-Apr.* This restaurant in a typical old Albi house 200m/220yd from the cathedral has an unusual interior decor designed like the inside of a barrel, with wooden beams. Prices are moderate and food is not heavy.

Le Table du Sommelier – *20 r. Porta -* ☎ *05 63 46 20 10 - closed Sun and Mon.* The proprietor sets the scene here perfectly, with cases of wine piled high in the entrance and rustic dining room with mezzanine floor. Beyond appearances, this wine-focused bistro serves refined cuisine using the freshest ingredients.

Le Robinson – *142 r. Édouard-Branly -* ☎ *05 63 46 15 69 - robinsonalbi@yahoo. com – closed Nov-Feb, Tue noon and Mon.* This isle of green on the banks of the Tarn is acceible from the pont Neuf. Dating from the 1920's, the old-fashioned dance hall has an exuberant charm. The food is simple and the welcome warm. Dream away the evening!

Jardin des Quatre Saisons - *19 bd de Strasbourg -* ☎ *05 63 60 77 76 – closed Sun evening and Mon.* A friendly welcome from the owners awaits, along with a good selection of wines and traditional cuisine. A little away from the centre, this remains a reliable favourite.

Le Moulin de La Mothe – *R. de Lamothe -* ☎ *05 63 60 38 15 - restaurant_ moulin_delamothe@wanadoo.fr - closed school holidays in Feb and Oct/Nov, Tues evening from 15 Sep-30 Apr, Sun evening and Wed.* In fine weather, this restaurant on the banks of the Tarn attracts a crowd. It has a terrace overlooking the park and the river. In cooler weather, the light and airy dining room offers the same view.

WHERE TO STAY

George V – *29 av. du Mar.-Joffre -* ☎ *05 63 54 24 16 – info@hotelgeorgev.com – 9 rms.* It is worth searching out this cosy establishment with its typical local style in the station district. Rooms are a generous size and some have a fireplace. At the first sign of fine weather, make the best of the pleasant shade of the little courtyard.

Chambre d'hôte Le Moulin d'Ambrozy – *81120 Lombers - 14km/9mi south of Albi on the N112 and then the D71 -* ☎ *05 63 79 17 12 – – 3 rms.* This authentic 17C mill in open countryside is experiencing a new lease of life, its attractive rooms with many personal touches including fine furniture such as a four poster bed, plus pleasant gardens and swimming pool. Dinner draws inspiration from seasonal specialities.

Cantepau – *9 r. Cantepau -* ☎ *05 63 60 75 80 – closed 25 Dec-11 Jan -* 🅿 *- 33 rms.* Wicker furniture, subdued hues and fans give this hotel a colonial feel following its recent revamp.Friendly welcome.

Hôtel Mercure – *41 bis r. Porta -* ☎ *05 63 47 66 66 – h1211-gm@accor-hotels. com -* 🅿 *- 56 rms.* This modern hotel has an original setting, in an old 18C red-brick mill on the banks of the Tarn. The functional rooms offer a view of the river and cathedral. Guests can enjoy the same view from the dining room.

SIT BACK AND RELAX

La Berbie – *17 pl. Ste-Cécile -* ☎ *05 63 54 13 86 - Jul-Aug: daily 9.30am-11pm; Sep-Jun: Wed-Mon 9.30am-8pm.* This attractive tea room on Place Ste-Cécile, opposite the cathedral, serves a wide range of tea, coffee, home-baked pastries, ice-cream sundaes and pancakes. Luncheon menu.

ON THE TOWN

Albi "the red," named after its red-brick façades, is a beautiful city. Visitors might like to start their day at "la Berbie" on Place Ste-Cécile, opposite the imposing cathedral. Then we recommend dropping in to sample some local specialities at "Pâtisserie Galy." During the day, a boat trip on the Tarn is a must, in order to appreciate the beauty of the city at its best. At the end of the day, this student town offers plenty of pleasant places to spend the evening, such as the "Connemara," "Estabar" or "Shamrock."

SHOPPING

In the streets of the Old Town (especially *rues Mariès, Ste-Cécile et Verdrusse*) are a variety of antique shops and boutiques. Also, visitors cannot miss the many shops selling local food and drink.

L'Artisan Pastellier – *5 r. Puech-Bérenguier* - ☎ *05 63 38 59 18* - *artisan. pastellier@wanadoo.fr* – *Tue-Sat 10am-noon, 2-7pm, Mon mid-Jun to mid-Sep and Sun in Aug 3-6.30pm - closed 20 Jan-10 Feb, 14 Jul, 15 Aug, Sun and Mon out of season.* Near the Maison du vieil Alby, this shop is a poem in blue. Made from pastel leaves, this irresitable colour is used to shade local crafts and fabrics. Claire and her husband prepare artists' materials of quality including inks for caligraphy. The owners know everthing there is to know about pastel and are happy to answer questions.

Marché biologique – *Pl. F.-Pelloutier* – *Tue 5-7pm.* In addition to organic produce, local craftwarer and books are also on sale here.

Markets– *Pl. Ste-Cécile.* A big market is held on Saturday on place Ste-Cécile: fruit, vegetables, foie gras (in season), mushrooms, garlic from Lautrec, charcuterie from Lacaune et Gaillac wines.

Patisserie J.P. Galy – *7 r. Saunal* - ☎ *05 63 54 13 37* - *Tues -Sat 9.45am-7pm - closed 1 week in Feb and 4 weeks Sep-early Oct and holidays.* For 14 years, Galy pastrycooks have been supplying local people and visitors with fine pastries, many of which are local specialities (try out the following:

navettes, gimblettes, croquants aux amandes, jeannots à l'anis, croissants aux pignons). These delicacies sell like hot cakes and it is worth paying a visit early in the day to avoid disappointment.

RECREATION

Boat Trip on the Tarn – *Berges du Tarn* - ☎ *05 63 43 59 63* - *www.mairie-albi.fr* - *Jun-Sep: Sun, Tue and Thu 11.25am-noon, 2pm-6.30pm Fri and Sat 10.45am-noon, 2pm-6.30pm, Mon and Wed 10.45am-noon, 2pm-5.15pm. 5€ (for 30min, children under 12: 3€); 15€ (for 2hr, children under 12: 10€)* ⌒. The boat in question is in fact a flat-bottomed barge, a gabarre, used for transporting goods until the 19C and now used for pleasure trips. Leaving the old harbour at the foot of the ramparts of the Palais de la Berbie, the barge travels along the Tarn past the old Albi mills, and the locks at the Moulin de Gardès and Moulin de la Mothe.

CALENDAR OF EVENTS

Free organ concerts in the cathedral - *Wed and Sun afternoons in Jul and Aug.*

Le festival de théâtre - *early Jul,* ☎ *05 63 49 48 80.*

Carnaval - *Feb.*

Le Grand Prix automobile d'Albi - *Sep.*

---

because his abuse of power was so blatant it outraged the Pope. **Louis d'Amboise** (1473-1502) was compelled to step down in his turn, after a lengthy and luxurious period in office, because of incessant quarrels with members of his flock.

Albi was elevated to an archbishopric in 1678.

Henri de Toulouse-Lautrec – The famous artist was born son of Comte Alphonse de Toulouse-Lautrec Montfa and Adèle Tapié de Celeyran, a first cousin, at the Hôtel de Bosc in Albi in 1864. Two childhood accidents, in 1878 and 1879, left him crippled for life, a diminutive figure on stunted legs.

In 1882, Toulouse-Lautrec set up home in Montmartre, where he immersed himself in the seamier side of Parisian life. He frequented bars, nightclubs, brothels and racecourses, and quickly developed a unique artistic style as he sketched the scenes around him, capturing the atmosphere of a social milieu of poverty and loose living remarkably vividly. From 1891 onwards, his posters appeared on more and more Parisian walls, as his skill as a lithographer won him fame. By 1899, his alcoholism and debauched lifestyle had reduced him to such a state that he was interned for a while in a sanatorium in Neuilly. Once he had recovered, he was released but soon fell back into his old ways, despite the vigilance of his friend Paul Viaud. On the verge of collapse, he left Paris in 1901 and died in the family château at Malromé, near Langon in the Gironde, on 9 September of that year. He is buried at the cemetery in Verdelais.

Cathédrale Ste-Cécile★★★

The Catholic Church had to move fast to re-establish its authority in the wake of the Albigensian Crusade. Bishop Bernard de Combret began the construction of a bishops' palace in 1265, and Bernard de Castenet began that of the cathedral in 1282. This was intended to symbolise the Church's newly found grandeur and power. It took 200 years to build the great monument; successive bishops later contributed to the finishing touches.

To get a better idea of the massive proportions of the cathedral, take a look at it from a distance, from the bridge across the Tarn (the Pont du 22-Août), or from one of the streets of Old Albi which open onto the cathedral square.

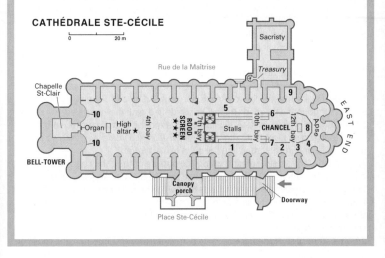

Exterior

The sheer, red-brick walls, once crowned by a tiled roof resting on the vaulting at the level of the windows (where there is now a row of white-stone gargoyles), have been surmounted since 1849 by a band of false machicolations, a rampart walk and bell turrets.

Doorway and canopy porch★– The main entrance is in the south side of the cathedral, through a 15C doorway, linking the building to an old defence tower, and up a grand flight of steps to an elaborate, carved stone canopy which forms the porch. This work of art was added under Louis I of Amboise (1520), and the extravagant, intricate decoration contrasts markedly with the austerity of the brick façade.

Bell-tower – The original tower was a square, keep-like structure about the same height as the nave. Between 1485 and 1492, Louis I had three more storeys added. The corners on the east side of the tower, where it adjoins the church, are adorned by two turrets running to the full height, whereas those on the west side have decorative turrets only up to the level of their first storey, giving the tower a somewhat lopsided appearance.

Interior

Nave – Turn left as you enter the cathedral and stand to one side of the organ at the west end, looking towards the east end. To picture what the original cathedral looked like, imagine the building without the ornate rood screen halfway down, or the gallery added in the 15C which cuts across the line of the side chapels. This would leave a vast nave with pointed vaulting, no transept and supported by interior buttresses with side chapels between them.

Cathédrale Ste-Cécile and Palais de la Berbie

Rood screen★★★ – The church was consecrated in about 1480. At around the same time, Louis I of Amboise decided to build the chancel, closed off by a carved stone rood screen. The resulting magnificent work of art, a consummate example of Late Flamboyant Gothic decoration, has often been compared with a piece of lacework. It is a mass of skilfully interlaced motifs, pinnacles and arches, with richly ornate pendant keystones.

The central and side doorways are elegantly carved from wood, with remarkably intricate iron door locks, beautifully wrought by hand. Of the 96 statues which adorned the rood screen until the French Revolution, only Adam and Eve remain. The three statues surmounting the rood screen (Christ crucified, with the Virgin Mary to his right and St John to his left) are late-19C replicas. Behind the central crucifix, on the side of the rood screen facing into the choir *(only visible from inside the choir)*, is a statue of St Cecilia, holding an organ and the palm of martyrdom.

The carved stone screen running round the outside of the choir consists of ornate ogee arcading with Flamboyant tracery and the Chi-Rho Christogram. Against each of the pillars between the arches stands the polychrome statue of an Old Testament figure. These statues in the chancel of Albi Cathedral are one of the best examples of the naturalism of Gothic sculpture in France. The influence of the Burgundian School can be seen in the realistic facial expressions, the slightly heavy folds of the clothing and the sturdiness of the figures. Particularly interesting statues include those of Judith (1), the prophets Zephaniah (Sophonias) (2), Isaiah (3) and Jeremiah (4), and, in the north ambulatory, Esther (5).

Chancel – ♿ ⏰ ☞ *Jun-Sep: 9am-6.30pm; Oct-May: 9am-noon, 2-6.30pm; guided tour (1hr 30min) available 1€. ☎ 05 63 43 23 43.)*– Inside the chancel, the statues of Charlemagne (6) and the Emperor Constantine (7) look down from above the entrance doorways. If you stand facing the high altar, the rich colours of the paintings on the walls of the ambulatory chapels can be seen through the openwork of the choir screen. The statues inside the chancel depict characters from the New Testament; the Virgin Mary (8), surrounded by angels, occupies place of honour behind the high altar. The pillars are decorated with the 12 Apostles. There are two rows of magnificently carved oak choir stalls, beneath a frieze of cherubim alternating with red or blue painted stone panels decorated with gilded arabesques.

The five tall stained-glass windows around the apse date from the 15C and were restored in the 19C. The side chapels are of mixed interest. Note in particular the chapel of the Sainte-Croix (9).

The monumental **organ**, built 1734-6 by Christophe Moucherel and last restored in 1981, is best admired while one is level with the rood screen. It consists of two distinct levels, one above the other, supported by a pair of atlantes. The elegant wooden organ loft is beautifully decorated with statues of cherubs playing musical instruments and, above them, St Cecilia and St Valerian.

Below the organ stands the new **high altar**⋆ (consecrated in 1980), a black marble creation by Jean-Paul Froidevaux. It is decorated with brightly coloured enamels, depicting a vine on three sides and St Cecilia on the fourth. A text from St Matthew's Gospel, on the mystery of the Eucharist, is inscribed around the altar.

Treasury – ⏰ ☞ *Jun-Sep: Sun 9am-noon (11.15am if mass); Oct-May: Sun 9am-noon (11.15am if mass), 2-6.30pm (6pm if mass), guided tour available. 3€ (children under 12: no charge). ☎ 05 63 43 23 43.* – This is located in a chapel intended, as far back as the 13C, to house the cathedral's archives and precious objects. Exhibits displayed in the first room include the 14C polychrome reliquary of St Ursula, a 13C crosier from the Limoges region, a 14C episcopal ring and a Sienese polyptych also from the 14C. Objects from other churches in Albi and from other parts of the diocese are displayed in the next room.

The Last Judgement (10) – This enormous mural painting at the west end of the cathedral, decorating the plaster wall beneath the organ, was executed in the late 15C, but was unfortunately stripped of its entire central panel, and most importantly of the focal image of Christ, when the chapel of St-Clair was added to the cathedral in 1693. The scene was painted in tempera, that is colour pigment ground and mixed with egg yolk and glue, unlike the fresco scenes painted on the cathedral vault. The brick wall beneath the painting, caught in the play of light from time to time, adds to the delicacy of touch and clarity of detail of the whole. It is possible that this painting was intended to compensate for the lack of sculpture on the west front, which is traditionally reserved for scenes of the Last Judgement in cathedral designs.

The composition is in three tiers. Across the top, heaven is represented by a band of angels. In the centre and to the right of where Christ would have been (ie to the left as you look at it) are the heavenly elect in three rows: on top, the Apostles wearing white robes and crowned with golden haloes; beneath them the saints, some of whom are obviously of quite high rank, who have been judged already and allowed to enter heaven; and below them, the newly resurrected dead judged fit to join the ranks

The last judgement

B. Kaufmann/MICHELIN

of the blessed, who are still facing the Judge Eternal holding out the books of their life story. In contrast to this serene group, the cringing damned (*to the right as you look*) are being hurled into the darkness of hell. Slightly higher, between them and the angels representing heaven, there is only a dark, cloudy void, symbolising the unbridgeable gap that their sins have created between them and the Heavenly Father. The bottom tier of the painting depicts, in vivid detail, the various punishments hell has to offer those who have broken any of the Seven Deadly Sins. The hideous tortures are clearly devised to reflect the particular vice to which the sinners were prone. From left to right, we see the proud, the envious, the angry, (the slothful disappeared when the opening to the chapel was made), the greedy, the gluttonous and the lustful.

Cathedral vault – Once this masterpiece was completed, the French artists left the cathedral of Ste-Cécile, so Louis II of Amboise called in Italians to decorate the walls and ceiling vault. The Bolognese artists who embellished the austere nave of the cathedral with dazzling paintings drew on the splendours of the golden age of the Italian Renaissance, the Quattrocento (15C). The effect of the white and grey ornamental foliage, highlighted in gold, on an azure background is most striking.

Many portraits of saints and Old Testament figures adorn the vault, which consists of 12 bays, each divided by the ribbing into four concave triangular sections (a real challenge to the artists' techniques of perspective). In the fourth bay along from the bell-tower, the triangular section to the west depicts Christ showing his wounds to Thomas, whereas that to the east contains the Transfiguration. In the seventh bay along (*above the rood screen*), to the east of St Cecilia and St Valerian, there is the Annunciation. The 10th bay along (*above the great choir*) is sumptuously decorated with the Parable of the Wise and Foolish Virgins (*west*) and the Coronation of the Virgin against the backdrop of a magnificent gold glory surrounded by cherubim and seraphim (*east*). Finally, above the beginning of the apse *(12th bay along)* the Christ of the Apocalypse is depicted in a gold mandorla, surrounded by angels, cherubim and seraphim and the symbols of the four Evangelists.

Palais de la Berbie★

The initiative to build a bishops' palace near the 12C cathedral (no longer extant) was taken by Bernard de Combret in about 1265. The name "Berbie" is derived from bisbia or "bishopric" in local dialect. Bernard de Castenet transformed the original building into a fortress, adding a massive keep and a fortified curtain wall. The size of this is best appreciated from the terrace on the banks of the Tarn. Although designed initially to protect the entrance to the keep, the wall has undergone alterations over the centuries. In the late 17C, the old parade ground was turned into a French-style garden, designed by Le Nôtre, and a hexagonal roof was added to the west tower. The rampart walk was transformed into a shaded path lined with marble statues of Bacchus and the Four Seasons (18C). The eastern wing of the building, with a slate roof, dates from the end of the 15C. Louis I of Amboise added pepper-pot roofs to the turrets, with elegant stone dormer windows to let in the light. All but one of these have disappeared.

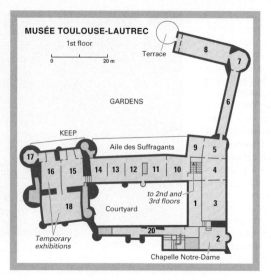

After the proclamation of the Edict of Nantes in 1598, there was no further need for a fortress. The west curtain wall was demolished and the north tower of the keep reduced in height. Prelates subsequently concentrated on the interior. Since 1922, the palace has housed the Musée Toulouse-Lautrec, a museum founded by his cousin, Gabriel Tapié de Celeyran and his lifelong friend, Maurice Joyant.

Musée Toulouse-Lautrec★★

Extensive restoration work is underway; it is however possible to see all the works, but some of them are liable to be moved to a different part of the museum.

A grand 17C staircase leads *(left)* to a gallery of archaeological exhibits (20) on the first floor; note the tiny, 20 000-year-old *Vénus de Courbet* (Upper Perigordian Era) discovered at Penne in the Tarn *département* (*3rd display case on right*).

The 13C chapel of Notre-Dame (2) has ribbed vaulting and colourful decor by the Marseille artist Antoine Lombard.

The following series of rooms were fitted out in the 17C. Gallery 1 contains copies of works by Georges de la Tour. The spacious Salon Daillon du Lude (3) has a handsome French style ceiling, where the beams and rafters are left visible and are enhanced with painted decoration, and contains among others a painting by Guardi and works by La Tour.

However, the main interest of the museum lies in the **Toulouse-Lautrec collection** itself; among the portraits of the artist by his contemporaries note in particular the full-face portrait by Javal, which captures the dignity in Toulouse-Lautrec's gaze. The museum at Albi houses the most comprehensive collection of the artist's works, bequeathed to the city by the Comtesse Alphonse de Toulouse-Lautrec, his mother, in 1922 and augmented by donations from other members of his family. Room 5 and the long gallery 6 contain early works, which bear witness to the artist's overriding

This Was Indeed Paris

Room 11 is dominated by one of Toulouse-Lautrec's most famous works: *Au Salon de La Rue des Moulins*. The pastel study and finished painting of 1894 are displayed on opposite walls. The artist's supreme skill as a draughtsman and his keen observational powers are well illustrated in pictures such as this, in which he relentlessly records the often harsh reality of the scenes he saw. The pencil lines are left visible beneath the paint. Other subjects are taken from the world of Parisian music halls and theatres, where Toulouse-Lautrec would go every night and draw numerous portraits: Valentin "le Désossé" ("boneless") who used to come and dance with La Goulue at the Moulin de la Galette; the singer-songwriter Aristide Briant, who would perform numbers in slang at his cabaret Le Mirliton; Caudieux, a café-concert artist; Jane Avril, whose wild dancing earned her the nickname "Le Mélinite," and whose delicate features and elegant posture are captured in several of Toulouse-Lautrec's works; and the singer Yvette Guilbert, who was passionately pursued by the artist but who forbade him to publish his portraits of her, as she found them unflattering.

interest in animals and people. *Artilleur sellant son cheval*, of a soldier saddling his horse, is an outstanding example of work executed by Toulouse-Lautrec at the age of only 16. Many of the works evoke his mother's estate at Celeyran (near Narbonne), where the artist often went to stay. During the course of the visit, notice the variety of signatures he used: Henri de Toulouse-Lautrec, Montfa, monograms like HL or HTL, Tréclau (anagram of Lautrec) written in an elephant, a mouse or a cat. The circular room at the end of the gallery (7 – drawings) and the following large room (8 – paintings) contain famous portraits and works, mainly evoking Toulouse-Lautrec's life in Montmartre. *L'Anglaise du Star*, one of Toulouse-Lautrec's most famous portraits, is a reminder of one occasion in Le Havre, when the artist had to send to Paris for his painting materials in order to capture the smile of blonde "Miss Dolly," a pretty English barmaid he had met in one of the bars by the port, before catching his usual boat to Bordeaux. The portrait of *La Modiste* (Mlle Louise Blouet d'Enguin) is an interesting departure from Toulouse-Lautrec's usual work with its use of an almost chiaroscuro technique. The artist's friend and cousin, Dr Gabriel Tapié de Celeyran, who kept a watchful eye on him, is also depicted. The drawings of circus scenes are reproductions of those executed from memory by Toulouse-Lautrec while he was being treated at the sanatorium at Neuilly in 1899. At the end of the room, a door leads onto a terrace (*closed out of season*) from which there is a pretty view of the River Tarn, the Pont Vieux and the formal, French style gardens of the Palais de la Berbie.

Room 9 contains a number of sketches of *"le jeune Routy,"* a ploughman at Celeyran, showing the amount of preparation Toulouse-Lautrec put into his portraits.

In rooms 10 to 14, along the north wing of the palace where visiting bishops were lodged, several famous works stand out, including a study for the poster for *La Revue blanche* (1895), a charcoal sketch given added depth by the use of colour, which pays homage to the beauty of Missia Godebski, wife of one of the Natanson brothers who edited *La Revue blanche*.

Room 23 contains the hollow walking cane, complete with miniature glass, used by Toulouse-Lautrec during and after his cure in Neuilly; he could fill it with brandy, thus deceiving Paul Viaud, the friend looking after him.

On the third floor is a collection of modern and contemporary art, including drawings of Verlaine by Louis Anquetin, sculptures by Maillol and Bourdelle, and paintings by Yves Brayer, Matisse, Marquet and Dufy.

From the rotunda there is a good **view** of the Tarn, with the bridges and old mills.

Old Albi★★

▷ *From place Ste-Cécile, take rue Ste-Cécile and then rue St-Clair (2nd on the right).*

1hr. A covered passage on the left offers glimpses of the **Saint-Salvy cloisters** which will be visited at the end of the town walk.

Hôtel Séré de Rivières

This 15C-18C mansion was the residence of a family of dyer's woad merchants who were ennobled in the 18C. The most distinguished member of the family was General **Raymond Séré de Rivières** (1815-95), who designed the defensive system based on a string of half-buried polygonal forts along the new borders of France after the loss of the eastern provinces to Prussia in 1870-71.

Maison du vieil Alby

This brick and timber house, restored to the medieval design, stands at the forked junction between the pretty streets of Croix-Blanche and Puech-Berenguier (good view of the bell-tower of Ste-Cécile from the end of the latter). The first floor is corbelled out over the street, and there is a solelhièr, or woad drying room, beneath the eaves. The house hosts local craft exhibitions and contains a variety of literature on the town of Albi.

Rue Toulouse-Lautrec

At no 8, the **Hôtel Decazes** features a handsome courtyard in a transitional architectural style from Renaissance to Classicism, with a balustraded staircase and galleries with basket-handle arches. On the right as you follow this street are the Maison La Pérouse, named after a famous French seaman (1741-88) (👁 *see also Musée La Pérouse*), which houses a **waxworks museum**, and the Hôtel du Bosc, where Toulouse-Lautrec was born. This house was built on the site of the 14C fortifications, part of which can still be seen (two towers and a section of rampart walk).

▷ *Turn left onto rue de Verdusse then right onto rue Saunal.*

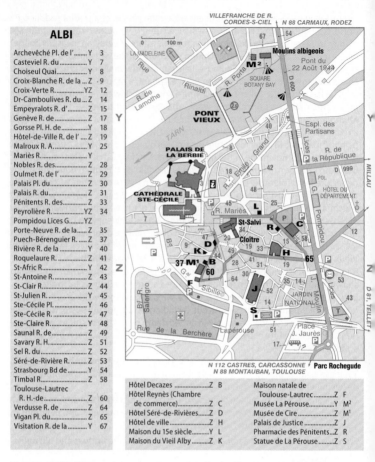

VILLEFRANCHE DE R.
CORDES-S-CIEL ✦ N 88 CARMAUX, RODEZ

N 112 CASTRES, CARCASSONNE ✦ Parc Rochegude
N 88 MONTAUBAN, TOULOUSE

Note a wealthy 16C woad merchant's mansion, flanked by a tower, and, farther on, on the corner of rue des Pénitents and rue de l'Hôtel-de-Ville, the fine 17C town hall.

Rue de l'Hôtel-de-Ville leads to the restored place du Vigan with its 81 fountains and the Jardin National.

▶ *Follow rue Timbal.*

Hôtel de Reynès★

Headquarters of the local chamber of commerce. This Renaissance stone and brick mansion once belonged to a wealthy merchant family. The courtyard is decorated with two galleries one above the other, next to a 14C corner tower. The mullions of the windows on the inner façade are ornately decorated with mermaid figures. The courtyard also features two busts of François I and Eleanor of Austria.

Pharmacie des Pénitents★ (or Maison Enjalbert)

This 16C house (now a chemist's shop) features timbering and crisscross-pattern brickwork typical of the Albi region. The decoration of the façade is characteristic of the Renaissance period.

▶ *Take rue Mariès towards the cathedral.*

Note no 6 on the right, an attractive 15C timber-and-brick building.

Collégiale St-Salvi

St Salvi began his working life as a lawyer, before taking holy orders and finally becoming Bishop of Albi in the 6C. He introduced Christianity to the region and is now buried on the site of this church, which has a turbulent history. Its layout and foundations date from the Carolingian period. In the 11C a church and Romanesque cloisters were built; then work was interrupted by the Albigensian Crusade and not restarted until the 13C, when it was continued in the Gothic style. The bell-tower on the north of the building reflects the different stages of construction: the Romanesque stone tower (11C) with Lombard bands has a Gothic storey (12C) on top of it, and there is a 15C brick construction on top of that. The crenellated turret known as "La Gacholle," on one side of the main tower, is decorated with the coats of arms of the city of Albi and the chapter. It originally served as a watchtower.

Interior

▶ *Enter the church by the north door.* All that remains of the Romanesque doorway, rather spoiled by a classical style appendage, is the archivolt, the arch mouldings and two capitals. The first four bays inside are Romanesque and still have their 12C capitals. Two apsidal chapels in the chancel also remain from the first stage of construction, offset from the line of the side aisles.

The chancel and the remaining bays of the nave are in the Flamboyant Gothic style. At the end of the nave, beneath the organ, is a group of Christ surrounded by six statues depicting priests, scribes and elders of the Sanhedrin (the supreme court of justice in Jerusalem). In the first, south side chapel, note the 15C statue of Christ chained to a pillar, and a beautiful, primitive painting on wood of the Entombment. A replica of a 12C wooden statue of St Salvi stands above the baldaquin, in the chancel.

The **cloisters** (*access via a doorway in the south side*) were rebuilt by Vidal de Malvesi in the 13C. All that is left is the east gallery, in which there are Romanesque historiated capitals and Gothic ones decorated with plant motifs. The artist and his brother are buried in a mausoleum with a funerary niche backing onto the church.

▶ *Return to place Ste-Cécile.*

Berges du Tarn★★

▶ *Follow the Azure circuit (see the Address Book), starting from the tourist office.*

The banks of the River Tarn offer splendid **views**★★ of the town and the old fortifications as well as a peaceful stroll far from the bustle of the town.

Additional Sights

Musée de Cire

Mid-Jun to mid-Sep: audio tours daily except Sun and Mon 10am-noon, 2.30-6pm; mid-Sep to end May: daily except Sun and Mon 2.30-5pm. Closed Dec-Feb, 1 May. 3.20€. ☎ 05 63 54 87 55. – 12 rue Toulouse-Lautrec.

The waxworks museum occupies the cellars of a house which was once the property of Lapérouse. Tableaux with wax characters evoke famous Albi residents – Toulouse-Lautrec, St Salvy and Lapérouse *inter alia* – and significant episodes in the town's history. Once-important local activities such as mining or the cultivation and extraction of dyer's woad are also depicted.

Musée La Pérouse

Apr-Sep: daily except Tue 9am-noon, 2-6pm, Sat-Sun 9am-noon, 2-7pm; Oct-Mar: daily except Tue 10am-noon, 2-5pm, Sat-Sun 2-6pm. Closed 1 Jan, 1 May, 1 Nov, 25 Dec. 2.50€. ☎ 05 63 46 01 87. – Entrance in rue Porta.

Set out in a series of handsome vaulted rooms, this museum recalls the naval expeditions of Admiral Jean-François de Galaup de La Pérouse, who was born in the Manoir du Go on the outskirts of Albi in 1741. In 1785, Lapérouse set off on a scientific expedition on board two frigates, the *Boussole* and the *Astrolabe*, but perished when the latter was shipwrecked off the island of Vanikoro, north of the New Hebrides. His last port of call had been Botany Bay in Australia in 1788.

Navigational instruments, maps, charts and scale models of ships give an insight into what it was like to sail the seas in the 18C. A video film covers four centuries of maritime adventures in the Pacific. The last investigations of the wreck of the *Astrolabe* were carried out by an international team of experts in 1986.

Statue of La Pérouse

This memorial to the famous seaman stands in the square which bears his name.

Excursions

Lescure, Église St-Michel★

▶ *5km/3mi NE towards Carmaux-Rodez, then right at the signpost to Lescure.* Jul and Aug: 2.30-6.30pm. Contact the town hall. ☎ 05 63 60 76 73.

The old priory church in Lescure cemetery was built by Benedictine monks from Gaillac Abbey in the 11C. The Romanesque doorway, which dates from the 12C, is one of its most interesting features. Four of the capitals are decorated with narr depicting the Temptation of Adam and Eve and Abraham's Sacrifice of Isaac, to the left, and the Damnation of the Moneylender and two scenes featuring Lazarus the beggar in heaven and the rich man in hell, to the right. There is a marked similarity between these capitals and those of the basilica of St-Sernin in Toulouse and the church of St-Pierre in Moissac.

Notre-Dame-de-la-Drèche

Guided tours by request. No charge. ☎ 05 63 53 75 00.– 5km/3mi N on the road to Carmaux-Rodez, then left towards Cagnac-les-Mines.

Perched on a little plateau in the Tarn countryside is a strikingly large shrine with warm rose-coloured brick walls. It was built in the 19C, on the site of a 13C church, and consecrated to the "Vierge d'Or de Clermont," a mid-10C gold statue of the Virgin Mary in Majesty from the Auvergne which inspired a number of imitations. The name of the church means "Our Lady of the sunny hillside" (adrech is the local dialect for a slope exposed to the sun). The upper walls of the interior of this octagonal rotunda are decorated with mural paintings depicting the Life of the Virgin Mary, designed by Bernard Bénézet and executed by Father Léon Valette.

A small museum, the **musée-sacristie**, contains among other things a remarkable altar hanging in gold brocade on the same theme as the murals, made by nuns of the Order of St Clare in Mazamet.

Castelnau-de-Lévis

▶ *7km/4.5mi W. Leave Albi on the road to Cordes-sur-Ciel, then take D 1 left.*

All that remains of the 13C fortress is a narrow square tower and some ruins. There is a good view of Albi, with the cathedral's silhouette towering above it, and the surrounding Tarn Valley.

▶▶ **St-Juéry (6km/3.7mi E)**, **Musée culturel du Saut du Tarn** – *May-Oct: guided tours (1hr30min) daily except Sat 2-7pm; rest of the year: daily except Sat 2-6pm. ◑ Closed mid-Dec to mid-Jan. ⌔ 4€ (children under 10: 2€). ☎ 05 63 45 91 01.)*, located in a former hydroelectric power station, and **Ambialet** (20km/12.4mi E) situated on a peninsula formed by a meander of the river.

ALÈS

POPULATION 76 159

MICHELIN LOCAL MAP 339: J-4

Situated at the heart of an old mining and silkworm farming region, Alès is a typical town of the Cévennes plain, with broad, bustling streets and esplanades. In high season, the town offers a full festival programme.

▶ **Orient Yourself:** The town (known as "Alais" until 1926) derives its name from Alestum, probably of Celtic origin. Founded at the junction of roads linking Nîmes and the Auvergne region, it spread out from a hillock enclosed in a meander of the Gardon. The hillock is now the site of Fort Vauban. There was once an oppidum on the hill to the south-west, the Colline de l'Ermitage (3km/1.9mi along D 50). From the chapel (viewing table) there is a panoramic view of Alès.

Don't Miss: Musée minéralogique de l'École des Mines, Musée-Bibliothèque Pierre-André Benoît.

Alès is also the departure point of the long-distance footpaths, GR 44C and GR 44D, which form part of the network covering the Cévennes from Mont Lozère to Mont Aigoual.

A R... istory

...y of Alès – Alès is where the Edict of Grace between Louis XIII and ...s signed in 1629. Under the terms of the Treaty, the Protestants ...ir right to play an active political role in the state, and they were ...sses. The freedom of worship granted in the **Edict of Nantes** ...d.

ALÈS

Albert-1er R.	B	2	Lattre-de-Tassigny Av. de .	B	6
Audibert R. Cdt	A	3	Leclerc Pl. Gén.	B	8
Avéjan R. d'	B		Louis-Blanc Bd	B	
Barbusse Pl. Henri.	B	4	Martyrs-de-la-		
Docteur-Serres R.	B		Résistance Pl.	B	9
Edgar-Quinet R.	B		Michelet R.	B	10
Hôtel-de-Ville Pl. de l'	A	5	Paul R. Marcel	B	12
			Péri Pl. Gabriel	B	13
			Rollin R.	A	14

St-Vincent R.	B	15
Semard Pl. Pierre.	B	16
Soleil R. du Faubourg du ...	B	17
Stalingrad Av. de	B	18
Taisson R.	B	19
Talabot Bd	B	20
Ancien évêché	A	B
Statue de Pasteur	A	E

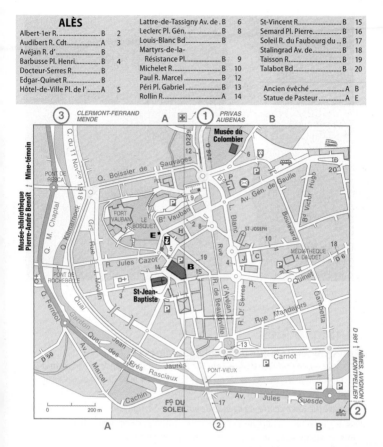

Louis Pasteur at Alès – In 1847, an epidemic disease called pebrine, about which little was known at the time, attacked the silkworms which were the region's traditional source of income. The epidemic worsened from year to year, until people began cutting down their mulberry bushes in despair. By 1865, 3 500 silkworm breeders were sending out distress signals loud and clear, at which point Pasteur accepted to try and find a remedy for the public good. The four years he spent studying the silkworm disaster at Alès were among the most exciting, but also emotionally charged, of his illustrious career.

The great scientist had barely arrived at Alès, when he learned of the death of his father, and in the course of the following year, two of his daughters died. Pasteur nonetheless managed to continue his studies, despite his great personal grief, and by January 1867 he had found a remedy: all the farmers had to do was to examine the breeding butterflies under a microscope and destroy any eggs which exhibited certain characteristics typical of the disease. Tests were carried out to check the theory, and in 1868 results showed Pasteur's preventive method to be a resounding success. Pasteur continued to oversee the work of his colleagues at Alès, despite suffering a stroke, until he was sure the problem had been resolved definitively.

The town of Alès put up a **statue** in the Bosquet gardens to mark its gratitude to the great scientist.

Industrial development – From as early as the 12C, Alès prospered from textile manufacturing and the cloth trade. In the 19C, the town became a major industrial centre fed by coal mines in Alès itself, the Grand'Combe and Bessèges, as well as mining for iron, lead, zinc and asphalt.

Nowadays, coal is only mined in open-cast mines. The Alès population is still a major industrial centre in the Languedoc region, specialising in metallurgy, chemistry (at Salindres) and mechanical engineering.

Ph. Delgado/Mine-témoin, Alès

Coal mine

Mining in Alès

Musée minéralogique de l'École des Mines★

&.◐ *Mid-Jun to mid-Sep: daily except Sat-Sun and public holidays 2-6pm; mid-Sep to mid-Jun: by request.* ↻ *4€.* ☎ *04 66 78 51 69.– 6 avenue de Clavières, in the Chantilly district.*

▷ *Leave the town centre via avenue de Lattre-de-Tassigny and avenue Pierre-Coiras.*

This museum has a collection of more than 1 000 minerals from all over the world. Some of the exhibits are quite outstanding (opal from Australia, chalcedony from Morocco, morion quartz – black cairngorm – from Aveyron in France). A 3-D audio-visual presentation sets off the brilliance of the stones and the diversity of their shapes and colours to good effect.

Mine-témoin★

&.◐ *Jul and Aug:* ↝ *guided tours (1hr, last departure 1hr30min before closing) 10am-7.30pm; Jun: 9am-6.30pm; Apr and May: 9am-12.30pm, 2-5.30pm. 6.50€ (children under 6: no charge).* ☎ *04 66 30 45 15. www.ales.cci.fr.*

▷ *3km/2mi W. Take the Rochebelle bridge over the Gardon and carry on north on rue du Faubourg-de-Rochebelle. Turn left onto chemin de St-Raby, then right onto chemin de la Cité-Ste-Marie. Temperature: 13-15°C/55-59°F. 20min audio-visual presentation on the formation of coal and mining technology.*

The mining museum comprises 650m/710yd of shafts hollowed out of the hillside, from which Benedictine monks extracted coal as early as the 13C. The exhibition covers the history of mining in the Cévennes region from the beginning of the Industrial Revolution to the present. Machinery, tools and the backdrop of the mine shafts themselves are used to illustrate changes in the various working practices within the mines: coal cutting, transporting ore, supporting the mine shafts, and ensuring safety.

Sights

Cathédrale St-Jean-Baptiste

↝ *Guided tours by request at the cathedral reception desk.*

The west front of the cathedral is Romanesque, with a Gothic porch dating from the 15C. The rest of the building dates from the 17C (nave) and 18C (great choir). Inside, the nave is vaulted in neo-Gothic style and there is a neo-Classical colonnade in the apse.

Next to the cathedral, in rue Lafare-Alès, stands the **Ancien Évêché**, the old bishops' palace dating from the 18C.

Address Book

🔸 *For coin ranges, see the Legend at the back of the guide.*

EATING OUT

🍽️ **Le Guévent** – 12 bd Gambetta - ☎ 04 66 30 31 98 - closed 18 Jul-23 Aug, Sun evening, Tue evening and Mon. Located a little away from the centre, this small local restaurant has a welocming ambience with a bright decor in which yellow predominates. Traditional Cévennes cuisine lovingly prepared by a passionate chef.

🍽️ **Riche** – 42 pl. Semard - ☎ 04 66 86 00 33 - riche.reception@leriche.fr - closed 1-25 Aug. This hotel-restaurant opposite the station boasts interesting decor from 1900, with decorative woodwork, mouldings and fine high ceilings. It has traditionally set tables with plenty of room in between them and varied menus. Rooms are modern and functional.

🍽️ **Auberge de St-Hilaire** – 30560 St-Hilaire-de-Brethmas - 3km/2mi SE of Alès on N 106 - ☎ 04 66 30 11 42 – auberge desainthilaire@hotmail.com - closed Sun evening and Mon. This welcoming inn stands at the exit to Alès in a garden courtyard, making a pleasant place to stop on the way to Nîmes. The terrace leads into an airy room decorated in warm Mediterranean colours. Several attractive menus featuring modern cuisine.

🍽️ **Auberge des Voutins** – 30340 Méjannes les Alè - ☎ 04 66 61 38 03 – closed 1-15 Sep, Sun evening and Mon except public holidays. This country dwelling is shielded from the road by trees. Traditional cuisine served by the fire or outside on a shady terrace.

WHERE TO STAY

🏕️ **Camping Domaine des Fumades** – Near the spa complex – 30500 Allègre-les-Fumades - 17km/10.5mi NE of Alès on D 16 then D 241 - ☎ 04 66 24 80 78 – domaine. des.fumades@wanadoo.fr - open 17 May-7 Sep – reservations required - 230 sites. This camp site on the outskirts of Alauzène, is laid out around a beautiful building with a magnificent patio. Amid well preserved natural surroundings, the site offers three swimming pools, restaurants and shops for the convenience of holiday-makers. Children's club.

SHOPPING

Jean-Luc Billard – 21 r. de la Montagnade - 11km/6.6mi S of Alès – 30720 Ribaute-les-Tavernes - ☎ 04 66 83 67 35 - gard@ orpailleur.com. This "gold-digger" promises to find gold by panning in the River Gard. Afternoon tours are organised Mon-Fri in Jul-Aug.

Musée du Colombier

🕐 Jul and Aug: 2-7pm (last admission 30min before closing); Sep-Jun: daily except Mon 2-6pm. 🕐 Closed 1 Jan, 1 May, 1 Nov, 25 Dec. 🎟️ No charge. ☎ 04 66 86 98 69.

This museum occupies the 18C Château du Colombier, in a pretty public park, next to the dovecot (French: *colombier*) after which the château and museum are named. The art collection housed here covers the 16C-20C, and some of the more notable works include a triptych of the Holy Trinity by Jean Bellegambe (early 16C) and paintings by Van Loo, Mieris, Bassano, Velvet Brueghel, Masereel, Mayodon, Marinot, Benn and others. There is also an interesting collection of local archaeological exhibits, and ironwork and other items from old Alès.

Musée-Bibliothèque Pierre-André Benoît★

▶ *Take the Rochebelle bridge over the Gardon, then follow the signposted route.*

Montée des Lauriers, Rochebelle. 🕐 Jul and Aug: 2-7pm (last admission 30min before closing); Sep-Jun: daily except Mon 2-6pm. 🕐 Closed Feb, 1 Jan, 1 May, 1 Nov, 25 Dec. 🎟️ No charge. ☎ 04 66 86 98 69.

The restored 18C Château de Rochebelle, once the residence of the bishops of Alès, houses a gift from Pierre-André Benoît to his native town and to the Bibliothèque Nationale. Benoît (1921-93) was a printer, publisher, writer, painter and draughts-man. He built up these interesting collections in the course of his encounters and correspondence with famous people, for example Char, Claudel, Tzara, Seuphor, Braque, Picasso, Miró, Jean Hugo and Villon.

Benoît published illustrated books, often in small format and limited editions. At the same time he collected works of art and books by his friends.

To save them from wear and tear, the graphic art works and the books are displayed in rotation or during temporary exhibitions, which are held on the ground floor, or in the library decorated by Benoît (*2nd floor*). The rooms on the first floor house the art collection: beautiful oil paintings on canvas by Camille Bryen, paintings from the years 1946-53 by Picabia, compositions with birds by Braque, landscapes by L Survage and miniatures.

Excursions

Château de Portes★

▹ *20km/12.5mi NW. Leave Alès on D 904 towards Aubenas, then turn left onto D 906. Park the car at the pass to explore the castle ruins on foot.*

🕐☞ *Jul and Aug: guided tours (1hr) daily except Mon 10am-1pm, 3-8pm (last admission 1hr before closing); Feb and Easter school holidays: daily except Mon 2-6pm; early Sep to mid-Nov: Sat-Sun and public holidays 2-6pm. Mid-Nov to end Jan: by appointment (2 days in advance)* ⊗ *3.50€.* ☎ *04 66 34 35 90 (M. Bonnet.)*

The old stronghold of Portes is perched on the ridge separating the Gardon valleys and Luech Valley, overlooking a wide expanse of surrounding land. For many years it provided protection for pilgrims travelling to St-Gilles through the Cévennes.

The medieval fortress, now in ruins, has a square ground plan. The lords of Budos, to whom the castle belonged from 1320 to the 17C, had an extra building added during the Renaissance, which gave the whole a slightly strange outline. The polygonal layout and carefully shaped projection shaped like the prow of a ship are architectural feats of note.

Inside the Renaissance building (used for exhibitions and concerts) are some beautiful monumental chimney-pieces with mantelpieces formed of a single slab of stone.

From the top of the castle, the **panorama**★ stretches to the north over the Chamborigaud Valley, beneath Mont Lozère and the Tanargue foothills.

Parc ornithologique des Isles

▹ *21km/13mi NE. Leave Alès on D 904 towards Aubenas then turn right to Les Mages. Go through the village and take D 132 to the right. The bird sanctuary is 800m/870yd beyond the turn-off to St-Julien-de-Cassagnas.*

♿🕐 *Early Jun to mid-Sep: 10am-7pm; Mar-May: 9am-noon, 2-6pm; mid-Sep to end Feb: 2-5pm.* ⊗ *5€ (children: 3.50€).* ☎ *04 66 25 76 70.*

Kids The sanctuary is home to hundreds of birds from all over the world: wild fowl, web-footed species, waders, birds of prey and climbing birds (good collection of parrots and budgerigars) among others.

Château de Rousson

▹ *9km/5.6mi N. Leave Alès on D 904 towards Aubenas then take the third road on the right after Les Rosiers (D 131).*

🕐☞ *Jul and Aug: guided tour (45min) 10am-7pm.* ⊗ *5€.* ☎ *04 66 85 60 31.*

The robust castle, protected by four corner towers, has not undergone any substantial modifications since it was built (1600-15). The main façade faces southeast and features a series of mullioned windows and an impressive Louis XIII door with bosses. Inside, there are various well-preserved old **tiled floors** which are most attractive. The kitchen on the ground floor has a huge fireplace and bread oven. The gallery on the first floor contains an old sea chest. The castle terraces give good views of the Aigoual and Ventoux ranges.

Préhistoram★

▹ *11km/6.8mi N. Leave Alès along D 904, towards Aubenas. Turn left onto a path signposted "Prehistorama."*

♿🕐 *Jun-Aug: 10am-7pm; Feb-May and Sep-Nov: daily except Sat 2-6pm.* 🕐 *Closed Dec and Jan.* ⊗ *5€.* ☎ *04 66 85 86 96.*

Kids This centre retraces the evolution of life on earth (mouldings of fossils) and of man in particular with tableaux peopled by fairly subjective reconstructions of the earliest human beings.

Bambouseraie de Prafrance

▹ *17km/10.5mi SW. Leave Alès on N 110, turn right on D 910A then right again on D 129.*

♿🕐 *Early Apr to mid-Sep: 9.30am-7pm; Mar and mid-Sep to mid-Nov: 9.30am-6pm. 6.50€.* ☎ *04 66 61 70 47. www.bambouseraie.fr.*

Kids This exotic bamboo plantation, not what one would expect in the heart of the Cévennes, was founded in 1855 by Eugène Mazel, who came from the Cévennes area. When Mazel was in the Far East studying the mulberry trees essential for silkworm breeding, he became fascinated by bamboos and brought back some cuttings. At Prafrance, where they reaped the benefits of a soil enriched by the alluvial deposits of the Gardon, a high water table and a suitable micro-climate, the bamboo forest soon became a spectacular jungle.

Laos huts at the Prafrance Bamboo Plantation

The park of about 40ha/100 acres has a magnificent avenue running right through it of 20m/65ft tall bamboos and Californian sequoias. Another avenue, lined with palm trees, boasts a superb Virginian tulip tree. A leisurely stroll round the gardens reveals a Laotian bamboo village, the maze and the arboretum planted with trees from Japan, China and America, among which are magnolias, banana trees, tropical conifers and the remarkable "ginkgo biloba" or "maidenhair tree," so-called because of the bright gold of its leaves in autumn. In the water garden, home to Japanese carp, lotuses and Egyptian papyrus plants flourish.

The bamboo plantation at Prafrance covers about 10ha/25 acres and comprises more than 100 varieties. A bamboo grows from 30-35cm/12-14in a day, soon reaching its final height, but it takes three years to thicken to the consistency of wood. In Asia, it is used for ladders, irrigation pipes, scaffolding and the construction of houses. Certain bamboos, easily recognisable by their yellow trunks, are used for making musical instruments. The rhizomes (underground stems) are transformed into basket or umbrella handles. The exotic scenery of Prafrance has been used as a set for several films, for example *The Wages of Fear* and *The Heroes are Tired*.

The Bambouseraie even supplies fresh foliage for the panda in the Berlin zoological gardens.

Le Mas Soubeyran, Musée du Désert★

▶ *15km/9mi SW along D 50 via Générargues to Luziers then right.*

🕐 *Jul and Aug: 9.30am-7pm; Mar-Jun and Sep-Nov: 9.30am-noon, 2-6pm.* ⊚ *4€.* ☎ *04 66 85 02 72.*

Le Mas Soubeyran overlooks the River Gardon. A few houses, huddled close together, stand on the small plateau surrounded by mountains. The countryside is bleak and rugged. The hamlet, with its **Musée du Désert**, is a Protestant Mecca. It will also interest any tourists with a love of history.

This little place is redolent with the history of the Protestant struggle, particularly in the Cévennes, from the time of the revocation of the Edict of Nantes (1685) to the Edict of Tolerance (1787).

Beneath the oak and chestnut trees near the museum, an annual "general assembly" is held in early September which attracts 10 000 to 20 000 Protestants.

The tour of the museum concentrates mainly on the Maison de Roland and the Mémorial. Illustrations of the Reformation and a video are on show in two reception rooms.

The **Maison de Roland** (Roland's house) is the same as it was in the 17C and 18C. Note the *"jeu de l'Oye"* (a type of snakes and ladders) designed to teach Roman Catholic principles to young Huguenots imprisoned in convents.

Various documents, declarations, orders, edicts, old maps and paintings retrace the period preceding the persecutions, the struggle of the Camisards, the restoration of Protestantism and the triumph of the ideology of tolerance.

In the kitchen is the Bible owned by the Camisard leader and the hiding place he used when the dragoons arrived. Roland's bedroom still contains its original furniture.

One room recalls the clandestine "Désert" religious meetings organised by the Protestants in remote ravines; exhibits include a Désert pulpit that could be turned into a grain barrel. The Bible room contains numerous 18C Bibles, a remarkable series of psalters and paintings by Jeanne Lombard.

Inside the **Memorial**, two rooms have been given over to the memory of the *"Désert Martyrs"* – executed ministers and preachers, refugees, galley slaves and prisoners. The display cases contain Huguenot crosses and an interesting collection of collapsible communion chalices.

The Salle des Galériens commemorates the suffering of the 2 500 Protestants condemned to the galleys. It also contains models of galleys and paintings by Labouchère and Max Leenhardt.

The tour ends in a reconstruction of the interior of a Cévenol home, in which the family is gathered together to listen to Bible readings, and with a memorial to the prisoners of the Tour de Constance in Aigues-Mortes.

Grotte de Trabuc★★

▶ *16km/9.9mi SW along D 50 to Luziers via Générargues then right to Trabuc.*

◷ *Jul and Aug: guided tours (1hr) 10am-6.30pm; Mar-Jun and Sep-Nov: 10am-noon, 2-6pm.* ◉ *7€ (children: 3.50€).* ☏ *04 66 85 28 60.*

Trabuc cave, the largest in the Cévennes, was inhabited in the Neolithic period and used by the Romans at the beginning of our era. More recently, during the Wars of Religion, the Camisards took refuge in its labyrinthine galleries, which proved an excellent hiding place. It was even used as a den by a band of brigands known as the Trabucaires, after the name of the type of gun they used, which in turn became the name by which the cave was known.

A 40m/130ft-long artificial corridor, drilled by miners from Alès 120m/390ft above the natural mouth of the cave, leads into the cave.

The visit reveals such treasures as the Gong chamber, with a great drapery like an elephant's ear which resonates like a gong, the *gours*, or underground lakes or hollows formed by weirs of calcite, the pipe-like concretions in the great corridor, the petrified calcite torrents coloured with oxides known as the "red cascades," and the strangely beautiful aragonite crystallisations, tinted black by manganese. Perhaps the most impressive sight of all is the remarkable underground landscape formed by the **"Hundred thousand soldiers"**★★, extraordinary concretions formed in *gours* reminiscent of the Great Wall of China. Their origin remains a mystery, but they are certainly a magnificent spectacle – the concretions stand only 1 or 2in high, packed close together, just like an army of foot soldiers besieging a fortified city. On the way back up to ground level, linger a while in the Lake chamber, which contains a beautiful pendant concretion shaped like an enormous butterfly, various jellyfish-shaped concretions, some eccentrics, and last but by no means least the underground lake itself – "Midnight lake" – in which the level of the green-tinted waters can vary by about 25m/82ft.

St-Christol-lès-Alès, Musée du Scribe

▶ *2km/1.2mi S towards Anduze and Montpellier; follow the signposting on the right before reaching the "pyramid" where the two roads separate. 42 rue du Clocher.*

♿◷ *Jul and Aug: guided tours (1hr15min) 10am-7pm; Jun and early to mid-Sep: daily 2.30-7pm; mid-Sep to end May: Sat-Sun 2.30-7pm.* ◉ *4€.* ☏ *04 66 60 88 10.*

A tastefully restored village house is the setting of this museum dedicated to the art of writing, in particular to the instruments used for writing: an impressive collection of quills, nibs and penholders, oddly shaped inkwells, writing material through the ages (papyrus, parchment and paper). Your enthusiastic guide will give you fascinating explanations and the visit will end with the reconstruction of a 19C classroom.

Vézénobres

▶ *11km/7mi S. Leave Alès on N 106.*

Vézénobres occupies a pleasant site on a hillside overlooking the confluence of the Gardon d'Alès and the Gardon d'Anduze. There is still some evidence of the medieval town: the Sabran gateway, remains of the old ramparts, ruins of a fortress and several houses dating from the 12C, 14C or 15C. Take a stroll through the picturesque stepped alleyways and enjoy the view from the top of the village.

AMÉLIE-LES-BAINS-PALALDA

POPULATION 3 475

MICHELIN LOCAL MAP 344: H-8

Amélie was originally called Bains-d'Arles and then renamed after Queen Marie-Amélie, wife of Louis-Philippe who, in the 19C, made the **southernmost spa town in France** fashionable. Mediterranean plant life, such as mimosas, oleanders, palm trees and agaves, in the local gardens reflects the mild climate. The air here is particularly pure, there are hardly any strong winds and the sun shines brightly for much of the time. *22 av. du Vallespir, 66110 Amélie-Les-Bains-Palalda, ☎ 04 68 39 01 98. www.amelie-les-bains.com.*

The Spa

Spa centres

The sulphur-rich spa waters at Amélie-les-Bains-Palalda, 230m/748ft above sea level in the Vallespir region, are widely renowned for their effective treatment of rheumatic complaints and diseases of the respiratory tract (people come all year round to take the waters). Amélie has one military spa centre and two for the public: the baths at Le Mondony, at the mouth of the Mondony gorge, and the Roman baths, in which there is a restored Roman swimming pool.

Address Book

For coin ranges, see the Legend at the back of the guide.

EATING OUT

Carré d'As – Q4 av. du Dr Bouix - ☎04 68 39 20 00 – casino.ameliemoliflor.com - closed 15-28 Feb, 1-28 Mar, Mon and Tue except public holidays. Local specialities in the restaurant, pasta and pizzas in the brasserie: the choice is yours.

WHERE TO STAY

Ensoleillade La Rive – R. J. Coste - ☎04 68 39 06 20 – 🖬 - 14 rms. Simple family hospitality by the Tech. Airy rooms with rustic furnishings; some with cooking facilities.

Rousillon – Av. Beau-Soleil - ☎04 68 39 34 39 - closed 28 Nov-20 Mar – 🖬 - 30 rms. Situated on the way into town, this accommodation offers bright and spacious rooms. A fine 19C building adjacent houses the rest of the hotel.

SHOPPING

Marché aux légumes – Pl. de la République - daily 7am-noon. Fruit and vegetables.

Les Caves du Roussillon – 10 r. des Thermes - ☎ 04 68 39 00 29 - daily 9am-12.30pm, 4pm-7.30pm. Those who love fine wines can taste one or two local vintages here including: Banyuls, Collioure and Rivesaltes. There are more than 300 Roussillon wines and a hundred or so Banyuls, so it would be difficult to know what to choose without the sound advice of the owner, M Reynal.

BARS AND CAFÉS

La Rosquilla Fondante Séguéla (Pâtisserie Pérez-Aubert) – 12 r. des Thermes - ☎ 04 68 39 00 16 - daily except Wed 8am-12.30pm, 3pm-7pm and holidays – closed 3 weeks Jul and 2 weeks Feb. It was here, in 1810, that Robert Séguéla, pastrycook by trade, invented the rousquille, a lemon-flavoured iced biscuit. The establishment is now a light, peaceful tea room, where visitors can taste the famous rousquille along with a couple of dozen varieties of tea, ice cream and chocolates made on the premises.

ON THE TOWN

Bar le Chateau – Rte d'Arles-sur-Tech - ☎ 04 68 39 31 71 - Thu and Sat 9pm-1am, Sun 3pm-7pm - closed Oct-May. A mature clientele cut the rug to the old-fashioned beat of musettes, tangos or popular waltzes. A charming spot.

Grand Café de Paris – 19 av. du Vallespir - ☎ 04 68 39 00 04 - daily 5.30am-2am - closed 2 weeks in Jan. Large café-brasserie where clients can eat a meal at a reasonable price and then dance the waltz or other old favourites in a back room. Mature clientele who know how to have fun, creating a lively and enjoyable atmosphere.

SPORTS AND RECREATION

Golf - Compact – Parc des Sports – ☎ 04 68 39 37 66 – daily – closed 15 Dec-15 Feb, 15 Aug and 1 Nov. 1 7-hole course.

Gorges du Mondony

30min round-trip on foot. Leave from the Roman baths and walk past the Hôtel des Gorges as far as the terrace which overlooks the mouth of the gorge. Take the cliff path and the galleries clinging to the rock face.

The gorge is a cool, pleasant place for a walk.

Palalda★

3km/2mi from the centre of Amélie.

The medieval town of Palalda, overlooking the Tech, is twinned with the spa town for administrative purposes. It is a fine example of a Catalan village. The tiny, often quite steeply sloping streets, bright with flowers, below the mairie are well worth exploring. The little square surrounded by the **church of St-Martin**, the museum and the town hall is particularly pretty. The church contains a lovely altarpiece depicting the life of St Martin.

Vallée du Mondony★

6km/3.5mi as far as Mas Pagris. Spectacular cliff road (passing places over the last 2km/1.2mi).

The road to Montalba leads off from avenue du Vallespir to the south of the town, before climbing the rocky spur of Fort-les-Bains and leading along the clifftops overlooking the Mondony gorge. It then crosses a series of stepped terraces, in full view of the jagged Roc St-Sauveur and of the deserted valley below, uniformly carpeted with green oak trees. Leaving the Montalba aerial tower to the left, it carries on through the granite gorge as far as the small valley of Mas Pagris. This is a good departure point for walks in the upper valley of the Terme.

Additional Sight

Palalda Museum

May-Sep: daily except Sun 10am-noon, 2-7pm, Mon, Sat and public holidays 2-7pm; mid-Feb to end Apr and early Oct to mid-Dec: daily except Sun 10am-noon, 2-5pm, Mon, Sat and public holidays 2.30-5.30pm. 2.50€. 04 68 39 34 90.

The museum is divided into two sections:

Museum of Folk Arts and Traditions

This section displays tools used in professions which either are no longer practised or have been mechanised. One room is devoted to the manufacture of espadrilles. Note the Catalan card game known as truc. Some 20m/22yd farther down the hill on place de la Nation are two rooms reconstructed as an early-20C kitchen and bedroom. Gourmets will take particular note of the *cargolade*, a local dish of grilled snails, eaten with *aïoli* (garlic mayonnaise) and washed down with *vins doux naturels* (sweet wine) such as Rivesaltes or Banyuls.

Roussillon Postal Museum

This section exhibits pictures, literature and other items tracing the history of the local postal service. There is a reconstruction of a late-19C post office and a display on the Roussillon lighthouse system (*tours à feu*), a code based on smoke signals which could alert the entire region within 15min to the threat of enemy invasion. Among the machines on display note the rare example of a "Daguin" franking machine. Finally, pause to admire the postman's uniform, in particular his smart boots.

Principat d'ANDORRA★★

POPULATION 65 844

MICHELIN LOCAL MAP 343: G-I, 9-10

This small independent state has a total area of 468km²/180sq mi (about one and a third times the area of the Isle of Wight). Andorra lies at the heart of the Pyrenees and has remained curiously apart from its neighbours, France and Spain. Visitors are attracted by its beautiful rugged scenery and picturesque villages.
🛈 R. Dr-Vilanova, Andorra La Vella, ☎ 82 02 14. www.tourisme-andorre.net.

👁 **Don't miss:** Valira d'Orient and Valira del Nord valleys.

A Bit of History

"Charlemagne the great, my father, delivered me from the Arabs" begins the Andorran national anthem, which then continues proudly, "I alone remain the only daughter of Charlemagne. Christian and free for 11 centuries, Christian and free I shall carry on between my two valiant guardians, my two protecting princes."

From co-principality to independent sovereignty – Until 1993, Andorra was a co-principality under a regime of dual allegiance, a legacy from the medieval feudal system. Under such a contract, two neighbouring lords would define the limits of their respective rights and authority over a territory that they held in common fief. Andorra was unusual, however, in that its two lords came to be of different nationality, but left the status of the territory as it was under feudal law, with the result that neither of them could claim possession of the land. This dual allegiance to two co-princes was established in 1278 by the Bishop of Urgell and Roger Bernard III, Count of Foix. However, while the bishops of Urgell remained co-princes, the counts of Foix passed their lordship on to France (when Henri IV, Count of Foix and Béarn, became king in 1589) and thus eventually to the President of the French Republic.

On 14 March 1993 the Andorrans voted in a referendum to adopt a new democratic constitution making the principality a fully independent state. The official language of the country is Catalan. The principality has signed a treaty of cooperation with France and Spain, the first countries to officially recognise its independence. It has also become a member of the U.N.

A taste for liberty – Andorrans pride themselves above all on seeking and fiercely defending their liberty and independence. A longstanding system of representative government and 11 centuries of peace have given them little incentive to alter the country's administration. The country is governed by a General Council, which holds its sessions at the "Casa de la Vall" and ensures the proportional representation of the various elements of the Andorran population and the seven parishes.

Andorrans do not pay any direct taxes, nor do they have to do military service. They also have free postal services within their country. Most of the land is communally owned, so there are very few private landowners.

Work and play – Until recently this essentially patriarchal society traditionally made a living from stock rearing and crop cultivation. In between the high summer pastures and the hamlets you can still see the old cortals, groups of barns or farmhouses, which are gradually becoming more accessible as the tracks leading up to them are made suitable for vehicles. The mountain slopes exposed to the sun are cultivated in terraces. Tobacco, the main crop in the Sant Juliá de Lòria Valley, is grown up to an altitude of 1 600m/5 200ft.

Rapid transformation – In less than half a century, the Andorran way of life has evolved remarkably rapidly; the first roads suitable for vehicles linking it with the outside world were not opened until 1913, on the Spanish side, and 1931, on the French. The influx of foreign visitors, attracted by its rugged high plateaus, ski slopes and ancient customs, is having a profound impact on the Andorran economy and tra-

The Valley's coat of arms

A. Thuillier/MICHELIN

Address Book

For coin ranges, see the Legend at the back of the guide.

EATING OUT

Don Pernil – *Av. d'Enclar 94 - Santa Coloma - 3km/2mi SW of Andorre-la-Vieille - ☎ (00-376) 86 52 55 - closed Jan.* The queues here are long to sample the meats barbecued over a wood fire and the regional dishes prepared by the owners. Guests are welcomed warmly into two rooms decorated with rustic local furniture.

Can Manel – *R. Mestre-Xavier-Plana 6 - Andorre-la-Vieille - ☎ (00-376) 82 23 97 - closed 1-15 Jul and Wed.* A small family-run restaurant a short distance from the town centre but extremely pleasant. From one of the two rooms decorated in regional furniture there is a view of the ovens where simple but fine food is prepared with the emphasis on locally grown fare.

Borda Estevet – *Rte de La Comella 2 - Andorre-la-Vieille – ☎ (00-376) 86 40 26 – bordaestevetandorra.ad .* This old stone-walled house a short distance out of town welcomes its clients into several rooms with quite typical rustic decor. At table, the local Pyrenean cooking and in particular the dessert trolley will send food-lovers into ecstasies.

WHERE TO STAY

Hôtel Cerqueda – *R. Mossen-Lluis-Pujol - Santa Coloma - 3km/2mi SW of Andorre-la-Vieille - ☎ (00-376) 82 02 35 – closed 7 Jan to 6 Feb -* 🅿 *- 65 rms.* This simple family-run hotel offers a peaceful stay. All the bathrooms have been recently decorated, even though some of the rooms still have slightly old-fashioned decor. Friendly welcome. Swimming pool.

Espel – *Pl. Creu-Blanca, Escaldes Engordany - ☎ (00-376) 82 08 55 - closed May – 102 rms.* Systematically renovated, the hotel's bathrooms have water from the Andorra's underground lakes. Pleasant local atmosphere and simple accommodation offering respite from the liveliness of the town.

Hôtel Coma Bella – *Sant Julià de Lòria - 7km/4mi au SW of Andorre-la-Vieille - ☎(00-376) 84 12 20 - comabellamyp.ad - closed 2-18 Nov -* 🅿 *– 30 rms.* This hotel in La Rabassa forest boasts a particularly peaceful location. There are two kinds of rooms: some are decorated with contemporary Andorran style furniture; others are more functional.

Font del Marge – *Baixada del Moli 49, Andorre-la-Vieille - ☎(00-376) 84 14 43 - margeandorra.ad - closed Nov – 42 rms.* A family ambience pervades this hotel located in a quiet steep alley. Meat lovers will enjoy the rotiserìe, while seafood predominates in the restaurant.

ON THE TOWN

Topic – *Carretera Général, Ordino - ☎ (00-376) 73 61 02 – 8-2am.* The bar-restaurant of the hotel Coma boasting futurist interiors and a terrace, serving drinks, tapas, salads, sandwiches, pizzas, and grilled meat and fish dishes

SHOPPING

Andorra is popular with die-hard shoppers. There are many luxury products available at duty-free prices. As with duty-free goods, the amount of liquor, cigarettes, perfume etc that you may bring home is restricted. Usual store hours are 9am-1pm and 4-8pm (9pm during holiday periods).

---

ditional way of life. Andorra shows signs of a somewhat haphazard development with the mushrooming of residential and office blocks, in the Gran Valira for instance. The population of Andorra numbered 76 900 in 2004, most of whom speak Catalan. The state is divided into 7 "parishes" or administrative units: Canillo, Encamp, Ordino, La Massana, Andorra la Vella, Sant Juliá de Lòria and Escaldes-Engordany.

Recreation

Soldeu El Tarter Ski Area
Alt 1 710-2 560m/5 610-8 398ft.

52 trails for skiers of all levels – 241 snow-making machines ensure permanent coverage of 14km/9mi of trails.

Pas de la Casa-Grau Roig Ski Area

Pas de la Casa and Grau Roig are linked together and accommodate more than half of all skiers in Andorra. Two small zones (Abelletes and Pessons) are reserved for beginners. There are 80km/48mi of downhill trails for moderate-to-good skiers, all offering beautiful views of the surrounding granite outcroppings. There is a special area for snowboarding; night skiing is possible twice a week.

Caldea

1 000m/3 250ft above sea level. 🕐 *Aug and Easter school holidays: 9am-midnight; rest of the year: 10am-11pm.* 🕐 *Closed 1 Jan (morning), from mid to end May, first week in Nov, 25 Dec.* 🎫 *24.50€ (3hr), 65.50€ (3 days), 98€ (5 days).* ☎ *00 376 80 09 99.*

🧒 This major water sports complex, designed for keeping fit and having fun is fed by the Escaldes-Engordany spa waters pumped from the ground at 68°C/155°F. The complex, designed by French architect Jean-Michel Ruols, takes the form of a gigantic futuristic cathedral entirely of glass. There is a wide range of activities available: Indo-Roman baths, Turkish baths, jacuzzis, bubble beds, hot marble, spray fountains etc. Restaurants, snack bars, shops and a panoramic bar some 80m/260ft above the ground all contribute to the happy atmosphere of this aquatic paradise.

Andorra la Vella

The capital of the Andorran valleys, huddled on a terrace (alt 1 209m/3 967ft) above the Gran Valira Valley, is a bustling commercial town. Once away from the busy main axis, however, the heart of Andorra la Vella has kept its peaceful old streets.

Casa de la Vall

🕐 ⚑ *Guided tours daily (30min) except Sun afternoon 9.30am-1pm, 3-7pm. Book one week in advance on* ☎ *00 376 82 91 29.* 🕐 *Closed on days when parliamentary sessions take place and certain public holidays.* 🎫 *No charge.*

The Casa is both Andorra's Parliament building and its Law Courts. The General Council holds session here. The massive stone building owes its overall appearance to the period of its construction, in the 16C, but it was heavily restored in 1963, when a second watch turret was added to the south corner. The main doorway is framed by long heavy archstones, characteristic of Aragon architecture. The interior owes its elegance chiefly to the ceilings and wood panelling. The reception room, once a refectory, on the first floor is decorated with 16C murals. The council chamber still has the famous "cupboard with the seven keys," fitted with seven different locks to which the seven parishes each had one of the keys, in which the national archives are kept.

Excursions

Valira d'Orient Valley★ 1

▷ *From Andorra la Vella towards the Puymorens Pass – 36km/22.5mi – allow 1hr 30min.*

🌨 *The Envalira Pass can be blocked by snow, but it is always reopened within 24hr. In bad weather, the Puymorens Pass road may be open only in the direction of Porté and the Cerdagne.*

The road leaves the outskirts of Escaldes and climbs the increasingly steep and rugged valley, leaving behind it the Andorra radio station with its startling neo-Romanesque bell-tower.

After Encamp, the road negotiates a sharp defile before reaching the hamlet of **Les Bons**, which occupies an eye-catching **site**★ perched on a rocky spur beneath the ruins of its once-protective castle and the chapel of Sant Roma. A little farther on to the right stands the striking black and white form of Andorra's national shrine, the **chapel of Our Lady of Meritxell** (♿ 🕐 *Daily except Tue 9.15am-1pm, 3-6pm;* ⚑ *Jul and Aug: possibility of guided tours;* 🎫 *No charge.* ☎ *00 376 85 12 53*), rebuilt in 1976.

Canillo

The church in this village has the tallest bell-tower in Andorra (27m/88ft). Not far off stands a white charnel house, in which the cells are funerary niches; such buildings are a common sight in countries of Iberian culture.

Sant Joan de Caselles

🕐 *Jul and Aug: 9am-1pm, 3-6pm. Rest of the year by request.* ☎ *03 376 85 11 15 or* ☎ *00 376 85 14 34.*

This lone church, with its three-storeyed bell-tower, is a particularly fine example of Romanesque Andorran architecture. The altarpiece (1525) behind the attractive wrought-iron parclose screen separating it from the chancel is the work of the Master of Canillo and depicts the Life of St John and his apocalyptic visions. During the last restoration (in 1963) a Romanesque **Crucifixion**★ was found; the stucco fragments of the Christ figure were fixed back onto the wall in their original setting, where a fresco completing the Calvary scene was also found (sun, moon, Longinus, the soldier with the lance, and Stephaton, the soldier who offered the sponge soaked in vinegar).

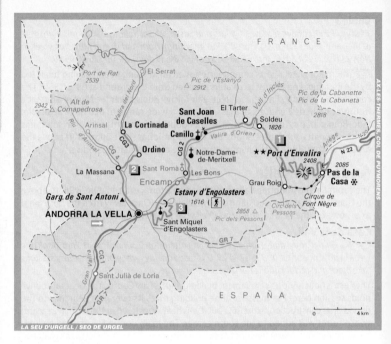

As the road climbs up to the Envalira Pass, the Pessons cirque is visible away to the right of the road and, a little farther on, the ski resort of Grau Roig.

Port d'Envalira★★

Alt 2 407m/7 823ft. This is the highest pass in the Pyrenees and has a good road over it. It marks the watershed between the Mediterranean (Valira) and the Atlantic (Ariège). There is a **panorama** taking in the Andorra mountains, which reach an altitude of 2 942m/9 653ft, stretching away to the west as far as Coma Pedrosa.

As the road drops down to Pas de la Casa, it offers spectacular views of the **Font-Nègre** cirque and lake.

Pas de la Casa※

Alt 2 091m/6 861ft. This frontier village, the highest in Andorra, has become a major ski resort.

▷ *Road N 22 runs through a desolate landscape as far as N 20, which leads to the Puymorens Pass.*

Valira del Nord Valley★ 2

▷ *From Andorra La Vella to La Cortinada – 9km/5.5mi.*

The old Andorran way of life and traditions are still to be found in this isolated upper valley. The road climbs quickly up out of Andorra-Escaldes.

Gargantas de Sant Antoni

From a bridge across the Valira del Nord you can see over to the right the old humpback bridge, once used by muleteers. The Coma Pedrosa peaks loom in the distance beyond the Arinsal Valley.

▷ *Go through the pleasant holiday village of La Massana to Ordino.*

Ordino

⊛ *Leave the car in the upper village in the square near the church.*

Downhill from the church this village has a network of picturesque streets well worth exploring. The church has attractive wrought-iron gates, which are commonly found in churches near the old Catalan forges. Near the church is another example of this craft, **Casa museu Areny-Plandolit** (◷ *9.30am-1pm, 3-6.30pm, Sun 10am-1.30pm in summer;* ≈ *2.40€;* ◷ *Closed 14 Mar, 8 Sep;* ℡ *00 376 83 69 08)*, "Don Guillem's" house, which boasts a splendid, 18m/59ft-long wrought-iron balcony.

La Cortinada

Village in a pleasant setting. Downhill from the church and graveyard with charnel house is an attractive house with galleries and a dovecot. The **church of Sant Marti** (⏱ *Jul and Aug:* 🚶*guided tours 9am-1pm, 3-6pm; Rest of the year by request;* ☎ *00 376 84 41 41)* contains Romanesque frescoes and Baroque altarpieces.

▷ *The road continues northwards. There are plans to link it up eventually with Vicdessos, via the Port de Rat (alt 2 539m/8 330ft).*

Estany d'Engolasters

9km/5.5mi, then 🚶 *30min round-trip on foot.*

▷ *Leave Escaldes E of Andorra, on the road to France, and at the outskirts of the village turn right, doubling back slightly, to follow the Engolasters mountain road.*

On the Engolasters plateau, where there are pastures as well as sports grounds used by the residents of Andorra la Vella, the outstanding landmark is the lovely Romanesque bell-tower of **Sant Miguel**.

At the end of the road, cross the crest under the pine trees and start downhill *(on foot)* to the dam, which has raised the level of the lake *(alt 1 616m/5 272ft)* by 10m/33ft. The waters of the lake reflect the dark forest which lines its shores. In the distance, opposite, stand the aerials of the Andorra radio station.

Engolasters – Church of Sant Miguel

A. Thuillier/MICHELIN

ARGELÈS-GAZOST

POPULATION 3 241

MICHELIN LOCAL MAP 342: L-4 – ALSO SEE LA BIGORRE

Argelès-Gazost developed into a residential spa town and resort in the 19C. The town nestles in a pleasant mountain-valley setting known for the mildness of its climate. The Argelès basin, meeting point of the main valleys of the Lavedan region is endowed with many attractive villages and picturesque sanctuaries. Isolated by the gorges of the upper Bigorre to the north and the high valleys of Cauterets and Luz to the south, it is an example of the internal basins in the Greater Pyrenees which benefit from mild weather conditions.

👁 **Don't Miss:** The Pibeste Peak.

Upper Town

The oldest and busiest district stands above the fast-flowing Gave de Pau and the resort proper with its thermal cure centres. From this part of Argelès, the dramatic **panorama** which unfolds on every side is heightened by the jagged teeth of the Viscos, between the Luz and Cauterets gorges, and the nearer peaks of the Néouvielle Massif. There is a particularly fine view of the valley of the Gave d'Azun and the surrounding mountains from the viewing table on the Terrace des Étrangers (Foreigners' Terrace), off place de la République.

Parc animalier des Pyrénées "La Colline aux marmottes"

Situated at the entrance of the town, coming from Lourdes along N 21.

Kids An hour-long walk will enable you to discover nine typically Pyrenean species, including: izards, ibexes, bears and marmots. The museum has three exhibition rooms dedicated to African, American and European wildlife. Plaster stage settings and light and sound effects bring the 150 stuffed and mounted animals to life. The visitor will discover animals from the American Far North (bears, lynx, beavers), Europe (wild boar, stag, wildlife from the Pyrenees) and Africa (antelopes, leopards and impalas).

Address Book

🪙 *For coin ranges, see the Legend at the back of the guide.*

EATING OUT

🍽 **Lac d'Estaing** – *Au Lac - 65400 Estaing – ☎ 05 62 97 06 25 - closed 16 Oct-30 Apr.* This small unpretentious inn not far from the lake has flowers growing up its façade. It occupies an enchanting setting and visitors will be spellbound by the view of the mountains from here. Classic cuisine. One or two modest rooms in case of emergency.

🍽 **Auberge de l'Arrioutou** – *Rte du Hautacam - 65400 Beaucens – 14.5km/9mi SE of Argelès on D 100 - ☎ 05 62 97 11 32 - open during school holidays and public holidays.* 1 350m/4 428ft above sea level, these old summer stables converted into a restaurant still have their original loose-box. In summer, walkers can take a break on the terrace with its cart-wheel tables. In the afternoon, pancakes are served with home-made jam.

🍽🍽 **La Châtaigneraie** – *65400 Salles-Argelès - 4km/2.4mi N of Argelès on D 102 - ☎ 05 62 97 17 84 – closed Jan and Mon. Reservataion required.* Take the time to appreciate the warm atmosphere of this nicely restored grange; the old furishings glow in the candlelight. In winter, meats are grilled on the central fireplace. In summer, you can sit outdoors under the shade of the pergola.

WHERE TO STAY

🏠 **Camping Les Trois Vallées** – *Sortie Nord - ☎05 62 90 35 47 - open Easter-Sep – reservation recommended - 380 sites.* This camp site has plenty to offer: a water sports complex, a small shopping centre and a rich display of floral plant life. We were captivated by it all.

🏠 **Chambre d'hôte Mme Vermeil** – *3 r. du Château – 65400 Arcizans-Avant - 5km/3mi S of Argelès on D 101 then D 13 - ☎05 62 97 55 96 - 🍽 - 3 rms.* Visitors will be captivated by the view of the valley from this fine 19C residence typical of the local (Bigorre) region. The rooms have been set up beneath the eaves with pine floors, panelling and furniture. Walkers should be sure to ask the advice of the owner, who is a mountain guide.

🏠 **Chambre d'hôte M. and Mme Domec** – *65400 Gez - 2.5km/1.5mi NW of Argelès on D 918 then a B-road - ☎05 62 97 28 61 – closed Oct-Apr - 🍽 - 5 rms.* This old stone barn, typical of the Pyrénées, has been converted into functional guestrooms with a view of the mountains. Garden with flowering plants and a barbecue. The house becomes available for hire during the winter (*gîte*).

🏠🏠 **Chambre d'hôte Eth Béryè Petit** – *15 rte de Vielle – 65400 Beaucens - 8.5km/5mi SE of Argelès on D 100 and a B-road - ☎05 62 97 90 02 - contactberyepetit. com - closed 15 Dec-15 Jan - 🍽 - 3 rms.* This fine 1790 family mansion typical of the local (Bigorre) region has been restored in line with artistic requirements. The rooms are tastefully decorated and overlook the valley, offering a splendid view. Breakfast is served in the fine lounge with its fireplace or on the terrace.

🏠🏠 **Hôtel Picors** – *Rte d'Aubisque - 65400 Aucun - 10km/6mi W on the rte du col d'Aubisque road - ☎05 62 97 40 90 - hotelpicors@aol.com - P - 48 rms.* Behind the impressive facade is functional accommodation with fine views of the Pyrénées. The pleasantly furnished lounge is comfortable. Indoor pool, sauna, tennis and minigolf.

🏠🏠 **Chambre d'hôte Le Belvédère** – *6 r. de l'Église - 65400 Salles-Argelès - 4km/2.4mi N of Argelès on D 102 - ☎ 05 62 97 23 68 - le-belvedere@wanadoo.fr – closed Nov - 🍽 - 4 rms.* This big house in the traditional regional style takes its name from the view extending out over the valley and all the way to the Pyrénées. In the summer months, enjoy your breakfast under the arbour in the park.

RECREATION

Les Gaves Sauvages – *2 av. des Pyrénées - ☎ 05 62 97 06 06 or 06 13 79 09 58 – 9am-7.30pm – closed Nov – 28€.* Whether you are a beginner or have experience, take advantage of the services of a licensed guide to discover the waterways from a canoe, kayak or raft.

Le Lac-Vert – *Village - 65400 Agos-Vidalos 6km/3.6mi SW of Argelès on N21 - ☎ 05 62 97 99 99 – from mid Jun-mid Sep: daily 10am-6pm.* This old quarry has been converted into a water sports park (*base de loisirs*) beneath trees. Facilities include pedalos, rafting, fishing, swimming pools with large water chutes. Picnic areas and a bar.

SHOPPING

Nyffénegger Dominique – *8 r. Bousquet - 65400 Agos-Vidalos - ☎ 05 62 90 37 72 – Open Jul-Aug daily 10am-noon, 2-6.30pm; rest of the year Tue-Sat 10am-noon, 2-6.30pm. Closed mid-Dec to mid-Feb.* This is the workshop of a glassblower and sculptor. Admire the lamps, vases and other decorative objects, all beautiful and unique. A good place to shop for a special gift.

Hiking Tour

Pic de Pibeste★★★

4.5km/2.5mi N via N 21 and D 102 (left) as far as Ouzous. Car park near the church. Allow at least 4hr 30min round trip on foot. It is essential to have sturdy shoes or boots, warm clothing and a supply of food.

🚶 The Pibeste Peak, despite its relatively modest height (alt 1 349m/4 426ft), offers one of the finest viewing points in the whole of the central Pyrenees. The footpath, identified with yellow markers, rises gently as far as the panorama over Ouzous, near an arboretum in which different species of pine are being developed; the following section, climbing in hairpin bends, is tougher – and steeper. Beyond Col des Portes (alt 1 229m/4 032ft) the path separates into two branches which join up again farther on to arrive at Pibeste after crossing a beech wood. At the upper station of the old cableway, staircases climb to the television transmitter.

From the summit there is a magnificent **panorama** southwards towards Pic du Midi de Bigorre on the left, the Luz and Cauterets mountains in the centre separated by the Vicsos peak and, in the distance, several peaks rising to more than 3 000m/9 850ft (Monte Perdido, Vignemale, Balaïtous). To the north the view extends towards Lourdes, Pau and the Tarbes plain.

Excursions

Beaucens, Donjon des Aigles

6.5km/4mi SE. ▶ *Take D 100 and then D 13 as far as Beaucens. There is a car park at the far end of the village at the foot of the castle.* 🕑 *1st Sun in Apr to end Sep: 10am-noon, 2.30-6.30pm. Birds of prey in flight (45min) every afternoon.* 🌐 *8€ (children: 5€).* ☎ *05 62 97 19 59.*

👶 The **Beaucens ruins** provide a fitting setting for the display of indigenous birds of prey (vultures, eagles, falcons, kites, buzzards, owls etc) and other exotic species (condors from the Andes, African vultures, American eagles). The highlight here is seeing the **birds of prey in flight**★ *(twice a day).*

Route du Hautacam★

20km/12mi E. ▶ *Leave Argelès via D 100, which crosses the Azun and climbs, after Ayros, the eastern slope of the Argelès basin.*

Artalens

Beyond the village, at an altitude of 800m/2 625ft, the road crosses a small valley where the stream is flanked by five former watermills; the last mill downstream still has its wheel. Hundreds of these small family concerns could be found all over the Bigorre district in the 19C.

After Artalens, the road leaves the summer grazing pastures and takes on a more panoramic aspect, offering distant **views**★ including, to the southwest, the Vignemale beyond Vallée de Cauterets, and Balaïtous which towers above the mountains surrounding Vallée d'Arrens. **Hautacam-Ski**, a picturesque winter sports resort and hang-glider's paradise, can be seen to the right.

Hautacam-ski area

Alt 1 500-1 800m/4 900-5 900ft. 🎿 11 lifts, 18 downhill slopes, for all levels, in a forest conservation area. 🎿 Some 15km/7mi of cross-country trails take you past beautiful views of the Argelès Valley and the Pyrenees. This resort area is very popular with hang-gliders. Heads up!

The road climbs above Hautacam to the mountain ridge overlooking the rugged foothills of the Pic du Midi de Bigorre, with an area of pastureland encompassing the Vallée de Gazost below.

Arrens-Marsous

12km/7.5mi SW. D 918, which follows the picturesque Azun Valley, leads to Arrens-Marsous on the edge of the Parc national des Pyrénées.

Monument des Géodésiens (Surveyors' Monument)

This tower, on the outskirts of Argelès-Gazost, is in the form of a geodetic instrument. It was built in 1925, on the hundredth anniversary of the first ascent of the Balaïtous crest. The successful climb was made by a team of military surveyors.

The peaceful little town of **Arrens-Marsous**, nestling in the valley, is both a holiday resort and a centre for high-altitude rambles to the Balaïtous massif.

ARGELÈS-PLAGE ☼ ☼ ☼

POPULATION 9 069

MICHELIN LOCAL MAP 344: J-7

This lively resort marks the point where the lower Roussillon coast runs into the first few rocky creeks of the Côte Vermeille. The immediate hinterland still has its irrigated gardens and orchards in which the most delicate of fruit trees thrive, along with nettle trees and eucalyptus. In summer, tens of thousands of holidaymakers descend on the resort looking for fun. About 60 camp sites and canvas villages within a radius of 5km/3mi make Argelès-Plage the camping capital of Europe.

A bus shuttle service operates from Jun to Sept between Argelès-sur-Mer (the town) and Argelès-Plage.

Address Book

For coin ranges, see the Legend at the back of the guide.

EATING OUT

Salamandre – *3 rte de Laroque - 66690 Sorède - 9km/6mi W of Argelès-Plage on D 2 - ☎ 04 68 89 26 67 - closed 15 Jan-13 Mar, 5-20 Nov, Tues lunchtime 15 Jul-15 Sep, Sun evening and Mon.* Leave the beach for a little trip into the hinterland. This simple village restaurant tempts the appetite of tourists passing through and local people with dishes cooked in front of the client. In summer try to get a table in the air-conditioned room at the back.

L'Amadeus – *Av. des Platanes - ☎ 04 68 81 12 38 - closed Dec-12 Feb, Tues, Wed and Thur in Feb-Mar and Mon except Jul-Aug.* This restaurant with the welcoming façade is not far from the Argelès tourist office. It boasts a light and airy dining room with panelled walls, round tables and white cane chairs. Nicely phrased menu. Terrace.

WHERE TO STAY

Camping Pujol – *☎ 04 68 81 00 25 - open Jun-Sep - ✂ - reservations required - 249 pitches.* This shady camp site offers pitches on the site of a sailing base with a jacuzzi and a health club. Children's entertainment and evening dances.

Camping La Sirène and l'Hippocampe – *☎ 04 68 81 04 61 - open 7 Apr-29 Sep - reservation recommended - 903 pitches.* Beautiful setting with trees and top-range equipment. Visitors can do whatever water sports they choose, including scuba diving. Children's club and free shuttle bus to Andorra and Barcelona. Mobile homes, chalets and bungalows also for hire.

Grand Hôtel du Lido – *Bd de la Mer - ☎ 04 68 81 10 32 - closed 1 Oct-27 Apr - 66 rms. 9.15€.* Direct access to the beach, swimming pool and shady garden. This hotel with its understated architecture is an ideal holiday venue. The spacious rooms have a living area and balconies overlooking the pool. Local cooking and brasserie-style menu by the pool.

SHOPPING

Marché artisanal – *Parking des Platanes - daily 5pm-midnight.* Local crafts.

SPORT

Antares Sub – *Quai Marco-Polo - ☎ 04 68 81 46 30 / 06 14 98 31 37 - www.antares-sub. com - Jul-Aug: daily 8am-noon, 2pm-8pm; Sep-Jun: daily 8am-noon, 2pm-6pm.* This is the oldest scuba diving school in Argelès. Magali, Gilbert and their team, experienced divers, teach courses from level 1-4, from basic introductions to exploring wrecks.

ON THE TOWN

Carnaval Café – *14 av. des Mimosas - ☎ 04 68 81 02 06 - Apr-Sept: daily 5pm-2am.* This bar-restaurant is undeniably delightful with its patio and terrace overlooking the pinewoods. Music on offer here goes from Latino to techno by the end of the evening. After one or two tapas or a main meal, the owners will offer you a Chupito, a very fruity liqueur.

Pub Flowers – *Av. du Gén.-de-Gaulle - ☎ 04 68 95 79 96 - www.flowers.fr - Jun-Aug: daily 8.30am-2am; Sep-May: Tues-Sun 4pm-2am - closed Nov.* In summer this bar hosts African and South American music groups. Add to that a good selection of cocktails and beers (150), and you get wild evenings and a great atmosphere. Billiard table and a large terrace.

Argelès beach

A. Thuillier/MICHELIN

Beaches

🧒 Argelès-Plage has been nominated a "kid" resort for its activities and facilities specially intended for children. There are several supervised beaches (June to September): Plage Nord, Plage des Pins and Plage Sud totalling 7km/4.3mi of fine golden sand. In addition, Le Racou (south of the harbour) offers 3km/1.9mi of rocky creeks.

A 2km/1.2mi-long promenade runs along the seafront between umbrella pine trees and Mediterranean plants (aloe, mimosa, olive and oleander).

Château de Valmy

&.🕐*Jul and Aug: 1.30-6.30pm; early Mar to end Sep: daily except Mon 1.30-6.30pm. Sound and light show in Jul and Aug: Tue, Wed and Thu at 9pm. 7.50€ (children: 6€). Dogs are prohibited. ☎ 04 68 81 67 32.).*

🧒 Various activities centred on birds of prey take place in the grounds of the Château de Valmy. There is a discovery trail and an hour-long falconry show in which **eagles**, kites, vultures and other birds of prey can be seen in full flight. There is also a demonstration of Pyrenean dogs looking after sheep.

Argelès-sur-Mer

2.5km/1.5mi W along D 618.

Situated at the heart of the old town, the **Casa de les Albères** (🕐 *Daily except Sun and public holidays 9am-noon, 3-6pm, Sat 9am-noon; 2€; 👣 May-Oct: guided tours (2hr); 4€; ☎ 04 68 81 42 74)* is a Catalan museum of folk art and traditions which displays tools used for trades once commonly plied in the Albères: cork (bottle-top) making, barrel manufacture, wine making, and also the manufacture of espadrilles (rope-soled sandals) and toys made from the wood of nettle trees.

Excursion

At the foot of Monts Albères ③

32km/20mi – allow 3hr – &. see Le BOULOU.

▸ *Drive W of Argelès-Plage along D 2 to Sorède. On reaching the centre of the village, turn left onto a road signposted "Vallée des tortues" and drive 2km/1.2mi to the parking area.*

Sorède

This village, traditionally involved in the manufacture of whips from nettle-tree wood, is now a centre for the breeding and study of tortoises.

Vallée des tortues - 🕐 *Jun-Aug: 9am-6pm; Mar-May and Sep: 10am-4pm; early Oct to mid-Nov: 11am-3pm; mid-Nov to end Mar: Sun and school holidays 11am-3pm. 7€ (children 3-10: 4€). ☎/fax 04 68 95 50 50.* 🧒 The 2ha/5-acre park houses some 40 tortoises, representing both land and water species from around the world. Informative panels answer all the questions you might wish to ask about these peaceful reptiles.

▶ *Return to Sorède and continue left along D 2 to Laroque-des-Albères then follow D 11 to Villelongue-dels-Monts. In the centre of the village, pick up the Cami del Vilar and drive 2km/1.2mi to the priory.*

Prieuré Santa Maria del Vilar

🕐 *Daily 3-6pm.* 🎫 *4€.* ☎ *04 68 89 68 35 (morning),* ☎ *04 68 89 64 61 (afternoon).*

The 11C priory stands in pleasant surroundings shaded by olive trees, holm oaks and cypresses; the overgrown site, abandoned for several centuries, is being cleared by an association which has undertaken the restoration of the priory. A fine Romanesque doorway leads into the church, characteristic of primitive Catalan Romanesque architecture; 11C and 12C frescoes can be seen in the apse. The charming cloisters have already been restored and an opera festival (started in 1996) gives music lovers a chance to appreciate the remarkable acoustics of the place.

▶ *Return to Villelongue-dels-Monts, turn left onto D 61A then right onto D 618 to St-Génis-des-Fontaines.*

Saint-Génis-des-Fontaines

The marble decoration of the parish church and cloisters testify to the importance of the former Benedictine abbey. Note in particular the white-marble lintel above the church doorway (dating from 1020), representing Christ surrounded by two groups of Apostles, and the colourful decoration of the cloisters (pink marble from Villefranche-de-Conflent, white and grey marble from Céret).

▶ *Continue E along D 618.*

Saint-André

🅿 *Leave the car in the shaded square to the right of the village high street. Reach the church by walking through an archway.*

The outside of the 12C church has important pre-Romanesque fishbone features. The marble lintel of the main doorway is technically similar to the St-Génis lintel. Inside, the foiled altar table is decorated with the same motifs as the lintel.

▶ *Continue E to return to Argelès.*

Aven ARMAND★★★

MICHELIN LOCAL MAP 330: I-9

The Aven Armand is undoubtedly one of the wonders of the underground world. The vertical entry shaft or chimney leads beneath the Causse Méjean, a vast tract of deserted heathland stretching away on all sides as far as the eye can see.

A Bit of History

Discovery of the Aven Armand – The famous speleologist E-A Martel began his exploration of the *causses* in 1883, going underground to explore in detail every pothole he discovered. He was accompanied on these dangerous expeditions by **Louis Armand**, a locksmith from Le Rozier. On 18 September 1897 Armand returned from an outing to the Causse Méjean in a state of great excitement, claiming to have discovered one of the most promising chimneys he had ever come across, which he believed might lead to a more tremendous underground cavern than any they had yet discovered. An expedition set off the very next day to investigate the enormous crevice, known by local farmers as *l'aven* ("the swallow-hole"). Initial soundings revealed a depth of 75m/244ft, but Armand got to the bottom without any problems and was enraptured at the forest of rock formations he found down there. Martel and another colleague, Armand Viré, went down the following day in their turn. Immediately after the discovery, Martel acquired ownership of the chimney for his devoted assistant and named it the "Puits Armand" ("Armand's well-shaft") after him. A consortium was set up to oversee the refitting and commercial exploitation of the underground chasm. Work on it began in June 1926 and a year later Aven Armand was opened to the public.

A. Cassaigne/MICHELIN

Stalagmites

Visit

🕐 ☞ *Jul and Aug: guided tours (1hr) 9.30am-6.15pm; Apr-Jun, Sep and Oct: 9.30am-noon, 1.30-5.15pm.* 🎫 *8€ (children: 5€).* ☎ *04 66 45 61 31. www.aven-armand.com. 1hr. temperature: 10°C/50°F.*

Viewing platform – A 200m/220yd-long tunnel has been excavated for easier access to the cavern and leads almost to the foot of the 75m/244ft-deep chimney down which the first explorers came. Subtle electric lighting gives a fairy-tale atmosphere to this land from the Arabian Nights. The tour takes you round the vast subterranean gallery. From the viewing platform (*accessible to everyone*) at the end of the tunnel there is an impressive view of the gallery below, which measures 60×100m/195×325ft and is 45m/146ft high.

The "Forêt Vierge" – Some spectacular concretions have built up on the scree that has fallen from the roof of the cavern, forming a sort of petrified forest. These fantastically shaped rock trees, in stands of varying density, can have bases measuring up to 3m/10ft in diameter, and some have grown up to 15-25m/50-80ft in height. Their "trunks" resemble those of palm trees or cypresses, and large, jagged "leaves" sprout from their crowns, some measuring two or three feet across. The stalagmites are no less intriguing, as they explode into a riot of arabesques, needles, palm branches and elegant pyramids topped with fat domes. In all there are 400 of them, a strange burgeoning over the centuries into this luxuriant virgin jungle glistening with calcite crystals.

As you walk through the gallery (*the steps have handrails, but some steps are slippery*), you can appreciate the variety of concretions it contains: elegant candles many feet high; bizarre figures with monstrous, club-shaped heads; curly cabbages and delicately engraved fruit; and most magnificent of all, the 30m/97ft-high corbelled column supported by a narrow pedestal, in the shadow of the great stalagmite.

A new lighting system has recently been installed, which picks out the various concretions in better detail and makes still more of the surprises that the Aven Armand has in store for visitors easier to see.

AUBRAC★

MICHELIN LOCAL MAP 338: J-3

Situated at 1 300m/4 225ft above sea level, Aubrac is a small holiday resort which offers plenty of sunshine and fresh air during the summer months, but which is popular also with winter sports enthusiasts. Parisians with roots in the Auvergne return here to enjoy local treats such as *aligot*, a potato dish made with lashings of local Tomme cheese. After a few days of good cooking and fresh air, they depart homewards sufficiently revitalised to cope with city life again.

Aubrac is also the name of the most southerly of the volcanic uplands of the Auvergne. It is a region of ponderous, rolling hills, with vast stretches of countryside covered in pastureland on which herds of cattle, named after the region, graze during the summer (Fête de la Transhumance in late May). While travelling through the area, keep an eye out for the **drailles**, trails occasionally lined with low drystone walls along which animals are herded from one seasonal pasture to another.

In winter, cross-country skiers arrive at the resorts of the **Espace Nordique des Monts d'Aubrac**, set up in 1985 (Aubrac, Bonnecombe, Brameloup, Lacalm, Laguiole, Nasbinals, St-Urcize).

> ⚬ *For coin ranges, see the Legend at the back of the guide.*
>
> ## WHERE TO STAY
>
> ⚬⚬ **La Dômerie** – ☎05 65 44 28 42 - *closed Nov-27 Apr* - 🄿 – *23 rms:* ▭ *7.62€.* Classic comfortable rooms are on offer in this 1870 inn. Madame is in charge of the ovens and serves up local recipes. Monsieur is at front of house and welcomes you into a timbered dining room. He also gives advice on walks and trips in the region.

Visit

A great square tower, a Romanesque church and a 16C building which has been turned into a forester's lodge are all that remain of the estate of the Brothers Hospitaller of Aubrac, an order of monastic knights who, from the 12C to the 17C, took it upon themselves to escort and protect pilgrims crossing these desolate regions on their way to Rocamadour or Santiago de Compostela.

Western Aubrac

Round-trip of 117km/73mi leaving from Aubrac – allow 4hr.

▷ *Take D 533 S into the delightful Boralde de St-Chély Valley. Turn left onto D 19 to Bonnefon, a hamlet dwarfed by a 15C square granary tower built by the monks of Aubrac. On leaving Bonnefon, take D 629 left and then turn right.*

The road twists its way uphill offering beautiful views of the Lot Valley and the Sévérac plateau. Just past a forester's lodge, it enters the forest of Aubrac, a tall beech wood dotted with pines.

Brameloup

This small winter sports resort has a number of wide pistes through the forest.

▷ *Turn back and take D 19 to the left.*

Prades-d'Aubrac

The 16C church in this village features a sturdy octagonal bell-tower. From the far side of the village there is a fine view of the Lot Valley.

As the road drops down towards the Lot, giving views over the Rouergue plateaux, it passes through a rapid succession of different landscapes. The vast pastures of the plateaux, with here and there a stunted beech tree, give way to moorlands, a

Winter in the Aubrac

A. Kumurdjian

few meadows and the odd field of crops. The Boralde Valley cuts off to the right. More and more land is given over to crops, and the road begins to go through groves of chestnut trees, and then orchards.

St-Côme-d'Olt★

The houses of this small fortified town have now spread beyond the limits of the old curtain wall; 15C and 16C houses line the narrow streets. The church features an unusual spiral bell-tower in the Flamboyant style (16C) and a panelled door sculpted in the Renaissance style.

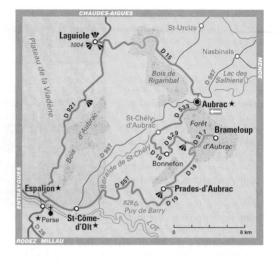

Espalion★   *See ESPALION.*

▶ *Leave Espalion on D 921 N.*

The road climbs towards Laguiole giving views of the Aubrac mountain range to the right and the Viadène plateau to the left.

Laguiole   *See LAGUIOLE.*

▶ *Take D 15 from the entrance to Laguiole.*

To the east of Laguiole, the road crosses expanses of pastureland and the odd beech wood. The views of the Viadène and Rouergue plateaux give way to that of the Margeride. This is one of the highest roads in the Aubrac region.

AUCH★

POPULATION 21 838

MICHELIN LOCAL MAP 336: F-8

Auch an important cross-roads since Roman times, on the busy trade route linking Toulouse to the Atlantic before traffic was diverted along the River Garonne, was revived in the 18C by the administrator Étigny and embellished during the Second Empire. The bustling street life and busy Saturday markets underline its position as administrative capital of Gascony. The main streets converge on place de la Libération. The Episcopal district stands apart above the River Gers.

Old Town

Escalier monumental

The 232 steps of this monumental staircase link place Salinis, the square next to the cathedral which overlooks the Gers Valley, with the quays below; the statue of d'Artagnan, dating from 1931, is halfway down. Climbing back up the steps, you have a fine view of the 14C **Tour d'Armagnac** (the 40m/130ft-high watchtower of the municipal prison) and the arrangement of abutments and double-course flying buttresses around the cathedral.

Cathédrale Ste-Marie★★

🕔 *Closed at lunchtime (except mid-Jul to end Sep). Pre-recorded commentaries on the building available at the entrance. Audio tour of the gallery and windows available* ⊚ *2€, identity document retained as guarantee.*

Construction of the cathedral of Ste-Marie started in 1489 with the east end but work was not completed until two centuries later. The solid 16C and 17C **façade**, with its recessed upper levels producing a slightly tapered effect, presents a carefully balanced relationship between pilasters, columns, cornices, balustrades and niches. The doorways are sheltered by a vast porch offering a good view of the interior with its dividing arches, constructed to look like the triumphal arches of Antiquity. The quadripartite vaulting, dating from the mid-17C, lends the interior a stylistic

Stained-glass windows of the cathedral of Ste-Marie

A. Thuillier/MICHELIN

unity. The style is the first of what became known as French Gothic – the nave is higher than the side aisles and the triforium set between large arcades and clerestory windows.

The axial chapel is flanked on the north side by the Chapel of the Holy Sepulchre, which houses an enormous early-16C *Christ Entombed* and, on the south side, by St Catherine's Chapel, with a 16C stone altarpiece.

The chancel, as vast as the nave, is graced by two extremely fine features – the stained-glass windows and the choir stalls. These are best admired by starting a tour of the ambulatory on the north side.

Stained-glass windows★★ – Eighteen works by the Gascon painter Arnaud de Moles embellish the windows of the ambulatory chapels. The early-16C windows are noted for their rich colours, unusually large panes and big, expressive figures. Some of the men's faces are almost caricatures and the decorations incorporating medallions and brace-like ornamentation with Flamboyant Gothic canopies, combine to produce one of the great masterpieces of early-16C French art. Vignettes of daily life adorn the lower parts of the windows.

The subject matter is drawn from the prevailing theological doctrines of the time, linking the Old and New Testaments and even the pagan world. Note the sibyls, prophetic women of Antiquity.

Address Book

TOURIST INFORMATION

1 r. Dessoles, 32000 Auch, ☎ 05 62 05 22 89. www.mairie-auch.fr.

Guided tour of the town – The historical centre (monumental stairway, statue of d'Artagnan, les Pousterles) is scheduled for visits Tue-Sat (Jul-Aug 11am and during school holidays 3pm.

For coin ranges, see the Legend at the back of the guide.

EATING OUT

La Table d'Hôtes – *7 r. Lamartine - ☎ 05 62 05 55 62 – closed 2-9 Mar, 30 Jun-6 Jul, 21-28 Sep, 21-31 Dec, Sun and Wed – reservations required – 15/20.50€*. This modest rustic restaurant on the corner of a narrow street in the old town, opposite the covered market and cathedral, is a very pleasant venue with its courtyard backing on to the covered market. Local country cooking which is a good value for money.

Le Café Gascon – *5 r. Lamartine - ☎ 05 62 61 88 08 – closed 1 week Feb school holidays, 1 week at Easter, 1 week early Jul, 1 week at Christmas, Sun, and Mon-Tue evenings*. This small restaurant has two rooms separated by an old spiral staircase. Be patient, for the authentic local fare is freshly prepared for your order. At the end of the meal, the speciality café gascon is prepared at your table.

WHERE TO STAY

Chambre d'hôte Le Castagné – *Rte de Toulouse - ☎ 05 62 63 32 56 - lecastagne@wanadoo.fr - 4 rms*. This restored 19C house is a good choice for active families. Mountain biking, minigolf, fishing and pedal boats on the lake – plenty to choose from! The rooms are furnished like the rest of the family home and offer views of the countryside. Exceptionally welcoming.

Hôtel Le Robinson – *Rte de Tarbes - ☎05 62 05 02 83 – closed 24 Dec-2 Jan and Feb school holidays - P - 23 rms; 5.50€*. This 1960s hotel looking like an outsize chalet is set back from the road in a park. The rooms are functional and overlook trees. Choose those with balconies.

Chambre d'hôte Le Houresté – *32360 Jégun - 3km/1.8mi W of Jégun on D 103 rte de Vic-Fézensac - ☎ 05 62 64 51 96 - 4 rms*. Located on a working farm, the 19C house bathes in the fragrance of wisteria and roses. The guestrooms are small but well appointed; one is in a mini-chalet and another in the old dovecot. The flower garden, orchard and barnyard animals add to the charm, while the owners are happy to share their lifestyle with guests.

Chambre d'hôte Mme Mengelle – *Au village - 32360 Jégun - ☎ 05 62 64 55 03 – closed Nov-Mar - 5 rms*. Antique furnishings, tapestries and wall hangings in muted tones, a few touches of African art create the ambience in this restored family mansion. One of the rooms has a canopy bed. Discreet service.

Chambre d'hôte Mme Vouters – *Engaron, on D 939 – 32350 Biran - 4km/2.5mi W of Biran towards Le Brouilh then Vic - ☎05 62 64 41 74 - closed Oct-Easter - 3 rms*. Recommended for lovers of peace and quiet, and nature. This old 1840 farmhouse welcomes adults (no children) in colourful rooms with furnishings from another era. Escorts for rides, loose-boxes and fodder are available for your horses.

SHOPPING

Boutique Claude-Laffitte SARL – *34-38 r. Dessoles - ☎ 05 62 05 04 80 or 05 62 05 04 18 – Sun and Tue 9.30am-12.30pm, Wed-Sat 9.30am-12.30pm – closed afternoons on public holidays*. Claude Laffitte is an unforgettable character and his restaurant, full of painting, photographs and scupture, lives up to his personality. In the shop, you can buy armagnac, foie gras, confit, rillons and other regional specialities.

Groupement Agricole de la Gouardère – *Chemin d'Esparebent – Follow the yellow duck - 32810 Roquelaure - ☎ 05 62 65 56 51 - www.ferme-lagouardere.com – daily 9am-6pm*. Here, the duck is king! The farm-raised fowl is served on site in the summer months (nice country-style dining room); the rest of the year, you can carry home *foies gras, magrets, rillettes, pâtés* and *confits* from the shop. Visits of the force-feeding and preserving workshops.

Maison de Gascogne – *R. Gambetta - ☎ 05 62 05 12 08 - Jul –Aug: Mon-Sat 10am-1pm, 2.30pm-7.30pm, Sun 2.30pm-7.30pm*. Every summer traders gather here to display and sell their wares, which are specialities of the region: *foies gras*, Armagnac, *croustade*, local crafts and cabinet-making.

SPORT AND RECREATION

Aéro-club Gascon – *Aérodrome d'Auch-Lamothe - ☎ 05 62 63 37 23 - www. acgascon.asso.fr – duty office: Mon-Fri 9am-noon, 2pm-6pm - closed holidays*. This flying club organizes initiatory flights in an aircraft. Other companies on the same site offer flights in a hot-air balloon or a glider.

Golf d'Embats – *Rte de Montesquiou - ☎ 05 62 61 10 11 - christian.carrere@ wanadoo.fr – daily 8.30am-6pm. 18 holes, very hilly*.

d'Artagnan, the Real Musketeer

The statue in the town honouring d'Artagnan represents him as the famous musketeer immortalised by the novelist Alexandre Dumas. The real-life character, Charles de Batz (born c 1615), borrowed the name d'Artagnan from the Montesquiou family on his mother's side as he was about to join the French Guards, and the name of d'Artagnan was more suitable for court use.

As a young soldier, he was already favoured by Cardinal Mazarin (1602-61), Richelieu's successor, and divided his time between battle campaigns, diplomatic missions and the bawdy life of the back streets. Having gained the confidence of Louis XIV, he was entrusted with the arrest of the powerful Finance Minister Jules Fouquet, who had grown extremely rich at the State's expense. D'Artagnan is said to have carried out his mission "with great delicacy." By then a Captain-Lieutenant in the 1st Company of the King's Musketeers, he died a hero's death, during the siege of Maastricht in 1673.

In 1700, an apocryphal autobiography, *Mémoires de Monsieur d'Artagnan*, was published, which pandered to the public taste for news of indiscretions in high places. The book had lain forgotten, gathering dust on library shelves, when Dumas (1802-70) rediscovered it and used it as background for his world-famous novel. So with *The Three Musketeers*, d'Artagnan lived again as the great Gascon hero.

Statue of d'Artagnan

Choir Stalls★★★ – ⊙ *Early Apr to mid-Jul: 8.30am-noon, 2-6pm; mid-Jul to end Sep: 8.30am-6pm; Oct-Mar: 9.30am-noon, 2-5pm.* ⊗ *1.50€.* This huge artistic project took the woodcarvers of Auch 50 years (c 1500-52) to complete. The 113 stalls – 69 of which are high-backed beneath Flamboyant canopies – are decorated with over 1 500 figures exquisitely carved from seasoned oak. The general theme again demonstrates the theological symbolism seen in the stained-glass windows. Motifs drawn from the Bible, secular history, myths and legends all have their place.

The statues crowning the apse side of the 1609 reredos closing off the chancel, originally adorned a rood screen demolished in the 19C. Noteworthy among them is a scene representing the four Evangelists around a table.

The splendid tones of the great organ (1694), constructed by Jean de Joyeuse, can be heard from May to September during the many **concerts** (*Festival Claviers en Pays d'Auch [May] and Claviers d'Été [Jul and Aug: Sun at 6pm, organ concerts in the Ste-Marie Cathedral on an instrument built in the 17th century by Jean de Joyeuse]*) which are given in the cathedral.

▸ *Place de la République leads to place de la Libération.*

Place de la Libération

This is the hub of activity in the upper town. The square is closed on the northwest by the town hall and allées d'Étigny, which were both built between 1751 and 1767 by the benevolent administrator whose statue stands at the top of the stairs.

From the tourist office housed in the 15C half-timbered **Maison Fédel** (off place de la République), take rue Dessoles, which was the town's main street before d'Étigny laid out his great thoroughfares.

▸ *Turn right onto rue Salleneuve (stone steps).*

The route through the square containing the Halle aux Herbes (covered fruit and vegetable market) leads back to the north side of the cathedral. On the left, the *préfecture* is located in the **Ancien Palais Archiépiscopal** (former Archbishop's Palace). Built between 1742 and 1775, it has a Classical façade, punctuated by tall fluted pilasters.

▸▸ Housed in the nearby former Couvent des Jacobins is the **Musée des Jacobins:** (⊙ *May-Sep: 10am-noon, 2-6pm; Oct-Apr: daily except Mon 10am-noon, 2-5pm* ⊙ *Closed 1 Jan, Easter Sunday and Monday, 1 and 11 Nov, 25 Dec.* ⊗ *3€.* ☎ *05 62 05 74 79.*) Gallo-Roman archaeology; South American colonial art.

▸ *At the south-west corner of the cathedral take rue d'Espagne.*

At the end of this street two historical houses (nos 20 and 22) form a picturesque ensemble.

▸ *Turn left onto rue de la Convention.*

Les Pousteries

The street, lined with historical houses, leads to the Pousterles, a series of narrow stair alleyways. In medieval times pousterles was a word used to designate the posterns set in the walls of the fortified upper town. At the end of the road, a left turn and a few steps lead to **Porte d'Arton**, which was once the main entrance to the town. Beyond this, rue Fabre-d'Églantine skirts the ancient walls of the lycée – formerly a Jesuit college founded in 1545 – before joining place Salinis. From there, the monumental staircase leads back to the embankment.

Excursions

Pavie
5km/3mi S via N 21.

Originally a Gallo-Roman villa, Pavie became a *bastide* in 1281. Little remains of the irregular outer curtain wall other than a 14C watchtower now part of a house. The town is built on a geometrical plan, with the streets intersecting at right angles. Rue d'Étigny and rue de la Guérite contain beautiful examples of old half-timbered houses. The 13C church, restored in the 19C, has kept its 14C square belfry. A Gothic bridge with three arches spans the River Gers.

The heart of Gascony
Round-trip of 72km/45mi – allow half a day.

▷ *Leave Auch via N 21 N and after 8km/5mi turn left on D 272. Passing to the right of Roquelaure, take D 148 along the ridge road. Continue beyond Mérens along D 518 to Lavardens.*

The road runs through a gentle, undulating landscape, offering a fine **view** ★ of Lavardens.

Lavardens

This picturesque village with narrow streets is noted for its imposing castle and attractive church belfry. Remains of the ramparts and the towers which were part of its fortified enclosure may also still be seen.

The **castle** (🕐 *Jun-Aug: 10am-7pm; Apr-Jun, Sep and Oct: 10.30am-12.30pm, 2-6pm; Feb, Mar, Nov and Dec: 10.30am-12.30pm, 2-5pm.* ✆ *5€.* ☎ *05 62 58 10 61.*) was razed in the 15C and its rebuilding never completed. The structure standing today is pierced with mullion and transom windows, and juts out boldly to the west where the façade is flanked with square towers.

A stairway hewn out of stone leads up to the main vaulted rooms, some of which have their original 17C floors of brick and stone laid in geometric designs. From the top floor, there is a panoramic **view** of the neighbouring hills.

▷ *Continue along D 103 W.*

A. Thuilier/MICHELIN

Lavardens

Jegun

The village, once Church property, stands on a rocky spur within the recognisable ground-plan of a bastide. Along the main street, stand the old market and various old houses, one with fine half-timbering. To the east is the 13C collegiate church of Ste-Candide, supported by powerful buttresses.

▶ *Continue W.*

Vic-Fézensac

This town holds busy markets and *féria*, traditional festivals which include bullfighting. The church of St-Pierre, with its octagonal belfry crowned by a lantern, contains a Romanesque oven-vaulted apse and traces of 15C frescoes (south apsidal chapel). The marble font, left of the entrance, is a graceful 18C sculpture of three children holding up a basin.

▶ *Leave Vic-Fézensac heading SE via N 124 towards Auch. At St-Jean-Poutge turn right on D 939 towards L'Isle-de-Noé.*

After about 4km/2mi, before turning left on D 374, note the unusual **Gallo-Roman pier** with a niche. Its purpose remains uncertain.

Biran

This small *castelnau* is built on a spur; a single road links the fortified gateway to the remains of the keep. The **church** (🕐 *10am-noon, 3-7pm, Sun 4-6pm. ☎ 05 62 64 68 96.*) shelters a monumental stone altarpiece, carved with scenes depicting the Pietà, the Deposition and the Entombment.

▶ *Continue along D 374 and rejoin N 124 to return to Auch.*

Other local *bastides* of interest include Fleurance *(24km/15mi N),* St-Clar *(35km/21mi NE via Fleurance),* Cologne *(39km/24mi NE via Mauzevin)* and Beaumont-de-Lomagne *(50km/31mi NE via Mauzevin).*

East of Auch

Round-trip of 57km/35mi – allow half a day.

▶ *Leave Auch heading E via N 124 and follow signs to Château de St-Cricq.*

The 16C **Château de St-Cricq** is now the town's reception and conference centre.

▶ *Continue along N 124 towards Toulouse.*

After 7.5km/4.5mi there appears, on the left, beyond a meadow, the long south façade of the **Château de Marsan** (18C-19C), owned by the Montesquiou family.

Gimont

See L'ISLE JOURDAIN.

▶ *Leave Gimont heading SW via D 12 and continue for 12km/7mi to Boulaur.*

Boulaur

This village perched above the Gimone Valley has a monastery founded in the 12C by sisters from the religious community at Fontevraud Abbey. Nowadays, it is inhabited by Cistercian monks. The abbey church has a tall east end of stone and brick, and a series of blind arcades which run under the roof of the south wall.

▶ *The twisting D 626 leads to Castelnau-Barbarens.*

Castelnau-Barbarens

This little village founded in the 12C has houses standing in concentric arcs radiating from the church-topped hill. All that remains of the old castle is a tower which now serves as the belfry. The terrace offers a panoramic **view** of the Arrats Valley and the neighbouring hills.

▶ *Drive towards Auch.*

On reaching the plateau, D 626 offers a fine **panorama**★ of the Pyrenees. The route crosses **Pessan**, an old *sauveté* (a rural township founded by a monastery as a sanctuary for fugitives), which developed around an abbey, founded in the 9C.

AX-LES-THERMES⚓

POPULATION 1 441

MICHELIN LOCAL MAP 343: J-8

Ax lies in the valley at the point where the River Oriège and River Lauze flow into the Ariège. It is a spa town, both a summer holiday destination and a winter sports resort.

The Spa

Its 80 mineral springs, at temperatures ranging from 18-78°C/64-172°F, supply three pump rooms: the Couloubret, the Modèle and the Teich. The main afflictions treated here are rheumatism, respiratory disorders and some skin problems. The focal point of the resort is the Promenade du Couloubret.

Bassin des Ladres

On place du Breilh, a jet of steam marks the site of this hot water basin which is filled in the morning and can be used as a public wash-house. St Louis had it built for soldiers returning from the Crusades suffering from leprosy – hence its name "Lepers' Basin." The hospital of St-Louis (1846), easily recognised by its bellcote, is a typical example of 19C "spa town" architecture.

Ski Areas

Ax-Bonascre-le-Saquet

Alt 1 400-2 400m/4 600-7 870ft. The ski area is spread out over a wide area. There are 70km/44mi of Alpine ski runs for all levels of skiers in these beautiful high mountains, partly forested; some of the slopes are quite steep. The **gondola** (*Mid-Jun to mid-Sep: 1.30-6pm, Dec to mid-Apr: 9am-5pm. 6€ round-trip. 05 61 64 20 06.*) to the Saquet plateau (beginners' slopes) is the main approach. There is grass skiing in the summer.

Ascou-Pailhères

Alt 1 500-2 030m/4 921-6 660ft. This family resort offers 15 Alpine ski runs for all levels: gentle slopes for young children, various runs for beginners and experienced skiers. An ideal choice for a family holiday!

Le Chioula

Alt 1 240-1 650m/4 068-5 413ft. Some 60km/36mi of cross-country trails wind through a lovely natural site and 6km/3.6mi of free trails are open for those who wish to learn cross-country techniques. There is lodging right next to the trails.

Address Book

For coin ranges, see the Legend at the back of the guide.

EATING OUT

L'Orry Le Saquet – *Rte d'Andorre - 05 61 64 31 30 – closed Wed lunchtime.* This inn by the road to Andorra is a good place to stop for brief refreshment in the rustic style dining room with an open fireplace. The cooking uses local produce. Some modest rooms available.

WHERE TO STAY

Chambre d'hôte Adret – Les Bazerques - *4km/2.5mi S of Ax-les-Thermes on N 20 then D 222 - 05 61 64 05 70 – closed Nov - 5 rms.* Escape from the centre of Ax-les-Thermes and discover the charms of this old late 19C barn. Rustic style rooms, two of which overlook the valley. Terraced flower garden with barbecue.

SHOPPING

La Boutique de la Ferme – *3 pl. des Platanes - 09310 Les Cabannes - 05 61 64 91 36 - www.lafermeduquiedeverdun.com – Tue-Sat 9.30am-12.30pm, 3.30-7pm; Sun 9.30am-noon.* "The Farm Shop" is a pleasant, old-fashioned place selling fresh produce including meats, fowl, foie gras, confits, charcuterie, honey from l'Ariège, cheeses and gift items typical of this mountainous region.

The Izard

About 40 years ago, the izard, a variety of wild goat found in the Pyrenees, had been all but killed off by hunters' bullets. Nowadays it is a protected species. There are over 1 000 in the Orlu Valley, which has consequently been designated a nature reserve since 1981. The izard is usually to be found between 1 600-2 500m/5 250-8 200ft above sea level, but it does venture below 900m/2 950ft. It is gradually taking over those areas which have been abandoned by man. The izard's coat changes colour depending on the season: it is red-gold in the summer and dark brown with patches of white in the winter, when it also becomes much thicker to combat the cold. The animals are not that timid and can be observed quite easily, especially during spring or autumn. The summer heat and winter cold force them to take refuge in the undergrowth. Izards are perfectly suited to their environment and can climb up and down even quite steep slopes with impressive agility.

Mijanès-Donézan

Alt 1 530-2 000m/5 019-6 561ft. Known as the "Québec of Ariège", the Donézan plateau offers nine downhill slopes 🎿 and 36km/22mi of cross-country trails 🎿, with two departure points. This is a family resort, which offers services for children including initiation sessions, play groups and a sledding area.

Hiking Tour

Réserve nationale d'Orlu

8.5km/5mi to the starting point of the footpath.

▶ *Leave Ax on the road to Andorra and turn off towards Orlu just before the bridge over the Oriège; stay on the north bank of the river.*

The road runs along the **Orlu Valley**★ and the shore of the reservoir contained by the Orgeix dam, with Orgeix manor house reflected in the waters. The old Orlu ironworks is surrounded by rocky slopes riddled with streams. Take the road on the left before the ironworks. Leave the car in the parking area of Pont de Caralp and walk along the track closed to motorised traffic.

🚶 *This hike (3hr round-trip) is suitable for all walking enthusiasts.*

The path climbs alongside the west bank of the Oriège to the En Gaudu shelter intended for shepherds, located downstream from the Jasse d'en Gaudu (cattle pen). Here you will be able to see marmots and izards, especially early in the morning or at the end of the day.

Farther up (an additional 2hr round-trip), the path crosses a stream, then, from Pas de Balussière, it continues along the east bank of the Oriège. Farther up still, the **Étang de Beys** comes into view. It can be reached via the Beys shelter.

Signal de Chioula★

45min on foot round-trip.

▶ *Leave Ax on D 613 N, following the Ariège Valley in a series of hairpin bends.*

🚶 At the Chioula Pass, a wide footpath leads to the beacon (alt 1 507m/4 898ft; 45min round-trip), from where there is a view of the peaks framing the upper Ariège Valley.

Excursions

Maison des loups

8.5km/5.3mi. ▶ *Leave Ax on the road to Andorra and turn towards Orlu just before the bridge on the Oriège; drive to the end of the valley as far as Les Forges.*
🕐 Jul and Aug: 10am-7pm (feeding of the wolves 3pm, 5pm); Apr-Jun: 10am-5.30pm (feeding time: 3.30pm); Sep to Oct: daily except Mon and Tue 11am-5pm. 🎫 5.70€ (children under 12: 4€). ☎ 05 61 64 02 66.

🧒 Observation platforms scattered across a magnificent woodland site, with mountain streams rushing through it, offer an opportunity to see different species of wolves roaming around in vast enclosures and being fed (explanations are given about the life and behaviour of these mythical animals). Children will also be attracted by the enclosures where donkeys, goats, lambs and young pigs are kept as well as by the "Sentier des traces" (the tracks trail).

Plateau de Bonascre★

8km/5mi. ▶ *Leave Ax on N 20 to Tarascon and turn off left almost immediately onto D 820.*

The road climbs steeply in a series of hairpin bends, giving a good view of the three river valleys which converge on Ax: the Ariège (towards Tarascon); the Orlu, with the Dent d'Orlu Peak towering on the skyline; and the upper Ariège Valley. At the top is the Bonascre plateau, home to the ski resort of **Ax-Bonascre-le-Saquet**, equipped with the basic facility of a gondola leading to the **Plateau du Saquet** (alt 2 030m/6 598ft).

▶ *Drive on past the "Sup-Aéro" holiday hostel and turn off left across the mountain side, on the Route forestière des Campels. Follow this road for about 1.5km/0.9mi.*

Take in the superb **view**★★ stretching from the valley cut by the upper reaches of the Ariège as far as the mountains on the border with Andorra. In the valley the main road and the railway line run side by side, crisscrossing one another from time to time.

Col du Pradel★

30km/18.5mi. ▶ *Leave Ax to the E on the road to Quillan. 3.5km/2mi out of town, turn left onto D 22.* 🚫 *The narrow pass road is closed from 15 November to 14 May*

The **Dent d'Orlu** (alt 2 222m/7 222ft), with its distinctive pointed outline making it the best known of the mountain peaks in the upper Ariège Valley, can be seen to the southeast. The road leads up the pass (alt 1 680m/5 460ft) along a series of tight hairpin bends. There is a lovely view of the mountains surrounding the upper reaches of the Ariège.

The Donézan

66km/41mi round-trip – allow half a day. ▶ *Leave Ax-les-Thermes E along D 613 towards Le Chioula and, 3.5km/2.5mi farther on, turn right onto D 25 towards Ascou-Pailhères.*

The road runs through the **Donézan** region, one of the wildest areas of the Pyrenees, where villages lie at an altitude of about 1 200m/3 936ft. The region is set in a hollowed-out basin in the granite plateaus of the Quérigut, from which the rivers flow into the Aude. The Donézan used to belong to the County of Foix, which has become the département of Ariège.

▶ *In Mijanès, turn left onto a minor road leading to Usson.*

Usson-les-Bains

The imposing ruins of the castle set high up on an isolated rock to the left of the road stand guard over the confluence of La Bruyante, which has flowed down from the Donézan region, and the Aude.

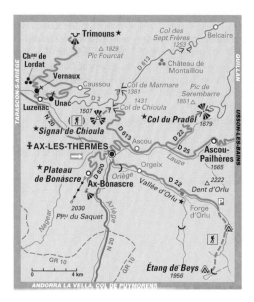

Trimouns quarry

The Climb to Trimouns★★
39km/24mi round-trip – allow 3hr.

▶ *Leave Ax-les-Thermes NW along N 20 towards Tarascon.*

Luzenac
This village has been famed since the end of the 19C for the nearby deposit of French chalk, which is quarried at the **Carrière de Trimouns**★, cut into the middle of the St-Barthélemy mountain massif between 1 700-1 850m/5 577-6 070ft above sea level. The raw French chalk is transported in skips to the factory in the valley, where it is dried, crushed and packaged.

▶ *Leave Luzenac across the bridge spanning the Ariège and follow D 2 towards Caussou.*

Unac
Note the fine Romanesque church towering above the valley. Inside, the two capitals at the entrance to the chancel are carved with a profusion of detail.

▶ *Carry on along D 2, the "Route des Corniches," admiring the bird's-eye views of the Ariège Valley, then turn left towards Lordat.*

Château de Lordat
Interesting castle ruins camped on a limestone outcrop.

▶ *Return to the Route des Corniches crossroads and go straight on towards Trimouns.*

Carrière de Trimouns★
🕐☁ *Jul and Aug: guided tours (1hr) daily except Sat-Sun 10am, 11am, 2pm, 3pm and 4pm; mid-May to end Jun and early Sep to mid-Oct: daily except Sat-Sun 4pm.* 🕐 *Closed Whitsun, 14 Jul, 15 and 16 Aug.* ☜ *5€ (5-12 years: 2.50€).* ☎ *05 61 64 68 07.*

🖐 *Leave the car in the visitors' car park.* The quarry at Trimouns is one of the largest operations of its kind in the world. Not only is the **view**★ of the huge white seam of French chalk itself impressive, but there is a magnificent **panorama**★★ of the upper Ariège mountains from the quarry.

▶ *Drive back to Lordat, then onto Luzenac via Vernaux.*

Vernaux
Below the village, the road runs past the isolated Romanesque church built from tufa.

▶ *Take N 20 back to Ax-les-Thermes.*

BAGNÈRES-DE-BIGORRE ⚓

POPULATION 8 423

MICHELIN LOCAL MAP 342: M-4

This picturesque spa lies in attractive pastureland, north of the Vallée de Campan, on the west bank of the River Adour. The waters of the cure centre, which are rich in calcium and sulphur salts, are drawn from 13 bores. These are used in the treatment of respiratory, rheumatic and psychosomatic disorders.

Bagnères-de-Bigorre is also a nucleus around which much Pyrenees folklore is centred, and was the home of a well-known 19C literary society, specialising in works inspired by the mountains. A choral society, known as the Chanteurs Montagnards, which travelled to London, Rome, Jerusalem and Moscow in the mid-1800s, still survives today. ☐ *3 allée Tournefort, 65200 Bagnères-de-Bigorre.* ☎ *05 62 95 50 71. www.bagneresdebigorre-lamongie.com.*

⊙ **Don't Miss:** Parc thermal de Salut, and the local-produce market on rue des Thermes *(every morning except Mon).*

Visit

Parc thermal de Salut★
45min round trip on foot.

🚶 A gateway at the end of avenue Noguès *(south of the town plan)* marks the entrance to this 100ha/247 acre park, offering pleasant walks under fine, shady trees. The central avenue crosses the park and skirts the garden leading to the former Établissement thermal de Salut – the old spa centre.

Old town

Among the attractions of this area (bordered to the east by the busiest part of the town, allées des Coustous) are **St Vincent's**, a 16C church with a belfry-wall pierced by three rows of arcades, **Tour des Jacobins**, a tower which is all that remains of a 15C monastery destroyed during the Revolution, and the **cloister ruins** on the corner of rue St-Jean and rue des Thermes. The charming **half-timbered house** at the junction of rue du Vieux-Moulin and rue Victor-Hugo dates from the 15C.

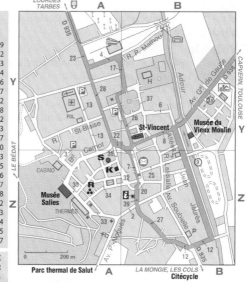

BAGNÈRES-DE-BIGORRE

3-Frères-Duthu R.	BZ	39
Alsace-Lorraine R. d'	BZ	2
Arras R. du Pont d'	AZ	3
Belgique Av. de	AY	4
Costallat R.	BY	6
Coustous Allée des	BZ	7
La-Fayette Pl.	ABY	22
Foch R. Maréchal	BY	8
Frossard R. Émilien	BZ	12
Gambetta R.	AY	13
Joffre Av. Mar.	AY	17
Jubinal Pl. A.	BZ	20
Leclerc Av. Gén.	AY	23
Lorry R. de	BZ	25
Pasteur R.	BY	26
Pyrénées R. des	BZ	27
République R. de la	AY	28
Strasbourg Pl. de	BZ	32
Thermes Pl. des	AZ	33
Thermes R. des	AZ	34
Victor-Hugo R.	AZ	35
Vignaux Pl. des	BY	37

Maison à colombage	AZ	K
Ruines du cloître St-Jean	AZ	R
Tour des Jacobins	AZ	S

Address Book

For coin ranges, see the Legend at the back of the guide.

EATING OUT

Le Bigourdan – 14 r. Victor-Hugo - ☎ 05 62 95 20 20 – closed Sun evening and Mon. The entrance to this little restaurant, next to the tour des Jacobins, leads to an old wooden stairway that climbs to the first-floor dining room. The decor is tasteful, the service efficient and the cooking based on local products.

Aux Berges de l'Adour – 65200 Hiis – 8km/4.8 mi N of Bagnères de Bigorre on D 935, rte de Tarbes and a narrow lane to the right. - ☎ 05 62 91 53 30 – closed Sun evening, Tue evening and Wed. The atmosphere in this restaurant, set up in a traditional old house, is pleasing: exposed beams, wooden furnishings, bright tablecloths, a wardrobe and a big dining table in front of the fireplace. Regional specialities.

WHERE TO STAY

Hostellerie d'Asté – Rte de Campan - 3.5 km/2.2mi S of Bagnères de Bigorre on D 935 - ☎ 05 62 91 74 27 - hotel@hotel-aste. com - closed 12 Nov-12 Dec. - 🅿 - 21 rms. Guests may wish to try a little fishing in the river running at the bottom of the hotel's large garden, or enjoy a game of tennis. A friendly welcome, with small but well presented rooms, some of which have balconies.

SHOPPING

Les Halles – Rue des Thermes – Tue and Sun mornings. About 50 stalls offer an appealing selection of the finest, freshest local products. Lively and fun. In the summer moths, local farmers set up for business on Wednesday.

SPORTS AND RECREATION

Établissement thermal de Capvern - ☎ 05 62 39 00 02 – May-Oct. Capvern-les-Bains has two spa treatment centres, Hount-Caoute and Bouridé, specialising in the treatment of kidney problems, hepatits, rheumatism and disorders of the metabolism. Weight-loss programme.

Musée Salies

🕐 May-Oct: 3-6pm; guided tour 1hr 15min: daily except Mon and Tue 3-6pm. 🚌 4€. ☎ 05 62 91 07 26.

The Fine Arts department of this museum includes an interesting collection of ceramics, and paintings by Joos van Cleve, Chasseriau, Jongkind, Picabia and others. There are also temporary natural history and photography exhibits.

Musée du Vieux Moulin

🕐 Daily except Sat-Sun and Mon 10am-noon, 2-6pm. 🕐 Closed Oct and public holidays. 🚌 2€. ☎ 05 62 91 07 33.

The old watermill is now used as a museum focusing on the crafts and folk traditions of the Bigorre mountain region (traditional tools used in weaving and the wool trade, agricultural implements etc).

Citécycle

On the outskirts of town, on the way to La Mongie. 🕐Jul-Aug: daily 10.30am-12.30pm, 2-6.30pm; Sep-Jun: daily except Tue 10.30am-12.30pm, 2-6.30pm. 🚶 Guided tour. 🚌 5.50€ (children: 3.80€). ☎ 05 62 95 53 11.

🎒 This is a museum, a showroom and a training centre entirely dedicated to cycling. It provides information on the history, the future and the industrial production of bikes.

Excursions

Gouffre d'Esparros★★

29km/18mi E along D84 and D26. 🕐🚶Jun-Sep: guided tours (1hr) 10am-noon, 1.30pm-6pm (Jul-Aug: booking advised); Jun and Sep: 10.30am-11.30pm, 2.30-5.30pm; rest of the year: during school holidays: 10am-12pm,1.30-5.30pm; Sat-Sun and public holidays: 10am-12pm,1.30-5pm, Tue 1.30-5pm; Jan: Sat on request (1 day's notice). 🕐 Closed Nov to mid-Dec, 1 Jan, 25 Dec. 🚌 6.50€ (children: 5€). ☎ 05 62 39 11 80. www.gouffre-esparros. com. Access is limited and bookings are recommended.

This recently opened site offers visitors exceptionally fine aragonite formations which look like snow crystals. The **Salle du Lac gallery** is particularly attractive.

Grotte de Médous★★

2.5km/1.5mi S by D935. ⏱ ⚓ *Jul and Aug: guided tours (1hr) 9am-noon, 2pm-6pm; Apr-Jun: 9-11.30am, 2-5pm; early Sep to mid-Oct: 9-11.30am, 2-5pm.* ⚓ *6.40€ (children: 3.20€).* ☎ *05 62 91 78 46.*

In 1948 three speleologists from Bagnères-de-Bigorre, exploring a gallery which did not penetrate very far into the rock, discovered a blow-hole which suggested the existence of a substantial cavern close by. The site, not far from Bagnères, was near a resurgent spring watering the pools in the grounds of Médous Château. The cavers gouged a larger hole in the rock wall, squeezed through an opening not much bigger than a cat flap and found themselves in a series of galleries full of marvellous rock formations.

The 1km/0.6mi route twists through an enchanted land of stalactites, stalagmites and broad petrified flows of calcite (carbonate of lime) which have hardened over the ages into fantastic forms evoking waterfalls, hanging draperies, a magnificent church organ etc; the chambers have subsequently been given suitably fanciful names. After the Gallery of Marvels, the Hindu Temple, the Cervin Halls and the Great Organ Chamber, the visit includes a boat trip along a short subterranean stretch of the River Adour: the caverns have been hollowed out over the millennia by waters siphoned off from the main river through a tunnel near Campan, only emerging into the open air again in the grounds of Médous Château.

Hiking Tour

Le Bédat★

1hr 30min round trip on foot.

▶ At the junction of three by-roads, north of the casino, a path to the left leads to the Fontaine des Fées (Fairy Fountain) and a statue of the Bédat Virgin. Behind the statue, another path follows the crest as far as the viewing table (alt 881m/2 890ft). The impressive view stretches over the Baronnies and the Lannemezan plateau (*east*) and across the Vallée de Campan to the summits of the Central Pyrenees (*south*).

BAGNÈRES-DE-LUCHON⚒⚒

POPULATION 4 439

MICHELIN LOCAL MAP 343: B-8

Bagnères-de-Luchon or Luchon as it is more commonly known, is a lively spa lying in a beautiful setting half way along the scenic Route des Pyrénées, ap- preciated for the restorative virtues of the fine climate as well as the waters. It is the busiest and most fashionable cure resort in the region, and also a tourist and winter sports centre with a wide choice of ski runs, climbs and excursions. In the winter, the town serves as a base for skiers attracted by the slopes at Su- perbagnères, the resort's high-altitude annex, and slopes around other resorts such as Peyragude and Le Mourtis. ▯ *Allées d'Étigny, 31110 Bagnères-de-Luchon,* ☎ *05 61 79 21 21. www.luchon.com.*

A Bit of History

Baths of Ilixo – In Gallo-Roman times, the Vallée d'One (the land of the Onesii) was already famous for its healing waters. Ilixo, the centre's divine custodian, presided over the magnificent baths which were second only to those in Naples, according to an inscription in Latin on the wall of the bath house. Excavations have revealed traces of enormous pools lined with marble, and systems for circulating warm air and steam. A Roman road linked the baths to Lugdunum Convenarum (St-Bertrand-de-Comminges).

The Great Intendant – In 1759, **Baron d'Étigny**, who lived at Auch, visited Luchon for the first time. The baron, who was Intendant (Royal Steward) of Gascony, Béarn and Navarre, was so impressed with the spa that he determined to restore it to its former glory. By 1762, a carriage road linked Luchon to Montréjeau in the north. The splendid avenue – which today bears the nobleman's name – was officially inaugu- rated, and planted with rows of lime trees which had to be guarded by soldiers as the inhabitants were hostile to such innovations.

Address Book

ⓘ *For coin ranges, see the Legend at the back of the guide.*

EATING OUT

🍽🍽 **Le Clos du Silène** – *19 cours des Quinconces -* ☎ *05 61 79 12 00 - colliourey@ aol.com – closed 17 Nov-10 Dec, Tue noon and Mon except public and school holidays.* Across from the spa centre, this new restaurant has made a name for itself. The two dining rooms are elegant – parquet floors, white tablecloths and colourful tableware – and the cuisine is refined. The desserts are especially good.

🍽🍽 **Ferme d'Espiau** – *31110 Billière - 9km/5.4km outside Bagnères-de-Luchon -* ☎ *05 61 79 69 69 – closed Mon-Wed except school holidays.* This mountain farm has a shaded terrace with a splendid view over the Peyresourde region. Enjoy hearty dishes and grilled meats in the pretty, country-style dining room.

WHERE TO STAY

🛏 **Deux Nations** – *5 r. Victor-Hugo -* ☎ *05 61 79 01 71 - hotel2nations@aol.com - 28 rms.* Laid out over two buildings, this establishment has been in the same hands since 1917, and offers clean, simple accommodation. The restaurant has its own access and opens onto an attractive planted terrace.

🛏 **Chambre d'hôte Le Poujastou** – *R. du Sabotier - 31110 Juzet-de-Luchon -* ☎ *05 61 94 32 88 - info@lepoujastou.com - closed Nov. -* 🅿 *- 5 rms.* Facing due south towards the Luchonnais peaks, this 18C establishment is the village café, and nowadays also provides up-to-date accommodation painted in ochre hues. Tasty country cuisine served in a typical pyrenean dining room.

🛏 **La Petite Auberge** – *15 r. Lamartine -* ☎ *05 61 79 02 88 - closed late Oct-26 Dec -*

🅿 *- 30 rms.* A hotel since the 1960s, this historic residence is strategically located mid-way between the Baths and the cable car for Superbagnères. The rooms are not large but are well equipped. Very pleasant terrace.

🛏🛏 **Rencluse** – *St-Mamet - 31110 Bagnères-de-Luchon -* ☎ *05 61 79 02 81 - closed 5 Mar-30 Apr and 7 Oct-2 Feb -* 🅿 *- 23 rms.* On the road for Spain, this friendly establishment has the ambience of a country family home. The rooms are airy and comfortable (those in the annex are quietest). Pleasant rustic feel to the dining room, which serves simple classic cuisine.

SPORT AND RECREATION

Domaine skiable de Luchon-Superbagnères - *Alt. 1 440-2 260 m.* 14 lifts. 24 runs cover a vast area benefitting from plenty of sun and snow cannons. At lower altitude, the Coumes section has easy slopes ideal for beginners. The Lac sector has pleasant intermediate runs through forestry, and those seeking the thrill of black runs should head for Arbesquens. To the west, the Céciré sector offers intermediate skiing against a backdrop of beautiful mountain scenery.

Golf club de Luchon – *Rte de Montauban - 31110 Montauban-de-Luchon -* ☎ *05 61 79 03 27 - golfluchon@wanadoo.fr - 9h-18h - closed Nov-Mar.* Founded in 1909, this 9 hole course is the region's oldest. Fine mountain backdrop, clubhouse with restaurant and tearoom.

Rafting, Canoeing and kayaking centre – *31110 Antignac -* ☎ *05 61 79 19 20 – www. antignac-rafting.com - Jul-Aug: 9am-7.30pm; Apr-Nov : Tue-Sat 9.30am-12.30pm, 2-6pm - closed 1 Jan, 25 Dec.* This watersports centre offers a variety of activities including canoeing, kayaking and air-boats, plus a host of other activities.

D'Étigny then replaced the original common pool with nine double troughs made of wood, each with a removable cover which had a hole for the bathers' heads.

This was a substantial improvement, though those taking the waters still had to undress in the open air, screened only by a board fence. D'Étigny was also the first person to think of appointing a regular doctor to a thermal spa.

The next step was to advertise the town. D'Étigny persuaded the governor of the province, Maréchal Duc de Richelieu, to take a cure. The duke, enchanted by the Roman ruins, was delighted. He extolled the merits of the spa back at the palace in Versailles and returned for a second cure. From then on, the town's success was assured. Even the premature death of Baron d'Étigny, in 1767, did not halt Luchon's development.

The Spa

Life in Luchon centres on **allées d'Étigny**, the main avenue leading to the baths. The mansion at no 18, built in the 18C, was where the Duc de Richelieu resided. It now houses the tourist office and local museum.

Cures – Water from some 80 springs is piped from Superbagnères mountain to the spa. Combining the effects of sulphur and radioactivity to treat respiratory disorders,

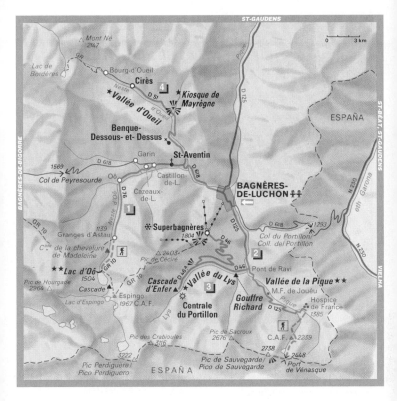

the Luchon cures have long been favoured by famous singers, actors, lawyers and preachers. More recently, there has been increasing success in treating rheumatic complaints and physiotherapy, by combining alluvial mud steeped in colonies of algae and bacteria giving off sulphur, found only in extremely hot water, with sulphurous emanations in a specially fitted out grotto or **Radio-Vaporarium**, where the temperature is 38-42°C/98-109°F. The Radio-Vaporarium is located in Luchon's most luxurious **spa treatment centre**.

Musée du Pays de Luchon

🕐 *9am-noon, 2-6pm.* 🕐 *Closed Nov and public holidays.* 👛 *1.60€.* ☎ *05 61 79 29 87.*

The ground floor of this regional museum displays the *Plan Lézat*, a three-dimensional relief map of the mountains around Luchon on a scale of 1:10 000, dated 1854. The upper floors are devoted to mementoes of famous visitors, distinguished Pyrenees climbers, and winter sports practised on the neighbouring massifs of Maladetta, Lys, Oô and Aran. Iron Age artefacts, statues and votive altars from the Gallo-Roman period show man's long-standing presence in the region. Photographs and reproductions in another room relate to the more recent history of the town, local casino and thermal cures. The arts, crafts and folk traditions of the surrounding valleys are represented by a rich and varied collection of weavers' looms, shepherds' crooks, farming tools and religious items.

Hiking Tours

Lac d'Oô★★ 1

▶ *Leave Luchon via D 618, the road to Col de Peyresourde. At Castillon, fork left onto the Vallée d'Oô road (D 76), which skirts the base of the huge moraine on which the villages of Cazeaux and Garin are perched.*

📷 *2hr 30min round trip on foot along the footpath marked GR 10. Alt 1 504m/4 934ft.*

The lake lies in a magnificent setting with the torrent from Lac d'Espingo, in the background, cascading down a spectacular 275m/902ft. The lake (covering 38ha/94 acres; maximum depth 67m/220ft) fuels the Oô hydroelectric power station *(consequent lowering of the lake's water level may render the scene less attractive)*.

Lac d'Oô

Vallée de la Pique★★ [2]

▶ *Leave Luchon via D 125.*

The road follows the Vallée de la Pique upstream, rising first through meadows and then through splendid beech forests. After crossing the river, turn left onto the road (D 125) leading to the Maison Forestière de Jouéu. The lodge, surrounded by conifers, belongs to the University of Toulouse and is a specialised botanical laboratory used to study the flora of the fields and forests.

▶ *Park the car and continue on foot.*

⚑ The Hospice de France sits at an altitude of 1 385m/4 544ft. This group of low buildings lies amid beautiful, high pastureland, typical of the Pyrenees, and is an excellent base for ramblers. The surrounding forest, abundance of waterfalls and majestic landscape all beckon invitingly.

☙ Walkers in good physical condition, who wish to have a closer view of the highest point in the Pyrenees, should leave the Hospice very early and take the mule track leading to **Port de Vénasque** (*alt 2 448m/8 032ft*). From the foothills on the Spanish side of the pass (*4hr 30min round trip on foot*), or better still from Pic de Sauvegarde, which rises to 2 738m/8 983ft (*6hr round trip on foot*), there is a superb view of the entire Maladetta massif.

Vallée du Lys★ [3]

32km/20mi S from Luchon to Superbagnères – allow 2hr 30min.

▶ *Leave Luchon S along D 125 then turn right onto D 46. Park the car 2km/1.2mi beyond the second Pont de Ravi.*

The full name of this valley is *Bat de Lys* (*bat* is the Gascon word for valley).

Gouffre Richard

From the base of an electricity pylon (*left*), there is a good view of a fast-flowing waterfall which plunges down into a rocky cauldron below.

After the turnoff to Superbagnères on the left, the road veers southwards, revealing a **panorama**★ of the highest peaks encompassing the cirque at the top of the valley.

☙ *Park in the (free) car park provided by the restaurant Les Délices du Lys.*

Centrale du Portillon (Portillon Power Station)

The hydroelectric station is powered by water falling from a maximum height of 1 419m/4 656ft, a drop considered sensational when the station was opened in 1941.

Cascade d'Enfer (Hell's Waterfall)

This is the last leap of the Enfer stream.

▷ *Return to D 46 and take the turnoff to Superbagnères on the left. The road runs through beech woods.*

Luchon-Superbagnères ski area

Alt 1 440m/4 723ft-2 260m/7 413ft. This ski complex features 14 lifts and 24 downhill slopes; it also has snow-making equipment. There are slopes for all levels, some on sunny hillsides, but also in the forest.

Superbagnères ✳

The skiing centre of Superbagnères stands well above the tree line, and can be reached by cableway from Bagnères-de-Luchon. The impressive Grand Hôtel, built in 1922 and bought by the Club Méditerranée, is the centre of the resort. From the orientation table on the south side of the hotel, there is a **view**✱✱ of the Pyrenees on the Luchon side with the glaciers of the Maladetta massif in the background.

Vallée d'Oueil★ 4

15km/9mi NW from Luchon to Cirès – 30min.

▷ *Leave Luchon by D 618.*

After several sharp bends, beyond a chapel commemorating the martyrdom of St Aventin, turn right on D 51. About 2km/1mi along, a track (*left*) leads to **Benque-Dessous-et-Dessus**. The church in the upper village contains 15C murals.

The lower **Vallée d'Oueil**✱ is noted for its charming pastureland and clustered villages.

Kiosque de Mayrègne★

Free access to the viewing table on the café terrace.

There is a fine **panorama** of the peaks along the Spanish border, from the sombre Vénasque massif, to the glacier-coated peaks of the upper cirque of the Portillon d'Oô. In the background, between Pic de Sacroux and Pic de Sauvegarde, the Maladetta range is visible once more, culminating in the 3 404m/11 168ft Pic d'Aneto, the highest point in the Pyrenees.

Cirès

The houses in this tiny, picturesque hamlet are packed into a mini-amphitheatre below a church isolated on its promontory. Like all the houses in the valley, their pointed roofs contain high lofts, enclosed by lattice work, to store the abundant hay.

BANYULS-SUR-MER ⌂

POPULATION 4 532

MICHELIN LOCAL MAP 344: J-8

ALSO SEE CÔTE VERMEILLE

Banyuls the most southerly seaside resort in France, has a delightful yachting harbour. The resort is developing without detriment to its charm, set against a pretty backdrop of vineyards around a bay divided into two coves by the promontory on which the old town stands. This site is sheltered from the harsh north-westerly gusts of the *tramontane*, with the result that a number of tropical plants have been introduced here (carob, eucalyptus, and various palm trees), originally by the biologist Charles-Victor Naudin (1815-99), and propagated along the Mediterranean coast as far as the Riviera. A sea-water therapy centre has recently been opened. 🛈 *Av. de la République, 66650 Banyuls-sur-Mer,* ☎ *04 68 88 31 58.*

⊙ **Don't Miss:** The view from Cap Réderis.
🧒 **Especially for Kids:** The Aquarium.

The Resort

The beach – The main beach lies in the shelter of the cove which is closed off to the east by a pair of islands, the Île Petite and the Île Grosse (on which there is a war memorial by Maillol), linked to the mainland by a dike.

Côte Vermeille and vineyards of Banyuls

The sea – The coastal waters along the Côte Vermeille are deep and clear and well-stocked with fish. They have attracted the attention of scientists because of their wealth of biological interest, to the extent that the Laboratoire Arago (Université de Paris VI)—a research and teaching centre specialising in oceanography, marine biology and land ecology—has been established at Banyuls.

Laboratoire Arago

Kids The centre's **Aquarium** offers a clearly presented display of Mediterranean fauna in its reconstructed natural environment (🕐 *Jul-Aug : 9am-1pm, 2-9pm; rest of the year 9am-noon, 2-6:30pm; 4.20€, children: 2.10€; ☎ 04 68 88 73 39)*.
A fine collection of 250 birds is on display in the entrance.

Réserve marine naturelle de Banyuls-Cerbère

Created in 1974 along the only rocky stretch of the Languedoc-Roussillon coastline, this conservation area was France's first marine reserve and remains the only one to be exclusively dedicated to a marine ecosystem. It extends 6.5km/4mi along the coast and covers an area of 650ha/1 606 acres; its aim is to protect marine species endangered by intensive fishing, by pollution due to waste water and by tourist activities (pleasure boats and underwater fishing).

Écrin bleu: Underwater Trail *(underwater trail of the Banyuls-Cerbère Marine Nature Reserve)* 🕐 *Jul and Aug: noon-6pm. Equipment rental from noon to 5pm (including waterproof information sheets). Meeting point on the Peyrefite beach and information area on the yachting harbour. No charge. ☎ 04 68 88 56 87.*
You start on this 250m/273yd trail with relevant information supplied on waterproof material; there are five observation stations along the way at depths not exceeding 5m/16ft. Each station marked by a buoy enables you to observe a different biotope and to get a glimpse of a variety of fish (red mullets, bass, rainbow wrasse…) and, if you're lucky, a dolphin, a loggerhead turtle or even a spotted sea horse.

The trail is supervised by swimming instructors and buoys are fitted with hand rails.

Vineyards and Mountains

Vineyards reign supreme over the last slopes of the Albères, covering the final outcrops of the Pyrenees and the steep hillsides of the Baillaury Valley. The schist slopes have been cut into terraces, supported by low stone walls, and reinforced to prevent the more exposed slopes being washed away by rainwater with a system of crisscrossing ditches.

Banyuls Wine

The grapes are vinified according to traditional methods developed by the Knights Templar. After a lengthy maturing process in oak casks in cellars or in the open air, the result is the famous **Banyuls**, a dry, medium or sweet wine capable of gracing the best of tables. It can be drunk as an apéritif, or with dessert, and is the ideal accompaniment to foie gras, strongly flavoured cheeses and game, among other things.
Several cellars, or **caves**, are open to the public, including two on the vertiginous cliff road (Route des Crêtes). The **Grande Cave** (🕐 *Apr-Oct: guided tours (45min) 10am-7.30pm ; Nov-Mar: 10am-1pm, 2.30-6.30pm.* 🕐 *Closed 1 Jan and 25 Dec; No charge; ☎ 04 68 98 36 92)* shows a video on the history of Banyuls and organises a guided tour

Address Book

For coin categories, see the Legend.

EATING OUT

Al Fanal and Hôtel El Llagut – *Av. Fontaulé -* ☎ *04 68 88 00 81 - closed 4 Jan-10 Feb and Wed from 15 Sep-15 Jun - alfanal@wanadoo.fr -* This house opposite the harbour once housed the garages for the Grand Hôtel but is now a restaurant with a good reputation. The well prepared cuisine characterized by local flavours is served amid nautical decor or on the terrace. One or two reasonably priced rooms available.

WHERE TO STAY

Villa Miramar – *R. Lacaze-Duthiers -* ☎ *04 68 88 33 85 – ange.st@wanadoo.fr - closed 16 Oct-31 Mar -* ⓟ *- 16 rms.* This 1960s villa is on a hillside slightly outside the town centre. The shady garden and swimming pool provide ample opportunity for relaxation. Inside, the room decor inspired by the Far East will lend an exotic touch to your holiday.

SIT BACK AND RELAX

La Paillotte – *14 r. St-Pierre -* ☎ *04 68 88 30 30 - www.la paillote.com - Tues-Fri noon-2.30pm, 6.30-10.30pm, Sat noon-2.30pm, 6.30-11.30pm, Sun 10am-3pm; Jul-Aug: daily until 2am - closed mid-Sep to mid-Mar.*

Small tea room awaiting discovery during a stroll in the streets of Old Banyuls. Visitors are welcomed by a tempting menu of fresh fruit juice cocktails and ice cream sundaes. There is also a choice of background music.

SHOPPING

Foire à la Brocante – *Allée Maillol - Jun-Aug: Fri 7am-1pm.* Bric-à-brac.

Les Ruchers de Banyuls – *Rte des Mas -* ☎ *04 68 88 09 36 - mielsdebanyuls@ europost.org - Mon-Sat 9am-8pm, Sun 3pm-8pm.* The Centène family have been wine-growers for centuries, but diversified in 1992 to bee-keeping. A variety of honeys are on sale: rosemary, white heather, sea lavender, thyme, mountain flowers.

Marché artisanal – *Av. de la République - Jul-Aug: daily 9pm-1am.* This local crafts market provides the main focus of activity in Banyuls during the summer months.

RELAXING

Thalacap Catalogne – *Av. de la Côte Vermeille - A 9 Perpignan Sud exit towards Argelès -* ☎ *04 68 98 36 66 - www.thalacap. com – 7am-10pm – closed 4 Jan- 1 Feb.* This seawater spa is in the upper part of town, facing the sea. Residential hotel with panoramic restaurant.

of the place where the oak barrels are kept, where the wines are left to mature in the sun and of the cellars with their antique casks. The **Cellier des Templiers-cave du Mas Reig** (♿ ⊙ ⏱ 🍷 *Jul and Aug: guided tours (45min) 10am-7.30pm;* ⊖ *No charge;* ☎ *04 68 98 36 92)* is also open to the public. This wine cellar dates from the days of the Knights Templar (13C), whose feudal castle and sub-commandery (Mas Reig) are next door (⚷ *closed to the public).*

Additional Sight

Métairie Maillol

5km/3mi SW. Follow the road to the Col de Banyuls. The road runs along the Baillaury Valley. ⊙ *May-Sep: 10am-noon, 4-7pm; Oct-Apr: 10am-noon, 2-5pm.* ⊙ *Closed public holidays. 3.10€.* ☎ *04 68 88 57 11.*

Aristide Maillol (1861-1944) was born in Banyuls. At the age of 20 he "went up" to Paris, where he began learning painting and more importantly, in line with the trend set by the "Nabis," interesting himself in the revival of crafts such as pottery and tapestry. He was over 40 by the time he had established himself as a sculptor of great talent, basing his groups of sturdy nude figures on earlier sketches. While as a painter and draughtsman he may have worked from models, as a sculptor he is distinguished by his unwavering observation, his quest for fluid movement and by his sense of the grandiose, which led him to produce some outstanding works, in which his figures exude both grace and power.

Visit

The artist liked to retire to his little country house at the bottom of a valley which gets scorching hot and dusty in the summer. This now houses the Musée Maillol which displays numerous sculptures, terracotta, paintings and drawings. The artist was buried at his request in the garden.

BÉZIERS ★

POPULATION 77 996

MICHELIN LOCAL MAP 339: E-8

Capital of the Languedoc vineyards stretching as far as Carcassonne and Narbonne, Béziers is a city that takes festivals and merrymaking very seriously. The year is punctuated by numerous events, such as the the Wine Festival or the Feria d'Été (summer festival) with a definite Spanish flavour. The oldest of the festivals is held in honour of Aphrodise, the first Bishop of Béziers and patron of the city, to which he bequeathed his heraldic device – a camel (legend attributes Egyptian origins to the saint). The local rugby team (ASB) and its achievements have also helped to spread the city's name abroad. 🏢 *29 av. St-Saëns, 34500 Béziers*, ☎ *04 67 76 47 00. www.ville-beziers.fr.*

▶ **Orient Yourself:** To get a better overview of the city, take a guided tour (*Jul and Aug, 1hr 30min; 4.50€*); enquire at the tourist office.

◉ **Don't Miss:** Cathédrale St-Nazaire.

A Bit of History

A Roman presence– Béziers was already a thriving city when the Romans arrived and colonised it in 36 or 35 BC. It was renamed Julia Baeterrae and fell within the Narbonensis province. Modern Béziers still occupies the original site on a plateau on the east bank of the Orb, overlooking the river, which it occupied before the arrival of the Romans. The Roman forum was probably located in front of the present town hall, where it would have been surrounded by temples and a market. Between rue St-Jacques and place du Cirque, the old houses are laid out in an elliptical pattern which reflects the presence, beneath the neat urban gardens and garages, of Béziers' Roman amphitheatre. The site is currently being excavated. In the 3C, under threat of Barbarian invasion, stones from the amphitheatre were used to build a fortified wall around the city.

The cost of backing the Cathars – During the Albigensian Crusade, the Crusaders laid siege to Béziers in 1209. The resident Roman Catholics were given the opportunity to leave the town before battle commenced, but they refused. Side by side with their Cathar neighbours, they fought outside the city walls to defend Béziers from the intruders, but eventually they were routed. The Crusaders pursued them into the town, and the ensuing massacre was bloody in the extreme, sparing neither old nor young. Even those who sought refuge in the churches were butchered, and Béziers itself was finally pillaged and put to the torch until not a creature there remained living.

The city did eventually manage to rise from its ashes, but for many years it was a sleepy, backward community. It was not until the vineyards were developed in the 19C that it rediscovered its old wealth and vigour.

...aire and the Pont Vieux

Address Book

For coin categories, see the Legend.

EATING OUT

Le Bistrot des Halles – *Pl. de la Madeleine -* ☎ *04 67 28 30 46 - reservation recommended Sat evening - 14.48/22.87€.* Local people rub shoulders with their neighbours in this bistro style restaurant with an old wooden bar and marble tables in the covered market district. The cooking has flair and there is a mouth-watering dessert buffet!

Le Val d'Héry – *67 av. du Prés.-Wilson -* ☎ *04 67 76 56 73 - closed 15-30 Jun, Sun and Mon.* Work up an appetite with a stroll in the plateau des Poètes, a pretty park in the centre of town, before heading for this restaurant with its decorative wall paintings, some of which are the chef's own work. His creativity is also evident in the fine cuisine.

La Potinière – *15 r. Alfred-de-Musset -* ☎ *04 67 11 95 25 - closed 27 Jun-27 Jul and Sun evening.* Popular with the locals, this restaurant in a little street has a cosy ambience and appealing menu, with sophisticated dishes guaranteed to meet with your approval.

L'Ambassade – *22 bd de Verdun (across from the station) -* ☎ *04 67 76 06 24 – lambassade-beziers@wanadoo.fr - closed 25 May-15 Jun, Sun and Mon.* The contemporary decor is a good setting for the appetizing dishes on offer and the exceptionally good wine list. A big favourite locally.

WHERE TO STAY

Champ de Mars – *17 r. Metz -* ☎ *04 67 28 35 53 – closed 12-20 Feb -* 🅿 *- 10 rms.* Small family run hotel in a quiet alley close to the square where the large Fiday market is held. Rooms are of average size and have been recently renovated to offer full facilities.

Chambre d'hôte Les Arbousiers – *34370 Maureilhan – 9km/6mi NW of Béziers towards Castres on D 112 -* ☎ *04 67 90 52 49 - ch.d.hotes.les.arbousiers@wanadoo.fr -* 🖂 *- 6 rms.* The owners of this large establishment with Mediterranean style rooms greet guests as friends. Every evening the menu includes home-made cold cuts, home-grown vegetables, and of course their own wine.

De France – *36 r. Boïeldieu -* ☎ *04 67 28 44 71 - 21 rms.* Quiet yet centrally situated in the heart of Béziers with attractively renovated rooms decorated in bright colours and furnished with wrought iron pieces

Château de Lignan – *34490 Lignan-sur-Orb - 7km/4mi NW of Béziers on D 19 -* ☎ *04 67 37 91 47 - chateau.de.lignan@wanadoo.fr -* 🅿 *- 49 rms.* This old bishops' palace in the village is set in a 6ha/15 acre park. The well equipped rooms have been tastefully renovated.Jacuzzi, sauna, swimming pool and restaurant with fine views.

ON THE TOWN

Béziers is a city where tradition and rugby hold sway. The main focus of activity is on the Allées Paul-Riquet. The delightful Friday flower market, large brasseries and department stores draw the crowds, strolling through the alleys. **Les arènes** *(av. Émile-Claparède)* for bullfighting, opera and musical shows; the le **théâtre municipal** for theatre, classical music and opera, dance; the **théâtre des Franciscains** for plays and exhibits.

Le Mondial – *2 r. Solferino -* ☎ *04 67 28 22 15 - Oct-Jun: Mon-Fri 7.30am-1am, Sat 7.30am-2am; Jul -Aug: Mon-Sat 7.30am-2am - closed 20 Aug-3 Sep.* With its Latino music, its wine bar with great sides of Bayonne ham hanging from the ceiling and its tapas, le Mondial attracts a very varied clientèle. At the back of the bar is a billiard table. Concerts on Wed, Fri and Sat.

SHOPPING

Markets – The central covered market is open Tue-Sun. Other food markets: Tue morning pl. Émile-Zola, Wed morning in the Iranget neighbourhood, Fri morning pl. David-d'Angers.

Antolin Glacier – *21 r. Martin-Luther-King -* ☎ *04 67 62 03 10 - glaces.antolin@wanadoo.fr - Mon-Fri 8am-6pm - closed public holidays.* Antolin has been part of the local landscape since 1916. Customers can choose from over 120 different flavours of ice cream and sorbets..

Les caves de Béziers – *3 rte de Pézenas -* ☎ *04 67 31 27 23 – lescaves.debeziers@wanadoo fr - Mon-Sat 9am-noon, 2-6.30pm (7pm in summer).* Local wines for sale.

Béziers was the home town of **Pierre-Paul Riquet**, who designed the Canal du Midi, and of **Jean Moulin**, an outstanding figure of the Resistance movement during the Second World War. A monument dedicated to him stands in the town's large public park known as the "Plateau des Poètes."

Walking Tour

▶ *Leave the car in the Jean-Jaurès car park. This walk starts from the statue of Pierre-Paul Riquet (see Canal du MIDI) standing in the centre of the avenue of the same name. Walk NW towards the theatre.*

Allées Paul-Riquet

This broad, 600m/650yd-long avenue, shaded by plane trees, positively bustles with life. In the centre of the avenue stands a statue of Riquet by David d'Angers. The theatre was built in the mid-19C and its façade is decorated with allegorical low-relief sculptures, also the work of David d'Angers.

▶ *At the end of the avenue, turn left onto boulevard de la République then right onto rue Casimir-Péret and left again onto rue Vannières.*

Basilique St-Aphrodise

The church is dedicated to the town's patron saint. Inside, beneath the gallery, is the font, a handsome 4C-5C **sarcophagus** on which the scene of a lion hunt has been carved. Opposite the pulpit is a 16C polychrome wood Crucifix. The Romanesque crypt houses a lovely sculpture of the head of Christ.

▶ *Turn back along rue Casimir-Péret then, just before reaching boulevard de la République, take rue Trencavel on the right.*

Église de la Madeleine

This Romanesque church remodelled during the Gothic period, then again in the 18C was one of the sites of the 1209 massacre (see A Bit of History).

▶ *From place de la Madeleine, follow rue Paul-Riquet, walk across place Semard to the right and take rue Tourventouse.*

A vaulted passageway leads to rue du Capus where you can see the **Hôtel Fayet**, an annexe of the Fine Arts Museum.

▶ *Turn right onto rue du Gén.-Pailhès then left onto rue du Gén.-Crouzat leading to place des Bons-Amis (note the charming small fountain), then to place de la Révolution.*

Ancienne cathédrale St-Nazaire★

Perched on a terrace above the River Orb, the cathedral symbolised the might of the bishops of Béziers between 760 and 1789. The Romanesque building was badly damaged in 1209, and repairs were carried out on it from 1215 until the 15C.
In the west front, which is flanked by a pair of fortified towers (late 14C), there is a beautiful rose window 10m/32ft in diameter. The fortifications on the east end are also a decorative feature: the arches between the buttresses are in fact machicolations. Go around the south side of the cathedral to the **cloisters**. The corbels supporting the ribs of the vaulting are decorated with beautiful 14C sculptures. Take a flight of steps into the Jardin de l'Évêché, from which there is a pretty view of the church of St-Jude and the River Orb spanned by a 13C bridge, the Pont Vieux (the Pont Neuf dates from the 19C).

▶ *Enter through the doorway in the north transept.* The bay directly in front of the chancel contains some 11C sculpted capitals. The colonnettes on top of them, decorated with crocketed capitals, and the cross-ribbed vaulting were added in the 13C, when this part of the cathedral was made higher. Note the lovely chancel apse which was built in the 13C and modified in the 18C.

The terrace near the cathedral gives an interesting view of the region around Béziers. In the foreground you can see the Orb flowing through vineyards, the Canal du Midi between tree-lined banks and the hill fort of Ensérune. In the distance are Mont Caroux, the Pic de Nore to the west and, on a clear day, Canigou.

Where wine once flowed

Studio Tref/Musée du Biterrois

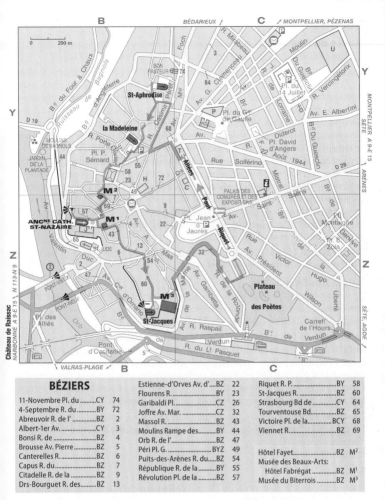

From place de la Révolution, follow rue de Bonsi: the **Hôtel Fabrégat** standing on the corner houses the Fine Arts Museum. Take rue Massot to your right then continue along rue des Dr-Bourguet.

▶ *From place St-Cyr, follow rue St-Jacques.*

You are now in the district known as *"quartier des arènes romaines,"* a reminder that the town was once a Roman colony forming part of the Narbonensis province (c 35 BC).

Église St-Jacques

This church is interesting in spite of being in a bad state of disrepair; its unusual 12C five-sided apse is remarkable, but the interest lies mainly in the unexpected **view**★ of the cathedral from the church gardens.

▶ *Walk past the Musée du Biterrois and follow avenue de la Marne to place Garibaldi then turn right onto avenue du Mar.-Joffre.*

Plateau des Poètes

This delightful, hilly landscaped park runs on from allées Paul-Riquet. It was laid out by the Bühler brothers in the 19C and contains tree varieties such as the Caucasian elm, the Californian sequoia, the magnolia and the Cedar of Lebanon. The busts of poets which line the paths are what earned the park its name. The fountain is by Injalbert (Fontaine du Titan).

▶ *Return to place Jean-Jaurès along allées Paul-Riquet.*

Additional Sights

Musée du Biterrois★

🕐 *Same hours as the the Musée des Beaux-Arts (below).* ☎ *04 67 36 71 01.*

This museum, in the old St-Jacques barracks built in 1702 to designs by Charles d'Aviler, contains substantial collections on local archaeology, ethnology and natural history: display of fauna from land, sea and lake, presented in the form of dioramas; collection of Greek, Iberian and Roman amphorae discovered on the seabed nearby at Cap d'Agde, site of many a shipwreck. Various galleries covering a range of topics lead off from the main foyer *(begin to the right of the entrance)*; the first ones look at geology and volcanic activity in the Languedoc region, and life during the Bronze and Iron Ages.

A major part of the museum is given over to the region's Gallo-Roman heritage, in the form of numerous finds made during excavation digs in the city. There is sigillated pottery from the workshops at La Graufesenque (🕐 *see MILLAU*) and milestones which once lined the Via Domitia. The high spot of the exhibition is the "Trésor de Béziers", consisting of three large chased silver platters discovered in 1983 in a vineyard on the outskirts of the city. Exhibits such as cippi, steles and votive altars give an insight into 1C and 2C funerary rites.

Various aspects of local economy are also illustrated, eg fishing, wine-growing and the construction of the Canal du Midi.

Musée des Beaux-Arts

🕐 *Jul and Aug: daily except Mon 10am-6pm; Apr-Jun, Sep and Oct: daily except Mon 9am-noon, 2-6pm; Nov-Mar: daily except Mon 9am-noon, 2-5pm.* 🕐 *Closed 1 Jan, Easter Sunday, 1 May, 25 Dec. 2.35€.* ☎ *04 67 28 38 78.*

The museum of fine art occupies two old private mansions near the cathedral. The **Hôtel Fabrégat** contains works by Martin Schaffner, Dominiquin, Guido Reni, Pillement, Languedoc painter J Gamelin, Géricault, Devéria, Delacroix, Corot, Daubigny, Othon Friesz, Soutine, Chirico, Kisling, Dufy and Utrillo, among others. There are also 100 or so drawings by J-M Vien, the complete collection of Jean Moulin's drawings, and a large bequest by Maurice Marinot (paintings, drawings, glassware).

The **Hôtel Fayet** houses 19C paintings, a bequest by J-G Goulinat (1883-1972) and the contents of the workshop of Béziers sculptor **J-A Injalbert** (1845-1933).

Excursions

Sérignan

11km/7mi S on D 19 towards Valras. The old **collegiate church**, dating from the 12C, 13C and 14C, stands on the south-west bank of the Orb. There are still traces of the fortifications visible on the exterior, including loopholes, machicolations and the remnants of watch turrets. Inside, the nave has a coffered ceiling and on either side of it a side aisle with ribbed vaulting. It ends in an elegant heptagonal apse. In a small chapel to the north of the chancel there is an ivory Crucifix attributed to Benvenuto Cellini.

Valras-Plage⌂

15km/9.5mi S on D 19. This fishing port and yachting harbour at the mouth of the Orb has a fine sandy beach stretching as far as the Grau de Vendres at the mouth of the Aude to the west. The Théâtre de la Mer hosts various shows during the summer.

Abbaye de Fontcaude

18km/11mi NW via D 14. 🕐 *Jul-Aug: 10am-7pm, Sun and public holidays 2.30-7pm;Jun and Sep: 10am-noon, 2.30-7pm, Sun and public holidays 2.30-7pm: Oct-May: 10am-noon, 2.30-5.30pm, Sun and public holidays 2.30-5.30pm.* 🕐 *Closed Jan (except Sun afternoon), 25 Dec. 4€.* ☎ *04 67 38 23 85.)*–

This Romanesque Premonstratensian abbey reached the peak of its influence during the Middle Ages, but it was destroyed during the Wars of Religion. It has been the object of a number of restoration projects and the abbey buildings are now used to host concerts. All that remains of the **abbey church** are the transept and the east end, which is best appreciated by walking round the church. The apsidal chapel is oven-vaulted and has three large windows framed by colonnettes with capitals. In the large scriptorium, where the monks copied out and illuminated manuscripts, there is a **museum** containing fragments of the **capitals** from the cloisters, executed with remarkable craftsmanship in the 13C to depict a variety of scenes. The old foundry, in which the original 12C bell was cast, has also been discovered on this site.

La BIGORRE★★★

MICHELIN LOCAL MAP 342: M-3 TO N-3

Bigorre is a former regional and historical entity which, together with the neighbouring Pays des Quatre Vallées (Four Valleys Region) forms part of the Central Pyrenees – the most attractive sector of the range with the remnants of ancient glaciers and the tallest summits, including Vignemale (3 289m/10 817ft), Pic Long (3 192m/10 469ft) and Balaïtous (3 146m/10 322ft). Visitors' favourite haunts include Lourdes, Gavarnie and Cauterets.

⊙ **Don't Miss:** Pic du Midi de Bigorre, Col d'Aspin, Massif de Néouvielle

Geographical Notes

This is a region of wild and craggy landscapes, of enormous cirques among the peaks, and of foaming, fast-flowing mountain streams, lying within the boundaries of the Parc national des Pyrénées.

The few border *ports* (small passes) which allow communication with Spain are scarcely lower than the summits. Some can only be used by local mountain people and their mules. Since 1976, the Bielsa Tunnel, at the head of Vallée d'Aure, has provided access in summer to traffic between Gascony and Aragon in Spain.

The busiest parts of the Bigorre region lie between the mountain area and the flatlands – in the basins of Lourdes and Bagnères and on the Tarbes plain. The prosperity here contrasts with the poverty of the Lannemezan and Ger plateaux, which are vast areas of debris piled up over thousands of years by the rivers, extending to the north next to the fan-like formation of the hills of Gascony.

Address Book

⌚ *For coin categories, see the Legend.*

EATING OUT

⊖⊖ **Ferme-auberge La Couriole** – 65380 Layrisse - 4.5km/3mi Nw of Loucrup on D 937, D 407 then a B-road - ☎ 05 62 45 42 25 - closed 2-15 Jan and Sun evening to Thu evening - ⌁ - reservations required. The stunning view from this farmhouse inn takes in the majestic summits of Midi de Bigorre, Montaigu and Vignemale. This is a new house with 19C window frames and doors. On the menu: garbure, magrets aux pêches and home-made pastries.

WHERE TO STAY

⊖⊖ **Chambre d'hôte Maison Buret** – 67 Le Cap-de-la-Vielle - 65200 Montgaillard - 5km/3mi N of Pouzac on D 935 - ☎05 62 91 54 29 - glcazaux@tiscali.fr – closed 1 week early Jun and 1 week end Oct - ⌁ - 3 rms. Built in 1791, this fine farmhouse still exudes its original character, from the traditional old furniture in the rooms to the dining room with its large fireplace. Note too the sculpted staircase, the pigeon-loft, the stables. A small Folk Museum is also housed here. Warm welcome and good value for money.

⊖⊖ **Chambre d'hôte Domaine Véga** – 65250 St-Arroman - 11km/7mi N of Sarrancolin on D 929 then D 26 - ☎05 62 98 96 77 – closed Nov-Feb - ⌁ - 5 rms. Fine 16C manor house at the centre of a park planted with cedars, giant thuyas and lime trees. The rooms are simple and comfortable, overlooking the landscaped swimming pool and surrounding countryside. Pigeons from the estate are on the menu.

⊖⊖ **Hostellerie du Val d'Aure** – Rte de St-Lary-Soulan - 65240 Cadéac - 3km/2mi S of Arreau on D 929 - ☎05 62 98 60 63 - hotel@hotel-valdaure.com - closed 27 Sep-19 May, Sat-Sun, Feb school holidays and Christmas- ▣ - 23 rms. What could be more relaxing than a few leisurely lengths of the pool in full view of the mountains. This is an option at this peaceful hotel set amid trees. Rooms are classic in decor and well looked after. Dining room with terrace overlooking the garden.

⊖⊖ **Hôtel Catala** – 65710 Beaudéan - 4.5km/3mi S of Bagnères-de-Bigorre on D 935 - ☎05 62 91 75 20 – closed 3-31 Jan, Sun evenings and Mon - ▣ – 22 rms. This hotel in a quiet spot in a small village might easily be overlooked. The same cannot be said for the original frescoes adorning the doors of some of the otherwise functional rooms, on the theme of art, sport or history. View of the church (listed) from the terrace.

SHOPPING

Filature Artisanale de Laine – 9 r. Ste-Quitterie - 65410 Sarrancolin - ☎ 05 62 98 77 21 – tours Mon-Fri 2-6pm (Jul-Aug Mon-Fri 10am-noon, 2-6pm). This is the last spinning mill of its kind in operation in the Pyrenees. The machines, dating from 1900, are used to turn out wool cloth for eiderdown coverlets and skeins of wool for knitting. The shop sells pure wool sweaters, jackets and coats.

A Bit of History

Comté de Bigorre – In 1097 Count Bernard II promulgated the fors de Bigorre – local laws confirming the two-way relationship between the people and their overlord.

The Salic Law – which in the north prevented women succeeding to the French Crown – did not apply in the Pyrenean States, which meant that several countesses ruled the region, many of them quite formidable women. In the 13C, Countess Petronilla had five husbands in 13 years – and had daughters by each one of them. The problems of succession must have been extremely complicated.

In 1292, Philippe le Bel sequestered the fief. However, the Treaty of Brétigny in 1360 confirmed it as an English possession, and in 1406, the intruders took flight after a war of attrition waged by the people of Bigorre. The region then passed to the House of Foix, and through them, eventually, to Henri de Navarre. Bigorre was united with the French Crown in 1607.

Lavedan – The mountainous part of the Bigorre region, from south of Lourdes to the Spanish border, was known as the Seven Valleys of the Lavedan. In the 10C, it was administered by viscounts, who were direct vassals of the Comtes de Bigorre. In

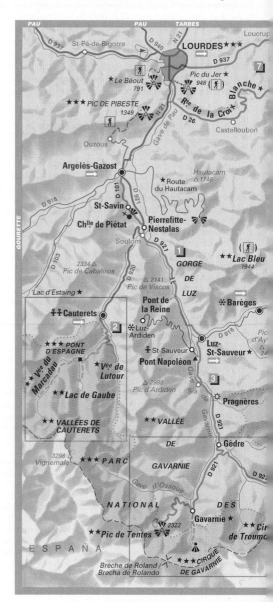

practice, however, the valleys were autonomous. The largest of these, known then as the Vallée de Barèges, lies in the middle (Luz). Four other valleys – Azun, Estrem de Salles, Bats-Surguère and St-Savin (Cauterets) – were on the western side of the Gave de Pau. The remaining two, less important, were on the east – Davant-Aygue and Castelloubon (Vallée du Néez). On his accession, the Comte de Bigorre would visit each valley to swear an oath to the Lavedan people to respect their customs. They would swear loyalty to him in return. As a precaution, hostages taken from the most prosperous families in the community were detained in the château in Lourdes until the safe return of the Earl.

Fighting spirit – The mountain dwellers of Bigorre, who are characteristically small, dark and wiry, are a robust people, who used to boast of being "always kings in our own country".

Men from the Vallée de Barèges helped to storm the castle in Lourdes and drive the English out of Castelnau-d'Azun in 1407. Warriors from Bigorre were just as ruthless with their own countrymen; in the 15C, a king's officer whose zeal had exasperated the inhabitants was thrown over a cliff.

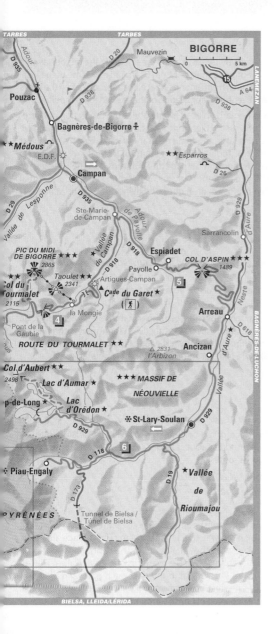

Lac Bleu

Colbert provoked several revolts by trying to apply the salt tax in the region – where the population, in any case, obtained their salt from Béarn or Spain. One of the local gentry, Audijos, enrolled 7 000 men from Bigorre under his banner and defied the king's commissioners for 12 years. Eventually application of the tax had to be modified.

Religious Bigorre – When Bernard I placed his fief under the protection of Notre-Dame du Puy-en-Velay (south-east of Clermont-Ferrand) in 1062, he could not have foreseen that, eight centuries later, the fame of a sanctuary in Bigorre would far outshine that of his patroness. Today, millions of faithful from all over the world have been to visit Lourdes, honouring Bernadette Soubirous and the Holy Virgin. Other abbeys have also played an important role in defining the special spiritual identity of the region of Bigorre: St-Pé-de-Bigorre, St-Savin and St-Orens *(south-east of Condom)*.

Hiking Tour

Lac Bleu★★

▶ *Leave Bagnères S along D 935 and, beyond Baudéan, 1km/0.6mi before reaching Campan, turn right onto D 29.*

🚶 *Hike through the Lesponne Valley, starting from Bagnères-de-Bigorre. Allow 4hr there and back. Alt 1 944m/6 378ft.*

The road runs along the charming **Vallée de Lesponne**★, which offers views of Pic du Midi de Bigorre and Pic de Montaigu, especially attractive in spring and autumn when they are snow-capped. The Chiroulet inns, near the top of the valley, are the starting point of the walk to **Lac Bleu**, a lake-reservoir in a splendidly isolated spot.

Excursions

Gorge de Luz 1

18km/11mi. From Argelès-Gazost to Luz-St-Sauveur– allow 1hr.

At Pierrefitte-Nestalas, the itinerary can be extended to include excursions into the valleys around Cauterets (Pont d'Espagne, Lac de Gaube, Marcadau) – the great classics of the Pyrenees tourist routes.

Argelès-Gazost – ♿ *See ARGELÈS-GAZOST.*

▶ *Drive S out of Argelès along D 101.*

St-Savin

This village, at one time one of the most popular religious centres in Bigorre, is now an interesting place to stop on the way to Cauterets or Luz. The **terrace** alongside the main square offers good views of the Argelès basin. The **church** here was once part of a Benedictine abbey, its abbots were the overlords of St-Savin Valley. The 11C and 12C building, fortified in the 14C, still has its internal watch-path, and a lantern-belfry crowns the 14C tower. The west front has a fine Romanesque doorway with a tympanum carved with a rare depiction of Christ, surrounded by Evangelists in priestly garments. Inside, the small 12C Romanesque font with caryatids was possibly reserved for the untouchables, locally known as cagots. The organ loft (16C) is decorated with masks whose eyes and mouths used to move when the organ was played. Next to it is a fine Spanish carved wooden figure of Christ (13C and 14C).

The **treasury** contains capitals from the old cloisters, Romanesque representations of the Virgin Mary and a particularly fine 14C silver-plated copper shrine.

▷ *Beyond the village, Chapelle-de-Piétat, perched on its rock, comes into view.*

Chapelle-de-Piétat

🚗 *Cars can only be parked just before the bend in the road skirting the spur.* The sanctuary is set in an extremely poetic **site** ★. From a small terrace shaded by lime trees, on the edge of a short but steep escarpment plunging towards the green Argelès basin, there is a fine view of St-Savin Church emerging from a thicket of chestnut trees. Among the orchards on the far bank of the river are the reddish ruins of Beaucens Castle, once the favourite residence of the viscounts of Lavedan. In the distance, Pic de Viscos *(alt 2 141m/7 024ft)*, at Pierrefitte-Nestalas, dominates the Cauterets and Barèges valleys.

Pierrefitte-Nestalas

At the northern end of this small town stands the **Musée Marinarium du Haut-Lavedan** *(&🕘 9.30am-noon, 2-6.30pm, Sun and Mon 2-6.30pm; 7€ (children: 5€); ☎ 05 62 92 79 56)*. Here, unexpectedly, is a collection of tropical marine fauna from all over the world, including an aquaium teeming with the life of a coral reef.

Beyond Pierrefitte there is the awe-inspiring Luz gorge, with its dark walls of vertical shale, supporting little plant life. Waterfalls tumble down here and there.

Before this route was established in the middle of the 18C, the only way to reach Luz was via an extremely precarious mule track known as **Les Échelles de Barèges** (the Barèges Stepladders) – which explains why well-heeled visitors usually preferred (to the dismay of their toiling porters) a longer detour via Le Tourmalet.

Pont de la Reine marks the end of the enclosed section. Beyond the bridge is Pays Toy (Luz basin), with its villages nestling among the trees. The foothills of the Néouvielle massif soon appear to the left of Pic de Bergons. Then, shaded by ash trees, the route finally reaches Luz or, if you keep to the west bank of the river, St-Sauveur.

Luz-St-Sauveur★ – 🕰 *See LUZ-ST-SAUVEUR.*

Vallées de Cauterets★★ ☐2

Excursions from Cauterets – 🕰 See CAUTERETS.

Vallée de Gavarnie★★ ☐3

Itinerary from Luz-St-Sauveur – 🕰 See Vallée de GAVARNIE.

Route du Tourmalet★★ ☐4

From Barèges to Bagnères-de-Bigorre. 48km/30mi – about 3hr.

Impressive mountain road on the slopes near Barèges. *Col du Tourmalet (Tourmalet Pass)* 🚗 *is usually blocked by snow from Nov to Jun.*

Barèges ✳

This pleasant ski resort (at 1 250m/4 100ft also the highest) was the cradle of the Pyrenean ski school. Today it is linked to three ski areas, Le Tourmaket, La Mongie and Super-Barèges.

The road crosses the desolate Vallon d'Escoubous, where the stream winds through stony pastures. After Pont de la Gaubie, look back through the opening of a small valley, for a view of Pic de Néouvielle, with its craggy, glacier-flanked pyramid. Before long, a line of bold rocky crests appears to the south. To the north, left of the road, Pic du Midi de Bigorre is visible, crowned by its television transmitter and observatory.

Col du Tourmalet★★

Alt 2 115m/6 937ft. From the pass, the mountain **panorama** is remarkable for the ruggedness of the summits, especially towards Barèges. In the distance, beyond the minor Ardiden range, rises the great mass of Balaïtous and its glacier.

Starting from the pass is the old road which leads ramblers to the summit of Pic du Midi in 2hr 30min, covering a difference in height of 700m/2 297ft. Waiting for them at the top is a free panoramic viewing terrace; after visiting the site, it is possible to return by cable car.

Pic du Midi de Bigorre★★★ – 🕐 *See Pic du MIDI DE BIGORRE.*

After a detour to see Pic du Midi, the road beyond Tourmalet Pass drops down through grassland which contrasts vividly with the rocky crags and ravines of the mountain's western side. Above the road, on the left, a series of hairpin bends looping across the mountainside marks the course of the old track followed by the sedan chairs of the Duke of Maine and his governess Madame de Maintenon when they went from Bagnères de Bigorre to take the waters at Barèges. Below the road, at an altitude of 1 800m/5 905ft, the pyramids of La Mongie-Tourmalet residential area mark the entrance to the winter sports resort of La Mongie.

La Mongie✳

This high-altitude (1 800m/5 900ft) winter sports resort enjoys a superb setting in a mountain amphitheatre and benefits from continuous snow from December to late April. It is the most specialised centre in the Pyrenees, offering downhill runs, cross-country ski trails and guided ascents which connect with the ski slopes above Barèges.

There is a gondola lift link to **Le Taoulet**★★ (alt 2 341m/7 681ft), a spur off Pic du Midi de Bigorre, which offers splendid **views**★★ of the Néouvielle massif, the Arbizon massif and the Vallée de Campan. Another cable links Le Taoulet and **Pic du Midi de Bigorre**★★★ (🕐 *see Pic du MIDI DE BIGORRE).*

Beyond the resort, the road drops more steeply through terraced woodlands, before sweeping through the valley of the Garet tributary, after which it crosses Tourmalet stream and the Arises, which cascades down in a series of waterfalls. The Artigues plateau, a scenic stretch of pastureland, partly covered by a reservoir, opens out down below, on the right.

Cascade du Garet★

Park by the Hôtel des Pyrénées in Artigues. Walk through the hamlet and cross a small bridge upstream from the power station.

🚶 A footpath rises into the valley of the Garet tributary and then passes into a wood of fir trees. Steps cut in the rock lead down to a viewpoint, from which the falls can be admired.

The road then follows the delightfully cool **Vallée de Campan**★, bordered by lush, green meadows. Houses and barns with Flemish style stepped gables and thatched roofs can be seen dotted here and there in the fields. Scattered buildings continue as far as Campan.

After Ste-Marie-de-Campan, the road (D 935, north) drops into the Vallée de l'Adour, providing occasional glimpses of the massive summit of Pic du Midi de Bigorre, always identifiable by the tall pylon of its television transmitter.

> **CATCH OF THE DAY**
>
> **Pêche Sportive Pyrénées** – *65710 Campan* – ☎ *05 62 91 83 38.* Take a course in trout fishing in a river or a mountain lake and learn all the techniques!

Campan

The small town includes a 16C covered market, an 18C fountain and a 16C church. Left of the porch, leading into the old cemetery (galleries with marble columns), stands a 14C Christ from an old abbey in the region. Inside the church, there is fine 18C woodwork.

Grotte de Médous★★ – 🕐 *See BAGNÈRES-DE-BIGORRE.*

▶ *Beyond Médous, D 935 continues to Bagnères.*

Bagnères-de-Bigorre⌂ – 🕐 *See BAGNÈRES-DE-BIGORRE.*

Route du Col d'Aspin★★★ ⑤

From Campan to St-Lary-Soulan. 61km/38mi – about 3hr.

⚠ From Decto Apr, Col d'Aspin (Pass) can be closed to traffic for anything from 12 to 48hr as snow clearing is not a matter of priority.

Beyond Ste-Marie-de-Campan, the run south through the attractive Vallée de l'Adour de Payolle is similar to that of the Vallée de Campan, though the highlands are somewhat more rugged. In front and to the right, the 2 831m/9 288ft-high Arbizon massif remains almost constantly in sight. Pic du Midi reappears, in the background, as the road passes through the **Payolle** basin (🎿 cross-country ski centre).

Espiadet

This is a hamlet at the foot of the famous Campan marble quarry. The red and white-veined green stone was used for the columns of the Grand Trianon in Versailles and, in part, for those of Garnier's Opera House in Paris.

Beyond Espiadet, the road rises continuously all the way to Col d'Aspin. At first offering occasional glimpses of the Arbizon massif, the road snakes through beautiful pine woods. The trees then thin out to reveal mountain pastures.

Col d'Aspin★★★

Alt 1 489m/4 884ft. Despite being at a considerably lower altitude than the other three passes (Tourmalet, Aubisque, Peyresourde) along Route des Pyrénées, the Col d'Aspin offers an incomparable and much wider **panorama**. The attractive grouping of the mountain masses and the contrast between snowy peaks and the blue distant forests combine to form an unforgettable landscape.

Beyond the pass, the narrow road drops steeply in hairpin bends, and in less than 13km/8mi falls from 1 489m/4 884ft to 704m/2 309ft. To the right is a bird's-eye view of the well-ploughed valley, sheltering the village of Aspin. The southern slopes are highly suitable for farming. There are views, again, of the Arbizon massif and the Arreau basin.

Arreau

This is a pleasant little town of slate-roofed houses, ideally situated at the junction of the River Aure and River Louron, and at the intersection between the Vallée d'Aure road and the Route des Pyrénées, on the threshold between the Peyresourde and Aspin passes. It was once the capital of the Four Valleys Region.

Note the 16C corbelled **Maison du Lys** and its half-timbered upper floor over a stone-built lower floor with carved lintels. The **halles** (covered market) with their basket-handled arches (now in concrete) form the ground floor of the timber-framed town hall.

The chapel, situated on the east bank, boasts a Romanesque doorway with small marble columns and storiated capitals. Downriver, near the confluence, stands a vast traditional manor typical of the Bigorre region, which houses the tourist office.

Beyond Arreau, the road follows the **Aure Valley**★. At one time, there was a Viscounty of Aure, under the sovereignty of the kings of Aragon. In the 14C, it was combined with the valleys of Magnoac, Neste and Barousse to form the Four Valleys Region **(Pays des Quatre Vallées)**, which fell to the House of Armagnac in 1398. It became part of the kingdom of France in 1475.

The road (D 929) follows the River Neste d'Aure upstream along the floor of a wide and pleasant valley.

Ancizan

A group of 16C houses recalls the former prosperity of what was once a small town. A long time ago, this part of the valley supported 1 000 weavers, all producing the local *cadis* (a coarse, thick cloth of undyed wool).

The **Musée de la Vallée d'Aure** (&⊘ *Jul and Aug: 10am-noon, 2-7pm; Sep-Jun: Wed, Fri and Sat-Sun 10am-noon, 2-6pm; 4.50€ (children under 15: 2.30€).* ⊘ *Closed early Nov to Dec school holidays;* ☎ *05 62 39 97 75.)* gives an insight into the life of the valley's inhabitants during the 19C (washerwomen, smugglers, etc.).

Beyond Ancizan, the valley floor is studded with hillocks – called *pouys* locally – which are the remnants of an ancient glacial moraine.

Just before Guchan, the road crosses the River Neste d'Aure affording a fine view of the mountain horizon, pierced by the sharp pyramid-like formation of Pic de Lustou (due south).

Massif de Néouvielle★★★ [6]
From St-Lary-Soulan to Pic De Néouvielle – & *See Massif de NÉOUVIELLE.*

Route de la Croix Blanche★ [7]
Round-trip from Lourdes – & *See LOURDES.*

Le BOULOU ⚓

POPULATION 4 428

MICHELIN LOCAL MAP 344: I 6-7

This spa resort, an ideal point of departure for exploring the Roussillon, lies at the foot of the Albères mountains on the north bank of the Tech, at the intersection of the main routes between Perpignan-Spain and Argelès-Amélie-les-Bains. Located on the fringes of a cork-oak wood, Le Boulou has two sizeable cork-making factories. 🅸 Pl. de la Mairie, 66160 Le Boulou. ☎ 04 68 87 50 95. www.ot-leboulou.fr.

▶ **Orient Yourself:** Guided tours (1hr 30min) leave at 3pm on Thu from the tourist office. ⌾ 4.50€.

Visit

The town still boasts remnants of its medieval past, in the shape of a quadrangular tower, part of the 14C curtain wall, and the early-15C chapel of St-Antoine.

Église Notre-Dame d'El Voló
🕐 9am-noon. ☎ 04 68 87 51 00

Of the original 12C Romanesque church, the beautiful white-marble **portal** by the Master of Cabestany has survived. Above the arch decorated with knot-work, seven carved corbels support a frieze illustrating scenes from Christ's childhood. Note, inside, the Baroque altarpiece adorning the high altar and, on the north wall of the nave, a 15C predella surmounted by two panels (15C) depicting St John the Baptist on the left and St John the Evangelist on the right.

Excursions

Monts Albères 🗆
49km/30mi round tour - allow half a day.

The Albères mountain range is the last outcrop of crystalline rocks on the eastern flank of the Pyrenees. Before it sinks into the Mediterranean trench, this barely indented

---

Address Book

⌾ For coin categories, see the Legend.

EATING OUT

◷◷ **Hostalet de Vivès** – 66490 Vivès - 5km/3mi W of Le Boulou on D 115 and D 73 - ☎ 04 68 83 05 52 - closed 11 Jan-6 Mar, Tue (except summer) and Wed. This pretty village inn occupies a 12C Catalan house. It serves well prepared local specialities in generous portions. Decor is simple. Some of the rooms have kitchen areas.

◷◷ **Le Canigou** – 6 6160 Le Boulou - ☎ 04 68 83 15 29 – closed Sun evening and Mon (except summer). The family atmosphere, bright dining room and terrace make this a popular spot, so book in advance to enjoy this gourmet favourite. Small well presented rooms.

◷◷ **Belladona** – Mas d'En Baptiste - 66480 Maureillas - 4km/2.5mi S of Le Boulou towards Barcelona on N 9 - ☎ 04 68 83 41 65 – closed Sep, Dec-Feb, Mon, Tue. May-Aug: open Fri evening to Sun lunchtime - ; - reservations required. Why not take a culinary journey back in time? This restaurant serves dishes only from ancient recipes found in old books. The menu features dishes based on aromatic herbs

grown by the proprietors, who have something of the enlightened hippy about them.

WHERE TO STAY

◷◷ **Relais des Chartreuses** – 106 av. d'En-Corbouner – 66160 Le Boulou - 4.5km/3mi SE of Le Boulou on N 9, D 618 and B-road - ☎04 68 83 15 88 – relais.des. chartreuses@wanadoo.fr - closed 3 Nov-11 Mar - 🅿 - 10 rms. Peacefulness is one of the main assets of this villa set in a delightful garden in a residential area. Neat and tidy rooms with floral fabrics and stylish furniture have less character than the building itself which originally dates back to the 17C.

RECREATION

Casino – RN 9 - Espace des Thermes - 66160 Le Boulou - ☎ 04 68 83 01 20 – casino. leboulou@moliflor.com - daily 11am-4am. Slot machines, roulette, black-jack.

Thermes du Boulou – Rte du Perthus - 66160 Le Boulou - ☎ 04 68 87 52 00 – ot-leboulou.fr/thermalisme – Feb-Dec: daily 7am-1pm. The spa centre offers 6-day sessions or, if you are passing through, a "quick fix" package of 4 spa treatments.

massif separates two areas of subsidence – to the north Roussillon, and to the south (in Spain) the Ampurdan, old gulfs which were filled in with alluvial deposits in the Tertiary Era up to several hundred metres deep (800m/2 500ft in Roussillon). The highest peak, Pic Neulos, towers 1 256m/4 120ft above sea level.

▷ *Leave Le Boulou W on D 115.*

Céret★ – See CÉRET

▷ *Leave Céret heading SW on D 13F towards Fontfrède.*

This pleasant road climbs through chestnut groves, offering many pretty views.

Turn right off the Las Illas road at the Col de la Brousse (alt 860m/2 820ft) into a very winding road through undergrowth to the **Col de Fontfrède** (June 1940-June 1944 stele – it was through these mountains that people escaped from France to join the Liberation Army). There is a fountain and picnic area at the pass.

▷ *Return to the Col de la Brousse and turn right towards Las Illas.*

The road winds through dense vegetation initially, followed by terraced gardens and farmhouses scattered over the hillside, each with its own private access. The tinkle of goat bells at every turning is a reminder of an unseen human presence. The Case Nove mas or farmhouse, to the left of the road, in a wide bend, followed almost immediately by the Mas Liansou, to the right, are characteristic examples of traditional Albères dwellings.

After passing through Las Illas, the road follows the river of the same name, clinging to the rock face and affording excellent views of the river gorge. The rocks themselves are scarcely visible beneath the dense vegetation, making the countryside appear very green.

Maureillas-Las-Illas

In this pleasant holiday village in the midst of cork-oak groves and orchards, a group of former cork-cutters have set up a cork museum, **Musée du Liège** (*Mid-Jun to mid-Sep: 10.30am-noon, 3.30-7pm; mid-Sep to mid-Jun: daily except Tue 2-5pm. Closed 1 Jan, 1 May, 1 Nov, 25 Dec. 3€. 04 68 83 15 41)*, which explains the transformation of this material from when it is stripped from the tree to the marking of the finished corks. The exhibition is enhanced by some astonishing cork sculptures and six magnificent oak casks acting as a showcase for local handicrafts.

Chapelle St-Martin-de-Fenollar

Mid-Jun to mid-Sep: 10.30am-noon, 3.30-7pm; mid-Sep to mid-Jun: daily except Tue 2-5pm. Closed 1 Jan, 1 May, 1 Nov, 25 Dec. 3€. 04 68 87 73 82.

This modest chapel, founded in the 9C by Benedictines from Arles-sur-Tech, contains some interesting 12C **mural paintings★** in the chancel, illustrating the mystery of the Incarnation. The lower tier depicts the Annunciation, the Nativity, the Adoration of the Magi and the Return of the Magi to their own country; the tier above this, the 24 old men of the Apocalypse;

Wise Man Bearing a Gift – Fresco in the Chapelle St-Martin-de-Fenollar

L. Campion/MICHELIN

and the vault, Christ in Majesty, surrounded by the four Evangelists, shown as angels each holding a book and the appropriate symbol.

▷ *N 9 leads back to Le Boulou.*

The Rome Valley [2]

53km/33mi from Le Boulou to Pic des Trois Termes – allow half a day.

▷ *Leave Le Boulou on N 9 S towards Le Perthus.*

Guided tours of the Rome valley leaving from Boulou are organised by the Association pour le patrimoine de la vallée de la Rome (heritage association). Information and reservations: Maison de l'Histoire, 1 r. des écoles, 66160 Le Boulou, and Le Boulou tourist office, 04 68 87 50 95.

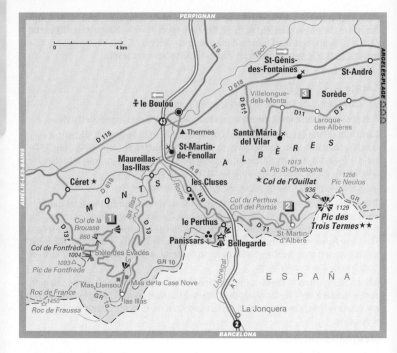

The **Vallée de la Rome** traversed for more than 2 000 years by the Via Domitia (built between c 120 BC), is still a very important communication route between France and Spain. Leaving behind the "Catalane" motorway, the amateur historian and archaeologist will discover a series of megalithic, Gallo-Roman and medieval sites in a superb landscape, against a background of vegetation composed of every possible shade of green.

Chapelle St-Martin-de-Fenollar – ♿ See above.

▶ Go back to N 9.

Les Cluses

This name is given to a series of hamlets on either side of the narrow gorge (or *clusa* in Latin) followed by the Via Domitia and the Rome Valley. There are a number of remains of 3C-4C Roman fortifications: on the west bank, **Château des Maures** or "Castell dels Moros" and on the east bank, **Fort de la Cluse Haute.** The viewing platform that has been set up on the "Dressera" (the old Roman crest road) overlooks the ruins of a gateway, perhaps an old toll gate where the "Gaul's one-fortieth levy" was collected on goods in transit between the Narbonensis and the Tarraconensis regions.

Next to the fort, the **church of St-Nazaire** (🕐 *9am-noon, 1.30-5pm*, 🕐 *closed Sun, book in advance at town hall;* ☎ *04 68 87 77 20)* is a pre-Romanesque construction with three naves (late 10C-early 11C), ending in oven-vaulted apses, the central one of which still bears traces of frescoes depicting Christ Pantocrator in a mandorla with a winged angel. The composition and colours used have led to the frescoes being attributed to the Master of Fenollar.

Le Perthus

Since prehistoric times, Le Perthus (from the Latin for "hack open with a pick") has been the scene of continual comings and goings of nomadic hordes, armies, refugees and, most recently, tourists. The original hamlet of customs huts finally reached the size of a town in the late 19C.

▶ From the centre of Le Perthus, turn left towards the Fort de Bellegarde.

Fort de Bellegarde

🕐 *Jun-Sep: 10.30am-6.30pm (last admission 30min before closing).* ⬚*3€.* ☎ *04 68 83 60 15.*

This powerful fortress, which stands in proud isolation on the top of a rock overlooking the town of Le Perthus from 420m/1 380ft above sea level, was rebuilt by Saint Hilaire, and then by Vauban between 1679 and 1688 on the site of a Spanish fort. The lower room of the stronghold of St-André still contains the well used by the garrison from the 18C onwards, entirely dug out of the rock and surfaced for 50m/165ft of its depth.

From the large terrace, a vast **panorama**★★ encompasses to the west the Canigou and Fontfrède peaks, to the north the Rome Valley and its bottleneck through Les Cluses, Ricardo Bofill's pyramid on the edge of the motorway (symbolising the meeting here of the two Catalonias) and the sprawling village of Le Perthus, and to the south the Panissars archaeological site and (in Spain) the Rio Llobregat Valley, with the town of La Jonquera in the background.

Site archéologique de Panissars

In the days of the Roman occupation, the Panissars Pass, or "Summum Pyrenaeum" as it was then called, was the main route over the Pyrenees. The pass marks the Atlantic-Mediterranean watershed, the Franco-Spanish border and the junction of the Via Domitia and the Via Augusta (which leads to Cadiz in Spain). In 1984, the large-scale masonry foundations of a Roman monument, which would once have straddled the road cut out of the rock, were discovered on the site; they are thought to be the remains of the Trophy of Pompey, erected when he returned from his victorious campaign in Spain against Sertorius (71 BC).

▶ *Turn back and, N of Le Perthus, turn right onto D 71 to the Col de l'Ouillat.*

Initially shaded by chestnut trees, the road lingers a while on the cultivated terrace (rye) of St-Martin-de-l'Albères (magnificent oaks). There is a good view of the Canigou and the southern slopes of the Albères; to the north, the St-Christophe summit looks like a human face lifted skywards.

🅐 From a right-hand bend, there is a view of Trois Termes Peak.

Col de l'Ouillat★

Alt 936m/3 070ft. A cool stopping place on the edge of the carefully maintained Laroque-des-Albères Forest of Laricio pines *(viewing terrace).*

The road winds through beeches and pines to the foot of the rocky outcrop of Trois Termes.

Pic des Trois Termes★★

Alt 1 129m/3 703ft. The **panorama** of the gullies and ridges of the Albères mountains, the plain of Roussillon with its string of coastal lagoons, and the valleys of the Conflu-ent and Vallespir can be viewed from here.

Towards Spain, there is a view of the Costa Brava, beyond Cape Creus, as far as the sweeping bay of Rosas.

▶ *Turn back.*

It is also possible to get to the Roussillon plain via Sorède, but the unsurfaced road between the Pic des Trois Termes and Sorède is accessible to four-wheel-drive vehicles only.

The Foot of Monts Albères ③

32km/20mi round tour from St-Genis-des-Fontaines – 🅑 *See ST-GENIS-DES-FONTAINES.*

BOZOULS★

POPULATION 2 329

MICHELIN LOCAL MAP 338: I-4

Bozouls famous for its canyon (trou), can be distinguished from afar by its modern church (1964), south of D 20. The sanctuary, in the shape of a ship's prow, houses a statue of the Virgin Mary by local sculptor Denys Puech. *Pl. de la Mairie, 12340 Bozouls. ☎ 05 65 48 50 52. www.bozouls.com.*

Don't Miss: trou de Bozouls

Visit

Trou de Bozouls★

The terrace just next to the war memorial, both works by Denys Puech, affords the best view of this 800m/2 600ft canyon, hollowed out of the Causse de Comtal by the River Dourdou. The sheer cliffs are pitted with caves. On the promontory encircled by the river, a Romanesque church and the convent of St-Catherine are perched on the very edge of the precipice.

Ancienne Église Ste-Fauste

▷ *From the town hall, walk round the south side of the "Trou".*

Inside this old church are a number of rather curious capitals. The 12C nave, with its raised, semicircular barrel vaulting, was originally roofed with heavy limestone slabs (lauzes), made heavier still by a thick layer of earth. Under this enormous weight, the pillars sagged and in the 17C, the old roof had to be replaced by a timber-frame one.

Bozouls canyon

From the shady terrace to the left of the church, there is an attractive view of the Dourdou gorge.

Excursion

Montrozier

▷ *10km/6mi. Leave Bozouls S. Drive 3.5km/2.2mi along D 988 then turn left onto D 126.*

On the banks of the Aveyron lies the picturesque village of Montrozier; an old Gothic bridge crowned by a calvary spans the river. The 15C-16C castle (⚷ *not open to the public*) is in good condition; note the machicolated rectangular buildings and the massive five-storey round keep.

The **Musée archéologique de Rouergue** (⏱ *Jul and Aug: 10am-12.30pm, 2-7pm; Jun and Sep: 2-6pm. Guided tour (1hr 15mins). 3€. ☎ 05 65 70 75 00; www.chez.com/aspaa*) houses thematic temporary exhibitions (supported by lectures and audio-visual presentations) devoted to the region's archaeological heritage.

Abîme du BRAMABIAU★

MICHELIN LOCAL MAP 339: F-4

ALSO SEE MASSIF DE L'AIGOUAL

The River Bonheur, which rises at the foot of Mont Aigoual at the Sereyrède Pass, used to flow across the small Causse de Camprieu, before cascading into its lower reaches.

Geographical Notes

The Bonheur left its surface bed to bury itself in the *causse*. After a subterranean course of more than 700m/2 300ft, it emerges through a high, narrow cleft and bursts into a rocky cirque called the "Alcôve" as a glorious waterfall. When the river is in spate, the deafening noise of the waterfall is not unlike the bellowing of a bull – hence the name "Bramabiau" (Brame-Biâou: singing bull) given to the river from its resurgence until it flows into the Trévezel farther downstream.

Visit

▶ *From the kiosk signposted "Bramabiau", follow the gently sloping path down through the undergrowth to the river.*

Jul-Aug: guided tours (50mins): 9am-7pm; Apr-Jun and Sep: 9am-6pm; late Oct-early Nov: 10am-5.30pm. 6.50€. ☎ 04 67 82 60 78 – temperature: 8°C/46°F.

There are lovely views of the opposite bank, carved out by the old canyon of the Bonheur on the edge of the causse. On arriving at the river bank, cross the bridge and climb up to the **Alcôve** at the foot of the cliff, where a spectacular waterfall gushes forth.

Visitors enter the underground world at the point where the river emerges from it. After crossing the Bramabiau between the first waterfall (in the open) and the second (underground), called the "*Échelle*" (ladder), the path leads along an impressively high gallery, with deep crev-

A. Thuillier/MICHELIN

Le Bonheur resurgent spring

ices caused by subterranean erosion, to the "*Salle du Havre*" (harbour chamber). From this gallery, a recent modification gives access to the **"Grand Aven"** (swallow-hole), where visitors can admire the work of cave painter Jean Truel. A path along a ledge more than 20m/65ft above the river, leads back up the Martel gallery, overlooking the "Pas de Diable" (devil's footprint), to a mineral seam. At this point some 200m/220yd of the cavern's length are dug out of a whitish barite seam, opening up into the "Petit Labyrinthe". A few steps lead to the **"Salle de l'Étoile"** (star chamber), with an unusual roof made up of rocks bound together with calcite. From some steps leading out of the underground chasm, there is a magnificent view from a height of more than 50m/160ft against the light down onto the river.

BRUNIQUEL★

POPULATION 561

MICHELIN LOCAL MAP 337: F-7

ALSO SEE ST-ANTONIN-NOBLE-VAL

With the bold outline of its castle rising like a crown above the town, Bruniquel lies in a picturesque setting★ at the mouth of the great gorges that the Aveyron has cut through the limestone of the Causse de Limogne. ▯ *Prom. du Ravelin, 82800 Bruniquel, ☎ 05 63 67 29 84.*

A Bit of History

According to Gregory of Tours (bishop, theologian and historian 538-594), Bruniquel has its origins in the founding of a fortress on this site by **Brunhilda**, daughter of the king of the Visigoths and wife of Sigebert, King of Austrasia. The memory of this princess is perpetuated by the castle tower that bears her name. The bitter rivalry between her and her sister-in-law Fredegund caused war to break out between Austrasia and Neustria in the 6C. The brutality of Brunhilda's own death is legendary; she was bound by her hair, an arm and a leg to the tail of an unbroken horse and smashed to pieces.

Visit

Old town★

Bruniquel is a pleasant place for a stroll, past the remains of its fortifications, town gateways and the old belfry, along steep and narrow streets lined with old houses roofed in half-cylinder tiles. Look out for rue du Mazel, rue Droite-de-Trauc and rue Droite-de-la-Peyre which are particularly pretty.

Château

🕐☛ *Jul and Aug: 10am-7pm; Apr, Jun and Sep: 2-6pm, Sun and public holidays 10am-12.30pm, 2-6pm; May and Oct: Sun and public holidays 10am-12.30pm, 2-6pm; All Saints 2-6pm. Unaccompanied visits: 2.50€ (children: 1.50€); guided tours: 3.50€ (children: 2€). ☎ 05 63 67 27 67.*

The various parts of the castle, built in attractive yellow stone on foundations said to date from the 6C, were built from the 12C to 18C. The barbican, which defended the approaches to the castle from the side of the village, stands on the esplanade in front of the main buildings. The massive 12C square tower is named after Brunhilda.

Inside, the decor of the 12C-13C Knights' Hall features colonnettes with capitals. Stairs lead to the first floor where the guard-room boasts a beautiful 17C chimney-piece with Baroque ornamentation.

In the seigneurial wing of the castle, a Renaissance loggia overlooks the sheer cliff, in which numerous rock shelters have been hollowed out, giving an open **view**★ of the bend in the river below.

Maison Payrol

🕐 *Apr-Sep: 10am-7pm. 3€. ☎ 05 63 67 26 42.*

This town house, the property of the influential local family Payrols, was built over several centuries, from the 13C to the 17C. Note the 13C **murals**★ and the imposing Renaissance ceiling on the first floor. Collections of locally made objects on display include cards, candlesticks, glassware and faience.

CANET-PLAGE ≋ ☼ ☼

POPULATION 10 182

MICHELIN LOCAL MAP 344: J-6

This long-established seaside haunt of the inhabitants of Perpignan, lying only 15km/9mi inland, owes its lively atmosphere to its busy marina (yachts), its sports facilities and the activities of its casino. The resort owes its name to the nearby Étang de Canet lined with reeds (canna in Latin means reed). 🛈 *Av. de la Méditerranée, 66140 Canet-Plage, ☎ 04 68 73 61 00. www.ot-canet.fr.*

Especially for Kids: The Aquarium.

Sights

Beaches

🚹 *See Getting to the beach in the Address Book.* North of the harbour lies Plage Sardinal, ideal for camping (camp site nearby). Seven beaches with sunshade and lilo hiring facilities are lined up along the coast south of the harbour: Plage des Enfants, Plage du Roussillon, Place Centrale, Plage du Grand Large (with a minigolf nearby), Plage de la Marenda, Plage Sud and Plage du Marestang. Volleyball and other team sports can be practised on all the beaches except Plage du Sardinal, Plage Sud and Plage du Marestang. Sailing clubs and/or sailing schools are available on Plage du Sardinal, Plage des Enfants, Plage du Grand Large, Plage du Marestang and Plage Sud.

Canet lagoon and Canigou Mountain

A. Thuillier/MICHELIN

Address Book

🚹 *For coin categories, see the Legend.*

EATING OUT

🍽 🍷 **Le Don Quichotte** – *22 av. de Catalogne -☎ 04 68 80 35 17 – ledonquichotte@wanadoo.fr – closed 10 Jan-9 Feb, Tue noon, Wed noon in Jul-Aug, Mon-Tue (except evenings in Jul-Aug).* The dining room of this restaurant near the post office has been painted a vibrant salmon pink. The recipes are however classic, attracting a clientele of regulars and tourists. Paintings on exhibit.

WHERE TO STAY

🍽 🍷 **Hôtel La Lagune** – *66750 St-Cyprien - 9km/6mi S of Canet on D 81A – ☎ 04 68 21 24 24 - contact@hotel-lalagune.com – closed 1 Oct-7 May - 🅿 - 36 rms.* A holiday hotel between land and sea. The pleasures of the beach await guests, whether alone or in a family, at the end of the flower garden. Rooms are plain and functional, opening onto the two swimming pools and beach.

RECREATION

Getting to the beach - *tram and train operates in Jul-Aug from Canet -* ☎ 04 68 61 01 13.

Club nautique Canet-Perpignan – *Zone technique - Le Port -* ☎ 04 68 73 33 95 - *cncp66@wanadoo.fr - daily 9am-noon, 2-6pm - closed 20 Dec-24 jan.* Sailing club.

Aqualand – 🧒 - *66750 St-Cyprien -* ☎ 04 68 21 49 49 - *mid-Jun to mid-Sep - south of Les Capellans.* Aquapark.

Club Omnipêche Plaisance – *Quai Rimbaud - capitainerie - 66750 St-Cyprien -* ☎ 06 09 54 78 12 - *Jun-Sep.* Halfday fishing trips and fishing lessons

Aéro Service Littoral – *Rte de Ste-Marie - 66440 Torreilles -* ☎ 04 68 28 13 73 - *www. ulm-torreilles.com - daily 8am-12.30pm, 2pm-7pm – first flight 30P.* ULM and motorized hang-gliding courses.

Aquarium

Boulevard de la Jetée, at the harbour. 🚸🕐 *Jul and Aug: 10am-8pm; Sep-May: 10am-noon, 2-6pm. 5.50€ (children: 3.50€).* ☎ *04 68 80 49 64. www.scerem.fr.*

🚸 Colourful display of local and tropical species that children will enjoy.

Étang de Canet

W of Canet-Plage along D 81 towards St-Cyprien. Accessible by car (parking area), on foot or by bus. Binoculars can be hired from the reception area (in high season) situated in one of the fishermen's huts. 👀 *Possibility of guided tours.* ☎ *04 68 80 89 78.*

Canet lagoon, covering 956ha/3.7sq mi, has been designated a protected natural environment. A village of fishermen's huts made of plaited reeds is still to be seen on the banks of the lagoon. A footpath (2.5km/1.5mi) enables visitors to discover some of the lagoon's flora and fauna (including 300 species of bird).

Excursion

St-Cyprien

9km/5.6mi S. This small yet elegant residential town, with its palm-tree-lined streets, is quieter in summer than the neighbouring resorts; it has retained, in its centre, the original Catalan village.

Musée François-Desnoyers

Rue Émile-Zola, near the town hall. 🕐 *10am-noon, 2-6pm:* 🕐 *closed Mon-Tue from mid-Sep to mid-Jun. Closed 1 Jan, 1 May, 11 Nov, 25 Dec. 2€.* ☎ *04 68 21 06 96.*

This museum, dedicated to local painter François Desnoyers (1894-1972), contains a selection of works which follow his artistic development *(⌖ note in particular Jousting in Sète)*; it also houses paintings and drawings from his personal collection by Gleizes, Picasso, Pierre Ambroggiani etc.

St-Cyprien-Plage ♨♨

The seaside resort comprises three districts: a residential district to the north, the harbour and the artificial water expanse at Les Capellans, separated from the sea by a string of beaches.

The hub of activity is concentrated around the marina, the second most important of Mediterranean France, and at Les Capellans, where, back in the 1960s, buildings of five to 10 storeys were erected and marinas developed. Sand beaches extend over a distance of 3km/1.8mi, offering swimming and water sports activities.

Le CANIGOU★★★

MICHELIN LOCAL MAP 344: F-7

Canigou towers above the orchards of Roussillon. This mountain peak is revered by Catalonians from France and Spain alike, who still come to light the first of their Midsummer Eve bonfires on its summit. Snow-capped for most of the year, the peak is clearly delineated on three sides by the ravine of the Têt (Conflent), the Roussillon subsidence plain, and the Tech Valley (Vallespir).

🍃 **When to Climb:** The northern slopes retain a few patches of snow until the beginning of summer, although rhododendrons are already in bloom fairly high up. Autumn is a pleasant season, temperatures are mild and visibility from the summit is perfect. Summer is to be avoided by those who dislike hot weather and crowds.

A Bit of History

Even in the time of Louis XIV, the geographers responsible for determining the Paris meridian were aware that Mont Canigou was only a few minutes of a degree out (7'48" to the east) from it and had thus calculated its altitude above sea level. In the absence of such precise data for the other massifs, Canigou was for a long time thought to be the highest peak in the Pyrenees.

One feat after another – Ever since the very first ascent of Canigou, reputed to have been in 1285 by King Peter of Aragon, Catalonian sportsmen have vied with each other to conquer the peak in every imaginable manner. The Chalet des Cortalets was

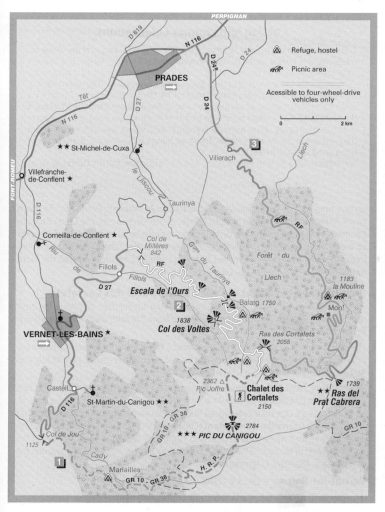

reached by bicycle in 1901, and on skis and then on board a Gladiator 10 CC automobile in 1903. In 1907, a lieutenant of the military police reached the summit on horseback without setting foot to the ground. The project to build a rack-and-pinion railway had to be discarded on the outbreak of the First World War. Vernet-les-Bains and Prats-de-Mollo are linked only by forest roads.

Canigou Mountain Roads★★★

From Vernet-les-Bains via Mariailles 1

12km/7.5mi – allow 45min by car and 10hr on foot there and back – for experienced hikers only.

Vernet-les-Bains★ – 👌 *See VERNET-LES-BAINS.*

▶ *Take D 116 to the Col de Jou via Casteil and park the car at the pass. Follow the GR 10 footpath to the summit, via Mariailles, where there is a refuge. Continue along the footpath designated Haute Randonnée Pyrénéenne to the Canigou peak.*

Pic du Canigou★★★ – *Alt 2 784m/9 131ft.*

🚶 The Canigou summit is crowned by a cross and the remains of a stone hut used in the 18C and 19C for scientific observations. To the south, the tinkling of bells can be heard from the animals grazing in the Cady Valley below. From the viewing table, there is an immense **panorama** to the north-east, the east and the south-east, towards the Roussillon plain and the Mediterranean coast. Canigou has been seen from as far away as the church of Notre-Dame-de-la-Garde in Marseille, 253km/157mi as the crow flies, when the mountain peak stands out clearly against the setting sun at

Catalan Midsummer Celebrations

Every summer on the feast of St John, or Midsummer Day, Canigou is the venue for celebrations in honour of the continuing brotherhood between French and Spanish Catalans. On 24 June a flame is lit in the Castillet at Perpignan and then carried to the Canigou summit where Catalans from Spain gather to receive it. The same evening, the flame is used to light fires all over Catalonia. It is then returned to the Castillet, via other parts of Perpignan where fires are to be lit. Celebrations continue all through the night until dawn, when people go to gather flowers associated with St John in the foothills of Canigou (Les Aspres) – vervain, St John's wort, walnut flowers – which they arrange in the form of crosses. These are hung on the doors of their homes to bring good luck and protection.

For details of the St-Jean celebrations, contact **Perpignan Tourist Office**: ☎ *04 68 66 30 30*.

certain times of the year *(around 10 February and 28 October)*. Even with the much lower Albères range forming a slight barrier in the foreground, the Costa Brava in Catalonia can still be seen in the distance. To the north-west and west the view takes on a sort of layered effect, with the ponderous secondary chains of the crystalline foundations of the eastern Pyrenees (Madrès, Carlit etc), contrasting with the more rugged limestone ridges of the Corbières (Bugarach).

From Vernet-les-Bains via the Chalet-hôtel des Cortalets ②

23km/14.5mi – about 1hr 30min by car and 3hr 30min on foot there and back. The track starting from Fillols is ⊛ closed on the way up from 1 to 6pm and on the way down from 8am to 3pm.

The old Cortalets road, built for the Club Alpin by the Water and Forestry Department in 1899, is a picturesque but very uneven mountain road, accessible only in July and August and dry weather, in a four-wheel drive or Jeep.

Excursions in Jeeps or Land-Rovers are organised from **Vernet-les-Bains** *(Garage Villacèque, ☎ 04 68 05 51 14. Taxi de la gare, ☎ 04 68 05 62 28. Tourisme Excursions, ☎ 04 68 05 54 39. Consult the municipal Tourist Office for other possibilities. ☎ 04 68 05 55 35.) or from* **Corneilla-de-Conflent** *(Cullell - ☎ 04 68 05 64 61. Mid-Jun to end Sep: departures by four-wheel drive at 8am and 11am. 16€ there and back). Beware of the poor condition of the road. The trickiest part, a very narrow 21% gradient, is protected by a parapet. There are 31 hairpin bends.*

Vernet-les-Bains★ – ⓒ *See VERNET-LES-BAINS.*

▸ *Take D 27 in the direction of Prades. After Fillols, turn right.*

Beyond Col de Millères, alt 842m/2 762ft, the road winds in tight hairpins along the rocky crest separating the Fillols and Taurinya valleys. On the left, there are views of Prades and St-Michel-de-Cuxa. The road follows a switchback route through larch trees and between rocky outcrops. A sweeping left bend affords a stunning view of the Cerdagne and Fenouillèdes regions. The road climbs steeply through magnificent undergrowth (beautiful tree trunks).

Canigou in spring

J.-D. Sudres/PHOTONONSTOP

Escala de l'Ours

This vertiginous cliff road is the most spectacular on the trip. It cuts a narrow tunnel through the rock itself, overlooking the Taurinya gorges several hundred metres below *(viewpoints at various stages along the tunnel)*. Beyond the Baltag forest hut, the increasingly bare trees (Arolla pines) thin out considerably. The surrounding countryside becomes a pastoral one with open meadows.

Col des Voltes

Alt 1 838m/6 029ft. From the pass there is a view of the northern slopes of Canigou and the Cady basin.

▶ *At the Ras dels Cortalets (alt 2 055m/6 740ft; picnic area), turn right.*

Chalet-hôtel des Cortalets

Alt 2 150m/7 050ft. Hotel-chalet at the mouth of the cirque formed by the Canigou, Joffre and Barbet peaks.

🚶 *West of the hotel-chalet, follow the path waymarked by red and white flashes along the banks of a lake and then up the eastern face of the Joffre peak. Leave the path when it starts going back down to Vernet and continue the ascent on the left below the ridge. A zigzag path winding between the rocks leads to the summit (3hr 30min there and back).*

Pic du Canigou★★★ – 👣 See 1 above.

From Prades via the Chalet-hôtel des Cortalets 3

20km/12.5mi – allow 2hr by car and 3hr 30min on foot there and back.

🚗 *The road, which is accessible only during the summer in dry weather, is very rough along the Llech gorge; a 10km/6mi stretch of the road is cut into the rock face. Excursions by Jeep or four-wheel drive are organised from Prades.*

Prades – 👣 See PRADES.

▶ *Leave Prades on N 116, towards Perpignan, then turn right onto D 24B.*

Beyond Villerach, D 24 goes through the Conflent orchards and then drops down into the Lech gorge. The road, cut into bare rock, overlooks the Llech gorge 200-300m/700-1 000ft below. It then continues over more rugged ground as far as the La Mouline forest hut *(alt 1 183m/3 880ft; picnic area)*.

Ras del Prat Cabrera★★

Alt 1 739m/5 704ft. This is a delightful stopping place *(with a bench seat)* above the unspoiled La Lentilla Valley. The ridges of the Serra del Roc Nègre block the upstream view. Enjoy the panorama of the Roussillon plain, the Albères mountains and the Mediterranean.

The road opens out in the upper cirque of the Llech Valley which is thick with silver pines. The **views**★★★ are stupendous; to the north lies the southern border of the Corbières, with the deep gash made by the Galamus gorge clearly evident.

The road leads through the orchards of the Lower Conflent to the foothills of Canigou.

▶ *Follow the "Balcon du Canigou" road W to the Chalet des Cortalets (👣 see 2 above).*

Pic du Canigou★★★ – 👣 See 1 above.

Le CAPCIR★

MICHELIN LOCAL MAP 344: D-7

Forming a plateau at an altitude of 1 500m/4 920ft, the Capcir is the highest region of northern Catalonia. Its mountains – covered with pine forests and spangled with lakes – provide many ski runs as well as numerous paths for walking or horse riding and fascinating encounters with wild animals such as izards and moufflons. Moreover, the Capcir has the largest course for Nordic skiing in the Pyrenees. The forest of La Matte has really beautiful Scotch firs, with long and even trunks that often reach over 20m/65ft. They can be admired from D 118 and D 52, between Formiguères and Les Angles. 🏠 *Maison du Capcir, 66210 Matemale.* ☎ *04 68 04 49 86.*

Lac des Bouillouses

A Bit of History

Between France and Spain – The two border countries, which used to fight over Catalonia, divided the Capcir between them for a long time, as they did Cerdagne, a region with which the Capcir shares much of its history. During the Middle Ages, the Capcir used to be governed by Catalan administration and, although it became an annexe of Roussillon in the 17C, its Catalan customs and traditions have survived over the centuries and are still very much alive today.

Ski Areas

Espace nordique du Capcir

A wide, forested area, covering 20 000ha/49 422 acres, with cross-country skiing trails as well as sled-dog runs and footpaths around Les Angles, Puyvalador, Formiguères, La Quillane and Matemale.

Les Angles*

Av. de l'Aude, 66210 Les Angles. 04 68 04 32 76. www.les-angles.com.

Alt 1 600-2 400m/5 260-7 874ft. The skiing area, which lies on the slopes of Le Roc d'Aude and Le Mont Claret, provides sportsmen with 40km/25mi of downhill ski runs, accessible to skiers of different levels (beginners on the Plateau de Bigorre; Pla del Mir, Balcère and Jassettes for the more experienced).

The four areas of La Matte, Calvet, La Llose and Le Galbe offer 102km/63mi of cross-country skiing as well as husky tracks and hiking trails. The area is very sunny, so snow-making equipment is used to keep the trails opens (255 snow cannon).
The resort also has a unique offer of "extreme sports": diving under the frozen surface of a lake, skiing pulled along by a horse or holding on to a kite or a sail for propulsion and ice surfing. Several major competitions in these extreme sports are held here every year.

Formiguères

1 pl. de l'Église, 66210 Formiguères, 04 68 04 47 35. www.station-formigueres.com.

Alt 1 700-2 100 m/5 577-6 890ft. The Formiguères resort has 18 downhill slopes, for all levels, with two chair-lifts and six drag-lifts. The cross-country trails are part of the Espace Nordique du Capcir.

Puyvalador

Alt 1 700-2 400m/5 577-7 874ft. Facing Lake Puyvalador, the 16 downhill slopes go through a pine forest. Off-piste skiing and snowshoe outings are organised by local guides.

Lakes

Lac des Bouillouses★

14km/8.7mi NW of Mont-Louis (see MONT-LOUIS) along the Quillan road (D 118). 300m/328yd beyond the bridge spanning the River Têt, turn left onto D 60. Leave the car in the parking area and go up to the lake by shuttle. Road covered with snow in winter, access with cross-country skis or with snowshoes. Access road closed in Jul and Aug at the "Pla de Barrès" locality from 7am-7pm. Access to the site on foot, by the Font-Romeu / Pyrénées 2000 and Formiguères chair-lifts or by the road shuttle service Information: Jul and Aug. ☎ *04 68 04 24 61.*

After 8km/5mi, the road leaves the bottom of the wooded furrow formed by the Têt to climb up to the threshold which marks the lower terrace of the Bouillouses plateau. A dam has turned this mountain lake (alt 2 070m/6 790ft) into a reservoir containing 17 500 000m³/618 million cu ft, which supplies water to the irrigation canals and hydroelectric plants in the Têt Valley.

The worn-down, rather bleak Bouillouses plateau is dotted with about 20 small lakes and pools, apart from the Lac de Bouillouses itself, which are of glacial origin, at an altitude of more than 2 000m/6 560ft, within the natural amphitheatre lying between the Carlit, Péric and Aude peaks.

🚶 A hiking trail to Pic Carlit starts from the lake *(14km/9mi; allow 3hr).*

Lac de Matemale

This 240ha/593-acre reservoir provides various water sports, hiking, riding and fishing facilities. The nearby forest offers relaxation in invigorating natural surroundings.

Lac de Puyvalador

This smaller 100ha/247-acre reservoir is ideal for wind-surfing or taking it easy on a pedalo.

Excursion

From Mont-Louis to Puyvalador

26km/16mi – allow half a day.

Mont-Louis★ – 🕭 *See MONT-LOUIS.*

▸ *Leave Mont-Louis heading N on D 118.*

As it climbs gently, the road offers an attractive view of the citadel, emerging from a wreath of trees with the Cambras d'Azé mountains in the foreground, in which an old glacial cirque has been hollowed out.

La Llagonne

Located at a crossroads, this village of the Haut-Conflent *(alt 1 680m/5 511ft)* takes its name from an old Catalan term that means "the lagoon". We can still see the signal tower with its surrounding wall. The fortified church of St-Vincent houses an outstanding Romanesque-Byzantine Christ made of wood.

▸ *From the Col de la Quillane, the pass which marks the watershed and the mouth of the Capcir, take D 32F to the left.*

Les Angles✳

This important Pyrenean resort, overlooking the Capcir plateau, was created in 1964 around an old village that has preserved its bell-tower.

Parc animalier des Angles – *Early Jun to mid-Sep: 9am-6pm; late Sep to late May: 9am-5pm. 8€ (children: 6.50€).* ☎ *04 68 04 17 20. www.faune-pyreneenne.com.*
At the southern end of the village of Les Angles, a road leads off to the Pla del Mir, where a zoological park has been laid out.
🔠 Two tours of the park (3.5km/2mi and 1.5km/1mi) enable you to meet various examples of the wildlife unique to the Pyrenees, in their mountain surroundings (moufflons, wild boars, ibexes, brown bears etc).

Formiguères

Passing along the forest of La Matte, you can reach this little winter sports resort, in which the church houses a Romanesque Christ.

▸ *Take D 32B to the left and follow the signposts for "Grotte de Fontrabiouse".*

Grotte de Fontrabiouse

🕐 *Jul-Aug: Guided tours (1hr) 10am-7pm; Sep-Jun:10am-noon, 2-5pm.* 🚫 *Closed mid-Nov to mid-Dec. 6€ (children: 3.50€).* ☎ *04 68 30 95 55.*

This cave was discovered in 1962 during the excavation of an onyx quarry, from which comes the floor covering that decorates the Palais de Chaillot in Paris and the Palais des Rois de Majorque in Perpignan. Well laid-out (⚐ *the disabled have access to a part of the route),* the tour of the cave reveals tubular structures, clusters of "organ pipes".

frozen falls, cascades of "jellyfish" and disc-columns, as well as finer forms resembling cauliflowers or bunches of flowers made of aragonite. A butterfly-shaped piece of aragonite stands for the logo of the cave.

Puyvalador

This village (a winter sports resort) which watches over the Aude gorge well deserves its Catalan name, which means "mountain sentinel".

Le CAP D'AGDE ♨ ♨ ♨

POPULATION 19 988

MICHELIN LOCAL MAP 339: G-9

This promontory, formed by a lava flow from Mont St-Loup, has been lengthened by the Richelieu breakwater, which was originally intended to connect Le Cap d'Agde to the island of Brescou to form one long roadstead. This enterprise was abandoned on the death of Richelieu. The decision to build a seaside resort goes back to 1963, when development began along the whole length of the Languedoc coastal area. Created in 1970, Le Cap d'Agde is today one of the most popular resorts of the Languedoc-Roussillon region and a favourite haunt of kite-flying enthusiasts. 🛈 *Bulle d'accueil, 34305 Le Cap-d'Agde,* ☎ *04 67 01 04 04. www.capdagde.com.*

▶ **Orient Yourself:** The resort occupies one of the best sites on the Languedoc coast. Dredging has opened up a vast, sheltered harbour, with no fewer than eight marinas, both public and private, along its shores, giving a total capacity of 1 750 berths. The architectural style of the town centre is inspired by traditional Languedoc architecture. The pastel walls and tiled roofs of some of the three or four storey blocks of holiday apartments are reflected in the waters of the harbour, whereas others line shady, winding streets leading to "piazzas."

👁 **Don't Miss:** The Cathédrale St-Étienne.

👶 **Especially for Kids:** The Aquarium, Aqualand and Île des Loisirs. Cap d'Agde has been nominated a "kid" resort for its activities and facilities specially intended for children.

Beaches

The resort's beaches – Footpaths known as "ramblas" give access to 14km/8.7mi of fine golden sand; this means that there is no road running alongside the beaches.

Plage **Richelieu** is the most extensive beach, Plage du **Môle** the most popular, Plage de Rochelongue the farthest to the west whereas **Plagette**, near the cliffs is the smallest; Grande Conque is a black-sand beach and Plage de la **Roquille** is covered with seashells. The beaches have facilities for hiring pedalos and wind-surfing boards, for playing volley ball and they also have clubs specially intended for children.

Nearby beaches – Le **Grau-d'Agde** *(5km/3mi W beyond the harbour)* offers a fine sandy beach ideal for families.

Plage de la **Tamarissière**, located on the other side of the Grau-d'Agde canal, is backed by a pine grove.

The small Plage de **Saint-Vincent** shelters inside a creek to the east of Grau-d'Agde.

Sights

Île des Loisirs

👶 This appropriately named "leisure island" offers children and adults a wide choice of entertainment: mini golf, amusement park, discotheques, casino, cinema, bars and restaurants.

A～ ～um

～nd Aug: 10am-11pm; May, Jun and Sep: 10am-7pm; Oct-Apr: 2-6pm, Sun and ～days 11am-7pm. 🕐 *Closed 1 Jan.* 6€ *(children: 4€).* ☎ *04 67 26 14 21.*

Address Book

For coin categories, see the Legend.

WHERE TO STAY

Camping Neptune – *34300 Agde - 2km/1mi S of Agde near the Hérault -* ☎ *04 67 94 23 94 – info@campingneptune.com - le.neptune@wanadoo.fr - open Apr-Sep - reservation recommended - 165 sites: 24.50€.* This camp site near the Hérault, planted with trees and flowering plants, leaves nothing to chance, least of all the gardening! Swimming pool surrounded by a pleasant beach. Games for young and old. Mobile homes for hire. Moorings possible.

Camping Californie-Plage – *34450 Vias - 3km/2mi SW of Vias on D 137E and road to left, along the beach -* ☎ *04 67 21 64 69 - californie.plage@wanadoo.fr - open 5 Apr-10 Oct – reservation recommended - 371 sites: 30.60€ –* food service. Pleasant shady spot situated by the sea. Swimming pool and free entry to the water sports area at Cap Soleil, another camp site 100m/110yd away. Mobile homes, chalets, bungalows and studios for hire.

Les Grenadines – *6 imp. Marie-Céleste - 34300 Agde -* ☎ *04 67 26 27 40 - hotelgrenadines@hotelgrenadines.com - closed 16 Nov-28 Feb -* ▣ *- 19 rms: 84/111€ -* ▭ *5.34€.* At the end of a no-through road not far from Richelieu beach, this hotel benefits from the peace and quiet of the residential area in which it is located. Clean and tidy rooms with whitewashed walls and tiles. A swimming pool shared with the neighbouring house. Simple meals provided.

ON THE TOWN

La Guinguette – *Rte de Mareillan - 34300 Agde -* ☎ *04 67 21 24 11 - May: daily 8am-8pm; Jun-Sept: daily 8am-midnight.* M Dubois has been running this delightful open-air café-bar by Prades lock near the Canal du Midi and the Hérault on the Mareillan road for 11 years. It is difficult to resist the magical spell of the accordeon playing tangos, waltzes and other popular dance tunes.

Le Palma – *Pl. de l'Arbre - Quai du cap d'Agde - 34300 Agde -* ☎ *04 67 01 24 83 - Apr-end Sep: daily 11pm-5am; winter: Fri-Sat and nights before holidays.* With its Art Deco style decor, its columns covered in mosaics and its red plaster curtains, Le Palma is one of the few discos outside the Île des Loisirs, and it is the nicest. A good

DJ mix of techno, house and other varieties that go together to create a great atmosphere. As the owner says, *Que viva la fiesta!*

Mamita Café – *41 quai Jean-Miquel - 34300 Agde -* ☎ *04 67 26 92 84 – May-Dec: daily 11am-2am; Jan, Mar-Apr: weekends 11am-2am; Apr-Sept. 11am-2am - closed Dec-Jan except weekends.* Latino-salsa music, a simple friendly welcome, and the café's air of being on first name terms offer an ideal venue for a break over one or two tapas and a rum cocktail. Terrace.

Restaurant-bar Casa Pepe – *29 r. Jean-Roger - 34300 Agde –* ☎ *04 67 21 17 67 - daily 8am-midnight (except Wed Sep-Jun) - closed Nov.* Small popular bar at the centre of Agde. Clientele of regulars, fishermen, rugby players and jousters make it their headquarters. The proprietor, Aimé Catanzano, a fisherman by trade, is a well known figure about town. Behind the bar, in a small but charming room at the far end of a courtyard, there is a small restaurant operation offering fish and seafood. Very welcoming atmosphere.

RECREATION

Canal du Midi boat trips – ☎ *04 67 94 08 79. 10€ (children under 10 : 6,50€) - Les Bateaux du Soliel.* 2hr trips on horse-drawn canal boats, the traditional method used until around 1960.

SARL Trans.Cap.Croisière – *Quai Jean-Miquel-cap d'agde BP 631 - 34300 Agde -* ☎ *06 08 47 22 32/ 06 08 31 45 20 – from mid Jun-mid Sept: daily 10.30am, 2.30pm, 4pm, 5.30pm, 9pm, 10.30pm; from Apr-mid Jun, and mid-Sept-early Nov: 2.30pm and 4pm - closed mid Nov-Mar.* All aboard the catamaran Cap'Nemo for a sea trip around Fort Brescou. A holiday excursion with a difference! The captain's explanations of the fort used as a prison in the 17C and 18C are fascinating.

Centre international du tennis – *Av. de la Vigne -* ☎ *04 67 01 03 60 - www.ville-agde - 9am-8pm - closed 1 Jan, 25 Dec.* In addition to tennis, visitors can also enjoy badminton, squash, gymnastics, plus the restaurant with terrace.

Golf – *4 av. des Alizés - 34300 Agde -* ☎ *04 67 26 54 40 - www.ville-agde.fr - Open all year - 42€ out of season ; 52€ in summer .* Attractive 18 hole course by the sea, with bar, restaurant and accommodation also available.

Come in for a moment of peace and quiet: squids, sharks, sea breams, and colourful corals are the silent occupants of some 30 pools. In summer, various activities are organised for children.

Aqualand

🕐 *Jun-Aug: 10am-6pm. 18.50€ (children: 15.50€).* ☎ *08 92 68 66 13*

This 4ha/10-acre aquatic leisure park, includes swimming pools with wave machines into which breathless daredevils are shot from the mouths of giant water chutes.

The park offers a wide range of aquatic entertainment for young and old alike, as well as shops, a cafeteria, a snack bar etc.

Musée de l'Éphèbe
(Underwater Archaeology Museum)

♿🕐 *9am-noon, 2-6pm (last admission 30min before closing).*
4€. ☎ *04 67 94 69 60.*

This museum contains the finds of excavations carried out for more than 25 years both out at sea in the Mediterranean and in the coastal lagoons of the Hérault delta.

In the entrance is a display on the techniques used in underwater archaeological excavation work. This is followed by an exhibition of Ancient Greek and Roman boats and Antique amphorae (displayed according to type and date) illustrating maritime trade during Greek and Roman occupation of the area.

The display of Antique works of art is dominated by the magnificent **Éphèbe d'Agde**★★, a bronze statue of a young Greek man, in the Hellenistic style, found in the Hérault in 1964.

The visit ends with a look at a Roman shipwreck and studies of seafaring in the Middle Ages and from the 16C to the 18C.

Éphèbe d'Agde

Musée de l'Éphèbe, Le Cap d'Agde

Excursion

Agde

5km/3mi N along D 32E. Agde is characterised by the dark grey (almost black) lava used in many of its buildings, which comes from the nearby Mont St-Loup, an extinct volcano. The town shares with neighbouring Sète the tradition of *joutes nautiques*, or jousting in boats, and the annual tournaments are enthusiastically followed by the townspeople.

Ancienne cathédrale St-Étienne★

🕐 *Jul and Aug: guided tours available, ask at the tourist office.* ☎ *04 67 94 29 68.*

This fortified church was rebuilt in the 12C, probably to replace an earlier 9C Carolingian building. The walls are 2-3m/6.5-10ft thick and are crowned with crenellations and machicolations above small decorative arches. The 35m/113ft-high bell-tower is a solid square machicolated keep, with a turret and bartizans at each corner (14C). The interior of the church consists of a nave covered with broken-barrel vaulting supported on a single transverse arch. Note the small round window in the vault through which those defending the church in times of siege could haul food and ammunition on a rope. The rectangular chancel contains a 17C polychrome marble altarpiece.

Musée agathois

🕐 *Jul and Aug: 9am-noon, 2-6pm; Sep-Jun: daily except Tue 9am-noon, 2-6pm. 3.80€.*
☎ *04 67 94 82 51.*

This museum of local folk art and traditions occupies a Renaissance mansion which was converted to a hospital in the 17C – the hospital's old dispensary forms part of the exhibition. The extensive display of various artefacts, paintings, glazed earthenware and costumes (including a collection of local lace headdresses known as sarrets) illustrates traditional livelihoods (seafaring, fishing, viticulture, crafts etc) and aspects of daily life in Agde. The exhibition also incorporates reconstructions of the interiors of local houses, model boats, works by local artists, memorabilia of local seafarers, liturgical exhibits, votive offerings and a sizeable collection of amphorae from the ancient Greek port.

CARCASSONNE★★★

POPULATION 43 950

MICHELIN LOCAL MAP 344: F-3

To visit the fortified town of Carcassonne is to be transported back seemingly to the Middle Ages. One of the most memorable events held here is a dramatic annual **fireworks and illuminations** display, in which the entire citadel appears to go up in flames, in honour of Bastille Day (14 July). It is hardly surprising that the romance and excitement conjured up by this impressive, lovingly restored fortress tend to eclipse the more day-to-day businesslike lower town, the Ville Basse, on the west bank of the Aude, for Carcassonne is in fact the commercial centre of the Aude *département's* **wine-growing industry. The town has been on UNESCO's World Heritage List since 1997.** 🔋 *15 bd Camille-Pelletan, 11000 Carcassonne,* ☎ *04 68 10 24 30. Also at : Tour narbonnaise (cité médiévale), Carcassonne,* ☎ *04 68 10 24 36.*

▸ **Orient yourself:** Tour of the ramparts by miniature railway – May-Sep. : 20min trip with guide to explain system of defences, departs Pte Narbonnaise: 10am-noon, 14-6.30pm. 5,50€ (children : 3€). ☎ 04 68 24 45 70.

😊 **Don't Miss:** The "Cité" of Carcassonne, Basilique St-Nazaire.

A Bit of History

The outcrop on which the fortified city of Carcassonne is built commands the main communication route between the Mediterranean and Toulouse.

The crusaders arrive – For 400 years, Carcassonne remained the capital of a county, then of a viscountcy under the suzerainty of the counts of Toulouse. Its prosperity was interrupted in the 13C by the Albigensian Crusade.

The crusaders from the north, who came down the Rhone Valley, arrived in Languedoc in July 1209, to stamp out the Cathar heresy. Since Count Raymond VI of Toulouse was bound by his excommunication, the weight of the invasion fell on the shoulders of his nephew and vassal **Raimond-Roger Trencavel**, Viscount of Carcassonne, who had publicly offered his protection to all those being hounded by the northern invaders.

After the sacking of Béziers, the crusading army, led by Papal Legate Arnaud-Amaury, besieged Carcassonne on 1 August. Despite the dynamic leadership of the youthful Trencavel, only 24, lack of water forced the town to surrender after two weeks.

The Army Council then appointed Simon de Montfort, Viscount of Carcassonne, in place of Trencavel. Before the year was out, Trencavel was found dead in the tower in which he was being held prisoner.

Rebellion – In 1240, Trencavel's son tried in vain to recapture his inheritance by laying siege to Carcassonne. However, although his missiles and mines breached the walls, the royal army forced his retreat. St Louis IX then had the small towns which had grown up around the foot of the ramparts razed, and the town's inhabitants paid for their rebellion with seven years of exile, at the end of which they were allowed to build a town on the opposite bank of the Aude – the present Ville Basse. The walled city was repaired and reinforced – work which was continued by Philip the Bold. From then on the town was so well fortified that it was considered to be impregnable.

Decline and restoration – After the annexation of Roussillon under the Treaty of the Pyrenees, Carcassonne's military importance dwindled to almost nil, as some 200km/125mi separated it from the new border, over which Perpignan stood guard in its stead. It was abandoned and left to decay. There was even talk of demolishing the fortifications altogether.

However, the Romantic movement brought the Middle Ages back into fashion. **Prosper Mérimée**, appointed general inspector of Historical Monuments, made a particular study of ruins in his travel document, *Notes d'un voyage dans le Midi de la France – 1835*. A local archaeologist, Jean-Pierre Cros-Mayrevieille, was passionately committed to defending the interests of his native town and persistently demanded its restoration from the authorities. **Viollet-le-Duc** was sent to visit Carcassonne and returned to Paris with such an enthusiastic report that the Commission of Historical Monuments agreed to undertake the restoration of the Cité in 1844.

A. Thuillier/MICHELIN

Ramparts of Carcassonne

The Cité★★★*2hr*

Tour of the ramparts aboard a **tourist train** *(& ☉ May-Sep: tours (20min, leaving from the Porte Narbonnaise) with explanation of the defence system 10am-noon, 2-6.30pm; 5€, children: 3€; ☎ 04 68 24 45 70.) or a* **horse-drawn carriage** *(☉ Apr to Nov: discovery of the ramparts in a caleche (20min), with historical commentary. 5.50€ (children: 4€). 3 r. Prés.-Fallières. ☎ 04 68 71 54 57).*

The "Cité" of Carcassonne, on the east bank of the Aude, is the largest fortress in Europe. It consists of a fortified nucleus, the Château Comtal, and a double curtain wall: the outer ramparts, with 14 towers, separated from the inner ramparts (24 towers) by the outer bailey, or lists *(lices)*.

There is a resident population of 139, with facilities such as a school and a post office etc, which saves Carcassonne from becoming a ghost town, entirely dependent on tourism for animation.

▷ *Leave the car in one of the car parks outside the walls in front of the gateway to the east, Porte Narbonnaise.*

Porte Narbonnaise

This is the main entrance, the only one wide enough to admit carts. A crenellated redoubt, built on the bridge across the moat, and a barbican peppered with arrow-slits stand in front of the two massive Narbonne towers, on either side of the gateway, with beak-shaped spurs designed to deflect missiles and to enable the defending soldiers to repel attackers more easily. Between the towers, above the archway, there is a 13C statue of the Virgin Mary.

Inside, the 13C rooms restored by Viollet-le-Duc house **temporary exhibitions** of modern art.

Rue Cros-Mayrevieille

This street leads directly to the castle, although visitors might well prefer to take a less direct route through the medieval town, with its narrow, winding streets and many interesting shops (crafts, souvenirs etc). To the right of place du Château is a large well, nearly 40m/145ft deep.

Château Comtal

☉✎ Apr-Sep: guided tours (30min) 9.30am-6pm; Oct-Mar: 9.30am-5pm. ☉ Closed 1 Jan, 1 May, 1 and 11 Nov, 25 Dec. 5.50€, no charge 1st Sunday in the month from Jan-Mar. ☎ 04 68 11 70 70. www.monum.fr. Can only be visited as part of a guided tour.

Built in the 12C by Bernard Aton Trencavel, with its back to the Gallo-Roman fortified wall, the castle was originally the palace of the viscounts. It was converted to a citadel after Carcassonne was made part of the royal estate in 1226. Since the reign of St Louis IX, it has been protected by a large semicircular barbican and an immense moat which make it a formidable internal fortress.

Address Book

⚭ For coin categories, see the Legend.

EATING OUT

A QUICK BITE

⚭**Le Bar à Vins** – *6 r. du Plo - ☎ 04 68 47 38 38 - mhrc@wanadoo.f – daily 9am-2am - closed Nov-Feb.* Situated at the heart of the medieval Cité, this wine bar boasts a charming shady garden offering a view of the St-Nazaire basilica. Tapas and fast food.

A LEISURELY MEAL

⚭⚭ **La Tête de l'Art** – *37 bis r. Trivalle - ☎ 04 68 47 36 36 - tilcke@tele2.fr – closed Sun in winter - 🍴 - reservation recommended at weekends.* Food and art go hand in hand in this restaurant specializing in pork dishes, which are served in rooms displaying works of modern painting and sculpture, in between figurines of the mascot itself.

⚭⚭ **Auberge de Dame Carcas** – *3 pl. du Château - ☎ 04 68 71 23 23 - closed Jan, noon and Wed.* A friendly establishment in the medieval Cité. The good-natured atmosphere and generous menu no doubt contribute to its success – the dining rooms on four levels are regularly packed with people. Carvery on ground floor.

⚭⚭ **Che⚭ Fred** – *31 bd O.-Sarraut - ☎ 04 68 72 02 23 - contact@chez-fred.fr – closed 9 Feb-2 Mar, 20 Oct-3 Nov, Sat noon, Tue evening and Wed in winter.* This modern bistro not far from the station in the lower town is full of life. The cuisine vascillates between Andalousian dishes and daily menus. Food is served in a white-washed room or on the terrace in summer.

⚭⚭⚭ **L'Écurie** – *43 bd Barbès - ☎ 04 68 72 04 04 - closed Sun evening.* This restaurant serving fine fare is located in magnificent old stables, where the old horses' stalls now separate the guests. This original setting and the garden-court, which is pleasant in summer, are popular with local residents, who count it among their favourite places to go.

WHERE TO STAY

⚭⚭ **Montségur** – *27 allée d'Iéna - ☎ 04 68 25 31 41 – reservation@hotelmontsegur. com – closed 20 Dec-3 Feb - 🅿 - 21 rms.* This late 19C family mansion is characterized by beautiful old furniture. Breakfast is served in the lounge or on the terrace. 150m/160yd away is the restaurant Le Languedoc, run by the same family.

⚭⚭ **Chambre d'hôte La Maison sur la Colline** – *Lieu-dit Ste-Croix - 1km/0.6mi S of la Cité on rte de Ste-Croix - ☎ 04 68 47 57 94 - closed 1 Dec – 15 Feb - 🍴 - reservation recommended in season - 5 rms.* Perched on top of a hill, this restored old farm offers a spectacular view of the Cité from its garden. Rooms are spacious and furnished with old dyed objects, in a different colour for each room: blue, yellow, beige, white.. Breakfast is served by the pool in summer.

⚭⚭ **Hôtel Espace Cité** – *132 r. Trivalle - ☎ 04 68 25 24 24 - infos@hotelespacecite. com - 48 rms.* Modern hotel with attractive façade at the foot of the citadel. It offers a "budget accommodation" formula. Rooms are functional and clean, without grand luxury but with plenty of light. Warm welcome. Breakfast buffet.

⚭⚭⚭ **Hôtel Le Donjon and les Remparts** – *2 r. du Comte-Roger - ☎ 04 68 11 23 00 - info@bestwestern-donjon.com - 🅿 - 62 rms.* Partly occupying a 15C orphanage at the heart of the Cité, this hotel combining old stonework and renovated decor offers three kinds of rooms to choose from: with white or rustic furniture in the main building, and modern style in the "Remparts" annex. Brasserie.

ON THE TOWN

Le Métronome – *3 av. du Mar.-Foch - ☎ 04 68 71 30 30 - daily 10-2am - closed 1 week Jan.* Le Métronome is one of Carcassonne's trendiest spots with its canalside terrace, large central bar and comfortable beige moleskin benches. Frequent concerts and a long list of tapas.

SHOPPING

Cabanel – *72 allée d'Iéna - ☎ 04 68 25 02 58 - cabanel@wanadoo.fr - Mon-Sat 8am-noon, 2-7pm.* This liqueur specialist has been here since 1868, selling a wide variety of unusual brews including Or-Kina (made from spices and plants), Micheline (its origins lost in medieval times), and Audoise (called the Cathars' liqueur). Selection of regional wines also available.

Marché aux fleurs. légumes and fruits – *Pl. Carnot - ☎ 04 68 10 24 30 – Tues, Thu and Sat 8am-12.30pm.* Flowers, fruit and vegetables

CALENDAR OF EVENTS

Spectacles médiévaux "Carcassonne, terre d'histoire" – *Aug.* Medieval festival.

Tournois de chevalerie – *Aug.* Jousting tournament.

CARCASSONNE

Château Pl. du	C	
Combéléran Mtée G.	D	21
Cros-Mayrevieille R.	D	24
Gaffe R. de la	C	
Grand-Puits R. du	CD	30
Marcou Pl.	D	
Médiévale Voie	D	36
Nadaud R. G.	CD	
Plô R. du	CD	
Pont Pl. A.-P.	C	
Porte-d'Aude Mtée de la	C	
Porte-d'Aude R.	C	
Prado Pl. du	D	
St-Jean Pl.	C	
St-Jean R.	C	46
St-Louis R.	C	
St-Saëns R. C.	D	48
St-Sernin R.	D	49
Trencravel R. R.-R.	C	
Trivalle R.	CD	
Viollet-le-Duc R.	C	56

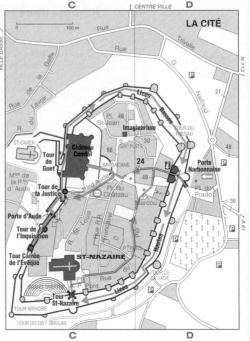

From the drawbridge, note the wooden hoardings protecting the walls to the right.

▶ *The tour begins on the first floor of the castle, which has been converted into an archaeological museum.*

Musée lapidaire

Archaeological remains from the fortified town itself and the local region are exhibited: 12C marble lavabo from the abbey of Lagrasse; a late-15C stone **calvary**★ from Villanière; the recumbent figure of a knight killed in battle; beautiful Gothic windows from a Franciscan convent; small, finely carved figures; alabaster low-relief plaques; commemorative stone tablets; disc-shaped stone crosses from the Lauragais, commonly though not always accurately called Cathar tomb stones etc. There is a collection of old prints of the fortified town, showing it as it was before Viollet-le-Duc's restoration.

Cour d'honneur

The main courtyard is large, with its surrounding buildings largely restored. To the south, the building has an interesting façade in which the three window levels reflect the different styles and periods of its construction: Romanesque below, Gothic in the middle and Renaissance above. To the right are doors to the dungeons.

Cour du Midi

In the south-west corner of the southern courtyard stands the tallest of the fortress' towers, the Tour de Guet, a very well-preserved watchtower. From the top, which was reached by a single wooden staircase, it was possible to see up to 30km/19mi away.

▶ *Leave the castle and follow rue de la Porte-d'Aude on the left.*

Porte d'Aude

This is the main feature of the outer bailey. A fortified path, the Montée d'Aude, weaves its way from the church of St-Gimer at the bottom of the hill (on the side of the Ville Basse) up to this gateway, which is heavily defended on all sides: various gates, large and small fortified buttresses, and a completely enclosed central space in which any attackers who had managed to penetrate that far would have been easy targets for those defending from the surrounding battlements.

The "lices basses"

Access via the Porte d'Aude on the right. This is the name given to the west and north section of the outer bailey. To the north-west the lices run from the Porte d'Aude to the Porte Narbonnaise; to the west, they get narrower and narrower until the dead end at the Tour carrée de l'Évêque.

First comes the **Tour de l'Inquisition**. As its name indicates, this tower was the seat of the Inquisitor's court. A central pillar, with chains, and a cell on the floor below bear witness to the tortures inflicted upon heretics.

Farther along stands the **Tour carrée de l'Évêque**. This square tower is built across the outer bailey, thus blocking any communication between its northern and southern parts. Since, with the exception of the upper watch-path, it was reserved for the bishop, it was fitted out more comfortably. There is a good view of the castle from the second room.

▶ *Return towards the Porte d'Aude and continue along the Lices Basses.*

The itinerary takes you past the **Tour de la Justice**. The Trencavels, as viscounts of Béziers and Carcassonne and protectors of the Cathars (*see above*), sought refuge here with the count of Toulouse during the Albigensian Crusade to escape the army of Simon de Montfort. This tower, rebuilt under St Louis in place of a Gallo-Roman tower, is circular, with round-arched doorways and brick inlays to level out the stone courses. The window openings were protected by tilting wooden shutters which enabled those inside the tower to see (and drop things on) anybody trying to attack the foot of the walls, without themselves being seen.

The outer bailey leads past the Château Comtal and along the northern, or Visigothic, inner curtain wall, which is the oldest stretch of the ramparts. The curtain walls and towers are very high at this point (note the later underpinning), and the original flat, Mediterranean tile roofs can be clearly seen on the towers of the outer curtain wall (whereas those rebuilt by Viollet-le-Duc are pointed and slate-covered, as in northern France).

▶ *Walk beneath the drawbridge by the Porte Narbonnaise and continue SE.*

The "lices hautes"

This is the name given to the stretch of outer bailey to the east of the fortified Cité, heading south from the Tour du Trésau. The gap between the inner and outer ramparts is very wide here (it was used for weapons practice and jousting), and it is edged with moats. Some way past Porte Narbonnaise, note the Tour de la Vade on the outer curtain wall to the left; this three-storey tower, almost entirely projecting outside the curtain wall, is a fortified keep in itself, designed to keep watch on the whole of the eastern ramparts. Carry on along the southern part of the bailey as far as the Tour du Grand Brulas, which stands on the corner opposite the Tour Mipadre.

Tour St-Nazaire

This handsome square tower was built to protect the church, located at the far end of the fortified town, away from the entrance. The tower's postern, masked by a corner bartizan, was only accessible up ladders. There are still a well and an oven in evidence on the first floor, and a viewing table has been installed at the top of the tower.

▶ *Enter the Cité through the Porte St-Nazaire*

Basilique St-Nazaire★

All that remains of the original church, the building materials for which were consecrated by Pope Urban II in 1096, is the Romanesque nave; the Romanesque apse and apsidal chapels were replaced by a Gothic transept and east end. The west front was modified by Viollet-le-Duc, who, in the mistaken belief that the church was

Stained-glass window of Basilique St-Nazaire

A. Thuillier/MICHELIN

part of a fortified "Visigothic" curtain wall, took it upon himself to add a row of crenellations along the top of the belfry-wall.

Once inside the church, it is easier to appreciate the contrast between the central nave, typical of Mediterranean French Romanesque architecture with its simple, austere lines beneath a barrel vault, and the much more ornate east end, all openwork and stone dappled with coloured light through the windows of the apsidal chapels and six transept chapels. The perfect proportions, uncluttered delicacy of line and tasteful decoration make this a remarkable piece of architectural design.

The basilica's **stained-glass windows**★★ (13C-14C) are considered the most impressive in the south of France. Remarkable **statues**★★ – reminiscent of those in Reims and Amiens – adorn the pillars in between the windows around the chancel walls. There are a number of eye-catching bishops' tombs, in particular that of Pierre de Roquefort (14C) in the chapel on the left.

▷ *Return to the Porte Narbonnaise via rue du Plô.*

Additional Sights

Musée des Beaux-Arts

Entrance: rue de Verdun. ⊙ *Mid-Jun to mid-Sep: 10am-noon, 2-6pm; mid-Sep to mid-Jun: daily except Sun 10am-noon, 2-6pm.* ⊙ *Closed public holidays. No charge.* ☎ *04 68 77 73 70.*

On display are 17C and 18C paintings (principally French, Flemish and Dutch masters) together with a varied collection of faience (from Moustiers, Marseille and elsewhere). A collection of the work of Carcassonne painter Jacques Gamelin (1738-1803) adds local flavour. Note the painting by Chardin, *Les Apprêts d'un déjeuner.*

The museum has a collection of memorabilia of the Chénier family, Languedoc by adoption: portraits of André Chénier, and of his mother in her Greek national costume – André Chénier's father was consul in Constantinople, and married there.

Likewise, 19C painting is well represented, with works by Courbet and a number of artists from the French Academy.

Maison des Mémoires Joë-Bousquet

53 rue de Verdun. ♿⊙ *Daily except Sun, Mon and Public holidays 9am-noon, 2-6pm. No charge.* ☎ *04 68 72 50 83 or 04 68 72 45 55 (reception).*

Paralysed after being shot during the First World War, Joë Bousquet lived here from 1918 to 1950 and never left his closed-shutter bedroom on the first floor (included in the visit), where he spent his time writing (poetry and a vast amount of letters) and receiving the well-known writers and artists of his time (André Gide, Paul Valéry, Aragon, Michaux, Paul Éluard, Max Ernst). He founded the Carcassonne Group with two local writers and published articles in the literary magazine Cahiers du Sud.

Excursion

Cabardès Region★ [1]

Round trip from Carcassonne. Local map see LA MONTAGNE NOIRE.

▷ *Leave Carcassonne along N 113 towards Castelnaudary. After Pezens, turn right onto D 629.*

Montolieu★

This village in the Cabardès region, overlooking the confluence of the River Dure and River Alzeau, is devoted to books and their related industries. It is home to 20 or so bookshops, craft workshops (bookbinder's, copyist's, engraver's) and a **Conservatoire des Arts et Métiers du livre** (♿⊙ *10am (9am in low season)-12.30pm, 2-6.30pm (6pm in low season) Sat-Sun and public holidays.* ⊙ *Closed 1 Jan, 1 May and 25 Dec. 1.50€.* ☎ *04 68 24 80 04)* dedicated to the art of book design and production.

▷ *A small road (D 64) S of the village leads to Villelongue Abbey.*

Ancienne abbaye de Villelongue

⊙ *May-Oct: 10am-noon, 2-6.30pm. 4€.* ☎ *04 68 76 92 58.*

The abbey flourished in the 13C but then fell into decline. One or two interesting parts of the monastery complex have survived: the refectory, a large room roofed with ribbed vaulting and with three windows surmounted by an oculus in the south wall; the south gallery of the cloisters; and the chapter-house.

The old abbey church was built to a Cistercian design and was rebuilt in the late 13C and early 14C. Of the original building, the chancel with its flat chevet, flanked with rectangular chapels, two transepts and the square of the transept crossing remain. Note the keystone depicting the Paschal lamb and the heads on the south-west pillar in the nave.

▶ *D 164 on the right leads to Saissac.*

Saissac

The village is perched high above the Vernassonne ravine over which tower the ruins of a 14C castle. A small road, skirting the village to the north, offers an attractive view of this picturesque site.

To appreciate the panorama over a wider area, go up to the platform of the largest tower in the old curtain wall. The tower houses a **museum** (🕐 *Early Jul to mid-Aug: 9am-1pm, 2-6pm; Apr-Jun and mid-Aug to end Sep: Wed, Thu, Sat-Sun 9am-1pm, 2-6pm.* 🕐 *Closed 1 May. 2.50€.* ☎ *04 68 24 47 80)* displaying various objects and tools evoking the history of Saissac and the traditional crafts practised there.

▶ *Drive E along D 103.*

Brousses-et-Villaret

An 18C **paper mill** (🕐👣 *Early Jul to mid-Sep: guided tours (1hr) at 11am, 3pm, 4pm, 5pm and 6pm (mid-Jul to end Aug 10am-7pm); mid-Sep to end Jun: at 11am and 3.30pm, Sat-Sun and public holidays at 11am, 2.30pm, 3.30pm, 4.30pm and 5.30pm.* 🕐 *Closed 1 Jan and 25 Dec. 4€, children under 7: no charge;* ☎ *04 68 26 67 43)* open to the public continues to manufacture paper the traditional way. Its Gutemberg Museum relates the story of printing techniques.

▶ *Continue along D 103 to D 118 and turn right. Beyond Cuxac-Cabardès, turn right onto D 73 then follow D 9 towards Mas-Cabardès.*

Mas-Cabardès

🕐 *9am-noon.* ☎ *04 68 26 30 77.*

The village stands proudly below the ruins of its fortified castle.

The narrow streets lead to the **church** whose belfry, topped by an octagonal tower, still has a somewhat Romanesque appearance, even though it dates from the 15C. The church itself was rebuilt in the 16C, over a 14C building. Remains of this are to be found inside (on the left of the entrance): a Romanesque capital and a low relief.

By going down the street to the left of the church you come to a junction with a second street, where there is a 16C stone cross. This is adorned with a carving of a shuttle, the emblem of weavers and witness to the textile industry in the Orbiel Valley.

▶ *Drive S along D 101.*

Châteaux de Lastours★

Departure from the village centre, at the "Accueil Village". 🕐 *Jul and Aug: 9am-8pm; Apr-Jun and Sep: 10am-6pm; Oct: 10am-5pm; Nov-Mar: Sat-Sun and school holidays 10am-5pm.* 🕐 *Closed Jan and 25 Dec. 4€.* ☎ *04 68 77 56 02.*

The ruins of four castles stand in this rugged setting on a rocky ridge between the deep valleys of the Orbiel and the Grésillou. The castles, called **Cabaret**, Tour Régine, Fleur d'Espine and Quertinheux, made up the Cabaret fortress in the 12C. Their lord,

Châteaux de Lastours

E. Larribere/MICHELIN

Pierre-Roger de Cabaret, was an ardent defender of the Cathar cause. During the **Albigensian Crusade**, Simon de Montfort was forced to withdraw from these stern walls in 1210, whereas both Minerve and then Termes *(SE of Carcassonne)* capitulated. Refugees came to seek protection at Cabaret, which resisted every attack. Simon de Montfort only took possession of it in 1211 after the voluntary surrender of Pierre-Roger de Cabaret.

For a particularly beautiful **view** of the Châteaux de Lastours ruins, their slender silhouettes rising harmoniously from the hillside dotted with tapering cypresses (and wild irises in the spring), drive up to the viewpoint on the opposite side of Grésillou Valley.

▶ *Follow D 701 to Salsigne.*

Salsigne

Mining has been the source of livelihood in this area for centuries. Roman and Saracen invaders extracted iron, copper, lead and silver. In 1892, gold was discovered here. At present, there are mining concessions at Salsigne, Lastours and Villanière. Since 1924, they have extracted 10.5 million tonnes of ore which has produced 92t of gold, 240t of silver, 30 000t of copper and 400 000t of arsenic. Since 1992, the mine has produced gold and silver only.

▶ *From Salsigne, follow the signs to the Grotte de Limousis.*

Grotte de Limousis

🕐☀☁ *Jul and Aug: guided tours (1hr) 10am-6pm; Apr-Jun: 10am-noon, 2-6pm; Sep: 10am-noon, 2-5.30pm; Oct and mid to end Mar: 2-5pm.* 🕐 *Closed 1 Jan and 25 Dec. 6.10€ (children: 3,05€).* ☎ *04 68 77 50 26.*

The entrance to this cave is set in arid, bare limestone countryside where only vines and olive trees grow. Discovered in 1811, the cave comprises a series of chambers extending for about 663m/2 179ft, in which curiously shaped concretions alternate with mirrors of limpid water. In the final chamber, an enormous **chandelier**★ of remarkably white aragonite crystals, 10m/33ft in circumference, is the main feature of the cave.

▶ *Return on D 511 to D 111 and there, follow the signs to Villeneuve-Minervois. Go through the village, which earns a living mainly from wine-growing, and take D 112 towards Cabrespine.*

Gorges de la Clamoux

These gorges show the striking contrast between the two slopes of Montagne Noire. As far as Cabrespine, the road runs along the floor of the valley, covered with orchards and vineyards.

▶ *Take the small road on the left which climbs steeply to the Gouffre de Cabrespine.*

Gouffre de Cabrespine

♿🕐☀☁ *Jul and Aug: guided tours (45min) 10am-7pm; Mar-Jun and Sep-Nov: 10am-noon, 2-6pm. 7€ (children: 3.50€).* ☎ *04 68 26 14 22.*

The upper part of this chasm consists of a huge network of subterranean galleries drained by the River Clamoux. The chasm has been described as "gigantic" and its dimensions fully justify this epithet. In the chasm proper, the "Salle des Éboulis" (chamber of fallen earth), the cavern reaches 250m/820ft in height. The tour of the cave follows a long balconied walkway, from which there is a spectacular overall view, while the concretions adorning the walls of the cavern can be appreciated from closer up. These form characteristic features such as solidified calcite flows coloured differently by mineral oxides, stalactites and stalagmites some of which have joined to form tall and slender columns, mini-shrubs or dazzling curtains of aragonite crystals, eccentrics apparently defying the laws of gravity and many more. The tour ends in the "Salles Rouges" (red galleries) and the "Salle aux Cristaux" (crystal gallery).

▶ *Return to D 112.*

The road reaches Cabrespine, overlooked by the Roc de l'Aigle to the left, then winds rapidly up a series of hairpin bends between groves of chestnut trees, overlooking deep ravines in the bottom of which a few tiny hamlets are huddled.

▶ *At Pradelles-Cabardès, take D 87 to the right towards the Pic de Nore.*

Pic de Nore★

Alt 1 211m/3 973ft. The highest point of the Montagne Noire, the Pic de Nore towers above the surrounding gently undulating countryside, which is covered with heathland. Not far from the television transmitter station, a viewing table offers a **panorama**★ which stretches easily from the Lacaune, Espinouse and Corbières mountains, to Mont Canigou, the Carlit massif and the Midi de Bigorre summit.

▶ *Return to Pradelles-Cabardès and turn left onto D 89 towards Castans then right onto D 620 towards Caunes-Minervois.*

Lespinassière

Built on an isolated peak inside a mountain cirque, Lespinassière is overlooked by its castle which still retains an impressive 15C square tower.

Gorges de l'Argent-Double

The River Argent-Double, which springs up near Col de la Salette, flows through a deep and sinuous gorge.

Caunes-Minervois

The village is known for the red-marble with grey and white veins quarried nearby. Sought after in the 18C, this marble was used to decorate the Grand Trianon in Versailles, the Palais Garnier in Paris and the St-Sernin Basilica in Toulouse.

Two fine mansions stand round the town hall square: Hôtel Sicard (14C) with its corner mullioned window and **Hôtel d'Alibert** (16C) which opens onto a charming Italian-style Renaissance courtyard – its superposed galleries are adorned with busts inside medallions.

The **abbey church** (♿ ⏱ *Jul and Aug: 10am-7pm; Apr-Jun, Sep and Oct: 10am-noon, 2-6pm; Nov-Mar: 10am-noon, 2-5pm. ⊘ Closed 1 Jan, 24, 25, 30 and 31 Dec. 3.50€. ☎ 04 68 78 09 44.*) of the former Benedictine abbey has retained its 11C Romanesque east end decorated with engaged columns and blind arcading. The square bell-tower surmounting the north transept comprises three tiers of twin bays; some of these are resting on Merovingian capitals.

▶ *Drive SW along D 620. Beyond Villegly, turn right onto D 35.*

Conques-sur-Orbiel

This pretty village still boasts traces of its earlier fortifications, such as the 16C south gateway surmounted by a statue of the Virgin Mary. The church belfry-porch, which spans a street, has all the air of a fortified building.

▶ *Follow D 201 S to return to Carcassonne.*

CASTRES ★

POPULATION 43 496

MICHELIN LOCAL MAP 338: F-9

This busy city stands on the banks of the Agout, which is still plied by passenger barges *(coches d'eau)*. It is an excellent point of departure for excursions to the Sidobre region, the Lacaune mountains and the Montagne Noire. Castres boasts a remarkable fine arts museum devoted to Spanish painting and in particular to the works of Goya.

Local economy is dominated by the wool industry. With Mazamet and Labastide, Castres has kept up the tradition of peyrats which started in the 14C. These weavers, who also worked on the land, used the wool from their own sheep and the dyers used the madder and woad cultivated on the neighbouring plains. The industry's evolution was interrupted during the Wars of Religion and the turbulent period which followed the revocation of the Edict of Nantes, but in the 18C the Languedoc Fairs led to renewed growth.

Nowadays, Castres and the surrounding area is the leading centre in France for carded wool and the second most important centre for the wool industry after Roubaix-Tourcoing. It encompasses a large number of textile mills, specialised spinning mills, dyeing and dressing workshops.

A Bit of History

A self-governed city – Castres grew up on the west bank of the Agout, around a Benedictine monastery founded c810. At the end of the 9C veneration of the relics of St Vincent, one of the preachers who took the Gospel to Spain, made Castres a stopping place on the pilgrim route to Santiago de Compostela. In the 10C, the town came under the rule of the viscounts of Albi and Lautrec. In the 11C, the viscount of Albi granted Castres the right to self-government by a college of "consuls" or *capitouls*.

The town managed to keep out of trouble during the Cathar heresy by submitting to Simon de Montfort.

The Reformation – From 1563, the Reformation attracted numerous followers. Once the city's *capitouls* had renounced Roman Catholicism, Castres became one of the strongholds of Calvinism in Languedoc. It was caught up in the Wars of Religion, which the Peace Treaty of Alès, Henri IV's ascent to the throne and the promulgation of the Edict of Nantes eventually brought to an end. In the 17C, the city hosted one of the four chambers set up by the Edict of Nantes to regulate differences between Protestants and Roman Catholics. This was a prosperous period during which local magistrates and merchants built luxurious town houses and the bishopric a magnificent episcopal palace.

However, the confrontations between Protestants and Roman Catholics persisted after the revocation of the Edict of Nantes until the French Revolution, forcing numerous Huguenots to flee into exile.

Jean Jaurès – The famous Socialist leader was born in Castres on 3 September 1859 and spent part of his childhood in Saïx, a little village on the banks of the Agout, southwest of Castres. He was a student at the *lycée* that now bears his name, and went on to train as a teacher at the École Normale Supérieure in Paris, after which he taught philosophy at the *lycée* in Albi and at the University of Toulouse. Attracted by politics, he was elected Republican Member of Parliament for the Tarn in 1885, then Socialist Member for Carmaux, where he took up the miners' cause in 1893. At the next elections, however, Jaurès was defeated, largely because of his support for Dreyfus, victim of what was eventually proved to be a military conspiracy which led to his being falsely convicted of selling sensitive information to the Germans, an affair which provoked bitter controversy throughout France. Jaurès nonetheless became head of the United Socialist Party (SFIO) not long after its foundation in 1905. As war approached, he put his influential voice to the service of promoting peace and devoted himself to the cause of international brotherhood. He was assassinated at the Café du Croissant in Paris on 31 July 1914. War was declared two days later. In 1924, his remains were transferred to the Panthéon, Paris.

Address Book

🪙 *For coin ranges, see the Legend at the back of the guide.*

EATING OUT

🍴 **Le Mandragore** – *1 r. Malpas - ☎ 05 63 59 51 27 – closed Sun-Mon.* This little restaurant in Old Castres offers traditional cuisine amid light and spacious contemporary decor. Menus are reasonably priced, and the ambience is family-style.

🍴 **Le Victoria** – *24 pl. du 8-Mai-1945 - ☎ 05 63 59 14 68 – closed 10-24 Aug, Sat lunchtime and Sun.* Those who like old stonework should definitely pay this restaurant a visit. The three vaulted cellars are said to have been part of a monastery. Seasonal cuisine.

WHERE TO STAY

🏠 **Camping Le Plô** – *81260 Le Bez - 5km/3mi SW of Brassac on D 53 then D 30 – ☎ 05 63 74 00 82 - info@leplo.com – Open Jul-Aug - ✂ - 60 sites. 🖙 15€.* Isolated in the Montagne noire, on the edge of a forest, this camping area is not only in a beautiful site, but it is also well kept and very clean. Not fancy, but immaculate.

🏨 **Hôtel de l'Europe** – *5 r. Victor-Hugo - ☎05 63 59 00 33 - 35 rms; 🖙 7€.* This is a hotel with character which will not burn a hole in your pocket. Three 17C mansions are linked by a pleasant patio with a staircase, trinkets and antiques. Brickwork, half-timbering and modern furniture are tastefully combined in the bedrooms. Simple cuisine.

🏨 **Hôtel La Renaissance** – *17 r. Victor-Hugo - ☎05 63 59 30 42 - closed 21 Dec-3 Jan - 20 rms; 🖙 7€.* This 17C house with its typical brickwork and half-timbering occupies a quiet site on a pedestrian street in the old town. The rooms have original decoration and furniture of different styles.

🏨 **Le Castel de Burlats** – *8 pl. du 8-Mai-1945 - 81100 Burlats - 7km/4mi NE of Castres on D 89 then D 58 - ☎ 05 63 35 29 20 – le.castel.de.burlats@wanadoo.fr – closed 15-22 Feb and 25-31 Aug - 🅿 -* 10 rms; 🖙 10€. This fine 14C and 16C palace opposite the abbey of Burlats stands in a wooded park and a formal French style garden. Comfortable spacious rooms, in which traditional and modern decor are combined, overlook the hill. The Renaissance style salon is charming.

SIT BACK AND RELAX

Signovert – *5 r. Émile-Zola - ☎ 05 63 59 21 77 – Mon 2.30-6.30pm; Tue-Sat 8.30am-12.15pm, 2.30-7.15pm, Sun 8.30am-1pm.* This pastry shop and chocolatier has been selling sweet delights since 1928, including the house speciality, *le Granit du Sidobre*, a kind of local nougat. Tempting petits fours to take home or enjoy in the tea room.

ON THE TOWN

Dixi's Café – *3 bd Gambetta - 81290 Labruguière - ☎ 05 63 50 20 47 - Tues -Sun 9am-2am, Mon noon-2am.* Formerly called the Moonlight, and founded 60 years ago by M Gayraud (a ballroom musician who created the atmosphere of an open-air music café), this disco-bar has been taken over by his son and has now embraced rock'n roll (music) and the American Dream (decor). It is still a success and the crowds still keep coming.

RECREATION

Le Coche d'eau – *R. Milhau-Ducommun - ☎ 05 63 62 41 72 – leaves from the city centre: Jun, Sep daily at noon, 2.20, 3.40pm; Jul-Aug daily at noon, 2.20, 3.40, 5.10pm – closed Oct-May - 4€ (child: 1.60€).* To take a ride on the Agout, board the Miredames, a fine wooden boat inspired by the old "water coaches" pulled along the river by horses. You will have another persepctive on the town of Castres and the Gourjade park.

Gourjade recreation area – North of town, the park has a golf course, walking paths, picnic areas, an orienteering trail, children's play areas, and a swimming pool (skating rink in winter).

Old Castres *1hr 30min*

▶ *Start from the theatre.*

Opposite are the superb **formal gardens** (Jardin de l'Évêché) designed by Le Nôtre in 1676.

Hôtel de Ville

The town hall occupies the **former bishops' palace** (Castres was the seat of a bishopric from 1317 to 1790), built in 1669 following Mansart's designs. To the right on entering the courtyard stands the **Tour St-Benoît**, a massive Romanesque tower with an elegant main doorway. It is all that remains of the former abbey of St-Benoît.

Quai des Jacobins

Cathédrale St-Benoît

This cathedral, dedicated to St Benoît de Nursie, was built on the site of an abbey church founded in the 9C by the Benedictine Order. It was designed by the architect Caillau in 1677; after completion of the chancel, Eustache Lagon took charge of construction work in 1710.

The most striking thing about this Baroque edifice is its enormous size. Above the high altar, which has a baldaquin supported on Caunes marble columns, is a painting depicting the Resurrection of Christ by Gabriel Briard (1725-77).

Around the chancel are four late-17C marble statues. The side chapels contain a rich collection of paintings from the charter house in Saïx. Most are the works of the Chevalier de Rivalz, an 18C painter from Toulouse.

▷ *Cross place du 8-mai-1945.*

Quai des Jacobins

The Pont Neuf and the quay afford attractive views of the houses lining the banks of the Agout. These used to be the homes of weavers and dyers in the Middle Ages and are built over vast stone cellars which open directly onto the water. Their bright colours reflected in the water make an attractive scene, particularly pretty when seen from a passenger barge.

Place Jean-Jaurès

The houses around this square feature Classical façades carved from sandstone (most of the buildings date from the first half of the 19C) and form an attractive group. The statue of Jean Jaurès by Gaston Pech dominates the square, and the fountain opposite is a scaled-down reproduction of one of the fountains at place de la Concorde in Paris.

▷ *Cross place Jean-Jaurès and turn right onto rue Henri-IV, then left onto rue du Consulat.*

Hôtel de Nayrac★

12 rue Frédéric-Thomas. This beautiful brick and stone mansion dating from 1620 is typical of 16C Toulouse-style civil architecture. The façades on three sides of the courtyard have mullioned windows and are connected by two corner towers on pendentives.

▷ *Take rue Émile-Zola and rue Victor-Hugo.*

Église Notre-Dame-de-la-Platé

This Baroque style building was rebuilt between 1743 and 1755. In the centre of the high altar is a very beautiful Assumption of the Virgin in Carrara marble, which was executed by the Italian artists Isidora and Antonio Baratta (Bernini School). In the chapel containing the font there is a Baptism of Christ. Opposite the altar is a fine 18C organ.

▷ *Retrace your steps and turn left onto rue de l'Hôtel-de-Ville.*

At no 31, admire the doorway with its round arch on fluted columns surmounted by a carved pediment depicting various types of weapon (pistol, sabre, cannon, and so on).

▷ *Turn left onto rue de la Platé leading to rue Chambre-de-l'Édit.*

Hôtel de Viviès

No 35. A monumental door leads to a courtyard surrounded by a 16C building with a square corner tower. It houses the **Centre d'Art contemporain** (🕐 *Jul and Aug: 10am-6pm; Sep-Jun: Sat-Sun and Mon 3-6pm, Tue 10am-noon, 2-7pm, Fri 10am-noon, 2-5.30pm.* 🕐 *Closed public and Christmas school holidays.* ⮕ *1€.* ☎ *05 63 59 30 52)*.

◗◗ **Hôtel Jean-Leroy** (*no 31, 16C*) and **Hôtel de Poncet** (*rue Gabriel-Guy, 17C*).

▶ *Rue Chambre-de-l'Édit goes back to the theatre.*

Additional Sights

Musée Goya★

🕐 *Jul and Aug: 10am-6pm; Apr-Jun and Sep: daily except Mon 9am-noon, 2-6pm, Sun and public holidays 10am-noon, 2-6pm; Oct-Mar: daily except Mon 9am-noon, 2-5pm, Sun 10am-noon, 2-5pm.* 🕐 *Closed 1 Jan, 1 May, 1 Nov, 25 Dec.* ⮕ *3€ summer, 2.30€ winter, no charge 1st Sunday in the month.* ☎ *05 63 71 59 30.*

This museum is located on the first floor of the Hôtel de Ville (🕐 *see Old Castres above*) in the former bishops' palace. It specialises in Spanish painting and is particularly famous for its exceptional collection of works by **Goya★★**, bequeathed in 1893 by the son of the collector Marcel Briguiboul, a painter from Castres.

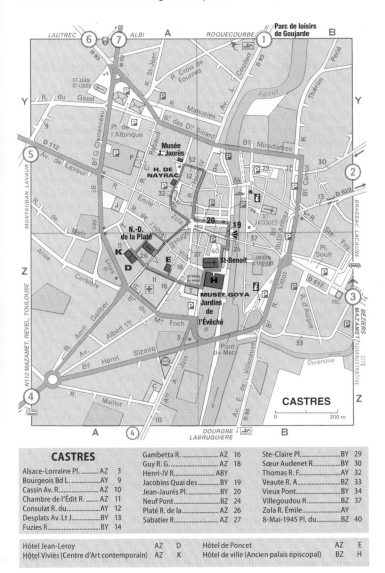

Admire the works of 14C Spanish Primitives, then spend some time in three rooms given over to the Spanish "Golden Age," the 17C, represented by Murillo, Valdès Leal and Ribera.

Goya's works are displayed in three rooms. Francisco de Goya y Lucientes was born in Fuendetodos, south of Zaragoza, in 1746, and was appointed court painter in 1786. He was commissioned to paint the portraits of numerous high ranking figures. The paintings and engravings on display here correspond to specific periods of his development as an artist.

J.-C. Ouradou/Musée Goya, Castres

The first room is dominated by *The Junta of the Philippines Presided over by Ferdinand VII*, a painting of exceptional dimensions, painted in about 1814, with a composition bathed in an atmosphere

Goya – Self-portrait

of dust. By emphasising the oval shape of the chair backs, the painter has frozen the king and his councillors in attitudes devoid of any sign of humanity; the impression of heavy immobility is accentuated even more by large, coldly geometric spaces, while the assembly dozes, yawns with boredom and tries to look important.

Goya's **self-portrait** with glasses and the portrait of Francisco del Mazo illustrate the expressiveness of Goya's painting. Two small rooms contain his etchings.

Show cases display Goya's series of etchings entitled *Los Desastres de la Guerra* (The Disasters of War), inspired by the Spanish War of Independence (1808-14).

On the walls the second edition of his 1799 series of etchings reinforced with aquatint, *Los Caprichos* (Caprices), expresses the isolation and inward contemplation provoked by the onset of the artist's deafness in 1792. The ephemeral nature of youth and beauty, the vanity of feminine coquetry, the injustice of a society in which fools trample over the poor, the alienation of men hounded by the Inquisition, chained to all sorts of superstitions – these are the themes depicted by Goya in his drawings peopled with witches and monsters. As such audacity could have been detrimental to the career of the court painter, Goya gave the copper plates for *Los Caprichos* to Charles IV, thus preventing the sale of the etchings.

Centre national et musée Jean-Jaurès

&. ⊘ *Jul and Aug: 9am-noon, 2-6pm, Sun 10am-noon, 2-6pm; Apr-Jun and Sep: daily except Mon 9am-noon, 2-6pm, Sun 10am-noon, 2-6pm; Oct-Mar: daily except Mon 9am-noon, 2-5pm, Sun 10am-noon, 2-5pm.* ⊘ *Closed 1 Jan, 1 May, 1 Nov, 25 Dec.* ⊛ *1.50€.* ☎ *05 63 72 01 01.*

This museum devoted to the life and work of the politician, as well as society in the late 19C and early 20C, also has an information centre with literature on the history of socialism. Seminars and temporary exhibitions are held here.

Purple Garlic From Lautrec

Purple garlic has been cultivated for centuries in and around Lautrec *(15km/9.5mi NW of Castres)* and is widely considered to be the best garlic in the world, with a particularly pleasant flavour and long storage-life. It is said to have been brought to Lautrec by Spanish pedlars in the 17C. Nowadays, purple garlic from Lautrec carries a quality label, the Label Rouge, and annual production exceeds 4 000t. Besides growing it, local people hold celebrations in its honour: on the first Friday in August every year there is a competition of sculpture using garlic as medium, followed by the tasting of a special garlic soup, then the culmination of the festivities with local residents gathering round at the end of the day to enjoy an enormous pot of *cassoulet* accompanied by *confit de canard*.

Naturally, garlic plays a leading role in local cuisine. It is crushed into sauces, used to stud meat, rubbed onto croutons and added to soups, vegetable dishes and stews. Even so, this represents something of a come-down compared with the prominence it once held in the local diet: in its heyday, the most popular packed lunch with local workers was a handful of raw garlic cloves eaten with a chunk of bread.

Excursions

Montredon-Labessionné

▷ *21km/13mi NE along D 89 then left 5km/3mi beyond Roquecourbe.*

Zoo de Montredon

🕐 *Jun to mid-Sep: 10am-7pm (last admission 5pm); Apr, May and mid-Sep to mid-Nov: 1-6pm (last admission 4pm).* ⊷ *10€ (children: 6€).* ☎ *05 63 75 11 11.*

Kids Camels, kangaroos and monkeys roam around in relative freedom–a real treat for children!

Planétarium-Observatoire

🕐 *Shows in Jul and Aug: daily except Mon at 3.30pm and 5pm; Sep-Jun: 1st and 3rd Sunday 3.30pm. 5€ (children: 3.50€). Evening show with advance booking. 7.60€ (children: 4.60€).* ☎ *05 63 75 63 12.*

Kids This planetarium stages two shows for children: the "Théâtre des étoiles" focuses on the solar system, constellations and the legends they gave rise to *(ages 4 and older)*; "*La Planète aux mille regards*" deals with satellites and the discoveries they led to, about earthquakes and the weather forecast for instance *(ages 8 and older)*.

Le Sidobre★ *53km/33mi round tour – allow 3hr*

To the east of Castres lies the Sidobre, a granite plateau delimited by the River Agout, cutting through a deep gorge, and its tributary, the Durenque.

This massif, which falls within the perimeter of the Parc naturel régional du Haut Languedoc, is interesting for two reasons. On the one hand, it is pitted with huge quarries, at times with rather unfortunate consequences for the landscape, which are evidence of its economic importance. It is one of the most important deposits in Europe, and part of the output of the quarries is worked and polished locally for tombstones and monuments. On the other hand, the plateau offers tourists fascinatingly unusual landscapes of granite rocks sculpted into ball shapes by erosion. Enormous rounded boulders, balanced on top of each other, rivers of rocks and the **compayrés** – heaps of rocks formed by isolated blocks shifted by the running water beneath them – make it a renowned tourist attraction.

▷ *Leave Castres on D 622 to Brassac. Turn right at the hamlet of La Fontasse.*

Chaos de St-Dominique

This river of rocks, in a pleasant wooded setting, covers the real River Lézert for a stretch of some 4km/2.5mi *(rocks are slippery in rainy weather)*.

Grotte de St-Dominique

15min on foot round-trip. Not accessible to those with reduced mobility.

🚶 Go along the north bank of the river, then cross it. The cave overlooks a glade and once gave shelter, if not to St Dominic himself, to one of his distant disciples being hunted down during the Revolution.

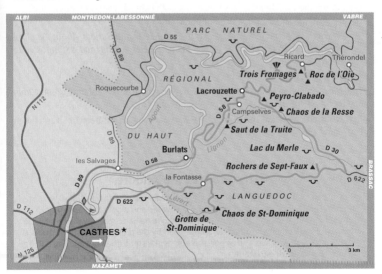

▶ *Return to D 622 and head back towards Brassac. After 5km/3mi, just past a café, turn left, then in the hamlet of Loustalou stop at the café-tabac "Au Rocher Tremblant".*

Rocher de Sept-Faux

This is the finest example of a rocking-stone in the Sidobre. Two blocks poised on top of one another, weighing 900t, can be rocked by simply pressing on a wooden lever.

▶ *Return to the Brassac road and turn left towards Lacrouzette.*

Lac du Merle

Large rounded blocks of rock break the surface of this fine lake, which is fed by the waters of the Lignon and surrounded by forests.

Chaos de la Resse (or "River of Rocks")

The roar of the Lignon, which is totally covered by this chaotic heap of rocks, is clearly audible to those nearby.

Peyro Clabado

The Peyro Clabado rock is the most impressive sight in the Sidobre. An enormous granite boulder, with an estimated weight of 780t, is balanced on a tiny pedestal of rocks. By an accident of nature, a chunk of the boulder is wedged between the pedestal and the rock, ensuring the stability of the whole structure.

Peyro Clabado

Lacrouzette

Most of the inhabitants of this small town earn their living from mining or working granite.

▶ *From Lacrouzette, take D 58 to Thérondel.*

This splendid road gives bird's-eye views of the Agout Valley.

▶ *Stop at the village of Ricard. Go through it on foot to take the footpath to the Trois Fromages and Roc de l'Oie.*

Trois Fromages; Roc de l'Oie

45min on foot round-trip.

🚶 *Follow the red and white flashes marking the GR footpath, a pleasant walk through the woods.*

The rock known as **Trois Fromages** ("three cheeses") is a single boulder fractured by erosion into three rounded fragments.

Further on, the **Roc de l'Oie**, seen from the path coming from Crémaussel, bears a striking resemblance to a goose – hence its name.

▶ *Return to D 58 and follow signposts to Lacrouzette and Burlats. About 2km/1mi beyond Lacrouzette, after the turnoff to Campselves, a little road is signposted to the left.*

Saut de la Truite

Stop the car near the River Lignon. 🚶 *Take a footpath to the right of the torrent. 10min on foot round-trip as far as the foot of the waterfall.*

At this gushing waterfall, the surrounding landscape, which has been fresh and green up to now, becomes more arid.

The Goose of the Sidobre

Legend has it that in those long-gone days when animals could talk, there was once a goose who lived in a cave with a tyrannical owner who would only allow her to go out at night-time to brood, insisting that she had to be back inside by daybreak. One morning, however, the sun had long since risen by the time the unfortunate goose made it back to her cave, and as punishment, her master turned her and the egg on which she was sitting to stone.

Burlats

At the point where the road leaves the Agout gorge stand the remains of a Bene-dictine abbey founded in the 10C, decorated with Romanesque doorways, capitals and mouldings and mullioned windows. Next to these is the **Pavillon d'Adélaïde,** a fine Romanesque house with beautiful windows, home in the 12C to Adélaïde de Toulouse and her court, where troubadours sang of courtly love.

▶ *Return to Castres via Les Salvages and D 89.*

CAUTERETS ⚹⚹

POPULATION 1 305

MICHELIN LOCAL MAP 342: L-5

ALSO SEE LA BIGORRE AND PARC NATIONAL DES PYRÉNÉES

Set amid high wooded mountains where the Gave de Cauterets meets the Gave de Cambasque, Cauterets is one of the main spas in the Pyrenees. The town is also a bustling summer resort, a popular excursion and mountaineering centre (Vignemale) and a booming winter sports resort.

Cauterets is a traditional base for holidaymakers, providing access to the neigh-bouring valleys of Cambasque, Jéret, Gaube and Lutour, with their foaming mountain streams right in the heart of the Parc national des Pyrénées.

A Bit of History

Birth and development of the resort – There is no known documentation on Cauterets before the 10C, although a 4C thermal pool was discovered in Pauze.

In the 10C, Raymond, Earl of Bigorre, bequeathed the Vallée de Cauterets to St-Savin Abbey, on condition that the abbot build a church to St-Martin Abbey and "always maintain buildings here for the use of thermal cures." It was not until the 11C that the abbot of St-Savin took effective control of the valley and carried out the prescribed tasks. Cauterets-Dessus was built on the slopes of Pic des Bains near Pauze.

By the 14C, the village was bursting at the seams, so the monks gave permission to found Cauterets-Debat, and transfer the church, houses and baths to the present site on the plateau, overlooking the stream. This is where the town stands today.

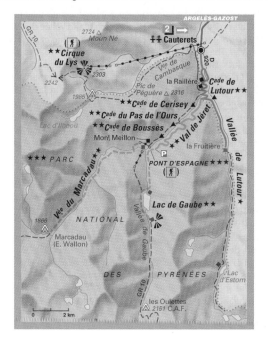

Address Book

For coin ranges, see the Legend at the back of the guide.

EATING OUT

L'Aragon – *R. de Belfort -* ☎ *05 62 92 54 94 – Sun-Thu 7.30am-2am; Fri-Sat 7.30am-3am.* This snack bar is a fun and lively spot, with tables set up on three levels and a wood fire providing warmth in the winter. The salads, cold cuts, soups and omlettes are inexpensive and just right when you want a quick bite to eat.

WHERE TO STAY

Chambre d'hôte les Ruisseaux – *Rte de Pierrefitte - 7km/4.2mi N of Cauterets, rte de Pierrefitte -* ☎ *05 62 92 28 02 - les-ruisseaux@ wanadoo.fr -* ⚲ *- 4 rms.* This bed and breakfast is in a house built in the 1920-30's and now owned by an English couple. The spacious rooms are newly furnished and immpeccable kept. There is a big, charming garden, surrounded by greenery.

Hôtel du Lion d'Or – *12 r. Richelieu -* ☎ *05 62 92 52 87 – hotel.lion.dor. wanadoo.fr - closed 1 Oct-20 Dec - 26 rms;* ⚲ *8€.* A nice family hotel only 100m/110yd from the Lys cable-car. The rooms are small but cozy. The patio is adorned with flowers in the warm months and is a pleasant place to relax a moment. Charming welcome.

Chambre d'hôte Grange St-Jean – *Rte de Lourdes, quartier Calypso -* ☎ *05 62 92 58 58 - igau.brigitte@wanadoo.fr – closed 2 weeks in May and 2 weeks in Nov -* ⚲ *- 3 rms.* The blue and yellow façade of this former barn makes this bed and breakfast easy to find. The rooms are decorated on a mountain theme. One room has its own terrace. Pretty garden facing a meadow.

SIT BACK AND RELAX

Aux Délices – *Pl. Georges-Clemenceau -* ☎ *05 62 92 07 08 – www.berlingots.com - daily 9am-12.30pm, 2.30pm-7.30pm – closed Nov.* Visitors can help to make *berlingots* (local speciality from Cauterets made with glucose syrup, sugar water and flavourings) at any time of day. Hand-made production has been going on for three generations.

Pavillon des abeilles – *23 bis av. du Mamelon-Vert -* ☎ *05 62 92 50 66 - Mon-Sat 10.30am-7.30pm – closed early Nov-late Dec.* This bee-keeper offers you his organic honey from the Hautes-Pyrénées (rhododendron, lime tree, marjoram and bilberry, heather) as well as cleansing and toiletry products (creams, balms, shampoos and soaps) and confectionery made from honey. There are introductory courses to bee-keeping for adults and children, and a gingerbread workshop.

SPA TREATMENT

Thermes de César – *Av. du Dr-Domer -* ☎ *05 62 92 51 60.* In the centre of town, the spa centre offers a range of package deals that may include: bubbling bath in an individual booth, water-jet therapy, mud packs, water massage, pool therapy.

The hot springs still remain the property of a group of surrounding municipalities, left over from the very old communal organisation of the Vallée de St-Savin (*see* **La BIGORRE** 1). Despite the discovery of the Raillère spring in the 17C, there was a dearth of activity. The opening of the Pierrefitte-Cauterets road in 1763 marked a major turning point in the prosperity of the resort, which reached a peak in the second half of the 19C. Construction of prestigious hotels and urbanisation of the left bank began in 1860. The inauguration of two electrified rail links in 1897-98 (*now closed*) increased the number of visitors.

Taking the waters became less popular in the 20C and the large 19C hotels have now been converted into apartments. Nevertheless, some thermal establishments have been revived including Thermes de César, which are open all year round, and offer skiers additional relaxation.

The sulphurous waters of the 10 springs which bubble out at temperatures between 36°C/97°F and 53°C/127°F have been proved effective in the treatment of respiratory and rheumatic disorders. Other specialised prescriptions also exist however, in accordance with the local saying, *A Cautarès, tout que garech* (At Cauterets, you can be cured of anything).

Famous visitors – The beneficial effects of the waters drew famous visitors. In the 16C, Marguerite de Navarre wrote a part of her *Héptaméron* while being treated for rheumatism. In 1765, a small building was constructed for Maréchal de Richelieu on the Raillère spring. During the Empire and Restoration, there was a new influx of celebrities. The most memorable visits were those of Queen Hortense de Beauharnais, the petulant Duchesse de Berry, George Sand, Vigny, Châteaubriand and Victor Hugo, who all found the setting appropriate for a few chapters in the novels of their whirlwind lives.

Visit

The Spa★

Thermal district

This is characterised by its narrow streets and high houses clustered on the right bank of the river, at the foot of Thermes de César, modelled on the thermal baths of Antiquity (triangular pediment and marble columns). Note, opposite the church, the lovely façade adorned with wrought-iron balconies and grey-marble window frames. There are other note-worthy façades along rue de la Raillère and rue Richelieu.

> **Shuttle** – There is a shuttle bus that runs every 10min between Cauterets (Lys gondola station, beginning at 9am) and the Courbet gondola. There is also a shuttle from the Cauterets bus terminal (another stop at the old Gare des Œufs) and the Pont d'Espagne. Schedule at the tourist office.
>
> **Skiers' special** – Ski passes are available at the cable-car departure points. Many hotels sell them as well, as some offer discounts on hotel-ski pass packages.

Early-20C town

On the left bank, boulevard Latapie-Flurin is bordered with luxury hotels built during Cauterets' heyday. Hôtel Continental and Hôtel d'Angleterre, founded by Alphonse Meillon (one of the gentlemen innkeepers synonymous with the popularity of the Pyrenees at the time), have impressive neo-Classical façades, lavishly decorated with cornices, pillars, caryatids and wrought-iron balconies.

Musée 1900

🕐 *Daily except Sun 10am-noon, 3-6.30pm.* 🕐 *Closed mid-Oct to mid-Dec.* 👓 6€. ☎ 05 62 92 02 02.

This museum depicts Cauterets at the end of the 19C and beginning of the 20C. It is housed in part of the Hôtel d'Angleterre. The former dining room decorated with stuccowork and large mirrors contains a fine collection of costumes recalling the sumptuous elegance of the guests one might have met in Cauterets at the time of the Belle Epoque. The other rooms, devoted to life in the mountains, contain costumes from the Pyrenees, tools (reconstruction of a clog-maker's workshop), skis and acces-sories used for practising winter sports at that time.

Esplanade des Œufs

Named after the Œufs spring, used in the former cure centre *(now the casino)*, this is pleasantly shady and lined with boutiques built from metallic structures left over from the Paris World Fair in 1889. The Gare des Œufs is also situated here; it provides a bus shuttle service to the Griffons spa centre. The sculpture of the bear was made by Stanko Kristic.

Railway station

At the entrance of the town.

This is an astonishing construction made of wood in an indefinable style believed to have formed part of the Norwegian pavilion at the 1889 World Exhibition. It is now a coach station.

The Winter Resort

Bringing relief to those who suffer from rheumatism is not the town's only asset for Cauterets is today one of the main winter resorts in the Pyrenees mountains.

Ski area

Alt 1 450-1 630m/4 757-5 348ft. The ski fields in Cauterets are divided into two parts. Cirque du Lys is the largest and has a constant snowfall from December through to May, with a wide variety of runs (25 in all) suitable for both beginners and experienced skiers. It has a chair-lift, a gondola lift and about 15 drag lifts. Weather permitting, it is possible to ski down to Cambasque (where the lift makes an inter-mediate halt).

At Pont d'Espagne, four ski lifts, including the Gaube chair-lift, offer skiers the pos-sibility of practising downhill skiing 🎿 in a relaxed atmosphere away from the crowds, in the very heart of the Parc national des Pyrénées, or of taking advantage of the 36km/22mi of cross-country skiing trails 🎿 divided into five loops in the Vallée du Marcadau.

Parc National des Pyrénées

Maison du Parc

Jun to mid-Oct and Dec-May: daily except Wed and Sun 9.30am-noon, 3-6pm (3-7pm in summer). Closed early Nov to mid-Dec, 1 Jan, 1 and 8 May, 25 Dec. No charge (projections; enquire on site). 05 62 92 52 56. www.parc-pyrenees.com.

At the entrance of the town. This information centre invites you to discover the natural environment protected in the nearby Parc national des Pyrénées, describing the different lifestyles, fauna and flora, and geological formation of the Pyrenees.

Cirque du Lys★★

*Access via the **Lys gondola lift** (Early to mid-Jul and mid-Aug to mid-Sep: 9am-12.15pm, 1.45-5.15pm (20min, departure every 30min); mid-Jul to mid-Aug: 9am-5.15pm. Closed from early May to end Jun. 7€ round-trip (chair-lift and cable-car for the crêtes du Lys: 9€). 05 69 92 50 27) and the **Grand Barbat chair-lift** (Mid-Jul to mid-Aug: 9.30am-5.10pm (20min, continuous); early to mid-Jul and mid-Aug to mid-Sep: 9.30am-12.10pm, 1.45-5.10pm. Closed from early May to mid-Jun. 4€ round-trip. 05 62 92 50 50). About 2hr.*

As you cross the Cambasque plateau, a superb **panorama** from Crête du Lys (2 303m/7 577ft) overlooks some of the most beautiful summits in the Pyrenees – Pic du Midi de Bigorre, Vignemale and Balaïtous (*viewing table*). It is possible to take one's mountain bike in order to ride back to Cauterets from the Grand Barbat chair-lift station.

It takes 1hr on foot to get to Ilhéou Lake (or Blue Lake) via the GR 10 rambling path.

Excursion

VALLÉES DE CAUTERETS★★ 2

Val de Jéret★★ *8km/5mi – about 2hr.*

▸ *Leave Cauterets by D 920, on the west bank behind the casino. After La Raillère cure centre (right), park in the official car park beyond Pont de Benquès (bridge).*

Another alternative is to follow **Chemin des Cascades**★ on foot from Cauterets (*5hr round-trip*) or from the car park by Pont de la Raillère (bridge), near the Griffons spa centre (*4hr round-trip; shuttle service between the Gare des Oeufs car park and La Raillère*). It is a beautiful forest walk, providing a closer view of the waterfalls, which are at their most attractive when the flowers are in bloom.

Cascade de Lutour★★

A footbridge spans the pool below the last four waterfalls of Gave de Lutour.

▸ *The road continues up the valley, which is narrow, steep and heavily wooded, strewn with huge boulders and embellished by waterfalls.*

Cascades de Cerisey, Pas de l'Ours and Boussès★★

These three attractive waterfalls are all very different. Above the Boussès waterfall, the river divides around Sarah Bernhardt's Island (*parking in the glade*).

Pont d'Espagne★★★

Park *in the Puntas car park (3€ per hour, 6€ per day; no charge after 9pm), and take the Puntas **cable shuttle** (15min – Jul and Aug: 8.30am-7pm; May, Jun and Sep: 9am-5.30pm. Closed Oct to early Dec. 2.50€ round-trip. 05 62 92 52 19) as far as Plateau du Clot (activity centre with cross-country ski trails and rambling paths) or go by foot to the bridge.*

This bridge does not, as its name implies, stand across the border between France and Spain; it gets its name from an ancient mule track leading to Spain a few centuries back. The site, marking the confluence of the Gave de Gaube and Gave de Marcadau, is magnificent. Several footbridges and viewpoints up and down river offer breathtaking views of the tumultuous waters of the two mountain streams forming a series of foaming cascades as they meet. The immediate surroundings are planted with firs and forest pines through which meanders a narrow path leading to the Pont d'Espagne from the Puntas parking area. Meadows dotted with mountain flowers stretch across the landscape, beyond the bridge. In winter, cross-country skiers make their way across these expanses.

Monument Meillon – *15min round trip on foot.*

Lac de Gaube

🚶 *Behind Pont d'Espagne Hotel, leave the road and take a stony footpath on the right. Further on, the path branches off to the right to the monument (Parc national des Pyrénées signpost).*

Through the fir trees, there is a glimpse of the main falls at Pont d'Espagne and of the Vignemale massif (south).

Hiking Tours

Pont d'Espagne is the starting point of several hikes.

Lac de Gaube★★

1hr 30min round trip on foot by GR 10 rambling path – departure immediately downstream from Pont d'Espagne. The **Gaube chair-lift** *(🕐 Jul and Aug: 8.45am-6.45pm; May, Jun and Sep: 9.15am-5.15pm. 🕐 Closed early Oct to mid-Dec. 🎫 5.50€ Round-trip (6€ for Puntas gondola and Gaube chair-lift). ☎ 05 62 92 52 19) from Plateau de Clots can be taken part of the way, followed by a 15min walk.*

At the top of the chair-lift, there are six nature information panels including information on forest flora and fauna and the izard, a local species of chamois.

The lake has become almost a ritual excursion for Pyrenees mountain climbers over the past 150 years. It occupies an austere and beautiful site, with a view of the distant walls of the Vignemale massif with its hanging glaciers.

A footpath along the west bank of the river, beyond the hotel complex, affords an excellent view of Pique Longue du Vignemale, 3 298m/10 820ft, one of the highest peaks in the Pyrenees.

Vallée du Marcadau★★

6.5km/4mi; 5hr round trip on foot from the Pont d'Espagne parking area.

An easy valley on foot, it was once a favourite route for crossing into Spain. Grass-covered shoulders, through which a limpid mountain stream meanders over beds of gravel, alternate with glacial thresholds in which the path climbs more steeply through groves of old, often twisted mountain pines. The Wallon refuge, at the end of the walk, stands at an altitude of 1 866m/6 122ft. Beyond it is a cirque of pastureland, with small lakes scattered in the upper reaches *(one-day excursion).*

Vallée de Lutour★

6km/3.6mi

▶ Take the Pont d'Espagne road as far as a series of hairpin bends. Beyond them, just before the thermal establishment called Le Bois, take a sharp left turn onto the narrow, very steep forest road leading to La Fruitière.

The track offers several glimpses, between the trees, of the upper Lutour falls, and then emerges from the forest into peaceful pastureland with grazing herds and occasional patches of rock and scree. Here and there, however, the pines continue up to an altitude of 2 000m/6 500ft.

La CERDAGNE★

MICHELIN LOCAL MAP 344: C-7 TO D-8

The Cerdagne region, *meitat de Franca, meitat d'Espanya* (half French, half Spanish), in the eastern Pyrenees lies in the upper valley of the Sègre, a tributary of the Ebre, between St-Martin gorge (alt 1 000m/3 300ft) and La Perche Pass (alt 1 579m/5 179ft).

The floor of this sheltered rift valley, as often as not bathed in golden sunlight, is a peaceful rural idyll, chequered with fields of crops and pasture between streams lined with alders and willow trees. Majestic mountains frame this valley: to the north, on the **sunny side** (*la soulane*), towers the granite massif of Le Carlit (alt 2 921m/9 581ft); to the south, the **shady side** (*l'ombrée*), lies the Puigmal range (alt 2 910m/9 545ft), with dark pine forests tucked into deep parallel ravines.

A Bit of History

The region earns its livelihood from stock breeding and winter sports (Font-Romeu).

The picturesque **Train Jaune** (*Regular service. Brochures available from local railway stations.* ☎ *08 92 35 35 35.*) runs through the region over a distance of 62km/38.5mi from Villfranche-de-Conflent to Latour-de-Carol (regular service, 21 stations along the line). The section between Mont-Louis and Olette is the most picturesque, crossing the Giscard Bridge and the Séjourné Viaduct. The train is painted in the colours of Catalonia – yellow and red – earning it the nickname "the canary" and it has been running since 1910.

Cradle of the Catalan State – After the Arabs had been driven out of Roussillon and Catalonia, the Cerdagne became essentially a small independent highland state, less and less subject to the Frankish administration of the Spanish border country.

In 878, one of the lords of the Cerdagne, **Wilfred le Velu** ("the hairy"), was invested with the counties of Barcelona and Gerona. By the 10C, his heirs, who had assumed overall rulership of their county, controlled the upper valley of the Sègre, Capcir, Conflent, the Fenouillèdes and the upper Roussillon plain. The dynasty died out in 1117 and the Cerdagne state, thereafter administered from Barcelona by the Catalan kings of Aragón, lost its original highland character.

The memory of the counts of Cerdagne has lived on in local religious and monumental history: **Wilfred le Velu** founded the abbeys of Ripoll and Sant Joan de les Abadesses and the bishopric of Vic (*see The Green Guide Spain*); in the 11C, Count Guifred extended the abbey of St-Martin-du-Canigou, and his brother, Abbot Oliva, a great builder and spiritual leader, turned Ripoll and St-Michel-de-Cuxa into incomparable centres of culture.

French Cerdagne – The 1659 Treaty of the Pyrenees did not define the new Franco-Spanish border precisely in Cerdagne, since an agreement had not yet been reached as to which mountains were to serve as natural borders. In 1660, experts signed a treaty for the division of the Cerdagne in **Llivia**, recognising Spain as owner of the county, except for the Carol Valley and a strip of land which would enable French

subjects to travel between the Carol Valley and the Capcir and Conflent regions. In all, 33 villages were annexed to France under the treaty. These were chosen from those closest to the border, but Llivia, with its official status of "city," was not included and remained under Spanish rule. It has formed a Spanish enclave on French territory ever since.

Ski Areas

Espace Cambre d'Aze

Alt 1 600-2 400m/5 249-7874ft. The resorts of Eyne and St-Pierre-del-Forçats combined their efforts to establish this winter sports centre, which comprises 27 Alpine ski runs for all levels of skiers spread across a picturesque forested area.

Err-Puigmal 2600

Alt 1 850-2 520m/6 070-8 268ft. Located on the slopes of Mont Puigmal. This peaceful winter sports centre offers 18 Alpine ski runs for all levels of skiers, including a few fine black runs, and 10km/6mi of cross-country ski tracks lower down on the edge of a fir forest.

Porté-Puymorens

Alt 1 615-2 500 m/5 298-8 202ft. Spread out over a large area, it includes 16 downhill slopes for all levels of skiers. There are 25km/15mi of cross-country trails in three loops. Snowboard and "ski-bike" activities are also popular. In March, the Grand Prix Porté-Puymorens, a downhill competition, is held.

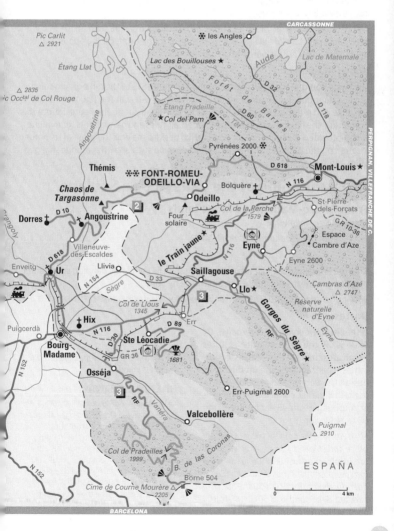

Vallée Du Carol★★

From the Col de Puymorens to Bourg-Madame 1
27km/16.5mi – allow 1hr.

After leaving the upper valley of the Ariège, with its relatively gentle slopes, the road enters a valley which gets deeper and deeper.

Col de Puymorens★
Alt 1 920m/6 300ft.

The pass lies on the Atlantic-Mediterranean watershed between the Ariège, a tributary of the Garonne which flows towards the Atlantic, and the Sègre, a tributary of the Ebre which flows towards Spain.

Above the entrance to the tunnel, on the French side, there is a 16m/52ft-high sculpture in coloured glass, the *Cascade de Lumière* (Cascade of Light), by Josette Rispal.

The road crosses a bridge over a gully scored by the passage of an avalanche and leads down into the Carol Valley, which shows more signs of human presence. There is a good view of the village of Porté-Puymorens, well placed to catch the sun, and of the glacial threshold beneath the reddish-brown ruins of the Tour Cerdane.

Beyond Porté, the road runs through a narrow ravine, the Défilé de la Faou. To the left there is an attractive view of the hamlet of Carol and two ruined towers beyond the viaduct. A stretch of road between tall, sheer valley walls brings you to the outskirts of Enveitg. In front stretches the Cerdagne, widening into a fertile mountain plateau (average altitude: 1 200m/3 400ft) which makes the surrounding peaks seem lower than they really are.

Before Bourg-Madame, the Grand Hôtel de Fort-Romeu can be seen on the left, with the Spanish enclave of Llivia in the foreground. To the right, on the Spanish side of the border, Puigcerdà is perched on top of a hill.

Bourg-Madame

The name Bourg-Madame was given to this village in 1815 by the duke of Angoulême, the last dauphin, in honour of Madame Royale his wife. On the fall of the Empire, the duke had returned to France from his exile in Spain along this route. Before this promotion, the hamlet was home to the open-air cafés and dance floors (*guinguettes*) which provided the night-life for nearby Hix, besides making the most of its border location on the banks of the River Rahur to develop such activities as industry, peddling and smuggling.

The Sunny Side of the Valley★ ("La Soulane")

From Bourg-Madame to Mont-Louis 2
36km/22.5mi – allow 2hr.

▶ *Leave Bourg-Madame heading N (N 20).*

Ur

Note the Romanesque east end of the church, with its Lombardy banding surmounted by a cogged frieze and, inside, the altarpiece by Sunyer.

▶ *At Ur, turn right onto D 618 and at Villeneuve-des-Escaldes take D 10 to the left.*

Dorres

In the **church** (*Contact the town hall ☎ 04 68 04 60 69*), the north side altar features a typical example of the Catalans' enduring penchant for dressing up their statues: an Our Lady of Sorrows (*soledat*). In the south chapel, closed off by a grille, is an impressive, somewhat bony looking Black Madonna.

😊 *If you take the path that runs at the foot of the hôtel Marty in Dorres, you will come to a* **sulphur spring** *(41°C/106°F) where the local people and summer visitors indulge in open-air thermalism.* 🕐 *8.30am-8pm (Jul and Aug: 8am-9pm).* 🚫 *3.50€.* ☎ *04 68 04 66 87. 30min round-trip on foot.*

🪙 *For coin ranges, see the Legend at the back of the guide.*

HILLTOP HIDEAWAY

🍴🍴 **Marty** – 66760 Dorres - ☎ 04 68 30 07 52 – closed 25 Oct-20 Dec - 🅿 - 21 rms. 🛏 5,80€. The atmosphere in this family-run guest house in this hanging village is popular with the regulars. The large dining room contains agricultural equipment, a mural fresco and exposed beams. Terrace. Some rooms have a veranda. Those on the third floor have an open view. Hearty regional meals.

▶ *Go back to D 618.*

Angoustrine

Walk up to the Romanesque **church** (🕐☀ *Jul and Aug: guided tours daily except Sat-Sun 10am-noon.*) at the top of the village to admire the **altarpieces**★, particularly that dedicated to St Martin, which depicts a knight in the central alcove and, on the painted panels, some of the saint's miraculous feats (including rescuing a sailor and a hanged man).

Chaos de Targasonne

This gigantic heap of granite boulders, of fantastically contorted shapes, was deposited by glaciers in the Quaternary Era.

A short distance (2km/1.2mi) on from the Chaos de Targasonne there is a view of the border mountains from Canigou to Puigmal, and of the more jagged Sierra del Cadi.

Odeillo

The church contains a 13C Virgin and Child, known as the Madonna of Font-Romeu, for most of the year (except during the grazing season from June to September). In the summer months, a 15C Virgin of the Hermitage takes its place.

Not far from the village stands the huge concave mirror of the **four solaire** (♿ *Jul and Aug: 10am-7.30pm; Jan-May and Oct-Dec: 10am-12.30pm, 2-6pm; Jun and Sep: 10am-6pm.* 🕐 *Closed 1 Jan and 25 Dec.* ☎ *6€ (no charge: children under 9).* ☎ *04 68 30 77 86)*, or solar furnace, which was inaugurated in 1969. The sunny slopes of this side of the valley can be seen reflected in the mirror's enormous parabolic surface (1 800m²/19 400sq ft), consisting of 9 130 smaller mirrors. The sun's rays are focused onto the mirror by 63 heliostats (flat mirrors

A. Thuillier/MICHELIN

Solar furnace

which can be positioned at various angles) arranged in rows up the hillside in front of the mirror. Solar energy (1 000 thermal kW) is thus concentrated into an 80cm/31in diameter space in which the temperature can exceed 3 500°C/6 300°F. The installation is used to process refractory and mineral ore components and to test materials for resistance to thermal shock.

Font-Romeu★★

♿ *See FONT-ROMEU.*

The road runs through the pine forest just above **Bolquère**, a picturesque village with a little church perched on a promontory, to the Mont-Louis plateau, leading into the Aude Valley and the Conflent region. At the junction with N 116, there is a monument to Emmanuel Brousse, a former member of parliament for Cerdagne.

Mont-Louis★

♿ *See MONT-LOUIS.*

LOOKING FOR A THRILL...

Compagnie des guides des Pyrénées catalanes – *Av. Serrat-de-l'Ours - 66210 Bolquère -* ☎ *04 68 30 39 66 or 06 14 84 92 99.* All-level courses and guided excursions: climbing, mountain biking, rambling, white-water sports, via ferrata.

...OR JUST A QUIET TIME?

Guide de pêche Marc Ribot – *16 av. des Lupins - 66210 Bolquère -* ☎ *04 68 30 30 93 or 06 89 99 22 64 - www.a-lamouche.com - closed early Nov-early Mar.* Explore the region while taking a course in fly-fishing.

The Shady Side of the Valley ("L'Ombrée")

From Mont-Louis to Bourg-Madame ③
112km/70mi – allow half a day.

From Mont-Louis (♿ *see MONT-LOUIS*), N 116 climbs steadily to the wide grassy threshold of La Perche Pass (*alt 1 579m/5 179ft*) linking the valleys of the Têt (Conflent) and the Segre (Cerdagne). To the south rises the Cambras d'Azó, with a very regular glacial cirque scooped out of it. Driving through the high moorland on the road to Eyne, there is an ever-broadening **panorama**★ of the Cerdagne: from left to right are the ragged outline of the Sierra del Cadi, Puigcerdà rising out of the bottom of the valley on its morainal base, the mountains on the Andorra border (Campcardos summit) and the Carlit massif.

▶ *Turn left onto D 29.*

Eyne

This attractive terraced village in a shell-shaped site is a small ski resort.

As you enter the village, you will see an annex of the **Musée de Cerdagne** (○ *Early Jul to mid-Sep: 11am-7pm; rest of the year, tours by request daily except Sat-Sun 8am-noon, 2-6pm. Guided tours of the botanical garden.* ○ *Closed public holidays except 14 Jul and 15 Aug.* ◎ *3.50€; children under 12: no charge).* ☎ *04 68 04 78 66.)* housed in old farm buildings. Water is the theme of the museum; there are plans for a botanical garden of endemic plants.

▶ *Follow D 33 S towards Llo.*

Llo★

This picturesque village is built on steep slopes at the mouth of a ravine through which a tributary of the Sègre flows. A watchtower dominates the scene. Further downhill is a Romanesque church, which features a doorway with the middle arch moulding decorated with bosses shaped like, inter alia, faces and spirals.

Gorges du Sègre★

▶ *Leave from the church in Llo.*

The Sègre flows down from the Puigmal massif through a gorge which can be followed back up as far as the third bridge over the torrent. On the way, admire a beautiful rock which is needle-shaped when seen from downstream.

Saillagouse

One of the production centres for the famous Cerdagne charcuterie.

▶ *Continue along N 116 towards Puigcerdà.*

Ste-Léocadie

Kids Cal Mateau farm houses the **Musée de Cerdagne** (○ *Guided tours mid-Jul to end Sep.* ◎ *3.50€ (children: 1.50€).* ☎ *04 68 04 95 54) (annex in Eyne,* ċ *see above).* This fine 17C-18C building is the setting of various exhibitions about shepherds, *la matança* (slaughtering of a pig), traditional horse-breeding and making flasks out of animal skins among other things.

▶ *Turn left onto D 89 leading to the Puigmal ski resort; when you come to the edge of the forest, take the surfaced forest road to the right just after a hairpin bend.*

Table d'orientation de Ste-Léocadie

Alt 1 681m/5 513ft. The viewing table is on the left, at the beginning of a bend, below road level. There is a **panorama**★ of the Cerdagne, opposite the gap formed by the Carol Valley through which Fontfrède summit can be seen.

▶ *Go back to D 89 and turn right.*

The mountain road leads up the Err Valley.

▶ *Go back to N 116, turn left and a little further on left again (D 30).*

Routes forestières d'Osséja★

Just above Osséja, leave the Valcebollère road to follow the route forestière, which forks at the edge of one of the largest forests of mountain pines in the Pyrenees. Take the right fork, which, after crossing the Col de Pradeilles on the brow of Puigmal, leads to boundary post 504 (Courne Mourère summit, about 2 205m/7 232ft above sea level). There are **views**★ of the

---

SPA BREAK

Les Sources de la vallée de Llo – *Rte des Gorges de Llo - 66800 Llo - ☎ 04 68 04 74 55 - Jul-Aug: daily 9.30am-8pm; Sep-Jun: daily 10am-7.30pm - closed early Nov-mid Dec - adults: 6€, children: 4€.* Take a bath in sulphurous springs at 35° and 37°C. Snack bar with freshly squeezed fruit juice, pancakes and waffles.

ċ *For coin ranges, see the Legend at the back of the guide.*

FAMILY STYLE

La Brasserie – *66800 Saillagouse - ☎ 04 68 04 72 08.* At the Hôtel Planes, occupying an old coaching stop in the centre of Saillagouse village, La Brasserie offers a simpler menu than its restaurant, which is very successful. Family cuisine.

Cerdagne, the mountains on the Andorra border and, to the south, the sierras of Catalonia.

▷ *Go back down to Osséja via the other branch of the fork in the road (completing a loop) and turn left onto N 116.*

Hix

Once the residence of the counts of Cerdagne and commercial capital of the region until the 12C, Hix declined to the rank of simple hamlet when King Alfonso of Aragón had the town transferred to the less vulnerable site of "Mont Cerdan" (Puigcerdà) in 1177, and more particularly once the collection of guinguettes nearby had been made the centre of local administration under the name of Bourg-Madame in 1815.

The little Romanesque **church** *(Other than in high season, guided tours by request at the Bourg-Madame tourist office. ☎ 04 68 04 55 35.)* houses two interesting works of art. On the right, the large altarpiece painted in the early 16C and dedicated to St Martin incorporates a 13C seated Madonna. The Romanesque Christ with dishevelled hair exudes a certain air of gentleness.

Bourg-Madame

  See 1 *above.*

CÉRET

POPULATION 7 291

MICHELIN LOCAL MAP 344: H-8

ALSO SEE LE BOULOU

The town of Céret in the Vallespir region is the lively hub of Catalan tradition in the northern Pyrenees, with activities such as bullfights and *sardana* dancing. It is a major fruit growing area thanks to well-irrigated orchards – local cherries ripen in mid-April and are among the earliest to reach the French markets. The town is becoming increasingly popular as an arts and crafts centre.

Sights

Old Céret

Huge majestic plane trees offer plenty of often welcome shade to those strolling between place de la République and place de la Liberté. Remnants of the original ramparts include a fortified gateway, the Porte de France, in place de la République and a restored section of another gateway, the Porte d'Espagne, in place Pablo-Picasso.

Address Book

For coin ranges, see the Legend at the back of the guide.

EATING OUT

Le Chat qui Rit – *À la Cabanasse, 1.5km/1mi from Céret on rte Amélie -* ☎ 04 68 87 02 22 - jean-paul.vander-elst@tiscali.fr *- closed 7 Jan-5 Feb, 26 Nov-3 Dec, Sun evening except Jul -Aug and Mon.* This unpretentious restaurant in a traditional house beside the road appeals to those with a healthy appetite, who will meet their match in the hors-d'œuvre and dessert buffets. As if these were not enough, there is a main course too.

Brasserie Le Carré – *1 bd La Fayette -* ☎ 04 68 87 37 88 - contact@les-feuillants.com *- closed Sun evening and Mon except between 16 Jun-14 Sep.* The second restaurant under the sign Les Feuillants greets its guests with a contemporary style veranda where *La Corrida*, a painting by Michel Becker, captures the attention of guests. Brasserie fare and regional theme menus at set times.

Hostal dels Trabucayres – *66480 Las Illas - 17km/10.5mi SE of Céret on D 618 and D 13 -* ☎ 04 68 83 07 56 - *closed 1 Jan-20 Mar, 25-30 Oct, Tues and Wed Sep-Jun.* This country inn in a charming village in the middle of the cork-oaks has been taking in travellers since the mid 19C. Rooms are modest and the fare is simple and typical of the region. It is a good stopover for those walking the GR10. Gîte for hire.

WHERE TO STAY

Hôtel Les Arcades – *1 pl. Picasso -* ☎04 68 87 12 30 - *closed 21 Dec-4 Jan -* 🅿 *- 30 rms;* 6€. This family-run hotel at the heart of the village is owned by two brothers and houses an amusing collection of posters, lithographs, and

paintings left by artists passing through. The rooms at the back are quieter than those on the façade.

ON THE TOWN

Bigaro Bar – *14 r. Mirabeau -* ☎ 04 68 87 09 04 - bigaro@club-internet.fr - summer: 4pm-5am; winter: 6pm-5am – closed Mon in winter. Pierre and Nathalie extend a warm welcome to visitors to the oldest bar in Céret (1928). They organise painting exhbits and concerts here.

La Chunga – *6 pl. des Tilleuls -* ☎ 04 68 87 34 68 - Jul -Aug: Mon-Thu 9pm-6am, Fri-Sun 6.30pm-6am; Jun-Sept: Tues-Thu 9pm-6am, Fri-Sun 6.30pm-6am - tapas at 3.05€ and draught from 2.29€. This music bar transforms itself into a disco every evening. Musical offerings include: rock and funk, flamenco, French popular music and others. With its roughcast stone walls and plain decor the style is essentially rustic. Clientele aged 20-35 years. Good party venue.

SOMETHING DIFFERENT

Usine Sabaté – *Espace Tech Ulrich -* ☎ 04 68 87 20 20 - daily except weekends and holidays 9am-5pm by appointment - closed Aug. Guided tour of the factory which turns out 500 million corks a year.

Delta Club Aude et Po – *64 rue de la République -* ☎ 04 68 87 25 54. Hang-gliding and paragliding.

Céret de Toros – This is the name of the local festivities which take place during the 2nd weekend in July: young cows let loose in the streets, various street shows, bullfighting.

Sardana Folk festival – Teams of dancers meet and compete at night in the bullring during the 2nd fortnight in July.

The "Céret School"

At the beginning of the 20C, the Catalan sculptor, Manolo Hugué (1872-1945), a friend of Picasso, came to live in Céret. He was joined by the composer Déodat de Séverac (to whom there is a monument with a medallion by Manolo next to the tourist office), Picasso himself, Braque, Juan Gris, Herbin, Kisling and Max Jacob, the poet and painter.

After an interruption due to the First World War, Manolo, Pierre Brune and Pinkus Krémègne encouraged visits from other artists; among many others, Masson and Soutine came in 1919 and Chagall in 1928-29. Brune was responsible for founding a museum of modern art, which opened in 1950 with an exhibition of works donated by artists who had stayed in the town. Since 1966, Céret has hosted important exhibitions of contemporary art, making the town something of a Mecca for artistic creativity.

A monument has been erected opposite the bullring (*arènes*) in honour of Picasso – *Sardane de la Paix* (1973). It is made of wrought iron welded to stainless steel and based on a drawing by the artist.

Like several towns in Roussillon, Céret commissioned Aristide Maillol to design its First World War Memorial.

Old Bridge★ (Vieux pont)

The old bridge more than holds its own in comparison with the nearby modern road and railway bridges. The 14C "devil's leap" spans the Tech in a single 45m/150ft arch, 22m/72ft above the river. There is a lovely view on one side of the Canigou massif and, on the other, the Albères range, sloping down to the Perthus Pass.

▶ *Walk downstream to the sawmill for a good view of the bridge.*

Musée d'Art moderne★★

&. ⏱ *Early Jul to mid-Sep: 10am-7pm; mid-Sep to end Jun: 10am-6pm (Oct-Apr: daily except Tue).* ⏱ *Closed 1 Jan, 1 May, 1 Nov, 25 Dec.* ✍ *5.50€ (children under 12: no charge).* ☎ *04 68 87 27 76.*

This modern building, with a sober main façade off boulevard Maréchal-Joffre, was designed by Barcelona architect Jaime Freixa. The entrance doorway is flanked on either side by a mural diptych by Antoni Tàpies on enamelled lava blocks.

Inside, spacious galleries are harmoniously arranged around patios which let in the beautiful Mediterranean light to enhance the works on display. As well as temporary exhibitions, the ground floor is home to ceramics by Picasso, works from the Céret period (1909-50) and contemporary works of art from 1960 to 1970.

The first floor is given over to contemporary art: Tony Grand, Joan Brossa, Perejaume, Viallat, Tàpies, Dominique Gauthier, Jean-Louis Vila, Susana Solano and Jean Capdeville.

Grotte de CLAMOUSE★★

MICHELIN MAP 339: G-6

ALSO SEE GANGES

The Clamouse cave is hollowed out of the Causse du Sud Larzac, near where the gorge of the River Hérault opens onto the Aniane plain. It was explored in 1945, during an exceptional summer drought, and opened to tourists in 1964.

A Bit of History

The **cave** takes its name from the resurgent spring which bubbles out below the road, cascading noisily into the Hérault after very heavy rain, amply justifying its dialect name of Clamouse ("howler"). However, there is a poignant popular legend according to which the origin of the name is a mother's cry of grief. The story goes that there was once a peasant family living in the Hérault gorge. The parents s~ their eldest son up onto the causse to work as a shepherd. One d~ was visiting his family, he recognised to his surprise a carved stick a swallow-hole out on the *causse*. His mother had found it in the h regularly came to collect water, and they deduced it must have bee

218

Crystallisations

an underground river. After this, the shepherd boy regularly sent things to his parents using this route. But one day, he was pulled into the swallow-hole by a more than usually vigorous sheep, and his poor mother saw the body of her son come floating down on the peaceful waters of the stream.

Tour *allow 1hr; temperature: 17°C/62.5°F*

The guided tour leads through various natural galleries to the Gabriel Vila chamber, also called the sand chamber because of the layers of sand the river deposits on it each time it floods. At first the route leads through various caverns, following the old river bed, along which water still runs when the river is in spate. These initial galleries, in which the chiselled, jagged rock forms a ghostly backdrop, are a good illustration of the effects of the slow corrosive action of water on the easily dissolved dolomitic limestone of which the cave is made.

The cave deposits formed at a time when the upper cave galleries were completely submerged with water. Then the Hérault scoured out a deeper bed for itself, the flow level of underground water dropped and the galleries through which the tour leads dried out and became fossilised. This was when the first rock deposits formed – several million years ago.

The next galleries contain two types of formation: the classic calcite stalagmites, stalactites, columns, discs and draperies, in some cases coloured by mineral deposits; and **delicate crystallisations**, relatively young formations (several thousand years old), sparkling white and much more rarely found in caves than the former – **crystalline "flowers"** of aragonite arranged in "bouquets," showers of **tube-like formations** which sway in the slightest draught, weird and wonderful **eccentrics, crystalline dams** transforming subterranean lakes into beautiful jewellery caskets containing **"cave pearls"** (pisolites). The Couloir Blanc (White Corridor) and Cimetière (Graveyard) feature a particularly impressive number and variety of formations. At the exit of the Cimetière is a huge translucent white concretion made of several discs run together, known as the "Méduse" (jellyfish).

A man-made exit tunnel leads back to the open. There is a picturesque view of the Hérault Valley and an exhibition on life in prehistoric times at Clamouse.

Delicate Crystallisations

The Grotte de Clamouse is renowned for the great number and variety of delicate crystalline formations it features. Unlike the calcite formations usually found in caves, those at Clamouse are made of aragonite, calcite or a mixture of these two different forms of calcium carbonate crystallisation. Their clear white colour, another particularity, indicates that they contain hardly any impurities or mineral deposits.

The underground network at Clamouse provides a set of conditions well-suited to the development of such crystallisations: dolomitic rocks which lend themselves to the formation of aragonite; porous rock walls; plentiful supply of water; above average temperatures; and a permanent slight draught.

Grotte de la COCALIÈRE ★

MICHELIN LOCAL MAP 339: J-K 3

This cave northwest of St-Ambroix on the Gard plateau, contains a network of explored galleries, running for over 46km/29mi underground. In addition, the site of La Cocalière has shown itself to have been a densely populated prehistoric settlement between the Paleolithic period (40000 BC) and the Iron Age (400 BC).

▷ *From St-Ambroix, follow D 904 towards Aubenas then turn right onto a minor road beyond the intersection with the Courry road.*

Tour

🕐 ☞ *Jul and Aug: guided tours (1hr) 10am-6pm; mid-Mar to end Jun and early Sep to mid-Oct: 10am-noon, 2-5pm. ☞ 7€ (children: 5€). ☎ 04 66 24 34 74. Guided tour 1hr; temperature 14°C/57.2°F.*

At the end of the entrance tunnel, a path leads for about 1 200m/1 310yd along the bottom of a horizontal gallery linking the various chambers.

The cave contains a remarkable number and variety of deposits and formations. These are reflected in pools of water, some fed by tiny waterfalls, on either side of the path. Numerous discs – concretions with impressive diameters whose formation continues to mystify experts – are suspended from or attached to the overhanging rockface often growing upwards in an irregular way. Some of the rocky roofs feature a sort of geometric coffering of fragile stalactites which are white, if made of pure calcite, or of varying colours, if bearing metal oxides. A small underground lake enclosed by a natural dam contains some cave pearls still in the process of being formed. After the speleologists' camp, walk through the Chaos chamber beneath roofs covered with evidence of erosion to get to a gallery of frozen falls and eccentrics which overlooks an imposing, sparkling waterfall and wells linked to the lower levels where underground rivers flow. Pass a prehistoric deposit before taking a small train back to the entrance.

Outside, in the immediate surroundings of the cave, note: a dolmen, some tumuli (piles of earth or stones built above graves), small drystone constructions like the *bories* of Provence, prehistoric shelters and a variety of karst phenomena (caves, sinkholes, faults).

🖋 *For coin ranges, see the Legend at the back of the guide.*

"THE FRAGRANT BASTIDE"

🍽🍽 **La Bastide des Senteurs** – *30500 St-Victor-de-Malcap - 8km/5mi from the Grotte de la Cocalière on D 904 and D 51C - ☎ 04 66 60 24 45 - subileau@bastide-senteurs.com – Feb-Oct daily (evenings only Jul-Aug except Sun and holidays); Oct-Apr: closed Sun evening and Mon.* The young owners have made a charming stopover point from this abandoned country house. The food is good, the decor plain but elegant and the welcome friendly. Everything here reflects the flavours and colours of the Mediterranean. Pretty rooms, swimming pool and pleasant terrace.

COLLIOURE★★

POPULATION 2 763

MICHELIN LOCAL MAP 344: J-7

ALSO SEE LA CÔTE VERMEILLE

Collioure is an extremely attractive small town on the Côte Vermeille, against the backdrop of the foothills of the Albères range. It has much to offer, in terms of both charm and amenities, and attracts huge crowds of tourists every year.

With its fortified church, so close to the coast that it seems to be actually in the Mediterranean, its old royal castle separating the two little ports, with their fishing nets, brightly coloured Catalan boats and characteristic masts, its old streets with colourful, flower-bedecked balconies and picturesque flights of steps, its seaside promenade and its outdoor cafés and boutiques with their inviting window displays, this little fortress town has a very distinctive character.

Numerous painters, attracted by its colourfulness, have chosen to immortalise it on their canvases. As early as 1910, the first of the "**Fauves** had made it their meeting place – Derain, Braque, Othon, Friesz, Matisse and others. Later, it was the turn of Picasso and Foujita.

Boramar beach is still a favourite subject for numerous modern artists.

A Bit of History

Origins of the town – Medieval Collioure was first and foremost the trading port for Roussillon, from where the famous "ornate" cloth from Perpignan was exported. This was when the Catalan naval forces ruled the Mediterranean as far as the Levant. In 1463, the invasion of Louis XI's troops marked the beginning of a turbulent period for the town. The castle was built on the rocky spur separating the port into two coves, around the square keep built by the kings of Majorca. Charles V and Philip II converted it to a citadel, reinforced by Fort St-Elme and Fort Miradou. After the Peace Treaty of the Pyrenees, Vauban put the finishing touches to the defences – the enclosed town was razed to the ground in 1670 to make way for a vast glacis. The lower town then became the main town.

Sights

▶ Walk to the old port or "Port d'Amont" via quai de l'Amirauté on the banks of the "Ravin du Douy", which is usually dry.

Chemin du Fauvisme

A waymarked route has been laid out through the streets of Collioure, leading past some of the views painted by Henri Matisse and André Derain. Each stage (20 in all)

L. Campion/MICHELIN

Collioure

Address Book

For coin ranges, see the Legend at the back of the guide.

EATING OUT

La Frégate – 24 quai Camille-Pelletan - ☎ 04 68 82 06 05 – closed 6 Jan-7 Feb. The inside of this restaurant is the focus of interest. The walls of both dining rooms are covered with pretty azulejo style tiles made by Spanish and Portuguese craftsmen. There is no view of the sea, but the terrace is pleasant nonetheless. As far as the cuisine is concerned, the influence is Mediterranean. Some rooms available.

Neptune – Rte de Port-Vendres - ☎ 04 68 82 02 27 – closed 2-31 Jan, 8-19 Dec, Mon in Jul-Aug; Sep-Jun: closed Tue-Wed. There is an unimpeded view of the old harbour from the two terraces of this restaurant, which offers a "moulerie" (mussels) option for those wanting to admire the countryside on a budget. Inside, the elegant decor is typical of the local region. Seafood and local specialities.

WHERE TO STAY

Ambeille – Rte d'Argelès - ☎ 04 68 82 08 74 - closed Oct-Mar – 🄿 - 21 rms; ⌁ 6€. 1970s building housing a simple family-run hotel. Rooms are generous in size and those on the façade have a pleasant view of the sea and the rooftops of the picturesque Catalan village.

SHOPPING

Le Dominicain Cave – Pl. Orphila, Port d'Avall - ☎ 04 68 82 05 63 – 8am-noon, 2-6pm. In a former Dominican convent dating from the 13C, this wine cooperative sells Banyuls and Collioure wines. Friendly welcome, tasting encouraged!

Anchois Desclaux – RN 114 - ☎ 04 68 82 05 25 – 9am-noon, 2-6pm (9am-8pm in summer). A visit here will show you the traditional techniques for salting and preserving anchovies – and you can sample the results.

Maison Roques – Rte d'Argelès - ☎ 04 68 82 04 99 - roque.collioure@wanadoo.fr - daily 8am-7.30pm – workshop visits Mon-Fri 8am-noon, 2-5pm. Since its foundation in 1923, Maison Roque has prepared its anchovies to its own recipe, handed down from father to son. The shop downstairs is great, but try to include a visit to the workshop upstairs for plenty of tips on what can be done with anchovies.

ON THE TOWN

Le Petit Café – Bd du Boromar - mid Jun-Sep: daily 9am-2am; Oct-Dec, mid Feb-mid Jun: Thu-Sun 9am-2am. This charming little cocktail bar was decorated by a local painter in a style drawing heavily on Mucha. It is quite common to meet some of Collioure's resident artists here. Muted music provides a suitable background to discussion and socializing.

Bar des Templiers – 12 quai de l'Amirauté - ☎ 04 68 98 31 10 - info@hotel-templiers.com - daily 7.30am-2am. The Templiers hotel is Collioure's leading address, and it has accommodated some famous figures from the art world (Derain, Picasso, Matisse). The walls of the bar are covered with paintings from this period. Regulars and tourists rub shoulders in this authentic and romantic bar.

Le Piano piano – 18 r. Rière - ☎ 04 68 98 07 23 - Apr-end Oct: daily 6.30pm-1am - closed Oct-Apr. Very lively, friendly bar where flamenco and world music are popular. At the back there is a small room with leather benches and a piano. The menu lists more than 50 varieties of beer and tapas. Clientele made up of regulars with the occasional tourist.

SPORT

C.I.P. de Collioure – 15 r. de la Tour-d'Auvergne – 25km/15mi S of Perpignan on RN 114 - ☎ 04 68 82 07 16 - www.cip-collioure.com - daily 9am-noon, 2pm-6pm. Diving, sailing and wind-surfing centre which provides equipment and professional training for these activities.

---

is indicated by the reproduction of the relevant painting on a panel. (Guided tours are also available, contact the tourist office for details: ☎ 04 68 98 07 16).

Église Notre-Dame-des-Anges

This church was built between 1684 and 1691 to replace the church in the upper town which had been razed on Vauban's orders. The distinctive bell-tower with its pink dome used to be the lighthouse for the old port.

The dark interior houses nine surprisingly ornate carved wooden, gilded **altarpieces**★ (explanation provided on the left of the chancel). That of the high altar is the work of Catalan artist Joseph Sunyer and dates back to 1698. It is an immense three-storey triptych occupying the whole of the retrochoir and, as a result, completely hiding the apse. All the statues are finely carved and well worth admiring. Also by Joseph Sunyer, note the Holy Sacrament altarpiece on the left of the chancel, more modest in size, but just as delicately carved.

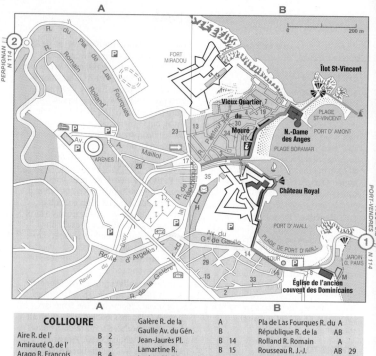

Treasury – The sacristy houses a beautiful Louis XIII vestment cupboard, 15C paintings, a 16C reliquary and a 17C Madonna, which is thought to have belonged to the older church.

Ancien îlot St-Vincent

The former island is connected to the church by two beaches back to back. Behind the little chapel, a vast panorama encompasses the Côte Vermeille. A sea wall leads to the lighthouse.

▶ *Go back.*

Old district of Mouré

This old district near the church is a very pleasant place for a stroll with its steep, flower-filled back streets.

▶ *Cross the Douy, at the end of the marina.*

The path along the quayside skirts the impressive walls of the Château Royal.
From the western car park, towards the Douy, there is an excellent **view** of the town and port; in the background are the Albères mountains, towering above the sea.

▶ *Continue to the Port d'Avall beach called the "Faubourg."*

Anchovies From Collioure

Anchovies, a speciality from Collioure, have been preserved in the same way for generations. Once brought to harbour, the anchovies – minus heads and guts – are left to pickle in vats of brine for a few months *(May to August)*. They are then rinsed, their backbones removed and they are left to drain. Finally, the anchovies are put into glass jars or tins filled with oil, either arranged flat or carefully rolled around a caper.
To compete with foreign competition, anchovies imported from Morocco for example, local producers have diversified, adding tubes of anchovy paste and olives stuffed with anchovies to their product lines. Collioure anchovies feature prominently in many Catalan dishes. *Anchoïade*, a paste of anchovies mashed with olive oil, garlic and basil, is delicious spread on French toast as an accompaniment to apéritifs.

On the way, admire the delightful coloured boats. It is also pleasant to stop for a while beneath the palm trees, perhaps to watch one of the many lively games of boules taking place.

Église de l'ancien couvent des Dominicains

This old church now houses the local wine cooperative.

Château Royal

🕐 *Jun-Sep: 10am-6pm (last admission 45min before closing); Oct-May: 9am-5pm.* 🕐 *Closed 1 Jan, 1 May, 25 Dec.* 🎫 *3€.* ☎ *04 68 82 06 43. www.cg66.fr.*

The imposing bulk of this castle, built on a former Roman site, juts into the sea between the Port d'Amont and the Port d'Avall. It was the summer residence of the kings of Majorca from 1276 to 1344 before being taken over by the kings of Aragón. Vauban had the outer wall added and the village sprawling at its feet demolished to make room for a glacis. The visit includes the underground passages, the parade ground, the 16C prison (in which there is a Catalan forge), the 13C chapel, the main courtyard, the Queen's bedchamber, the upper rooms and the ramparts with their sentry path. The 17C barracks house exhibitions on grape vines, cork, the manufacture of Sorède whips and *espadrilles* (rope-soled sandals) and Catalan boats. Several rooms are reserved for temporary exhibitions.

Le COMMINGES★★

MICHELIN LOCAL MAP 343: C-6 AND 7 TO D-6

The region of Comminges, historically and ecclesiastically a province of the ancient kingdom of Gascony, lies at the centre of the Pyrenees, halfway between the Atlantic and the Mediterranean. It was at one time attached to the Couserans area and Val d'Aran. Geographically, Comminges extends from the heights of the Upper Garonne basin to the mild alluvial plains irrigated by the river after it emerges from the mountains. The southern limits include the peaks of the Maladetta massif (Pic d'Aneto, at 3 404m/11 164ft, is the highest peak in the Pyrenees). The northern flatlands stretch as far as Muret, 19km/12mi from Toulouse, taking in grandiose landscapes, a renowned spa (Bagnères-de-Luchon) and a famous artistic and spiritual centre (St-Bertrand-de-Comminges).

Geographical Notes

Granite and marble – The Luchon sector of the Pyrenees, still scoured by a number of glaciers, forms an east-west barrier of granite crests, all of them over 3 000m/ 9 800ft high. Within this massif lie the valleys of the Oô (Spijoles, Gourgs Blancs, Perdiguère) and the Lys (Crabioules, Maupas). The most marked depression, Port de Vénasque (Vénasque Pass), is still 2 448m/8 030ft above sea level.

Limestone foothills north of the Marignac basin, on the east bank of the Garonne, culminate in Pic de Cagire (alt 1 912m/6 272ft), which rises from the forest to form a striking landmark in front of the snow-covered crests in the distance. The forest, mainly beech, continues eastwards as far as Massif d'Arbas (Pic de Paloumère – alt 1 608m/5 276ft), which is honeycombed with subterranean cavities and frequently used as a training ground for speleologists.

The lower part of Gascony, for years ignored by sightseers and tourists, has revealed evidence, during the past century, of an important colonisation in Paleolithic times (Aurignac, Save and Seygouade Gorges, near Montmaurin), as well as the remains of Gallo-Roman villas (Montmaurin). It was here in the 5C, before the first barbarian invasions, that the golden era of large estates, furnished with marble from the quarries of St-Béat, drew to a close in Aquitaine.

Pyrenean Garonne – In Vallée d'Aran, on the Spanish side of the frontier, the word *garona* is used for several different mountain streams. The largest, Río Garona de Ruda, rises near Monte Saboredo (alt 2 830m/9 285ft), south of Puerto de la Bonaigua (Bonaigua Pass). Several tributaries flow into the river, notably Río Garona de Jueu, which appears in the middle of a forest as a spring gushing from rock fissures in a fan of cataracts 30m/100ft high. According to the speleologist Norbert Casteret, who made a study of the north face of the Maladetta in 1931, the waters are a resurgence of melted ice from glaciers higher up the massif.

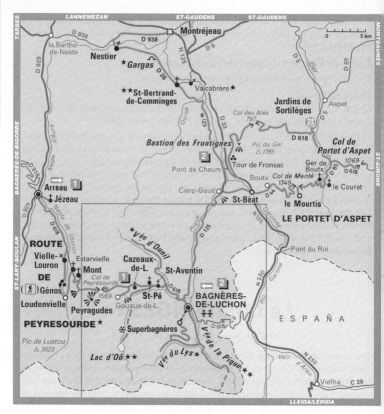

The Garonne reaches France at Pont du Roi. At this point, it is no more than a typical high mountain stream, with a steeply sloping bed and a variable flow, shrunken in winter and swollen in May and June. In the Comminges region, the Garonne is broadened by the Pique, the River Ourse and River Aure. At Montréjeau, flowing into a regular channel lying along the foot of the range from La Barthe-de-Neste to Boussens, it curves suddenly eastwards to cross St-Gaudens plain. The Boussens *cluse* (transverse valley) marks the Garonne's final exit from the Pyrenees.

A Bit of History

A creation of the Romans – In the year 76 BC, the Roman Triumvir, Pompey, on his way to a campaign in Spain, annexed the upper valley of the Garonne and incorporated it in the Roman province of Transalpine Gaul. On his return four years later, he founded the town of Lugdunum Convenarum (today St-Bertrand-de-Comminges) attracting a population of *convenae* (people of all origins) largely drawn from the ranks of brigands, mountain dwellers and shepherds. The town prospered and grew rapidly.

In the more remote valleys of the Pyrenees, local devotion to pagan deities was intense. These cults managed to survive for many years alongside both Celtic and Imperial divinities, dying out only gradually under the influence of Christianity. Most of the mountain churches in the Luchon area – especially in the Oueil and Larboust valleys – have stonework built into their walls which once formed part of the fabric of pagan temples.

Comté de Comminges – Comminges, which at first formed part of the Duchy of Aquitaine, was joined to Couserans in the 10C to create a fief under the suzerainty of the Comtes de Toulouse and reverted to France in 1454. However, the treaty of Corbeil, concluded between St Louis of France and Iago (James) I of Spain in 1258, reserved the claim of Aragón to the Vallée d'Aran, which today still forms part of Spanish Catalonia.

Failing agreement on the delineation of a new *département* to be called the Central Pyrenees, the Comminges district was incorporated into the Haute-Garonne département in 1790.

Painted Churches in the Vallée Du Louron

Several of the Romanesque churches in the Vallée du Louron have amazingly intricate paintings on their ceilings. They were decorated by French and Spanish artists in the 16C, benefiting from the newly acquired wealth of the Spanish after their discovery of the New World. The recurring theme in these churches is the Last Judgement – it can be seen in Vielle-Luron, Mont and Jézeau. The sometimes naïve representations of the devil and monstrous creatures are particularly evocative. Hell is a dominant theme in the Christian iconography of the time. On the eve of the Wars of Religion, local Christianity was strengthened by the assertion of Catholicism under the influence of the dioceses of Comminges and the Council of Trent.

These churches are not always open to the public. For further information, if you wish to visit them, contact the **Maison du tourisme de la vallée du Louron** in Bordères-Louron – ☎ 05 62 99 92 00.

Excursions★

Round tour from Arreau 1 *52km/32mi – 4hr.*

Arreau – ♿ *See La BIGORRE.*

▶ *Leave Arreau E via D 112.*

Jézeau

At the top of the village, the **church** houses a fine Renaissance **reredos**, of carved, gilded and painted wood. The wooden vault in the single nave is covered in paintings depicting the Last Judgement, a major theme in Christian iconography.

▶ *Go back to D 618 SE of Arreau.*

The road climbs up the valley of the River Louron, at first hemmed in by two wooded slopes and then running out, south of Avajan, into an upland basin scattered with villages, most of them in a damp environment and partly abandoned. This depression, closed off to the south, is overlooked on the left (east) by Pic de Hourgade (2 964m/9 724ft), a mountain broken up into sharp spines, separating snow-filled valleys.

Vielle-Louron

Église St-Mercurial is one of the most beautiful painted churches in the Vallée du Louron. The Tree of Jesse and Christ surrounded by the four Evangelists can be seen in the wooden vaulting. There are fine **paintings** in the 16C sacristy – sardonic demons torment the damned, who are being cooked in a cauldron or devoured by a monster.

Génos

15min round trip on foot. At the top of the hill, just before the entrance sign, take the road leading up to the church.

🚶 A path, skirting the cemetery on the left, leads to the castle ruins, attractively situated on a glacial threshold, overlooking a lake with various water sports facilities and providing a **view** of the valley with the mountains in the background.

▶ *Drive onto Loudenvielle on the other side of the lake.*

Loudenvielle

L'Arixo (🕐 *Jul and Aug: daily except Tue 10am-noon, 2.30-6.30pm; other school holidays: daily except Mon and Tue. 2.30-6.30pm; rest of the year: Sat 2-6pm, Wed, Thu and Fri by request at the town hall. ☜ 4.57€ (under age 18: 2.30€). ☎ 05 62 99 95 94 or 05 62 99 68 02)* offers an insight into life, traditional housing and religious art in the Louron Valley. Film, Italian theatre and interactive model illustrating painted churches.

▶ *Follow D 25 running along the opposite shore of Génos Lake and drive to Estarvielle via Armenteule.*

The church in **Estarvielle** contains paintings of the soldiers gambling for Jesus' clothes.

Mont

The Romanesque church has a square belfry, pierced with windows with small columns. A fresco is painted on the façade above the porch. Fine **paintings**, dating from 1574, and adorning the interior of the church, have been attributed to Melchior Rodigis – the Passion of Christ, the Prophet Isaiah announcing the coming of the Saviour, and the Evangelists.

Beyond the turn-off to Mont, there is a belvedere overlooking the Vallée de Louron. The road leads up through an anticlinal valley, the opposite slope of which is covered by the magnificent Balestas pine forest, and through Col de Peyresourde, at an altitude of 1 569m/5 148ft.

Peyragudes

This ski resort, which has developed on either side of the ridge separating the *départements* of Hautes-Pyrénées and Haute-Garonne, was created by the merger of two other resorts – Peyresourde and Les Agudes.

The hilltop just above the high altitude airport offers a **panoramic view**★ of the west face of the jagged, partly snow-covered Néouvielle massif. The descent on the Luchon side of the pass reveals all the natural splendour of the site.

It is worth leaving D 618 to take the cliff road to Gouaux-de-Larboust for the **views**★★ over the Vallée d'Oô and the slate roofs of Oô village. The fresh valley with its burgeoning ash and walnut trees gracefully rises to meet the high mountain landscape typical of the Luchon massif – mainly dark rock masses (Spijoles, Les Gourgs Blancs, Pic du Portillon d'Oô) where small glaciers glitter.

Ski area

Alt 1 600-2 400m/5 249-7 864ft. ⛷ *17 ski lifts.*

A total of 38 ski runs for skiers of all levels, especially down the impressively long Vallée Blanche run through a wide open cirque. 70 snow-making machines guarantee skiing at lower altitudes. The ski pass is valid in the other Haute-Garonne resorts. There are 4 loops of cross-country ski tracks totalling 15km/9mi. In January, the Peyragudes Rider's Cup snowboarding competition is a popular event.

Cazeaux-de-Larboust

The church is decorated with 15C **murals**, most of them restored with a heavy hand. Facing the entrance there is a curious Last Judgement showing the Virgin succouring Christ to lighten His suffering and calm His anger. The sword of justice falls from the hands of the Divine Judge.

Leaving Cazeaux there is a charming view of the church and houses of Castillon.

Chapelle St-Pé (St-Pierre-de-la-Moraine)

This is a pleasant place to stop. The walls of the chapel, and particularly the buttresses, incorporate many fragments of pagan funerary monuments. Here, as in all the upper parts of the Comminges district, there are many traces of ancient religions, notably Celtic and Roman.

Fresco in the church at Cazeaux-de-Larboust

St-Aventin

☞ *Leave the car 100m/110yd before the beginning of the ramp leading to the church.*

This hamlet boasts a majestic Romanesque **church** with some fine fragments of sculpture, including a 12C **Madonna and Child**★ (*on the pier right of the main door*). There is a remarkable bas-relief showing a furiously stamping bull uncovering the secret burial place of the martyr St Aventin, who had been beheaded by the heathens (*on a buttress, right*), and Gallo-Roman funerary monuments (*where the nave meets the apse*). Inside, note the pre-Romanesque font carved with symbolic animals (lambs, fish, doves) and the 12C mural paintings.

▶ *The tree-shaded road continues its descent towards the Bagnères-de-Luchon basin.*

LE PORTET D'ASPET

Round tour from Bagnères-de-Luchon ②
94km/58mi – 3hr

Bagnères-de-Luchon ⚕⚕

⚓ *See BAGNÈRES-DE-LUCHON.*

▶ *Leave Luchon N via D 125.*

Beyond Luchon, the first part of the route follows the Vallée de la Pique. Just before Cierp-Gaud, there are particularly fine views of the mountain mass forming the border (southeast), and the limestone Gar massif, surmounted by a large cross (northeast). The River Garonne (north) flows into the wide Marignac basin.

As it goes through the basin beneath the escarpments of Pic du Gar, D 44 passes several marble quarries and approaches St-Béat Gorge.

St-Béat

St-Béat, a former stronghold and the key to France – clearly displayed in the town's coat of arms – commanded the site where Val d'Aran opens out into Gascony. The grey houses splashed by the river form a semicircle at the bottom of the gorge. On the right bank, the 12C keep, used as a clock tower, along with a few crenellated ramparts, are all that remains of the 14C-15C citadel.

The local white and grey marble has made Béat famous since Roman times (⚓ *see MONTMAURIN*) and was used for many of the fountains and statues in the gardens of Versailles. The Roman quarry can be seen on D 44 just outside the village.

St-Béat is the homeland of Maréchal Gallieni (1849-1916). His family house can be seen in the side street, just after and opposite the post office. His statue stands on the promenade on the right bank of the River Garonne just beyond the church.

The road climbs quickly above the slate roofs of the village of Lez and the huddled roofs of Boutx.

Beyond, the road rises in a series of hairpin bends through a forest of conifers and arrives at **Col de Menté** (*alt 1 349m/4 426ft*).

Le Mourtis

Le Mourtis is a quiet and convivial winter sports resort. Chalets and apartment blocks, inhabited mainly during the skiing season, are scattered beneath a forest of age-old, lichen-covered fir trees – part of an enormous belt of woodland straddling the valleys of the Garonne and the Ger.

Descending the eastern slope of Menté Pass, the road passes through the narrow valley of the Upper Ger, strewn with isolated barns and villages perching on the slopes, their churches displaying unusual triple-spired belfry-walls **(Ger de Boutx, Le Couret)**. After passing the turn-off to Henne-Morte on the left, the route climbs again, more steeply.

Col de Portet d'Aspet

Alt 1 069m/3 507ft. From the slopes in front of the chalet-hotel by the pass, a mountain panorama opens out, with the dark, gently sloping pyramid of Mont Valier (*alt 2 838m/9 311ft*) in the background.

The Couserans district extends from the eastern side of the pass.

▶ *Turn back and continue the itinerary along D 618.*

The route follows the Vallée du Ger via a spectacular wooded gorge.

▶ *Turn right onto D 5 towards Sengouagnet.*

Jardins des Sortilèges

🕐 *Mid-Jul to mid-Sep: daily except Mon 10am-noon, 3-6pm; Jun and mid to end Sep: Sat-Sun 3-6pm.* 💰 *4.50€.* ☎ *05 61 88 81 08.*

These seven gardens are devoted to common plants and their secrets; for instance, did you know nettles have numerous benefits, or that certain weeds could be used in cooking?

▶ *Turn back then right onto D 618 again.*

From Col des Ares (alt 797m/2 615ft), the road continues to descend through the pretty Frontignes countryside.

Bastion des Frontignes

From the hairpin bend just before the village of Antichan there is a fine **view** of the Luchon massif and its glaciers. *Viewing table.*

Skirting Pic du Gar, the route now offers more and more extensive views, northwards over the valley of the River Garonne, and southwards to Bagnères-de-Luchon and the mountain cirque surrounding it. The ruins of the **Tour de Fronsac**, which appear on the left, are all that remains of an ancient fortress of the Comtes of Comminges. *At Pont de Chaum (Chaum bridge) turn right on N 125.*

St-Bertrand-de-Comminges★★

See St-BERTRAND-DE-COMMINGES.

▶ *Follow D 26.*

Grottes préhistoriques de Gargas

Jul and Aug: guided tours (45min) by appointment at the reception desk 9.30am-12.30pm, 2-7pm; Apr-Jun, Sep and Easter school holidays: 10am-noon, 2-6pm, Sun 2-6pm; Mar, Oct and Nov: 10am-noon, 2-5pm, Sun 2-7pm; Dec: 10am-noon, 2-4pm, Sun 2-4pm. Closed 1 Jan and 25 Dec. 5€ (6-12 years: 2.50€). 05 62 39 72 39.

These two-storey caves, inhabited by prehistoric man, contain many hand prints, carvings of animals, a few paintings and some fine concretions.

Nestier

The **calvary** standing on the slopes of Mont Arès is amazing! In 1854, the vicar of Nestier decided to build 12 stone chapels in a row on the slopes of Mont Arès. The tympanum of the 12th and largest of all has a ceramic decoration depicting the Crucifixion. An outdoor theatre added in 1990 stages various shows.

▶ *Drive N along D 75 to St-Laurent-de-Neste and turn right onto D 938.*

Montréjeau

Overlooking the confluence of the River Neste and River Garonne, this former *bastide* (stronghold) founded in 1272, is seen at its best on market days. Owing to its towering position, it offers several vantage points: place de Verdun (covered market and public gardens), place Valentin-Abeille (central fountain, arcading and fine timber-framed house at no 21), boulevard de Lassus (cliff road). **Views**★ extend to the Pyrenees of the Luchon area, beyond the wooded heights of the Barousse.

CONDOM

POPULATION 7 251

MICHELIN LOCAL MAP 336: E-6

Condom is the main town in the Armagnac region, an area with many attractive rural churches and manor houses. The old mansions of Condom itself give the town a typically Gascon appearance. Its economic activities – selling grain and Armagnac, flour-milling and the timber industry – are also the traditional activities of the region.

The River Baïse, stretching alongside the old quays, was channelled long ago to transport brandy to Bordeaux.

Town Centre *1hr 30min*

▶ *Start from place St-Pierre.*

Cathédrale St-Pierre★

The belfry, with its quadrangular tower, rises majestically above the cathedral, one of the last major edifices in the Gers region to be built (1507-31) in the Gothic style of South-West France.

The Flamboyant Gothic south door still has 24 small statues in the niches of the archivolt, including the lamb of John the Baptist, emblem of Jean Marre. Marre, the great building bishop of Condom (1496-1521), can be seen on the base of the empty niche in the central pier.

The nave is illuminated by windows with Flamboyant tracery. The stained glass in the chancel comes from a local workshop (1858) whereas that in the rest of the nave comes from a major workshop in Limoges (1969). The ribs of the vaulting are articulated around historiated keystones.

The neo-Gothic screen around the chancel has large statues of angels and saints made from terracotta moulded in 1844.

▶ *Walk round the chancel to the left.*

Above the door to the sacristy, a fine marble plaque commemorates the consecration of the cathedral in 1531. The Lady Chapel, at the east end, is a Gothic sanctuary which was once part of the old cathedral.

Cloisters★ – The cloisters were largely rebuilt in the 19C. St Catherine's Chapel (*now a public passageway*) off the eastern gallery of the cloisters, has attractive keystones on the polychrome vaulting.

Cloisters of St-Pierre Cathedral

A. Thuillier/MICHELIN

Chapelle des Évêques

🕐 *Mon-Thu 9am-noon, 2-5pm; Fri: 9am-noon, 1-4pm.*

Erected after the cathedral, the chapel was nevertheless built in Gothic style. Note, in particular, the Renaissance doorway surmounted by a baldaquin window.

▶ *Walk along rue Lannelongue to rue Jules-Ferry.*

On the right stand the former bishop's stables, which now house the Musée de l'Armagnac.

Musée de l'Armagnac

🕐 *Apr-Oct: daily except Tue 10am-noon, 3-6pm: Nov-Mar: daily except Tue 2-5pm.* 🕐 *Closed 1 Jan, 1 May, 25 Dec.* ⌾ *2.20€.* ☏ *05 62 28 31 41.*

This museum contains rare tools and machinery used in the old days by local vine-growers (18t press and a grape-crushing roller), a complete set of cooper's tools

Address Book

For coin ranges, see the Legend at the back of the guide.

EATING OUT

Moulin du Petit Gascon – *Rte d'Eauze* - *05 62 28 28 42 – closed 3 weeks in Nov, Sun evening and Mon mid Sept-mid Jun.* A little corner of the countryside that we would prefer to keep to ourselves. On the banks of the Baïse stand a delightful little lock, an old mill on one of the banks and, next to the old lock-keeper's lodge, a restaurant. The terrace and classic cuisine of the patron are also worth a mention.

WHERE TO STAY

Hôtel Continental – *20 r. du Mar.-Foch* - *05 62 68 37 00 - lecontinental@ lecontinental.net – closed 2 weeks in Jan and 20-28 Dec - 25 rms; 8€.* Recently renovated, this hotel once again has the spit and shine of its heyday in the early 1920s. Located near the river, the hotel provides rooms with a balcony or a terrace. Rooms on the courtyard are the quietest. Pretty garden.

Chambre d'hôte au Vieux Pressoir – *St-Fort - 32100 Caussens - 11km/6.6mi E of Condom on D 7 and a lane on the right -* *05 62 68 21 32 – auvieuxpressoir@ wanadoo.fr – closed Feb school holidays – reservations required - 4 rms.* The large 17C manor has an exceptional view over the countryside and the vineyards. The rooms, with antique furnishings, are comfortable and well kept. Farm-fresh products are on the menu. Try the duck!

SOMETHING DIFFERENT

Gascogne navigation – *05 62 28 46 46.* From April to October, take a boat trip along the River Baïse. Discover the Barlet Mill, the green riverbanks in the Bouquerie district and the Teste boat lock. And, if you feel like going farther, the river is open to traffic as far as Valence-sur-Baïse via three more locks.

Theatre Festival – If you are in the area around 14 July, you can enjoy this festival, held in the cloisters, which spotlights productions by universities and students fresh out of drama school.

From above! – *Aéro-club de l'Armagnac, Aérodrome du Herret* - *05 62 28 09 06.*

---

and of bottle samples produced by Gascon gentlemen-glassmakers and various stills. The old Armagnac export routes along the River Adour and the Garonne are shown on a map.

Hôtel de Polignac, Hôtel de Cugnac – **Maison Ryst-Dupeyron** (*Jul and Aug: guided tours (1hr) 9am-noon, 2-6pm, Sat-Sun 2.30-6pm; Sep-Jun: daily except Sat-Sun 9am-noon, 2-6pm.* *Closed 1 Jan.* *No charge.* *05 62 28 08 08.*), 18C cellars – and **Hôtel de Riberot** (fine 18C mansions).

Excursions

La Romieu★

11km/6.6mi E on D 931 and D 41.

The entrance to the late-12C to early-13C **collegiate church**★ is through the cloisters, with their interesting (though damaged) decorative motifs and through a doorway beneath a machicolated arch. The octagonal **eastern tower** stands apart. 14C murals may still be seen in the sacristy – 16 angels adorn the vaulting. A spiral staircase (153 steps) leads up to the platform which provides good views of the rooftops of the village, the belfry-tower and the cloisters.

Lectoure★

21km/13mi E along D 7.

The capital of the Lomagne region occupies a remarkable **site**★ on a promontory overlooking the Gers Valley. The resort's appeal is enhanced by the Lac des Trois Vallées (*3km/1.9mi SE*) offering a choice of outdoor activities. Not to be missed are the **cathedral** remodelled several times but still representative of the regional Gothic style and the **Musée gallo-romain**★ housed in the cellars of the former 17C bishops' palace; the museum contains interesting archaeological collections including a group of 20 taurobolia, pagan altars discovered in 1540 beneath the cathedral adorned with bulls' or rams' heads.

The ancient rue Fontélie lined with ochre-coloured houses, runs down to the 13C **Fontaine Diane** enclosed by a 15C wrought-iron railing.

Vallée de L'ossé and Vallée d'Auzoue

Round trip 40km/25mi W of Condom – allow half a day.

▶ *Leave Condom via D 15 towards Montréal.*

Larressingle★

This 13C fortified village is protected by walls surrounding a keep, a church and a few restored houses. A bridge straddling the moat and a fortified gate lead into the village. The ruined keep consists of three storeys linked by a spiral staircase. The fortified Romanesque church has been reduced to two adjoining chancels. A path outside the ramparts leads around the fortifications. On your way you will discover the **Cité des machines du**

Fortified entrance in Larresingle

A. Thuillier/MICHELIN

Moyen-Âge (♿🕐💬⤴

Jul and Aug: 10.30am-7pm (guided tours possible at 11.30am, 3pm, 4.30pm and 5.30pm); Apr-Jun and Sep: 11am-5.30pm; Jan-Mar and Oct-Dec: 1-5pm. ⊙ 4.60€. ☎ 05 62 68 33 88), the faithful reconstruction of a 13C siege camp, including several machines used in siege warfare such as a trebuchet which could throw cannon balls weighing over 100kg/220lb at a target 220m/240yd away.

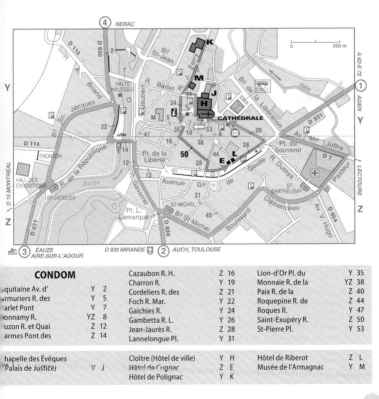

Montréal

This *bastide*, one of the earliest to be built in Gascony (1256), stands in a picturesque site, above the valley of the River Auzoue. Though severely damaged during the Wars of Religion, it still has a fortified Gothic church and a main square bordered by houses with arcades, one of which houses the **Musée archéologique** (♿ ○ *Jul and Aug: 10am-12.30pm, 2.30-7pm; Sep-Jun: daily except Sat-Sun 9am-noon, 2-6pm.* ○ *Closed Jan and public holidays (except 14 Jul and 15 Aug).* ◎ 4€. ☎ 05 62 29 42 85; *access through the tourist office*). Inside, there are several exhibits (pottery, iron objects, and Merovingian buckles) found at Séviac, including the Tree Mosaic, a harmonious composition of fruit trees and fleur-de-lis.

The ruins of Église St-Pierre-de-Genens (*2.5km/1.5mi S*) boast a Romanesque porch surmounted by the Greek letters *chi* and *rho*, representing Christ, in white marble dating from the 7C-8C.

▷ *Follow signs W of Montréal to reach Séviac.*

Séviac, Gallo-Roman villa

○ *Jul and Aug: 10am-7pm; May, Jun, Sep and Oct: 10am-noon, 2-6pm.* ◎ 4€, *ticket includes access to the Montréal Archeological Museum.* ☎ 05 62 29 48 57 or 05 62 29 48 43.

The archaeological excavations carried out on the site since the last century have revealed the foundations of a large, well-appointed Gallo-Roman villa from the 4C, intermingled with the vestiges of paleo-Christian and Merovingian buildings, all of which indicate permanent occupation here from the 2C to the 7C. The main residence, on a slightly elevated chalky plateau, is arranged around a square courtyard, surrounded by galleries with mosaic floors opening out onto a courtyard through marble colonnades. To the southwest, another courtyard separates the living quarters from a vast thermal complex, the largest to be discovered in a private home. It consists of rooms heated by hypocausts (a hot-air circulation system under the floor), a pool and baths richly decorated with coloured marble and many remarkably ornate, well-preserved mosaics.

▷ *D 29, N out of Montréal, follows the course of the River Auzoue.*

Fourcès★

A small bridge across the Auzoue, bordered by a 15C and 16C castle, leads to this picturesque *bastide* founded by the English in the 13C. The unusual village with its circular ground plan still has half-timbered houses, with stone or wood arcades, grouped around a large shaded main square with a stone cross in the centre. The scattered remains of the old town walls and a clock tower can still be seen. Fourcès is a riot of colour during the Spring Flower Market, held the last weekend in April.

▷ *Return to Condom via D 114.*

Wine Country

Round trip 50km/31mi – allow half a day.

▷ *Leave Condom via D 931 SW.*

This tour, recommended in autumn when the vines are golden brown, gives a brief glimpse of the wine country of Armagnac and a few châteaux where visitors can taste and buy.

Mouchan

The village has a lovely little Romanesque **church** (○ *3-7pm by appointment.* ☎ 05 62 28 40 33 (town hall) or 05 62 28 40 56 – Mme Nicole Castaing), the oldest part of which dates back to the 10C (*base of the existing belfry*). Some of the architectural features are

---

Armagnac

There are three main grades according to age: the 3-star or 3-crown Armagnac spends at least 18 months in a cask; the VO (Very Old) and VSOP (Very Superior Old Pale) a minimum of four and a half years and the XO, Hors d'âge, Napoléon and Extra must be over five and a half years old. It goes without saying that the longer Armagnac is allowed to mature in a cask the better it tastes.

Armagnac must be served after a meal, at room temperature, in special glasses which are wider at the base so that the content can be warmed with the palms of the hands in order to release the aromas.

worth noting – outside, the east end with its three bays framed with small columns, surmounted in turn by a cornice with sculpted modillions, and the walled-up north door, with a chequered pattern on its archivolt; inside, the archaic quadripartite ribbed vaulting in the transept, and the billet and ovolo moulding which runs around part of the church. In the oven-vaulted chancel, there is an attractive series of arches with smooth foliated capitals and, more rarely, historiated capitals.

▶ *Go to Cassaigne Château via D 208.*

Château de Cassaigne

&ⓒ☜ *Jul and Aug: guided tours (1hr) 10am-7pm; mid-May to end Jun and early to mid-Sep: 10am-noon, 2-7pm; Mid-Sep to mid-May: daily except Mon 10am-noon, 2-7pm.* ⓒ *Closed Feb, 1 Jan, 1 Nov, 25 Dec.* ☜ *No charge.* ☎ *05 62 28 04 02.*

The 13C castle was the country residence of the bishops of Condom and has undergone many transformations over the centuries. The present façade has harmonious, Classical 18C contours. After a visit to the cellars where Armagnac is aged in oak barrels, a slide-show presents the history of the castle, vine-growing and production of the prestigious spirit. The 16C kitchen, with an unusual flattened brick dome, like a baker's oven, is filled with an array of tin and copper kitchen utensils, earthenware and solid wood furniture. The exit via the north steps looks out over the vineyards. The visit is rounded off with a tasting session.

▶ *Take D 229 towards Lagardère, then turn right after 4.5km/3mi.*

Château du Busca-Maniban

ⓒ☜ *Apr-Oct: guided tours (1hr) daily except Sun 2-6pm (last admission 1hr before closing).* ⓒ *Closed public holidays.* ☜ *4€ (children: 3€).* ☎ *05 62 28 40 38.*

An immense courtyard leads to the two-storey castle. The hall is remarkably majestic (notice the two oak cupboards from the Morlaàs School), with a monumental staircase leading up to a gallery supported by colonnades – half-stone, half painted wood – with Doric capitals. On the first floor, the so-called Italian Room has some fine pieces of furniture. On the ground floor, the two former kitchens are filled with utensils and furniture. Notice the 15C chapel decorated with 17C Italian paintings. From the terrace, on a clear day, you can see as far as the Pyrenees.

▶ *Return to Cassaigne.*

On the way down, the vine-covered hillsides can be seen, overlooking the ruins of Mansecôme Castle.

▶ *At Cassaigne, turn right on D 142.*

Abbaye de Flaran★

ⓒ *See Abbaye de FLARAN.*

Valence-sur-Baïse

The *bastide* of Valence is the result of a feudal contract, drawn up in 1274, giving equal rights to the Abbot of Flaran and Comte Géraud V d'Armagnac. The town is situated at the junction of the River Baïse and River Auzoue. It is laid out on an orthogonal plan on either side of the main street. A 14C church, refurbished in the 19C, stands on one side of the covered square.

▶ *Leave Valence via D 232 N to visit the ruins of Château de Tauzia on a small road to the left.*

Château de Tauzia

The castle, standing in ruins in the middle of a meadow, was once a modest fortress with two side towers built in around the 13C. The mullion windows are from the 16C.

▶ *Go back to D 142 via Maignaut-Tauzia. Turn left on D 42 to St-Puy.*

Château Monluc

ⓒ☜ *Jun-Sep: guided tours (1hr) daily 10am-noon, 3-7pm; Oct-May: daily except Mon 10am-noon, 3-7pm, Sun 3-7pm.* ⓒ*Closed Jan, 1 May and 25 Dec.* ☜ *No charge.* ☎ *05 62 28 94 00.*

For centuries, France and England fought over the medieval fortress of St-Puy, once owned by the illustrious Maréchal Blaïse de Monluc, an army commander and a man of letters. Château Monluc is the birthplace of **pousse-rapière** (rapier thrust), a liqueur made by soaking fruit in Armagnac. Mixed with a sparkling dry wine, it makes a delicious cocktail. The vaulted cellars are used as a backdrop to explain how the precious drink is made. The tour includes a large furnished room, once the dining room, which had floor heating using the Roman hypocaust system, an old winepress, wine-making equipment for dosing and corking, and an exhibition on Blaise de Monluc and the estate.

▶ *Follow D 654 towards Condom then turn right onto D 232 to St-Orens.*

St-Orens

St-Orens is a fortified village perched on a hill. A gateway in the ramparts leads to the end of the promontory on which the castle, with its mullion windows, is located.

▶ *Return to Condom via D 654.*

CONQUES

POPULATION 302

MICHELIN LOCAL MAP 338: G-3

Conques is a peaceful little village occupying a stunningly beautiful site★★ on the steep slopes of the Ouche gorge. It is home to a splendid Romanesque church with a magnificent treasury, the remains of an abbey which for many years offered shelter to the interminable stream of pilgrims on their way to Santiago de Compostela.

A Bit of History

St Faith – The abbey only became famous after the relics of St Faith, known to the French as Sainte Foy, came into its possession in a rather dubious manner. This young Christian girl, no more than 13 years old, was martyred in about 303 in Agen, where her relics were subsequently kept and jealously guarded. In the 9C, the legend goes, one of the monks from Conques held them in such veneration that he decided to steal them. He left for Agen, where he passed himself off as a pilgrim and joined the community of St Faith. Over a period of 10 years, he won the confidence of the community to the extent that he was put in charge of guarding the relics, whereupon he promptly stole them and took them back with him to Conques. Once there, the saint doubled the number of miracles she performed – at the time, they were known as the "japes and jests of St Faith."

Pilgrimages – Construction of the present church began in the 11C. Its architecture is similar to the other famous sanctuaries of the day – Santiago de Compostela, St-Sernin in Toulouse, St-Martin in Tours and St-Martial in Limoges (the last two of which have been destroyed). Between Le Puy and Moissac, Conques was the stopover recommended in the guide book written for pilgrims on their way to Santiago de Compostela.

From the 11C to the 13C, the endless stream of pilgrims to Santiago de Compostela made this the Golden Age for Conques. It is quite extraordinary to think how popular this long, difficult journey was, but it was practically the only equivalent of modern tourism available in the Middle Ages. People went to absolve themselves of their sins or were motivated by simple devotion. Jugglers and tumblers followed the route taken by the pilgrims and, in the evening, in the hostelry of some monastery, would entertain the weary travellers. When the pilgrims arrived at their journey's goal – not without one or two potentially life-endangering adventures on the way – they would gather large quantities of the scallop shells to be found in plenty on the coasts of Galicia (still known in French as *coquilles St-Jacques*), which are one of the symbols of St James the Great. They would return home absolved of their sins and having considerably broadened their experience.

The monastery was eventually converted into a collegiate church of canons. In 1561, the Protestants reduced it to ruins. The church was partly burned down, then sank into obscurity. It was on the point of complete collapse when Prosper Mérimée, during one of his tours of inspection of historic buildings, discovered it and gave such a heart-rending account of its plight that he saved it.

Visit

Centre européen d'Art et de Civilisation médiévale

🕐 *Daily except Sat-Sun 9am-noon, 2pm-6pm.* 🕐 *Closed public holidays.* ⊶ *No charge.*
☎ *05 65 71 24 00. www.conques.com.*

Housed in an underground complex on the hillside overlooking the site of Conques, this new complex is a cultural reference centre for the historical period from 476 to 1453. Its unique documentary collection forms the basis for a complete programme of cultural activities (seminars, national heritage classes, presentations, concerts) aimed at researchers, the general public and anyone else interested in western medieval civilisation.

Abbatiale Ste-Foy★★

Allow half a day. This magnificent Romanesque abbey church was begun in the mid-11C, but most of it dates from the 12C. Two towers, which were rebuilt during the 19C level with the façade, and an octagonal lantern tower over the transept crossing, rise above the church's roofline.

Tympanum above the west door★★★

The tympanum (*best seen in the late afternoon towards sunset*) is in a remarkable state of repair. Its originality and dimensions make it a masterpiece of 12C Romanesque sculpture. Any pilgrim arriving on the parvis in front of the church could not fail to be impressed by this image of the Last Judgement, made up of 124 figures representing the dramatic juxtaposition between souls at peace and souls in torment described in St Matthew's Gospel. This iconographical scene arranged around the figure of Christ is carved in yellow limestone, and a few remaining traces of paint remind us that it used to be painted in bright colours.

Bands reserved for inscriptions delimit three superposed tiers divided into sections. On the left of the figure of Christ is Hell, and on his right Paradise, clearly indicated by His left hand pointing downwards to the condemned, while His right hand is raised towards the Elect. Christ sits enthroned in a mandorla surrounded by five layers of clouds. In the tier above, two angels carved on the spandrels are blowing their horns to herald the Last Judgement while two others are carrying the Cross. In the middle tier, the procession of the Elect is making its way to the Lord, led by the Virgin Mary followed by (*right to left*) St Peter, then important figures in the history of Conques, including Charlemagne, a legendary benefactor of the abbey.

On the other side of the figure of Christ, angel knights are fending off the hordes of the damned, who are pursued by the fires of hell; the sinners include errant monks captured in a net and a drunken man hung by the feet. The central and upper section of the lower tier is devoted to the weighing of souls; the Archangel St Michael is opposite a devil who is trying to tip the scales. To the left of this, angels are opening coffins in an image of the resurrection of the dead and, farther still to the left, tiny arcades represent the church of Conques next to which St Faith is prostrating herself to receive God's blessing. Beneath her, on the bottom tier, is Paradise with Abraham welcoming the Holy Innocents into his arms, surrounded by wise Virgins, martyrs and prophets. The entrance to this celestial Jerusalem is guarded by an angel reaching out his hands to greet the Elect, while to the right, the antechamber of Hell is marked by a devil pushing the damned into the gaping jaws of Leviathan. On the far right, Satan is seen presiding over the chaos of Hell where mortal sins are being punished; Pride is shown being unseated from its horse, Greed being hung high and dry, and Slander having its tongue pulled out by a devil.

All this must have made quite a strong impression on pilgrims making their

The towers of the abbey church

H. Payelle/MICHELIN

way to Santiago de Compostela. The stern face of the Eternal Judge must have struck fear into many a heart. The peace of Paradise (once painted blue), emphasised by the almost monotonous alignment which is designed to convey order and serenity, contrasts strongly with the violence and confusion of hell (painted red), which is treated altogether differently. The sculptors at Conques achieved an exceptional degree of mastery which never fails to amaze those who visit this example of Romanesque genius.

The medieval sculptors were not without a sense of humour, however – if you take a closer look at the outside edge of the archivolt, curious little faces can be seen peeping over the rim of the moulding (*les curieux de Conques*).

Go round the church to the right, along the south façade with its 12C funerary niches, one of which still bears the epitaph of Abbot Bégon (1087-1107), and enter the church through the door in the south arm of the transept.

Interior

The inside of the church makes a striking impression because of its enormous height (22m/72ft) and general simplicity of line, which verges on the austere. As in other churches frequented by pilgrims, the chancel is wide and surrounded by an ambulatory to allow the faithful to process past the relics of St Faith, which used to be displayed there. On the walls of the sacristy are traces of frescoes (15C) depicting the martyrdom of St Faith. The ornate 12C railings in front of the choir replaced a screen which was said to have been made from the fetters of prisoners released by St Faith. Above the passage which connects the galleries, in the central bay of the north transept, there is a beautiful sculpture group of the Annunciation. Note the contemporary stained-glass windows made of a brand new type of glass which diffuses light entering the church, lending it an interesting quality. They are the work of Pierre Soulages, from Aveyron.

Cloisters

In 1975, the ground plan was reconstructed with paving stones. All that is left of the cloisters themselves is a series of arcades opening onto what used to be the refectory and a very beautiful serpentine marble basin which was once part of the monks' lavabo.

Six twin windows open into the refectory where a number of lovely capitals from the original arcades are now on display.

Trésor de Conques★★★ (Treasury)

 Apr-Sep: 9.30am-12.30pm, 2-6.30pm; Oct-Mar 10am-noon, 2-6pm. *Closed 1 Jan and 25 Dec.* *5.50€* *0 820 820 803.*

The treasury of the abbey of Conques houses a collection of silver and gold plate which is the most comprehensive display of the evolution of church plate in France from the 9C to the 16C. It includes a particularly interesting set of reliquaries, produced by a goldsmithing workshop set up in the abbey in the 11C. Listed below, in chronological order, are the most important exhibits (*some of which have a switch beneath them so that they can be rotated and admired from all sides*).

9C – Reliquary of Pepin, gold leaves embossed on a wooden core – thought to be a gift from Pepin, this exhibit is inlaid with numerous precious stones, including an antique intaglio depicting the god Apollo.

10C – Reliquary statue of St Faith (**Statue-reliquaire de Sainte Foy**), the main piece in the collection, gold and silver gilt plating on a wooden core – over the years the statue has had numerous precious stones added to it as well as, in the 14C, the monstrance through which the relic can be seen (in

 For coin ranges, see the Legend at the back of the guide.

COUNTRY CHARM

 Ferme-auberge Domaine des Costes Rouges – *Combret - 12330 Nauviale - 13km/8mi S of Conques on D 901 then B-road* - *05 65 72 83 85 – closed Oct-Mar -* *- reservations required.* A rustic inn run by a friendly couple who prepare a selection of old traditional local favourites: saucisse à l'huile, canards à la broche flambés au capucin, home-baked pastries. all washed down with locally produced wines. Three guest rooms in a house in the village.

 Auberge St-Jacques – *05 65 72 86 36 info@aubergestjacques.fr – closed 2 Jan-2 Feb - 13 rms;* *6.80€.* This house is several centuries old, but guests will sleep peacefully in the comfortable rustic style rooms, watched over by the hotel's patron saint, no doubt! Traditional local cuisine served in a dining room with rustic decor, or a brasserie on the ground floor.

the middle of her chest, just behind the head of the little figure in her lap). This unique piece of craftsmanship is also adorned with cameos and antique intaglios. The figure of the saint is holding tiny tubes designed to take flowers between her fingers.

11C – Portable alabaster altar, known as the *autel de Sainte Foy*, featuring embossed silver and enamel work; reliquary thought to be of Pope Pascal II, in silver on a wooden core, reworked several times; the *A de Charlemagne*, in gold-plated silver on a wooden core – tradition has it that the Emperor, wishing to assign all the abbeys in Gaul with a letter of the alphabet, according to their order of importance, awarded Conques the letter "A."

12C – St Faith's reliquary chest – this leather chest decorated with 31 enamel medallions still contains the remains of the saint; portable altar of the Abbot Bégon, consisting of a red porphyry plate in an engraved, niello silver mounting; reliquary known as the Lanterne de Bégon III or "St Vincent" reliquary, silver on a wooden core; five-and six-sided silver, gilt and enamel reliquaries, made in the 12C with much older fragments.

13C – Arm reliquary thought to be of St George, in silver on a wooden core, the hand making a sign of blessing; embossed and gold-plated silver triptych; Virgin and Child, in silver on a wooden core – this type of reliquary statue was very popular during the reign of St Louis.

14C – Head-reliquaries of St Liberate and St Marse, silver and painted canvas – small silver shrine of St Faith.

16C – Gilt gospel bookbinding; processional cross, made from embossed silver leaf on a wooden core with a relic of the true cross beneath the figure of Christ.

Trésor II (Musée Joseph-Fau)
Entrance through the tourist office.

This old house, located opposite the pilgrims' fountain, contains 17C furniture, statues, neo-Gothic reliquaries and Felletin tapestries from the abbey (*ground and first floors*). The basement contains a lapidary museum with a beautiful collection of Romanesque capitals and abaci, which are remains of the old cloisters.

Village★

The steep little streets are lined with lovely old houses in red stone which harmonises with their limestone roof slabs (*lauzes*).

Above the church of Ste-Foy, the village is spread out on the hillside along rue Charlemagne, the path once climbed by the pilgrims on their way to the abbey. From this street, a rocky path leads to a hillock topped by the chapel of St-Roch and a calvary. From here there is a beautiful view of Conques clustered around the abbey church. Above the church, more streets lead to the remains of old fortifications.

▸ *At the war memorial, turn left towards place du Château.*

In the square stands the fine Château d'Humières (15C-16C) with its carved consoles. Farther on is one of the three remaining 12C gates, the Porte de Vinzelle.

From the cemetery, a corner of which is occupied by the funerary chapel of the abbots of Conques, there is a pretty view of the Ouche.

▸▸ **Château de Pruines** – *15km/9.3mi SE via D 901 to St-Cyprien-sur-Dourdou, then D 502.* ○ *Jul and Aug: guided tours (1hr) 11am-12.30pm, 2.30pm-6.30pm; Apr-Jun, Oct and Nov: Sun and public holidays: 3-5.30pm; Sep: daily except Tue and Wed 3-6pm.* This pink-sandstone 17C manor houses an unusual **collection of ceramics**★.

Les CORBIÈRES★★

MICHELIN LOCAL MAP 344: D-J. 4-6

The Corbières massif forms a roughly square plateau sloping gently northwards from the eastern Pyrenees. At the heart of the massif, a core of primary deposits in the Orbieu Valley has resulted in a dramatically jumbled relief with colour contrasts heightened by the uniquely luminous Mediterranean light. Much of the countryside is covered in the spiny and sweet-smelling scrub known as *garrigue*.

However, it is above all for two of its features that the Corbières is best known: ruined castles and wine.

A Bit of History

The perfect spot for a vineyard – The *garrigue* has been ousted increasingly by vines, which have taken over every available clay dip and valley east of the Orbieu and, around Limoux, the slopes of the small region that produces *blanquette* (a sparkling white wine). For many years dismissed as a region which concentrated on quantity not quality, the **Corbières** has relatively recently been awarded the *Appellation d'Origine Contrôlée* for its fruity, full-bodied wines (mainly red, some white and rosé) with their bouquet so evocative of the fragrant local flora. The widely differing soil types in the region dictate that a corresponding variety of grape types is cultivated (the grape varieties most commonly used in Corbières wines are Carignan, Cinsaut and Grenache). This has the happy result that any tour of *dégustation* taken in the region turns into a real voyage of discovery, as local wines can vary enormously even between neighbouring vineyards.

The wines (red only) of neighbouring **Fitou**, also an *Appellation d'Origine Contrôlée*, are dark, robust wines with a hint of spiciness.

Many of the local villages have their own wine cooperative (*cave coopérative*) and these, with many local private wine-growers, are only too willing to allow potential customers to taste their wares (some private producers, however, require prior reservation, so a wine guide listing telephone numbers comes in useful).

The battlefield of the Languedoc – Towering above the Fenouillèdes on rocky limestone ridges (such as the Pic de Bugarach – alt 1 230m/4 030ft) are numerous vertiginous feudal fortresses, almost all of which are now in ruins. The Corbières region was initially a fall-back position for the Visigoths after they had been driven south from the Haut-Languedoc, then later a battlefield bloodied by epic combats between the Franks and the Saracens, before finally becoming border territory under the Carolingian Empire, subject to the vicissitudes stemming mainly from rivalries among neighbouring vassals. However, after integration of the region into the French royal estate in 1229, capture of the fortresses which had supported the Cathar cause, and the King of Aragón's renunciation of his feudal rights over the territories north of

Cucugnan and its vineyards

E. Larribère/MICHELIN

Address Book

For coin ranges, see the Legend at the back of the guide.

EATING OUT

Auberge du Vigneron – *11350 Cucugnan -* ☎ *04 68 45 03 00 - auberge. vigneron@ataraxie.fr - closed 13 Nov-28 Feb, Mon noon in Jul-Aug; Sun evening and Mon.* A village house where guests can sample the delights of simple cooking, a glass or two of Corbières wine and cosy little rooms. The restaurant occupies an old wine store, but moves to a fine terrace with a view of the mountains in summer.

Cave d'Agnès – *11510 Fitou -* ☎ *04 68 45 75 91 – closed 16 Nov-14 Mar, Thu noon and Wed – reservations required.* This resoundingly popular restaurant occupies an old barn at the top of the village. The food is fit for a king and the setting is very pleasant: an authentic barn shown off effectively with modern lighting effects.

Le Merle Bleu – *Pl. de l'Église - 11350 Paziols -* ☎ *04 68 45 02 48 – lemerlebleu@ hotmail.com - ✉ - reservations required.* Tucked at the top of the village, this little restaurant with white walls and blue furniture offers a good view of the plain and Château d'Aguilar from the terrace. Claude Nougaro, who knew the area, dedicated a poem to it, which can be read on the menu. Mediterranean family cuisine.

WHERE TO STAY

Chambre d'hôte Les Ginestous – *11330 Palairac - 12km/7.5mi N of Tuchan on D 39 -* ☎ *04 68 45 01 24 - a-lacaze@ wanadoo.fr - closed 1 Nov-Easter - ✉ - 4 rms.* Guests can recharge their batteries in this little house by the village fountain, off the beaten track. The rooms are rustic in style with white walls. A small roof terrace enables guests to take breakfast in the sunshine. Regional specialities on the main menu.

CATHAR SITES

Centre d'Études Cathares – *Maison des Mémoires - 53 r. de Verdun - BP 197 - 11004 Carcassonne Cedex -* ☎ *04 68 47 24 66 - www.cathares.org.* Research and information centre devoted to Cathar history; open to the public.

Carte intersites – This card gives reductions on visits to 16 Cathar sites: the châteaux of Lastours, Arques, Quéribus, Puilaurens, Termes, Villerouge-Termenès, Saissac, Peyrepertuse, Usson, the Château comtal de Carcassonne, the abbeys of Caunes-Minervois, Saint-Papoul, Saint-Hilaire, Lagrasse, Fontfroide and the Musée du Quercorb in Puivert. It also gives free admission for one child. It is on sale at all the sites at a price of 4€.

"Pays Cathare" – This is a trademark acquired by the Conseil Général de l'Aude. The logo guarantees the authenticity and the "extra" quality of the certified food products, hotels and restaurants.

the Agly in 1258, the border between France and Spain settled down. For the next five centuries the "five sons of Carcassonne" – Puilaurens, Peyrepertuse, Quéribus, Termes and Aguilar – served as royal garrisons ready to confront any threat of invasion posed by the Spanish. They were deprived of their strategic importance by the annexation of Roussillon to France and subsequently for the most part fell into disuse.

Monasteries – The Corbières massif attracted numerous monastic institutions with their various associated outbuildings – priories, granaries, oil and wheat mills and almshouses. The Benedictines settled in Alet, St-Polycarpe, St-Hilaire (northeast of Limoux; Romanesque church remains of what was an 8C Benedictine abbey) and Lagrasse; the Cistercians in Fontfroide whereas their sisters went to Rieunette. The large number of sanctuaries, easy to spot because of the cypress trees growing in their graveyards, is striking in such a depopulated area.

Excursions

CATHAR CASTLES★★

Round-trip from Duilhac-sous-Peyrepertuse [1]
117km/73mi – allow an overnight stopover.

Numerous castles and castle ruins, including the "Five Sons of Carcassonne" (*see above*), dot the landscape of the Corbières region. Perched on rocky limestone ridges, these vertiginous feudal fortresses were often places of refuge for Cathars fleeing from the Inquisition.

Duilhac-sous-Peyrepertuse
As you leave the upper town to the north, note the village fountain, which is fed by a spring with a surprising volume of flow for the region.

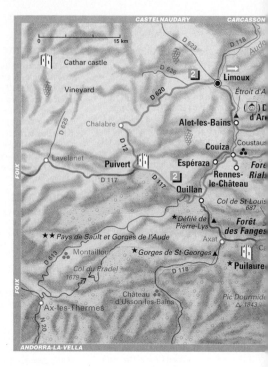

Château de Peyrepertuse★★★

🕐 *See Château de PEYREPERTUSE.*

▶ *Return to Duilhac and drive to Cucugnan.*

Cucugnan

This pretty village is well known from the tale of *Le Sermon du curé de Cucugnan*, presenting an anthology of Oc folklore in the form of a sermon by Cucugnan's parish priest, which was adapted into French by Alphonse Daudet in the second half of the 19C. A Provençal version by Roumanille and an Occitan version in verse by **Achille Mir** (the original) are also extant. The tiny Achille-Mir theatre on place du Platane hosts a virtual theatre performance on the theme of the **"Sermon du curé de Cucugnan"** (🕐 *Jul and Aug: 10am-9pm; Apr-Jun and Sep: 10am-8pm; Oct: 10am-7pm; Mar: 10am-7pm; Feb: 10am-6.30pm; Nov: 10am-6pm. 🕐 Closed 3 weeks in Jan, 1 Jan and 25 Dec. ⊛ 4€ (ticket combined with the château de Quéribus). ☎ 04 68 45 03 69)* following Achille Mir's version, with the voice of writer Henri Gougaud.

▶ *Continue along D 14.*

Padern

20min on foot round-trip. ⚠ *Be careful; the ruins are dangerous in places.*

▶ *To reach the castle, follow the yellow-marked "sentier cathare."*

🏰 The Château de Padern, owned by the abbots of Lagrasse until 1579, was completely rebuilt in the 17C. The remains of a round tower, leading to the upper part of the keep now in ruins, can still be seen. Fine view of the village and the River Verdouble.

▶ *At the end of D 14, turn left onto D 611.*

Tuchan

Production centre for Fitou wines (AOC). The picturesque D 39 winds through the Tuchan Valley, between the vibrant splashes of colour formed by the vineyards – green or bronze, depending on the season – at the foot of the imposing, but desolate, Tauch mountain.

▶ *East of Tuchan, a surfaced path going through vineyards branches off D 39 to the left and leads to Aguilar Castle.*

Château d'Aguilar

10min on foot from the parking area. Enter the enclosure from the SW.

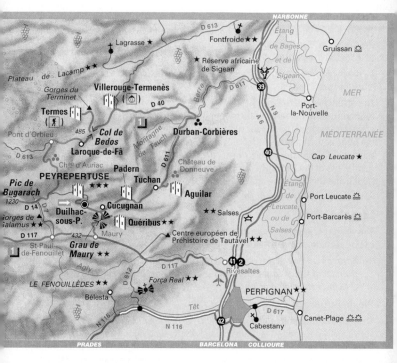

The Château d'Aguilar stands on a very exposed site on top of a small rounded hill, the only outcrop for some distance around. The fortress was reinforced in the 13C, on the orders of the king of France, with the addition of a hexagonal curtain wall flanked by six round towers open to the gorge and reinforced by a stone glacis. Besides the wall, a Romanesque chapel with its interior architecture remains intact, apart from the vault which has caved in.

There is an attractive view of the vineyards in the Tuchan basin.

▷ *Return to Tuchan and turn right onto D 611 to Durban.*

Durban-Corbières

The castle overlooking the village includes a crenellated rectangular two-storey building with 13C twin bays and 16C mullioned windows. In addition there are remains of curtain walls and towers.

▷ *Drive W out of Durban along D 40.*

Villerouge-Termenès

Kids At the heart of the medieval village stands the **castle** (🕐 *Jul and Aug: 9am-7.30pm; Apr-Jun and Sep to mid-Oct: 10am-6pm; Feb and Mar, mid-Oct to endDec: certain Sat-Sun, public holidays and school holidays: 10am-5pm. 🕐 Closed Jan. ⊜ 4€. ☎ 04 68 70 09 11*) (12C-14C) flanked by four towers. It was owned by the bishops of Narbonne and in 1321 was the scene of the burning at the stake of the last Cathar Parfait, Guilhem Bélibaste. The three floors of the east wing, which has been restored, house audio-visual exhibitions on Bélibaste's life and works (*ground floor*), on the archbishop of Narbonne, Bernard de Farges, and the administration of his diocese (*first floor*) and on the daily life of Villerouge and its inhabitants in the Middle Ages (*second floor*). From the sentry walk there is a view of the village and its surroundings. The south wing is home to the great banqueting hall and the west wing to a medieval spit-roast.

Every year during the summer months, Villerouge is the scene of medieval banquets and various other events evocative of life in Languedoc in the Middle Ages.

▷ *Follow D 613 SW of Villerouge to Col de Bedos then turn right onto D 40.*

Col de Bedos

Bedos Pass is located on D 40, a **ridge road**★ winding through wooded ravines. In the dip formed by the lower gorge of the Sou, the ruins of the Château de Termes are clearly visible on their rock.

Château de Termes

🕒 *Jul and Aug: 10am-8pm; Apr-Jun and early Sep to mid-Oct: 10am-6pm; Mar and mid-Oct to end Dec: Sat-Sun, public and school holidays, 10am-5pm.* 🕒 *Closed Jan and Feb.* ☎ *3.50€.* ☎ *04 68 70 09 20. Leave the car at the foot of the hill, beyond the bridge.*

⬛ *30min on foot round-trip; follow a steep track up then climb a succession of tiers that mark the curtain walls.*

The castle was held by Raymond de Termes, a notorious heretic, and only succumbed to Simon de Montfort after a four month siege (August to November 1210), the hardest of the first stage of the Albigensian Crusade. The site, on a promontory defended by the huge natural trench of the Sou Valley (Terminet gorge), is more interesting than the ruins of the fortress itself, which once covered 16 000m²/172 224sq ft. There are good views of the **Terminet gorge** from near the northwest postern (⚠ *dangerous slopes*) and the top of the rock.

▶ *Return to Col de Bedos and turn right onto D 613.*

Laroque-de-Fâ

The village occupies a picturesque site on a fortified spur, watered by the Sou, which can be seen dropping towards the Orbieu in the distance.

▶ *Beyond Mouthoumet, as you reach Orbieu bridge, turn left onto D 212 and drive past the ruins of Auriac Castle. In Soulatgé, turn right onto D 14 to Cubières. Turn left onto D 45 just before Bugarach.*

Pic de Bugarach

The Bugarach summit (*alt 1 230m/4 030ft*) can be seen from a number of charming yet virtually deserted valleys which surround it, giving good views of the different faces of the mountain with its rugged slopes. The ascent to the Col du Linas, winding through the upper Agly Valley, is particularly impressive. Looking back (east) from the pass, the ruins of St-Georges – the western spur of the citadel of Peyrepertuse – seem to merge with the rocks on which they stand.

▶ *Turn left onto D 46 before St-Louis; it leads to D 9 heading for Caudiès-de-Fenouillèdes.*

Forêt domaniale des Fanges

This forest massif covers an area of 1 184ha/2 924 acres and is home to some exceptional Aude firs. The **Col de St-Louis** (*alt 687m/2 253ft*) is a good departure point for ramblers (rocky, often very uneven ground).

▶ *Drive on to Caudiès and turn right onto D 117 to Lapradelle.*

Château de Puilaurens★

🕒 *Jul and Aug: 9am-8pm; Apr-Jun and Sep: 10am-6pm; Oct: 10am-5pm; Feb, Mar and early to mid-Nov: Sat-Sun and school holidays 10am-5pm.* ☎ *3.50€.* ☎ *04 68 20 65 26.*

▶ *From Lapradelle, take the small road S (D 22) and then the uphill road to the right 800m/875yd beyond Puilaurens.*

⬛ *Leave the car and continue on foot; 30min round-trip.*

The castle high above the upper Aude Valley has remained more or less intact; the crenellated curtain wall with four towers and projecting battlements defending the approach to the keep can be seen from some way off. From the Treaty of Corbeil in 1258, Puilaurens was the most advanced position held by the king of France towards the Kingdom of Aragón. A zigzag path leads up to the main gateway and into the lower courtyard. Go through a postern at the foot of the eastern tower to a rocky spur from which the strength of the fortress' site can best be appreciated; it is impregnable from the north. Note also the embossed stonework. There is a view of the Pic de Bugarach to the north-east and the Boulzane Valley to the south.

▶ *Rejoin D 117 and turn right to Maury then left onto D 19.*

Grau de Maury★★

🕒 *Jul and Aug: 9am-8pm; Apr-Jun and Sep: 10am-6pm; Oct: 10am-5pm; Feb, Mar and early to mid-Nov: Sat-Sun and school holidays 10am-5pm.* ☎ *3.50€.* ☎ *04 68 20 65 26.*

There is a fine panorama from this little pass, the southern gateway to the Corbières. The mountain chains stretch back in steps from the jagged ridge which overlooks the dip formed by the Fenouillèdes to the south.

▷ *A steep narrow road to the right leads up from the Grau de Maury to the ruined fortress of Quéribus.*

Château de Quéribus★★

⚙ *See Château de QUÉRIBUS.*

▷ *Head back to Cucugnan and turn left onto D 14 to return to Duilhac.*

RAZÈS REGION ②

120km/75mi round-trip from Limoux. ⚙ *See LIMOUX: Excursions.*

CORDES-SUR-CIEL★★★

POPULATION 996

MICHELIN LOCAL MAP 338: D-6

Cordes-sur-Ciel occupies a remarkable site★★, perched on top of a rocky outcrop, the Puech de Mordagne, overlooking the Cérou Valley. On a bright day, it looks quite charming with the sunlight enhancing the soft pink and grey hues of the old façades. The village may owe its name to the textile and leather industry which prospered here in the 13C and 14C, as in the case of Córdoba in Spain.

A Bit of History

Fortified town – In 1222, during the Albigensian Crusade, the Count of Toulouse, Raymond VII, decided to build the fortified town of Cordes in response to destruction of the stronghold of St-Marcel by Simon de Montfort's troops.

The charter of customs and privileges enjoyed by the inhabitants of Cordes included, among other things, exemption from taxes and tolls. The town-cum-fortress rapidly became a favourite haunt of heretics, and the Inquisition found rich pickings during its work here.

The end of the Cathar disturbances ushered in a period of prosperity. In the 14C, the leather and cloth trades flourished; craftsmen wove linen and hemp cultivated on the surrounding plains, whereas the dyers on the banks of the Cérou used the **pastel** (blue dyer's woad) and saffron which grew so abundantly in the region. The beautiful houses built during this period bear witness to the wealth of the inhabitants.

Decline and revival – The quarrels among the bishops of Albi, which affected the entire region, the resistance of Cordes to the Huguenots during the Wars of Religion and two plague epidemics put an end to this golden age in the 15C. After a brief burst of life at the end of the 19C, due to the introduction of mechanical embroidery looms, Cordes, which had originally been designed to be isolated, finally fell into decline, cut off as it was from the main communication routes. Fortunately, the threatened demolition of its Gothic houses spurred the population into action and a number of measures to classify some of its buildings as historic monuments were taken in 1923. But those most susceptible to the charm of Cordes were the artists and craftsmen who rallied to the cause and helped to put the town back on the map.

Restoration is still being carried out, preserving the original character of Cordes. In 1970 the town also became a venue for musical entertainment.

The winding, steeply sloping, stone streets are home to an ironmonger, an enameller and a sculptor of figurines, not to mention weavers, engravers, sculptors and painters, who practise their crafts in the beautiful old houses whose original appearance has been so successfully conserved.

Upper Town★★

Traffic is banned in the upper town in summer. You can park the car (fee charged) near the Porte de la Jane or at the bottom of Grande Rue de l'Horloge, but expect problems finding a space in season. The climb to the old town is not so steep from the former as it is from the latter. Alternatively, the upper town can be reached by a shuttle (every 15min in season).

The main attraction of Cordes, besides its exceptional setting, is undoubtedly its beautiful **Gothic houses**★★ (13C-14C), in particular, the **sculpted decoration of the façades**. The largest and best-preserved houses line the Grand-Rue (or rue Droite). The façades, built of warm pinkish Salles sandstone with hints of grey, open through great arches at street level, surmounted by two storeys with ogive windows, some of which have unfortunately been replaced by simple rectangular openings.

In several houses, iron bars ending in a ring project from the façade on the second floor. These were to support a wooden or iron rod, placed horizontally through each of the rings, on which material was probably draped to act as blinds, following a medieval custom popular in Italy and Provence. However, since the sun does not penetrate very far into the narrow streets, the rings may have been used to hang banners during festivals.

Address Book

⏱ For coin ranges, see the Legend at the back of the guide.

EATING OUT

◇◇ **Auberge de la Bouriette** – *Campes - 4km/2.5mi NE of Cordes-sur-Ciel on D 922 then D 98 -* ☎ *05 63 56 07 32 – closed during week 1 Dec-15 Mar.* This arable farm is still in operation. The dining room occupies the old barn and gives a view of the surrounding countryside. Simple fare using local produce. B&B accommodation possible. Terrace and swimming pool.

WHERE TO STAY

◇ **Camping Moulin de Julien** – *1.5km/1mi SE of Cordes-sur-Ciel on D 922, road to Gaillac -* ☎*05 63 56 11 10 - open 15 May-15 Sep -* ⏱ *- reservation recommended - 130 sites.* Come and pitch your tent at the foot of the medieval city. This camp site is typical of the area: it has a water chute coming out of an old dovecot to plunge into the pool. Children's play area. Chalets for hire.

Chambre d'hôte Aurifat – ☎*05 63 56 07 03 – aurifat@wanadoo.fr - closed Jan and Feb -* ⏱ *- 4 rms.* This is an enchanting spot! The old 13C brick and half-timbered watch tower, with a dovecot standing next to it, has been well restored. The rooms are charming, and the terraced garden has a good view of the fields. Good swimming pool. Cordes is but a stone's throw away on foot!

SHOPPING

Pâtisserie Andrieu – *Grand Rue de l'Horloge -* ☎ *05 63 56 01 02 – 8am-8pm.* Oublies (waffles) and croquants de Cordes are specialities in this shop.

Art'Cordes - ☎ *05 63 56 14 79 – 10.30am-12.30pm, 2.30-6pm – closed Jan.* Inside the Grand Fauconnier house, you will find displays of the work of about 20 local artists.

L'atelier du Laguiole – *26 R. Raymond-VII -* ☎ *05 63 56 10 83 – 10am-noon, 2-6pm.* Here you will find every form of the famous Laguiole knife: for professional use, as a collector's item, for your pocket, the dinner table and more. Each item made here is unique and the workshop visit is very instructive.

LEISURE ACTIVITIES

Jardin des Paradis – ☎ *05 63 56 29 77 – Jul to mid-Sep: 10.30am-6.30pm (last entrance 30min before closing); mid-Sep-Jun: Sat, Sun and holidays 11am-6pm. 5.40€ (children under 12 free of charge).* Paths have been set out on the old terraces of the lower town, starting from place du Théron. Guided tours can be arranged, with special themes, such a s a candlelight visit to study the stars, a visit including the discovery of aromatic plants, tasting jellys made from flowers or learning the art of floral composition.

Fêtes du Grand Fauconnier – *Around 14 July.* These festivities offer you a journey back to medieval times: admire the costumes, the troubadours, jugglers and archers, but you will have to pay for a stroll through the upper town.

"Musiques sur Ciel" – *ACADOC -* ☎ *05 63 56 00 75 - last fortnight in July.* Chamber music festival. Violin and bow makers meet musicians from all over Europe.

Porte de la Jane

Cordes, which is laid out in a diamond-shape, had two curtain walls built around it in 1222. These had the strongest fortifications at their weakest points of access open to attackers, the east and west ends. This portcullis gateway, a remnant of the second curtain wall, doubled the Porte des Ormeaux.

Porte des Ormeaux

Assailants thinking they had penetrated the town's defences, having fought their way past the Porte de la Jane, were surprised to find themselves confronted by the massive towers of this second fortified gateway.

Chemin de Ronde

The southern wards (Planol haut), and those of rue du Planol, offer attractive views of the surrounding countryside.

Porte du Planol or du Vainqueur

This gateway is the eastern counterpart of the Porte de la Jane.

Barbacane

This barbican, below the Porte du Planol, is part of a third curtain wall which was built around Cordes when the town was extended at the end of the 13C.

Maison Gorsse

The façade of this house features some beautiful Renaissance mullioned windows.

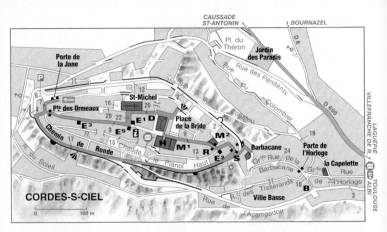

CORDES				
	Fontourniés R.	7	Le Planol	17
Boucarié ou du Tuadou R. de la	2	Grand-Rue Raymond-VII	9	Portal Pl. Charles	16
Bouteillerie R. de la	3	Horloge Pl. de l'	10	St-Louis R.	19
Brayer Pl. Yves	4	Lices Promenade des	12	St-Michel Pl.	22
Fontourniés Pl.	6	Mitons R. des	13	St-Michel R.	20
	Obscure R.	15	Trinité Pl. de la	24

Escalier du Pater Noster	B	Maison du Grand Veneur	E⁵
Halle et puits	D	Maison du Grand Écuyer	E³
Maison Fonpeyrouse d'Alayrac	E¹	Musée d'Art et d'Histoire Charles-Portal	M²
Maison Gorsse	E²	Portail peint	R
Maison Prunet	M¹	Porte du Planol	S
Maison du Grand Fauconnier (Hôtel de ville)	H		

Portail peint

The name of this gateway (Painted Gate) probably comes from the painted Madonna which once adorned it. It is the partner of the Porte des Ormeaux to the east and houses the **Musée Charles-Portal** (⚑ see Additional Sights).

▶ Grand-Rue, which is cobbled and very steep, leads to the heart of the fortified town.

Along the street stands the **Maison Prunet** which houses the Musée de l'Art du Sucre (⚑ see Additional Sights).

Maison du Grand Fauconnier★

This beautiful old mansion, in warm golden stone, now houses the town hall. The roof corbels were once decorated with falcons, which earned the mansion its name. The remarkably elegant façade with its lovely regular bond was restored in the 19C.

Covered market and well

Twenty-four octagonal wooden pillars (renovated several times since the 14C) support the roof structure (reconstructed in the 19C) over the market place which once rang to the sound of cloth merchants and is today the hub of the city. Fixed to one of the pillars, behind a handsome 16C wrought-iron cross, a marble plaque commemorates the assassination of three inquisitors (an episode dismissed as hearsay by scholars). Nearby there is a **well** 113.47m/372ft deep.

Place de la Bride

This is a welcome rest area shaded by trees. There is a sweeping view of the peaceful Cérou Valley to the northeast, against the slender silhouette of the Bournazel belfry to the north.

Église St-Michel

This church, which has been refurbished many times over the centuries, still has its original 13C chancel and transept, with pointed intersecting rib vaulting, and a splendid 14C rose window set in the wall. The interior buttresses separating the side chapels are similar to those in the cathedral at Albi. Likewise, the 19C paintings are an imitation of the decoration on the vault of Ste-Cécile. The organ (1830) comes from Notre-Dame in Paris (the cathedral's first choir organ).

There is a vast panorama from the top of the watchtower adjoining the belfry.

Kids North of place Charles-Portal, the **Palais des Scènes** (🕐 Daily except Mon 10am-noon, 2-7pm. 🕐 Closed Feb and Mar. ⚲ No charge. ☎ 05 63 56 00 78) houses giant animated tableaux recounting the history of the fortified town.

Maison Fonpeyrouse d'Alayrac

The inner courtyard of this recently renovated late-13C house has a particularly interesting layout. Two timber galleries give access to the upper storeys. The mansion now houses the tourist office.

Maison du Grand Veneur★

This mansion, named after the Master of the Royal Hunt, has a distinctive three-storey façade, decorated on the second storey with a frieze of high-relief sculptures depicting hunting scenes. They include a huntsman on the point of stabbing a wild boar which has been chased out of the forest by a dog; a hare, with a dog in hot pursuit, about to be struck by a hunter's arrow (between the windows on the left); a hunter blowing his horn while two animals are escaping into the forest (between the right-hand windows). Note the protruding iron rings (see above), which are particularly well preserved.

Maison du Grand Écuyer

The elegant façade of this mansion is built of beautiful, regularly bonded, Salles sandstone and adorned with highly imaginative figures, sculpted in the round.

▶ *Return to the Porte des Ormeaux.*

Lower Town

As suburbs sprang up around the citadel, a fourth, then a fifth curtain wall were built in the 14C. East of the town the clock gateway, or **Porte de l'Horloge**, probably rebuilt in the 16C, is a picturesque remnant of the fourth wall. It can be reached from place de Lacampadou up a flight of steps known as the **Escalier du Pater Noster**, because it has as many steps as the prayer has words.

La Capelette

To visit, see the instructions posted on the door. The interior of this old chapel, built in 1511, was decorated by Yves Brayer (see Additional sights below).

Additional Sights

Musée d'Art et d'Histoire Charles-Portal★

Jul and Aug: daily except Sat 11am-1pm, 4-7pm; mid-Apr to end Jun and Sep to end Oct: Sun 3-6pm. 2.30€. ☎ 05 63 56 00 52.

The museum is named in honour of Charles Portal, keeper of public records for the Tarn *département* and great historian of Cordes. It is located inside the Portail Peint and contains items of local historical interest.

On the ground floor are some antique grain measures, a rather unusual sarcophagus from the Merovingian necropolis (6C) in Vindrac (*5km/3mi W of Cordes*), the beautiful studded door from the Maison du Grand Fauconnier and the falcons (*faucons*) to which this house owes its name.

A room on the first floor is entirely devoted to the various styles of architecture in Cordes (military, religious, civil).

The second floor houses interesting collections of local prehistoric exhibits, a set of earthenware typical of the end of the Bronze Age and some opulent Gallo-Roman furniture which belonged to the temple at Loubers.

Another room contains the *libre ferrat* or iron book, so-called because its binding incorporated an iron chain. This record book contains the town's regulations from the end of the 13C to the 17C. New consuls were sworn in on the Gospel extracts inside it.

The third floor displays objects found during excavation of the Vindrac necropolis: jewellery, buckles, a set of antefixes and earthenware from Gallo-Roman times.

Musée de l'Art du sucre

Jul and Aug: 9am-7pm, Apr to Jun and Sept to Oct: 10am - noon, 2-6.30pm, Nov to Dec and Feb to Mar: daily except Mon 10am-noon, 2.30-6pm. Closed Jan. 2.30€ (children: 1.55€). ☎ 05 63 56 02 40.

Housed in a lovely rose-coloured mansion, this unusual museum contains works of art made entirely of sugar, mostly displayed in glass cases.

In the second room, a 2.60m/8.5ft-high "arbour of a hundred roses" greets the visitor. The museum display also includes, at intervals, various paintings, reproductions of cars, trains and planes and miscellaneous exhibits (stamp album, Provençal market, musical instruments).

Musée Yves-Brayer
🕐 *Jul and Aug: 9am-7.30/8pm; Apr-Jun, Sep and Oct: 10am-12.30pm, 2-7pm; Nov, Dec, Feb and Mar: daily except Mon morning 10am-noon, 2.30-6pm.* 🕐 *Closed Jan and 25 Dec.* 🖚 *2.30€.* ☏ *05 63 56 02 40. Housed in the Maison du Grand Fauconnier.*

A 15C spiral staircase leads to the **Salle Yves-Brayer**, home to some of the painter's works: drawings, lithographs, etchings and watercolours.

The **Salle de la Broderie cordaise** offers embroidery demonstrations on a tambour frame. The mechanical embroidery frames, from St-Gall in Switzerland, brought Cordes prosperity in the late 19C and early 20C.

A third gallery, the **Salle de la Fresque**, which owes its name to the 14C murals decorating part of the walls, contains works of modern and contemporary art (paintings, stained glass and ceramics).

Excursions

- ▶▶ **Le Cayla** – *11km/7mi SW on D 922 towards Gaillac (signposted).* **Musée du Cayla** commemorates writers and poets **Maurice de Guérin** (1810-39) and his sister **Eugénie** (1805-48).

- ▶▶ **Monestiés** – *15km/9mi E on D 922 towards Villefranche, then D 91 to Carmaux.* **Chapelle St-Jacques** (🕐 *Jul and Aug: 10am-1pm, 2-7pm; mid-Mar to end Jun, Sep and Oct: 10am-noon, 2-6pm; early Jan to mid-Mar, Nov and Dec: 2-5pm.* 🕐 *Closed 1 Jan and 25 Dec.* 🖚 *3.50€ (combined ticket with the Bajén-Vega centre: 5€).* ☏ *05 63 76 19 17)* contains some beautiful sculpture groups, in particular a marvellous 15C **Entombment**★★. Take a look at the **Centre contemporain Bajén-Vega** (🕐 *Jul and Aug: 10am-1pm, 2-7pm; mid-Mar to end Jun, Sep and Oct: 10am-noon, 2-6pm; early Jan to mid-Mar, Nov and Dec: 2-5pm.* 🕐 *Closed 1 Jan and 25 Dec.* 🖚 *3.50€ (ticket also valid for the tour of the Chapelle St-Jacques)* ☏ *05 63 76 19 17.)* which houses paintings by Spanish political refugees Martine Vega and Francisco Bajén.

CÔTE VERMEILLE★★

MICHELIN LOCAL MAP 344: J-7 TO K-8

The resorts along this rocky stretch of coast, tucked inside narrow little bays, owe much of their character to their old vocation as small maritime fortresses. The "vermilion" coast is named after just one of the vivid colours which make up the natural palette of the local landscape, which is further enhanced by the bright, clear light of this region.

Two roads offer tourists a chance to explore the Côte Vermeille: Route des crêtes (N 114), the mountain road, and Route du littoral, the coast road, via Collioure and Port-Vendres (*heavy traffic in summer*).

The Mountain Road ☐1

37km/23mi from Argelès-Plage to Cerbère – about 2hr 30min.

Argelès-Plage ♨♨♨
👁 *See ARGELÈS-PLAGE.*

Beyond Argelès and the long flat stretch of beach to the north, the coast suddenly becomes much more dramatic. The road (N 114) climbs into the first foothills of the Albères range, continually cutting across the rocky headlands lapped by the Mediterranean.

▶ *At the roundabout just before Collioure, take D 86 left.*

The road heads uphill, initially through the Collioure vineyards.

▶ *Turn left again at the first intersection, onto a downhill road.*

Notre-Dame-de-Consolation
🕐 *Early Apr to mid-Nov: 8am-10pm.* 🖚 *No charge.* ☏ *04 68 82 17 66.*

This hermitage is well known throughout Roussillon. The chapel contains numerous votive offerings from sailors.

Address Book

For coin ranges, see the Legend at the back of the guide.

EATING OUT

La Côte Vermeille – *Quai Fanal – 66660 Port-Vendres - ☎ 04 68 82 05 71 - closed 5 Jan-5 Feb, Sun and Mon*. This building by the fishing harbour, just before the fishmarket, houses a restaurant run by two brothers. Seafood features on the menu, of course! It is served in a modern setting with a good view of the harbour.

⊜⊜ **Les Clos de Paulilles** – *66660 Port-Vendres - 3km/2mi N of Banyuls on N 114 - ☎ 04 68 98 07 58 – daure@ wanadoo.fr - open in evening Jun-Sep and Sun lunchtime - reservations required*. This restaurant at the heart of a wine-growing property serves good country cooking, and washes each course down with a different home-produced wine! So as not to get tipsy too soon, sit on the shady terrace where a refreshing sea breeze may come to your rescue!

WHERE TO STAY

⊜ **Ermitage Notre Dame de Consolation** – *66190 Collioure – ☎04 68 82 17 66 – closed 11 Nov-31 Mar - ⇥ P - 12 rms*. This pilgrimage site in a little oasis of greenery welcomes guests in basic but fresh and colourful rooms. Some are in old monks' cells. It is possible to visit the chapel. There is a picnic area reserved for guests' use in the evening.

▷ *Turn back to D 86 and turn left (note: this stretch of mountain road has no safety barriers or other protection).*

Cork-oaks become more prevalent, in between patches of exposed black rock – flaky schist.

▷ *Follow the signs for the wine route, "Circuit du vignoble," through the vineyards towards Banyuls.*

This spectacular mountain road leads to a viewing table. On the roadside opposite are the ruins of some old three-storey brick and schist barracks built in 1885.

▷ *Take the steep, narrow track to the right leading up to Tour Madeloc (note: extreme caution required: gradient of 1:4, with tight hairpin bends and no space for passing).*

The road passes two more fortified constructions before reaching a small level plateau.

Tour Madeloc

Alt 652m/2 138ft. 15min on foot round-trip.

An old signal tower which, together with the Tour de la Massane to the west, was part of a network of lookout posts during the reign of the kings of Aragón and Mallorca. Tour de la Massane surveyed the plain of Roussillon whereas Tour Madeloc kept watch out to sea. In front of the tower is a postern forming a lookout point with a splendid **panorama**★★ of the Albères mountains, the Vermeille and Roussillon coasts. The tower itself is round, made of schist and crowned with machicolations.

The track back down to D 86 gives breathtaking, unrestricted **views**★ of the sea and the town of Banyuls.

▷ *Turn right onto D 86.*

The road, with its many pretty views of the surrounding slopes, leads to Banyuls. It goes past the underground wine cellar of Mas Reig, situated in the oldest vineyard in the Banyuls area, as well as the modern cellar in which wines from the Cave des Templiers are aged.

Banyuls

See BANYULS-SUR-MER.

Cap Réderis★★

See below.

Cerbère

This small seaside resort lies well sheltered in a little cove and has a pebble beach. It is the last town on French soil before Spain and the Costa Brava, and the international railway line from Paris to Barcelona has a stop here. The railway viaduct can be seen as you arrive along the tortuous road. White houses, outdoor cafés and narrow pedestrian streets all lend charm to the scene.

The Coast Road ②

33km/21mi from Cerbère to Argelès-Plage – about 2hr.

Beyond Cerbère, the cliff road winds through vineyards – including several terraces which have been abandoned – overlooking a vast seascape. Beaches follow in quick succession, separated by sharply pointed promontories.

Cap Réderis★★

Where the road is nearest to the edge of the cliff, walk a few paces towards the edge for a better view. A magnificent **panorama** encompasses the coasts of Languedoc and Catalonia, as far south as the Cabo de Creus.

Farther along, the whole of the bay of Banyuls comes into view on the left, from a wide bend in the road. This is a particularly spectacular sight at high tide. The road twists and turns along the coast, with the sea in full view close at hand. Down below, there are numerous tempting little bays and rocky coves. As the road drops down towards Banyuls, there is a clear view of the town with its schist pebble beach and palm trees.

Banyuls ☆

🕭 *See BANYULS-SUR-MER.*

As it leaves Banyuls, the road goes past a seaside sanatorium specialising in helio-therapy. In the distance, on the left, Tour Madeloc rears its proud head.

Port-Vendres

Just before you reach Port-Vendres, there is an excellent view of the port complex on the right.

▶ *Turn right towards Cap Béar then, after the Hôtel des Tamarins, cross the railway line and drive round to the south of the bay.*

Cap Béar

The narrow cliff road climbs steeply in a series of tight bends. From the lighthouse at the tip of the headland, the coast can be seen all the way from Cap Leucate to Cabo de Creus.

Port-Vendres ⌂

Otherwise known as the Port of Venus, it grew up around a cove which offered excellent shelter for galleys. The town's development as a naval port and stronghold really took off in 1679, under Vauban's influence.

Once a major port for trade and passengers to and from Algeria, Port-Vendres has become increasingly popular for pleasure boating, and the fishing fleet is the most active on the Roussillon coast.

Collioure★★

ℹ *See COLLIOURE.*

The road leaves the foothills of the Albères before reaching Argelès.

La COUVERTOIRADE★

POPULATION 153

MICHELIN LOCAL MAP 338: L-7

This tiny fortified town with its striking military features, in the middle of the Causse du Larzac was once the property of the Knights Templars, under orders from the commandery at Ste-Eulalie-de-Cernon. The curtain wall was built in about 1439 by the Knights of St John of Jerusalem (who took over possession of the *causses* on dissolution of the Order of the Templars).

La Couvertoirade, like other villages on the Larzac plateau, rapidly became depopulated. By 1880, the village had only 362 inhabitants. A few craftsmen now live here (enamel work, pottery, weaving).

ℹ *For coin ranges, see the Legend at the back of the guide.*

SAVOURY OR SWEET

🍴 **La Crêperie Montes** – R. Droite - ☎ 05 65 62 25 89 - closed 15 Nov through Easter school holidays - ✉ - 6.30/18.30€. The menu features crêpes of course, but with herbes de Provence and olive oil! Take a break from exploring the historic old town and enjoy one. The pretty vaulted dining room is decorated with woodcuts, drawings and old tools.

Sights

▶ *Park the car near the north gate, outside the ramparts.*

Ramparts

🕐 *May-Aug: 10am-7pm; Apr: 10am-noon, 2-6pm; early Sep to mid-Nov and Feb school holidays: 10am-noon, 2-5pm; end Feb school holidays to end Mar: Sat-Sun 10am-noon, 2-5pm.* 3€. Guided tours possible by request. 5€. ☎ 05 65 58 55 59.

Go through the north gateway and take the flight of steps (*no handrail*) leading up from the foot of a Renaissance house. The tall, square north tower would appear to have been used as a watchtower.

The "Cardabelle"

Many of the doors in La Couvertoirade and other villages in the area are adorned with a curious dried plant, resembling a sunflower surrounded by ragged spiny leaves – this is the *Carlina acanthifolia*, a type of thistle known locally as the **cardabelle**. It has the characteristic of opening or closing according to the degree of humidity, making it the local equivalent of seaweed hung outside to forecast the weather.

La Couvertoirade

Following the watch-path round to the left as far as the round tower, you have an interesting view over the town and its main street, rue Droite.

▶ *Return to the foot of the north tower and go into the village, bearing left.*

Church

🕐 *Apr-Aug: 10am-7pm; Feb, Mar and early Sep to mid-Nov: 10am-noon, 2-5pm. By request at the information desk or at the town hall. ☎ 05 65 58 55 59.*

This fortified 14C church built on the edge of the parade ground was an integral part of the town's defences. Inside, at the entrance to the chancel, there are two disc-shaped steles showing different representations of the cross. The tiny graveyard by the entrance to the church contains some unusual disc-shaped gravestones.

Château

This fortress was built by the Templars in the 12C and 13C; the two upper floors have since disappeared.

▶ *Keep left until you reach a large square, once a village pond, where you walk round a block of houses to the right to reach rue Droite.*

Rue Droite

The houses in the main street are very attractive, with straight flights of stone steps outside leading up to a balcony and the door into the living area, beneath which a vault protected the ground floor where the sheep were kept.

Go through the south gateway, bereft of its tower, which collapsed. To the left, just past the corner of the town wall, there is a fine example of a *lavogne*, or village sheep pond, a common feature in the *causses*.

▶ *Walk along the outside of the ramparts, round to the right, to get back to the car.*

Grotte de DARGILAN★★

MICHELIN LOCAL MAP 330: I-9

In 1880 a shepherd called Sahuquet was chasing a fox when he saw it slip between a crack in the rocks. The shepherd enlarged the crack to follow his quarry and found himself in a huge dark underground chamber. Thinking it to be the antechamber to hell, he fled and the first complete exploration was not carried out until 1888, when E A Martel and six companions took four days to examine it. Once "officially" discovered, it was not long before the cave began to attract visitors, but little was done to adapt it for them. Dargilan then became the property of the Société des Gorges du Tarn which, under the management of Louis Armand, fitted iron steps, ramps and railings so that the cave could be visited safely. In 1910, electric lighting was installed in all the galleries.

Visit

Allow 1hr; temperature: 10°C/50°F. ○ ⌖ Jul and Aug: guided tours (1hr) 10am-6.30pm; Apr-Jun and Sep: 10am-noon, 2-5.30pm; Oct: 10am-noon, 2-4.30pm. ⌖ 8€ (children: 4€). ☎ 04 66 45 60 20.

Visitors first enter the **Grande Salle du Chaos**, a gallery 142m/465ft long by 44m/114ft wide and 35m/115ft high. This sinkhole was formed later than the rest of the cave. It looks like a chaotic underground heap of rocks on which concretions are slowly building up.

At the back of the Grande Salle, the smaller Salle de la Mosquée contains a large number of beautiful stalagmites. The "Mosque," a mass of stalagmites with glints of mother-of-pearl, is flanked by the "Minaret," a lovely column 20m/66ft high.

The "Salle Rose" adjoining the "Mosque" takes its name from the colour of its concretions (pink). Go back into the Grande Salle from where a number of staircases lead down into the depths of the cave.

A natural shaft leads to the "corridor of petrified cascades" in which there is a magnificent calcite drapery, reddish-brown flecked with yellow ochre and white, stretching 100m/330ft long and 40m/130ft high.

The Salle du Lac owes its name to a shallow stretch of water. It is decorated with thin, folded translucent draperies. After going through the "labyrinth" and a chamber of gours (natural underground lakes), left as a mark of its passage by the water that once flowed here, the visitor reaches the Salle du Clocher with, in its centre, a slender pyramid 20m/66ft high – the "Belfry." Beyond this, the Salle du Cimetière leads to the Salle des Vasques (hand basins) and then the "gallery of the two wells." The visit ends in the Salle du Tombeau, which contains a fine stalagmitic frozen fall.

Visitors retrace their steps to leave the cave via a semi-artificial gallery and an overhang path from which there is a beautiful panorama of the Jonte Valley.

Grotte des DEMOISELLES★★★

MICHELIN LOCAL MAP 339: H-5 – ALSO SEE GANGES

This cave was discovered in 1770, and properly examined and documented 10 years later. E-A Martel, who explored it in 1884, 1889 and 1897, revealed the cave to be in fact an old swallow-hole, the mouth of which opens onto the **Plateau de Thaurac**. In the imagination of the local rural community, this gaping chasm was home to fairies or demoiselles.

ⓒ *For coin ranges, see the Legend at the back of the guide.*

EATING OUT

⊜ **Restaurant des Grottes** – *34190 St-Bauzille-de-Putois - 2.5km/1.5mi W of the Grotte des Demoiselles - ☎ 04 67 73 70 28 - closed end Sep-early Oct and in the evening except Jul-Aug - ⌖. After the darkness of the cave, come and sit on the terrace in the shade of the century-old chestnut and local variety of elm tree. Inside, time seems to have stop... at the moment the restaurant was launched in 1951. Good value for the mo...*

▶ *At St-Bauzille-de-Putois, take the hairpin road (one-way) up to two terraces (parking facilities) near the entrance to the cave. From the terraces there is an attractive view of Séranne mountain and Hérault Valley.*

Visit

Allow 1hr; temperature: 14°C/57°F. ⏱ 🎧 *Jul and Aug: guided tours (1hr, last departure 30min before closing) 9am-7.30pm; Apr-Jun and Sep: 9.45am-6.30pm; Oct-Mar: 9.45am-noon, 1.30-5.30pm.* ⏱ *Closed 1 Jan and 25 Dec.* ✆ *7.50€ (children: 3.90€).* ☎ *04 67 73 70 02. www.demoiselles.com.*

From the upper funicular station, hollowed out of the mountain and level with the roof of the cave, a series of chambers leads to the natural mouth of the swallow-hole. The most striking thing about the cave is the number and size of the concretions thickly covering its walls. The magnificent "architecture" of their surroundings cannot fail to impress visitors throughout the tour.

From the swallow-hole, a series of narrow corridors leads to a sort of platform overlooking the central part of the cave itself: an immense chamber, 120m/394ft long, 80m/262ft wide and 50m/164ft high.

The huge space, the enormous columns seeming to support the roof, the awesome silence and the light mist which seems to hang in the air from time to time all combine to give the impression that one is in a gigantic cathedral.

Walkways lead all round this spectacular chamber, gradually dropping down to the elegant stalagmite resembling a Virgin and Child, perched on a white calcite pedestal. At this point look back to admire the fantastic set of "organ pipes" adorning the north wall of the cave.

The walkway leads on through beautiful draperies, some of which are translucent, whereas others form mini-stages for the strangest performers.

A number of viewpoints above the cavern enhance the impression of passing through some dream world of rock right until the end of the tour.

A. Cassaigne/MICHELIN

Grotte de la DEVÈZE ★

MICHELIN LOCAL MAP 339: B-8

This cave was discovered in 1886, when a tunnel was being drilled through Devèze mountain to carry the Bédarieux-Castres railway line, and explored in 1893 by a team including Louis Armand, Martel's faithful assistant. From 1928 to 1930, it was explored in more detail by Georges-Milhaud and his team and, in 1932, part of the cave was opened to visitors. It lies beneath the railway station at Courniou and is a trace of the old course of the Salesse, a tributary of the Jaur.

🚶 A waymarked path (*yellow markings*) starting near the entrance to the cave leads (*1hr 15min*) to seven *capitelles*, drystone shepherd huts.

Visit

Allow 1hr; temperature: 12°C/54°F.

The cave

The tour begins on the middle level, from where there is a view of some fine mineral draperies of various shapes and colours. All along the cave walls are slender, white ...ons forming delightful bouquets of aragonite flowers. At the end of the ... is a large petrified fall dropping down onto the lower level.

In the middle of a pile of boulders resulting from a rockfall are a number of rocks of varying shapes and forms, the most impressive of which is a huge stalagmite known as the "Cenotaph" or "Bridal Cake," an architectural structure on a pedestal beneath a roof covered with tubular shapes and draperies.

The upper chamber 60m/195ft above (*access via a flight of steps*) is full of eccentrics, draperies and discs.

The tour ends in the Georges-Milhaud chamber which is dotted with dazzling white crystallisations.

Musée français de la Spéléologie

This museum houses collections of documents and items related to cave exploration and famous French speleologists, including: Édouard-Alfred Martel, Robert de Joly, Norbert Casteret and Guy de Lavaur de la Boisse. Displays also concern paleontology, the protection of the underground environment and cave fauna.

ELNE★

POPULATION 6 410

MICHELIN LOCAL MAP 344: I-7

Elne was known, during the days of the Iberians, as "Illiberis" and was named after the Empress Helen, Constantine's mother. At the end of the Roman Empire, it was the true capital of the Roussillon area. Its status of bishopric from the 6C to 1602 entitled it to call itself a "city", the term originally applied to administrative divisions of Roman provinces, whereas its wealthier rival, Perpignan, was never more than a "town". The superb cathedral cloisters testify to Elne's former splendour.

Set 6km/3.5mi from the coast between apricot and peach orchards lining the roads east and west (*D 4 and D 612*), Elne is a major stopping point on the road to Spain.

Sights

Cathédrale Ste-Eulalie-et-Ste-Julie *1hr*

Building work began on the cathedral in the 11C. The six chapels in the south aisle were built from the 14C to the mid-15C; their ribbed vaulting reflects the three stages in the evolution of Gothic architecture. The original plans provided for two bell-towers, but only the square, stone tower on the right was built.

In the chapel beside the south entrance (chapel 3), there is an altarpiece painted by a 14C Catalan artist depicting the visions and miracles of St Michael. Opposite the southeast entrance beneath the Passion Crucifix known as the "Improperia Cross," there is an interesting fluted marble stoup made out of an ancient basin decorated with a large acanthus leaf.

Cloisters★★

🕐 *Jun-Sep: 9.30am-7pm; Apr, May and Oct: 9.30am-6pm; Nov-Mar: 9.30am-noon, 2-5pm.*
🕐 *Closed 1 Jan, 1 May, 25 Dec.* ⊜ *4€ (children: 1.50€).* ☎ *04 68 22 70 90. To enter the cloisters, walk round the chevet to the left.*

Kids The south cloisters backing onto the cathedral were built in the 12C; the other three date from the 13C and 14C. Nevertheless, there is a high level of architectural uniformity since the Gothic construction copied its Romanesque predecessor.

The superb **capitals** on the twin columns supporting the rounded arcades are decorated with narrative carvings, imaginary animals, biblical and evangelical figures,

B. Kaufmann/MICHELIN

Cloisters seen from the north gallery

and plants. The carvings are particularly descriptive beneath the abaci of the quadrangular pillars. The Romanesque south gallery is the most outstanding of all. Capital 12, depicting Adam and Eve, is the most remarkable work in the cloisters.

From the east cloisters (where some 6C and 7C sarcophagi are on display), a spiral staircase rises to a terrace from which there is a view over part of the cloisters, the towers (note the larger of the two) and the cathedral roof. On the horizon is the Albères range.

Musée d'Archéologie

Entrance up the staircase at the end of the east cloisters. The archaeological museum occupies the old chapel of St-Laurent and exhibits 15C, 16C and 17C earthenware, Attic ceramics (4C BC) and sigillated ceramic ware from Illiberis (Elne under Roman rule). At the back there is a display on Véraza culture (Aude region) with reconstructions of huts made of wood and reeds.

Musée d'Histoire

Entrance via the west cloisters. The historical museum occupies the old chapter-house and contains archives, a variety of literature and the town seals. In one of the display cases are two statues of the Virgin Mary, the Vierge des Tres Portalets (13C) and the Vierge du Portail de Perpignan (14C).

Musée Terrus

  🕐 *Jun-Sep: 10am-7pm; Apr and May: 10am-6pm; Oct: 10am-12.30pm, 2-6pm; Nov-Mar: 10am-noon, 2-5pm.* 🕐 *Closed 1 Jan, 1 May, 25 Dec.* ✆ *1.80€ ticket combined with the Elne cloister).* ☎ *04 68 22 88 88.*

This museum, housed in a modern building, is named after a local artist, Étienne Terrus (1857-1922) and displays works by him and by the artists whose company he kept, such as Luce, Maillol and G de Monfreid (woodcuts). Terrus was influenced by the Impressionists and the Fauves but nonetheless developed a style of his own which is evident in his Roussillon landscapes (*View of Espira-de-Conflent or Mas d'Adel*) and his still-life pictures.

Le Tropique du Papillon

Entrance via avenue Paul-Reig, at the intersection with the Argelès-Perpignan road (N 114). 🕐 *Jul and Aug: 10am-7pm; May: 10am-12.30pm, 2.30-7pm (6pm in Apr).* ✆ *5€ (children: 3.50€).* ☎ *04 68 37 83 77.*

Butterflies and moths flutter freely around this tropical hothouse; there is a nursery and an educational area.

Oppidum d'ENSÉRUNE ★★

MICHELIN LOCAL MAP 339: D-9

The Ensérune hill fort stands 120m/390ft above the Béziers plain. Its decidedly Mediterranean geographical location and wonderful pine wood are quite out of the ordinary, and its archaeological site is also of particular interest. It was here, in 1915, that traces of an Iberian-Greek settlement and a crematorium dating from the 4C and 3C BC were uncovered.

A Bit of History

Ensérune was a settlement from the 6C BC until the beginning of the Christian era and its remains are an indication of the type of civilisation that preceded the arrival of the Romans. In the 6C BC, huts probably built of pisé, or mud, were strung out across the hilltop. Nothing remains of this period except the food stores dug into the tufa stone. Ensérune had trading links with Greece via Marseille and enjoyed an economic boom. The old village evolved into a town with stone houses set out in a chequerboard pattern. A large earthenware jar (*dolium*) was sunk into the floor of every house to serve as a pantry. A town wall was built and to the west of the town there lay a vast area used for funeral pyres.

From the middle of the Second Iron Age, Ensérune underwent further change. It expanded and the hillsides were laid out in terraces. A grain store was built to the south, consisting of a number of silos. At the end of the 3C BC, the hill fort was probably razed by Hannibal. It was rebuilt and regained its erstwhile prosperity after the arrival of the Romans who, in 118 BC, founded their first colony in Narbonne. Tanks were built, a sewage system was installed, paving stones were laid, and the walls were plastered and painted. Then the population gradually moved away from the hill fort, and it finally fell into a total decline in the 1C AD when *Pax Romana* enabled people to settle safely on the plains.

Visit

About 1hr 30min. ◷ *May-Aug: 10am-7pm (last admission 1hr before closing); Sep and Apr: daily except Mon 10am-12.30pm, 2-6pm; Oct-Mar: daily except Mon 9.30am-12.30pm, 2-5.30pm.* ◷ *Closed 1 Jan, 1 May, 1 and 11 Nov, 25 Dec.* ◷ *4.60€ (under age 18: no charge).* ☎ *04 67 37 01 23.*

> ◷ *For coin ranges, see the Legend at the back of the guide.*
>
> ### CHÂTEAU DINING
>
> ◷ **Restaurant du Château de Colombiers** – *R. du Château – 34440 Colombiers - 2.5km/1.5mi E of the oppidum of Ensérune on B-road -* ☎ *04 67 37 06 93 - closed Jan and Mon – reservations required off-season.* This castle was built on top of 12C vaulted cellars in the 16C and 17C. A floating landing stage awaits amateur sailors on the nearby Canal du Midi. There is a pleasant terrace beneath the chestnut trees. The restaurant has a lord of the manor atmosphere about it.

Museum★

Built on the site of the antique city, the museum houses items found during excavations which illustrate daily life from the 6C to the 1C BC.

Displayed on the ground floor is a collection of *dolia* (jars) found buried beneath houses, ceramics, vases, amphorae, pottery of various origins (Phocaean, Iberian, Greek, Etruscan, Roman as well as local).

First-floor exhibits include funerary objects found in the necropolis, dating from the 5C to the 3C BC: Greek vases and urns used for cremation or to contain offerings. Note the famous "Procris and Cephalos" cup from Attica exhibited in a small glass case. In the Mouret room, the central glass case contains an egg found inside a grave, which symbolises the renewal of life.

Panorama

Viewing tables set out at all four cardinal points of the compass around the hill fort provide an opportunity to enjoy a vast panoramic view stretching from the Cévennes to Canigou and across the entire coastal plain. In the foreground are archaeological finds that have been left in place, such as dolia, remains of columns, and the foundations of ancient walls.

The **view**★ is particularly unusual to the north. It takes in the **old Montady Lake** which was drained in 1247. The plots of land radiate out from the centre because of the channels that drain the water off into a collector. From there, an aqueduct passes under the hill and takes the water to the floor of the old Capestang Lake, which was drained in the 19C.

Oppidum d'Ensérune

L. Campion/MICHELIN

ENTRAYGUES-SUR-TRUYÈRE★

POPULATION 1,267

MICHELIN LOCAL MAP 338: H-3

Entraygues, which was founded in the 13C by the Count of Rodez, is well situated at the confluence of the River Lot and River Truyère, between hillsides covered with meadows, fruit trees and vines which produce an excellent wine.

The town has become a sports and leisure resort (canoeing, rambling). There is an excellent view of the village and the Truyère Valley from the Condat viewpoint to the northwest, on the Aurillac road.

Sights

Gothic bridge★ (Pont gothique)
One-way traffic in summer.
The bridge dates from the end of the 13C.

Old town

To see the covered passageways known locally as *"cantous"* and the picturesque houses with over-hanging upper storeys and flowers at every window, start from the tiny place Albert-Castanié or place de la Croix; on the corner of the old Sabathier mansion, marks on the wall indicate the highest levels reached by the River Lot and River Truyère when in spate. Walk down Rue Droite. On the right is a fine 16C entrance with a knocker above

Gothic bridge

the door so that riders did not have to dismount. Turn left on Rue du Collège then follow **Rue Basse★**, the best preserved of all the streets in Entraygues. Continue along the water's edge (quai des Gabares) to the confluence of the two rivers. From this spot, there is a fine view of the castle (o━ *not open to the public*). Only the two towers date from the 13C; the central section was rebuilt in the 17C.

Excursions

Puy de Montabès★
11km/6.8mi NE along D 34 then right on D 652. 🚶 *15min on foot round-trip.*
Superb **panoramic view**★ over the mountains of Cantal, Aubrac, and Rouergue (the cathedral in Rodez is visible in clear weather). Downstream from Entraygues, the view encompasses the Lot Valley and Châtaigneraie plateau. Viewing table.

Vallée du Lot★★
👣 *See ESPALION.*

Gorges de la Truyère★
80km/50mi round-trip – allow 3hr.
▷ *Leave Entraygues heading N along D 34.*
Among the granite plateaux of upper Auvergne, the River Truyère flows through deeply sunken, narrow, sinuous gorges, in which the landscape is tree-covered and rugged. The gorges constitute one of the finest natural sights of central France.

Dams, built as part of a hydroelectric power scheme, have transformed extensive stretches of the river into reservoirs, which have of course altered the appearance of the gorges, happily without spoiling their picturesque character, except when water levels are low. There is no road leading along the entire length of the valley, but many roads cut across it, providing some fine viewpoints over the river and its gorges.

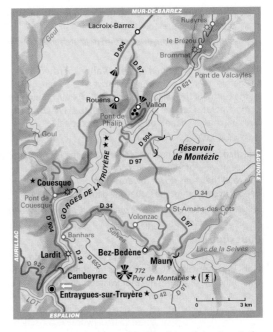

Barrage de Cambeyrac

The 14.5m/47ft-high Cambeyrac dam, which regulates the flow of the river, is the last of the Truyère Valley hydroelectric installations just before the river flows into the Lot. A little farther upstream, after a bend in the river, the Lardit hydroelectric power station can be seen on the opposite bank.

▷ *In the hamlet of Banhars, turn left onto D 34. Beyond the bridge over the Selves, continue right along D 34.*

The road winds through the picturesque Selves Valley before reaching the tiny Volonzac plateau.

▷ *In Volonzac, turn right onto a narrow road leading to Bez-Bedène.*

Bez-Bedène

This typical Rouergue-style village occupies a harsh, isolated setting and consists of a few houses strung out along a rocky ridge enclosed within a meander of the Selves. Of note are the small 12C church with a bellcote, and the 14C single-span bridge.

▷ *Continue along the same road to the crossroads with D 34, into which you turn right towards St-Amans-des-Cots. D 97 leads to the Maury dam.*

Barrage de Maury

The Maury dam was built in 1948 at the confluence of the Selves and Selvet. Its reservoir, covering an area of 166ha/410 acres, lies in a varied, colourful landscape.

▷ *Drive back to St-Amans-des-Cots along D 97.*

Réservoir de Montézic

Situated on the granite Plateau de la Viadène, the Montézic reservoir is formed by two dams on the Plane rivulet. With a surface area of 245ha/605 acres,

⚅ *For coin ranges, see the Legend at the back of the guide.*

EATING OUT

🍲 **Ferme-auberge de Mejanassère** – *4km/2.5mi E of Entraygues on D 42 -* ☎ *05 65 44 54 76 - closed Oct-end Mar and Mon-Fri Oct-Mar -* 🍽 *- reservations required.* The terrace of this farm-inn overhangs vines that date back to Ancient Roman days; there is a view of the whole valley from here. The charm of this spot is irresistible. The food served is typical of the region and the bread baked over a wood fire completes the picture. Good guest rooms and a gîte.

WHERE TO STAY

🛏 **Camping Les Tours** – *12460 St-Amans-des-Cots - 6km/4mi SE of St-Amans on D 97 and D 599 -* ☎ *05 65 44 88 10 - camping-les-tours@wanadoo.fr - open 17 May-7 Sep - reservation recommended - 250 sites: food service.* Water sports lovers and nature addicts will love the setting of this camp site by Selves lake. Wind-surfers, canoes and pedalos can be hired. There is a swimming pool and a children's club.

it serves as an upper reservoir to that at Couesque and supplies the underground plant through high pressure tunnels.

▶ *Return to D 97 and drive across the Phalip suspension bridge spanning the Couesque reservoir.*

The road skirts the ruined castle of **Vallon**, perched on a spur above the valley. At the hamlet there is a fine viewpoint over the Truyère gorges.

At the centre of the village of **Lacroix-Barrez**, a monument was erected in 1949 to commemorate Cardinal Verdier, archbishop of Paris, who from 1930 to 1940 had over 100 churches or chapels built around the capital.

▶ *Follow D 904 S.*

The road reaches the hamlet of **Rouens** on the left. Downhill from the church, there is a scenic view of Couesque reservoir and Phalip bridge.

The road then runs down towards the floor of the valley, offering fine views of the deep Truyère gorges, the Couesque dam and its reservoir.

▶ *Before the Couesque bridge on the Goul, take a road to the left which leads to the Couesque plant and dam.*

Couesque dam★

This narrow-vault dam overhanging the river on the downstream side is 60m/196ft high. The reservoir stretches as far as the confluence of the Bromme and the Truyère, where the tail-race from the Brommat underground plant emerges.

Located in the hydraulic power station, the **Espace Truyère** (*Affected by the "Vigipirate" security plan, opening dates and times uncertain (*o━ *closed in 2003);* ☎ *05 65 44 56 10*) traces the development of the valley's hydroelectric scheme and explains how the various plants work by means of models, presentations and video films.

As the road travels south, the valley gradually offers a landscape of meadows, vineyards and orchards.

Lardit hydroelectric power station

This power plant uses water from the Selves and its tributary the Selvet, retained by the Maury dam on the Selves, south of St-Amans-des-Cots. The water is carried to the Lardit power station through a 6km/3mi-long tunnel followed since 1985 by a pressure pipeline.

▶ *Return to Entraygues via the Cambeyrac dam.*

ESPALION★

POPULATION 4,360

MICHELIN LOCAL MAP 338: I-3 – ALSO SEE AUBRAC

Espalion lies in pleasant surroundings in a fertile basin crossed by the River Lot. Above the town are the feudal ruins of Calmont d'Olt.

Walking Tour

Vieux pont (Old bridge)

From the marketplace, this 11C bridge forms part of a picturesque view that encompasses the Vieux Palais and the old tanneries with timber balconies lining the river banks.

Vieux palais (Old palace)

The palace was built in the 16C and used to be the residence of the governors of Espalion.

Église de Perse★
1km/0.6mi SE along avenue de la Gare.

This fine, pink sandstone Romanesque building dates from the 11C and is reminiscent of the abbey church at Conques. Indeed, this was once one of the daughter-houses of Conques Abbey. It is dedicated to St Hilarian, Charlemagne's confessor, who is said in holy legend to have retired to Espalion and been beheaded by the Moors.

Tanners' houses by the old bridge on the River Lot

On the south side is a **portal**★ including a tympanum depicting Pentecost. The lintel is decorated with carvings of the Apocalypse and the Last Judgement.

Above and to the left are three naïve carvings of the Adoration of the Magi. Inside the church, note the historiated capitals, among them a lion hunt and Christ in Majesty, either side of the apse. There are traces of frescoes on the transept vaulting.

Additional Sights

Musée Joseph-Vaylet

◷ *Jul and Aug: 10am-noon, 2-7pm; May, Jun, Sep and Oct: daily except Mon and Tue 10am-noon, 2-6pm; Dec-Apr: Sat-Sun and public holidays 2-6pm.* ◷ *Closed Nov.* ⊜ *4€ (ticket combined with the Musée du Scaphandre).* ☎ *05 65 44 09 18.*

The museum, housed in the old church of St-Jean and adjacent buildings, has a large number of collections relating to folk arts, crafts and traditions, including weaponry, furniture, glassware, religious artefacts (450 holy-water stoups) and pottery.

There is also a **museum of diving suits** (*Same admission times and charges as the musée Joseph-Vaylet and combined ticket.* ☎ *05 65 44 09 18.*) in the same building. The exhibits are all on the theme of underwater diving and honour the memory of the three men from Espalion who, in 1860, invented the aqualung and the depressuriser (gas regulator).

Musée du Rouergue

◷ *Mid-Jul to end Aug: 10am-12.30pm, 2-7pm, Sat 2-7pm, Sun and public holidays 10am-12.30pm, 2-7pm.* ⊜ *3€.* ☎ *05 65 73 80 68.*

The cells of the former prison now house exhibits relating to local life and customs, including an extensive costume collection.

Excursions

Château de Calmont d'Olt

◷ *Jul and Aug: 9am-7pm; May, Jun and Sep: 10am-noon, 2-6pm; Feb, Easter and Nov school holidays: 2-6pm.* ⊜ *6€ Jul and Aug; 4.50€ Sep-Jun.* ☎ *05 65 44 15 89.*

▶ *Leave Espalion S along D 920 and follow the signs to the car park.*

🄺🄸🄳🅂 This medieval fortress stands on a spur of basalt from which there is a fine **view**★ of the Lot Valley, the Aubrac and the Causse du Comtal. It has not been used as a military stronghold since the 17C. A historic tour backed up by an audio-visual presentation gives information on the castle and the strategy and machinery of siege warfare used here in the 15C.

Vallée du Lot★★

54km/37mi – allow one day.

▶ *Leave Espalion W via D 556 (avenue de St-Pierre). At St-Pierre cross the bridge to the left. Then turn onto the track to the left.*

St-Pierre-de-Bessuéjouls

This unpretentious church in a rustic setting shelters beneath its bell-tower an outstanding little **Romanesque chapel** ★ *(access via a worn flight of steps)*. The pink chapel was built in the 11C. Each of its sides measures 6m/19ft and it is decorated with archaic motifs such as knotwork, palmettes, Maltese crosses and historiated capitals. Carved on the left side of the altar is a figure of the Archangel Michael slaying the dragon, and on the right side the Archangel Gabriel with an inscribed scroll.

Estaing★

⚐ *See ESTAING.*

Leaving Estaing, the road offers an attractive view of the Lot, the old bridge and the castle which dominates the little town.

Gorges du Lot★★

After widening for a few miles, and then being flooded by the Golinhac dam reservoir, the valley narrows into some very picturesque, rugged gorges about 300m/1 000ft deep, and rarely exceeding 1 500m/5 000ft across at the top of the valley walls. Rocky crests or points, with jagged or forbiddingly solid silhouettes, rise up out of the woods covering the sides of the gorges.

A few miles from Estaing is the **Golinhac dam**, which stands 37m/121ft high and, a little farther along on the opposite bank, stands the glass and metal structure of the hydroelectric plant, fed by the dam.

Entraygues-sur-Truyère★

⚐ *See ENTRAYGUES-SUR-TRUYÈRE.*

▶ *Follow D 107 W.*

The road offers a sweeping view of Entraygues and its castle, at the confluence of the River Truyère and River Lot.

The Lot Valley no longer has the harsh, forbidding character of the gorges upstream of Entraygues. At first, it is quite wide and very scenic. Vineyards which produce very good wine (VDQS Entraygues-le-Fel) grow in terraces on the well-exposed hillsides and the countryside is dotted with farmhouses. Farther on, the vineyards become scarcer, box grows among the rocks, which are closer together, and woods cover the slopes; several times, however, the valley widens into small cultivated basins where villages with picturesque houses nestle among fruit trees.

Vieillevie

Beautiful Renaissance castle, topped with protective defence walling *(can be visited in summer, please inquire)*.

▶ *Follow D 42 towards Decazeville.*

A minor road to the right leads steeply up to La Vinzelle, a tiny village hanging on to the mountain slope and affording a wide view of the Lot Valley.

▶ *Turn back to rejoin D 42 and continue towards Decazeville.*

St-Parthem

Here is your chance to learn all about the River Lot, sometimes called Olt. The **Maison de la rivière Olt** (⏱ Jul and Aug: daily except Friday 11am-1pm, 2-6pm (Wed evening 9pm); May, Jun and Sep: Whitsun; Oct-Apr: by request. ⏰ Closed Dec and Jan. ⊛ 4€ (children: 2.40€). ☎ 05 65 64 13 22.) is a very informative museum (audio-visual presentation, model, reconstructions) devoted to the River Lot which begins its journey in the Lozère region and covers 480km/298mi before flowing into the Garonne.

▶ *Continue along D 42 to Decazeville.*

ESTAING★

POPULATION 612

MICHELIN LOCAL MAP 338: I-3

The old houses in Estaing huddle round the foot of the castle, birthplace of the family of the same name, whose fame and fortune spanned several centuries until the 1789 Revolution. The Lot flows through Estaing, making it a pleasant holiday resort and an ideal centre from which to visit Entraygues and Espalion.

A colourful procession celebrating St Fleuret, a 7C local bishop, takes place on the first Sunday in July.

Sights

From the Entraygues road, there is a picturesque view of the Lot, the old bridge and the castle high above the village. From the Laguiole road, there is a delightful view, especially in the morning, of the other side of the castle, the chevet of the church and the old houses of the village.

Château

🕐 Jun-Sep: daily except Mon 9.30am-12.30pm, 2.30-7pm; Oct-May: 9am-noon, 2-6pm, Sat-Sun by request. ☜ 3€. ☎ 05 65 44 72 24.

Built over successive architectural periods (15C-16C) using a variety of building materials, the castle features a curious combination of styles and is dominated by its keep. From the west terrace, there is a superb view of the old town and the River Lot. The castle is occupied by a religious Order.

> 🪙 For coin ranges, see the Legend at the back of the guide.
>
> **FARMHOUSE B&B**
>
> ☜ **Chambre d'hôte Cervel** – Rte de Vinnac - ☎05 65 44 09 89 – closed 15 Nov -30 Mar - 🍴- 4 rms: 39/47€ – meal 15€. This farm on a hillside is run by a friendly couple who fell in love with this region. The rooms offer every comfort, and the menu features imaginative local cooking. Do not miss the kid (chevreaux) or the highly scented Aubrac tea.

Church

The 15C church opposite the castle contains the relics of St Fleuret. In front of the church are several fine Gothic crosses.

Gothic bridge

The bridge carries a statue of François d'Estaing, Bishop of Rodez, who had the superb bell-tower built on the town's cathedral.

Maison Cayron

This house is located in the old town. It still has its Renaissance windows and now houses the town hall (mairie).

Estaing

Le FENOUILLÈDES★★

MICHELIN LOCAL MAP 344: F AND G 6

The Fenouillèdes, the area whose name evokes the aromatic plant known as fennel, lies between the southern Corbières and the Conflent.

Geographically speaking, this area links the furrow hollowed out between the Col Campérié and Estagel (the more populated area, including the vineyards of Maury and the "Côtes du Roussillon") and a more rugged crystalline mountain range that becomes particularly arid between Sournia and Prades. However, here as elsewhere, extensive land clearance indicates the advance of the vineyards into the scrubland of holm-oaks and thornbushes.

Excursion

Round-Trip from St-Paul-de-Fenouillet

60km/37mi – about 4hr.

St-Paul-de-Fenouillet

This town lies on the east bank of the Agly, a short distance before its confluence with the Boulzane.

Clue de la Fou

This is a *cluse* or transverse valley gouged out by the Agly. There is always a strong wind blowing here whatever the weather. Cross the river and follow D 619 as it hugs the river bank.

The road consists of a picturesque succession of bends in sight of the Fenouillèdes furrow and its vineyards. In the background the ruined castle of Quéribus can be seen perched on its rocky pinnacle. The Canigou peak looms in the distance. The road runs close to the Roman aqueduct at **Ansignan**, which is well preserved and still in use, then, in an ever-increasing number of bends, it reaches Sournia via Pézilla-de-Conflent.

▸ *Turn right onto D 7 towards St-Prats-de-Sournia.*

The road offers a fine view of the Corbières to the north and of the Mediterranean Sea through the Agly Valley.

▸ *Beyond Le Vivier, turn left onto D 9 towards Caudiès.*

Notre-Dame-de-Laval

Previously a **hermitage**, this Gothic church stands on an esplanade lined with olive trees, its pink-roofed body flanked by a tower with an octagonal top section surmounted by a brick roof shaped like a candle snuffer. At the foot of the slope the

---

For coin ranges, see the Legend at the back of the guide.

EATING OUT AND WHERE TO STAY

◻◻ **Le Relais des Corbières** – *10 Ave. Jean-Moulin - 66220 St-Paul-de-Fenouillet - ☏ 04 68 59 23 89 – relais. corbieres@free.fr - closed 2-28 Jan, Sun evening and Mon except Jul-Aug and public holidays.* The road may be nearby, but visitors will not be disappointed here. There is a warm welcome and food free of frills awaiting guests in the dining room with rustic decor. Terrace to the side of the house. This establishment is a useful address to have in the valley.

◻◻ **Domaine de Coussères** – *66220 Prugnanes - 5 km NW of St-Paul-de-Fenouillet by D 117 and D 20 - ☏ 04 68 59 23 55 - Closed 1 Nov-15 Mar - 6 rooms.* Perched on a butte amid the vines, this superb *bastide* dominates a majestic landscape of mountains and *garrigues*. Large, tastefully decorated rooms, and a warm welcome in the dining room. Lovely garden, swimming pool and several terraces add to the charm of the place.

Fennel

This typical Mediterranean plant (*fenouille* in French) with its pretty parasol-like flowers can be found growing wild along the hedgerows and is also cultivated for its culinary and aromatic properties. Raw fennel may be offered in little slices to nibble on as a palate-cleanser and digestive aid between courses. It has a distinctly licorice taste and a faint sweetness that brighten salads. Braised, the stalks and bulb are tender and the sweet flavour is amplified. Fennel seed is used in Mediterranean cuisine in sausages and baked goods; the feathery fronds of fennel are used as a seasoning herb; the pollen is a potent ingredient for spicing up pork, poultry and salad dressings.

lower gate forms a shrine. It contains a statue of Mary and Joseph (15C). The upper gate, dedicated to Our Lady "the Bread-Giver" (Madonna and Child, also 15C) has Romanesque columns and capitals that have been brought here from another building and reused.

The road climbs to **Fenouillet**, a village in the shadow of the two ruins that has given the area its name, giving a succession of delightful views (*looking back*) of the hermitage of Notre-Dame-de-Laval and the Bugarach summit, on the horizon. It reaches **Caudiès-de-Fenouillèdes**, the gateway to the Fenouillèdes.

▷ *Continue N along D 9 to Col de St-Louis then turn right onto D 46 and right again onto D 45.*

Pic de Bugarach
& *See Les CORBIÈRES.*

▷ *Turn right onto D 14.*

Cubières
Near the old mill, some private land has been set out as a rest area with picnic tables in a cool site on the shady banks of the Agly.

▷ *Turn right onto D 10 which runs alongside the Cubières stream then the River Agly.*

Gorges de Galamus★★

The spectacular rugged road carved out of the rock and the hermitage clinging precariously onto the hillside give this narrow gorge all the atmosphere of a fantasy world, especially when bathed in the rays of the Catalan sun. The gorge is so narrow and steep that one only gets rare glimpses of the mountain stream foaming down below.

Ermitage St-Antoine-de-Galamus

▷ *Leave the car in the car park at the hermitage before the tunnel. 30min on foot round-trip.*

⚑ The path runs down from the hermitage terrace (view of Canigou). The hermitage building (*outdoor restaurant*) conceals the chapel in the dim depths of a natural cave.

On its way to St-Paul-de-Fenouillet, D 7 follows a sinuous course and runs through vineyards. From a wide bend, there is a view of Canigou to the right.

Hermitage of St-Antoine in the Galamus gorge

D. Hée/MICHELIN

Abbaye de FLARAN★

MICHELIN LOCAL MAP 336: E-6

The abbey was founded in 1151 as part of the expansion of the Cistercian Order throughout Gascony. Through the benevolence of local overlords, it prospered rapidly, before falling under the domination first of the English and then the French. It was spared neither by the Wars of Religion nor, later, by the demands of the Revolution.

Situated on the outskirts of Valence-sur-Baïse, it has now been turned into a regional **cultural centre** hosting concerts, exhibitions and seminars throughout the year.

Visit

1hr. ⏱ Jul and Aug: 9.30am-7pm; Feb-Jun and Sep-Dec: 9.30am-12.30pm, 2-6pm. ⏱ Closed 3 weeks in Jan, 1 May and 25 Dec. ◉ 3.80€, no charge 1st Sunday in the month Nov-Mar. ☎ 05 62 28 50 19.

From the main courtyard, bordered on the west side by the stables and outbuildings, visitors can admire the west front of the abbey church at close quarters. The upper part of the façade is pierced by a rose window encircled by a chequered pattern. The semicircular arched entrance below is unusual in that it has no tympanum above the door. The **living quarters**, constructed in the 18C for the use of the Prior and his guests, have the charm of a small Gascon château. The reception area and the living room are decorated with fine plaster mouldings.

The **abbey church**, built between 1180 and 1210, comprises a nave, flanked by single aisles and surmounted by broken-barrel vaulting. The ornamentation of the double capitals is very simple, following Cistercian tradition – either smooth foliage or scrolls and interlacing, all highly stylised. Note that the transept is longer than the nave. The semicircular east end and rows of blind arcades festooning the four chapels (best seen from the garden) are characteristic of early Romanesque art in the south. A foretaste of the Gothic style, however, can be seen in the ribbed vaulting above the transept crossing.

The **cloisters** are accessible from the church via a doorway surmounted by the Greek letters *chi* and *rho*, the "XP" monogram from the Greek for Christ, a favourite motif of Gascon artists during the Romanesque period. Of the four original cloister galleries, only that on the west side (early 14C) remains today. The framework of the structure resembles that favoured by contemporary architects in the Toulouse area – the pointed arches of the arcades rest on twinned columns, the capitals of which are decorated either with foliage or with human or animal faces.

The **monastic buildings** extend from the northern arm of the transept. The **armarium** or library is entered via the **chapter-house** in which the quadripartite vaulting is supported by beautiful columns of different-coloured Pyrenees marble. Three openings with arching, resting on small columns, give onto the cloisters.

Beyond a passageway leading to the garden, the former **monks' common room** and the **storeroom** house an exhibition on that part of the pilgrims' route to Santiago de Compostela which passes through Gascony. The exhibits include maps, sculptures, and pilgrims' funerary crosses.

The **sacristy** opens off the north transept. It is a very light, square room, notable again for the rib vaulting springing from a central column. A stone staircase outside the entrance leads to the **monks' dormitory** converted into separate cells in the 17C. The Prior's apartments are located in the northwest corner of the upper gallery of the cloisters, from which there is a fine view of the abbey as a whole.

In the centre of the northern wing stands the **refectory**, flanked by **kitchens** and the **calefactory**, originally the only heated room in the complex, where the monks would have gone to keep warm while reading and writing. The refectory was remodelled in the 18C. It is decorated with fine stuccowork, particularly above the chimney-piece where the motif is a phoenix rising from the ashes.

RETREAT TO THE FARM

◉◉ **Ferme de Flaran** – Rte. de Condom - 32310 Valence-sur-Baïse - 1km SE of the abbey by D 142 - ☎ 05 62 28 58 22 - hotel-flaran@wanadoo.fr - closed Jan and 15 Nov-15 Dec. - 🅿 - 15 rooms - 🍴 7€. Former Gascon farm maintains its charming country atmosphere. Small, simple rooms with exposed beams. Tranquil poolside terrace where you can prolong your dinner beneath the stars.

Flaran Abbey cloisters

A. Thuillier/MICHELIN

The **garden** is in two parts – a formal garden in the French style and, near an old mill, a herb garden stocked with medicinal and aromatic plants. There is a good view of the eastern wing of the monks' building and the east end of the abbey church.

Ferme de la Magdeleine

The farm buildings (barns, stables and farmer's quarters) adjoin each side of an old square tower, southwest of the abbey proper; they are all that remains of the 14C fortifications. Between the farm and the monastery, a 5C Roman mosaic, recently uncovered from a villa nearby, can be seen.

FLORAC

POPULATION 1,996

MICHELIN LOCAL MAP 330: J-9

ALSO SEE MONT LOZÈRE, LE PONT-DE-MONTVERT AND GORGES DU TARN

This small town lies in the Tarnon Valley at the foot of the dolomitic cliffs which make up the Rochefort rock. Florac is situated at the entrance to the Tarn gorges, on the edge of the Causse Méjean, the Cévennes, and Mont Lozère. Because of this location, it was chosen as the site for the head office of the **Parc national des Cévennes**.

Florac, which was the capital of one of the eight baronies in the **Gévaudan** area under the direct control of the bishop of Mende, has a very eventful history. It was subjected to a very tough feudal regime and was only too painfully aware of the truth in the saying, *pays du Gévaudan, pays de tyrans* (Gévaudan, land of tyrants). After the constant struggle against local noblemen came the Wars of Religion. Nowadays, though, this small town is a peaceful spot famous for its good food and outdoor leisure activities.

Every summer, the town hosts the *24 heures de Florac*, when riders complete a 160km/99mi circuit on horseback in the area around Florac, taking in Mont Lozère, Mont Aigoual and the Causse Méjean. 🛈 *33 Ave. Jean-Monestier, 48400 Florac*, ☎ *04 66 45 01 14. www.ville-florac.fr*

Town Walk

Château

🕐 *Jul-Aug: 9am-6.30pm; Easter-end Jun and November holidays: Sat-Sun and holidays 9.30am-12.30pm, 1.30-5.30pm; early Sep-Easter: daily except Sat-Sun 9.30am-12.30pm, 1.30-5.30pm.* 🎟 *3.50€.* ☎ *04 66 49 53 01 or 04 66 49 53 03. www.cevennes-parcnational.fr.*

This long 17C building flanked by two round towers now houses on the ground and first floors an interesting exhibition on the Parc National des Cévennes (landscape, flora, fauna, and activities linked with the park). The **Information Centre** provides a full range of information on hiking, guided tours, open-air museums (*écomusées*) in the park and overnight accommodation.

FLORAC		Monestier Av. J.	
		Palais Pl. du	8
Dides Pl. L.	3	Rémuret R. de	10
Église R. de l'	4	Serve R. de la	12
Julie R. A.	5	Souvenir Pl. du	13
Marceau-Farelle Esplanade	7	Tour Av. M.	15

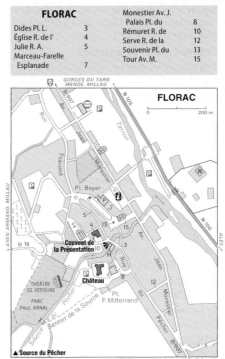

Address Book

For coin ranges, see the Legend at the back of the guide.

EATING OUT

La Source du Pêcher – *1 R. Remuret – ☎ 04 66 45 03 01 - closed 1 Nov-Easter and Wed except Jul -Aug -* . This restaurant stands at the heart of Old Florac, in a pedestrian zone, on the banks of the Vibron. It serves regional cuisine in a small Art Deco style dining room in ochre and green tones. The terrace stands in the shade of a great willow tree.

Auberge Cévenole – Chez Annie – *48400 La Salle-Prunet – 2km/1mi S of Florac towards Alès - ☎ 04 66 45 11 80 – closed mid Nov-early Feb, Sun evening and Mon out of season.* This old Cévennes house conceals a pretty, rustic style dining room with an open fireplace. The cuisine is firmly rooted in local produce; this is a good opportunity to try out the famous local dish, *aligot*. Pleasant terrace and a few basic but neat and tidy rooms.

WHERE TO STAY

Lozerette – *48400 Cocurès - 5.5km/3.5mi NE of Florac on N 106 and D 998 - ☎04 66 45 06 04 - lalozerette@ wanadoo.fr – closed 1 Nov – Easter -* - *21 rooms - 7.50€.* This charming mansion is in a small village at the heart of the Cévennes national park. Although it is by the road, it is quiet. The neat rooms are pleasantly furnished. Set menu is good value for money.

SHOPPING

Atelier du sucre et de la châtaigne – *64 Ave. Jean-Monestier - ☎ 04 66 45 28 41 – 9am-noon, 3-7pm – closed mid-Jan through Feb, Sun afternoon and Mon off-season.* Home-made specialities based on local ingredients: chestnuts, honey, berries. The *pain à la châtaigne* (chestnut bread) is especially good.

La Maison du Pays Cévenol – *3 R. du Pêcher - ☎ 04 66 45 15 67 - www. payscevenol.com - Tue-Sat 9.30am-12.30pm, 1-7pm, Jul-Aug: daily 9am-7pm - closed Jan-Feb.* Monsieur Digaro himself selects his suppliers, experts in the fabrication of honeys or the preservation of game products, snails and trout; his wines, cheeses and oils are all made with the finest ingredients the region has to offer. Jams, syrups and dried mushrooms are all produced in-house.

TRAVELS WITH A DONKEY

If you have fallen under the spell of Robert Louis Stevenson's account of crossing the Cévennes on the back of the humble Modestine, you might try a donkey ride of your own! Try the following:

Tramontâne - *La Rouvière - 48110 St-Martin-de-Lansuscle - ☎ 04 66 45 92 44 - chantal.tramontaine@nomade.fr.*

Nearby is the start of the "Spring Trail" (*Sentier de la Source*) along which the explanatory signposts give a full insight into the natural environment in which the River Pêcher rises.

Couvent de la Présentation

This convent used to be a commandery of the Knights Templar. Note the superb façade and monumental doorway dating from 1583.

Source du Pêcher

Situated at the foot of the Rochefort rock, this is one of the main resurgent springs on the Causse Méjean. The river bubbles and froths up from the spring during heavy rain or when the snow melts.

Excursions

Corniche des Cévennes★ 1

58km/36mi from Florac to St-Jean-du-Gard – allow 2hr.

To get the best out of this scenic road, you should make this trip in the late afternoon on a fine day, when the low-lying sun's rays throw the jagged outline of the ridges and the depth of the valleys into vivid relief. However, the landscape can leave an even stronger impression when seen beneath a stormy sky.

▶ *Leave Florac heading S on D 907.*

At first, the road follows the Tarnon Valley, at the foot of the escarpments of the Causse Méjean, before climbing to St-Laurent-de-Trèves.

St-Laurent-de-Trèves

On a limestone promontory overlooking this village, the remains of 190 million-year-old **dinosaurs** have been discovered. At that time, the area was covered by a lagoon, inhabited by dinosaurs of about 4m/13ft in height which walked on two legs.

A. Thuillier/MICHELIN

Corniche des Cévennes

Inside the old church, there is a display (Kids ⏱ *Jun and Aug: daily except Sat 10am-1.30pm, 2.30-6pm;* ⌖ *3.50€.* ☎ *04 66 49 53 01 or 04 66 49 53 03; www.cevannes-parc-national.fr.*) on dinosaurs in general and on this site in particular.

There is also a splendid **view**★ of the Causse Méjean, as well as of Mont Aigoual and Mont Lozère. The Corniche des Cévennes proper actually starts from the Col du Rey, leading through the windswept limestone plateau of the **Can de l'Hospitalet**, dotted with rocks, which was one of the assembly points of the Camisards in the 18C. The road then follows the edge of the plateau overlooking the Vallée Française through which the Gardon de Ste-Croix flows.

From **Col des Faïsses** (a *faïsse* is a local term for a bank of cultivated land), where the mountain drops away steeply on either side, there is a good view of the Cévennes. The road crosses the Can de l'Hospitalet plateau, a bare and rocky stretch of land with a stunning view of Mont Lozère, the little town of Barre-des-Cévennes, the Vallée Française and the Aigoual massif.

At Le Pompidou, limestone gives way to schist. The road then follows a ridge through chestnut groves and sparse meadows where daffodils bloom in the spring.

▷ *Before reaching St-Roman-de-Tousque, turn left onto D 140 then right onto D 983.*

The road enters the **Vallée Française** which Robert-Louis Stevenson went through when he toured the Cévennes with a donkey named Modestine; it is well worth reading his account of this unusual journey in *Travels with a Donkey*. The name Vallée Française goes back to pre-medieval times when it was a Frankish enclave within Visigoth territory.

Notre-Dame de Valfrancesque

This charming 11C Romanesque sanctuary is today a Protestant church.
The road runs down to St-Jean-du-Gard along the Gardon de Mialet riverbed, past the Marouls farm, now a useful stopover for hikers.

Round-trip in the Cévennes ②
75km/47mi – allow 3hrs.

This trip takes visitors through the Cévennes, a region crisscrossed by deep valleys in between serrated ridges, in which houses are roofed with schist slabs, roads lined with chestnut trees, and villages steeped in memories of the Camisard uprising.

▷ *Head S from Florac on D 907 and N 106 towards Alès.*

The road begins by following the Mimente Valley, where it is flanked by schist cliffs. Beyond the ruins of the Château de St-Julien-d'Arpaon perched on a hilltop to the left of the road, there is a view of Le Bougès, a mountain rising to an altitude of 1 421m/4 618ft, to the right.

▷ *At the Col de Jalcreste, turn right onto D 984 to St-Germain-de-Calberte.*

There is an interesting view of the mouth of the Gardon de St-Germain Valley. Beyond the pass, the road runs down to **St-Germain-de-Calberte** among chestnut trees, holm-oaks and broom. Cévennes-style houses with stone-slab roofs and decorative chimneys line the roadside.

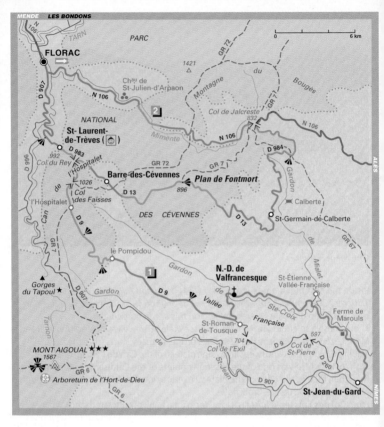

The Château de Calberte, perched on a spur of rock, comes into view in a bend of the road.

▶ *Beyond St-Germain-de-Calberte, turn right onto D 13.*

Plan de Fontmort
Alt 896m/2 912ft.

At a junction in the Fontmort forest is an obelisk which was inaugurated in 1887 to celebrate the signature of the Edict of Tolerance by Louis XVI. The memorial also serves as a reminder of the many battles fought by the Camisard rebels against the Maréchal de Villars in this region. There is a superb view to the east over the ridges of the Cévennes.

From the Plan de Fontmort to Barre-des-Cévennes, the road follows a narrow ridge that provides a number of fine views over the valleys of the Cévennes to the south and, in the foreground, the heather-clad moorland.

Barre-des-Cévennes

This small, austere village with its tall, bare house fronts overlooks all the roads running along the Gardon rivers. Its setting is particularly picturesque and its location made it a major defensive and lookout position during the Camisard uprising. The remains of entrenchments are still visible on the Colline du Castelas.

Along the Barre-des-Cévennes footpath (3km/2mi), walkers can find out about the village's past and discover its natural environment.

▶ *Join the Corniche des Cévennes at the Col du Rey and turn right onto D 983. There are views of the Mont Aigoual range to the left and the Mont Lozère ridge to the right.*

▶ *Return to Florac via St-Laurent-de-Trèves and the Tarnon Valley.*

FOIX★

POPULATION 9,109

MICHELIN LOCAL MAP 343: H-7

Situated at the mouth of the old Ariège glacial valley, Foix makes a striking impression on visitors with its rugged **setting**★ against a backdrop of jagged peaks and its skyline with three castle towers, proudly standing on their rock overlooking the river's final gully as it wends its way across the folds of the Plantaurel hills.

The old town has narrow streets radiating out from the crossroads at the corner of Rue de Labistour and Rue des Marchands adorned with a tiny bronze fountain "*de l'Oie*" (goose). This part of the town forms a stark contrast to the 19C administrative area laid out around vast esplanades consisting of the Allées de la Villote and the Champ de Mars.

The region around Foix forms the *département* of Ariège, named after the main river that tumbles down from the mountains to form a Pyrenean valley constituting the backbone of the *département*. ▯ 29 R. Delcassé, 09000 Foix, ☎ 05 61 65 12 12. www.mairie-foix.fr.

A Bit of History

Once part of the Duchy of Aquitaine before becoming part of the County of Carcassonne, the Foix region was raised to the status of county in its own right in the 11C. Under the terms of the Treaty of Paris (1229) putting an end to the Albigensian Crusade, which was particularly active in this region, the count of Foix was forced to acknowledge his position as vassal to the king of France. In 1290, the Foix family inherited Béarn and promptly settled there, preferring to be master of its own house than to submit to royal authority.

In 1607, the area was annexed to the crown by King Henri IV who inherited the county.

A family covered in glory – In his day, Gaston III (1331-91), the most famous of the **counts of Foix** and viscounts of Béarn, was the only one of the king of France's vassals to be in a sound financial situation. He took the name of Fébus c 1360, meaning "the Brilliant" or "the Hunter." **Gaston Fébus** was a man of many characters. He was a skilled politician who exercised absolute power and literate to the extent that he even wrote poetry and summoned writers and troubadours to his court. However, he also ordered the murder of his brother and killed his only son. He was an enthusiastic hunter and wrote a treatise on the art of hunting.

Among other representatives of the illustrious lineage of the counts of Foix worth a mention is Gaston of Foix, the famous "Italian thunderbolt," Louis XII's nephew, who was ordered to take command of the royal army in Italy. He won the Battle of Ravenna in 1512 but lost his life, cut down by 15 lances, at the age of only 22. Odet of Foix, his cousin, fought beside him at Ravenna and was also wounded. He survived, however, and went on to play a major role in the conquest of the Milan area (1515).

Gold-panners – The waters of the Ariège contain gold dust and, from the Middle Ages to the end of the 19C, there were large numbers of men called *orpailleurs* panning for gold in the sandy river beds. The River Ariège contained gold downstream from Foix; the largest nuggets were found between Varilhes and Pamiers, some of them weighing as much as 15g. This source of wealth, however, became too unreliable, and the race of professional gold washers died out.

Miners and blacksmiths – Pyrenean iron ore was highly reputed for its richness and was first extracted a very long time ago.

The mine at Le Rancié, finally closed in 1931, was still being worked in the 19C on a long-established cooperative basis and the people living in the valley were registered with the "Office of Miners." As such, they were partners rather than salaried staff. They were limited as to the quantity of ore they could extract every day. Often, miners would work alone and, once they had filled their hods, would carry them on their backs up to the mouth of the gallery and would then sell the ore for cash to muleteers. They in turn transported it down to Vicdessos where the managers of iron foundries would come and purchase the supplies they needed.

In 1833, seventy-four "Catalan" iron foundries were still getting their supplies from this mine. They processed the ore by means of reaction with charcoal (this was made possible by the fact that this ore, like the ore mined in Pyrénées-Orientales, contains the necessary flux), but this led to massive deforestation,

Address Book

For coin ranges, see the Legend at the back of the guide.

EATING OUT

Au Grilladou – *7 R. La Faurie -* ☎ *05 61 64 00 74 - closed Wed evening, Sat lunchtime and Sun from end Sep-late Jun.* This little restaurant situated on a pedestrian street at the foot of the château offers pizzas, salads and grilled dishes at very reasonable prices. Simple décor, efficient service and warm welcome.

Ferme-auberge Le Plantié – *09000 Vernajoul - 5km/3mi NW of Foix on D 1 (towards Grotte de Labouiche) -* ☎ *05 61 65 41 96 - closed Sun evening - reservations required.* This inn in the middle of the countryside, surrounded by fields and woodland, offers a respite from the hustle and bustle of the centre of Foix. It is a livestock breeding and force-feeding farm, so *foie gras* and poultry feature on the menu. The dining room has rustic decor. Produce is for sale.

Le Phœbus – *3 Cours Irénée-Cros -* ☎ *05 61 65 10 42 - closed 18 Jul-18 Aug, Sat lunchtime and Mon.* The owner offers a menu printed entirely in Braille for sight-impaired visitors. Comfortable dining room overlooks the Arège; traditional cuisine prepared with care.

Ferme-auberge de Mailhac – *Mailhac - 09000 Loubières -* ☎ *05 61 05 29 51 - info@mailhac.com - reservations required.* Exposed beams and stonework, antique furniture, peasants' tools: this 18C farm in the countryside has been beautifully restored. Family cuisine with traditional flair, served on the terrace in fine weather.

Ferme-auberge de Caussou – *09000 Cos - 2.5km/1.5mi au NW of Foix on D 117 -* ☎ *05 61 65 34 42 - caussou@voila.fr – closed 15 Dec-15 Mar -* 🖙 *- reservations required.* This cattle and sheep farm dates from the end of the 18C. The large dining room has stone and half-timbered walls and offers beef specialities such as *blanquette au "millas."* For a view of the garden and valley, stay in one of the first floor rooms.

WHERE TO STAY

Chambre d'hôte M. and Mme Savignol – *Chemin du Rec – 09000 St-Paul-de-Jarrat - 7km/4mi SE of Foix on N 20 then D 117 -* ☎ *05 61 65 14 26 - closed Oct-May -* 🖙 *- 3 rms.* This modern house offers plenty of space and every comfort. The owner is actually also the architect. The spacious rooms have panelling and furniture dating from the 1970s. A large terrace overlooks the swimming pool and flower garden.

Lons – *6 Pl. G.-Dutilh -* ☎ *05 61 65 52 44 - hotel-lons-foix@wanadoo.fr - closed 21 Dec-5 Jan - 38 rooms -* 🖙 *7€.* In the old town dominated by the château, this historic establishment features simple, practical rooms. Dining room overlooking the Arlège. High ceilings, cornices and mouldings lend charm to the restaurant.

Auberge Les Myrtilles – *At Col des Marrous - 19km/11.8mi W of Foix by D 17 -* ☎ *05 61 65 16 46 - aubergelesmyrtilles@wanadoo.fr -closed 3 Nov-3Mar, Tues from Sep-May, Wed from Mar-May and Mon. -* 📧 *- 7 rooms -* 🖙 *6€.* This little inn is just like a mountain chalet amid the fir trees and is worth the climb to the pass in itself. It is a very relaxing setting. Regional fare is served without pretention in the pleasant terrace garden or in the cheerful dining room with checkered table cloths. Modest rooms with pine furniture.

SHOPPING

Azema Bigou – *Campredon - 09600 La Bastide-sur-l'Hers -* ☎ *05 61 01 11 09 – Mon-Sat 10am-noon, 2-5pm.* This family-run business has been making traditional horn combs since 1820. It is the only such entreprise still in operation in all of Europe. The workshop visit is very interesting, and the tour ends in the shop.

SPORT

Golf Club de l'Ariège – *09240 La Bastide-de-Sérou -* ☎ *05 61 64 56 78 - golf-club-de-lariege@wanadoo.fr – 10am-4pm, (9am-7pm in summer) – closed 1 Jan.* An 18-hole course and a beginners' 6-hole course; bar and restaurant.

Centre équestre de Cantegril – *7km/4.2mi W of Foix on D 117 – 09000 St-Martin-de-Caralp -* ☎ *05 61 65 15 43 -open summer 9am-9pm, winter 9am-7.30pm – closed Mon except during school holidays – 11/15€, per hour's ride (beginners or advanced).* This centre is oriented towards families and offers introductory breaks or courses for perfecting techniques such as acrobatic riding, dressage, jumps and riding excursions. More sporty types may like to try out horse-ball and take part in competitions.

FILM FESTIVAL

Résistances – This is the theme of the European cinema festival (*2nd week in July*) which has seen its success grow steadily since 1997. Some performances take place in the open; discussions and workshops are also organised. ☎ *05 61 05 13 30.*

Château de Foix

Sights

Château

🕒 *Jul and Aug: 9.45am-6.30pm; Jun and Sep: 9.45am-noon, 2-6pm; Apr-May: 10.30am-noon, 2-5.30pm; Feb, Mar and Oct-Dec: daily except Mon and Tue (except school holidays) 10.30am-noon, 2-5.30pm.* 🕒 *Closed Jan, 1st Mon in Sep and 25 Dec.* ⊗ *4€ (6-18 years: 2€).* ☎ *05 34 09 83 83.*

Pont de Vernajoul, the bridge spanning the River Arget (at the end of Rue de la Préfecture) offers the best view of the castle.

The castle's history is closely linked to the history of France. In 1002, the Count of Carcassonne, Roger the Elder, bequeathed the castle of Foix and its lands to his son, Roger-Bernard, who took the title of Count of Foix.

The castle's earliest foundations date from the 10C. It is a sturdy stronghold which Simon de Montfort was careful not to attack in 1211-17 during the Albigensian Crusade. In 1272, however, the Count of Foix refused to acknowledge the sovereignty of the King of France, and Philip the Bold personally took charge of a military expedition to attack the town. With food supplies exhausted and seeing the rock beneath his castle being hacked at with pick-axes, the count finally surrendered.

After the union of Béarn and the County of Foix in 1290, the counts all but abandoned the town. Gaston Fébus was the last of them to live in the castle.

In the 16C, the castle lost any remaining military function. It was later taken over by Henri IV and turned into a prison. It remained a place of internment until 1864. Nowadays, it houses a museum.

The main interest of the castle is really its location, high above the town. Little now remains of the building itself apart from three towers and the museum, representing a quarter of the original complex.

Of the three watchtowers, the most interesting are the central tower and the round tower which have both retained their 14C and 15C vaulted rooms inside. The two towers used to be encased in a double ring of curtain walls, making the castle a particularly formidable target. From the terrace between the towers or, even better, from the top of the round tower, there is a **panoramic view**⋆ of Foix, the Ariège Valley, and the Pain de Sucre ("sugar loaf") in Montgaillard.

Musée départemental de l'Ariège

In the château; 🕒 *same hours as the château.*

In the large, lower room are collections of military and hunting weapons reminding visitors of the castle's original function. Archaeological exhibits are evidence of pre-historic Man's activities in the caves in Ariège (300 have been listed and 60 explored), from the Paleolithic Era to the Bronze Age. These include remnants of animals (most of them castings) including: cave bears, reindeer, hyenas and mammoths. There are also castings of human footprints. The museum also contains the remains of capitals from the cloisters at the church of St-Volusien.

Église St-Volusie

🕐 ⏱ 🚶 *Jul-Aug: possibility of guided tours 11am-12.30pm, 4-6pm; rest of the year: daily except Sat-Sun.* 🎫 *No charge.*

This fine Gothic church has a 14C nave and a raised early-15C chancel. Note the stalls, the large narrow windows and the Renaissance altar made of polychrome stone with scenes of the Visitation and the Last Supper. Opposite the church (*no 1 Rue de la Préfecture*) stands an elegant mansion decorated with caryatids.

Excursions

Route Verte and Route de la Crouzette★★

Round-trip 93km/58mi – allow 5hrs.

🚗 *The road is usually blocked by snow from mid-December to mid-June between the Col des Marrous and the Col de la Crouzette. It may also be blocked at the Col des Caougnous.*

▶ *Head W from Foix along D 17.*

Route Verte★★

The "green road" climbs gently as it runs up the **Arget** (or Barguillère) **Valley**, an area that was once famous for its metalworking (nails), wending its way through woodland. After La Mouline, the road becomes steeper and, in Burret, it parts company with the Arget, which rises in a small wooded corrie a little farther south. The landscape either side of the road becomes more pastoral.
en habillage avec le texte qui suit

Col des Marrous

Alt 990m/3 218ft. From the pass, there are extensive views to the south over the Arget Valley and Arize Forest.

The road continues to climb through a forest where beech trees predominate. From the first bend on this stretch of the road, there are some fine views of the Plantaurel area and La Bastide-de-Sérou. Beyond the Col de Jouels, the road clings to the upper slopes of the wooded Caplong cirque, in which the Arize rises, and the views of the surrounding countryside become ever more panoramic. In the background is the truncated pyramid of Mont Valier (*alt 2 838m/9 223ft*).

From **Col de Péguère** (*alt 1 375m/4 469ft*), there is an uninterrupted panorama.

Tour Laffon

15min on foot round-trip. 🥾 *Follow the path to the right behind the hut.*

Magnificent **panorama**★ of the central and Ariège Pyrenees, from the Pic de Font-frède (1 617m/5 255ft) to the Pic de Cagire (1 912m/6 214ft) beyond the Col de Portet d'Aspet.

Route de la Crouzette★★

This hilltop road runs along the rounded, bracken-covered crests of the Arize range and overlooks the forested cirques formed by the tributaries of the Arize to the north and the cool, gently hollowed out Massat Valley to the south.

Sommet de Portel★★

🥾 *15min on foot round-trip. Alt 1 485m/4 826ft.*

▶ *Leave the car in a wide bend on the road, at a mountain pass 3.5km/2mi beyond the Col de Péguère.*

Climb the grassy bank to the northwest, as far as the foundations of an old beacon. The **panorama** of the peaks in the upper Couserans region extends as far as the mountains on the border. From this summit, the old track drops down inside the line of the bend in the road, reaching the Coulat spring in just a few minutes. This attractive spot is ideal for a picnic or a stroll.

Beyond the Col de la Crouzette, during the steep descent to Massat via Biert and then D 618 to the left, there is a view of the upper Couserans region and the entire range of peaks below the Col de Pause, Aulus and the Garbet Valley.

Massat

This small local capital boasts a church with a gabled west front flanked by an elegant 15C octagonal tower. On the top level (the tower reaches 58m/190ft), the muzzles of decorative cannon project through diamond-shaped apertures. Above the entrance there is a fine wrought-iron grille.

▶ *Continue along D 618.*

To the east of Massat, the upper Arac basin widens out and the winding road provides some attractive views of the rural countryside around Massat. Farther on, the majestic Mont Valier range looms into sight. The road then climbs up to the Col des Caougnous.

Before reaching this pass, there is the gap formed by the Col de Port. To the right, beyond the rounded hills in the foreground, towers the jagged summit of the Pic des Trois Seigneurs.

The road passes a succession of hamlets, and the view of Mont Valier becomes most impressive. Leaving the last few houses behind, along with the upper limits of the pastures and forests, the road enters an area of moorland decked in ferns and broom. To the right is a wonderful pine forest.

Col de Port

Alt 1 250m/4 100ft. This pass seems to mark a natural boundary between the "green" Pyrenees on the side of the Atlantic watershed and the "sunny" Pyrenees towards the Mediterranean where the landscape is full of contrasts.

The road runs down through the Saurat Valley, an area of fertile land well exposed to sunshine. Beyond Saurat, in line with the road, is the Montorgueil tower. The road then runs between two enormous rocks named Soudour and Calamès, the latter crowned with ruins.

Grotte de Bédeilhac

800m/870yd from the village of Bédeilhac. 🏃*See TARASCON-SUR-ARIÈGE.*

Tarascon-sur-Ariège

🏃 *See TARASCON-SUR-ARIÈGE.*

▶ *Leave Tarascon N on the road to Mercus-Garrabet, along the east bank of the Ariège.*

On the left, beyond the Pic de Soudour (alt 1 070m/3 478ft), the Romanesque church of **Mercus-Garrabet** comes into view, set apart on a rocky outcrop in the middle of its graveyard. Other spurs farther down the valley on the opposite bank give the countryside a rugged, untidy appearance.

Le Pont du Diable

▶ *Keep following the road along the east bank of the Ariège. Leave the car just beyond the level crossing.*

This pretty bridge spans the Ariège at a point where the river flows fast but calmly. The lower projection of the main arch suggests that the height of the bridge was raised at least once in the 14C. Take a look at the bridge's system of fortification on the side of the west bank (door and lower chamber). The bridge struck terror into the hearts of the people of the region; building was restarted more than a dozen times as, legend has it, all the work done each day collapsed during the night – hence the bridge's name (*diable* = "devil").

A.Thuillier/MICHELIN

Pont du Diable

Mérens Horses

These small, bearded horses belong to an ancient local breed as depicted in the paintings on the walls of Niaux cave, which were painted over 10 000 years ago! The good-tempered, hardy little horses used to be put to work in the fields. An association (Syndicat Hippique d'Élevage de la Race Pyrénéenne Ariégeoise, or SHERPA) set up in 1933 has been promoting the role these horses can play in the tourist economy of the Ariège. Their gentle character makes them ideal for riding and pony-trekking holidays, of which there are many to choose from in this region. From May to October, they can be seen grazing at liberty in the mountain pastures of the upper Ariège Valley. There is an information centre about the breed at La Bastide-de-Sérou.

Beyond the turn-off to Lavelanet, a rocky outcrop called the **Pain de Sucre** ("sugar loaf") looms into view ahead, with the village of **Montgaillard** at its foot.

▶ *Drive into the village and follow signs for "Les Forges de Pyrène."*

Les Forges de Pyrène★

⚒ ⏱ *Jul and Aug: 10am-7pm; Jun and Sep: 10am-12.30pm, 1.30-6pm, Sun and public holidays 10am-12.30pm, 1.30-6.30pm; Apr-May and Oct: 1.30-6pm, Sun and public holidays 10am-12.30pm, 1.30-6.30pm; early-mid Nov, Christmas vacation and winter: 1.30-6pm.* ⏱ *Closed Jan, 8 Nov, 25 Dec.* ✆ *7€.* ☎ *05 34 09 30 60.*

Kids "The past brought back to life" could be an accurate description of the Forges de Pyrène, an open-air museum spread over 5ha/12 acres, devoted to more than 120 traditional crafts and occupations of bygone days, from the dairywoman with her team of dogs to the wax maker and his candles or the craftsman who made the first bowls used in the game of *pétanque*. In the various workshops located in barns, you can watch craftsmen demonstrate their skills (a smithy, a baker, a sculptor). Don't miss the old ironworks, the iron museum and the sawmill.

The Plantaurel Hills

58km/36mi from Foix to Montbrun-Bocage – allow half a day.

▶ *Leave Foix N along the west bank of the River Ariège to Vernajoul and turn left onto D 1.*

These medium-height foothills (*highest point 830m/2 723ft*) of the Pyrenees extend from east to west along the northern edge of the range. Several rivers (Touyre, Douctouyre, Ariège, Arize) have dug their way through the hills, forming transverse valleys.

Underground river of Labouiche★

⏱📷 *Jul and Aug: guided tours (1hr15min) by boat for 12 people (last departure 45min before closing) 9.30am-5.15pm; Apr-Jun and Sep: 10-11:15am, 2-5:15pm; beginning of Oct to mid-Nov: school holidays, Sat-Sun and public holidays 10-11.15am, 2-6.30pm.* ⏱ *Closed Mon.* ✆ *7.50€ (children: 5.50€).* ☎ *05 61 65 04 11.*

Kids The underground river of Labouiche has hollowed out a **subterranean gallery** in the limestone of the Plantaurel range (on the northern edge of the central Pyrenees), first explored in 1905.

Visitors will be enchanted with the boat trip along 1.5km/1mi of this "mysterious river", which includes two changes of craft, 70m/230ft below ground level through high and low-vaulted galleries, in which the lighting varies according to the effect required. Stalactites and stalagmites, standing out clearly against the limestone background, turn into strange beasts and flowers and other fantastic objects as the imagination runs wild.

A beautiful underground waterfall marks the end of the stretch of gallery open to visitors.

▶ *Continue along D 1, turn left onto D 11 and left again onto D 117.*

La Bastide-de-Sérou

The church, located in the old part of town, contains a 15C carved-wood crucifix from the Rhine region (*on the left as you enter*) and a late-15C Pietà (*in a chapel to the left of the chancel*). The market square (*note the stone corn measures*) and narrow streets south of the church have retained several old houses with interesting 18C doorways.

▶ *Continue along D 117 then turn right onto D 49 to Brouzenac.*

La Ferme des reptiles

♿ 🚭 *Mid-Jun to mid-Oct: guided tour 2-7pm (last admission 1hr before closing); early Apr to mid-Jun and mid to end Oct: Sat-Sun, public and school holidays 2-6pm.* 🕿 *6€ (children under 12: 5€).* ☎ *05 61 65 82 13. www.lafermedesreptiles.com.*

🧒 Thrilling hands-on guided tour of this zoo which houses all kinds of reptiles from the common grass snake to the mighty python not forgetting iguanas and tortoises.

▸ *Return to D 117 and turn right then right again onto D 15.*

Beyond Durban, the road follows the shaded Arize Valley towards Mas-d'Azil. On the way, note the small chapels clinging to the slopes.

Grotte du Mas-d'Azil★★

👁 *See Grotte du MAS-D'AZIL.*

▸ *Continue alongside the River Arize, which flows through a narrow gorge, to Sabarat then turn left onto D 628 to Daumazan-sur-Arize. In the village, turn left onto D 19.*

Montbrun-bocage

The small village **church** contains remarkable 16C **murals**★; in the chancel, note St Christopher, the Tree of Jesse and scenes from the Life of St John the Baptist. The north side is decorated with scenes from the Passion and Hell.

Abbaye de FONTFROIDE★★

MICHELIN LOCAL MAP 344: I-4 – ALSO SEE LES CORBIÈRES

The old **Cistercian abbey** of Fontfroide lies tucked almost out of sight deep in a little valley in the Corbières. This tranquil setting surrounded by cypress trees could almost be somewhere in Tuscany. The fine flame-coloured shades of yellow ochre and pink in the Corbières sandstone used to build the abbey enhance the serenity of the sight, particularly at sunset.

A Bit of History

In 1093 a Benedictine abbey was founded on land belonging to Aymeric I, Viscount of Narbonne, which embraced the Cistercian Order in 1145. In 1150, Fontfroide sent 12 Cistercian monks to found the monastery at Poblet in Catalonia. In the 12C and 13C, the abbey enjoyed a long period of prosperity. Pope Pierre de Castelnau's legate, whose assassination sparked off the Albigensian Crusade, stayed here after his trip to Maguelone. Jacques Fournier, who was elected Pope in Avignon in 1334 and who reigned under the name of Benedict XII, was abbot here from 1311 to 1317.

Visit *1hr*

The welcome centre is situated in the nearby abbey farm (13C), and houses the ticket office, bookstore, winery and a restaurant. ⏱ *Mid-Jul to end Aug: guided tours (1hr10min) 9.30am-6pm; early Apr to mid-Jul: 10am-12.15pm, 1.45-5.30pm; Nov-Mar: 10am-noon, 2-4pm.* 📷 *7.25€.* ☎ *04 68 45 11 08. www.fontfroide.com.*

Most of the abbey buildings were erected in the 12C and 13C. The conventual buildings were restored in the 17C and 18C. The present owners live in the buildings overlooking the north side of the cloisters.

The setting is delightful, with floral courtyards, well-maintained paths, and superb terraced gardens.

The tour begins in the Cour d'honneur, built by the commandery abbots in the 17C.

The guard-room (13C) has ribbed vaulting, and features a fine 18C wrought-iron doorway and a monumental chimney-piece. This room was the refectory for the lay brothers and pilgrims.

🪙 *For coin ranges, see the Legend at the back of the guide.*

BED & BREAKFAST

😊😊 **Chambre d'hôte Domaine de St-Jean** – *11200 Bizanet - 2.5km/1.5mi NW of the abbey on D 613 towards Lagrasse then B-road -* ☎*04 68 45 17 31 -* 🍴 *- 4 rooms.* This large 19C wine-grower's house set amid vines and pine trees makes an ageeable place to stay. The rooms are well kept. There is a view of the Fontfroide massif from the garden. Ample breakfasts.

Abbaye de Fontfroide

B. Kaufmann/MICHELIN

The tour then moves on to the medieval buildings, which are beautiful, not least because of their exceptionally regular bonding.

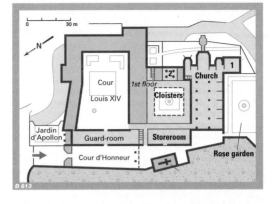

Cloisters – The cloister galleries have ribbed vaulting. The oldest gallery is that adjacent to the church (mid-13C). The gallery opposite underwent alteration in the 17C.

All the galleries have arcades supported on pairs of slender marble colonnettes, in different colours, decorated with capitals carved with ornate plant motifs and framed by a relieving arch. The tympana of these feature several oculi or a single larger round window. As a whole the cloisters are a consummate example of architectural elegance.

Terraced roofs run above the galleries.

Abbey church – Building work began on the church in the mid-12C. The spacious interior is imposing and perfectly in proportion; it is a particularly beautiful and moving example of the elegant simplicity of Cistercian architecture. The ribbed, barrel-vaulted nave is flanked by side aisles with half-barrel vaulting. Note the bases of the pillars, which have been raised in order to leave room for the choir stalls. The south chapels were added in the 14C-15C. In the funeral chapel (13C) (1), there is a fine stone Calvary dating from the 15C. The north transept has a gallery from which monks who were ill were able to follow services.

Chapter-house (2) – The chapter-house is roofed with nine Romanesque vaults supported on decorative ribs that spring from slender marble colonnettes.

Monks' dormitory – The dormitory is located above the storeroom. It is roofed with fine ribbed barrel-vaulting dating from the 12C.

Storeroom – This fine late-11C room, separated from the cloisters by a narrow alley-way, was probably given a vaulted roof in the 17C.

Rose garden – The rose garden contains about 3 000 rose bushes (11 varieties). Various footpaths enable visitors to walk around the abbey and fully appreciate the charms of its setting.

FONT-ROMEU ✳ ✳

POPULATION 2,003

MICHELIN LOCAL MAP 344: D-7 – ALSO SEE LA CERDAGNE

Font-Romeu is a man-made holiday resort dating from c 1920, built at an altitude of 1 800m/5 850ft on the sunny side of the French Cerdagne, higher than any other mountain village. The resort occupies a wonderful site protected from northerly winds on the edge of a pine forest. There is a superb panoramic view across the valley.

Besides its altitude, Font-Romeu's higher than average exposure to sunshine and exceptionally dry climate meant that, from the very outset, it was seen as a mountain-top health resort. Its impressive sports facilities (including a swimming pool, an ice rink and stables) attract athletes from all over the world who come to follow altitude training programmes here

Address Book

For coin ranges, see the Legend at the back of the guide.

EATING OUT

Complexe Casino – 46 Ave. Emmanuel-Brousse - ☎ 04 68 30 01 11 - closed Oct, Mon and Tue in off-season. Casino, movie theatre, discotheque and restaurant await you in this modern building located downtown. Savory, traditional dishes in the pleasant restaurant. Reasonably priced lunch menu.

La Cerdagne – 8 Ave. d'Espagne - ☎ 04 68 30 80 30 - carlit.hotel@wanadoo.fr - closed 1 Nov-9 Dec and 16 Apr-7 May. This restaurant within the Hôtel Carlit (which also has its own brasserie, El Foc) serves as a local culinary institution of the French Cerdagne, as demonstrated by its menu of traditional specialties with a catalan flair.

WHERE TO STAY

Hôtel de la Poste – 2 Ave. Emmanuel-Brousse - ☎ 04 68 30 01 88 - reservations suggested - 6€. The facade of this family hotel features paintings of mountain animals. Well-kept rooms offer calm and comfort. Generous portions of regional cuisine in the restaurant.

Sun Valley – Ave. d'Espagne - ☎ 04 68 30 21 21 - pierre.mitjaville@wanadoo.fr - closed 20 Oct-3Nov - 41 rooms 9€. Every single room features a balcony facing south, allowing plenty of sunlight throughout. Salon with fireplace to complete the mountain experience.

SPORTS AND RECREATION

Bureau des Guides – 90 Ave. Emmanuel-Brousse - ☎ 04 68 30 23 08 - Mon-Sat 10am-noon, 4pm-6.30pm. The Bureau des guides organizes rafting, hydrospeed, canyoning, pot-holing and rock-climbing at Font-Romeu.

Ozone 3 Montagne et Loisirs – 40 Ave. Emmanuel-Brousse - ☎ 04 68 30 36 09 – ozone3-montagne.com. Outings organised for mountain bikers, hikers and climbers. White-water sports on the River Aude.

Centre européen canin en altitude – Les Airelles - ☎ 06 84 84 05 00 or 06 17 03 67 11. After a guided tour of the park where dogs are bred and raised, you can try your hand at dog-sledding.

Winter Resort

Font-Romeu and Pyrénées 2000 ski areas✶✶
Accessible by road or by gondola from the centre of Font-Romeu (2.5km/1.5mi via the route des pistes leading off from the calvary).

The two areas together rise 1 600-2 250m/5 249-7 382ft through a pine forest. Snow-making equipment (460 snow cannon) covers 85% of the area, so skiers are never in want of the white stuff. All in all 40 downhill slopes provide pleasure for skiers of all levels, from the Airelles plateau, ideal for beginners, to the Bouillouses, more challenging. One slope is lit for night skiing. At the Pyrénées 2000 resort, there are instructors specialised in ski techniques for people with physical handicaps.

In addition, the area has one of the vastest cross-country trail systems. In February, Pyrénées 2000 welcomes the Transpyrénéenne, a cross-country race open to all comers.

At the **Centre Européen d'Entraînement Canin en Altitude** of Font-Romeu (Airelles plateau), dog-sledding instruction is available year round.

La Fontaine du Pèlerin

Between the resort and the secondary school (*lycée*) lies a hermitage bearing witness to the famous Catalan pilgrimage that gave Font-Romeu its name (from *fontaine du Pèlerin* or "pilgrim's fountain").

Ermitage★

The hermitage contains a statue of Our Lady known as the "Vierge de l'Invention". Legend has it that Our Lady of Font-Romeu was "discovered" (*inventée* in French) by a bull. One day the beast refused to move away from a spring, scraping the earth with its hooves and bellowing loudly. The herdsman, intrigued and in the end fed up with the noise, eventually took a closer look and found a statue of the Blessed Virgin Mary in a crack in the rock.

During certain festivals, or *aplechs*, crowds flock to the hermitage. On 8 September, the festival *del Baixar* ("of the Carrying Downhill"), the statue of the Virgin Mary is solemnly carried downhill to the church in Odeillo where it remains until Trinity Sunday (*el Pujar*: "the Carrying Uphill"). It is then brought back to the hermitage, in a similarly solemn procession. Other *aplechs* are held on the third Sunday after Whitsun (*cantat*: "of the sick") and on 15 August (Feast of the Assumption).

The **chapel**★ (🕐 *Jul and Aug: 10am-noon, 3-6pm; ⌣guided tour Tue and Thu 5-6pm.* ☎ *04 68 30 68 30.*) dates from the 17C and 18C. The miraculous spring set into the wall to the left provides the water supply for the pilgrims' bathing pool inside the building with the gable facing the mountain.

Inside, there is a magnificent **altarpiece**★★ by Joseph Sunyer dating from 1707. The central niche contains the statue of Our Lady of Font-Romeu or, when the statue is in Odeillo, the statue of the so-called Virgin Mary of the Hermitage (15C). On the predella are three detailed scenes depicting episodes from the "Invention". Take the staircase to the left of the high altar leading to the **camaril**★★★, the Virgin Mary's small "reception room", a typically Spanish construction that is touching for the devotion that inspired it.

Angelic musician, Camaril

This is Sunyer's masterpiece. The altar has painted panels and is topped by a statue of Christ flanked by the Virgin Mary and St John. Two delicate medallions depicting the Presentation in the Temple and the Flight into Egypt adorn the wall above the door. The four corners are decorated with pretty statues of angel-musicians.

Calvary

Alt 1 857m/6 035ft. Some 300m/325yd from the hermitage on the road to Mont-Louis, turn right onto a path lined with stations of the cross. From the calvary scene at the top, there is an extensive **panorama**★★ over Cerdagne and the surrounding mountains.

Excursions

Col del Pam★

▶ *From the calvary, drive along the road to the ski slopes then continue on foot.*

🚶 *15min round-trip. Alt 2 005m/6 516ft.* From the observation platform above the Têt Valley, there is a **view** of the Carlit range, the Bouillouses plateau, the Capcir (upper Aude Valley) and the Canigou summit.

Llivia

9km/5.6mi S along D 33E. This Spanish enclave on French territory (🔊*see La CERDAGNE*) boasts picturesque lanes, the remains of a medieval castle perched on a hill overlooking the town and a few old towers.

Musee municipal

🕐 *Apr-Sep: daily except Mon (other than Jul and Aug) 10am-1pm, 3-7pm, Sun and public holidays 10am-2pm; Oct-Mar: daily except Mon 10am-1pm, 3-6pm, Sun and public holidays 10am-2pm. 0.90€.* ☎ *(00-34) 972 89 63 13.*

This local museum houses the famous **Pharmacie de Llivia**★ (Llivia chemist's shop), one of the oldest of its kind in Europe. Ceramic jars and an assortment of 17C and 18C objects commonly found in an apothecary's shop are of particular interest.

The **fortified church** boasts a fine doorway with Catalan wrought-iron decorations; inside note the beautiful altarpiece dating from 1750.

GAILLAC

POPULATION 11,073

MICHELIN LOCAL MAP 338: D-7

Gaillac lies at a crossroads on the north bank of the Tarn. For many years, its wealth came from trade based on the river boat traffic on the Tarn. The old town still has some charming squares with fountains and narrow streets lined with old houses that are a happy combination of timber and brick work. *Pl. St-Michel, 81600 Gaillac, ☎ 05 63 57 14 65. www.ville-gaillac.fr.*

Sights

Abbatiale St-Michel

In the 7C, Benedictine monks founded an abbey in Gaillac and dedicated it to St Michael. Building work began on the abbey church in the 11C and went on until the 14C, with a number of interruptions. Inside the church is a fine polychrome wooden statue of the Madonna and Child (14C).

Next to the church are the abbey buildings, which now house the **Maison des Vins de Gaillac**, as well as the **Musée des Arts et Traditions populaires** (& ⓘ *Jul and Aug 10am-1pm, 2-7pm, rest of the year 10am-noon, 2-6pm. ⓘ Closed 1 Jan, 1 May, 1 Nov, 25 Dec. 2.30€. Combined tickets are available for the 3 museums: 3€, valid 1 year ☎ 05 63 41 03 81)* with tools and master-works illustrating the work of journeymen (*compagnons*), displays evoking work in local vineyards, and various objects of local historical interest.

Tour Pierre de Brens

This charming brick tower dates from the 14C and 15C and underwent alterations during the Renaissance. It still has a few gargoyles, mullioned windows and a delightful bartizan.

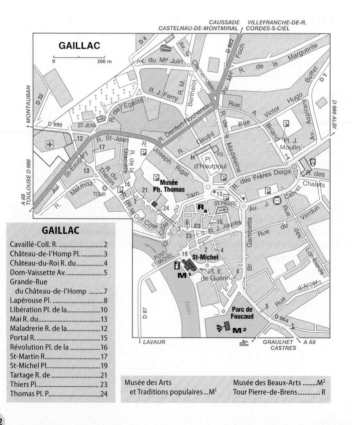

Address Book

✦ *For coin ranges, see the Legend at the back of the guide.*

EATING OUT

🍴 **La Table du Sommelier** – *34 Pl. Thiers - ☎ 05 63 81 20 10 - closed Sun (except in Jul and Aug) and Mon*. Warm, rustic décor incorporating heavy tables, wood trimming and winegrowers' tools. Regulars enjoy the small appetizer plates and the interesting selection of wines.

🍴🍴 **Les Sarments** – *27 R. Cabrol (behind the Abbaye St-Michel) - ☎ 05 63 57 62 61 - closed 25 Apr-3 May, 19 Dec-10 Jan, 21 Feb-7 Mar, Sun evenings, Wed evenings and Mon*. This former wine storehouse (the red brick vaults date from the 14C-16C) sits in the heart of the old town, just steps from the Maison des Vins. A wine list featuring Gaillac vintages accompanies the selection of regional dishes.

WHERE TO STAY

🛏 **L'Occitan** – *Pl. de la Gare - ☎ 05 63 57 11 52 - hotel.occitan@wanadoo.fr - closed Sat-Sun Nov-Mar -* 🅿 *- 12 rooms -* 🍴 *6€*. Former typical station hotel features clean, comfortable, spacious rooms. The former bar now serves as the breakfast-room.

🛏🛏 **Hôtel Verrerie** – *R. de l'Égalité - ☎ 05 63 57 32 77 - contact@la-verrerie. com -* 🅿 *- 14 rooms -* 🍴 *7.50€*. This old glass-making factory was built in the 19C and stands in the middle of a pretty park with a stand of bamboo. This is the landscape that greets you from the window of your room, which for its part is fitted with contemporary furniture. The dining room is modern and opens onto a terrace facing the lawn.

WINE SHOPPING

Maison des Vins de Gaillac - Caveau St-Michel – *Abbaye St-Michel - ☎ 05 63 57 15 40 - maisons.vins.gaillac@wanadoo.fr – Jul-Aug: 10am-1pm, 2.30-7pm; rest of the year: 10am-noon, 2-6pm – closed Christmas, 1 Jan, 1 May and 1 Nov*. This wine centre on the banks of the River Tarn sells products from 82 different vineyards and 3 cooperatives producing Gaillac wine. Tastings, presentation of the vineyards and sales.

Cave coopérative de Labastide-de-Lévis – *B.P. 12 - 81150 Marssac-sur-Tarn - ☎ 05 63 53 73 73 - www.cave-labastide. com - mid Jun-mid Sept: 9am-12.30pm, 2pm-7pm; rest of the year: 9am-noon, 2pm-6pm - closed Sun and public holidays*. This wine cooperative represents 1 400ha/3 458 acres and about 15% of Gaillac vineyards. 50% of its production is classified AOC, including the famous Gaillac "perlé" (very slightly sparkling). A tour covers every stage of wine production up to bottling. Free tastings.

Domaine du Moulin – *Chemin de Bastié - ☎ 05 63 57 20 52 - domainedumoulin@ libertysurf.fr - Mon-Sat 9.30am-noon, 2pm-7pm, Sun by appointment*. This estate has been voted best red Gaillac in the barrel for the last 8 years at the Gaillac and Paris wine competition. The Hirissou family has tended the vines for 9 generations, and these vineyards have found favour with stars such as Charles Aznavour, Johnny Halliday and Claude Chabrol, as well as enlightened wine lovers. Tastings.

Château Raynal – *La Brunerie - 81600 Senouillac - ☎ 05 63 41 70 02 - www.ville-gaillac.fr - museum: daily guided tour by appointment - closed mid to late Aug*. After visiting a small museum on the history and evolution of farming in the Gaillac region, it is time to sample some good local wine: dry or sweet white, and a red that could be laid down for a few years (*vin de garde*). Hospitable welcome from this family of winegrowers.

Château de Mayragues – *- - 81140 Castelnau-de-Montmiral - ☎ 05 63 33 94 08 - www.chateau-de-mayragues.com - Mon-Sat 9am-7pm; closed Christmas*. There are many reasons to visit this château: the 14-16C fortified architecture, the hilly setting, the vineyards and, of course, the Gaillac wines (red, rose, dry and sweet whites, sparkling).

Les vins de Robert et Bernard Plageoles – *Domaine des Tres Cantous – 11km/6.6mi N of Gaillac on D 988. - 81140 Cahuzac-sur-Vère - ☎ 05 63 33 90 40 - robert-bernard-plageoles@wanadoo.fr – Jun-Aug: 8am-noon, 3-7pm; Sep-May: 8am-noon, 2-4pm, Sat-Sun and holidays by appointment only*. The vineyard owned by Robert and Bernard Plageoles is a good place to taste a variety of white wines such as the unusual vin de voile, aged in an open cask for seven years, or mauzac nature, a sparkling wine. Red wines are made with duras and syrah grapes. Knowledgable and passionate, Robert Plageoles waxes poetic on the subject of his wines.

RECREATION

Plan d'eau d'Aiguelèse – *Planète Obade – 81600 Rivières - ☎ 05 63 41 50 50 - planete. obade@wanadoo.fr – May-Oct: daily 9am-noon, 2-6pm; Nov-Apr: daily 9am-12.30pm, 2-6pm - closed off-season*. Leaving from this marina, take a motor boat trip up the Tarn valley. On the lake itself, you can have fun with canoes, pedalos and wind-surfers.

The Gaillac Vineyards

The vineyards cover an area of 20 000ha/49 400 acres, from which red, rosé, white and sparkling wines are produced.

The south bank of the Tarn is where the grape varieties used to make red wines are grown: Gamay, Braucol, Syrah and Duras. The better-positioned vineyards on the north bank grow not only grapes for red wine (Duras, Braucol, Syrah, Cabernet and Merlot) but also the Mauzac, Loin de l'œil and Sauvignon (also found on the plain around Cordes-sur-Ciel) grape varieties used to produce white wines.

The traditional techniques used in modern wine-growing guarantee the good quality of Gaillac wines, all of which are AOC *(Appellation d'Origine Contrôlée)*. The efforts made over the last 10 years in the Gaillac vineyards have ensured that they now rank among the foremost wine producers in South-West France.

Parc de Foucaud

The delightful terraced gardens above the Tarn were laid out by the famous 17C French landscape gardener, André Le Nôtre (whose masterpiece was the garden at the palace of Versailles).

The château, an 18C residence belonging to the family of Counsellor de Foucaud d'Alzon, houses the **Musée des Beaux-Arts** (🕐 *Early Apr to mid-Oct: daily except Tue 10am-noon, 2-6pm; rest of the year: Fri and Sat-Sun and public holidays 10am-noon, 2-6pm;* 🕐 *closed 1 Jan, 1 May, 1 Nov, 25 Dec. 2.30€* ☏ *05 63 41 03 81)*, an art museum with works by local artists (painters and sculptors).

Musée d'Histoire naturelle Philadelphe-Thomas

🕐 *Same hours as for the Musée des Beaux-Arts*. This museum houses extensive mineral and paleontological collections.

Excursions

Lisle-sur-Tarn

9km/5.5mi SW via N 88.

This town on the north-west bank of the Tarn boasts a vast **square** with covered arcades and a fountain, a reminder of the days when this was a *bastide* (1248).

The historic town centre has a few old-brick and timber houses dating from the 16C, 17C and 18C. Some of them are linked to their outbuildings by pountets, little bridges one storey up across the narrow streets and alleyways. The church of **Notre-Dame de la Jonquière** has a Romanesque portal and a bell-tower built in the Toulouse style.

In the **Musée Raymond-Lafage** (🕐 *Apr to mid-Oct: daily except Tue 10am-noon, 2-6pm; rest of the year: Thu and Fri 10am-noon, 2-6pm; possibility of guided tour (45min); 2€, no charge 1st Sun in month;* ☏ *05 63 40 45 45; www.ville-lisle-sur-tarn.fr)*, named after a 17C draughtsman who was born in Lisle, there are not only drawings and engravings by Lafage himself, but also collections relating to Gallo-Roman and medieval archaeology, works of sacred art and portraits by Victor Maziès (1836-95).

From the bridge, there is a pleasant view of the town and its retaining walls.

Château de Mauriac★

▶ *11km/7mi N on D 922. Turn right just before Cahuzac.*

🕐 *May-Oct: guided tour (1h) 3-6pm; rest of the year: weekdays and Sat on request, Sun 3-6pm. 6€ (children: 4€). Inquire with M. Emmanuel Bistes,* ☏ *05 63 41 71 18. www.bistes.com*

This castle, parts of which date from the 14C, has a beautiful, uniform façade. Two large corner towers flank a main building in which the central entrance is itself flanked by two smaller towers.

On the ground floor are a number of rooms displaying works by Bernard Bistes, painter and owner of the castle.

The first-floor rooms have all been restored and refurbished in different styles and colour schemes. The furniture blends well with the wall coverings and the French-style ceilings redecorated by Bernard Bistes and his students. Note the room known as the "Polish Room". It has a French-style ceiling decorated with 360 panels depicting a beautifully fresh-looking **herbarium**★.

Castelnau-de-Montmiral

13km/8mi NW on D 964. This is a picturesque village perched on a spur of rock high above the Vère Valley and Grésigne Forest (*outdoor leisure park*). Castelnau-de-Montmiral is an old bastide, founded in the 13C by Raymond VII, Count of Toulouse, to replace the stronghold razed during the Albigensian Crusade. Its eventful past is still visible in its old houses, all of which have been enhanced by a skilful restoration programme.

Place des Arcades, as its name suggests, is flanked by arcades topped with corbelled half-timbered houses. On the west and south sides are two 17C houses.

In the 15C **parish church**, note the polychrome stone statue of Christ Bound (15C), the Baroque altarpiece and, above all, to the left of the chancel the **gem-encrusted cross-reliquary**★ of the counts of Armagnac known as the Montmiral Cross, a fine example of 13C religious gold and silver work.

GANGES

POPULATION 3,502

MICHELIN LOCAL MAP 339: H-5

This small industrial town is situated on the confluence of the Hérault and the Rieutord and is a good base for trips into the surrounding area. The old town and the avenues lined with plane trees make a pleasant place for a stroll. Ganges made its fortune from the manufacture of fine silk stockings during the reign of Louis XIV. Natural silk was replaced by artificial silk then nylon, and the cottage industry by factories, of which half a dozen or so still produce high quality stockings. ▮ *34190 Ganges,* ☏ *04 67 73 00 59.*

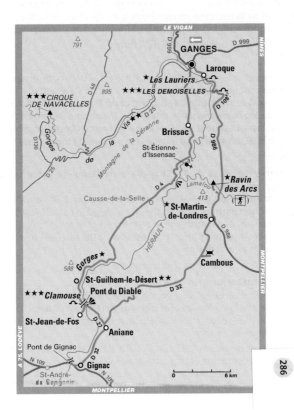

Vallée de l'Hérault★

94km/58mi round-trip – allow one day.

▶ *Leave Ganges SW along D 4.*

Brissac

There is a good view of this picturesque village as you arrive. The oldest district stands in the shadow of a castle dating from the 12C and 16C.

D 4 rejoins the Hérault as it flows between limestone scarp slopes. From the road, you can see the Romanesque chapel of **St-Étienne-d'Issensac** to the left and a 12C bridge spanning the river.

Shortly after Causse-de-la-Selle, the road leaves the plateau and enters a coomb hollowed out by a river that has now disappeared. On very hot days at the height of summer, this dried up rocky gully exudes an atmosphere of intense desolation.

Gorges de l'Hérault★

Overlooked by steep slopes, the river gorge, which remains fairly open as far as St-Guilhem-le-Désert, gradually becomes narrower by the time it reaches the Pont du Diable. The Hérault cuts a deep, enclosed course along the floor of the valley between sheer rock faces adorned with tenaciously clinging, scrubby trees. Here and there one sees a small terrace supported by a wall, a few lines of vines, a tiny meadow or one or two olive trees clinging onto the hillside above the river – these are the only forms of cultivation possible here.

St-Guilhem-le-Désert★★ – ⚬ *See ST-GUILHEM-LE-DÉSERT.*

Grotte de Clamouse★★★ – ⚬ *See ST-GUILHEM-LE-DÉSERT.*

The road crosses the river via a modern bridge near **Pont du Diable**, an early-11C bridge built by Benedictine monks. There is a view of the Hérault gorge and the aqueduct which supplies vineyards in the St-Jean-de-Fos area with water.

▶ *Drive down D 27 to the small town of Aniane.*

Aniane

Aniane is a quiet wine-growing town which has lost all trace of the prosperous abbey founded here in the 8C by St Benedict. A stroll through the narrow streets takes in the church of St-Jean-Baptiste-des-Pénitents, built in a mixture of architectural styles and now used to house temporary exhibitions. There is also the church of St-Sauveur, with the austere west front so characteristic of French Classical architecture in the 17C, and the 18C town hall with rounded bay windows at the corners.

Gignac

Towering over the village, the 17C **Chapelle Notre-Dame-de-Grâce** has an unusual Italian-style west front.

The road (N 109) crosses the Hérault over **Pont de Gignac**. Built from 1776 to 1810 to plans by architect Bertrand Garipuy, this is considered to be the finest 18C bridge in France because of its daring design and the beauty of its architectural lines.

A flight of steps leads to a platform downstream on the east bank from where there is an admirable view of the bridge.

▶ *Return to Aniane and follow D 32 to St-Martin-de-Londres.*

Village préhistorique de Cambous

🕐 *Jul and Aug: daily except Mon 2-6pm; Sep-Oct: Sat-Sun and public holidays 2pm-6pm; Apr-Jun and Easter holidays: Sat-Sun and public holidays 2-6pm. 2.50€. ☎ 04 67 86 34 37. The access road is rather bumpy. Leave the car in the Cambous car park and walk to the prehistoric village.*

Kids This site, discovered in 1967, revealed remains of stone dwellings dating from 2800-2300 BC: four groups of huts, each comprising 8 to 10 adjacent buildings with 2.5m/8ft-thick drystone walls and openings forming corridors. A house has been reconstructed to look exactly as it would have done then.

⚬ *For coin ranges, see the Legend at the back of the guide.*

DINNER ON THE FARM

🍴 **Auberge Domaine de Blancardy** – *34190 Moulès-et-Beaucels - 7km/4mi E of Ganges on D 999 and B-road - ☎ 04 67 73 94 94 - closed Jan, Feb, Wed and Thu noon.* This wine-growing farm, dating from the 13C and 14C, supplies its kitchens with poultry, rabbits and *foie gras* from its own grounds. Supper is served in an old vaulted wine cellar, or in the inner courtyard during summer. Some rooms available.

LEISURE ACTIVITIES

The Outsider France – *15 Pl. des Halles - ☎ 04 67 73 01 01 - www.aupalya.com – 9am-6pm.* Climbing, canyoning, hiking, canoeing, via ferrata and other outdoor adventures.

St-Martin-de-Londres★

This charming old village has retained traces of its 14C defensive wall and, in its centre, stands the parish close fortified in the 12C. The 11C **church**★, nestling among old houses, is reached via some steps. Like other early Romanesque churches in Languedoc, it features harmonious proportions, an oven-vaulted semicircular east end and Lombard-band decoration.

▶ *Follow D 986 N towards Ganges.*

Ravin des Arcs★

Stop the car by the bridge spanning the Lamalou. *Take a path on the left leading to the Ravin des Arcs. It rises as far as a wall then veers to the left. From that point the path is clearly waymarked in red and white (GR 60). Allow 2hr round-trip.*

The path goes through scrubland dotted with holm-oaks then runs down towards the Ravin des Arcs, a narrow canyon reaching a depth of 200m/656ft in places. This owes its name to the many natural arches formed by the eroding power of the Lamalou; the finest of these is known as the **Grand Arc.**

Grotte des Demoiselles★★★ – 🕯 *See Grotte des DEMOISELLES.*

The road runs through an impressive sheer-sided gorge, a canyon really, gouged out by the River Hérault.

Laroque

Wander through the paved streets and discover in turn the belfry topped by a campanile, the castle and the former silkworm-breeding establishment overlooking the river.

Grotte des Lauriers★ – ⊶ *Closed for renovation work.* Discovered in 1930 by E-A Martel, this cave is decorated with rock carvings dating from the Magdalenian period *(not visible at present).* The cave is in two parts: one part contains fossils (Salle de l'Éboulis, Salle du Lac), the other part, where water continues its eroding process, contains an amazing variety of limestone concretions.

La GARDE-GUÉRIN★

MICHELIN LOCAL MAP 330: L-8

An impressive tower is the first indication of this old fortified village lying on the Lozère plateau, at the tip of a scarp slope overlooking the Chassezac gorge. Its geographical location is interesting, situated as it is between the Gévaudan and Vivarais regions where the granite of Mont Lozère meets the schist of the Ardèche.

A Bit of History

Road safety in the Middle Ages – The old Régordane Roman road was, for many years, the only means of communication between Languedoc and Auvergne. In the 10C, in order to free the region of its highway robbers, the bishops of Mende decided to set up a guard post in the wildest part of the plateau. It is this guard post that has given the village its name.

A community of noblemen, the pariers, was established here and, in return, enjoyed special civic status. There were 27 of them in all and they escorted travellers in return for a toll. Each of them had his own fortified house in La Garde and the village, encircled by a curtain wall, was defended by a fortress.

La Garde Guérin

Visit

The village

The population is made up of a small number of stock breeders. The houses are built of large granite ashlars and are characteristic of an architectural style common in mountainous areas. The few taller houses with mullioned windows are the former residences of the pariers. The mountain church with its bellcote is particularly well built.

The Keep

The entrance is under a porch to the left of the church. This is the largest remaining section of the original fortress. From the top, there is a view of the village and the Chassezac gorge. The **panorama**★ stretches as far as Mont Ventoux.

Belvédère du Chassezac★★

Leave the car near the signpost "belvédère" to the left of D 906. 15min on foot round-trip. A path leads to a narrow terrace.

The site is impressive: the bird's-eye view of the Chassezac gorge below, the thundering noise of the water gushing through, amplified by the steep rock face, the jagged rocks and the sheer depth of the abyss leave a lasting impression.

For coin ranges, see the Legend at the back of the guide.

ROOMS WITH A VIEW

Auberge Régordane – ☎04 66 46 82 88 - closed 4 Oct-9 Apr - 15 rooms - 7€. This picturesque 16C residence with solid grey granite walls is in a village overlooking stunning natural scenery. Small neat rooms in pastel colours. Restaurant tables move outside to the courtyard in summer. For those who are keen: fishing, canyoning, rock-climbing.

GAVARNIE ★

POPULATION 164

MICHELIN LOCAL MAP 342: L-6

ALSO SEE LA BIGORRE

The Vallée de Gavarnie and the Cirque de Gavarnie (a great geological amphitheatre, which has been on UNESCO's World Heritage List since 1997) are known all over the world. The landscape is so forbidding that it provoked the visiting Baroness Dudevant (the author George Sand) to write, not without exaggeration: "From Luz to Gavarnie is primeval chaos; it is hell itself." Victor Hugo described the track through the neighbouring Chaos de Coumély as "a black and hideous path". 🄸 *65120 Gavarnie,* ☎ *05 62 92 49 10. www.gavarnie.com.*

🅿 **Parking**: Gavarnie, the highest village in the Pyrenees, is very crowded in the summer. Leave your car outside the town, and walk to the town. Private and municipal lots charge the same fee: about 4€ for the day.

🚲 From the village, you can reach the Cirque de Gavarnie astride a donkey or a horse. You will find them near the parking area closest to the path leading up *(16€ round trip).*

Sights

The Village

In the summer season the small village experiences a phenomenal influx of visitors: strictly the end of the road as far as wheeled traffic is concerned, Gavarnie has since 1864 provided a large and varied assortment of mounts for the trek to the Cirque. Once the day-trippers have gone, however, and the mules, donkeys and ponies have been returned to their pastures, Gavarnie resumes its identity as a climbers' centre, a base for mountaineers.

Cemetery

Besides the tombs of local inhabitants in the upper section of the cemetery, a fervour for commemoration exists in the village and surrounding area, turning a visit into sort of pilgrimage. There's a statue of Russell, a medal of Béraldi, a plaque commemorating locals who died in the war, and by the side of the road going back towards Luz, the tomb of the geographer Schrader not far from the entrance to the amphitheatre.

Church

The 14C church was once part of a priory founded by the Hospitallers of St John of Jerusalem, and stands on the old pilgrims' route to Port de Boucharo (Boucharo Pass,

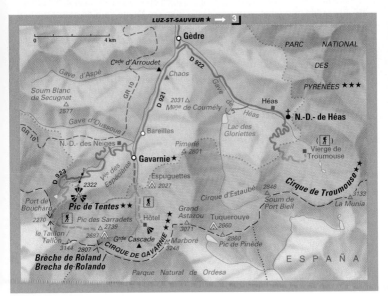

Address Book

  For coin categories, see the Legend at the back of the guide.

WHERE TO STAY AND EAT

⊜⊜ **Hôtel Marboré** – ☎05 62 92 40 40 - hotel@lemarbore.com - closed 4 Nov-20 Dec - 🅿 - 24 rooms - ⊡ 7.50€ - restaurant ⊜⊜. This hotel at the heart of the Parc national des Pyrénées is an ideal departure point for walks to the cirque or others. Rooms are basic but well kept. The dining room is part bistro in style, part open-air chic with cane furniture on the veranda.

SUMMER FUN

The Cirque makes a grand open-air auditorium for the annual festival of music, theatre and dance, the last two weeks of July. It is a 20min walk from the village to the field. Dress warmly!

WINTER SPORT

Domaine skiable de Gavarnie-Gèdre – *Alt. 1 350-2 400m.* 11 lifts, 22 runs for all levels. The longest beginners trail in the Pyrenees. 7.5km/4.5mi of cross-country trails. In January or March, the "Derby Gavarnie 3000" takes place – a cross-country contest between Gavarnie and the Brèche de Roland.

---

alt 2 270m/7 448ft). The three 17C gilt wood statues at the entrance represent the Virgin Mary, St Joseph and John the Baptist. To the left of the high altar at the entrance to the Chapelle du Bon Port stands a polychrome statue of St James of Compostela. Inside the chapel, two statuettes of Compostela pilgrims flank the 14C statue of Notre-Dame-du-Bon-Port. The Virgin Mary holds a pilgrim's water flask.

Hiking Tours

Cirque de Gavarnie★★★

🚶 *2hr on foot there and back.* At the end of the village, take the unsurfaced path then follow the left bank of the *gave* (mountain stream). Cross over an old stone bridge and walk up through the woods, leaving the river to your right. As you go down again towards the river, the landscape brightens up, the Cirque gets nearer against a background of fir trees. On the left a few waterfalls can be seen. The last part of the journey consists in climbing through mixed vegetation (trees and bushes such as wild roses in June-July) to reach the first rocky folds marking the approach of the Cirque itself. Shortly before arriving at the Hôtel du Cirque, the river rushes through a narrow gorge.

Then the **Cirque de Gavarnie** suddenly comes into view – three superimposed layers of horizontal strata rising in giant steps from the floor of the blind valley. Snow-covered ledges separate the tiered formations one from the other, gleaming white against the ochre cliff faces.

The amphitheatre was formed by glacial action on a previous degradation of Secondary Age sediments, when waters released from the Monte Perdido massif pushed back the head of the valley and undermined the surrounding cliffs. Subsequently the glacier – of which only fragments remain on the upper ledges – pierced out the amphitheatre and carried away the debris of the earlier erosion.

Gazing with wonder at the majesty of the sheer rock walls and tiered snow platforms, Victor Hugo exclaimed: "It is both a mountain and a rampart; it is the most mysterious of structures by the most mysterious of architects; it is Nature's Colosseum – it is Gavarnie!"

The Cirque is 3.5km/over 2mi wide at its base and 14km/9mi around the crest line (from Astazou in the east to Pic des Sarradets in the west). The floor level is, on average, 1 676m/5 503ft above sea level; the surrounding summits rise to more than 3 000m/10 000ft.

The mounted excursions end at the Hôtel du Cirque but it is possible to continue, on foot (*1hr there and back*), as far as the Grande Cascade. This, the most impressive of the innumerable waterfalls silvering the walls of the circus, is fed by melt-water overflowing from the frozen lake 2 592m/8 500ft up on Monte Perdido on the Spanish side of the frontier. The cascade drops a clear 422m/1 385ft into the void.

From the hotel there is a spectacular view of the Cirque and its surroundings, one of the most magnificent mountain landscapes in all Europe.

Brèche de Roland (Roland's Breach)

🚶 *4hr on foot there and back for experienced hikers: beware of the névés from September to early July. Follow the marked path starting E of Port de Boucharo.*

The path follows the Haute Route des Pyrénées. At the foot of the Taillon glacier, it fords a waterfall (*carefully follow the red arrows painted on the rocks; névés may render your crossing more difficult*). From the pass preceding the Sarradets refuge, there is a good view of the Grande Cascade of the Cirque de Gavarnie. Beyond the refuge, the climb to the breach is longer and more difficult because of the snow and *névés* one encounters. As you reach the breach, there is a **view** of the barren Spanish side and of Monte Perdido. According to legend, the vast fracture in the rock face was made by Roland (a gallant 8C knight who was a nephew of Charlemagne) when he tried to break his trusty sword Durandal to prevent it from falling into the hands of the Saracens. The *Chanson de Roland (Song of Roland)* was the first of the epic French *chansons de geste* (epic poems).

Excursions

Pic de Tentes★★
11km/7mi, by the Port de Bouchoro road.

▶ *Leaving Gavarnie in the direction of Luz (north), turn left just before the bridge. The road skirts the statue of Notre-Dame-des-Neiges at the mouth of the Vallée d'Ossoue, then enters the Vallée des Espécières.*

▶ *When you reach Col de Tentes, leave the car at the saddle and continue on foot to the rounded summit of Pic de Tentes (alt 2 322m/ 7 618ft), to the NE.*

From the summit there is a breathtaking **panorama**★★ of the peaks surrounding the Cirque de Gavarnie (the valley floor is not visible from here). Among the most remarkable is Pic du Marboré, gashed by the course of the Grande Cascade glacier. Farther west the rocky spine of Les Sarradets, in the foreground, slightly masks the Brèche de Roland (*see above*) before the frontier crest reappears at Le Taillon and the peaks of Les Gabiétous. More distant still, far off to the north-west, rises Le Vignemale, which shoulders the Ossoue glacier. To the north-east the Néouvielle massif stands in front of Pic du Midi de Bigorre (recognisable by its television transmitter).

③ Vallée de Gavarnie★★
20km/12mi itinerary from Luz-St-Sauveur - 3hr 30min - for a full map of the itinerary, see La BIGORRE.

Great hollows – the Pragnères, Gèdre and Gavarnie basins – were gouged out by glaciers during the Quaternary Age; the waters then sliced through the rock between the basins to create narrows, the most typical of which is St-Sauveur Gorge. Temporary dwellings perch on the resulting ledges; torrents rush down in cascades from the tributary valleys.

Luz-St-Sauveur★ – See LUZ-ST-SAUVEUR.
▶ *Leave the town via D 921.*

Pont Napoléon
Avoid, in the holiday season, the line of excursion coaches which forms at around 3pm near the Pont Napoléon. The single arch of this bridge, built on the orders of Napoleon III in 1860, spans the gorge channelled by the Pau Torrent; a marble memorial column surmounted by an eagle stands at its eastern end. The bridge offers an impressive view over the sunken stream and the scrub-covered gorge.

The road, carved from the bed-rock, twists through another gorge; passing through the hamlet of Sia (bridge) it approaches the service cable-way which rises alongside the pipelines supplying the power station.

Centrale de Pragnères (Pragnères Power Station)
Visits cancelled due to the government "Vigipirate" security plan. ☎ 05 62 92 43 12.

This is the most powerful hydroelectric plant in the Pyrenees. The turbines are fuelled by waters collected from the Néouvielle massif and from the west bank tributaries of the Pau Torrent – the former with a water-head of 1 250m/4 101ft, the latter with a fall of 900m/2 953ft. The Néouvielle water supply is stored in Cap de Long reservoir, more than half of which is filled with the help of two pumping stations.

When tours are permitted, visitors to the power station are shown the machine room with its turbines, and a model, illustrated with illuminated circuits, of the complex and its supply lines.

Just before Gèdre, the jagged peak of Pimené (alt 2 801m/9 190ft) appears, beyond and to the right of the Montagne de Coumély (streaked with another hydroelectric pipeline). Pimené is the final peak before the Cirque de Gavarnie.

Gèdre

This village lies in a basin of green meadows cut by long lines of poplar trees, at the confluence of the Héas and Gavarnie torrents. Gèdre makes a charming halt on the route to the Cirque de Gavarnie and is also a starting point for excursions to the Troumouse and Estaubé cirques. From the Hôtel de la Brèche de Roland there is a view of the legendary Brèche de Roland in the mountain wall and, farther to the right, the snow-filled hollow of the "False Breach", from which a single pillar of rock known as *Le Doigt* (the finger) points upwards.

▷ *Follow the toll road to the Cirque de Troumouse (15km/9mi), usually obstructed by snow from December to April.*

The road climbs through the pastures of the Héas Valley, the grassy slopes of which are punctuated by a chaos, a scattering of boulders which have tumbled from the Montagne de Coumély and, higher up, a second chaos in which the largest rock serves as a pedestal for a statue of the Virgin Mary.

Héas

Its dome rising amid the last clump of trees in the valley, the **chapel** (🕐 *May-Oct: 8am-7pm, service Sun at 11am*) is the site of regular pilgrimages (*15 August, 8 September, Fête of the Rosary, 1st Sunday in October*). The original building was swept away by an avalanche in 1915 and rebuilt 10 years later. The north aisle of that original chapel still remains, along with statues, paintings, the 1643 bell, a stoup and an 18C processional Cross. The venerated statue of Notre-Dame-de-Héas, recovered intact from the debris of the avalanche, now stands in the chancel.

From the road winding up the southern slope of the valley there are interesting views of the "trough" hollowed by the ancient Héas glacier. The escarpment on the northern side above Héas chapel is notched by a mountain torrent falling from a pool at the bottom of a swallow-hole.

To the south a semicircle of mountain crests appears – a rock formation notable for the extraordinary wave-like structure of its pale, tightly folded strata.

Cirque de Troumouse★★

Toll road from Héas: 3.50€ per vehicle. The best view of this amphitheatre is from a rocky spur, in the centre of which stands a statue of the Virgin Mary, the Vierge de Troumouse *(45min there and back on foot).*

🚶 The amphitheatre is enormous – large enough, it is claimed, to accommodate three million "spectators". Carpeted in meadow grass and flowers, slightly convex on the whole, it is enclosed by an almost unbroken rampart of mountains 10km/6mi around. The highest point is Pic de la Munia (alt 3 133m/ 10 279ft), identifiable by the remains of its hanging glacier.

Below this, on the left, are twinned rock pinnacles known locally as "the Two Sisters".

▷ *Return to Gèdre and continue along D 921.*

The scenery again takes on a wild aspect. Above, to the right, is the glacier-created hanging valley of the Aspé Torrent. The stream dashes down into the main valley via the spectacular Cascade d'Arroudet. The road crosses the rock-strewn Chaos de Coumély (chaos is a French geological term referring to an accumulated scattering of irregular rocks and boulders) at the foot of the **Montagne de Coumély** and begins the final ascent towards Gavarnie.

Beyond and to the left of the Fausse Brèche and Pic des Sarradets (*in the foreground*) the upper reaches of the amphitheatre with its snow-covered ledges come into view, together with the summits of Le Casque, La Tour and Pic du Marboré.

The hamlet of Bareilles appears next (*right*) and then, on the Turon de Holle, at the mouth of the Vallée d'Ossoue, the monumental statue of Notre-Dame-des-Neiges.

La GRANDE-MOTTE

POPULATION 6,458

MICHELIN LOCAL MAP 339: J-7

The coastal plain south-east of Montpellier is the setting for the tall, eye-catching pyramids of La Grande-Motte, a highly original man-made seaside resort set in moorland and sand dunes on the Mediterranean coast. Thanks to the wide roads which link it to the A 9 motorway, the resort can take advantage of its proximity to Nîmes and Montpellier. Vast car parks in the town centre leave the seafront free for pedestrians. The Palais des Congrès (conference centre) overlooks the yachting marina. *Allée des Parcs, 34280 La Grande-Motte, ☎ 04 67 56 42 00. www. ot-lagrandemotte.fr.*

Kids **Especially for Kids:** Aquarium panoramique and Espace Grand Bleu.

The Resort

It was designed as a complete complex by a team of engineers and architects under the leadership of Jean Balladur. The main buildings, with their resolutely modern designs, form honeycomb **pyramids**, all of them south facing.

The **villas** have been built in Provençal style or around inner courtyards.

The resort is continuing to develop westwards into the pedestrian district of the Motte du Couchant, where the

Address Book

For coin categories, see the Legend at the back of the guide.

EATING OUT

La Cuisine du Marché – 89 R. du Casino - ☎ 04 67 29 90 11 - closed Mon and Tue from Sep-Jun - reservation recommended. This little restaurant behind its modest façade is an address to remember. The owner uses top quality produce in his creations and limits the number of covers in the two small dining rooms so as to offer his clients the best service. Fixed price menus are particularly interesting.

WHERE TO STAY

Golf – 1920 Ave. du Golf - ☎ 04 67 29 72 00 - golfhotel34@wanadoo.fr - 𝕻 - 44 rooms - 11€. Rooms overlook the golf course or Ponant lake, take your pick. All have a balcony where you can lounge in the sun and enjoy some peace and quiet. Decor is contemporary and the furniture is regularly updated.

SPORT

This seaside resort, which rose from the sands 40 years ago, offers a full range of

sport and leisure activities for the holidaymaker. Tourists can choose between relaxing walks by the sea or the thrill of hurtling down the giant Grand Bleu water chutes.

Blue Dolphin – 71 Quai Eric-Tabarly, Le Miramar shopping centre - ☎ 04 67 56 03 69 - www.bluedolphin.fr - daily 9am-noon, 2pm-7pm - closed Jan and Tue. Diving club: trained by professionals and given a good briefing by Pascal Jard, experienced diver and in charge of operations here, visitors can then go and admire the spectacle of the deep. All levels taught, from initiation to level 4.

Étrave croisière – Quai d'Honneur - ☎ 04 67 29 10 87 - www.etrave-crosieres.com - daily 7am-8pm - closed Nov-Feb - For nigh on thirty years, Étrave Croisières has been taking passengers on voyages of discovery around the coast. There are also sea-fishing trips and boats for hire, with or without a licence.

SHOPPING

Marché provencal – Pl. de la Mairie - Sun 8am-12.30pm. Provençal market.

Port and Pyramidal holiday homes at La Grande-Motte

buildings take the form of rounded shells facing the sea, and northwards around Ponant Lake. Many green open spaces are available for pedestrians.

Kids La Grande-Motte has been nominated a "kid" resort for its activities and facilities specially intended for children and awarded the Pavillon bleu d'Europe for the quality of the sea water.

Beach

The entire complex faces the sea and has been laid out in relation to the vast fine sandy beach stretching over a distance of 6km/4mi and fitted with toilets and showers. Dogs are not allowed on this beach; however another beach welcomes them.

Marina and sports amenities

Framed by the pyramids, the marina can accommodate 1 410 yachts. The main attractions of La Grande-Motte for visitors are the water sports facilities on Ponant Lake and the possibilities for angling in Or Lake.

Aquarium panoramique

Jul and Aug: 10am-11.30pm; mid to late Jun and mid to late Sep: daily 10am-12.30pm, 2-7.30pm, 8.45-10.30pm; mid-Sep-late Dec and Feb: daily except Sun morning 10am-noon, 2-6pm; Jan: Sat-Sun and public holidays 2-6pm. 5€ (14 and under: 3.50€). ☎ 04 67 56 85 23.

Kids Gurnards, sea-horses, sea eagles, groupers, sharks, octopuses and more than 300 species of fish and invertebrates from the French coast and Camargue lagoons swim around the different pools.

Espace Grand Bleu

Mid-Jun to mid-Sep: 10am-8pm, Sat-Sun 10am-7pm; mid-Sep to mid-Jun: Tue and Thu noon-2pm, 4-8pm, Mon and Wed noon-8pm, Fri noon-2pm, 4-10pm, Sat-Sun public holidays and school holidays 10am-6pm. 4€ off-season, 9.50€ high season ☎ 04 67 56 28 23.

Kids This is an aquatic theme park with water slides for all ages, Jacuzzi, wave pools, sauna etc.

Excursion

Carnon-Plage

8km/5mi. This "lido"-style beach situated between La Grande-Motte and Palavas-les-Flots and separated from the road by a string of dunes is particularly popular with people from Montpellier. The marina is linked to the Rhône-to-Sète canal.

GRUISSAN ⌂

POPULATION 3,061

MICHELIN LOCAL MAP 344: J-4

ALSO SEE LES CORBIÈRES

Today linked to the sea by a channel, Gruissan used to be isolated in the middle of lagoons and served as a point of defence for the port of Narbonne. The new resort has grown next to the old village, on the shores of the Grazel lagoon. The coastline is characterised by houses set high on stilts. ▯ *Bd. du Pech-Meynaud, 11430 Gruissan, ☎ 04 68 49 09 00. www.ville-gruissan.fr.*

The Resort

The resort of Gruissan grew up after a channel was opened linking Le Grazel lagoon with the sea. Small blocks of flats laid out around the main basin in the new marina (yachts, fishing boats) have formed the heart of the resort since 1975. They are characterised mainly by their yellow ochre pebble-dash and their multi-ridge cradle-shaped roofs.

The popularity of the new resort lies not only in its position, wide open to the sea, but also its geographical location as an ideal centre from which to explore the Massif de la Clape, one of the lesser-known beauty spots in Languedoc (*see NARBONNE*).

Salins de l'Île St-Martin

♿🕐 *Late Jun to early Sep: discovery tour (1hr30min) daily 9.30am, 11am, 2.30pm, 4pm, 5.30pm; early Mar-late June and early Sep-late Oct: 10:30am, 2.30pm. 6€. ☎ 04 68 49 59 97. Rte. de l'Ayrolle.*

Sea water penetrates through this salt marsh along 35km/22mi of channels. The salt harvest takes place in September.

Gruissan-Plage

This seaside resort still has a strange estate of chalets (as seen in the film *Betty Blue*, shot here) built on piles to protect them from the floods that are always a possibility at the equinoxes.

The Old Village

Once the home of fishermen and salt-pan workers, the old village features houses set out in concentric circles around the ruins of the Barbarossa tower. Set some distance from the coast, amid the sleepy waters of inland lagoons, the village seemed to have resolutely turned its back on the sea. Yet this was once a sizeable harbour, with boats that set out to fish off the shores of Spain and Algeria. The fishermen still celebrate the festival of St Peter at the end of June.

P. Blot/MICHELIN

Gruissan

Address Book

For coin categories, see the Legend.

EATING OUT

Le Lamparo – *In the village -* ☎ *04 68 49 93 65 - closed 15 Dec-28 Jan, Mon and Tue off season.* A modest little restaurant in this fishing village surrounded by lagoons. Simple bistro style dining room and menu with the emphasis on fish. Reasonable prices.

Le Souquet's – *Domaine de la Pierre Droite - 5.5km/3.5mi au NW of Gruissan towards Narbonne on D 32 and B-road -* ☎ *04 68 49 13 23 - closed 1 Oct-15 Apr and lunchtime except weekends –.* This restaurant is in an old wine-grower's

house in the middle of the countryside at the foot of La Clape mountain. Fish and meat grilled over vine shoots are served on the superb terrace surrounded by vines with a view of the mountain. Two gîtes for hire for those wishing to prolong their stay.

WHERE TO STAY

Hôtel de la Plage – *On the beach -* ☎ *04 68 49 00 75 - closed mid Sept-Easter -* 🅿 *- 17 rooms.* This hotel occupies a small 1960s building. The well kept modestly furnished rooms are quite cheap. From the terrace you can see the famous beach chalets on stilts that featured in J-J Beineix's film, Betty Blue.

Excursion

Cimetière marin

4km/2.5mi, then 30min on foot there and back. Leave Gruissan on D 32, the Narbonne road. At the crossroads beyond the tennis courts, take the road signposted to Notre-Dame-des-Auzils into the Massif de la Clape and keep left all the way. Leave the car in the car park (in front of the Rec d'Argent nursery) and walk up to the chapel. If you prefer, you can drive the 1.5km/1mi of forest track signposted to Les Auzils, leave the car on a piece of rough ground and continue on foot (20min there and back).

All along a stony path that winds here and there between the broom, umbrella pines, holm-oaks and cypresses are moving memorials to sailors lost at sea. From the **chapel of Notre-Dame-des-Auzils** at the top of the hill in the heart of a thicket, there is an extensive view over Gruissan and the Massif de la Clape.

ILLE-SUR-TÊT

POPULATION 4,995

MICHELIN LOCAL MAP 344: G-6

This little town in the Roussillon plain is situated between the Têt and its tributary the Boulès. It is an important fruit and vegetable market and the departure point of the Conflent road to Prades and the Aspres road to Amélie-les-Bains. In 1834, Prosper Mérimée, then on a tour of inspection of Historic Monuments, drew attention to Ille-sur-Têt by choosing the town as the setting of one of his most famous short stories, The Venus from Ille. *Sq. de la Poste, 66130 Ille-sur-Têt,* ☎ *04 68 84 02 62.*

Walking Tour

Walking through the town, note the imposing Baroque façade of the **Église St-Étienne-del-Pradaguet,** a medieval sculpture – **"Les Enamourats"** – on the corner of Rue des Carmes and Rue Deljat, and a magnificent 15C sculpted **Gothic cross** on Place del Ram.

Église des Carmes

Easter holidays and Jul-Aug: guided tours daily except Sat-Sun on request at the Hospici d'Illa, 10 R. de l'Hôpital, 66130 Ille-sur-Têt, ☎ *04 68 84 83 96.*

THE OLD MILL

Domaine du Moulin – *66300 Caixas - 6km/4mi from the church of Fontcouverte towards Fourques -* ☎ *04 68 38 87 84 - closed late Nov-Mar, in the evening, Mon, Tue and Wed - reservation recommended.* In the mountains, this old miller's house is a favourite meeting place for food lovers. There are 23 dishes on the menu – the owner really wants to help you discover local cuisine! To aid digestion, how about a walk beneath the cork-oaks or a siesta in the garden.

The Organ Pipes of Ille-sur-Têt

The Carmelite church, built in the 17C, houses a collection of paintings from the studio of the Guerras, a family of Baroque artists from Perpignan.

Sights

Hospici d'Illa

🕐 *Mid-Jun to end Sep: 10am-noon, 2-7pm, Sat-Sun and public holidays 2-7pm; Oct: daily 2-6pm; early Feb-mid June: daily except Tue 2-6pm.* 🕐 *Closed, 1 May. 3.20€ (children under 13: no charge).* ☎ *04 68 84 83 96.*

Kids The former Hospice St-Jacques (16C and 18C main building) houses a permanent exhibition of Romanesque and Baroque paintings, sculpture and gold and silver plate displayed in a series of alcoves on the ground and first floors. Some 11C frescoes from the church at Casesnoves are on display in the sacristy. The centre also runs Catalan cooking workshops. At the end of the garden, there is the Romanesque church of La Rodona (11C, 12C and 14C) with a pointed-arch doorway. The museum also organises visits to some of the other Baroque Catalan churches of the region, at Espira-de-Conflent, Joch and Finestret for example.

Les Orgues d'Ille-sur-Têt★

Just north of Ille-sur-Têt; 15min on foot. 🕐 *Jul and Aug: 9.30am-8pm; Apr-Jun and Sep: 10am-6.30pm; Feb and Mar: 10am-12.30pm and 2-5.30pm;, school holidays 10am-5.30pm; Oct: 10am-12.30pm, 2-6pm; Nov-Jan: 2-5pm; last entry 45min before closing.* 🕐 *Closed 1 Jan, 25 Dec. 3.50€.* ☎ *04 68 84 13 13. www.ille-sur-tet.com*

Kids The road (D 21), after passing the river, bends back into a little valley dominated by amazing geological formations consisting of earth pillars (cheminées de fées or "fairies' chimneys"), columns of soft rock capped with hard conglomerate, known as the "Organ Pipes". These phenomena are grouped on two sites, one of which, to the east, is accessible to the public. It is a wonderful cirque with craggy white walls, in the centre of which stands an impressive earth pillar known as "the Sybil". Farther west, towards Montalba, more formations of a deeper ochre colour can be seen to the left of the road. About 1km/0.6mi higher, after a series of bends, a **look-out point** (*viewing table*) takes in the site of the "Organ Pipes", with Ille-sur-Têt on the horizon.

Excursions

Saint-Michel-de-Llotes

3km/1.9mi S along D 2. The **Musée de l'Agriculture catalane** (🕐 *Mid- Jun to mid-Sep: daily except Tue 10am-noon, 2-7pm, Sat-Sun and public holidays 2-7pm; mid-Sep to mid-Jun: daily except Tue 2-6pm.* 🕐 *Closed 1 Jan and 25 Dec. 3€.* ☎*04 68 84 76 40*) illustrates all the aspects of local farming, wine-growing, cattle-breeding etc. A great variety of tools is on display.

Les Aspres★

56km/35mi from Ille-sur-Têt to Amélie-les-Bains – allow 3hrs.

This is a rugged region, where inhabitants are few and far between and nothing breaks the overall stillness. A major part of the attraction for visitors lies in the beauty of an essentially Mediterranean landscape, covered mainly by olive groves and cork oaks, against a backdrop of schist or granite rocks, and in the discovery of Serrabone priory standing in solitary splendour against this somewhat unforgiving backdrop.

▶ *Leave Ille-sur-Têt S on D 2, then turn right onto D 16 to Bouleternère.*

D 618 (*turn left in Bouleternère*) leaves the orchards in the Têt Valley for the garrigues (scrubland) along the Boulès gorge.

▶ *After 7.5km/4.5mi turn right to Serrabone.*

Prieuré de Serrabone★★ – ⏱ *See Prieuré de SERRABONE.*

Col Fourtou

Alt 646m/2 100ft. The view looking back from the pass is of the Bugarach, the highest point in the Corbières (1 230m/3 998ft), and that looking forward is of the Vallespir mountains on the Franco-Spanish border – the Roc de France and, farther to the right, the Pilon de Belmatx with its jagged crest. To the right of these is the Canigou range.

Prunet-et-Belpuig

The **Chapelle de la Trinité** (🕐 *Daily except Tue 9am-6pm*) has a door with scrolled hinges. Inside, there is a 12C robed Christ and a Baroque altarpiece depicting the Holy Trinity, with the Holy Ghost as a youth, Christ as an adult and God the Father as an old man.

Château – 🚶 *30min walk (there and back) from the Chapelle de la Trinité.*
Across the moor, the brooding ruins of this castle occupy a prime site on a rocky spur overlooking a wide **panorama**★, taking in Mont Canigou, the Albères, the Roussillon and Languedoc coasts and the Corbières (Bugarach).

After the Xatard Pass the road drops down to Amélie, passing only two villages on its way – St-Marsal and Taulis – and skirting the upper Ample Valley. Holm-oaks and chestnut trees grow on the surrounding slopes.

L'ISLE-JOURDAIN

POPULATION 5,560

MICHELIN LOCAL MAP 336: I-8

Situated at the intersection of the Gers and Haute-Garonne départements, Isle Jourdain was once a stopover on the road to Santiago de Compostela, commemorated by the statue of St James at Halte St-Jacques (avenue de Lombez). Bertrand de l'Isle, founder of Saint-Bertrand-de-Comminges, was born here (*See ST-BERTRAND-DE-COMMINGES*). There is a lake with water sports facilities and a restaurant at the western end of the town alongside N 124. 🛈 *Au bord du lac, 32600 L'Isle-Jourdain,* ☎ *05 62 07 25 57.*

Town Centre

The main attraction, in place de l'Hôtel-de-Ville (the town hall was inspired by the *Capitole* in Toulouse), is the house of Claude Auge built at the turn of the 20C and featuring a number of stained-glass windows, including the well-known emblem of the Larousse publishing house (a woman with a dandelion flower, seeds blowing in the wind), and sculptures on the façade. The 18C Collegiate Church (*access from the east side of the square*) has arresting neo-Classical architecture with frescoes painted inside.

Musée d'Art Campanaire★

♿🕐 *Mid-Jun to mid-Sep: daily except Tue 10am-noon, 2.30-6.30pm; mid-Sep to mid-Jun: daily except Tue 10am-noon, 2.30-5.30pm.* 🕐 *Closed early to mid-Jan, public holidays.* 4€ *(no charge 1st Sun in month).* ☎ *05 62 07 30 01.*

This bell museum is housed in a former grain store (note the beautiful timber frame). A collection of more than 1 000 bells from every period of time and corner of the world is exhibited on two floors. On the ground floor, the "foundry" exhibit explains how bells are made. One of the rooms contains a huge clock with a visible mechanism from the Bastille Prison in Paris; in another room, there is an immense, very beautiful mid-19C clock, with four jaquemarts, figures with hammers for chiming out the hours, from Meung-sur-Loire. The first floor features several carillons and their keyboards which the visitor is invited to play (*a green sticker indicates which instruments can be used*). There is a magnificent collection of dinner bells used at table (note the engraved rock-crystal bell from the Second Empire), bells used in playing various games, and an exhibit entitled *Cloches du Monde* – bells from Europe, America, the South Pacific, Asia and Africa, including miniature bells from Nigeria whose handles are carved with wooden figures, and a Chinese jade bell from the Ch'ing Dynasty (18C). The *Sonnailles* exhibit features a selection of cow-bells. A number of **subrejougs** (harness bells from Vallée de la Save), remarkable for their polychrome decorations, are displayed in the last room.

J.-C. Salles/Musée d'Art Campanaire

Nigerian iron bell (19C-20C)

Le Gimontois

Round trip of 21km/13mi – allow 2hr 30min.

▶ *Leave L'Isle-Jourdain to the W on N 124.*

Gimont

This *bastide*, founded in 1266 and built on a typical grid pattern, closely hugs a tall, slender hill. The main street of the village, which lies along the crest, runs in a straight line through the old covered market place. The **church**, an excellent example of single-nave southern Gothic architecture, is surmounted by a brick tower in the style of Toulouse. Inside, the first chapel on the left contains a Renaissance triptych of the Crucifixion. On each side of the high altar, note the two monstrance-reliquaries shaped like Renaissance towers with lanterns on top, sacred vessels for holding the Eucharist and relics.

Foie gras and bullfighting are local specialities.

▶ *Leave Gimont W on D 12, route de Saramon.*

Chapelle Notre-Dame-de-Cahuzac

This 16C brick and stone chapel is dedicated to the Virgin Mary who is said to have appeared to a local shepherd. Note the Gothic doorway, with its door leaves carvings representing the 12 Apostles, and the 400 marble plaques, medallions and ex-votos left here by pilgrims.

▶ *Continue along D 12.*

Abbaye de Planselve

🕐 *By request at the tourist office in Gimont; only the entry hall and the pigeon houses are accessible to visitors. 2€. ☎ 05 62 67 77 87.*

This 12C Cistercian abbey, occupied until it was almost completely destroyed in 1789, has recently been partly restored. The abbey is surrounded by an impressive brick wall which runs alongside the road. The Gothic porch has two bays covered with ribbed vaulting. Remains of the site include the lay brothers' building with its ten 12C Romanesque bays and two dovecots. Below one of the pigeon houses is a space the monks used for storing ice; the other is decorated with a keystone depicting an abbot with his cross.

STAGE COACH INN

🍽 **Le Relais de la Diligence** – *32490 Monferran-Savès - 6km/4mi W of l'Isle-Jourdain towards Auch on N 124 - ☎ 05 62 07 80 14 - closed Mon except holidays reservations recommended weekends.* This well restored old farmhouse is not far from one of the pilgrimage routes to Santiago de Compostela in Spain. The dining room on a slope has rustic decor in which wood and stone blend harmoniously. Traditional fare. Collection of miniature horses.

HILLTOP HIDEAWAY

🍽 **Chambre d'hôte au Soulan de Lourange** – *32200 Gimont - 5km/3mi SW of Gimont, Rte. de Saramon (D 12) and a lane to the right - ☎ 05 62 67 76 62 – closed 1 week in Jan -* 🚭 *- 4 rooms.* Set upon a little hill, this 18C manor house looks like it would be at home in Tuscany. There is a pretty view over the Gers countryside, Gascony and the distant Pyrenees. The spacious rooms have old-fashioned furnishings and the flower garden is very pleasant.

LAGRASSE

POPULATION 615

MICHELIN LOCAL MAP 344: G-4

ALSO SEE LES CORBIÈRES

On the final descent to Lagrasse on the road (D 212) from Fabrézan, there is a sweeping view of the town, with its bridges, intermittent ramparts, historical houses and abbey. The abbey, one of the outposts of the Carolingian civilisation near the Spanish March (Frankish Catalonia) and well endowed with large estates in both Roussillon and Catalonia, owes its majestic appearance to the fortifications added in the 14C and the embellishments of the 18C. Two bridges, including an 11C humpback bridge, link the abbey to the town, which is also fortified and has an attractive covered market. 🛈 6 Bd. de la Promenade, 11230 Lagrasse, ☎ 04 68 43 11 56. www.lagrasse.com.

La Cité Médiévale

The old medieval city developed around the monastery. Take a pleasant stroll along the narrow streets lined with medieval houses where craftsmen have set up their workshops.

▶ Enter the walled town via Porte du Consulat and follow the street of the same name before turning left onto Rue Paul-Vergnes.

Église Saint-Michel

This Gothic church has a single nave with ribbed vaulting, flanked by nine side chapels. Note the keystones decorated with the guilds' symbols.

▶ Retrace your steps and turn left onto Rue de l'Église, then walk across place de la Bouquerie and along Rue des Mazels (16C Maison Lautier).

Place de la Halle

In its centre stands the 14C covered market: 10 stone pillars supporting a timber framework. Medieval façades, some of them half-timbered, surround the square; note in particular the 14C **Maison Maynard**.

Take a look at the 16C Maison Sibra in Rue Foy, then follow Rue des Deux-Ponts leading to **Pont Vieux**, which gives access to the abbey.

For coin categories, see the Legend.

DINING AT THE INN

🍴 **Hôtel Fargo** – 11220 St-Pierre-des-Champs - ☎ 04 68 43 12 78 - lafargo@club-internet.fr - closed 16 Nov-26 Mar - 🅿 - 6 rooms - 🍽 6€ - restaurant 🍴. This former catalan forge, tucked away in a magnificent wooded park along the river bank, is entirely renovated. Colonial style furnishings. Warm welcome.

🍴 **Hostellerie des Corbières** – 9 Ave. de la Promenade - ☎ 04 68 43 15 22 - hostelleriecorbieres@free.fr - closed 1 Dec-1Feb and Tues except July-Aug - 6 rooms - 🍽 6€ - restaurant 🍴. This pleasant small house in the heart of town offers newly renovated and well-equipped rooms. The dining room terrace opens onto a lovely landscape of vines, olive trees and *garriques*. Traditional cuisine.

Abbaye Sainte-Marie-d'Orbieu

45min ⏱ Jul and Aug: 10.30am-7pm (last entry 6.15pm); Apr-Jun and Sep-Oct: 10.30am-12.30pm (last entry 11.45), 2-6.15pm (last entry 5.45); early Nov-mid Dec and mid Jan-late Mar: 2-5.30pm (last entry 5pm). 2.50€. ☎ 04 68 43 15 99.

Palais vieux

The buildings surround an unusual yet charming courtyard. Two covered galleries, resting on columns with reused Romanesque capitals, support an upper floor beneath the timber roof frame. An imposing cedar tree dispenses its generous shade over this romantic setting. In a corner of the courtyard is the **abbot's chapel**★ which has some rare late-14C ceramic paving and traces of mural paintings.

Although remodelled, the Palais Vieux includes the oldest parts of the abbey. On the upper floor, a lapidary museum houses a display of fragments from the original cloisters and from the doorway, believed to be the work of the Master of Cabestany; also on this floor is the monks' dormitory with its fine timber frame resting on stone arches. A staircase leads, via the "pre-Romanesque tower", to the lower level where the cellars, store rooms and bakery are located.

Cloisters

These were built in 1760, on the site of the original cloisters built in 1280, some of the remains of which are still visible.

Church

The abbey church, which has been altered many times over the centuries, is built on the foundations of a Carolingian church. Its present appearance dates from the 13C. In the nave, on the right, a door opens onto the Romanesque south transept, grafted onto the pre-Romanesque church in the 11C. There are three oven-vaulted apsidal chapels decorated on the outside with Lombardy banding.

Bell-tower

Built in 1537, and incorporated into the 14C fortifications, the 40m/131ft bell-tower is completed with an octagonal crown pierced with openings, but having no spire. A spiral staircase (*150 steps*) leads to the top from which there is an attractive view.

The Lagrasse church bell-tower

D. Pazery/MICHELIN

Excursion

Plateau de Lacamp★★
27km/17mi SW along D 23 and D 212.

Between Caunette-sur-Lauquet and Lairière, the Louviéro Pass on D 40 gives access to the "forest track" of the western Corbières. The Plateau de Lacamp, at an average altitude of 700m/2 300ft, forms a breakwater towards the Orbieu. For about 3km/2mi, the track runs along the southern edge of the causse, giving sweeping **views** of the Orbieu Valley, the Bugarach and Canigou peaks, St-Barthélemy, the threshold of the Lauragais and the Montagne Noire.

LAGUIOLE

POPULATION 1,248

MICHELIN LOCAL MAP 338: J-2

Laguiole (pronounced Laïole), once famous for its cattle fairs, is now widely reputed for its elegant pocket knives, with their distinctive handles made of horn, wood, aluminium and, more rarely, ivory. Laguiole is also a winter sports resort and the producer of an excellent Tomme cheese made from cows' milk. *Pl. du Foirail, 12210 Laguiole, ☎ 05 65 44 35 94. www.laguiole-online.com.*

Visit

Ski area

Situated above 1 000m/3 281ft, the Laguiole ski area forms part of the **Espace nordique des monts d'Aubrac**, a favourite haunt of cross-country skiing enthusiasts.

The Laguiole Knife

First manufactured in 1829, the Laguiole knife was originally designed as an all-purpose tool, to which a corkscrew and a pointed implement (otherwise known as a "hoof-pick") were eventually added. Production was revived at the beginning of the 1980s, and manufacture of Laguiole knives is now the town's leading industry. Recent years have seen an explosion in the number of local knife makers, whose workshops have practically taken over the entire main street. In order to regulate a situation that is becoming somewhat confusing, an official trademark – the "Laguiole Origine Garant'ʳ' – has now been adopted.

Address Book

A ROOM AT THE MILL

Auberge du Moulin – *12210 Soulages-Bonneval* - ☎ *05 65 44 32 36* - *closed Fri evenings Oct-Jun except school holidays.* – *5 km by D 541* - P - *12 rooms* - 🍴 *4.50€* - *restaurant* 🍴. Plain, modest comfort abounds at this quiet mill. Rooms are small, but several offer views of the waterfall. Regional dishes on the menu in the restaurant.

SHOPPING

Coopérative fromagère Jeune Montagne – ☎ *05 65 44 35 54* - *coop.jm@wanadoo.fr* – *Sep-Jun: Mon-Sat 8am-noon, 2-6pm, Sun and holidays 9am-noon; Jul-Aug: Mon-Sat 8am-7pm, Sun and holidays 9am-1pm, 2-6pm. Tour: 30-45 min.* A must for cheese lovers! This co-op produces Laguiole cheese and Aligot de l'Aubrac. Discover the secrets that make these cheeses great as you visit the maturing cellars and learn about the process. Tasting and sales.

Jean Bringuier – *11 R. de la Violette* - ☎ *05 65 44 31 15* - *Mon-Sat 7.30am-7.30pm, Sun 7.30am-12.30pm.* This family-owned gourmet grocer has been passed from father to son since the beginning of the century. Fine local meats and *charcuterie* products, plus cheeses, jams, conserves and condiments round out the selection.

Le Couteau de Laguiole – *8 R. de la Vergne* – ☎ *05 65 48 45 47* - *Mon-Fri 8am-noon, 1.30pm-7pm, Sat by prior appointment.* This craftsmen's factory founded in 1985 relaunched the Laguiole knife industry. Laguiole knives, which are entirely hand-made, have a distinctive handle of horn or wood, a fine steel blade and the slender sweeping lines of a swordfish. Workshops and shop.

Musée du Haut-Rouergue

Currently being restructured; contact the tourist office. ☎ *05 65 44 35 94.*

This regional museum, on three floors, houses a display of craftsmen's tools as previously used in the Aubrac area, as well as a reconstructed *buron* or cowherd's hut, inhabited during the summer months.

Musée du Couteau de Laguiole

♿🕐 *Jul and Aug: 9am-noon, 2-6pm; Jan-Jun and Sep-Dec: daily except Sun and public holidays 9am-noon, 2-6pm. 3.50€.* ☎ *05 65 51 23 47. Zone artisanale La Poujade.*

Kids This knife museum offers an insight into the manufacture of the famous Laguiole knife with the help of a craftsman who makes collector's items before your very eyes!

◗◗ **Château du Bousquet** – *5km/3mi SW.* 🕐 *School holidays: guided tours available 2.30-6.30pm, by request only mornings.* 🕐 *Closed Tue. 5€ (children: 3€).* ☎ *05 65 48 41 13.* Austere 14C castle built of volcanic basalt.

LAMALOU-LES-BAINS ⚓

POPULATION 2,156

MICHELIN LOCAL MAP 339: D-7

ALSO SEE OLARGUES

Most of the Lamalou springs were discovered in the 13C and their soothing powers were quickly appreciated. The present spa specialises in treating people with illnesses affecting their motor systems, such as poliomyelitis, or other mobility problems such as the after-effects of road accidents. Lamalou can boast a number of famous patients who have come to take waters here – Mounet-Sully, Alphonse Daudet, André Gide etc.

Lamalou-les-Bains is an excellent point of departure for excursions in and around the Caroux region. Seen from the surrounding hills, its site, spread out along the Bitoulet, is very picturesque. 🛈 *1 Ave. Capus, 34240 Lamalou-les-Bains,* ☎ *04 67 95 70 91.*

Visi...

301

...les★

...ided visit during the week; Feb-Nov: guided tours Wed 2.30pm.
... tourist office for access, ☎ *04 67 95 70 91. 200m/220yd W of*

Address Book

⚜ *For coin categories, see the Legend.*

EATING OUT

🍴 **Ferme Piscicole du Pont des 3 Dents** – *34610 St-Gervais-sur-Mare - 15km/9mi N of Lamalou on D 22 then the Castanet road -* ☎ *04 67 23 65 48 - closed Jan, Tues except Jul-Sep and Mon -* 🍴 *- reservations required.* The menu at this farm features freshwater trout, salmon, and crayfish. You can fish for them yourself, or simply await them at the table, where they are served grilled over charcoal. As the owner knows 29 ways of cooking trout, you are unlikely to get bored of it.

WHERE TO STAY

🛏 **Hôtel L'Arbousier and Paix** – ☎ *04 67 95 63 11 - arbousier.hotel@wanadoo.fr -* 🅿 *- 31 rooms -* 🍽 *7.50€ - restaurant* 🍴.

This large house slightly out of the town centre has a fresh-looking yellow painted façade and pale green woodwork. Pleasant, well lit reception area; neat and tidy rooms.

SPORTS AND RECREATION

Casino – *26 Ave. Charcot –* ☎ *04 67 95 77 54 – www.moliflor.com - Mon-Fri 10am-2am, Sat-Sun 10am-3am.* Slot machines, restaurant, bar, dinner-dance on Friday and Saturday evenings.

Balladânes – *Mas de Riols – 34260 La Tour-sur-Orb –* ☎ *04 67 23 10 53 – www.balladanes.com* – One-week walking tours (accompanied by donkeys or llamas, with or without guides) through the Parc naturel regional du Haut-Languedoc, across Monts de l'Espinouse, Monts d'Orb and around Lake Salagou

Safely tucked inside the cemetery walls, this old parish church in pink sandstone was built during the first half of the 12C. It is a fine example of rural Romanesque architecture in the south of France. Outside, note the elegant apse decorated with Lombard arcades. Speculation surrounds the identity of the archaic sculpted figure which also decorates the apse; it could be a pilgrim on the way to Santiago de Compostela, complete with staff and pouch, or, more probably, St Peter, the patron saint of the parish, with his crozier, cross and open Bible.

The lintel of the doorway on the south façade features the Chi Rho monogram worked several times in Arabic script, blossoming into a crucifix. This is surmounted by an ornate basalt tympanum. The church interior features Mozarabic capitals and two 12C low-relief sculptures by the Toulouse School: an impressive face of Christ in Majesty and a St Peter.

Excursions

Gorges d'Héric★★

In Mons-la-Trivalle, take D 14E to the NE. Leave the car at the mouth of the river gorge. A track runs along the gorge to the hamlet of Héric. 3hr on foot there and back.

🚶 The track first begins by following the course of the stream as it froths along between tall walls of rock, cascades into mini-waterfalls, and slackens its pace in natural swimming pools, the largest of which is the **Gouffre du Cerisier**. Farther on, on the right, is a majestic amphitheatre, the **Cirque de Farrières**, with a fringe of jagged needles of rock round its rim. The path leads past the slopes of Mont Caroux to the right before arriving in **Héric**, a tiny hamlet with stone slab-roofed houses.

The walls of the gorge are the finest rockfaces in the region and are therefore popular with rockclimbers, but the gorge itself is also frequented by swimmers, walkers and people out for a picnic.

Gorges d'Héric

Sanctuaire de Notre-Dame-de-Capimont
5km/3mi NE. Leave the car in the parking area and walk up to the sanctuary.

From this peaceful pilgrimage Chapel there is a fine view of the Orb Valley. From St-Anne's chapel situated behind Notre-Dame-de-Capimont, one embraces Monts de l'Espinouse to the north-west with Lamalou and the Bitoulet Valley in the foreground, whereas Pic de la Coquillade and the ruins of St-Michel can be seen to the south.

Monts de l'Espinouse★
80km/50mi round tour from Olargues. ⬤ See OLARGUES.

LANGOGNE

POPULATION 3,095

MICHELIN LOCAL MAP 330: L-6

Langogne lies in an attractive setting in the upper Allier Valley on the borders of the Lozère, Ardèche and Haute-Loire départements. The old part of Langogne is an interesting example of medieval urban planning, with its houses arranged in a circle around the church. Some of them have been built in the towers of the old curtain wall. Along the circular boulevard is an 18C corn market. ⬛ *15 Bd. des Capucins, 48300 Langogne, ☎ 04 66 69 01 38. www.langogne.com.*

⬤ A local-produce market takes place in the evening from mid-July to mid-August.

Sights

Halle (covered market)
Built in 1742 originally as a shelter for cattle, this later became a corn market. Its roof of heavy limestone slabs (*lauzes*), supported by 14 granite columns, still has its original overhanging ridge course.

Église St-Gervais-et-St-Protais
The exterior of this Romanesque church (10C), altered several times between the 15C and the 17C, is made of sandstone ashlar mixed with volcanic material. The interior is in fine granite bond. It was originally the church of a Benedictine priory. The façade, from the late 16C and early 17C, has a portal with a basket-handle arch and coving, surmounted by a bay in Flamboyant style.

Inside, numerous carved historiated **capitals**★, with a rich decoration of plant motifs, brighten up this austere building. The most remarkable are on the pillars in the nave, particularly the first bay on the left – guardian angels – and the third bay on the right – Lust. The first chapel on the right houses a statue of the Virgin and Child – Our Lady of Infinite Power. This Madonna figure, an object of secular veneration, was apparently brought back from Rome in the 11C.

Naussac reservoir
1km/0.6mi W. Leave Langogne on D 34. In order to control the River Allier, a dam was built which swallowed up the old village of Naussac. The resulting lake, 7km/4mi long, is ideal for water sports enthusiasts, drawn by its various facilities.

Filature des Calquières
⬤ *Jul-Aug: guided tour (1hr) 9am-noon, 1.30-6.30pm (last entry 45min before closing); Apr-Jun and Sep-Oct: 9am-noon, 2-6pm; Nov-Mar: daily except Sun 9am-noon, 2-6pm, Sat 2-6pm. ⬤ Closed 25 Dec-12 Jan, public holidays (except 14 Jul and 15 Aug). 5.50€. ☎ 04 66 69 25 56.*

This former wool-spinning mill has been turned into a museum illustrating wool processing from the fleece shorn off a sheep to the finished product ready to be knitted or woven.

Causse du LARZAC★

MICHELIN LOCAL MAP 338: K-M 6-8

ALSO SEE LES GRANDS CAUSSES

The Causse du Larzac rises between Millau and Lodève, for all the world like an enormous limestone fortress, dotted with villages and Knights Templars' estates. This is the area where Roquefort cheese is made from ewe's milk.

A Bit of History

The great cause – Covering nearly 1 000km2/400sq mi, the Causse du Larzac is the largest of the *causses* and its altitude ranges from 560m/1 840ft to 920m/3 020ft. It consists of a series of arid limestone plateaux and green valleys. On the plateaux, clayey depressions (sotchs) covered with red soil, are used to grow crops. The water that falls on the Causse du Larzac reappears at the bottom of the valleys that dissect it, in nearly 60 resurgent springs. Like the other causses, Larzac is full of "chimneys" in the limestone rock; that of **Mas Raynal**, west of Le Caylar, explored in 1889 by a team consisting of E-A Martel, L Armand, G Gaupillat and E Foulquier, proved to be an "inspection chamber" for the underground river which feeds the Sorgues.

Templars and Hospitallers – In the 12C, the Order of the Knights Templar received part of the Causse du Larzac as a gift and built a commandery, or local headquarters, at Ste-Eulalie-de-Cernon with annexes at La Cavalerie and La Couvertoirade. In 1312, after the dissolution of the Order of the Knights Templar, the Hospitallers of St John of Jerusalem (or Malta) took over the Templars' estates, including the fortress towns on the Causse du Larzac, which consequently became part of the most powerful military order of the time. In the 15C, which was a period of instability and unrest, the Hospitallers erected many fortifications; it is to these walls, towers and fortified gates that the Causse du Larzac owes its present rugged appearance.

Address Book

For coin categories, see the Legend.

EATING OUT

Ferme-auberge de Jassenove – 12100 Millau - 16km/10mi SE of Millau on N 9 then left on B-road towards Jassenove - ☎ 05 65 60 71 80 - closed for a fortnight in Sep and on Wed in Jul –Aug - ⊁ - reservations required. In an unspoiled wooded corner of the Causse de Larzac stands this charming farmhouse-inn. The atmosphere is friendly and welcoming. One of the specialities on offer is a Roquefort soufflé to die for!

WHERE TO STAY

Chambre d'hôte Domaine de la Barraque – 12230 Ste-Eulalie-de-Cernon - 4km/2.5mi from Ste-Eulalie on D 561 then follow signposts. – ☎ 05 65 62 77 33 - closed 1 Jan-Easter - 7 rooms - ⌑ 6.80€ – meals. This large farm in the middle of the countryside is full of character. The rooms are light and unfussy with old-fashioned furniture. There are dormitories for the budget conscious. Horses can be hired and stabled here.

Chambre d'hôte Le Barry du Grand Chemin – 88 Fa, St-Martin - 34520 Le Caylar - ☎ 04 67 44 50 19 - - 6 rooms – meals. This 1850 house with a stone façade has had a wing added to it in which the rooms at street level are very well kept indeed. The owners prepare grilled meat dishes for the buffet supper in the small vaulted dining room, which is pleasantly cool in summer.

Domaine du Luc – Hameau du Luc - 30770 Campestre-et-Luc - ☎ 04 67 82 01 01 - ⌁ - 8 rooms - meals. This group of stone houses (185) formerly served as an agricultural reform colony for children. The former dormitories have been attractively renovated as modern, functional guestrooms. Pleasant dining room graced with a handsome fireplace.

EVENTS

Route du sel – ☎ 05 65 76 56 26. Horse-riding tour from Valras to Rodez in July.

Les Estivales du Larzac – Cultural events throughout the area in July and August. Medieval camp and shows in La Cavalerie, Sainte-Eulalie de Cernon, Saint-Jean d'Alcas, Viala du Pas de Jaux, in August. Information: Conservatoire Larzac Templier et Hospitalier, ☎ 05 65 59 12 22, www.conservatoire-larzac.fr

Templars and Hospitallers

166km/103mi round tour from Millau – allow one day.

Millau★ – ⚐ *See MILLAU.*

▷ *Leave Millau along N 9 towards Béziers.*

The road runs through the Tarn *département* and climbs up the northern flank of the Causse du Larzac, offering superb panoramas of Millau, the Causse Noir and the River Dourbie gorge. After a bend in the road above the cliff face, the immense bare surface of the causse comes into view.

Maison du Larzac

♿ ⏱ *Early Jul to mid-Sep: 10am-7pm. No charge.* ☎ *05 65 60 43 58.*

To the right of N 9 is an enormous sheepfold roofed with limestone slabs (*lauzes*) also called La Jasse. It contains the reception area for the **Écomusée du Larzac**, an open-air museum of crafts and traditions whose exhibitions provide the visitor with an excellent introduction to the Causse du Larzac. This museum was founded in 1983 with the aim of presenting the natural, historical and cultural heritage of the causse through various elements distributed over an area 35km/22mi long and 25km/15.5mi wide. They include a traditional farm, an ultra-modern sheepfold with a "rotolactor" which can milk 700 ewes per hour, the Blaquière sheepfold built in the 1970s, and exhibitions on local architecture, archaeology, the Templars etc.

▷ *Carry on to La Cavalerie. The road runs alongside the Larzac Military Camp.*

La Cavalerie

⏱ ⚐ *Jul-Aug: 10am-7pm; Jun & Sep: 10am-noon, 2-6pm; Oct-May 10am-noon, 2-5pm. Guided tours 11am and 3pm (call for fee).* ☎ *05 65 62 78 73.*

Formerly the seat of a vice-commandery of the Templars and then the Hospitallers, this large village is a reminder of the age of chivalry, and still has its ancient ramparts. Local activity has been revived by the Larzac Military Camp whose installations can be seen from the road to Nant.

▷ *From N 9, take D 999 on the right towards St-Affrique. After 3.4km/2mi, take the road to Lapanouse-de-Cernon on the left.*

Ste-Eulalie-de-Cernon

⏱ ⚐ *as for La Cavalerie. Guided tours (call for fee)* ☎ *05 65 62 79 98.*

In the cool valley of the Cernon, Ste-Eulalie was the seat of the Templars' commandery to which La Cavalerie and La Couvertoirade were attached. In the 18C, the revolutionary orator Mirabeau often came here to visit his uncle, Admiral Riqueti-Mirabeau, the last of the commanders.

From its past as a medieval fortress, Ste-Eulalie has kept most of its ramparts, towers and gates (the one that opens to the east is remarkable) as well as some picturesque covered passageways. The church, with a main door surmounted by a 17C marble Virgin Mary, looks onto a charming square graced with a fountain.

▷ *Follow D 561 S then turn right onto D 23.*

The road goes through another village built by the Knights Templars, **Le Viala-du-Pas-de-Jaux** (⏱ *as for La Cavalerie. Guided tours* ☎ *05 65 58 91 89).*

Roquefort-sur-Soulzon★ – ⚐ *See ROQUEFORT-SUR-SOULZON.*

▷ *Drive S from Roquefort along D 93 towards Fondamente then turn right at the signpost "St-Jean-d'Alcas".*

St-Jean-d'Alcas

⏱ ⚐ *as for La Cavalerie. Guided tours (call for fee)* ☎ *05 65 97 61 07.*

The fortified Romanesque church is enclosed within the ramparts of this picturesque village. Some of the houses featuring round doorways and mullioned windows have been tastefully restored.

▷ *Follow D 516 and D 7, drive over the A 75 motorway, and continue straight on along D 185 to La Couvertoirade.*

La Couvertoirade★ – ⚐ *See La COUVERTOIRADE.*

▷ *Follow D 55 S and continue towards Le Caylar.*

The road, which climbs slightly, offers a good view of the curious village of Le Caylar and the Aigoual massif in the distance on the left.

Le Caylar

The name of this village means "rock", and it is indeed crowned by extremely jagged crumbling rock formations. From some distance away, it looks as though the village has impressive ramparts and fortified towers. As you get closer, however, you can see that the supposed "fortress" is actually rocks eroded by water.

The small Romanesque chapel of **Notre-Dame-de-Roc-Castel** (◑ *Easter to 1 Oct*), nestling among the rocks overlooking the village, contains a 12C stone altar. A lone section of wall reminds us that the chapel was part of the fortress demolished on Richelieu's orders. The highest of the rocks gives a very pretty view over the dolomitic rocks.

At the foot of the rocks, the old town has retained its **Tour de l'Horloge** (clock tower), all that remains of the ramparts. Some medieval houses still have their picturesque 14C and 15C doors and windows.

Inside the village **church**, there is a 17C Christ Wounded in wood and, in the Lady Chapel, a beautiful 14C carved stone altarpiece depicting scenes from Christ's childhood.

▶ *Leave Le Caylar S on the road past the cemetery and turn left onto a slip road that runs parallel with and then goes under the A 75 motorway. Take D 155E as far as St-Félix-de-l'Héras, where you turn left onto D 155. Where the road crosses over the motorway (the old N 9), leave the car and continue on foot to the Pas de l'Escalette.*

Pas de l'Escalette★

Alt 616m/2 021ft. This pass, a rocky cleft between towering cliffs, gives a good **view** of the Lergue waterfall. The name of the pass derives from the steps cut into the rockface, which led down from the Larzac plateau.

▶ *Return to the Caylar-Nord interchange and drive onto the A 75 motorway to Millau.*

LAVAUR

POPULATION 8,537

MICHELIN MAP 338: C-8

Lavaur located on the west bank of the Agout, at a crossroads linking Toulouse, Castres and Montauban, still has the charming old districts typical of a small fortified town in Languedoc. Lavaur was defended by the castle of Plo, the only remains of which are a few walls holding up the Esplanade du Plo, in the southern part of the town. *Tour des Rondes, 81500 Lavaur, ☎ 05 63 58 02 00. www.ville-lavaur.fr.*

A Bit of History

During the Albigensian Crusade, the town was besieged by the troops of Simon de Montfort and surrendered on 3 May 1211, after two months of resistance organised by Guiraude, a lady of the town, and 80 knights who had espoused the Cathar cause. They were hanged, other heretics were burnt at the stake, and Lady Guiraude was thrown into a well which was then filled with stones.

Sights

Cathédrale St-Alain★

The original Romanesque building, destroyed in 1211, was rebuilt in brick in 1254. On the south façade, at the top of a Romanesque tower with a stone base, is the famous painted wood **Jack-o'-the-clock** which strikes the hour and half-hour. The mechanism and clock were made in 1523. Walk right round the church to admire the apse overlooking the Agout. The interior is in the southern French Gothic style with an imposing single nave

---

"THE BARTIZAN"

🛏🍴 **L'Échauguette** – *81500 Giroussens - 10km/6mi NW of Lavaur on D 87 then D 12 - ☎ 05 63 41 63 65 - closed 2-23 Feb, 15-30 Sep, Sun evening and Mon.* This typical local house in the middle of a small village overlooks a meander of the Agout. The numerous ceramic items on display add to its rustic charm. One of the dining rooms features a fine fireplace. The food is good and inexpensive. Terrace for fine weather. Some rooms available.

(13C-14C) and a seven-sided apse (late 15C-early 16C), lower and narrower than the nave. The Romanesque door that leads to the first chapel on the right is part of the original building; the capitals on the colonnettes are decorated with scenes from Christ's childhood. In the third chapel, a funerary recess in the Flamboyant style houses a Pietà in wood and a lectern (both 18C).

In the chancel, the 11C white-marble altar-table (Moissac School) comes from Ste-Foy, the oldest church in Lavaur.

On the left side, a painting depicting Christ crucified and St Jerome is attributed to Ribera. The 16C organ was restored by Cavaillé-Coll in the 19C.

The west side of the nave leads to the porch underneath an octagonal belfry. On the central column of the Flamboyant doorway is the statue of St Alain and, on the lintel, the Adoration of the Magi. The doorway was damaged during the Wars of Religion and during the French Revolution.

Jardin de l'Évêché

This garden, on the site of the former bishops' palace, forms a terrace overlooking the Agout, to the north of the church. Its ancient cedars and carefully tended flower beds make it a pleasant place for a quiet walk.

Église St-François

Before the Revolution, the church of St Francis, located in the main street, was the chapel of the Franciscan convent founded in Lavaur in 1220 by Sicard VI of Lautrec, Baron of Ambres. This elegant church was built in 1328. To the right of the entrance, there is a fine brick and timber house.

Excursion

St-Lieux-les-Lavaur

10km/6mi NW on D 87 and D 631 to the left.

This charming site in the Agout Valley is the point of departure for the Tarn tourist **steam train** *(Earlu to mid-Aug: 2.30pm, 3.30pm, Sat-Sun, public holidays and Mon 2.30pm, 3.30pm, 4.30pm; mid-late Jul and mid-late Aug: Sat-Sun, holidays and Mon 2.30pm, 3.30pm, 4.30pm; Easter to mid-Jul and Sep-Oct: Sun and public holidays 2.30pm, 3.30pm and 4.30pm. Other departures; inquire at ticket office. 5€, children: 3.80€. 05 61 47 44 52; www.cftt.org)* running as far as Giroussens.

Giroussens, jardins de Martel★

 May-Aug: 10am-6pm; Apr, Sep and Oct: 1-6pm, Sat-Sun and public holidays: 10am-6pm; Mid to end Mar: Sat-Sun and public holidays 10am-6pm. 6€ (children under 10: 3.50€). 05 63 41 61 42. 9km/5.6mi NW along D 87 and D 631.

 These fine English-style gardens combine pools covered with water lilies, flower beds and woodland. There is also a mini-farm for children.

Saint-Sulpice-la-Pointe

 Jul-Sep: guided tours (45min) 3-7pm; rest of the year: by request. 3€. 05 63 41 89 50. 11km/6.8mi NW along D 630.

The ruins of Castela Castle tower above this bastide (fortified town). Beneath the ruins lies the **Souterrain du Castela**, four underground galleries (142m/466ft long) occupied successively by forgers, wool spinners etc.

Nearby is a 14C church with an impressive 40m/131ft-high belfry-wall.

LÉZIGNAN-CORBIÈRES

POPULATION 8,266

MICHELIN LOCAL MAP 344: H-3

Halfway between Carcassonne and the sea, between the Aude Valley, the Canal du Midi and the River Orbieu, Lézignan-Corbières is a small active town which relies on wine-growing and the Corbières wine trade. Promenades lined with plane trees, tiny squares and alleyways surround the church of St-Félix. 9 pl. de la République, 11200 Lézignan-Corbières, 04 68 27 05 42.

Address Book

EATING OUT

🍽 **Le Tournedos** – Pl. de Lattre-de-Tassigny - ☎ 04 68 27 11 51 - tournedos@wanadoo.fr - closed 24 Jan-7 Feb, 26-Sep-12 Oct, Sun evening and Mon. This family-run house has been given a lick of fresh paint. Amid Provençal style decor the food is served in quantities that will satisfy even the largest of appetites! Some basic rooms available for those wishing to break their journey in the Corbières region.

🍽🍽 **Auberge du Domaine des Noyers** – 11700 Montbrun-des-Corbières - 7km/4mi W of Lézignan towards Carcassonne, then to Conilhac on D 165 - ☎ 04 68 43 94 01 - closed 1 Nov-Easter - 🍴 - reservations required evenings. The proprietor is a wine-grower and his wife a cook. With a fairly plain dining room as a backdrop, guests can devote their full attention to farm chicken, garden vegetables or cassoulet all cooked over an open fire, and washed down with vin maison. Some rooms available. Swimming pool.

🍽🍽 **La Balade Gourmande** – Bd. Léon-Castel – RN 113 - ☎ 04 68 27 22 18 - closed Mon evening, Tue evening and Wed evening - reservations recommended. This contemporary pink building houses two dining rooms graced with Provençal décor (yellow walls, linens in colours of Provence). Traditional cuisine and fine regional specialties - cassoulet is a must! - for sampling in a warm, convivial atmosphere.

WHERE TO STAY

🏠🏠 **Chambre d'hôte M. and Mme Tenenbaum** – 5 Ave. du Minervois - 11700 Azillé - 16km/10mi NW of Lézignan, towards Homps then Carcassonne and D 806 - ☎ 04 68 91 56 90 - pierreetclaudine@tele2.fr – closed 1-15 Nov - 🍴 - 4 rooms. A charming welcome, a swimming pool surrounded by high walls and a terrace garden are just some of the things this place has to offer. This family residence dating from 1835 has simple rooms furnished in a variety of styles.

Visit

Musée de la Vigne et du Vin

♿🕐 9am-7pm. 5.35€. ☎ 04 68 27 07 57.

This vine and wine museum has been set up in an old vineyard. The main courtyard opens onto the saddle room, the stables and a winepress, whereas under an awning are displayed the tools of the now vanished cooper's trade.

The winemaking cellar contains a large vat for treading the grapes and scalding apparatus with a yoke so that it could be driven by a team of oxen.

On the first floor, the tools needed for vine growing are displayed by season. They include swing-ploughs, pruning shears, grafting knives, back-baskets, wooden tubs, funnels and branding irons.

A room, located near the information desk, is devoted to wine transport along the Canal du Midi from the 18C to the present time.

Excursion

The Lézignan Region

49km/30mi round tour; about 1hr

▷ From Lézignan drive along D 24 to Ornaisons then turn right onto D 123.

Gasparets

📷 Espace Octaviana houses the **Musée de la Faune** (♿🕐 9.30am-noon, 2-6pm. 🕐 Closed Mon (Oct-May), 1 Jan, 25 Dec. 5€ (children: 2€). ☎ 04 68 27 57 02), a museum containing a collection of stuffed animals from every continent including birds of prey, nightbirds and common species as well as the Pyrenean brown bear and wild boars from the region. The most interesting exhibits in this large collection, either due to their bright colours or size, are the golden pheasant, the capercaillie and the crested eagle.

▷ D 61, D 161 and D 611 via Boutenac and Ferrals lead to Fabrezan.

For several miles the road leaves the plain to cross the garrigue-covered hills.

Fabrezan

In this picturesque village with its narrow, winding streets overlooking the stony Orbieu Valley, the town hall houses the **Musée Charles-Cros** (🕐 Daily except Sat-Sun and public holidays 9am-noon, 2-6pm. No charge. ☎ 04 68 27 81 44), dedicated to the locally born inventor of the forerunner of the phonograph.

D 212, then D 111 on the left towards Moux. Just before reaching this village, turn right towards Lézignan. At Conilhac, take D 165 on the left.

The road climbs a hill, then comes to the vineyard of **Montbrun-des-Corbières**, which is spread out below. Continue towards Escales, perhaps with a brief stop at the Romanesque chapel of **Notre-Dame-de-Colombier**.

▶ D 127 and D 611 lead back to Lézignan.

LIMOUX

POPULATION 9,411

MICHELIN LOCAL MAP 344: E-4

ALSO SEE LES CORBIÈRES

The town's skyline is dominated by the distinctive outline of the Gothic spire and east end of St Martin's Church overlooking the river. The lively narrow streets are still partly enclosed within a fortified wall built in the 14C after the damage inflicted by the Black Prince, son of King Edward III of England. Limoux is the hub of production of **blanquette**, a sparkling AOC wine made from the Mauzac, Chenin and Chardonnay grapes, using the *méthode champenoise*. 🖪 *Prom. du Tivoli, 11303 Limoux, ☎ 04 68 31 11 82.*

Blanquette de Limoux sparkling wine

🅐 Limoux has gained quite a reputation for its carnival, which runs from January to April, during which processions of masked people, accompanied by musicians, dance along beneath the arcades on place de la République.

Address Book

🖕 *For coin categories, see the Legend.*

EATING OUT

🍽 **La Maison de la Blanquette** – *46 bis Prom. du Tivoli -* ☎ *04 68 31 01 63 – closed Oct and Wed.* The blanquette in question has nothing to do with veal casserole (blanquette de veau), but instead is the name of the local sparkling white wine (blanquette de Limoux)! This restaurant tucked behind the wine shop serves traditional fare, accompanied by local wines, of course.

WHERE TO STAY

🛏 **Le Mauzac** – *9 Ave. Camille-Bouche - RD 118 -* ☎ *04 68 31 12 77 -* 🅿 *- 21 rooms -* 🛏 *6€.* A convenient stop along the road to Carcassonne, this hotel on a hillside offers air-conditioned, soundproofed and very comfortable rooms fitted with pine furniture. Those at the back are preferable. Cute breakfast-room. Charming welcome.
🛏🛏 **Grand Hôtel Moderne and Pigeon** – *1 Pl. du Gén.-Leclerc -* ☎ *04 68 31 00 25 - grandhotelpigeon@wanadoo.fr – closed 15-20 Jan - 16 rooms -* 🛏 *12€ - restaurant* 🍽🍽. This 17C detached mansion on the market square (access can be rather a challenge) has retained several aspects of its original decor such as the frescoes and stained glass in its handsome staircase. The rooms have been renovated, and those on the top floor are larger. Restaurant with terrace.

SPORTS AND RECREATION

Alet Eau Vive – *Allée des Thermes - 11300 Alet-les-Bains -* ☎ *04 68 69 92 67 - aleteauvive@libertysurf.fr – 9am-7pm.* White water sports on the River Aude.

WINE CELLARS

Blanquette de Limoux – For the address of vineyards open to visitors, contact the Limoux tourist office or the *Syndicat des vins AOC de Limoux (20 Ave. du Pont-de-France -* ☎ *04 68 31 12 83).*

Les Vignerons du Sieur d'Arques *(av. du Mauzac -* ☎ *04 68 74 63 45)* provides a reservation service for vineyard tours.

Sights

Catharama

Jul-Aug: daily 10am-6pm; rest of the year: audio-visual show 10am, 11am, 2pm, 3pm, 4pm and 5pm. Closed Toussaint-Easter. 4.50€. ☎ 04 68 31 48 42. 47 Ave. Fabre-d'Églantine.

An audio-visual presentation of the Cathar heretic movement (from the Greek word *katharos* meaning pure) which spread through Languedoc during the 12C and 13C and was eventually eradicated by the Albigensian Crusade.

Musée Petiet

Prom. du Tivoli. Jul and Aug: 9am-7pm; Sep-Jun: 9am-noon, 2pm-6pm, Sat-Sun and public holidays 10am-noon, 2pm-5pm. Closed 1 Jan, 1 May and 25 Dec. 3€. ☎ 04 68 31 85 03.

Housed in the former workshop of the Petiet family, this museum displays various works dating from the second half of the 19C: local paintings such as *The Ironers* by Marie Petiet (1854-93), battle scenes from the 1870 Franco-Prussian War by Étienne Dujardin-Beaumetz, as well as works by Henri Lebasque (*Reading*) and Achille Laugé (*Notre-Dame de Paris*).

Excursions

St-Polycarpe

8km/5mi SE along D 129. The **fortified church** here was part of a Benedictine abbey which was dissolved in 1771. The Romanesque apse, with Lombard bands forming part of the building's actual framework, can be seen from the graveyard. Beneath the high altar various items from the treasury are on display: head reliquary (bare head) of St Polycarp, head reliquary of St Benedict and a reliquary of the Holy Thorn, all 14C works; as well as fabrics from the 8C. The two side altars feature Carolingian decoration carved with knot-work and palm leaves. On the walls and vault are the remains of 14C frescoes (restored).

Razès Region ②

120km/75mi round tour from Limoux – allow one day – local map see Les CORBIÈRES.

▸ *Leave Limoux S along D 118.*

Castles along this route are not perched very high unlike those of the Corbières mountains (*see Les CORBIÈRES*), yet their defences were quite efficient during the Albigensian Crusade.

On approaching Alet, the Aude Valley cuts across a fold in the Corbières mountain massif, before narrowing down again into a gorge, the **Étroit d'Alet**.

Alet-les-Bains

The **old town** of Alet, surrounded by 12C ramparts, is a charming place to explore with many interesting old houses, particularly on **place de la République**. Picturesque narrow streets branching off from the square lead to the city gates: Porte Calvière and Porte Cadène.

Not far from D 118 are the **ruins** (*Jul-Aug: daily except Sat-Sun and public holidays 10am-noon, 2.30-5.30pm; Jun-Sep: Sat-Sun and holidays 10am-noon, 2.30-5.30. Closed mid-Dec to mid-Jan, 1 May, 1 and 11 Nov, 25 Dec. 2.50€. ☎ 04 68 69 93 56. www.info.aletlesbains.free.fr*) of the 11C Romanesque abbey church which was raised to the status of cathedral from 1318. This was when the Romanesque chancel was replaced by a Gothic one complete with a vast ambulatory. Work was left unfinished, however, and what with the destruction of the cathedral by the Huguenots in 1577 and the construction of the road in the 18C, which cut off the ambulatory chapels, all that remains of the Gothic elements of the building is the north tower (*to the right as you look at the east end*). The polygonal **Romanesque east end**, built of beautiful red and ochre sandstone, has five buttress columns around the outside with Corinthian capitals incorporated into a wide, ornate cornice. A narrower, less ornate cornice runs right round the inside of the apse, linking the two Corinthian capitals supporting a triumphal archway. The door and windows of the chapter-house feature some interesting Romanesque capitals, whereas the south door of the abbey church (*in the nearby cemetery*) is decorated with high-relief sculptures.

▸ *Turn left off D 118 onto D 70 then right (on a bend) onto a minor road towards Arques.*

Hat-Making in the Aude Valley

In 1804, a few people from Bugarach in the Corbières returned from captivity in Upper Silesia, where they had learned about the hat trade, and decided to set up their own branch of the industry in their homeland. They moved to Espéraza in 1820, attracted by the plentiful water supply there, and soon new factories had been founded at Quillan, Couiza and Chalabre. Initially there were adequate resources of wool and rabbit fur locally, but before long the hat-making centres were importing their raw materials from elsewhere and exporting finished and semi-finished *(cloches)* hats.

Production had to bow to a drop in demand once the younger generations stopped wearing hats so much. There is now only one factory left, in Montazels, while most of the others have switched to making shoes, furniture, plastic foam (at Espéraza) or decorative laminates (such as Formica).

Donjon d'Arques

🕐 *Jul and Aug: 9.30am-8pm; Jun and Sep: 10am-7pm; Apr and May: 10.30am-6.30pm; Mar and Oct: 10.30am-noon, 1.30-5.30pm; mid-Nov-late Nov: 10.30am-noon, 1.30-5pm. 4€. ☎ 04 68 69 82 87. From Arques, 500m/550yd along D 613.*

Arques keep

🄺🄸🄳🅂 This keep, used as living quarters since the end of the 13C, stands inside a quadrangular wall now in ruins. It is built of beautiful gold-coloured sandstone and features a large number of arrow slits and a curious arrangement of corner turrets mounted on hollow bases. The upper section of the walls is of rusticated masonry. Inside, two rooms, one above the other, and a room with a high ceiling and the corners cut off, are open to the public. In Maison Déodat Roché in the village there is an audio-visual exhibition on the Cathar doctrine.

▶ *Slightly farther on to the left, a forest track leads through the Rialsesse Forest.*

Forêt de Rialsesse

This forest was planted a century ago. The transition from Austrian pines to deciduous trees can be seen clearly from the opposite side of the valley on D 613 which leads up to the Col de Paradis from the west.

D 613 runs through **Coustaussa**, past the ruins (inaccessible and dangerous) of its castle dating from the 12C.

Couiza

This town, essentially devoted to the shoe-making industry, is home to the old château of the dukes of Joyeuse. This well-preserved mid-16C building, flanked by round towers, is in a style typical of many buildings in the Languedoc and Cévennes regions. It has been turned into a hotel. A pitted rustic work doorway leads into an austere Renaissance courtyard. The arcade on the inside of the entrance façade is decorated with superimposed columns divided by an entablature.

Rennes-le-Château

The village of Rennes-le-Château stands on a plateau more than 25m/80ft above the Aude Valley. From the car park near the water tower there is a view to the west of the upper Aude Valley dotted with the red rooftops of tiny towns such as Espéraza and Campagne-sur-Aude.

Rumour abounds in Rennes-le-Château about the enigmatic figure of Father Béranger Saunière, parish priest here from 1885 to his death in 1917. How was the abbot suddenly able to fund from 1891 onwards the complete restoration of his church, which was in rack and ruin, the construction of a sumptuous mansion (the Villa Bétania), a bizarre, semi-fortified library-tower (the Tour Magdala) and a tropical greenhouse for himself, and in general a lifestyle fit for a prince for the next 20 years? Speculation has tended to agree that the secret of the abbot's wealth must have been the discovery of some hidden treasure, which has led to all sorts of hypotheses about the Knights Templar (despite the fact that they were never based locally), the Cathars, and even the treasure brought back from the Holy City itself by the Visigoths.

At the end of the 19C, the **Église Ste-Marie-Madeleine** was decorated with neo-Gothic murals and polychrome statues, some of which are, to say the least, unusual.

The **Espace Bérenger Saunière** (🕐 *early May to mid-Sep: 10am-7pm; mid-Sep to end Oct, Mar and Apr: 10am-6pm; Nov-Feb: 10am-5pm.* 🕐 *Closed 1 Jan and 25 Dec. 4.25€. ☎ 04 68 74 05 84)* includes a **museum** housed in the presbytery and devoted to local history (among exhibits is the Visigothic pillar said to have contained the famous treasure) and the **Domaine de l'abbé Saunière**, regrouping the priest's garden, his private chapel, the Villa Bétania and the Magdala tower, as well as a museum on what is known of the life of the priest.

▶ *Return to Couiza and follow D 118 towards Quillan.*

Espéraza

This small town on the banks of a tight meander in the Aude was once an important hat-making centre, a past which is commemorated by a museum, the **Musée de la Chapellerie** (👍🕐 *Jul and Aug: 10am-6pm; Sep-Jun: 10am-noon, 2-5pm.* 🕐 *Closed Jan, 25 Dec. ☎ 04 68 74 00 75.),* in the old goods depot. The museum is laid out like a factory, showing the 20 or so stages involved in the making of a felt hat. An exhibition of various types of headdress and a film add to the interest of the visit.

Espéraza's other claim to fame, the discovery locally at the end of the 19C of the fossils of prehistoric reptiles, also has a museum dedicated to it, the **Musée des Dinosaures** (👶 👍🕐 *Jul and Aug: 10am-7pm, last admission 1hr before closing; Feb-Jun: 10am-noon, 2-6pm; rest of the year by request;* 🕐 *Closed 1 Jan, 25 Dec. 6.50€ summer, 4.90€ offseason; ☎ 04 68 74 26 88; www.dinosauria.org),* next to the hat-making museum. The display includes panels retracing the discovery of the fossils, a reconstruction of one of the local digs, bone fragments (mostly remoulds) and semi-fossilised eggs, a video and the enormous skeleton of an unusual sauropod that researchers are currently studying.

Quillan – 👍 *See QUILLAN.*

▶ *Follow D 117 W to Puivert.*

Puivert

The valley in which Puivert lies is surprisingly green and fresh-looking after the wooded hills of Sault plateau. It lay under water until 1279, when the lake suddenly overflowed, with disastrous consequences for Chalabre and Mirepoix downriver. There is now a small reservoir south of the village. The local museum, the **Musée du Quercorb** (🕐 *Jul and Aug: 10am-7pm; Apr-Jun and Sep: 10am-noon, 2-6pm; Oct: 2-5pm. 4€. ☎ 04 68 20 80 98),* contains displays on local history, traditions and livelihoods. On the second floor there is an interesting collection of casts of medieval musical instruments, originally part of the ornamentation of the castle.

Puivert Castle (🕐 *Mar-Oct: 9am-8pm; Nov-Feb: 10am-5pm. 4€. ☎ 04 68 20 81 52)* (*east of the village*) was captured during the crusades of 1210, and given by Simon de Montfort to Lambert de Thury, before being handed back to the lords of Bruyères-le-Châtel (near Arpajon), who from then on settled in the region and enlarged the castle. All that remains of the castle, which dates from before the siege of 1210, are a few sections of wall to the west. Of the new 14C castle, part of which was destroyed, a square tower-gate decorated with the Bruyères lion on a coat of arms and a 35m/115ft-high keep are still standing. Visitors can see one of the lower rooms of the keep, with barrel vaulting, the chapel, with ogive vaulting and a "piscina" (or basin for ablutions) set into the wall, and finally the "Minstrels'" room in which ogive vaulting rests on *culs-de-lampe* carved to depict musicians playing their instruments (bagpipes, tambourine, viol, lute etc), evoking the splendour of court life at Puivert during the age of the troubadours.

▶ *Return to Limoux via D 12 to Chalabre then along D 620.*

LODÈVE ★

POPULATION 6,900

MICHELIN LOCAL MAP 339: E-6

Lodève stands surrounded by graceful hills at the confluence of the River Lergue and River Soulondres. It is close to the mountainous areas of Causse du Larzac and Monts de l'Orb as well as to the Hérault Valley and Lac du Salagou, a picturesque artificial lake framed by cone-shaped hills. The look-out point on the N 9 diversion coming from Millau offers a sweeping view of the site. *7 Pl. de la République, 34700 Lodève, ☎ 04 67 88 86 44. www.lodeve.com.*

A Bit of History

The history of Lodève goes back to Antiquity. It is here that Nero minted the coins needed for the pay and upkeep of the Roman legions. During the Middle Ages, the fortified town and diocese were ruled by bishops. In the 10C, a certain Bishop Fulcran was renowned for his holiness. This wealthy man gave food to the poor and cared for the sick. He was also a warrior who built fortresses and defended the town against brigands.

In the 12C, one of his successors introduced industry to Lodève, founding one of the first mills used to make paper from rags. During the following century, the cloth trade developed and, in the 18C, Lodève was granted a monopoly which brought prosperity to the town: the supply of all the cloth needed by the king's armies to make its soldiers' uniforms.

In the 19C, the authority of the bishops was replaced by that of the drapers, which was, however, short-lived.

Sights

The Gothic **Pont de Montifort** spans the Soulondres with a very pronounced humpback; there is an attractive view of it from the footbridge farther downstream.

Ancienne cathédrale St-Fulcran★

The original cathedral is now the crypt. The church was rebuilt for the first time in the 10C by St Fulcran, and again in the 13C, but most of it dates from the first half of the 14C. After the Wars of Religion, it required considerable restoration, but the original style was preserved. The buttressing and the two watchtowers framing the façade show its defensive function.

The interior features a short nave with side aisles and a vast chancel. The far end of the latter, surrounded by 18C panelling and a marble balustrade, is roofed with elegant ribbed vaulting. At the opposite end is an 18C organ.

The first chapel in the south side aisle is the final resting place for the 84 bishops of Lodève. The third chapel, devoted to Our Lady of the Seven Sorrows, has latticed vaulting which is characteristic of Late Gothic; from here, a door leads into the cloisters (14C-17C).

Musée de Lodève★

🕐 *Daily except Mon 9.30am-noon, 2-5pm.* 🕐 *Closed 1 Jan, 1 May, 1 Nov, 25 Dec. 3.50€.* ☎ *04 67 88 86 10. www.lodeve.com*

The museum, located in what used to be the cardinal's palace (17C-18C), contains several collections concerning Lodève and its region.

The Cloth Trade

Sheep raising has been the main activity of the Lodève region for many centuries. Not surprisingly, therefore, the wool industry began to prosper as early as the 13C. Later, Henri IV had cloth factories moved to Lodève from Semur, and locally produced fabrics were subsequently commissioned to clothe the royal troops. Under Louis XV, Cardinal Fleury granted his native town a monopoly in the field of military supplies.

The special status was a mixed blessing. Under such protection, factory inspectors closed their eyes to poor workmanship and the quality of Lodève fabrics deteriorated. By the mid-18C they were already attracting criticism. Manufacture stopped in 1960. This traditional industry has now been superseded by other branches of the textile industry, particularly hosiery.

The ground floor, devoted to geology and paleontology, has a rare collection of the fossilised imprints of flora and reptile (or batrachian) tracks from the end of the Primary Era as well as those of huge dinosaurs from the Secondary Era. A comparison between these animal tracks and similar ones in South Africa supports the continental drift theory.

The first floor contains prehistoric remains from the Lodève area (Paleolithic and Neolithic) and a presentation of local history from Gallo-Roman times to the

> ### "THE LITTLE WINE STEWARD"
>
> **Le Petit Sommelier** – *3 Pl. de la République - ☎ 04 67 44 05 39 - closed Oct/Nov school holidays, Wed evening and Mon except Jul -Aug*. This old family house on a small square near the tourist office has been transformed into a Parisian style bistro. The colourful dining room is the backdrop to traditional cuisine with innovative touches here and there.

present (mementoes of Cardinal de Fleury). A display is also devoted to Lodève art, with engravings by Barthélemy Roger (18C-19C) and sculptures by Paul Dardé (20C). In a second wing of the building there is an exhibition of **disc-shaped steles** from Usclas-du-Bosc, near Lodève (12C-15C). The use of these monolithic stones, fairly popular in the South-West in the Middle Ages, dates back to Antiquity; the disc then represented the sun, but with the coming of Christianity, this symbol came to symbolise the risen Christ. Two rooms also contain a display on the traditional textile industry in Lodève.

Manufacture nationale de Tapis

  Guided tour Tue, Wed, Thu 1.30-3.30pm. 3.20€. ☎ 04 67 96 40 40. Ave. du Gén.-de-Gaulle (Montpellier road).

This tapestry-weaving mill is the only annexe of the Gobelins in Paris; copies of ancient works intended for national monuments are woven in the workshops which can be visited.

Excursions

Prieuré St-Michel-de-Grandmont★

Daily 10am-7pm. Guided tours available by request (1hr30min). 5.40€. ☎ 04 67 44 09 31. www.grandmont.fr.st 8km/5mi E. Leave on N 9 towards Millau and turn right onto D 153 towards Privat.

This priory was founded in the 12C by monks of the Grandmont order, which flourished from the 11C to 14C, and is one of the remaining examples of the 150 Grandmont monasteries.

The priory complex comprises among other things a church, Romanesque cloisters topped by a charming bell-turret, and a vast chapter-house. The priory grounds are home to some interesting dolmens and give good views of the Languedoc plain.

Grotte de Labeil

Mid-Jun to mid-Sep: guided tours (45min) 10am-7pm; mid-Mar to mid-Jun, mid-Sep to Oct: 11am-5pm. 6.40€ (children: 3.20€). ☎ 04 67 96 49 47. 12km/8mi N. Leave on N 9 towards Millau. Turn off W at the junction for Lauroux and take D 151 to Labeil.

The **Cirque de Labeil** (natural amphitheatre) constitutes the southern foothills of Larzac plateau. From the entrance to the cave (*500m/550yd beyond Labeil*) there is a good view of Lauroux Valley which stretches away from the foot of the viewpoint. A track follows the bed of an underground river for about 300m/330yd. In this very damp cave, which was once used for the production of Roquefort cheese, the main features are stalactites, stalagmites and frozen falls, of which there is a particularly spectacular example coloured ochre and grey by the metal oxides it bears.

LOURDES★★★

POPULATION 15 203

MICHELIN LOCAL MAP 342: L-4

The town of Lourdes on the banks of the Pau torrent, is famous the world over as a religious pilgrimage centre. The great ceremonies, which take place from Easter to All Saints' Day, with processions of believers and invalids buoyed up by faith and hope, lend the town its particularly moving spiritual atmosphere. *Pl. Peyramale, 65100 Lourdes, ☎ 05 62 42 77 40. www.lourdes-infotourismefrance.com.*

The Pilgrimage

A few figures – Pilgrimages are mainly held at Easter and during Holy Week attracting over 5.5 million visitors a year, three-quarters of whom are French and 70 000 sick or handicapped. Considered to be the most important place of pilgrimage in the western hemisphere, among French towns, Lourdes is second only to Paris in providing tourist accommodation (350 hotels, 40 000 beds). The town has 600 shops, 80% of them selling religious objects.

Some 700 special trains and 400 planes service Lourdes every year (via the Tarbes-Ossun-Lourdes International Airport). The TGV Atlantique (high-speed train) has been coming here since 1993. A ring road links D 940 and D 937 (Pau-Lourdes) and N 21 (Tarbes-Argelès-Gazost), diverting traffic from the town centre.

Bernadette Soubirous (1844-79) – The Soubirous family was poor and the parents, millers, brought up their four children with difficulty. Bernadette, the eldest, was born in Lourdes but spent her first few months with a wet-nurse at Bartrès, not far from Lourdes. In early 1858, when she was 14, she was living with her parents in their single room and attending a school for poor children run by the Sisters of Charity. At weekends, preparing for her First Communion, she went to parish Catechism classes.

On Thursday 11 February, a school holiday, Bernadette was gathering wood on the river bank near a local landmark known as Massabielle Rock, accompanied by one of her sisters and a neighbour. It was then, in a grotto hollowed out from the rock, that she saw for the first time the vision of the Immaculate Conception; the beautiful Lady was to appear to her 18 times in total.

Massabielle Grotto – Although Massabielle Rock was not easily accessible at the time, a crowd of believers and unbelievers alike began to form around its cave, and increased daily as news of Bernadette's vision spread. During the ninth apparition Bernadette began to scrabble with her fingers in the earth floor of the cave and suddenly a spring, never before suspected, gushed forth and continued to flow in front of the startled spectators.

In 1862 the Church decided that a sanctuary should be built around the grotto. The first procession was organised in 1864 during which a statue dedicated to Our

Address Book

THE PRACTICAL PILGRIM

Tourist train – A small train runs from the end of March to early November; departures from place Mgr-Laurence every 20min between 9am-noon and 1.30-6.30pm; at night 8-11pm. Accessible to persons of impaired mobility. 5€ (children: 2.50€).

Discounts – With the Lourdes Pass, offered free of charge by the town, you can save money: after visiting five attractions of your choice, you can visit two more for free. With the Visa Lourdes pass, you can visit seven attractions for 34€ (children 17€).

Pilgrimage – Before 5am, only the path to the Calvary is open (Les Lacets entrance). At 9am, the faithful form a group on the Esplanade du Rosaire to celebrate the Queen of Heaven (Easter to 31 October). After this, the grotto is open. Thousands of votive candles flicker along the path and in front of the entrance. Nearby, 20 taps provide water from the sacred spring. There are blue marble pools where pilgrims in search of a miracle cure may be immersed. At 4.30pm, the Holy Eucharist is borne in procession from the Chapelle de l'Adoration to the Esplanade du Rosaire. Once all have gathered at the esplanade, the blessing of the sick begins. At 8.45pm, a torchlight procession is held from the grotto to the esplanade and the parvis of the basilica.

Lady of Lourdes, and lodged within the cave where the apparitions occurred, was officially blessed.

In 1866, Bernadette entered the St-Gildard convent belonging to the Sisters of Charity Order. She died in April 1879, was beatified in 1925 and canonised in 1933.

World's largest pilgrimage – The earliest visits, at first at parish and then diocesan level, were expanded in 1873 into a national event organised by the Fathers of the Assumption in Paris. A year later, a second event included arrangements for 14 invalids to be treated at Lourdes. From then on, attention to the sick and the lame became a priority.

Since the celebration of Bernadette's centenary in 1958 and the Vatican II Council, planning of organised pilgrimages has taken a new turn. All the great traditional events, such as the Holy Sacrament Procession and the Torchlight Procession, have been retained but there have been new initiatives concerning meetings, the reception of pilgrims etc. The grotto has been relieved of certain "accessories" and the Basilique du Rosaire, renowned for its organ and acoustics, now welcomes secular concerts and musical events.

The Vicinity of the Grotto

The two avenues leading to Esplanade du Rosaire are used for important church rites and processions. A large statue of the crowned Virgin Mary stands at the entrance to the plaza.

Sanctuaries and places of prayer – The neo-Byzantine **Basilique du Rosaire**, consecrated and blessed in 1889, occupies the lower level, between two curving ramps embracing the wide circular esplanade and leading upwards. The basilica (2 000m²/2 392sq yd) can accommodate a congregation of 2 000. Mosaics in the side chapels represent the Mysteries of the Rosary.

Between this building and the Upper Basilica lies the crypt, reserved in the daytime for silent prayer. Bernadette was present when the **crypt** was consecrated on 19 May 1866. The neo-Gothic **Basilique Supérieure**, slender and white, was dedicated to the Immaculate Conception and consecrated in 1871. The interior comprises a single nave divided into five bays of equal size. Twenty-one altars and numerous votive offerings decorate the walls. The vaulting in the side chapels carries inscriptions quoting the words Bernadette heard from the Virgin Mary.

Below the Upper Basilica, beside the river, is **La Grotte miraculeuse**, the cave where the visions appeared; a Virgin Mary in Carrara marble marks the spot.

Two bridges span the river to give access to the north bank meadow where the **Espace Ste-Bernadette** has been built. The church in this complex, echoing the shape of the esplanade's open circle, was consecrated in 1988. It is large enough to accommodate 7 000 worshippers. The Assembly of French Bishops meets here each year in plenary session. Larger still is the colossal **Basilique Souterraine de St-Pie X**, the underground

Carcarague/IMAGES TOULOUSE

Lourdes – Basilique du Rosaire

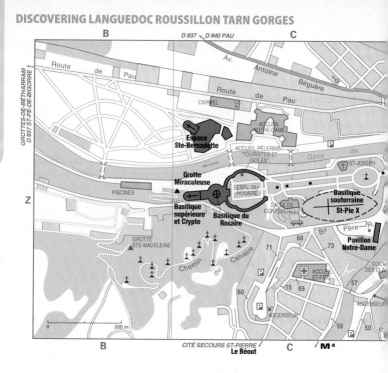

basilica consecrated on 25 March 1958 to solemnise the official centenary of the apparitions. The huge oval hall built beneath the esplanade, on the side of the southern avenue,
can hold up to 20 000 pilgrims – more than the entire population of Lourdes. It is one
of the largest churches in the world, measuring 201m×81m/660ft×266ft at its widest
point and covering an area of 12 000m²/14 350sq yd. Pre-stressed concrete supports
the low vaulting, with no need for intermediate columns.

The **Chemin du Calvaire** (Road to Calvary) starts beside the grotto and winds up
through the trees past 14 Stations of the Cross in bronze statuary. It ends at the Cross
of Calvary. Nearby are the grottoes of St Madeleine and Our Lady of Sorrows (Notre-
Dame-des-Douleurs), in the natural cavern on the flank of Mont des Espélugues.

Pavillon Notre-Dame

On the ground floor of this building is the **Musée Sainte Bernadette** (&🕐 Apr-Oct:
9am-11.45am, 2-5.45pm; Nov-Mar: school holidays 10am-noon, 2.30-5pm. No charge.
☎ 05 62 42 78 78) containing mementos of the young saint, together with pictorial
material on the site of the 18 apparitions and on the history of the pilgrimages.

The basement houses the **Musée d'Art sacré du Gemmail** (🕐 Mid-Apr to end Oct:
9am-noon, 2-7pm. No charge.) (Gemmail is a technique which involves the juxtaposition and superposition of coloured glass fragments illuminated from the interior by
artificial light, to produce a form of stained-glass window without the lead armatures).
The museum compares this contemporary expression of sacred art with more traditional examples in the same material throughout the ages.

A gallery annex opens on alternate (*odd*) years to display the work of the winner of
the biennial festival and competition devoted to religious art in this medium. The
laureate is authorised to use the title Painter of Light.

Commemorative Sites

Cachot

&🕐 Apr-Oct: 9am-noon, 2-7pm; Nov-Mar: 3-5pm; during short school holidays: 10am-
noon, 3-7pm. No charge. ☎ 05 62 94 51 30. 15 rue des Petits-Fossés.

The Soubirous family made their home in a disused prison; they were living there in
a state of penury at the time of the apparitions.

Centre Hospitalier

&🕐 Apr-Oct: 9am-noon, 2-7pm; Nov-Mar: 2-4pm. No charge. ☎ 05 62 42 42 42 or 05 62
94 40 11. Beneath the colonnade, follow the signs marked Visite Chapelle.

Formerly the hospice run by the Sisters of Charity, this hospital complex is where
Bernadette attended classes before being admitted as a boarder from 1860 to 1866.

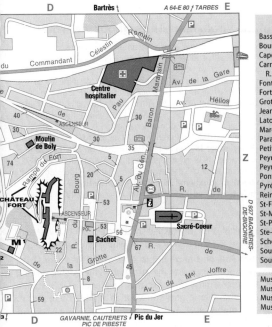

Photographs and personal souvenirs of the saint are on view in the parlour; in the small adjoining chapel where she made her first Communion are her communicant's cape, her Catechism and Holy Bible, and her prayer stool.

Moulin de Boly

🕐 Apr-Oct: 9am-noon, 2-6.30pm; Nov-Mar: 3-5pm, school holidays 10am-noon, 3-5pm. No charge. ☎ 05 62 42 78 78. Rue Bernadette-Soubirous.

This old mill, which was Bernadette's mother's dowry, was where Bernadette was born on 7 January 1844. It now contains an exhibit on the Soubirous family.

Église du Sacré-Cœur

The building of this parish church started in 1867 on the orders of Monseigneur Peyramale, pastor in Lourdes at the time of the apparitions. According to records it was at the font here – transferred from another sanctuary which was demolished in 1908 – that Marie-Bernard (Bernadette) Soubirous was baptised two days after her birth.

Bartrès

3km/1.8mi N. It was to the wet-nurse, Marie Aravant-Lagües, in this village that Bernadette was entrusted as a baby. She returned here occasionally either for health reasons or to help out with some minor chore. Mementoes of Bernadette's visits can be seen in **Maison Lagües** (♿ 🕐 Early Apr to mid-Oct: daily except Sun 8.30am-noon, 2-6pm. No charge. ☎ 05 62 42 02 03.). Period examples of country furniture are on display in the old kitchen.

Returning to Lourdes, park near the wayside shrine to St Bernadette and climb to the **bergerie** (sheepfold) where, until 1858, the young girl kept sheep.

Sights

Château Fort★

🕐 Apr-Sep: 9am-noon, 1.30-6.30pm (last admission 1hr before closing); Oct-Mar: daily except Tue 9am-noon, 2-6pm (Fri 5pm). 🕐 Closed 1 Jan, 1 and 11 Nov, 25 ⊶ Dec. 5€ (children: 2.50€). ☎ 05 62 42 37 37. Access via a lift, via the Saracens' Staircase (131 steps) or up the castle ramp from rue du Bourg. The third route passes the small Basque cemetery on the side of the slope, with its characteristic round headstones.

The castle is perched on the last boss constricting the ancient glaciated valley of the Lavedan. The glacier's terminal tongue, 400m/1 312ft thick, petered out where Lourdes is today. The fortress, guarding the gateway to the Central Pyrenees, imposed feudal law on the turbulent hill-men of the Lavedan region and was subsequently, in the 17C and 18C, used as a state prison.

Apparitions of the Virgin Mary Throughout the World

In the 19C and 20C, the Virgin Mary was seen about 100 times, but it seems as though the Middle Ages holds the record with 4 000 Marian apparitions between the year 1000 and 1515. Apparitions have been recounted in the Christian world since the 2C. By the 7C, so-called apocryphal texts (considered less authoritative than the Bible because of their late origins), relating many legends about Mary, had fired the imagination of believers. With so many apparitions reported, the Fifth Lateran Council established rules for the examination of revelations by the Holy See in 1516. Since the 19C, only 12 Marian apparitions have been officially recognised, namely:
11 February-16 July 1858 in Lourdes (Hautes-Pyrénées); 17 January 1871 in Pontmain (Mayenne); 15 February-8 December 1876 in Pellevoisin (Indre); 1877 in Gietzwald (Eastern Prussia/Poland); 21 August 1879 in Knock (Ireland); 13 May-13 October 1917 in Fatima (Portugal); 29 November 1932-3 January 1933 in Bauraing (Belgium); 15 January-2 March 1933 in Banneux (Belgium); 25 August-1 September 1953 in Syracuse (Italy); 2 April 1968 in Zeitoun (Egypt); 1973-1981 in Akita (Japan); 1976-1984 in Betania (Venezuela).

From Pointe du Cavalier (Rider's Bluff), at the castle's southern extremity, a vast panorama unfolds over the valley of the Pau torrent and the whole Pyrenean chain.

Inside the fortress a **Pyrenean Folk Museum**★ displays items from the regions lying between Bayonne to the west and Perpignan to the east. Among the exhibits on local customs and folk arts are costumes, musical instruments, fine ceramics, a Béarnaise kitchen and a collection of *surjougs* (harness bells on wooden frames). There are also sections on paleontology and prehistory.

The castle **chapel**, on the eastern side, contains woodwork, an altar and 18C polychrome statues from the original (*demolished*) parish church in Lourdes. On the esplanade several 1:10 scale models illustrate Pyrenean architectural styles from both sides of the Franco-Spanish frontier. The castle itself, with its square keep towering above the rock, is a fine example of medieval military architecture.

Musée Grévin de Lourdes★

&🕐 *Early Apr to 11 Nov: 9-11.40am, 1.30-6.30pm (late opening 8.30-10pm).* ⊕ *5.50€ (children: 2,75€).* ☎ *05 62 94 33 74.*

Housed on five floors, this museum traces the main events in the life of Bernadette Soubirous and that of Christ. The painting entitled The Last Supper after the work by Leonardo da Vinci attracts a lot of attention.
From the terrace there is a view of the château, the Pau torrent and the sanctuaries.

Musée du Petit Lourdes

&🕐 *Early Apr to mid-Oct: 9-11.45am, 1.30-6.45pm.* ⊕ *5€.* ☎ *05 62 94 24 36.*

Kids This is an open-air reconstruction of Lourdes and the surrounding area at the time of the apparitions (1858). From the Bartrès sheepfold to the Cagots district (👆 *read about life in the Basque Country in The Green Guide Atlantic Coast*), there are houses, historical monuments, mills lining the streets and on the river banks, reproduced at a scale of 1:20, based on 19C documents.

Musée du Gemmail

🕐 *Easter to end Oct: 9am-noon, 2-7pm. No charge.* ☎ *04 47 61 01 19.*

This museum is mainly dedicated to profane art, unlike the art from the Grotto. There is a collection of copies of works of art signed by Rembrandt, Manet, Van Gogh, Vuillard, Degas and Picasso.

Musée de Lourdes

&🕐 *Apr-Oct: 9am-noon, 1.30-7pm.* ⊕ *5€.* ☎ *05 62 94 28 00.*

The town centre as it was in 1858 has been reconstructed in life-size scenes with sound effects and a commentary (*portable headphones*). The scenes evoke the daily life and the traditional activities of the past: inside a traditional local house are artisans' workshops (shoemaker, cabinetmaker and basket-maker) and a pastoral scene (shepherd's hut).

Aquarium

&🕐 *Jul and Aug: noon-7pm; Jun: Wed, Sat-Sun and public holidays 2-6pm; Easter and Nov school holidays: daily except Mon 2-6pm.* ⊕ *7.50€ (children: 5.50€).* ☎ *05 62 42 01 00. At the entrance to the town, on the Tarbes road.*

Kids This aquarium is devoted to Pyrenean fish, from trout swimming in mountain streams to wels which can reach a length or 5m/16ft. The hands-on pool will delight youngsters.

Address Book

For coin categories, see the Legend.

EATING OUT

Pizza Da Marco – *R. de la Grotte -* ☎ *05 62 94 03 59 – closed Sun and Mon.* This is a pleasant place, decorated with photos and engravings. The pizzaïolo is set up in the front room, but it is nicer to sit in the other one. Crispy pizza and efficient service.

Brasserie de l'hôtel de la Grotte – *66 r. de la Grotte -* ☎ *05 62 42 39 34 - booking@hoteldelagrotte.com - 1 Apr-31 Oct.* Agreeable contemporary surroundings comprising ochre coloured dining room, veranda and terrace, and a menu to suit all budgets. Extravagant diners can decamp to the more formal adjacent restaurant.

Le Magret – *10 r. 4 Frères-Soulas -* ☎ *05 62 94 20 55 - pene.philippe@ wanadoo.fr – closed 5-26 Jan and Mon.* This little restaurant occupies a rustic style dining room with exposed beams and straw-bottomed chairs. Pilgrims and locals alike can enjoy traditional southwest cuisine without pretention.

WHERE TO STAY

Cazaux – *2 chemin Rochers -* ☎ *05 62 94 22 65 - hotelcazaux@yahoo.fr – closed end Oct-Easter - 20 rooms.* This small hotel just outside the town centre offers scrupulously kept, fresh-looking rooms, a friendly welcome and reasonable prices among other things. It is near the market.

Chambre d'hôte M. and Mme Vives – *28 rte de Bartrès – 65100 Loubajac - 6km/4mi NW of Lourdes on D 940 towards Pau -* ☎ *05 62 94 44 17 - nadine.vives@ wanadoo.fr - closed 11 Nov until Feb holidays -* 🖬 *- 6 rms.* If you like the countryside, peace and quiet and a farm atmosphere, then this is the place for you. Sheep, chickens and ducks are raised and consumed here against a stunning backdrop of the Pyrenees. Four rooms with beams and sloping ceilings, and two others with a terrace. Fine garden and children's play area.

Chambre d'hôte Le Grand Cèdre – *6 r. du Barry - 65270 St-Pé-de-Bigorre -* ☎ *05 62 41 82 04 - chp@grandcedre.com -* 🖬 *- 4 rms.* This lovely 17C manor is sure to charm you. Each room is in a different style: Art déco, Louis XV, Henri II, Louis-Philippe. Dining room, music room and superb park with a glasshouse and a vegetable garden.

Chambre d'hôte Les Rocailles – *65100 Omex - 4.5km/3mi SW of Lourdes on D 13 then D 213 -* ☎ *05 62 94 46 19 - muriellefanlou@aol.com - closed 1 Nov-Easter -* 🖬 *- 3 rms.* We fell in love with this sweet little place! The owner used to be a costume designer at the Paris Opera and has decorated this small stone house with taste and refinement. Warm woods blend harmoniously with shimmering fabrics.

Hôtel Solitude – *3 passage St-Louis -* ☎ *05 62 42 71 71 - contact@ hotelsolitude.com – closed 6 Nov-31 Mar - 281 rms.* This large imposing modern hotel on the banks of the Pau, a Pyrenean stream, has a small rooftop swimming pool. The dining room is a rotunda and has a terrace overlooking the river. The rooms with their little red armchairs are comfortable. We recommend those on the side of the river.

Hôtel Impérial – *3 av. du Paradis –* ☎ *05 62 94 06 30 - hotelimperial.lourdes. fr@gofornet.com – closed 16 Dec-31 Jan - 93 rms.* This 1935 hotel, which has been completely renovated in its original Art Deco style, is near the cave. The rooms are pleasant and furnished in soothing mahogany tones. Large classic style dining room and drawing room opening onto a small garden.

SIT BACK AND RELAX

La Louisiane – *13 r. Lafitte B.P. 20 -* ☎ *05 62 94 60 15 - Jul-Oct: Mon-Sat 8.30am-7.15pm; Nov-Jun: Mon-Sat 9am-7.15pm - closed holidays.* This coffee shop opposite the market square offers a peaceful interlude with top quality beverages. Try the coffee (12 varieties of different roast), or one of the 80 varieties of tea or 6 of hot chocolate on the menu.

LEISURE ACTIVITIES

Golf – *Chemin du Lac -* ☎ *05 62 42 02 06 - www.golfdelourdes.com - 9am-5pm (winter), 9am-6pm (summer).* Pleasant 18 hole course.

La Truite des Pyrénées – *65400 Lau-Balagnas -* ☎ *05 62 97 02 05 - Mon-Sat 9am-noon and 3-5pm; Jul-Aug: 9am-noon and 3-7pm.* Everything you need to know about trout fishing (equipment and instruction available). There is also an exhibition about fish-farming and a shop.

Sports Nature – *65270 St-Pé-de-Bigorre -* ☎ *05 62 41 81 48 - www.sport-nature.org – early Apr-15 Sep: open 24hrs a day; winter: every day 8.30am-5.30pm.* Outdoor activity center with camping and *gite* accommodation.

Lourdes Forest – *Leave town on D 937; just before St-Pé, cross the river to the left then turn right onto the forest road.* The woods, planted with maples, oaks and beeches, offer picnic facilities and are ideal for jogging.

Lac de Lourdes – *Leave town W along D 940 and turn left onto the path leading to the edge of the lake via l'Embarcadère restaurant.* Lying at an altitude of 421m/1 381ft, the 11m/36ft-deep glacial lake offers water sports facilities (non-supervised bathing), fishing and golf (Lourdes 18-hole golf course to the south). From the shores of the lake there are fine views of the Pyrenean foothills. A footpath runs round the lake.

Voie Verte des Gaves – This is a 17km/10.6mi-long cycle track between Lourdes and Soulom to the west. *Information from Association française de* *développement des Véloroutes et Voies Vertes - Délégation Grand Sud-Ouest - 9 rue Bourdon - 31200 Toulouse - ☎ 05 61 11 87 09.*

Excursions

Pic du Jer★

A **funicular railway** (🕐 *Easter to All Saints: 10am-6pm (10min, departure every 15min).* 🚡 *7.50€ there and back, 5.50€ one way.* ☎ *05 62 94 00 41.*) on the southern side of the town climbs this peak. A gentle 10min walk from the upper station leads to the 948m/3 110ft summit, which offers a fine **panorama** of the Central Pyrenees.

🚶 *The walk can be extended (30min round trip) by leaving the paved path to the observatory at the first right-hand bend on the way down. A narrow track (Promenade du panorama de Castelloubon) branches off to climb to the mountain's southern peak.* From here, the impressive view includes the junction of the Argelès and Castelloubon valleys.

Le Béout★

Alt 791m/2 595ft. Take the footpath from the Cité-Secours-St-Pierre rescue centre.

🚶 The **view** of Lourdes, Pic du Jer, Pic de Montaigu, the Argelès Valley and the valleys of Bat-Surguère and Castelloubon is splendid. Continue up along the ridge, where the scattering of huge, contorted boulders testifies to the power of the Quaternary Age glaciers under which the mountain was completely submerged. At the far end the view takes in Pic du Midi de Bigorre, the Lac de Lourdes, Pic Long in the Néouvielle massif, the highest point (alt 3 192m/ 10 473ft) of the French Pyrenees, the Marboré Cylinder and Monte Perdido.

Pic de Pibeste★★★ – 🕐 *See ARGELÈS-GAZOST.*

St-Pé-de-Bigorre

▶ *Leave Lourdes by D 937. Before reaching St-Pé, cross the river on the left then follow the road on the right which runs through Lourdes Forest and rejoins D 937 shortly before St-Pé-de-Bigorre.*

The small town, popular as a base for outdoor activities, grew up around an abbey dedicated to St Peter (from which the Gascon name Pé derives). The Romanesque abbey, built on the pilgrims' route to Santiago de Compostela by Cluniac monks, was at one time the finest and the largest religious monument in the Pyrenees; the Wars of Religion, however, and the earthquake of 1661 inflicted terrible, irreparable damage on it.

The west end of the abbey church included a transept with a tower above the crossing; all that remains today is a small wing below the tower with Romanesque decoration, which is used as the present baptistery (*left of the entrance*). A much-revered statue of Notre-Dame-des-Miracles dates from the 14C.

Route De La Croix Blanche★ 7️⃣

Round tour from Lourdes. 48km/30mi – about 2hr – 🕐 *local map see La BIGORRE.*

▶ *Leave Lourdes via D 937. It is a steep winding road through the foothills of the Pyrenees. Turn right on D 935 to Bagnères-de-Bigorre.*

Pouzac

The 16C church, protected by a fortified wall pierced with a Classical portal, contains an impressive 17C sculpted altarpiece by Élie Corau from Bagnères and Jean Ferrère from Asté. The late-17C wooden vaulting was painted by Jean Catau.

▶ *Continue along D 26.*

This road links the valley of the Ardour to that of Gave de Pau, running through cool valleys in among oak, birch and chestnut trees.

As the road climbs into the mountains, between the Oussouet and Castelloubon valleys, the views successively point southwards to Pic de Montaigu and Pic du Midi de Bigorre, north-east to the lava flow of the Adour and the lowlands, and south-west to Balaïtous Massif, easily identifiable by its glacier.

▶ *Return to Lourdes via N 21.*

Mont LOZÈRE★★

Between Florac, Génolhac and Villefort, this powerful granite massif, rising majestically above the Cévennes countryside, forms a geographical unit set off by the gorges of the Tarn, the Lot, the Altier and the Cèze. The area, crisscrossed by numerous GR footpaths, is ideal hiking country: a six-day hike round Mont Lozère is described in detail in the GR 68 topoguide; GR 7, on the other hand, runs across Mont Lozère, offering hikers the opportunity to discover typical landscapes and hamlets (particularly between Col de Finiels and Ferme de l'Aubaret). 🛈 *Information about the Mont Lozère area is available from the Parc national des Cévennes headquarters in Florac.*

Geographical Notes

"Mont Chauve" – Mont Lozère has earned its nickname ("Bald Mountain") from its 35km/22mi of bare, high-lying plateaux. The mountain culminates at the Finiels summit (alt 1 699m/5 573ft), the highest peak in the Massif Central which is not of volcanic origin. The eroded granite of which it is made up has been weathered into curious boulders forming scattered rocky outcrops amid heathland which still bears the remains of its ancient forest cover of beech groves. The mountain slopes, replanted over the last few decades, are covered once again in pines, firs and beeches to the south (Bougès mountain), to the east (Vivarois slopes) and to the north.

The robust architectural style of the houses blends in perfectly with the countryside. Granite boulders have at times been incorporated directly into the walls. Nowadays, most of the villages are deserted, as life is very harsh on these wind- and snow-swept plateaux. Storm bells, the sound of which was once the only means of finding one's way during a blizzard, are still to be found here and there. A few granite markers bearing the Maltese Cross are a reminder that part of the land was once owned by the Knights Hospitallers of St John of Jerusalem, who later became the Knights of Malta. In the past, flocks of sheep dotted the vast hillside pastures during the summer months. Estimated to have numbered about 100 000 head in the 19C, less than 10 000 are to be found grazing nowadays, and the sheep trails (drailles) of the past are slowly being overgrown. Sheep have given way to herds of cattle which come to graze on the high plateaux of Mont Lozère from villages on the southern slopes.

Rambling on Mont Lozère

A. Thuillier/MICHELIN

Ski Areas

Mont-Lozère-Le Bleymard ski area

Alt 1 350-1 560m/4 429-5 118ft. Vast open spaces lend themselves to cross-country skiing (22km/14mi of tracks) and snowshoeing. In addition, there are 8km/5mi of Alpine ski runs for all levels and 5 ski lifts. ☎ 04 66 48 66 48.

Mas de la Barque ski area

Alt 1 340-1 650m/4 396-5 413ft. A total of 38km/24mi of cross-country skiing tracks; snowshoeing tracks. Info station, ☎ 04 66 46 92 72.

Écomusée du Mont-Lozère

The aim of this open-air museum of local crafts and traditions, founded under the sponsorship of the **Parc national des Cévennes**, is to familiarise visitors with the natural and human environment of Mont Lozère. It consists of a headquarters, the

Maison du Mont Lozère at Pont-de-Montvert, and various sites of architectural and natural interest scattered throughout the massif. At the **Troubat** and **Mas Camargues** farms, the emphasis is on 19C rural architecture and the everyday running of a farm. An inventory has been made of all the storm bells and markers bearing a Maltese Cross in the area. Several footpaths have been laid out.

Most of the museum's sights are mentioned in the itineraries described below.

Eastern Part of Mont Lozère★ ⬚1⬚

Round tour from Le Pont-de-Montvert. 130km/80mi – allow one day.

▶ *Follow D 20 N and turn right immediately after leaving Le Pont-de-Montvert.*

The narrow road (⚠ *tricky in summer owing to increased traffic*) runs across barren pastures and heathland dotted with rocks.

L'Hôpital

This hamlet was a commandery for the Knights Hospitallers of St John of Jerusalem. One or two summer visitors have bought and are restoring some of its granite build-ings and the Écomusée has had the old-style thatched roofs put back on the watermill and the old grange.

▶ *The GR 7 footpath which crosses L'Hôpital leads to Pont-du-Tarn.*

Pont-du-Tarn

1hr on foot there and back from L'Hôpital.

🔲 The GR 7 follows the old Margeride sheep trail, making a very pleasant walk with lovely views of the surrounding Tarn plain, named thus as the young river flows across this plateau. A pretty bridge spans the river as it threads its way through polished rocks at the foot of the Commandeur woods.

Mas Camargues★

🕐 *Jul and Aug: 10.30am-12.30pm, 2.30-6.30pm.* 🕐 *Closed 14 Jul and 15 Aug (morning).* 🎫 *3.50€* ☎ *04 66 45 80 73.*

This family mansion is surprisingly large and has an unusually regular façade made of hewn blocks of granite. It has been restored by the Parc national des Cévennes. An **observation trail** has been laid out around it to explain various aspects of farming in this region – sheepfold, mill, small canal, reservoir – and the surrounding countryside (jumbles of granite boulders, beech groves).

🔲 It is possible to walk on as far as **Bellecoste** (*1km/0.6mi*), an interesting example of rural architecture with a communal oven and a traditional thatched shepherd's house.

▶ *Return to D 20 and turn right.*

The road, lined with service trees, climbs up the south face towards Finiels Pass. After the village of Finiels, it crosses wide expanses of deserted countryside, punctuated here and there with granite boulders. The horizon is blocked to the south by Bougès mountain and the hilly outline of the Causse Méjean.

Col de Finiels★

Alt 1 548m/5 077ft. From the area around the pass, and particularly from the peaks on either side of the road, the **view**★ in fine weather stretches as far as Mont Aigoual and the Causses.

At the beginning of the descent, the Tanargue massif (the Cévennes part of the Vivarais region) is visible ahead and to the right.

The stony skeleton of the world was here vigorously displayed to sun and air. The slopes were steep and changeful. Oak trees clung along the hills, well grown, wealthy in leaf, and touched by the autumn with strong and luminous colours. Here and there another stream would fall in from the right or the left, down a gorge of snow-white and tumultuary boulders. The river in the bottom (for it was rapidly growing a river, collecting on all hands as it trotted on its way) here foaming a while in desperate rapids, and there lay in pools of the most enchanting sea-green shot with watery browns. As far as I have gone, I have never seen a river of so changeful and delicate a hue; crystal was not more clear, the meadows were not by half so green; and at every pool I saw, I felt a longing to be out of these hot, dusty, and material garments, and bathe my naked body in the mountain air and water.

Robert Louis Stevenson: *Travels With a Donkey*

Sheepherding on Mont Lozère

Chalet du Mont Lozère

Newly planted fir trees surround the refuge chalet, a hotel, **information centre** (🕐 *Jul and Aug: 9.30am–noon, 1.30–6.30pm. No charge.* ☎ *04 66 48 66 48.*) for the Cévennes park and a large UCPA (French open-air sports centres association) building which welcomes ramblers and horse-riders in summer. From December to April, it is also a centre for skiing, particularly for cross-country skiing.

Sommet de Finiels★

3hr on foot there and back.

🚶 From Mont Lozère chalet, take the waymarked path between D 20 and the chapel, which follows a row of stones right up to the top of the ridge. Turn right towards the remains of a stone hut. From here, a sweeping **view**★★ to the south-east reveals a series of rounded peaks on the high plateaux as far as Pic Cassini, whereas to the north the horizon is hidden by the granite plateau of La Margeride. Follow the line of the ridge to the 1 685m/5 527ft marker and then join the "Route des Chômeurs" on the way down which leads back to the point of departure.

Beyond the Mont Lozère chalet, where D 20 leaves the ravine of the Altier to cross over to the side of the Atlantic watershed, the mountains of La Margeride can be seen stretching away to the north. Farther on, the village of **Le Bleymard** has solidly built houses with roofs of limestone slabs (*lauzes*) and a 13C church.

Le Mazel is the site of a now disused lead and zinc mine which was worked here from the beginning of the 20C to 1952.

▶ *Turn right onto D 901 towards Villefort.*

The scenery becomes increasingly bleak and rugged. The road leaves the Lot Valley, having crossed the Col des Tribes, to follow the winding, wooded Altier Valley. The towers of the **Château de Champ** (15C) can be seen downhill from the road on the right. A few miles past Altier, once a stronghold, the road reaches Lake Villefort. On its shores stand the ruins of the Renaissance **Château de Castanet**.

Villefort reservoir and dam

The dam, which is 190m/623ft long at its crest, rises to a height of 70m/230ft above the river bed. The reservoir supplies the Pied-de-Borne plant 9km/6mi downstream. Beyond the dam, along the road to Langogne, a water sports centre and a beach provide leisure activities for locals and visitors alike.

Villefort

This pleasant town at the mouth of the Phalère Valley has much to offer the holiday-maker, with its nearby reservoir, well equipped for water sports enthusiasts, and its ideal location as a base for trips on foot or by car into the Cévennes, Bas Vivarais and Mont Lozère. In season, the Syndicat d'Initiative at Villefort houses an **information centre** (♿ 🕐 *Jul-Sep: 9am-12.30pm, 3-7pm, Sun and public holidays 9.30am-1pm; Oct-Jun: daily except Sat-Sun 9am-noon, 3-5pm.* 🕐 *Closed 1 May. No charge.* ☎ *04 66 46 87 30.*) on the Parc national des Cévennes.

▷ *On leaving Villefort, take D 66.*

The road rises above a ravine shaded by chestnut trees, offering splendid views of Villefort and its valley. It goes through the villages of Paillères and Costeilades, surrounded by small terraced gardens. The houses are roofed with limestone slabs (lauzes), with finials on the roof ridges. Gradually, to the northeast, the plateaux formed by the Borne and Chassezac gorges come into view. As the road passes through a stretch scattered with granite outcrops, the Tanargue and Mézenc massifs can be seen, with the Alps on the horizon. The road reaches the Pré de la Dame ledge, covered with large granite boulders.

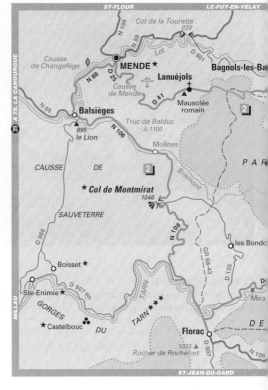

▷ *Just beyond Pré de la Dame, the road to Mas de la Barque leads off to the right.*

Mas de la Barque

This forester's hut, an overnight stop for hikers, stands in a peaceful setting of meadows and coppices surrounded by forest. In winter, it is also a ski centre.

An **observation trail** (*45min, currently inaccessible*), laid out by the Parc national des Cévennes as part of the Écomusée du Mont Lozère to give visitors the opportunity of exploring the forest environment, leads off from the hut.

A second path leads up to the Cassini summit from where there is a wonderful **panorama**★★, as far as the Alps and Mont Ventoux in clear weather (*2hr there and back*).

▷ *Return to Pré de la Dame and carry on towards Génolhac.*

Belvédère des Bouzèdes★

Alt 1 235m/4 051ft. At this viewpoint, the road makes a hairpin bend on open ground on the brow of a steep hill overlooking Génolhac, 800m/2 600ft below. This little village looks surprisingly Mediterranean with its tiled roofs.

Génolhac

Génolhac is a charming little town, bright with flowers in season, in a pleasant setting in the Gardonnette Valley. The Maison de l'Arceau houses an **information centre** (🕒 *Daily except Sat-Sun, Tue and Thu: 9am-noon, 1.30-5.30pm. No charge.* ☎ *04 66 61 19 97. www.cevennes.parcnational.fr*) on the Parc national des Cévennes and offers overnight accommodation.

▷ *Drive N along D 906 to La Banlève and turn right onto D 155.*

The road leads to Brésis, overlooked by the ruins of a medieval castle with a handsome crenellated keep.

▷ *Turn right onto D 51 which runs down towards Bessèges.*

Château d'Aujac

🕒 *Jul and Aug: guided tours (1hr) daily except Mon 11am-7pm; Mar-Jun and Sep-Nov: Sun and public holidays 2-6pm.* ☞ *5€.* ☎ *04 66 61 19 94.*

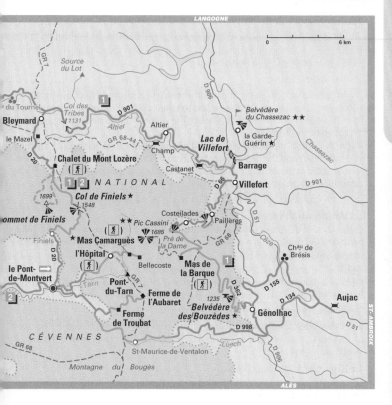

> *In Aujac, turn left onto a minor road climbing up to the castle. Leave the car in the parking area and walk up to the entrance (10min).*

Built on a rocky spur, on the borders of the Gard, Lozère and Ardèche départements, the castle was built in the 11C to keep watch over the Cèze Valley. With its round and square towers and L-shaped main building, it is one of the best-preserved castles in the area. The castle and the village lying at its foot are gradually being restored by a team of volunteers.

> *Follow D 134 W towards Génolhac, turn left onto the road to Alès, then right onto D 998 towards Florac.*

The road along the Luech Valley is particularly scenic as far as St-Maurice-de-Ventalon.

> *Continue 2km/1mi after Les Bastides, a road on the right leads to Troubat farm-house.*

Ferme de Troubat

🕐 🍴 *Jul and Aug: guided tours (45min) 10.30am, 2.30 and 6.30pm; May-Jun: daily except Tue 3-6pm.* ✆ *3.50€.* ☎ *04 66 45 80 73.*

This old farmstead in rose-coloured granite has been restored by the Parc national des Cévennes and has a stable barn, bread oven, mill and threshing area.

Ferme-fortifiée de l'Aubaret

This fortified farm on the Margeride sheep trail is dwarfed by the massive chaos of rocks behind it. The farm's sturdy pink-granite walls have mullioned windows.

> *Rejoin D 998 and turn right to return to Le Pont-de-Montvert.*

Western Part of Mont Lozère ★★ ②

Round trip from Mende. 100km/62mi – allow half a day.

> *Leave Mende on D 25 heading SE towards the airport. In Langlade, turn left onto D 41.*

Lanuéjols

The **Roman mausoleum**, situated on the way out of the village to the west, was erected by wealthy Roman citizens to the memory of their two young sons who apparently died of the same disease.

The Romanesque **Église St-Pierre** is built of attractive ochre-coloured stone. Its barrel-vaulted nave ends in an elegant oven-vaulted apse. Note the interesting capitals.

▷ *Continue along D 41 to Bagnols-les-Bains.*

Bagnols-les-Bains

This cure resort specialising in the treatment of rheumatism and ear, nose and throat complaints is built in a semicircle around the slopes of the Pervenche mountain, and stretches downhill to the banks of the Lot. The waters of the mineral spring were first exploited by the Romans.

Bagnols is first and foremost a holiday and leisure destination. Its altitude (913m/2 995ft) and the nearby pine forests contribute to the fresh, healthy mountain air. It is a particularly good remedy for the effects of overwork or stress, with its peaceful atmosphere and steady climate.

▷ *From Bagnols drive N along a road leading to Le Villaret.*

Le Vallon du Villaret

Early May to mid-Sep and Easter school holidays: 10am-6.45pm (last visit 4.30pm); mid-Sep to end Oct: Sat-Sun 10am-6pm; Nov school holidays: 10am-6pm (last visit 2hr before closing). 8€. 04 66 47 63 76.

Kids The leisure park is designed around the discovery of nature: trails and areas all have a dominant theme ("trunks," "sounds," "water"). The village (artist studio, exhibitions, concerts) is situated at the end of this interactive vale.

▷ *Return to Bagnols and turn left to Le Bleymard.*

The valley sides draw in, becoming steep rocky gorges, cloaked in woods. The ruins of Tournel Castle can be seen perched proudly on a rocky spur around the foot of which surges the river.

Le Bleymard – *See* 1 *above.*

▷ *Turn right onto D 20 to Le Pont-de-Montvert.* *This section of the tour is described in* 1 *above in the other direction.*

Le Pont-de-Montvert – *See Le PONT-DE-MONTVERT.*

▷ *Turn right onto D 998 to Florac.*

The road follows the upper Tarn Valley which later narrows into rugged gorges. Miral Castle, with the remains of its 14C fortifications, can be seen perched on a promontory.

Florac – *See FLORAC.*

▷ *Drive N along N 106 towards Mende.*

Beyond the intersection with the road leading to Ispagnac along the **Tarn gorge**★★★ (*see Gorges du TARN*), there is a spectacular cliff-edge passage uphill overlooking Florac.

Col de Montmirat★

Alt 1 046m/3 432ft. The pass cuts between the granite of Mont Lozère and the limestone of the Causse de Sauveterre. To the south there is a vast **panorama**★: in the foreground lie the *valats* or little troughs along which water drains down into the Tarn; beyond these loom the cliff edges of the Causse Méjean; farther left are the Cévennes ridges; and on a clear day the summit of Mont Aigoual can be seen.

The road goes down the Bramon Valley, which gradually narrows, offering views of the "Truc de Balduc," a small, steep-sided *causse*, and of the foothills of Mont Lozère in the distance.

Balsièges

To the south of this village tower the cliffs of the Causse de Sauveterre. High up on the skyline stand two huge limestone rocks, one of which is known as the "lion of Balsièges" because of its shape.

N 88 runs along beside the Lot between the steep wooded slopes of the Causse de Mende and Causse de Changefège before reaching Mende.

LUZ-ST-SAUVEUR★

POPULATION 1 098

MICHELIN LOCAL MAP 342: L-5

ALSO SEE LA BIGORRE AND PARC NATIONAL DES PYRÉNÉES

The villages of Luz and St-Sauveur face one another across the Pau torrent in a picturesque mountain setting.

The inhabitants of this valley, once fierce and unsociable by nature (the ruins of the castle wrested from the English have proved the point since 1404), were nevertheless unable to disguise their gratitude to Napoleon III and Empress Eugénie for the benefits showered on the town and its surroundings by the royal couple. A trip around the Luz basin from Pont de la Reine north of the town to Pont Napoléon in the south, via the Solferino Chapel, is virtually a Napoleon III tour. The chapel is used for an annual ceremony commemorating the foundation of the Red Cross.

LUZ★

Luz, the capital of a small mountain canton, which for centuries was cut off in winter from the lowlands by the hazardous route through the avalanche-prone Échelles de Barèges, is today a surprisingly busy and well-equipped tourist centre. Fashionable as a summer resort in the 18C and 19C, the small town boasts a number of distinguished houses dating from that period, white beneath their slate roofs and adorned with carved lintels, cornices and wrought-iron balconies.

Fortified Church★

🕐 Church: 9am-7pm. Museum: Jun-Oct: daily except Sun and public holidays 3-6pm; school holidays (Feb, Nov and Christmas): Tue, Thu and Sat 3-6pm. 👓 2€. ☎ 05 62 92 32 88.

Address Book

EATING OUT

🍽 **Auberge de Viella** – Pl. de la Mairie - 65120 Viella – 1.5km/1mi NE of Luz-St-Sauveur on D 918 rte de Barège and a lane to the right - ☎ 05 62 92 85 14 – closed Nov – reservations required – 11.50/17€. On the same square as the town hall, this cosy restaurant has a country-style decor, warmed in winter by an open fire. Friendly service, local specialities and delicious garbure soup.

WHERE TO STAY

🛏 **Chambre d'hôte La Munia** – 65120 Saligos - 3km/2mi N of Luz-St-Sauveur on D 921 then D 12 - ☎05 62 92 84 74 – closed 1 week in Jun - 🍴 - 3 rms: 23/24€ - meal 11€. This is the place to come if you are on a budget. The rooms are basic but pleasant and open onto the valley. If dining, be sure to sample the lamb raised by the proprietor and cooked in various ways by herself. Two gîtes available.

🛏 **Chambre d'hôte Le Palouma** – 65120 Chèze - 5km/3mi N of Luz-St-Sauveur on D 921 then D 12 - ☎05 62 92 90 90 – closed 15 Oct-1 Jan - 🍴 - 3 rms: 28/34€. This is a good departure point for rambles. The owner was once a mountain policeman and can advise you on your route. On your return, a good night's sleep in one of the wood-panelled rooms will soon recharge your batteries.

🛏 **Chambre d'hôte Eslias** – Les Cabanes - 65120 Viella - 2.5km/1.5mi E of Luz-St-Sauveur on D 918 then B-road - ☎05 62 92 84 58 - 🍴 - 3 rms: 30/40€ - meal 13€. The small house has a panoramic terrace with a view of the surrounding summits. Rooms are very peaceful and comfortable. One self-catering cottage available.

SPORTS AND RECREATION

Air Aventures Pyrénées – 65120 Viella - 1.5km/1mi NE of Luz-St-Sauveur on D 918 and a lane to the right - ☎ 06 08 93 62 02 or 06 80 65 85 00. Hang-gliding and paragliding.

Via ferrata – Located near Pont Napoléon, this via ferrata can be included in an adventure course which entails crossing the mountain stream by means of three suspended cables. Bureau des guides de Luz, ☎ 05 62 92 87 28.

SPA

Établissement thermal – Quartier thermal - ☎ 05 62 92 81 58. You can take a break and enjoy the facilities, which include a pool, jacuzzi, hammam, sauna, relaxing baths

The church, incorrectly called a Templars' church, was built in the 12C and fortified in the 14C by the Hospitallers of St John of Jerusalem. The defensive features included a watch-path running round beneath the roof, a crenellated wall enclosing an old cemetery, and two square towers. The Romanesque doorway is decorated with the figures of Christ the King surrounded by the Evangelists. (See illustration in Introduction, Architecture.)

Inside, note the 18C woodwork, the small **museum** of religious art in the Chapelle Notre-Dame-de-la-Pitié, and a **museum of ethnography** in the Arsenal tower.

Fortified Church

A. Thuillier/MICHELIN

St-Sauveur ✝

The town's single street, perched above the torrent, is named after the Duchesse de Berry, leading socialite of the 1828 season, on one end; and after Empress Eugénie, whose visits – particularly that of 1859 – ensured the resort's success, on the other.

Luz Ardiden ✳

A small mountain road from Luz-St-Sauveur leads to the ski resort of Luz Ardiden – alt 1 680m/5 527ft-2 450m/8 060ft. This superb **setting** has remained practically unspoilt by the construction of apartment blocks and chalets; skiers stay in the villages in the Vallée de Luz.

Ski area

The ski area is serviced by 19 lifts. The Aulian and Bédéret slopes, which are linked by ski lifts, offer a total 50km/31mi of downhill runs (32 runs in all) for all levels of expertise; competitive skiers will find them especially rewarding. Skiers can slalom around moguls, and schuss or monoski in Snowboard Space. Off-piste skiing is practised in the adjacent valley of Bernazaou, which will eventually be linked up with the other slopes.

The Ticket-Toy ski pass includes the neighbouring resorts of Barèges and Gavarnie-Gèdre.

MAGUELONE ★

MICHELIN LOCAL MAP 339: I-7

Located 16km/10mi south of Montpellier, Maguelone which stands in an unusual site on a sand spit that lies between the Golfe du Lion and the Pierre Blanche and Prévost lagoons, and is linked by a narrow road to the seaside resort of Palavas-les-Flots, is peaceful and charming. The vestiges of its cathedral stand on a slight hill, framed by umbrella pines, cedars and eucalyptus.

The Rhône-Sète canal, which passes through the lagoons between the sand spits and the Languedoc coast proper, cut across the road which, up until 1708, linked Maguelone to dry land. A gigantic arch was erected in the 19C to mark the boundaries of the Maguelone territory.

A Bit of History

Historical trials and tribulations – The origins of Maguelone are uncertain; it ... Phoenician trading post or a colony of Greek navigators. In any case, in ... o the Saracens. At that time, the harbour, south of the cathedral, was ... the sea by a channel.

Charles Martel recaptured the town from the infidels but, afraid that they would use it as a home base again, he immediately destroyed it (737). In 1030, Bishop Arnaud I rebuilt the cathedral on the site of the old church and added extensive fortifications. He built a path from Maguelone to Villeneuve, and a 2km/1.2mi bridge, and closed off the channel joining the Saracen harbour to the sea in order to protect it from attack.

In the 12C, the church was rebuilt to make it bigger and its fortifications were strengthened.

For Maguelone, the 13C to 14C was a period of expansion. A community of 60 canons lived here, reputed for their generosity and hospitality.

Like all the strongholds in the region, Maguelone, which found itself in the hands of the Protestants and Catholics in turn during the Wars of Religion, was finally demolished in 1622, on the orders of Richelieu. Only the cathedral and bishops' palace still remain.

During construction of the canal, Maguelone was bought and sold several times, its ruins dispersed or swallowed up by the surrounding lagoons. In 1852, Frédéric Fabrège bought the estate and set out to restore it. The church became a religious building again in 1875.

Former Cathedral★ 30min

🕐 *9am-7pm (early Jun to mid-Sep: visitors must park on the car park and continue their journey by tourist train – 🖕 see above). No charge.* ☎ *04 67 50 63 63.*

Access – *Out of season, via a road (cul-de-sac), 4km/2.5mi long, which begins at Palavas-les-Flots, at the end of rue Maguelone.*

During the summer season, park in the car park 2km/1.2mi away and take the tourist train to the cathedral, or take the ferry, and then the **petit train** *(Pilou car park:* 🕐 *Jun-Aug: 8am-8.30pm; May, Sep, Sat-Sun and public holidays 10am-6pm; Oct-Apr: 1-5pm.* ☎ *04 67 69 75 87.), from Villeneuve.*

Exterior – The church was attached to a continuous curtain wall, with fortified gatehouses and turrets, demolished under Richelieu at the same time as the three large towers. The high, very thick walls (the southern wall is 2.5m/8ft thick) have a small number of narrow arrow slits, placed asymmetrically. All that is left of the crenellated parapet that once surmounted the building are a few machicolations. A remarkable sculpted doorway leads into the church. The lintel is an antique Roman military column on which fine foliage was later sculpted and the date 1178 inscribed.

The white and grey tympanum with its slightly pointed arch and marble voussoirs is thought to date from the 13C; in the centre is the figure of Christ surrounded by St Mark, represented by a lion, St Matthew by a winged man, St John by an eagle and St Luke by a bull.

Interior – Fragments of tombstones have been set into the wall on the right; some are from the Roman era, whereas others from the 11C come from the burial places of wealthy Montpellier citizens. At that time, Pope Urban II absolved the sins of all those who asked to be buried in Maguelone.

Two bays of the rectangular nave, made of limestone blocks, are covered with a vast gallery that cuts it in half vertically and masks the broken-barrel vaulting.

The chancel is soberly decorated. The small apse is decorated with blind arches and three semicircular windows and is surmounted by a thin band with a cog teeth pattern.

F. Gégot/MICHELIN

St Paul on Maguelone cathedral detail

MARVEJOLS

POPULATION 5,501

MICHELIN LOCAL MAP 330: H-7

Well-situated in the pretty Colagne Valley, Marvejols has benefited from a favourable climate and setting which have lent themselves to the founding of numerous medical and pedagogical centres. Appointed a "Royal City" in 1307 by Philip the Fair, Marvejols went on to play an important role in the wars in the 14C and sided with Du Guesclin against the mercenaries of the Grandes Compagnies. A Protestant fortress town, it was destroyed in 1586 by Admiral Joyeuse. Its fortified gatehouses are reminiscent of its war-torn past. 🛈 *Pl. du Soubeyran, 48100 Marvejols,* ☎ *04 66 32 02 14.*

Fortified gatehouses

Consisting of two large round towers connected by a curtain wall used as lodgings, the fortified gatehouses commanded the three entrances to the old town. On the **Porte du Soubeyran**★, an inscription records how the town was rebuilt by Henri IV – to express their gratitude, the inhabitants had a highly original statue of their royal benefactor erected in the fortified square, which is closed off by the gatehouse on one side. It is the work of the sculptor Auricoste, who was also the author of the legendary "Beast of Gévaudan" on place des Cordeliers.

The other two gatehouses, the **Porte du Théron** and **Porte de Chanelles**, once known as the "Hospital Gatehouse," also bear inscriptions recounting the good deeds of Henri IV.

Eastern Aubrac

Round tour north-west of Marvejols. 97km/60mi – allow 4hrs – 🚗 *The Bonnecombe Pass is snowbound from December to April.*

▶ *Leave Marvejols NW along D 900.*

As it climbs, D 900 offers a broad view of Marvejols, La Margeride, Mont Lozère, the Causses and the Cévennes on the horizon, before passing through pine forests, then fields and meadows, and finally the pastureland so typical of the Aubrac region. It then reaches Nasbinals.

Nasbinals

Nasbinals is an active livestock market, with an interesting little Romanesque church. There are several lively agricultural **fairs** during the year. The village is also a ski resort. The **ski area** has facilities for both downhill (three runs) and cross-country skiing (15km/9.3mi of tracks), a husky track, two snowshoeing trails and a ski-lift.

Address Book

EATING OUT

🍴🍴 **Auberge des Violles** – *48100 Chirac - 14km/9mi W of Marvejols on N 9 and B-road -* ☎ *04 66 32 77 66 – closed Dec-Jan and Tue off-season -* 🍴 *- reservations required.* These typical houses with their lauze roofs at the end of a winding road are ideal for nature-lovers. The inn's rustic atmosphere is enhanced by solid wood tables made by the proprietor, who is a shepherd as well as a cabinet-maker. Food is fresh from the market. Swimming pool.

🍴🍴 **"L'Auberge" Domaine de Carrière** – *Quartier de l'Empery – 48100 Marjevols - 2.5km/1.5mi W of Marvejols, Montrodat road -* ☎ *04 66 32 47 05 - laubergedomainedecarriere@wanadoo.fr - closed 1-24 Jan, 1 week in Sep, Sun evening,* Wed off-season and Mon. This restaurant is set in the old stables of a delightful château. The fine dining room is decorated with furniture from different periods and has a partial mezzanine. In summer, lunch on the terrace can be followed by a stroll in the park or a swim in the pool.

SPORTS AND RECREATION

Les Ailes des Trucs Lozériens – *48100 Le Monastier –* ☎ *04 66 32 74 70 - bj.burlot@wanadoo.fr.* Hang-gliding, paragliding and kite-flying for experienced enthusiasts.

SHOPPING

Market – *Pl. du Soubeyran.* The town's weekly market for local products takes place on Saturday mornings.

At the end of the last century one of the village's inhabitants, a certain **Pierre Broude** nicknamed "**Pierrounet**," acquired quite a reputation for his skill in healing broken or dislocated limbs. News of his amazing medical prowess spread rapidly, and soon invalids of all kinds, not only the lame, were travelling from far and wide to consult him. He is said to have been seeing around 10 000 clients a year at the height of his fame. Nasbinals has a monument to him, the base of which is decorated with crutches.

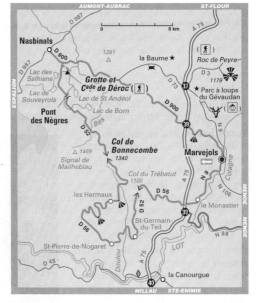

▶ *Turn back along D 900 to Montgrousset then take D 52 to the right.*

Grotte et Cascade de Déroc

30min there and back on foot. Park the car by D 52 and take a rough path lined with drystone walls to the left, towards a farm.

The path leads to a stream and follows its bank for a while, before crossing it to get to the edge of a gully down which a tributary of the Bès plunges. The waterfall tumbles over a granite ledge in front of a cave in which rock prisms form the ceiling vault. Before long D 52 reaches a barren region with lakes. It runs along the shores of Lake Salhiens before cutting across pastureland to the **Col de Bonnecombe**. Beyond the pass, the road drops down through Les Hermaux to St-Pierre-de-Nogaret, giving pretty **views**★ of the Lot Valley and the entire Causses region. It then follows a winding, scenic route through woodland and the Doulou Valley to St-Germain-du-Teil.

▶ *Take D 52 to the left to the Col du Trébatut. Turn right at the crossroads onto D 56, which leads to the Colagne Valley. In Le Monastier, take N 9 back to Marvejols.*

The Gévaudan

Round tour north of Marvejols. 52km/32mi – about 3hr 30min.

▶ *From Marvejols drive to the A 75 motorway and follow it towards Clermont-Ferrand. Leave at Exit 37, take the bridge across the motorway and follow signs to Château de la Baume.*

Château de la Baume★

🕐 *Jul and Aug: guided tours (45min) daily 10am-noon, 2-6pm; Sep-Jun: by request.* *5.50€.* 🕾 *04 66 32 51 59.*

The rugged appearance of this 17C residence, made of granite and covered with stone slabs, is softened by a shady park which is quite an unexpected sight in the middle of the surrounding plateaux. Inside, admire the main staircase with its Louis XIV balusters and the large fireplaces made of chestnut wood that had first been left to soak in the peatbogs of the Aubrac; this makes the wood rot-proof and accounts for its dark brown colour. The great hall has a beautiful parquet floor with different coloured timbers forming a geometric pattern around coats of arms. The study is decorated with painted wood panelling in pastel tones. Large paintings depicting mythological scenes complete the decoration.

▶ *Return to the motorway and take the bridge across it. At the second roundabout, take the third road to the right then turn right onto D 53 towards St-Sauveur-de-Peyre. Follow signs to Roc de Peyre.*

Roc de Peyre

15min on foot there and back.

⬛ From the top (1 179m/3 867ft, *viewing table*) of the rock, accessed by a path and a flight of steps, there is a remarkable panorama of the Aubrac, the Plomb du Cantal, the Margeride, Mont Lozère, Mont Aigoual and the Causses.

It is difficult to imagine, and no trace remains to suggest, that a fortress once occupied this rocky pinnacle of exceptional strategic interest. Nonetheless, no fewer than 2 500 cannonballs were needed by Admiral Joyeuse to destroy the keep of this Protestant fief in 1586. Time then took care of the rest.

▶ *Turn back and take N 9 to the left then a little road on the left towards Ste-Lucie, then turn right immediately onto a road going uphill (past a chapel).*

Parc à loups du Gévaudan★

Wolf feedings take place three times per week (Mon, Wed, Fri) and are open to the public. 🕐☀☁ *Jun-Aug: 10am-7pm; Apr, May, Sep and Oct: 10am-6pm; Nov-Mar: 10am-5pm; guided tours (45min) available on request.* 🕐 *Closed Jan.* ☞ *6.50€ (reduced Nov-Mar; children: 3.50€).* ☎ *04 66 32 09 22. www.loupsdugevaudan.com.*

Parc à loups du Gévaudan

🄺🄸🄳🅂 This 4ha/10-acre **wild animal reserve** is home to about 100 wolves from Europe, Canada and Mongolia, some of which were born in Ste-Lucie. A film shot in the park, with a commentary by J-P Chabrol and G Ménatory, can be viewed on request. A viewing table along the 30min walk provides an attractive vista. In summer, it is best to take a guided tour since the wolves are less visible than in autumn or winter.

▶ *N 9 leads back to Marvejols.*

Wolves in the Gévaudan

Grotte du MAS-D'AZIL★★

MICHELIN LOCAL MAP 343: G-6

This cave is one of the most interesting natural sights in the Ariège. It is also a famous prehistoric milestone in the scientific world as it is here that the Azilian culture was studied and defined.

A Bit of History

In 1887, as a result of methodical excavations, Édouard Piette discovered a new layer of evidence of human habitation dating from between the end of the Magdalenian (30 000 BC) period and the beginning of the Neolithic – this was the Azilian period (9 500 BC). Research continued under Abbé Breuil and Joseph Mandement, and others such as Boule and Cartailhac. The items excavated are exhibited in the cave and the town of Mas-d'Azil.

The Cave

The cave, hollowed out by the Arize underneath the Plantaurel mountain range, is 420m/1 378ft long with an average width of 50m/160ft. Upstream, the entrance forms a magnificent archway (65m/213ft high), whereas downstream, a flattened opening (8m/25ft or so) pierces a sheer rock 140m/460ft high. The path follows this passageway alongside a torrent, whose waters are gradually eroding the limestone walls, then under a majestic vault, shored up in the centre by an enormous pillar of rock.

DONKEYS FOREVER

Asinerie de Feillet "Asinus" – *Le Feillet - 09420 Castelnau-Durban -* ☎ *05 61 96 38 93 - www.asinus.fr - Jul-Nov: Mon-Sat 2-4pm or by appointment for groups.* This donkey breeding operation uses milk from the animals to make cosmetic products including fine soap. The internet site (in French) www.bourricot.com, has information about the virtues of these products and links to donkey-friendly sites around the world.

Tour

🕐 ☀ *Jul and Aug: guided tours (45min) 10am-6pm; Jun and Sep: 10am-noon, 2-6pm; Apr and May: 2-6pm, Sun, public holidays and Easter school holidays 10am-noon, 2-6pm; Mar, Oct and Nov: Sun and public holidays 2-6pm.* 🕐 *Closed Mon (except Jul-Aug, school holidays and public holidays).* ☜ *6.10€ (children: 3.10€), ticket combined with the museum.* ☎ *05 61 69 97 71.*

The four floors of excavated galleries run for 2km/1mi through limestone which is sufficiently homogeneous to prevent infiltration and propagation of moisture. The tour includes the **Salle du Temple**, a Protestant place of refuge, the intermediate floor of which was destroyed under Richelieu after the fruitless siege of 1625. Display cases contain exhibits dating from the Magdalenian (scrapers, chisels, needles, a moulding of the famous neighing horse head) and Azilian periods (harpoons made from antlers – the reindeer moved northwards as the climate became warmer – arrowheads, coloured pebbles and miniaturised tools).

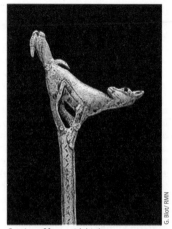

Carving of fawn with birds

The Salle Mandement contains the remains of animals (mainly mammoth and bear), coated in rubble and doubtless reduced to a heap of bones by subterranean flooding (the Arize, which was 10 times the volume that it is today, made the water level reach the roof).

Musée de la Préhistoire

🕐 *Jul and Aug: 11am-1pm, 2-7pm; Apr-Jun and Sep: daily except Mon 2-6pm; Mar, Oct and Nov: Sun and public holidays 2-6pm.* 🕐 *Closed 1 Jan and 25 Dec.* ☜ *4.60€ (children: 2.30€).* ☎ *05 61 69 97 22.*

This prehistory museum contains collections from the Magdalenian period, particularly the famous carving of a fawn with birds (*Faon aux oiseaux*).

MAZAMET

POPULATION 11,259

MICHELIN LOCAL MAP 338: G-10

Situated at the foot of the Montagne Noire, Mazamet is still thriving on the wool industry which brought prosperity to the area in the 18C. Specialising in the "pulled wool" technique, the town is also renowned for tawing the pelts once the wool has been removed. Today, sheepskins are mainly imported from Australia, South Africa and Argentina, wool is exported to Italy and skins to Spain, Belgium, Italy and the USA. ▯ *R. des Casernes, 81200 Mazamet.* ☎ *05 63 61 27 07. www.ville-mazamet.com.*

A Bit of History

Hilltop village – In the 5C, the Visigoths built **Hautpoul** clinging to a hilltop site to protect it from would-be attackers. Nonetheless, Simon de Montfort managed to storm the stronghold in 1212 and the Wars of Religion finished off what he left standing. In the valley below, the textile industry expanded, thanks to the supply of pure water from the Arnette ideal for washing wool. With the advent of machinery, the river was harnessed to provide the necessary power to drive it. The inhabitants of Hautpoul were thus persuaded to abandon their hilltop site to found Mazamet.

Centre of the wool industry – With the neighbouring plains producing valuable dyestuffs such as woad, madder and saffron, the nearby Montagne Noire specialising in sheep rearing, and the Arnette and Thoré providing an abundant supply of water, it is hardly surprising that Mazamet had become a major centre for the wool industry by the 18C. In 1851, the company of Houlès Père et Fils et Cormouls imported sheepskins from Buenos Aires and stripped them of their wool. This opened up a new branch of the industry for obtaining "pulled wool": wool is loosened (with soft water or chemical products) and removed from sheep's pelts (as opposed to wool obtained from fleeces sheared off living animals) and cleaned, then handed over to the textile industry for carding, combing, spinning and weaving; the sheepskins are sent to be dressed in the mégisseries or tawing workshops. Two marked trails *"Mazamet au fil de la laine"* start from the tourist office or the public park.

Visit

Maison Fuzier

🕐 *Jul and Aug: 9am-12.30pm, 2-7pm, Sun and public holidays 10.30am-12.30pm; Apr-Jun and Sep: daily except Sun and Public holidays 9am-noon, 1.30-7pm; rest of the year: daily except Sun and public holidays 9am-noon, 1.30-6.30pm.* 🕐 *Closed 1 Jan, Easter Monday, 1 and 8 May, Pentecost Mon, Ascension, 25 Dec. No charge.* ☎ *05 63 61 27 07.*

Situated in the town centre, this building houses the tourist office and a **museum on the Cathars**, retracing the history of Catharism and of the ruined castles which abound in this region. The museum also has an exhibition on the various types of local burial procedure dating back to earliest times.

Église du Sacré Cœur de Bonnecousse

Access via avenue Jean-Mermoz, heading towards Toulouse. Just north-west of Mazamet, in Aussillon-Plaine, stands the church of Sacré-Cœur, built in 1959 (lead statue of the Virgin and Child; sanctuary tapestry woven by Simone Prouvé; Dom Ephrem stained-glass window in baptistery).

Excursions

Hautpoul

4km/2.5mi S along D 54 then the first road on the right. Built on a spur which bears the ruins of its castle and church, this hamlet was the original site of Mazamet. Its setting, directly above the **Gorges de l'Arnette**, dotted with factories specialising in loosening wool from sheepskins, offers an attractive **view**★ of Mazamet and the Thoré Valley.

The **Maison du Bois et du Jouet** (🕐 *Jul and Aug: 2-7pm; mid-late Jun and early-mid Sep: daily except Mon 2-6pm; early Mar-mid Jun and mid-Sep-late Dec: Wed, Sat-Sun and school holidays 2-6pm.* 🕐 *Closed 1 Jan, 25 Dec.* 🎟️ *5€ (4-14 years: 3€).* ☎ *05 63 61 42 70.)* (a craft centre) will be appreciated by adults and children alike.

Lac des Montagnès

6km/3.7mi S along D 118. Set against a backdrop of hills and woodland, this beautiful man-made lake, the reservoir which supplies Mazamet with water, is popular with anglers, swimmers and walkers.

Causse MÉJEAN★

MICHELIN MAP 330: H-9 TO I-9

This is the "middle" plateau hence its name. The Tarn gorge separates it from the Causse de Sauveterre. The Causse Méjean is the highest of the plateaux, and its climate is particularly harsh. Winters are freezing cold, summers are scorching, and there are huge differences in temperature between day and night.

A. Cassaigne/MICHELIN

Causse Méjean

Geographical Notes

The plateau is a combination of dolomite and outcrops of pure limestone, in varying degrees of thickness. In the shallow depressions known as sotchs, where the decalcification of the rock has led to an accumulation of red earth, meadows and fields produce high yields. Numerous megaliths indicate that Stone Age people had adapted very well to local conditions.

The Causse Méjean has a very low population density. To the east, the landscape

> **COUNTING SHEEP**
>
> 🍴 **Auberge du Chanet** – *Hameau de Nivoliers - 48150 Hures-la-Parade - ☎ 04 66 45 65 12 - lechanet@cevennes.com – closed 20 Nov-25 Mar.* This old sheep farm at the heart of the causse is an oasis of peace and quiet. Traditional cuisine is served in the shelter of the vaulted dining room or in the sun on the terrace. Several accommodation options, from rooms to dormitories.

stretches vast and arid; to the west, like the Causse de Sauveterre, wooded plateaux are interspersed with ravines several hundred feet deep. The Causse Méjean is sheep (*brebis*) country and it is not unusual to come across flocks of more than 300. The dolomitic limestone landscape, not unlike a rabbit warren, is also dotted with collections of ruin-shaped rocks. Local people have left areas such as these to game and coniferous forests.

The griffon vulture, a species not seen in the region for some 50 years, was re-introduced to the area in 1970. Przewalski horses (the last surviving wild horse subspecies), which were threatened with extinction, have also been seen wild in the region recently.

Excursion

Round trip 87km/54mi starting from Florac – allow 3hrs.

▷ *Leave Florac W along D 16 (Causse Méjean is signposted in town) then turn left onto D 63.*

At the intersection of these two roads, the landscape is totally barren except for an airport and a gliding base. Farther on, D 63 runs through the hamlet of Le Villaret where a stud farm breeds Przewalski horses and these small wild animals, originally from Mongolia, can be seen galloping across the nearby fields.

Aven Armand★★★ – 👟 See AVEN ARMAND.

Hyelzas, a traditional Causses farmstead

🕐 *Jul and Aug: 10am-7pm; Apr-Jun, Sep and Oct: 10am-noon, 2-6pm.* 🕐 *Closed public holidays and from Toussaint to Easter.* 🎫 *4.80€.* ☎ *04 66 45 65 25. www.ferme-caussenarde.com*

This restored farmhouse is an excellent example of the traditional architecture of the Causses. The farmstead is built of drystone and consists of several buildings linked by flights of steps on the outside. The cowshed is on the ground floor. The upper vaulting supports a heavy roof of limestone slabs.

Birdlife

A great variety of birdlife is to be found inhabiting the dolomitic limestone scenery, coniferous woodland and vast empty spaces of the Causse Méjean: the rock thrush, the red-legged partridge, the jackdaw and, in winter, the alpine accentor and the snow finch. Birds of prey include the short-toed eagle, the golden eagle, the peregrine falcon, the kestrel, the hen harrier (or marsh hawk) and the griffon vulture, whose recent reintroduction into the area has been accompanied by the setting up of protected nesting sites mainly in the Jonte gorge, around the village of Le Truel.

The interior of the farmhouse is open to the public. The rooms are stone-flagged and the cows in the cowshed below provided the only source of heat. The tank in the scullery serves as a reminder of the importance of water in an area where it is in such short supply. The furniture and utensils have been returned to their original places. A shed contains farm machinery that shows the major stages in the development of agriculture.

An exhibition displays models of local monuments (Meyrueis clock tower, Millau bridge and old mill) and of traditional stone dwellings (Causses farmsteads, Lozère houses).

▶ *Return to the D 986 intersection and turn right.*

Meyrueis – 🖼 *See MEYRUEIS.*

▶ *Follow D 996 towards Florac.*

There is a striking contrast between the barren Causse Méjean (*on the left*) and the forested Aigoual massif *(on the right)*.

▶ *Turn left when you reach Col de Perjuret.*

Chaos de Nîmes-le-Vieux★

▶ *From the pass, head either towards Veygalier or to l'Hom or Gally; park the car. This walk is not recommended in rainy and foggy weather or when the wind blows hard in winter as the outside temperature may then fall to -15°C.*

Seen from a distance, the Chaos de Nîmes-le-vieux rises like a ruined city from the bare expanse of the Causse Méjean. It is said that during the Wars of Religion, the royal armies in pursuit of Protestants were sadly disappointed on their arrival here, having thought that they had at last reached their goal, "Nîmes."

From Veygalier

🕐 Apr-Sep: guided tours from Veygalier, unaccompanied tours from Hom or Gally starting points. 1.22€ guided tours (ticket combined with the small museum). In Veygalier, an attractive village typical of the causse, a house has been converted to display an exhibition on the geology of the *causse*.

From here a trail leads off through "streets" of stone overlooked by strangely shaped rock formations 10-50m/30-160ft high. From the hill above Veygalier, there are fine views over the cirque bristling with dolomitic rocks, where the stone houses blend in with their curious surroundings.

From l'Hom or Gally

1hr 30min on foot from Gally to Veygalier.

An interesting discovery trail has been laid by the Parc national des Cévennes. The different "explanation tables" enable visitors to appreciate the originality of this natural environment so typical of the Causses.

▶ *Drive back to Florac along D 907.*

Hiking Tours

Corniches du Causse Méjean★★★

Hiking tour from Le Rozier – allow 7hrs. This remarkably well laid out and well-maintained footpath should present few difficulties, although there are one or two particularly spectacular clifftop passages which require great care; the path is slippery in wet or cold weather and crowded in July and August. Wear hiking shoes and take enough food and water for one day.

▶ *Behind the church in Le Rozier, take the footpath which leads off from the junction of two roads (GR 6A waymarked in red and white).*

Half an hour's climb brings hikers to the pretty little hamlet of **Capluc**, now deserted.

Rocher de Capluc

Not recommended to those who suffer from vertigo. Bear left towards Capluc rock, easily identified by the metal cross on top of it. The rock forms the far end of a promontory on the south-west edge of the Causse Méjean. At the top of a flight of stone steps, to the right, there is a house leaning against the rock face. Take a metal ramp and another flight of stone steps up to the terrace around the rock. From here there is a dizzying climb to the summit of the rock up metal ladders. But the reward at the top is an exhilarating view plunging down to Peyreleau and the confluence of the River Jonte and River Tarn. Opposite, there is a fine view of the villages of Liaucous and Mostuéjouls perched high on the cliff.

▶ *Return to Capluc.*

Climb to the Col de Francbouteille

Corniches du Causse Méjean

200m/220yd past the hamlet of Capluc, there are two ways of reaching the Francbouteille Pass.

The path known as the "Ravin des Echos" (*accessible to all capabilities*), which runs along a section of the GR 6A footpath, winds gently uphill, offering fine views of the causse.

The Jacques-Brunet path (*steep, with vertiginous sections*), which is reached up a flight of steps, climbs through juniper bushes, boxwood and pine. It threads its way between little chimneys, reaches the top of a crest from which there is a magnificent view of the Tarn and Jonte canyons, then carries on along the slope overlooking the Tarn. It

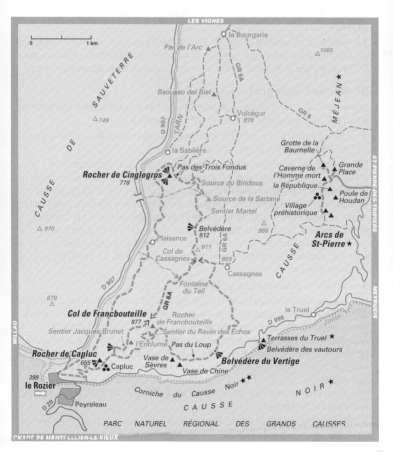

skirts the "Enclume" (Anvil) standing detached from the magnificent surrounding rock walls. After a passage through cool undergrowth from which there are numerous views of the Tarn Valley, the path reaches the pass.

Col de Francbouteille

This pass is still also known as the "pass of the two canyons." It is marked by a stele dedicated to the Club Alpin. The Francbouteille rock looms, to the right, like the prow of a colossal ship.

▷ *Follow the arrows to the GR 6A footpath.*

Soon, Teil spring comes into view on the left. Springs are few and far between on the plateau of the Causse Méjean, and this one is much appreciated by hikers.

▷ *At the Col de Cassagnes, leave the Martel footpath leading to Cinglegros rock (⟳ see below) to the left, and bear right towards the isolated village of Cassagnes.*

The footpath crosses the causse; only the cry of the griffon vulture, recently reintroduced to the Causse Méjean, breaks the monotonous silence. Leave a pine plantation to the right to follow the footpath along the cliffs overlooking the Jonte gorge.

Belvédère du Vertige

After about an hour's walk, there is a look-out point with a protective handrail, which gives an impressive view over the Jonte canyon, with the river flowing more than 400m/1 300ft below. A short distance upstream, the viewpoints called the "Terrasses" can be seen far below as pinpricks beside the valley road. In the foreground, an enormous rock stands completely detached from the cliff.

The footpath runs in front of a cave, once used as a sheep pen, then between two natural bridges. The steep descent, barred in the middle by a grille to stop the sheep from leaping into the ravine, is called **Pas du Loup** ("wolf's tread"). Immediately after negotiating this, two enormous monoliths – the **Vase de Chine**, at the mouth of the ravine, and then the **Vase de Sèvres** – come into sight, an incalculable reward for all the effort spent trying to reach them. In the distance, Peyreleau and Le Rozier, Capluc rock, and the cliffs of the Causse Noir above the south bank of the Jonte can be seen.

▷ *Return to the footpath which drops downhill amid a group of extraordinarily jagged dolomitic rocks. Leave the footpath to the Col de Francbouteille to the right, and return to Capluc and Le Rozier along the Ravin des Echos and Brèche Magnifique paths.*

Rocher de Cinglegros

Hiking tour from Le Rozier – allow one day. 🏃 *This hike is recommended only for those who are fit and nimble, and who do not suffer from vertigo.*

▷ *Follow the route of the Corniches du Causse Méjean described above as far as the Col de Cassagnes, then turn left to Cinglegros rock.*

This well laid out path offers excellent views of the cliffs overhanging the west bank of the Tarn opposite. After about a 20min walk, a natural **look-out point** made of rocks provides a view down into an impressive ravine. Then, the footpath reaches the source of the Sartane (sometimes dried up), and immediately after this it gets wider. Again, to the left of the path, there is a small spring – the source of the Bindous.

At the next fork, leave the path to Volcégure to the right to take the path to the left through the undergrowth, towards the Pas des Trois Fondus. Before long, a stretch of path leads downhill to a terrace, from which there is a gratifying view of the Cinglegros gap.

▷ *Take the steep path downhill to the left.*

The **Pas des Trois Fondus** leads down to the floor of the ravine where Cinglegros stands in splendid isolation. First there are two metal ladders, followed by a series of cramp-irons fixed into the rock face, and finally some steps cut into the rock.

A footpath leads through the undergrowth to the foot of the rock. The aids installed for climbing to the summit are very well maintained, and the ascent is most impressive. It is made up of nine metal ladders with six handrails, steps cut into the rock face and cramp-irons fixed to the rock in between. Once at the summit, relax and take a well-earned leisurely stroll on the terrace, from which there is an incomparable view over the Tarn gorges.

▷ *Return to base along a footpath leading down to the hamlet of Plaisance, then to Le Rozier on the path to La Sablière.*

Arcs de St-Pierre

1hr 30min on foot there and back.
There are two possible ways to get to the
Arcs de St-Pierre.

▷ *Either via D 63 which branches off D 986*
at Hures-la-Parade; after 3km/2mi,
take the little road on the right to St-
Pierre-des-Tripiers; 1km/0.6mi past
this village, take the small unsurfaced
road, again to the right, opposite the
junction for La Viale.

▷ *Or up the steep, narrow hairpin road*
branching off D 996 from Le Truel
towards St-Pierre-des-Tripiers, in the
Jonte Valley. Level with the junction
for La Viale, take the small unsurfaced
road to the left.

Arcs de St-Pierre

The "Arcs de St-Pierre" is a mass of eroded rock formations resembling ruins.

🚶 Take the footpath downhill (*waymarked in red*) to the **Grande Place**. In the middle of this rocky amphitheatre stands a 10m/32ft-high monolithic column. The footpath climbs to the left, up to the cave of **La Baumelle**.

Drystone walls, which for a long time were maintained by shepherds who brought their sheep here, can still be seen.

After returning to the Grande Place, follow the waymarked path leading from it to the Caverne de l'Homme mort ("Dead Man's Cave"); 50 skeletons similar to that of Cro-Magnon man were discovered here; most of them had had their skulls operated on with flint.

Farther along, on the left, huge boulders come into sight with shapes that have earned them evocative names such as **Poule de Houdan** ("Houdan's hen") or **La République** (looking for all the world as if it is wearing the Republicans' cap of liberty). The path bends to the left and, after about 300m/330yd, leads to the site of a **prehistoric village** of which only sections of ruined walls are left, some of them half buried. The cavities still visible in the rock face have been identified by historians as notches for fixing roof beams.

Finally the path arrives at the **Arcs de St-Pierre**, three natural arches, the first of which, with its overhanging spur, is regarded as one of the finest in the Causses. The second, very regular, opens out onto a space wooded with slender pine trees soaring towards the light. Some of them have been bent or broken by wind or rough weather, since the soil on the Causse Méjean is never very deep. The third arch has a huge vault.

MENDE ★

POPULATION 11,804

MICHELIN MAP 330: J-7

ALSO SEE MONT LOZÈRE

Mende, the capital of the least populated of all French *départements*, the Lozère, is a large rural market town dominated by an imposing cathedral inside a circle of boulevards. Its narrow winding streets are lined with lovely old houses with, here and there, a beautiful timber door, a portal or oratories. Mende's administrative, educational and commercial roles have stimulated a certain degree of development in recent years. ⓘ *Pl. du Gén.-de-Gaulle, 48000 Mende, ☎ 04 66 49 40 24.*

A Bit of History

Beautiful mansions already graced the north bank of the Lot as early as Roman times. In the 3C, St Privat, who converted the Gévaudan, sought refuge from the Barbarians in a cave on Mont Mimat. He was captured and killed however. The cave he had lived in and the crypt where he was buried became very popular centres of pilgrimage, around which the town developed over the centuries.

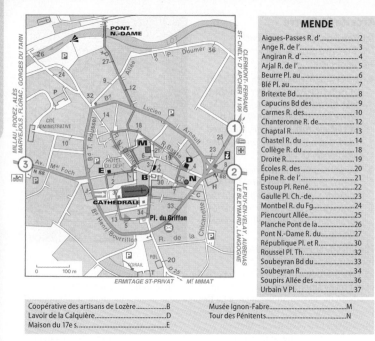

During the Wars of Religion, a particularly gruesome episode in the history of Mende occurred when Captain **Merle**, a fanatical Protestant, attacked the town on Christmas Eve in 1579, while all the inhabitants, including those defending the town, were in church celebrating Christ's birth. A few months later, the Roman Catholics, seeking to reclaim their home town, laid siege to Mende, but Captain Merle, something of an expert at nocturnal attacks, had them all cut to pieces during their sleep. Merle was not without enemies in his own camp, however, and another Protestant leader, Châtillon, took advantage of Merle's absence to seize Mende. Merle managed to recapture the town nonetheless and was appointed governor of it by the future Henri IV.

Town Walk

Cathedral★

Several churches predated the present cathedral, most of which was built in the 14C under Pope Urban V. The belfries date from the 16C. When Captain Merle seized Mende in 1579, he had the cathedral pillars blown up, leaving only the belfries, the north side walls and the apsidal chapels. The cathedral was restored in the early 17C.

Exterior – The west façade, in front of which is a porch built in 1900 in the Flamboyant style, is framed by two belfries. That on the left, the "Clocher de l'Évêque" ("Bishop's Belfry"), has a fine colonnade at the top which seems to have been inspired by the Italian Renaissance and contrasts strongly with the soberness of the belfry on the right, known as the "Clocher des Chanoines" ("Canons' Belfry").

Interior – Side doors lead into the cathedral which has three naves flanked by 15 side chapels.

The remains of the rood screen currently adorn the baptismal chapel (*second side chapel to the north*). The woodwork of the upper and lower chancel stalls, on either side of the bishop's throne, date from the same period (1692). They depict themes from religious history and various scenes from the Life of Christ.

Above the tall stained-glass windows in the chancel, eight Aubusson tapestries (1708) illustrate the main scenes from the Life of the Virgin Mary.

On either side of the high altar stand large candelabra in carved wood dating from the 16C. The Lady Chapel (*by the sacristy*), dedicated to Our Lady of Mende, houses the 11C carved Black Virgin which the Crusaders are said to have brought back from the Orient where Mount Carmel monks are reputed to have carved it out of very hard wood.

Mende Cathedral once had the largest bell in Christianity, the "Non Pareille" ("Unequalled"), weighing 20t. Broken by Merle's men in 1579, all that remains is the enormous clapper, 2.15m/7ft long, which is to be found under the 17C organ, next to the door of the bishop's belfry.

Under the nave are the tomb and crypt of St Privat (*light switch on the left as you go down*).

▶ *Take rue de l'Arjal, to the right of the cathedral.*

The street leads to **place Griffon** equipped with a fountain once used to clean the streets.

▶ *Turn left onto rue du Soubeyran then right onto rue de la Jarretière (opposite the east end of the cathedral) which leads to place au Blé.*

Tour des Pénitents

Remaining tower from the 12C fortified town wall which stood where the modern boulevards are.

▶ *Return to place au Blé and follow rue Charlier-Hugonnet on the right side of the covered market. Continue along rue Basse on the left.*

On the corner of rue Basse and rue d'Angiran stands the **Lavoir de la Calquière** (wash-house): it was used in the past for cleaning sheepskins with lime, hence its name.

▶ *Walk up rue Basse. Beyond place du Mazel, turn right onto rue du Chou-Vert then take rue de Chanteronne across the boulevard.*

Pont Notre-Dame

A. Thuillier/MICHELIN

Pont Notre-Dame★

This very narrow bridge, built in the 13C, has always managed to withstand the heavy flooding of the Lot, because of the width of its main arch.

▷ *Turn back; at the end of rue du Chou-Vert, turn right onto rue du Collège then left along rue Notre-Dame. In place René-Estoup, turn right onto rue d'Aigues-Passes.*

Note the **17C house** (no 7) with its windows decorated with fake balusters. The Pietà is a reminder of a bread-blessing procession which once took place here.

▷ *Return to place Urbain-V along rue de l'Ormeau on the left.*

MEYRUEIS

MICHELIN LOCAL MAP 330: I-9

This small town on the confluence of the rivers Bétuzon, Brèze and Jonte perches at the mouth of the River Jonte gorge, where the Causse Noir, the Causse Méjean and the Aigoual massif all converge. Its clear mountain air (due to its altitude of 706m/2 316ft) and the many and varied attractions which surround it make the town a popular holiday destination. *Tour de l'Horloge, 48150 Meyrueis, ☎ 04 66 45 60 33. www.meyrueis.office.tourism.com.*

Town Walk

While strolling along quai Sully beneath the plane trees by the river bank and exploring the network of smaller streets, look out for the Maison Belon, with its elegant Renaissance windows, and the **Tour de l'Horloge**, a clock tower once part of the town's fortifications.

Excursions

▷ *Drive out of town on D 986 and soon after leaving Meyrueis take a small road on the left as far as a car park. A 15min walk along a forest path brings you to the castle.*

Château de Roquedols

🕐 *Jul and Aug: daily except Sun and Mon, 10am-1pm. No charge. ☎ 04 66 45 62 81. 2km/1.2mi S.*

The massive 15C-16C square castle is flanked by four round towers. The pink and ochre tones of the stone stand out against the green backdrop of the Bétuzon Valley. Inside, there is a lovely Renaissance staircase and some fine antique furniture, as well as old horse-drawn carriages and a model of Mont Aigoual. The château is the property of the Parc national des Cévennes and houses an **information centre** overlooking the main courtyard.

Aven Armand★★★

11km/6.8mi then 45min tour. Leave Meyrueis N along D 986; the road leading to the underground chasm branches off 9.5km/6mi farther on. 🖇 See AVEN ARMAND.

Grotte de Dargilan★★

8.5km/5.3mi then 1hr tour. Drive 7km/4.3mi W along D 39 and turn onto D 139. 🖇 See Grotte de DARGILAN.

Gorges de la Jonte

Massif de l'Aigoual★★★ – ♿ See Massif de l'AIGOUAL.

Gorges de la Jonte★★

21km/13mi from Meyrueis to Le Rozier – allow 1hr. We recommend the route described below driving down along D 996 from Meyrueis to Le Rozier, rather than up the gorge, since the canyon becomes increasingly impressive as it nears the confluence of the Jonte and the Tarn.

The Jonte gorge can also be visited on foot along the clifftop footpaths over the Causse Méjean (♿ see Causse MÉJEAN) and the Causse Noir (♿ see Causse NOIR).

Downstream from Meyrueis, the road along the Jonte gorge follows the river's north bank all the way. The sides of the gorge are crowned with tall limestone cliffs worn into bizarre formations by erosion.

Some 5km/3mi from Meyrueis, the mouths of two caves in the Causse Méjean can be seen opening into the cliff on the right – the **Grotte de la Vigne** and the **Grotte de la Chèvre** Beyond the caves, the gorge becomes narrower and, in summer months, the Jonte disappears into the crevices along the river bed.

On the outskirts of the hamlet of Les Douzes, the river reappears after flowing for some distance underground. Here it enters a second gorge which is so deep that the huge poplar trees growing in it are scarcely visible.

The huge isolated **Roc St-Gervais** towering over the hamlet of Les Douzes is topped by the Romanesque chapel of St-Gervais.

Arcs de St-Pierre★ – *4.5km/3mi then 1hr 30min on foot there and back.*
Leave from Le Truel. ♿ See Causse MÉJEAN.

Le Belvédère des vautours
♿⏱☞ *Mid-Jun to late Aug: part guided visit (1hr) and part unaccompanied, 10am-7pm; mid-Mar to mid-Jun and early Sep to mid-Nov: 10am-6pm. Last entry 1hr before closing. ♾ 6.50€ (children: 3€). ☏ 05 65 62 69 69. www.vautours-lozere.com. 1.5km/1mi downstream from Le Truel.*

Vultures were reintroduced into the area in 1970; this exhibition tells you all about their way of life, feeding habits etc and it is even possible to watch these wild birds at close range on a giant screen, via a camera.

There is an observation platform at the viewpoint that affords a superb view of the Jonte gorge. The sides of the gorge consist of two levels of limestone cliffs separated by marl slopes. These are known as the **Terrasses du Truel**★.

On the rim of the cliffs on the edge of the Causse Méjean stands a most unusual, vase-shaped boulder called the "Vase de Sèvres."

The road comes into sight of the Capluc rock, to the right, followed by the village of Peyreleau, to the left, and finally the village of Le Rozier.

Le Rozier – ♿ See Gorges du TARN.

Canal du MIDI★

MICHELIN LOCAL MAP 343: H-4 TO I-4, J-5 TO K-5, 334: A-1 TO K-3 AND 339: A-9 TO F-9

Today's tourists who seek the calm and beauty of the Canal du Midi may find it hard to imagine that the Seuil de Naurouze (alt 194m/636ft) represented a major obstacle for civil engineers prior to Riquet, trying to design a canal linking the Atlantic and the Mediterranean. ⊡ www.canalmidi.com, or www.canaldumidi.fr.

A Bit of History

The idea of building such a canal dates back to the Romans. François I, Henri IV and Richelieu all commissioned studies to this end, none of which bore fruit. Finally **Pierre-Paul Riquet**, Baron of Bonrepos (1604-80) and state tax-farmer for Languedoc, successfully carried out the project, at his own expense. The construction of the port at Sète in Riquet's lifetime, and the opening of the canal from the Rhône to Sète and of the Garonne lateral canal in the 19C crowned his efforts.

A solo achievement – When the construction of a canal linking "the two seas" was first dreamt of, the Seuil de Naurouze was an insurmountable obstacle. After meticulously studying the site, Riquet, a man of imagination, found a solution: the Seuil de Naurouze was the site of a spring – the Fontaine de la Grave (no longer extant after the construction work) – whose waters divided into two streams, one flowing west and the other east; all that would be necessary would be to increase the flow of this spring in order to feed the canal and its locks on either side of the watershed. Riquet decided to tap the waters draining from the Montagne Noire. With the help of a hydraulic engineer from Revel, he harnessed the waters of the Alzeau, the Vernassonne, the Lampy and the Sor, directing them along two channels, the Rigole de la Montagne to the St-Ferréol reservoir, and then the Rigole de la Plaine to Naurouze.

In 1662, he succeeded in interesting Colbert in his project and was granted the necessary authorisation for it in 1666. Over a period of 14 years, 10 000-12 000 workmen were employed. Into this massive undertaking, Riquet sank money representing a third of the total cost of the project, namely 5 million livres, burdening himself with debts and sacrificing his daughters' dowries. He died exhausted in 1680, six months before the opening of the Canal du Midi. Under the Restoration his descendants regained their rights to a share of the profit from the canal and in 1897 they agreed to sell the canal to the State. Since that time it has been administered as a public enterprise.

Heritage and future projects – Riquet's 240km/150mi-long canal begins at Toulouse at the Port de l'Embouchure, the end of the Garonne lateral canal and runs into the Thau lagoon, at the Port des Onglous. It incorporates 91 locks, but there is a reach of 54km/33.5mi (a day's journey by boat) between Argens-Minervois and Béziers.

Commercial traffic no longer uses the canal, since its locks, which at the time were designed for the ships most commonly in use on the Mediterranean, cannot accommodate any vessel longer than 30m/98ft. Modernisation of the canal began on the section between Toulouse and Villefranche-de-Lauragais (43km/26.5mi). This historic canal follows a most attractive course, with numerous tight bends, locks with oval or round basins, elegant brick bridges, and reaches of water bordered, on the Mediterranean slopes, with plane trees, cypresses and umbrella pines.

After a century of decline, passenger traffic, which before the age of the railway was transported by light "stage boats" travelling at 11kph/7mph, has been picking up with the advent of riverboat tourism – numerous companies for hiring houseboats and or going on river cruises have been set up.

The Essential Canal

The Canal du Midi can be considered as a whole, comprising the waterway itself, as well as the landscape and engineering that go along with it, and the buildings that serve its operation.

Water feeds into the canal

There are several works that serve to bring water into the canal and make the flow regular.

Les rigoles – Water that is brought in from some distance from the watershed is carried by little canals known as *rigoles*. The Rigole de la Montagne ① feeds into the St-Ferréol basin.

Address Book

THE PRACTICAL CANAL

When to cruise along the canal – March to November is the best time. The peak season (July-August) engenders a few inconveniences: boats for hire are difficult to find, traffic through the locks is intense, prices are higher, etc. In May and June the banks of the canal are brightened up by irises and various water plants. In September and October, the weather is often quite settled, temperatures are mild and the countryside puts on the most beautiful russet mantle.

Locks operate between June and August from 9am-12.30pm and 1.30-7.30pm. Some of them operate automatically, others manually (average time: 15min).

Hiring a boat – No licence is needed; instruction is usually provided by the boat-hire company just before departure. Maximum speed allowed: 6kph/3.7mph. Boats can be hired for a week or a weekend, for a single journey only (if the company has several hiring points along the way) or for a return trip. If you wish to go cruising during the summer, book well in advance, if possible apply directly to your departure point.

Bikes are very useful to have on board if you wish to make the occasional excursion (some boat-hire companies also hire bikes).

For addresses of boat-hire companies, consult the *Planning Your Trip* section at the beginning of the guide.

What to take on board – Non-slippery shoes, a torch to find your way back at night, fishing tackle (it is compulsory to have a licence), suitable maps and guides, sold by boat-hire companies or available from:

Boat trips – Trips along the length of the Canal du Midi, lasting from 2 to 6hr, with or without lunch, are organised by several companies:

Béziers Croisières, BP 4052, 34545 Béziers Cedex, ☎ 04 67 49 08 23, offer cruises between Béziers and Poilhès; timetable, prices and bookings by phone.

Croisières du Midi, 35 quai des Tonneliers, BP 2, 11200 Homps, ☎ 04 68 91 33 00, 10€ (children 5.50€) offer trips aboard traditional *gabares*, starting from Homps, from late March to the end of October. Bookings essential.

On dry land – You may also visit the canal on foot or bicycle, along the 49km/30mi of towpath developed for such outings.

For coin categories, see the Legend at the back of the guide.

EATING OUT

◙◙ **Le Relais de Riquet** – *12 Espl. du Canal - 11320 Le Ségala - 10km/6.2mi W of Castelnaudary by N 113 then D 217 -* ☎ *04 68 60 16 87 - closed Mon.* You won't regret a mealtime halt at this retro-style bar/restaurant just steps from the canal. Try the house cassoulet.

◙◙ **Ferme-auberge du Pigné** – *11150 Bram/1.2mi SE of Bram toward Montréal -* ☎ *04 68 76 10 25/06 85 40 01 99 - reservations required.* This pretty farmhouse sits amid a vast farming property; the dining room occupies an outbuilding, and features a terrace overlooking a tree-filled garden. Dishes incorporate ingredients raised on site, plus housemade charcuterie and desserts.

WHERE TO STAY

◙◙ **Chambre d'hôte Bernard Fouissac** – *La Bastide-Vieille - 34310 Capestang - 13km/8mi W of Béziers on the Rte. de Castres by D 39 -* ☎ *04 67 93 46 23 - closed 1 Nov-1 Mar -* ⚘ *- 3 rooms - meals* ◙◙. Large, comfortable guest rooms outfitted in the structures of this 12C *bastide* among the vines. Idle away a few hours in the lovely library/salon. Meals are served in the former baking-room.

◙◙ **Chambre d'hôte Le Liet** – *11610 Pennautier - 5km/3.1mi NW of Carcassonne by N 113 then D 203 -* ☎ *04 68 11 19 19 - chateauleliet@francemultimédia.fr - closed Nov-Feb - 6 rooms and 4 self-catering cottages.* This 19C château sits in a wooded park blessed with varied plant and animal life. Rooms and suites look out into an unspoilt natural landscape; several have balconies. Magnificent breakfast-room.

◙◙ **Chambre d'hôte Abbaye de Villelongue** – *11170 St-Martin-le-Vieil - 5km/3.1mi NE of St-Martin-le-Vieil by D 64 -* ☎ *04 68 76 92 58 - closed late Oct -* ⚘ *- 4 rooms.* Silence and solemnity at this former cistercian abbey from the 12C, but the comfort is anything but monk-like: lovely antiques, private bathrooms, luxurious beds. Windows open onto a ravishing cloister and its pretty garden where breakfast is served in fine weather.

SHOPPING

Coopérative L'Oulibo – *Hameau de Cabezac - 11120 Bize-Minervois -* ☎ *04 68 41 88 88 - www.loulibo.com - winter: Mon-Fri 8am-noon, 2-6pm; summer: Mon-Fri 8am-noon, 2-7pm (Sat 9am and Sun 10am). closed Christmas and New Years.* Olive oil and olives, plus fine regional products including honey, wine, sweets, jams, crafts, etc. Free guided tours in summer.

Gailhousty

Reservoirs and basins – To collect water, artificial lakes were created, such as the one at Narouze, and reservoirs held back by dams, such as the one at St-Ferréol. Reservoirs provide water to the canal during dry periods. The Canal du Midi is located at a watershed: from the Narouze basin, water flows towards the Atlantic on the one side, and the Mediterranean on the other.

Spillways – These serve to evacuate overflow when the canal has too much water in it at certain times of year, or, when it is necessary, to empty a basin or reservoir to clear it out and make repairs or improvements. Located right at the high water level, spillways are generally made of cement, and provide a sloping surface down to a river or stream. In cases where this surface cuts across the tow path, a bridge is built above it, such as the one at Argent-Double ②. Another system in use empties out overflow from the bottom of the canal, by way of a sluice gate, as at Gailhousty; a combination of the two systems is used in a siphon spillway at Ventenac-en-Minervois.

Crossings

There are crossings that allow the canal to go over or around obstacles, and others that allow pedestrians or vehicles to go over the canal.

Aqueducts and Canal-bridges ③ – To cross a stream, the canal uses a vaulted aqueduct. To cross a river, a canal-bridge works better. The first such bridge ever built in Europe is the one at Répudre; there are others which cross over the River Cesse, River Fresquel and River Orbiel.

Underground passages – The canal goes underground to get through a mountain or hillside without raising its level. Examples are the tunnel at Malpas, near Ensérune, and the Cammazes *percée*, dug through the Montagne Noire, and allowing the water from the Montagne stream to feed into the St-Ferréol basin.

Bridges – There are many bridges that make it possible for people and vehicles to cross the canal. Most of them are made of stone, with flattened vaulting and curved parapets.

Locks ⑤

The use of locks makes it possible to pass from one reach of water to another, when each is at a different level. The boat that is travelling downstream enters into a lock which is full of water. The upstream gate then closes behind the boat and water is released so that the level lowers down to the level of the reach below. The downstream gate is then opened, and the boat passes through. The locks on the Canal du Midi are oval in form, to create better resistance to the pressure of the land mass. The first lock of this shape was built at Négra.

Stair-step locks – Made up of several locks, these are used to go up or down steep inclines. At St-Roch, outside Castelnaudary, there are four locks; at Fonséranes, there are eight.

Canal architecture

Around the canal, there are a number of buildings which were put up to house engineers and workers, or lock-keepers, as well as buildings necessary for technical and administrative tasks. Of course, there are also inns and mills set up along its banks.

Lock-keepers' houses ⑥ – On any canal, the lock-keeper's house will be a reflection of traditional regional architecture. Along the Canal du Midi, these houses are rectangular, with one or two rooms on the ground floor. The façade bears a plaque which indicates the distance separating the lock from the nearest locks upstream and downstream.

Ports – Ports are necessary to the operation of the canal. There is usually a stone pier, and often an inn. In the past, of course, there were stables for the draught-horses, a wash-house, a chapel and sometimes an ice house, as at Somail ⑦. Other ports offer dry docks for repairing boats; there is still one at Port St-Sauveur in Toulouse. Such ports require a lot of space, and create small harbours, such as the one at Castelnaudary.

Vegetation

All along its length, the canal is lined with great trees which are an integral part of its image. In addition to providing pleasant shade and beauty, they also have an effect of limiting the evaporation of canal water. Most of the species are fast-growing ones, such as plane trees, poplars, and maritime pines. There is a special service responsible for their care and supervision. At some of the more significant points, such as Narouze, landscaping has been carried out extensively, adding yet more charm to this wonderful site, where man and nature create a special harmony.

Discovering the Canal

From Toulouse to the Seuil de Naurouze ①

45km/28mi along N 113; allow a few extra miles for detours – about 2hr.

This itinerary goes through a fertile agricultural region dotted with fine brick-built houses, churches with belfry-walls characteristic of the Toulouse Gothic style and castles testifying to the prosperity brought about by the production of dyer's woad (👁 *see ST-FÉLIX-LAURAGAIS: Dyer's woad country*). A waymarked cycle path runs along the canal.

Écluse d'Ayguesvives

This picturesque lock in the centre of a hamlet is one of several along the Canal du Midi. Note the old mill (1831) opposite the lock. Lying 1.5km/0.9mi south is the village of **Ayguesvives**. Note the brick-built Gothic church and the monumental brick gateway leading to the castle.

▷ *N 113 crosses the canal. In Avignonet-Lauragais, take D 80 towards Baraigne.*

Foriserone lock

J. Malburet/MICHELIN

Aire de Port Lauragais

The rest area along the A 61 motorway (*accessible from either direction*), halfway between Villefranche-de-Lauragais and Castelnaudary, is on the site of Port Lauragais on the Canal du Midi.

Situated at the end of a peninsula that juts out into Port Lauragais, a vast building houses shops and a cafeteria. Beneath the roof extension is a harbourmaster's office to welcome boats passing through. At the entrance, a fountain by sculptor Sylvain Brino depicts the water supply system of the canal and the functioning of its locks.

▶ *Return to Avignonet and continue E along N 113, soon turning off to Montferrand.*

Montferrand

This hilltop village (alt 300m/984ft) was the site of a Cathar fortress which fell in 1211; all that remains today is the fortified gate. Note the 16C belfry-wall of the deconsecrated church.

▶ *Go back to N 113 and cross over via D 218.*

Obelisque de Riquet

Leave the car in the parking area near the monument. The obelisk, built in 1825 by Riquet's descendants, stands in an enclosure on a natural pedestal formed by the "stones of Naurouze," between the Naurouze Pass (N 113) and the canal. It is surrounded by a double ring of fine, stately cedar trees. Local legend has it that when the cracks in the stones close up, society will sink into debauchery and the world will end. View of the Montferrand hill to the west.

▶ *Walk to the Seuil de Naurouze.*

Harnessed water ②

114km/70mi from the Prise d'Alzeau to the Seuil de Naurouze – allow 5hr.
This itinerary follows the water-supply system of the Canal du Midi.
Ⓖ *See MONTAGNE NOIRE.*

From the Seuil de Naurouze to Carcassonne

50km/31mi along N 113 – allow 1hr

From the watershed ridge, N 113 runs along the north bank of the canal all the way to Carcassonne.

Seuil de Naurouze★

This is where water harnessed in the Montagne Noire flows into the Mediterranean and Atlantic sections of the Canal du Midi.

Walk round the reservoir to the left. A pleasantly shaded path runs round the octagonal reservoir built between 1669 and 1673. The tour successively reveals the pumping station, the spillway evacuating overflow to the River Fresquel, the watershed reach, the lock which feeds water brought down by the Montagne Noire *rigole* (small canal) to the Canal du Midi and the Ocean lock (1671). The reservoir is surrounded by an arboretum planted with Aleppo pines, nettle trees, sycamores, North-African cedars, wild cherry trees etc.

▶ *Return to the parking area along an alleyway lined with plane trees.*

Castelnaudary

The town, famous for its *cassoulet* (a thick stew of haricot beans, sausages, mutton and/or preserved goose) is an excellent stop-over for anyone cruising along the Canal du Midi; the Grand Bassin, which offers plenty of mooring space, acts as a reservoir for the four St-Roch locks picturesquely situated at its eastern end. Standing on a hill overlooking the Lauragais plain, the restored 17C Moulin de Cugarel testifies to Castelnaudary's once important flour-milling activity.

Carcassonne – Ⓖ *See CARCASSONNE.*

From Carcassonne to Béziers

120km/75mi; allow a few extra miles for detours – half a day.

Between Carcassonne and Béziers, the Canal du Midi takes a more sinuous course as, for a major part of the way, it runs alongside the River Aude. D 610 follows the canal as far as Homps. Just beyond Homps, turn right onto D 124 which skirts the towpath.

🚶 *Leave the car in Roubia and walk along the towpath towards Ventenac (2.5km/1.5mi there and back).*

Pont-canal de Répudre

This is the first canal-bridge built in France by Riquet in 1676.

From the castle overlooking the village of Venténac-en-Minervois, there is a fine view of the canal and the surrounding plain.

▷ *Drive N along D 26.*

Ginestas

In this village surrounded by vineyards there is a dimly lit **church** (🕐 *9am-noon. Possibility of guided tours by request at the town hall.* ☎ *04 68 46 12 06.*) containing some fine works of art: a 17C altarpiece in gilded wood, the statue of Notre-Dame-des-Vals, a very simply made Virgin and Child and a 15C naïve polychrome statue of St Anne.

▷ *Drive E for 2km/1.2mi to Le Somail.*

Nine locks

Le Somail★

The Canal du Midi flows through this peaceful hamlet, which has retained its humpback bridge flanked by a chapel and its inn dating from 1773. There is also a **Musée de la Chapellerie** (Headdress Museum 🕐 *Jun-Sep: 9am-noon, 2-7pm, Sun and public holidays 2-6pm; Oct-May: 2-6pm. Guided tours available on request.* ☎ *3.20€.* ☎ *04 68 46 19 26.*): hats and headdresses from all over the world from 1885 to the present.

▷ *From Le Somail, drive N to join D 5.*

The road runs east to Béziers, following the canal part of the way. Alternatively, make a detour via the hilltop village of Quarante to the north.

▷ *In Capestang, take D 37 S to Nissan-lez-Ensérune. From there, the Oppidum d'Ensérune is signposted.*

Oppidum d'Ensérune★★ – See Oppidum d'ENSÉRUNE.

Nearby, the canal goes through the Malpas tunnel.

▷ *Continue to Colombiers, turn E onto D 162E then left onto N 9 and follow signposts to Écluses de Fonséranes.*

Écluses de Fonséranes★

A sequence of eight locks makes up a sort of 312m/338yd-long staircase, which enables river craft to negotiate a drop in level of 25m/81ft. Nowadays the locks have been replaced by a single lock, lying parallel to the original system.

Pont-canal de l'Orb

Access via the towpath downstream from the locks.

Since 1857, a canal-bridge carrying the Canal du Midi over the Orb, provides an alternative to the somewhat daunting stretch of river.

Béziers★ – See BÉZIERS.

Pic du MIDI DE BIGORRE★★★

MICHELIN LOCAL MAP 342: M-5

ALSO SEE LA BIGORRE

This mountain peak a familiar landmark to the Gascons, is distinguished by a silhouette which stands clearly apart from the main Pyrenean chain. Ease of access, a series of outstanding views and a scientific installation of world renown had long established its importance before modern tourism set the seal on its fame.

Access – ⚹🕓 *Jun-Sep: departure from la Mongie 9am-4.30pm (last there and back trip 7pm); Oct-Sep: departure from la Mongie 10am-3.30pm (last there and back trip 5.30pm).* 🕓 *Closed Nov.* ⚌ *23€ (children: 12€).* ☏ *0825 002 877. www.picdumidi.com.*
The road from Col du Tourmalet to Les Laquets is closed to hikers, cyclists and motorists; therefore the summit of Pic du Midi de Bigorre can only be reached by cable-car from La Mongie (see La BIGORRE) or along waymarked footpaths (warm clothing, sunglasses and sunscreen are recommended; ⚹ *visits are discouraged for pregnant women, small children and visitors with cardiac conditions).*

Summit

Arrival: level 4. Alt 2 865m/9 400ft. A glassed-in gallery and several terraces offer the most impressive **panorama**★★★ in the Pyrenees. As the 19C climber and explorer **Henry Russell** (1834-1909) said, there are mornings here "which must make the Saints long to be on Earth!" Southwards, the Néouvielle massif stands out like an extraordinary real-life illustration of glacial relief.
The Pic du Midi **Observatory and Institute of World Physics** was founded in 1878 and attached to the University of Toulouse in 1902. One of the most important high-altitude scientific research centres in the world, it was open to tourists at the end of the 20C. Its **Vaisseau des étoiles**, an interactive museum, provides a fascinating view of Earth from outer space and an interesting insight into some of the mysteries of our universe.

MILLAU★

POPULATION 21,339

MICHELIN LOCAL MAP 338: K-6

This bustling town in a fertile green valley at the confluence of the Tarn and Dourbie is an excellent departure point for excursions, particularly for the Causses and the Tarn gorges. Nearby, the slopes of the Borie Blanque and the Brunas and Andan peaks are very popular for paragliding and hang-gliding. 🛈 *Av. Alfred-Merle, 12100 Millau,* ☏ *05 65 60 02 42. www.ot-millau.fr*

⚹ **Don't Miss:** From N 9, which climbs up the Causse du Larzac *(look-out point – reached via ③ on town plan),* there is a lovely view of Millau's picturesque **setting★**, the old mill and the ruined 12C bridge.

A Bit of History

A glove-making town– In this part of the Causses, where the traditional ewe's milk cheese-making industry is sufficiently provided for only at the expense of the lambs, it was natural that a leather industry should develop. Very early on, Millau became a centre of manufacture for lambskin gloves.
The glove-making process comprises three phases: tawing or softening the lambskin, dyeing it and then making it into the actual glove. Before completion, a glove changes hands about 70 times. Glacé-kid and suede gloves, washable tanned and lined sports gloves, protective gloves – Millau produces about 250 000 pairs of gloves a year which are exported all over the world.
After the war, when wearing gloves went out of fashion, other market outlets had to be found. Nowadays, the leather dressing factories of Millau, which tan and dye lamb and sheepskins, direct their production towards the manufacture of clothing (particularly haute couture), glove-making, shoe-making, leather goods and furnishing.

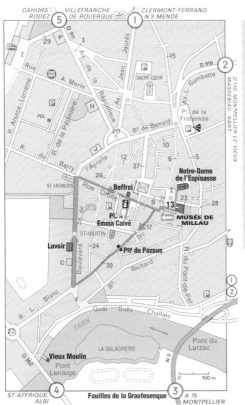

The Graufesenque potteries – During the 1C AD Condatomagus ("the market where the rivers meet"), the predecessor to Millau, was one of the main centres for the making of earthenware in the Roman Empire.

The site offered all the resources necessary for **earthenware** making – fine quality clay, a plentiful water supply and enormous reserves of wood from the forests on the causses.

The techniques used for making earthenware were imported by the Romans and involved the methods of moulding, firing and stamping with decorative designs or potter's marks used in the production of *terra sigillata* ware, bright-red pottery covered with a glaze. Some of the ware was thrown on a wheel and had a smooth surface, but on the whole it was cast in a mould and decorated with floral, geometric or historiated patterns of Hellenistic influence. More than 500 potters made millions of pieces which were then exported throughout Europe, the Middle East and even India.

The Graufesenque archaeological site is open to the public, and a large collection of earthenware is on display at the Musée de Millau.

Terra sigillata ware from Graufesenque

Sights

Fouilles de la Graufesenque

& May-Sep: 9am-noon, 2-6.30pm; Oct-Apr: 9.30am-noon, 2-6pm. Closed 1 Jan, 1 May, 1 and 11 Nov, 25 Dec. 4€, no charge 1st Saturday in the month Oct-Apr. 05 65 60 11 37.

▶ 1km/0.6mi S. Leave Millau towards Montpellier and Albi, then turn left after the bridge over the Tarn.

This archaeological site contains the foundations of a Gallo-Roman potters' village with central street, canal, workshops, slaves' houses and enormous kilns used to fire up to 30 000 vases at a time (*video presentation*).

Address Book

For coin categories, see the Legend.

EATING OUT

Auberge de la Borie Blanque – *Rte. de Cahors -* ☎ *05 65 60 85 88 - closed Feb holidays, weekday evenings Nov-Mar, Mon evening, Sat lunchtime and Sun except Jul-Aug.* Stunning natural setting. Vaulted dining room with exposed stonework for winter cosiness; pleasantly shaded terrace with panoramic views for summer. Cuisine incorporates fresh, regional ingredients.'

La Braconne – *7 Pl. du Mar.-Foch -* ☎ *05 65 60 30 93 – closed Sun evening and Mon.* This old house in the centre of Millau has a fine 13C vaulted dining room. We recommend the grilled dishes cooked in the fireplace at the back and local specialities cooked by the owner.

La Table d'Albanie – *23 R. Pont-de-Fer -* ☎ *05 65 59 16 87 - closed 5-25 Feb, 20-29 Oct, Tue evenings and Wed.* Young and energetic welcome at this pleasant establishment near the banks of the Tarn. Rustic furnishings done by a local woodworker. Flowered terrace in summer.

WHERE TO STAY

La Capelle – *7 Pl. Fraternité -* ☎ *05 65 60 14 72 - 45 rooms.* This hotel has two main advantages: reasonable prices and a peaceful location. Rooms are fairly plain and have 1960s decor.

Ferme-auberge de Quiers – *In Quiers - 12520 Compeyre - 12km/7.4mi N of Millau by N 9 and D 907 -* ☎ *05 65 59 85 10 - open early Apr-Toussaint -* - *6 rooms - meals* . In a quiet hamlet amid the crags, this old restored farmhouse offers comfortable rooms with charm of yesteryear, several with exposed beams and stonework. Rustic dining room, and a superb view over the valley.

Château de Creissels – *2km/1mi S of Millau St-Affrique road -* ☎ *05 65 60 16 59 - Jan-Feb, Mon lunchtime and Sun from Oct-Apr -* ☐ *- 30 rooms -* ☐ *8€ - restaurant* . This château is on the hillside above Millau. The rooms in the 12C building have old-fashioned style decor, while those in the 1971 building are furnished in the style of the 1960s. Dining room in vaulted cellar.

SHOPPING

Cave des Vignerons des gorges du Tarn – *Ave. Causses - 5km/3mi from Millau - 12520 Aguessac -* ☎ *05 65 59 84 11.* This co-op produces wines with the Vin délémité de qualité supérieure (VDQS) label côtes de Millau (red and rose). You will also find Cerno here, an apéritif made from Gamay flavoured with herbal essences.

J. Bonami – *4 R. Peyssière -* ☎ *05 65 60 07 40 - Mon-Sat 6am-1.30pm, 3.30-8pm – closed a fortnight in Feb, 3 weeks after 15 Aug and holidays.* The Bonamis make no bones about their sentiments: they are staunchly anti-artificial, anti-poor quality, and for tradition. Their attitude translates to the highest quality cakes, pastries and sweets made according to long tradition at this excellent *pastisserie*.

SPORTS AND RECREATION

Rambling – The main waymarked footpaths are the GR 62 ("Causse Noir-Lévezou-Rouergue") and several PR, "Causse Noir" (13 itineraries around Millau for rambling and mountain biking), "Millau et les causses majeurs," "St-Affrique-Vallée du Tarn-Pays de Roquefort" (footpaths around St-Affrique, Camarès and Roquefort). These paths are marked on the IGN maps to a scale of 1: 25 000 and on the PR "Aveyron Midi-Pyrénées" topoguide (ref 082).

Hang-gliding and paragliding – Millau is an international centre for this popular sport and many courses take place from April to November. An up-and-coming sport is Kite-boarding, using a kite for propelling yourself along. Below are some useful addresses:

Children – Millau organises many activities and workshops for children and publishes a brochure listing all the organisers who cater for children. For this reason the town was awarded the label Kid. Information is available from the tourist office.

PNR des Grands Causses – *71 boulevard de l'Ayrolle -* ☎ *05 65 61 35 50 – parc.gands. causses@wanadoo.fr – May-Sep: 9am-12.30pm, 2-6pm; rest of the year: 9am-noon, 2-5pm – closed weekends, holidays, and 1 week at the end of the year.* The Parc provides useful addresses for finding accommodation, practising unusual activities and discovering the local cultural heritage.

Horizons Loisirs sportifs – *6 Pl. L.-Grégoire -* ☎ *05 65 59 78 60 – www.horizon-millau.com – Mar-Nov: 10am-noon, 2-5pm; Jul-Aug: 9.30am-noon, 2-5pm.* Potholing, paragliding, canyoning, climbing, hiking.The centre is a member of the Fédération française de spéléologie et de parapente.

Évasion Parapente et Randonnées – *Chemin des Terrasses, Rte. de Paulhe -* ☎ *05 65 59 15 30 - www.millau-evasion.com. Open all year.*

Centre international de Vol libre – *Cabrières, 12520 Aguessac,* ☎ *05 65 59 84 44 – www.cabrieres.net*

Escapade – *Rte. des Gorges du Tarn, 12520 Aguessac -* ☎ *05 65 59 72 03 – high season: 8am-8pm; rest of the year by appointment.* Canoeing, kayaking, canyoning, climbing, potholing and mountain biking.

Centre Permanent d'Initiatives pour l'Environnement (CPIE) du Rouergue – *La Maladrerie -* ☎ *05 65 61 06 57.* The centre organises walks aimed at the discovery of nature and the local cultural heritage.

Roc and Canyon – *55 Ave. Jean-Jaurès - ☎ 05 65 61 17 77 - www.roc-et-canyon.com - Jul-Aug: daily 8am-8pm; reception: daily 9am-noon, 2pm-5pm.* Rock-climbing, pot-holing, cross-country cycling, rafting, hiking, canyoning, riding, canoeing, free flight, via ferrata, tandem paragliding, adventure circuit. All these activities are offered under the supervision of state-qualified instructors.

Musée de Millau★

🕒 *Jul and Aug: 10am-6pm; May, Jun and Sep: 10am-noon, 2-6pm; Oct-Apr: daily except Sun and public holidays 10am-noon, 2-6pm.* ✎ *5€, no charge 1st Saturday in the month.* ☎ *05 65 59 01 08.*

The museum is housed in the 18C Hôtel de Pégayrolles.

The **paleontology** section includes numerous fossils of flora and fauna from secondary marine sediments and the almost complete skeleton of a plesiosaurus from Tournemire, a 4m/13ft-long 180-million-year-old marine reptile.

The museum's vaulted cellars house a remarkable, extremely well-presented collection of Gallo-Roman **earthenware**★, found at Graufesenque – both smooth and decorated vases from every period of manufacture, moulds, potter's chisels and accounts books and a reconstructed kiln. There are also piles of vases which got stuck together during firing and were completely deformed. These "failures" were thrown into large pits.

The **Maison de la Peau et du Gant**★, on the first floor, presents Millau's two traditional industries – tawing, by which a perishable, raw skin is converted into a high quality product which will not rot (*10min video*), and glove-making. The exhibits include numerous tools, samples of leather and a presentation of the various stages in glove-making, from cutting out to the finishing touches (reconstruction of a 19C workshop), as well as a magnificent collection of evening gloves.

Town Walk

Place du Maréchal-Foch

This is the most picturesque part of the old town, with its covered square embellished with arcades (12C-16C) supported on cylindrical columns. The quadrangular stone still visible was once part of the stocks (*between the 2nd and 3rd column from the north*), and the capital of the column next to it to the north bears the very faint inscription "*Gara qué faras*" or "Watch what you are doing."

Église Notre-Dame-de-l'Espinasse

This church once possessed a thorn from the Crown of Thorns, whence its name. An important centre of pilgrimage in the Middle Ages, the building, originally Romanesque, was partly destroyed in 1582 and rebuilt in 17C. The frescoes that decorate the chancel (1939) are by Jean Bernard and the stained-glass windows in the nave (1984) by Claude Baillon.

▶ *From the square, follow rue des Jacobins.*

Continue straight on through **passage du Pozous**, a 13C fortified gateway. Rue du Voultre, which features several low-vaulted passageways, leads to boulevard de l'Ayrolle.

▶ *Turn right onto this boulevard.*

Lavoir

The semicircular shape of this unusual 18C wash-house is emphasised by a neo-Classical colonnade. The wash-house itself is surmounted by an elegant roof.

▶ *Continue along the boulevard to Église St-François then take rue Droite opposite the church.*

Beffroi (Belfry)

🕒 *Jul and Aug: guided tour 10am and 11am, unaccompanied visit 2.30-6pm; mid to end-Jun and Sep: guided tour only 3pm, 4pm and 5pm; rest of the year by request only.* ✎ *2€ unaccompanied visits.* ☎ *05 65 59 50 32.*

Standing in rue Droite, one of the main shopping streets, this Gothic tower is all that is left of the old town hall. The square tower (12C), used as a prison in the 17C, is topped by an octagonal one (17C). Good view from **place Emma-Calvé**.

▶ *Return to rue Droite and continue straight on to place du Maréchal-Foch.*

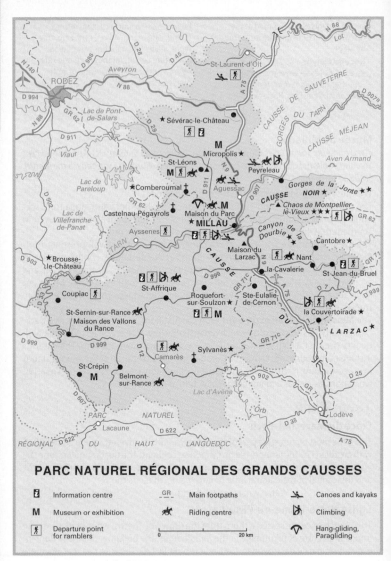

PARC NATUREL RÉGIONAL DES GRANDS CAUSSES

🛈	Information centre	GR	Main footpaths	🚣	Canoes and kayaks	
M	Museum or exhibition	🏇	Riding centre	🧗	Climbing	
🚶	Departure point for ramblers	0 ————— 20 km		🪂	Hang-gliding, Paragliding	

Parc Naturel Régional des Grands Causses

This regional park founded in 1995, covers 315 640ha/779 963 acres, roughly the whole of the southern part of the Aveyron *département*. It incorporates 94 towns or villages with a total population of more than 64 000.

The park's charter sets out various aims: enhancement of the region's natural and architectural heritage; support for agricultural methods designed to make best use of available land and local economy (conservation of local breeds of sheep threatened with extinction, development of accommodation facilities such as bed and breakfast offered by farms); promotion of locally grown foodstuffs and traditional crafts. As far as the preservation of the local architectural heritage is concerned, projects are already under way to save typical features which testify to the region's past way of life, such as village ovens, drystone shepherds' huts, village ponds, dovecots, wash-houses and fountains.

Parc naturel régional des Grandes Causses

Excursions

Prieuré de Comberoumal

🕐 *10am-6pm. No charge.* ☎ *05 65 62 02 28. 18km/11mi NW along D 911 then D 30 left to St-Beauzély. Park the car at the end of the path leading to the priory.*

The Prieuré is one of the best-preserved priories owned by the Grandmont Order founded in the 11C. Advocating poverty and meditation, the order was at the height of its fame from the 12C to the 14C; afterwards, it gradually declined and was dissolved during the 18C.

The priory, dating from the Romanesque period, consists of four buildings forming a square around some small cloisters that have unfortunately been destroyed. To the north is the church. The nave is lit by a single window, at the back, whereas the chancel is wider and pierced with three very splayed windows, flooding it with light. The west wing, which has been altered, was reserved for guests (Romanesque fireplace with a circular duct). The south wing, altered during construction of the first floor, still has its ground-floor refectory and kitchen (a service hatch can be seen in the passageway leading to the cloisters). To the east, there is a covered passageway leading to the cemetery, a chapter-house and a common room – or still room.

Sévérac-le-Château★

32km/20mi N along N 9. This village, which was once fortified, stands on an isolated hillock in the valley watered by the Aveyron and its tributaries. It is overlooked by a sheer outcrop of rock bearing the remains of an imposing castle.

The Sévérac barony, one of the oldest and most powerful in France, numbers among its ranks **Amaury de Séverac** (1365-1427), a Maréchal de France, who took part in countless daring feats of arms, and the composer **Déodat de Séverac** (1873-1921), born in St-Félix-Lauragais (👉 *see ST-FÉLIX-LAURAGAIS*).

In the little streets leading to the château are some **picturesque old houses** (15C-16C), with pretty window frames, their corbelled turrets and upper storeys overhanging the street.

A 17C entrance gate leads into the main courtyard of the **château** (🕐 *Jul and Aug: 9.30am-9.30pm;* 🎟 *6€, children: 3.50€; rest of the year unaccompanied visits;* ☎ *05 65 47 67 31. www.severac-le-chateau.com*). Older buildings (13C-14C) can be seen on the north side. On the south side are the Renaissance façade and the remains of a monumental double flight of stairs.

From the terrace, to the east of the main courtyard, there is a view of the town of Sévérac, the upper Aveyron Valley, the Causse de Sévérac and Causse de Sauveterre, the foothills of the Cévennes and, further to the right, the Lévézou. From the watchtower of the west wall, there is an extensive view over the Aveyron Valley, with, in the distance, the outline of Loupiac Castle flanked by four round towers.

MINERVE★

POPULATION 104

MICHELIN LOCAL MAP 339: B-8

Minerve occupies a picturesque site★★ on a promontory overlooking arid countryside crisscrossed by rugged gorges. 🚏 *9 R. des Martyrs, 34210 Minerve,* ☎ *04 68 91 81 43.*

🅿 **Parking:** There are several car parks around Minerve *(access to town for residents only).*

A Bit of History

In the Middle Ages, a proud fortress which stood atop this spur witnessed one of the most dramatic episodes in the Albigensian Crusade. In 1210 Simon de Montfort, at the head of 7 000 men, took his stand at the gates of the stronghold in which numerous Cathars had taken cover. After five weeks of siege, the

FAMILY INN

😋😋 **Relais Chantovent** – ☎ *04 68 91 14 18 - closed 18 Dec-18 Mar, Sun evenings and Mon – 15/35€.* This family inn is a welcome sight in this little Cathar village (access on foot). Regional cuisine is served in a white-washed dining room with beams or on the terrace for a view of the gorge. Ice cream and pancakes available in the afternoon. Basic rooms available in two separate buildings.

Minerve

townspeople, having run out of water, were forced to capitulate. They were given the choice of converting or being slaughtered. 180 "Parfaits" nonetheless refused to deny their Cathar faith (commemorative stele by J-L Séverac on place de la Mairie).

Walking Tour *allow 1hr 30min*

▷ *Take D 147 SW of the village. During droughts, it is possible to walk along the river bed. In summer, the Grand Pont is the setting of cultural events.*

Ponts naturels (Natural bridges)★

The road affords attractive views of natural bridges. These were formed at the beginning of the Quaternary Era when the Cesse abandoned the two meanders it once formed before flowing into the Briant, to attack the limestone cliff. As it forced its way through the many cracks in the wall, enlarging them gradually as it went, two tunnels were formed: the first, the **Grand Pont** spanning the river, 250m/820ft long ending in an opening about 30m/100ft high; and upstream, the **Petit Pont**, about 15m/50ft high, through which the Cesse flows for some 110m/360ft.

Climb up to the narrow, picturesque rue des Martyrs, lined with several craft workshops (Maison des Templiers: 13C door). It leads to the church and museums.

Église St-Étienne

This small Romanesque church has an 11C oven-vaulted apse and a 12C nave. On the high altar table, there is an inscription indicating that it was consecrated by St Rustique, Bishop of Narbonne, in 456. About a hundred 5C-9C graffiti can be made out on it.

▷ *Walk on towards the tower standing N of the village.*

Known as "**La Candela**," this 13C octagonal tower is, together with sections of the curtain wall overlooking the Briant Valley to the east, all that remains of the local fortress which once commanded the way to the causse and was dismantled by order of Louis XIII in 1636.

▷ *Go back down rue des Martyrs and turn left into a narrow alley, paved with rough stones, leading down to the ramparts.*

Parts of the double curtain wall which protected Minerve in the 12C still remain, including the southern postern with its pointed archway.

▷ *Follow the path to the left along the lower edge of the village.*

Puits St-Rustique

Connected to the ramparts by a covered path, this well was used to supply water to the townspeople during the siege of 1210. Simon de Montfort destroyed it with a powerful catapult from the other side of the river, forcing Minerve to capitulate.

Vallée du Briant

A narrow path skirts the village, following the steep-sided, narrow Briant Valley. It comes up under the ruins of the "Candela."

Additional Sights

Museum

🕐 *Mid-Mar-mid-Nov: 10am-12.30pm, 1.30-6pm; mid-Dec to Jan: 12.30-5pm; Feb-mid Mar: noon-5pm.* 👓 *1.70€.* ☎ *04 68 91 22 92.*

Mainly devoted to prehistory and archaeology up until the Roman and Visigoth invasions, the museum contains a moulding of human footprints discovered in 1948 in the clay of the **Grotte d'Aldène** (*see The Haut Minervois below*). The footprints are thought to date from the Upper Paleolithic Age (from the Aurignacian period about 15 000 years ago). The first floor houses paleontological collections – a number of fossils found in the Cesse Valley.

Musée Hurepel

🕐 *Jul and Aug: 10am-1pm, 2-7pm; Apr-Jun: 10.30am-12.30pm, 2-6pm; Sep and Oct: 10.30am-12.30pm, 2-5.30pm.* 👓 *2.50€.* ☎ *04 68 91 12 26.*
Dioramas of the main episodes in the Albigensian Crusade.

Haut-Minervois★

35km/22mi round tour.

▷ *Take D 10E1 W towards Fauzan. The road follows the narrow, steep-sided meanders of the Cesse.*

Canyon de la Cesse

At the beginning of the Quaternary Era, the waters of the Cesse hollowed out a canyon, enlarging existing caves and making new ones. Upstream of Minerve, the valley gets narrower and the water, leaving the impermeable rock of the Primary Era, runs for 20km/12mi underground, only flowing along its bed at ground level during heavy storms in winter.

▷ *Turn left onto the road to Cesseras which leads down to the plain and vineyards. Go through Cesseras and turn right onto D 168 to Siran. After 2km/1mi, turn right again.*

Chapelle de St-Germain

This Romanesque chapel, nestling in a grove of pine trees, is particularly interesting on account of the decoration of its apse.

▷ *Return to D 168 and carry on to Siran.*

After a little less than 1km/0.6mi, a hill with pine trees growing on it comes into view on the left.

🔲 *Stop the car beyond the bridge which crosses a track and take the footpath up to the top of the hill.* There, you will discover an interesting **dolmen** of the covered-alleyway type, called **Mourel des Fades** ("fairies' dolmen").

Chapelle de Centeille★

🕐 *Sun 3-5pm.* ☎ *04 68 91 50 07 (Mme Lignères). N of Siran.*

Surrounded by cypress trees, holm-oaks and vines, this 13C chapel, located on the border between the Causse de Minerve and the plain, encompasses a vast panorama of vineyards, La Livinière with the unusual domed bell-tower of its basilica and, on a clear day, the Pyrenees in the distance.

Inside, beautiful 14C and early-15C **frescoes**★ depict the Tree of Jesse, St Michael and St Bruno. The transept contains a 3C Roman mosaic excavated at Siran.

Around the chapel can be seen several drystone hut constructions known locally as capitelles.

▷ *Return to the village of Siran and, after the water tower, take a small road on the left which skirts the St-Martin peak and rejoins D 182 to the N, overlooking the Cesse gorge. Turn right towards Minerve. Just after the hamlet of Fauzan, take a small road to the left.*

After 1.5km/1mi, next to a disused factory, a vast flat stretch of land gives a view of the Cesse gorge and the **caves** which pepper the cliff face. It is in one of these caves – **Aldène** – that the human footprints from the Paleolithic Age were discovered (*see Musée de Minerve above*). A small path between two rocks leads to the **Grotte de Fauzan** in which traces of prehistoric footprints were also found.

▷ *Return to Minerve along the Cesse canyon.*

MIRANDE

POPULATION 3,568

MICHELIN LOCAL MAP 336: E-8

Mirande is a lively town, one of the most characteristic of France's south-western *bastides* – fortified towns. Since its founding in 1281 by the Abbé de Berdoues Bernard VII, Comte d'Astarac, and Eustache de Beaumarchés, the village has retained the chessboard symmetry of its ground plan, with separate 50m/164ft square blocks of dwellings and the centre of the grid marked by a place à couverts (a market place surrounded by arcades where business and trade could be carried out, shielded from sun or rain), named after the Astarac family. *R. de l'Évêché, 32300 Mirande, ☎ 05 62 66 68 10.*

Sights

A pleasant stroll through the town takes in **place d'Astarac** and adjacent streets, in particular **rue de l'Évêché** where several fine half-timbered houses have been preserved.

Église Sainte-Marie

The picturesque turreted belfry of this early-15C sanctuary served more than once as a shelter for the *bastide's* defenders. The tower is pierced by openwork Gothic bays, the fenestration becoming richer level by level. An outer porch attached to the belfry spans the street. Ribbed vaulting roofs the porch and the ensemble is shored up by two huge arches.

The Gothic nave in the interior was heightened in the 19C.

Musée des Beaux-Arts★

Daily except Sun 10am-noon, 2-6pm. Closed Sun and public holidays. 2€. ☎ 05 62 66 68 10.

Most of the carefully displayed works in this small Fine Arts Museum were donations or legacies from local enthusiasts.

A portrait of Joseph Delort, founder of the museum, hangs in the entrance hall where show cases contain antique ceramics and lustrous 17C-19C glazed earthenware and porcelain from such renowned centres as Moustiers, Samadet, Dax and Nevers.

Address Book

WHERE TO STAY

Chambre d'hôte au Château – *32230 Juillac - 4km/2.4mi E of Marciac on D 255 - ☎ 05 62 09 37 93 - deresseguier@marciac.net – closed 1 week in Oct - - 3 rms – meal.* At the heart of a working farm, this lovely 18C chartreuse offers spacious, tasetfully decorted rooms. In the dining room, you will enjoy farm-fresh produce. For fun: bike rental, fishing and strolling in the park.

Chambre d'hôte Le Moulin de Régis – *Near the EDF-GDF centre - ☎ 05 62 66 66 29 - - 6 rms.* This 12C watermill, perfectly restored, is really worth a visit. You reach the rooms by way of an unusual wooden lift. Tiled floors and fine old furniture add to the beauty. For relaxation: sauna, jacuzzi, horseback riding.

JAZZ AFLOAT

La Péniche – *Rte du Lac – 32230 Marciac - ☎ 05 62 09 38 46 - Tues-Sun 9am-10.30pm - closed 1 week at Christmas and 1 week at end of Jun.* This bar-restaurant floating on the village lake is much prized by the musicians who played at the Marciac jazz festival. It is packed to the gunwhales with charm. Service is friendly and efficient, but the owners are never too busy to tell you the story of the barge's epic journey from the port of Sète to Marciac.

LEISURE ACTIVITIES

Farm visit – *Ferme de Bordeneuve - 32320 Montesquiou - ☎ 05 62 70 94 20 - from 2pm.* This charming farm and the 3km/1.9mi marked footpath which surrounds it offer nature lovers a pleasant afternoon activity. After the visit, tea (including local produce) is served in the picturesque covered courtyard.

Flânerie – *65700 Castelnau-Rivière-Basse - ☎ 05 62 31 90 56.* Donkeys for hire for hiking through the Pyrenees. Possibility of staying on a farm breeding Pyrenean donkeys.

Paintings from the 15C to the 19C are exhibited in the Great Hall. Among a collection of small Flemish works painted on copper, note the exceptional 17C *Adoration of the Magi*. The Italian paintings from the same period include a somewhat truculent *Italian Masquerade* by Michelangelo Cerquozzi, whereas French painting from the 16C is distinguished by Claude Vignon's magisterial *Prophet Zacharia* in which the treatment of the subject, ardent and fiery against a contrast of light and shade, shows the influence of Caravaggio. Three 19C French seascapes, one of them painted on a flat stone, were inspired by Dutch masters of the 17C.

In the middle of the hall, beneath a pyramid roof, one work stands out from a group of interesting portraits; an extremely fine 18C *Study of a Head* from the school of Jacques-Louis David. There is also a display of beautiful gilded porcelain. Beyond, on a single panel, three different schools can be compared: 16C Italian, 17C Dutch and 17C Flemish.

In a smaller room, a slide show presents paintings from the reserve collection, most of them with a local connection.

Bastides and Castelnaux★

93km/58mi – allow 1 day.

▶ *Leave Mirande via N 21 NE towards Auch. After 3km/1.8mi turn left on D 939.*

The itinerary suggested below describes a triangle formed by D 943 to the north, D 3 and the Vallée du Bouès to the west and N 21 to the east. It includes a selection of *bastides* and *castelnaux*, the well-planned villages and towns built by seigneurs around their châteaux or strongholds, which are typical of this region.

The route crosses **L'Isle-de-Noé**, a village at the convergence of the River Grande Baïse and River Petite Baïse, where an 18C château can be seen.

▶ *Take D 943 on the right.*

Barran

The main curiosity in this *bastide*, built on the site of an earlier ecclesiastical settlement, is the extremely unusual spiral-shaped spire above the **church**. The village still has a fortified gateway on the east side, and the characteristic covered market in the main square.

▶ *Return to L'Isle-de-Noé and continue W.*

Montesquiou

This *castelnau* rises on a spur high above the Vallée de l'Osse. The village gave its name to the younger branch of the De Fézensac family, from which sprang the seigneurs of d'Artagnan and De Monluc. A gateway at the end of the main street is all that remains of the 13C outer wall; near it stands a picturesque row of half-timbered houses.

▶ *Continue W.*

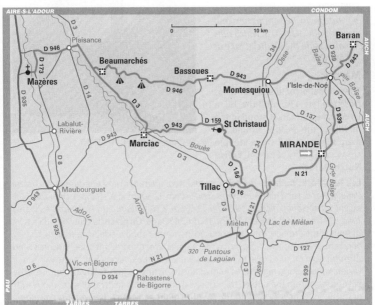

Bassoues

The 14C **keep**★ (◷ *Jul and Aug: 10am-7pm; Apr-Jun, Sep, Oct and school holidays: daily except Tue 10am-noon, 2-6pm; Nov-Mar: Wed, Sat-Sun and holidays 10am-noon, 2-5pm, school holidays 2-5. ◷Closed Jan, 25 Dec.* 3€. ☎ 05 62 70 97 34; www.bassoues. net), which can be seen from afar, is a magnificent example of military architecture. Its highly fortified south-eastern front (*restored*) contrasts with the well-appointed interior: latrines on each floor, a spiral staircase leading up to vaulted rooms on the first and second floors, a decorated chimney, a sink under an arch, and niches serving for storage space. Exhibitions in the rooms trace the birth and evolution of Gascon villages. The top-floor platform, where round watchtowers rise between the terrace and the top of the buttresses, offers a good **view**★ to the north-east.

The village **church** was remodelled in the 16C and the 19C; it has a single nave extended by a quadripartite-vaulted chancel and contains a fine 15C stone pulpit. D 946 now descends, via a 12km/7mi **crest route**★, to the Rivière Basse depression drained by the Arros. On the way, the view extends through the Adour gap as far as the Pyrenees.

Beaumarchés

This royal *bastide* was founded in 1288 as the result of a *contrat de paréage* between the Seneschal (Steward) of Beaumarchés and the Comte de Pardiac. The deal – whereby the lesser noble agreed to hand over a part of his revenue, in return for protection, to the greater noble – is illustrated in the **church** on one of the capitals adorned with an escutcheon bearing the arms of France. This Gothic church with its single nave is striking for its massive appearance and its 15C porch, which was planned to become a belfry but was never completed. An interesting frieze of carved male and female heads runs around the upper gallery.

▶ *Drive to Plaisance, turn left onto D 946 to Préhac-sur-Adour then left again onto D 173.*

Mazères

Note the Romanesque **church** (◷ *Tours by appointment.* ☎ *05 62 31 94 30.)* with its gable belfry flanked by buttresses surmounted by bartizans. Inside, the chancel has retained its Romanesque capitals and there is a curious marble reliquary (1342), mounted on a pedestal, under which pilgrims would crawl to ask for the protection of the saint (*apply to the presbytery*).

▶ *Return to Beaumarchés and continue along D 3, which runs alongside the artificial lake at Marciac.*

Marciac

The foundation of this *bastide* dates from the late 13C; until the 19C a large covered market stood in the middle of the arcades around the main square. A tall stone steeple crowns the belfry of the 14C **Église Notre-Dame**.

Romanesque church at Mazères

A. Thuillier/MICHELIN

Les Territoires du Jazz – &◷ *Early to mid-Aug: 10am-8pm (last entrance 45min before closing); Apr-Jul and mid-Aug to end Sep: 9.30am-12.30pm, 2.30-6.30pm; Oct-Mar: daily except Sat and public holidays 9.30am-12.30pm, 2.30-6.30pm, Sun 11am-1pm. ◷ closed 1 May, 24 Dec.* 5€ (under 18: 3€). ☎ 05 62 08 26 60. On place du Chevalier d'Antras, this out of the ordinary museum, housed in a former abbey, is dedicated to the history of jazz from its African origins to modern times. Wearing headphones, visitors swing through such mythical places as New Orleans and the Cotton Club, to the rhythm of Dixieland, blues and ragtime. In August, the town hosts a **jazz festival**. Supported by Bill Coleman from the outset, this convivial, high-quality festival attracts thousands of music-lovers every year, in the first fortnight of August, (*Information available* *from the festival office, ☎ 0 892 690 277; note: reserve accommodations well in advance)* drawing an eclectic crowd of enthusiasts (along with well-known performers) to this otherwise quiet, rural setting.

▶ *Head E towards Auch, following the picturesque D 943 which runs above the valley of the River Boûes. At the top of the climb turn onto D 159, a crest road with fine views of the Pyrenees.*

Northwards *(left)*, there are glimpses of the impressive keep rising above Bassoues.

▶ *Turn right onto D 156 to St-Christaud.*

Here the road crosses the Via Tolosane, which was once the route followed by pilgrims from Provence on their way to Santiago de Compostela.

St-Christaud

The village **church**, built of brick in the Transitional style, stands on a dominant site facing the distant Pyrenees. An unusual feature of the building is the square windows, between buttresses, set in a diamond shape.

▶ *9km/5mi further on, turn right onto D 16.*

Tillac

This small *castelnau* laid out on the plain has picturesque half-timbered houses with angle-posts along its main street, which links a fortified tower with the 14C **church**.

▶ *Return to Mirande along D 16 and N 21.*

MIREPOIX

POPULATION 3,061

MICHELIN LOCAL MAP 343: J-6

In the 13C, many Cathars settled in the town of Mirepoix, including the seigneur, Pierre Roger de Mirepoix who played an important role in the defence of Montségur during the 1243 siege. However, in 1209 Simon de Montfort had handed the city over to one of his lieutenants, Guy de Lévis. Shortly thereafter, Mirepoix was devastated by a flood from the waters of Lake Puivert. Jean, the son of Guy de Lévis, rebuilt the town in a safer place, at the confluence of the River Hers and River Countirou, and built the bastide we see today. *Pl. du Mar.-Leclerc, 09500 Mirepoix, ☎ 05 61 68 83 76. www.ot-mirepoix.fr.*

Visit

Place Principale★★ (Place Mar.-Leclerc)

The main square is surrounded by late 13C-15C houses, in which the first floor juts out over timber "**couverts**," or covered arcades. Note in particular the **Maison des Consuls** decorated with carved heads. With the public gardens, old-world shops and cafés, the square is a pleasant place to spend some time, particularly in the evening.

At the north-west and north-east corners, note the typical fitting together of the "valleys" where the couverts meet; only the smallest crack is left in the covering over the arcades below.

Cathedral St-Maurice

The layout of the building gives no inkling of the long drawn-out construction that went into it. The cathedral, surmounted by an elegant Gothic spire, was begun in 1343 and completed in 1865.

▶ *Enter through the north door.*

The nave (early 16C) is the widest (31.60m/104ft) of any built for a French Gothic church. It is flanked with chapels set between the interior buttresses, following Gothic tradition in the south of France.

Excursions

Camon

8km/5mi SE, on D 625, then D 7.

The little village of Camon, tucked close around its imposing **abbey** (*Contact the tourist office. ☎ 05 61 68 88 26.*), comes into view against a backdrop of the Ariège hills.

Having visited the fortifications, enter the village through the Porte de l'Horloge (note the handsome half-timbered corner house) to see the conventual buildings renovated by Philippe de Lévis, Bishop of Mirepoix, in the 16C. There are the remains of the old cloisters, the fine spiral staircase inside the round tower and the oratory decorated with 14C mural paintings.

Address Book

For coin categories, see the Legend.

WHERE TO STAY

Hôtel La Maison des Consuls – *6 Pl. du Mar.-Leclerc - ☎ 05 61 68 81 81 – hotel@maisondesconsuls.com - 8 rooms - 9€.* This picturesque 14C court house in the old part of town features half-timbering and exposed beams. Ask for one of the old-fashioned rooms named after prominent historic figures from Mirepoix, or the suite with a private terrace and telescope.

"THE WHEELBARROW"

La Brouette – *4 bis Rte. de Foix – 09100 Pamiers - ☎ 05 34 01 02 64 – www.labrouette.com – Mon-Fri 9am-12.30pm, 3pm-7.30pm, Sat 9am-7.30pm, Sun 9am-1pm - closed Sun afternoon and Mon.* An extensive choice of products selected from 120 local farms is what you will find in this bountiful shop selling everything from food to cosmetics to Mohair woollens. They often hold demonstrations and tastings of featured products.

A. Thuillier/MICHELIN

Mirepoix covered arcades

The church, which used to be the abbey church, houses a 17C altarpiece by the Spanish School and a 14C Crucifix.

Pamiers

21km/13mi E along D 922. Pamiers is situated on the east bank of the River Ariège, on the edge of a fertile plain well protected from floods. Its name is derived from that of a town in Asia Minor, in memory of the part played by the count of Foix, Roger II, in the First Crusade. It became a bishopric in 1295 and has since been home to four monastic communities. The **Cathédrale St-Antonin**, in place du Mercadel, has a handsome bell-tower in the Toulouse style, resting on a fortified base. All that remains of the original 12C church is the doorway. The church of **Notre-Dame-du-Camp** (🕐 *Daily except Sat-Sun: 9-11.30am, 3-6pm)*, in Rue du Camp, features a monumental brick façade with crenellations and two towers, and a single 17C nave inside. Pamiers has several interesting **old towers**: the Clocher des Cordeliers (*Rue des Cordeliers*), similar to the tower of this name in Toulouse; the Tour de la Monnaie (*near Rimbaud School*); the square Tour du Carmel (*Place Eugène-Soula*), originally a keep built by Count Roger-Bernard III of Foix in 1285; the tower of the Couvent des Augustins (*near the hospital*); and the brick and stone Porte de Nerviau (*near the town hall*). The **Promenade du Castella** is a walkway which follows the line of the old castle, the foundations of which are still visible between the Porte de Nerviau and the Pont-Neuf. At the top of the hill is a bust of the composer **Gabriel Fauré**, born in Pamiers in 1845.

Pamiers is a good departure point for trips to the rest of the Ariège and the Pyrenees.

MOISSAC★★

POPULATION 12,744

MICHELIN LOCAL MAP 337: C-7

The town of Moissac lies clustered around the ancient abbey of St-Pierre (a site of major interest for lovers of Romanesque art), in a fresh and pretty setting on the north bank of the Tarn and either side of the Garonne branch canal. A jazz festival brings life to the town in July and classical music concerts are given throughout July and August. The surrounding hillsides are covered with orchards and vineyards which produce the reputed Chasselas grape variety (a white grape). In 1991 a marina was opened on the banks of the Tarn. ▯ *Pl. Durand-de-Bredon, 82200 Moissac, ☎ 05 63 04 01 85. www.moissac.fr.*

▶ **Orient Yourself:** To get to the abbey by car, pay close attention to the signals, signs and especially the large orange arrows that point the way.

🕐 **Organising Your Time:** If you visit in July, plan to take in some of the great jazz and classical music concerts and street festivities.

⌓ **Don't Miss:** The opportunity to taste the famed Chasselas grape, considered of the highest quality in this region.

⌚ **Also See:** MONTAUBAN, ST-ANTONIN-NOBLE-VAL

A Bit of History

The golden age of the abbey – It was during the 11C and 12C that Moissac abbey was at its most influential. Probably founded in the 7C by a Benedictine monk from the Norman abbey of St-Wandrille, the young abbey of Moissac did not escape the pillage and destruction wrought by Arabs, Norsemen and Hungarians.

It was struggling to right itself again when, in 1047, an event occurred which was to change its destiny. On his way through Quercy, St Odilon, the famous and influential abbot of Cluny, who had just laid down the rules at the monastery at Carennac, affiliated the abbey of Moissac to that of Cluny. This marked the beginning of a period of prosperity. With the support of Cluny, Moissac Abbey set up priories throughout the region, extending its influence as far as Catalonia.

A series of misfortunes – The Hundred Years War, during which Moissac was occupied twice by the English, and then the Wars of Religion dealt the abbey some fearsome blows. It was secularised in 1628 and then suppressed altogether during the Revolution. In 1793, during the Reign of Terror, the archives were dispersed, the art treasures pillaged and numerous sculptures disfigured. In the mid 19C, it narrowly escaped complete destruction when there was question of demolishing the monastery buildings and cloisters to make way for the railway line from Bordeaux to Sète. The intervention of the Beaux-Arts commission saved it from ruin.

Abbey★★ *1hr*

Église St-Pierre★

This used to be the abbey church. All that remains of the original 11C building is the belfry porch, which was fortified c 1180 with the addition of a watch-path, a crenellated parapet, loopholes and a machicolated gallery.

From the outside, the two very different periods from which the nave dates are clearly distinguishable – one part, in stone, is Romanesque, whereas the other, in brick, is Gothic. The Romanesque part is to be found at the base of the walls of the nave and in the round-arched windows in the lower part of the walls. The rest of the nave was built in 15C in the southern French Gothic style.

South portal★★★

The tympanum above this doorway, executed c 1130, ranks as one of the finest examples of Romanesque sculpture in France. It is majestic in its composition, depicting a wide range of scenes and maintaining harmonious proportions between the various figures portrayed. The odd slightly awkward gesture or rigid posture in no way mars the overall beauty of this immensely moving work.

The theme of the tympanum is the Vision of the Apocalypse according to St John the Evangelist. Enthroned at the centre of the composition, Christ dominates the other figures: wearing a crown and with a halo around his head, he holds the Book of Life

Address Book

🪙 *For coin categories, see the Legend.*

EATING OUT

🍴🍴 **Le Chapon Fin** – *Pl. des Récollets –* ☎ *05 63 04 04 22 - closed 10 Nov-7 Dec, Mon between Nov-Easter.* A step away from the Romanesque abbey, this establishment on the market square tends to pamper its customers. The welcoming dining room in contemporary pastels serves classic cuisine. In season, try the delicious chasselas doré de Moissac grapes. A few renovated bedrooms.

WHERE TO STAY

🏠 **Le Carmel** – *5 Sente du Calvaire - ☎ 05 63 04 62 21 - accueil.cafmoissac@wanadoo. fr - 📠 - 28 rooms - 🍽 4€ - meals 🍽.* Guests are welcome to visit or stay over in this international centre built in a protected woodland. Once a Carmelite convent, the very well-maintained nuns' rooms still hint of the monastic life. The park, laid out in terraces, gives a splendid view of the city.

🏠 **Chambre d'hôte Ferme de la Marquise** – *Brassac - 82190 Bourg-de-Visa - 16km/10mi NW of Moissac on D 7 - ☎ 05 63 94 25 16 – mglamarquise@infonie.fr - 📠 - 4 rooms – meal 🍽.* This venerable working farm is your doorway to a glimpse of life in rural Quercy. The straightforward guest rooms feature handsome exposed beams and family furniture. Meals, prepared with farm produce, are a credit to the cooking of southwest France.

🏠🏠 **Chambre d'hôte Le Platane** – *Coques-Lunel - 82130 Lafrançaise - 10km/6mi E of Moissac on D 927, D 2 and D 68 - ☎ 05 63 65 92 18 - 📠 - 3 rooms - meals 🍽🍽.* This brick mansion, with its stables and dovecote, has been restored with comfort in mind. Relax by the pool in the shade of generous trees or enquire about the possibility of going horse-riding.

SHOPPING

Chasselas – The slopes of lower Quercy along the right banks of the Tarn and Garonne rivers, between Montauban and Moissac, boast an annual production of over 16,000 tons of prime chasselas grapes. True Moissac grapes grow in long bunches holding round, well-defined fruit of a lightly golden, pearly hue. Remarkably sweet and succulent, they are famous for their unusually fine flavour. Care to try some? At the end of the Promenade du Moulin, along the river Tarn, an *uvarium* (a health centre where a grape diet is followed) built in the 1930s, sells fresh grape juice to connoisseurs from September to early October.

Jacques Laporte – *6 R. du Marché - ☎ 05 63 04 03 05 - Tue-Sat 8am-12.15pm, 2pm-7pm, Sun 8am-1pm - closed 1 week at end of Jan and 2 weeks in Jul.* The cakes and other sweet treats sold in this pastry shop-chocolatier-ice cream parlour located a few steps from the market have a fine local reputation. The house speciality is the grain doré de Moissac, a delectable filled chocolate.

"La rue des Arts" – *9 R. Jean-Moura - ☎ 05 63 04 21 46 – daily from 9am.* Cross the porch to discover this appealing shop where handicrafts are in the spotlight. Antique frames, paintings, ceramics and porcelain are restored here; glass is blown and lace tatted as one watches. Each artisan is happy to share his enthusiasm and knowledge with interested visitors.

RECREATION

Moissac Navigation Plaisance – *Quai Charles-de-Gaulle - ☎ 05 63 04 48 28 - 06 16 01 13 88 – Mar-end Oct: daily 9am-noon, 2pm-7pm - closed for one month depending on schedule.* Leisurely barge trips on the Canal des Deux-Mers and on the Tarn along the famous Montech water slope allow day sailors to discover, among other attractions, the Moissac canal bridge.

---

in his left hand and is raising his right hand in benediction. Strongly defined features, penetrating eyes, and the neat arrangement of beard and hair in symmetrical curls all add to the intensity of his expression and accentuate the power and majesty which emanate from his figure.

Christ is surrounded by the symbols of the four Evangelists: St Matthew is represented by a young winged man, St Mark by a lion, St Luke by a bull and St John by an eagle, a truly magnificent scene. The rest of the tympanum is occupied by the 24 Elders of the Apocalypse, arranged in three tiers. Their faces, turned towards Christ, express amazement at the majesty of the sight. The effect of the scene on the onlooker is unusually intense, as the composition centres entirely around the main figure, who is the object of all the other figures' gazes. The beauty and elegance of form, the perfection of contour and drapery, the precision of detail and the facial expressions are remarkable.

The tympanum is supported by a remarkable lintel decorated with eight rosettes framed in a cable moulding coming out of the mouth of a monster at either end.

The central pier, vigorous in style, is a magnificent monolithic block decorated with three pairs of rampant lions, each pair forming an X one above the other. Finally, there are two strikingly lengthy figures carved on either side of the pier: St Paul, on the left, and Jeremiah, on the right. The engaged doorposts depict St Peter, patron saint of the abbey, and the Prophet Isaiah. On each side of the doorposts are historiated scenes carved on remnants of sarcophagi made of Pyrenean marble.

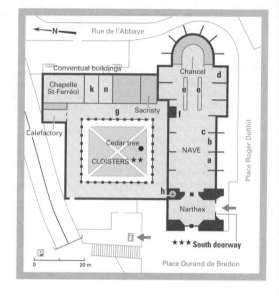

Interior

The entrance is through the narthex, in which the four intersecting pointed ribs of the vault spring from eight sturdy engaged columns decorated with highly stylised capitals (11C-12C). The nave still contains some of the original furnishings. Note an Our Lady of Pity from 1476 (**a**), a charming Flight into Egypt from the late 15C (**b**), a magnificent Romanesque **Crucifix**★ (12C) (**c**) and an Entombment (**d**) from 1485. The chancel is enclosed by a 16C carved stone screen, behind which a Carolingian apse has recently been uncovered. The choir stalls (**e**) date from the 17C. In an alcove beneath the organ, stands a white Pyrenean marble Merovingian sarcophagus (**f**).

Cloisters★★★

Jul and Aug: 9am-7pm; Apr-Jun and Sep: 9am-noon, 2-6pm, Sat-Sun and public holidays 10am-noon, 2-6pm; Oct-Apr: 10am-noon, 2-5pm, Sat-Sun and public holidays 2-5pm. Closed 1 Jan and 25 Dec. 5€, ticket combined with the museum. 05 63 04 01 85. Entrance through the tourist office.

These beautiful cloisters (late 11C) have remarkably delicate arcades with slender columns, alternatively single and paired, in harmonious tones of marble – white, pink, green and grey – and a rich wealth of sculpted decoration.

The four galleries, with timber roof vaults sloping down into the cloister garth, are supported by 76 arcades reinforced by piers at the corners and in the middle of each side. These piers, clad in blocks of marble taken from old sarcophagi, are decorated

Cloisters

L. Cazenave/MICHELIN

with low-relief sculptures, including nine effigies of the Apostles and, on the pier in the middle of the east gallery (the gallery opposite the entrance), that of Abbot Durant de Bredon (**g**), Bishop of Toulouse and Abbot of Moissac, who played a decisive role in the abbey's development; his effigy, executed only 15 years after his death, is so strikingly realistic that it is considered to be a true portrait.

The decoration on the capitals includes a huge variety of motifs – animal, plantl, geometric and historiated. Scenes represented are taken from the Old and New Testaments and include episodes from the Life of Christ, His miracles and parables, scenes from the Apocalypse and the Life of the Saints honoured in the abbey.

In the south-west corner, a staircase (**h**) leads to the first floor of the narthex and onto the roof which affords a fine view of the cloisters, the town and the Tarn Valley beyond.

The conventual buildings include the calefactory, St-Ferréol Chapel containing some 12C capitals, a room (**k**) in which a display of photographs illustrates the extent of Moissac's influence on sculpture in the Quercy region, and leading off from this a room (**n**) housing religious art (gold and silver work, note the late-15C Virgin of Sorrow) and liturgical vestments.

Additional Sight

Musée Moissagais

♿🕐 *Apr-Sep: daily except Sun morning and Mon 9am-noon, 2-6pm; Oct-Apr: 10am-noon, 2-5pm.* 🕐 *Closed Jan (except during Christmas school holidays), 1 Jan, 1 May, 25 Dec.* ⊷ *5€, ticket combined with the cloister.* ☎ *05 63 04 03 08.*

The museum is housed in what used to be the abbot's lodgings, a large building flanked by a 13C crenellated brick tower, which was destroyed during the Revolution.

Just inside the entrance, two maps show the importance of the abbey during the Middle Ages and the spread of its influence throughout the whole of South-West France. The vast 17C stairwell is used to display items of religious historical interest.

The various rooms contain collections on the history and traditions of the region – local ceramics (particularly from Auvillar), furniture, Moissac headdresses, reconstruction of a 19C kitchen from the Bas Quercy region, various examples of local craftwork and costumes.

◗◗ **Boudou** – *7km/4.5mi W.* Village with **panorama**★ of the Garonne Valley.

◗◗ **Castelsagrat** – *18km/11mi N.* Picturesque *bastide* with arcaded square, old well and 14C church containing a huge gilt-wood altarpiece.

La MONTAGNE NOIRE★

MICHELIN LOCAL MAP 338: E, F, G AND H-10 AND 344: E-2 TO F-2

The Montagne Noire or Black Mountain, forms the south-west tip of the Massif Central. It is separated from the Agout massif (Sidobre and the Lacaune and Espinouse ranges) by the furrow formed by the Thoré which is extended by the valleys of the Jaur and the upper Orb.

Geographical Notes

There is a strong contrast between its densely forested northern slope, which rises steeply above the Thoré, and its typically Mediterranean southern slope, which drops gently down to the Lauragais and Minervois plains, in sight of the Pyrenees. The northern slope culminates in the Pic de Nore (alt 1 210m/3 970ft).

This very diversified relief transforms the winds that arrive here: the violent and dry west winds become laden with rain, whereas the "sea" wind from the east, with a high moisture content, turns into the dry southerly wind (autan) bringing the thunderstorms of Haut Languedoc. This explains why rainfall in the Montagne Noire is more than 1m/33in per year.

The northern slopes, where most rain falls, are covered with dark forests (oak, beech, fir, spruce), whereas the southern slopes are rugged, with scant vegetation including a mixture of *garrigue*, gorse, sweet chestnut trees, vines and olive trees.

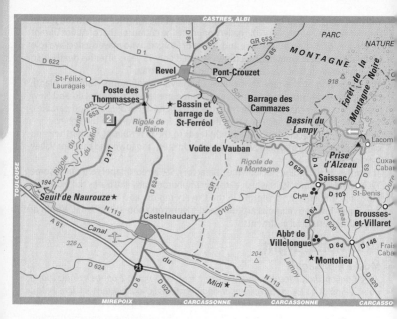

Way of life on the Montagne noire – Only a relatively meagre income can be made by raising stock or growing crops here, and it has been many years since anyone earned a living weaving wool and hemp. The gold mines in Salsigne are still operational, and marble is mined at Caunes-Minervois, but the Montagne Noire's greatest wealth nowadays lies in its abundant reserves of water and its beautiful countryside.

Hiking Tours

A **forest road** stretches from the Prise d'eau d'Alzeau to the Bassin du Lampy (15km/9.3mi). It is marked on the IGN 2344 Ouest map.

The **GR 7** long-distance footpath runs through woodland, skirting the Rigole de la Montagne from the Bassin du Lampy to the Cammazes dam (11km/6.8mi). Between the Conquet spillway and the Cammazes dam, the rigole is lined with bricks; between Le Conquet and Plo de la Jasse, it follows a steep course and was therefore built with 14 small spillways designed to regulate the current. You need the IGN 2244 Est and 2344 Ouest maps for this section.

The **GR 653** long-distance footpath, the "Pierre-Paul Riquet" variation of GR 7, starts from the Bassin de St-Ferréol, joins up with the Rigole de la Plaine in Revel, skirts it as far as the Poste des Thommasses (9km/5.6mi) then runs on to the Seuil de Naurouze (another 24km/15mi). For this itinerary, you need the IGN 2344 Ouest, 2244 Est and 2244 Ouest maps.

The Cabardès Region★ 1

Round tour from Carcassonne – & *See CARCASSONNE.*

Harnessed Water★ 2

From the Prise d'Alzeau to the Seuil de Naurouze. 114km/71mi – allow 5hr

This itinerary follows the water-supply system of the Canal du Midi devised in the 17C by Pierre-Paul Riquet then improved upon through the following centuries. The Montagne Noire holds considerable reserves of water and Riquet had the idea of harnessing water from several mountain streams and sending it via a small canal to the watershed reach at Naurouze.

▶ *From St-Denis, follow D 353 towards Lacombe then a forest road on the right.*

Prise d'Alzeau

A monument put up in memory of Pierre-Paul Riquet, who designed and built the Canal du Midi, retraces the various stages of construction of the canal. It marks the beginning of the Rigole de la Montagne, the channel which collects the waters of

the Alzeau (and other rivers on the way) and takes them to the Lampy reservoir. The beginning of this canal can be seen behind the forest lodge.

▶ *Turn back and continue to Lacombe. Turn left towards Lampy along forest roads.*

Forêt domaniale de la Montagne noire

This 3 650ha/9 000-acre forest, consisting mainly of beech and fir trees, includes the Ramondes and Hautaniboul forests. The road crosses the Alzeau at La Galaube in a lovely woodland setting.

Bassin du Lampy

This 1 672 000m³/60 000 000cu ft reservoir on the Lampy flows into the Montagne Noire channel, which stretches from the Alzeau offtake to the St-Ferréol reservoir. A pleasant footpath runs alongside the channel for 23km/14.5mi as far as the village of Les Cammazes.

The reservoir was built from 1776 to 1780 to supply the Canal du Midi, after the Robine de Narbonne branch canal was opened. Magnificent beech groves, crisscrossed with shady paths, make the Bassin du Lampy a popular place for a walk.

▶ *Follow D 4 towards Saissac then turn right onto D 629. Just before Les Cammazes, turn right onto a road leading to the dam.*

Cammazes Dam

The 90ha/220-acre reservoir retained by this 70m/230ft-high arch dam feeds the Canal du Midi, supplies 116 towns and villages with drinking water and irrigates the entire Lauragais plain east of Toulouse. Footpaths lead down to the edge of the Sor.

▶ *Return to D 629 and turn right.*

The road continues alongside the Rigole de la Montagne.

Voûte de Vauban

On the outskirts of Cammazes, the Rigole de la Montagne runs through the Voûte de Vauban, a 122m/133yd-long tunnel.

St-Ferréol reservoir

A. Thuillier/MICHELIN

Address Book

For coin categories, see the Legend.

Auberge des Mazies – Rte. de Castres - 31250 Revel - ☎ 05 61 27 69 70 - bienvenue@mazies.com. Exposed beams and a vast fireplace dominate two handsome dining rooms, one of which boasts a charming mezzanine. Sit on the terrace in summer to dine al fresco on regional specialties of the house.

Midi –34 Bd. Gambetta - 31250 Revel - ☎ 05 61 83 50 50 - contact@ hotelrestaurantdumidi.com. Former 19C post office renovated as a family hotel-restaurant. In the salon, cast an eye over the lovely fresco mural depicting St-Guilhem-le-Désert. Traditional French dishes incorporating regional ingredients marry beautifully with the local vintages on the wine list. Comfortable guestrooms.

WHERE TO STAY

Hôtel Le Pavillon des Hôtes – 81540 Sorèze - 6km/4mi E of Revel on D 85 - ☎05 63 74 44 80 - - 18 rooms - ☐ 10.50€ - restaurant . This hotel occupies the old abbey school founded in the 17C by Benedictine monks. The rooms are plain and peaceful. The very reasonable prices include a contribution towards maintaining the monument.

Hôtellerie Abbaye-école de Sorèze – R. Lacordaire - 81540 Sorèze - A 61 exit 20 or 21, to Revel then Sorèze – ☎ 05 63 74

44 80 - contact@hotelfp-soreze.com - ☐ - 70 rooms - ☐ 10,50€ - restaurant . This structure is full of history: founded in 754 by Pépin le Bref, pillaged and destroyed, then rebuilt in the 17C by Benedictine monks. Today the former monks' cells served as elegant guestrooms offering views of the park or the cloister. Lovely, contemporary restaurant in the former refectory.

Hôtellerie du Lac – 31250 St-Ferréol – 3km/2mi SE of Revel on D 629 - ☎ 05 62 18 70 80 – contact@hotellerie-du-lac.com – ☐ – 25 rooms - ☐ 7€ – restaurant . This 19C family mansion overlooking the lake is a haven of peace and quiet. Half of the recently fitted-out, functional rooms give onto the tranquil landscape. Between the flower garden, the heated swimming pool and the fitness room, a most relaxing sojourn.

Hôtel Demeure de Flore – 81240 Lacabarède - 18km/11mi E of Mazamet on N 112 - ☎ 05 63 98 32 32 - demeure.de. flore@hotelrama.com – closed 5 Jan-3 Fev, Mon off-season – ☐ – 11 rooms - ☐ 9.50€ – restaurant . Come in along the linden-lined alley and discover the charms of this 19C house where guests are made to feel quite at home. Pretty, personalized bedrooms; period pieces and artwork abound throughout. Appealing dining room with a terrace surveying the flower garden and its pool.

Bassin and barrage de St-Ferréol★

The reservoir stretches for 67ha/166 acres between wooded hillsides. The magnificent lake is ideal for sailing and swimming, and its shores make a pleasant place for a stroll. Located on the side of the Montagne Noire towards the Atlantic Ocean, it is the main supply reservoir for the Canal du Midi.

The St-Ferréol reservoir itself is fed by the upper Laudot and the Rigole de la Montagne linking it to the Lampy reservoir.

The **dam** was built by Riquet between 1667 and 1672; one thousand men, women and children worked on the site. It consists of three parallel walls: the upstream wall below the water level of the reservoir, the "great wall" (35m/115ft high) and the downstream wall. There are several service tunnels between the three walls.

The English-style **park** is crisscrossed by winding alleyways and planted with forest pines, cedars, maritime pines, sequoias etc.

Revel

Revel lies on the edge of the Montagne Noire and the Lauragais region. The manufacture of furniture, cabinetmaking, marquetry, bronze work, gold-plating and lacquer work are the town's main activities. Designed as a bastide, it has a geometric street layout around a main square surrounded by covered arcades or *garlandes*. The 14C **covered market** still has its original timber roof and its belfry (renovated in the 19C). Near the north-east corner of the square stands the **Conservatoire des Métiers du bois** (guided tours available (1hr30min) 10am-noon, 2-6pm; Fri, Sun and public holidays 2-6pm; 4.60€, under 8 no charge; ☎ 05 61 27 65 50; cmbois.free.fr), a museum offering an overview of the wood trade, from forestry to the many crafts using wood as a raw material; some of these have now disappeared (cartwright, clog-maker) others still keep traditional skills alive (carpenter, joiner, cooper, violin-maker). Various workshops display their skills (design and traditional furniture).

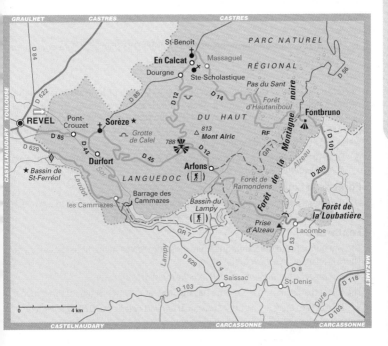

> *Follow D 85 E to Pont-Crouzet.*

Pont-Crouzet

The Rigole de la Plaine starts here. This canal collects water from the Sor and takes it to the Poste des Thommasses.

> *Return to Revel and follow D 622 S then D 624 towards Castelnaudary.*

Poste des Thommasses

This catches the water of the Laudot from St-Ferréol together with that of the Sor, which has been diverted from Pont-Crouzet via the Rigole de la Plaine. The water caught in this way is then sent onto the Seuil de Naurouze.

> *Turn right onto D 217 to the Seuil de Naurouze.*

Seuil de Naurouze★ – & *See Canal du MIDI.*

Round Tour From Revel

> *Leave Revel SE along D 629 then turn left onto D 44 running through the picturesque Sor gorge. See map above.*

Durfort

At the threshold of the deeply incised Sor Valley, Durfort has always been a centre of copper-smithing. Craftsmen continue this industry today, with coppersmiths working with the last tilt-hammer (15C) still in operation to produce various objects from copper. There is a **copper museum** (&⏰📷 *Jun-Sep: guided tour (30min) daily except Tue, 3-7pm;* 👛 *2€.* ☎ *05 63 74 22 77)* in one of the old coppersmith's houses.

> *Continue to Pont-Crouzet (see above) and turn right onto D 85 to Sorèze.*

Sorèze

The village developed in the 8C around an abbey, the only remains of which is the majestic 13C octagonal **bell-tower**.

The abbey's famous **college**★ (⏰📷 *Apr-Sep: guided tours (1hr): 10am-noon, 2-6pm; Oct-Mar: 10am-noon, 2-6pm;* 👛 *4€ (children: 2€)* ☎ *05 63 50 86 38; www.abbaye-desoreze.com),* founded in the 17C by Benedictine monks (originally as a seminary for children from poor families), became a royal military school during the reign of Louis XVI. Bought back by the Dominicans in 1854, its first head was Father Lacordaire, who died there in 1861. The famous preacher is buried in the parish church in the village, and there is a statue of him, in white marble, in the forecourt of the village school. The college closed down in 1991.

Sorèze was selected as one of the centres for the Parc naturel régional du Haut Languedoc.

▷ *As you leave Sorèze, turn right onto the pleasant D 45 then bear right again onto D 12.*

Arfons

Once the property of the Knights Hospitallers of St John of Jerusalem or of Malta, Arfons is now a peaceful mountain village with slate-roofed houses. On the corner of a house in the main street is a lovely 14C stone statue of the Virgin Mary.
🚶 Surrounded by forests, Arfons is the point of departure for a number of delightful walks (*GR 7 waymarked footpath*).

▷ *From Arfons, drive SE to Lacombe through the Montagne Noire Forest, then rejoin D 203 heading N across La Loubatière Forest.*

Forêt de la Loubatière

D 203 makes a particularly pleasant drive through the forest, winding through beech trees, the forest's predominant variety, as well as oak and fir.

Fontbruno

The war memorial to the Montagne Noire resistance forces stands here above a crypt. There is an attractive view of the plain.

▷ *Just past the monument, turn left into the forest of Hautaniboul.*

The forest road comes to a pass, the **Pas du Sant**, at the intersection of three roads.

▷ *Take D 14 to the left, and after Massaguel turn left again onto D 85 to St-Ferréol.*

En Calcat

Two Benedictine abbeys were established here by Father Romain Banquet on his personal estate. The **Monastère de St-Benoît**, for men only, was consecrated in 1896 and is still an active community. The artistic work carried out by the monks includes a workshop that produces cartoons for Dom Robert tapestries, which are then made in Aubusson, as well as crafts such as pottery, stained glass and zither making.
A little farther on, on the left, is the **Abbaye Ste-Scholastique** (founded in 1890), occupied by a contemplative order of nuns (weaving and binding workshops).
Carry on to **Dourgne**, a village which makes its living quarrying slate and stone.

▷ *Take D 12 to the left to return to Sorèze via Mont Alric.*

Mont Alric viewing table

Alt 788m/2 585ft. The view to the west stretches as far as the Revel plain, whereas the Pyrenees can be seen in the south. In the foreground, to the east, is Mont Alric (alt 813m/2 667ft).

▷ *Take D 45 right to Sorèze then D 85 back to Revel.*

MONTAUBAN★

POPULATION 51,855

MICHELIN LOCAL MAP 337: E-7

On the boundary between the hillsides of Bas Quercy and the rich alluvial plains of the Garonne and the Tarn, the old bastide of Montauban, built with a geometric street layout, is an important crossroads and a good point of departure for excursions into the Aveyron gorges. It is an active market town, selling fruit and vegetables from market gardens from all over the region. The almost exclusive use of pink brick lends the buildings here a distinctive character, found in most of the towns in Bas Quercy and the Toulouse area. 🚹 *4 R. du Collège (pedestrian access Pl. Prax), 82000 Montauban, ☎ 05 63 63 60 60. www.montauban-tourisme.com*

A Bit of History

A powerful stronghold – In the 8C, there were already several communities on the site of the modern suburb of Moustier, on a hillside overlooking the Tescou. A Benedictine monastery was later established, around which a village called Montauriol grew up. However, it was not until the 12C that the present town was founded. Fed up with being exploited by the Abbot of Montauriol and the neighbouring feudal lords, the town's inhabitants sought help and protection from their overlord, the Count of Toulouse, who founded a bastide, or fortified walled town, in 1144 on a plateau overlooking the east bank of the Tarn to which he accorded a very liberal town charter. Attracted by the advantages this new town offered, the inhabitants of Montauriol flocked there, contributing to its rapid expansion. Its name, *Mons albanus*, later became Montauban.

A Citadel of Protestantism – By 1561, most of the town had gone over to the side of the Reformists; the two town consuls were Calvinists and encouraged the inhabitants to pillage churches and convents. Catholic reaction did not manage to check the general trend in favour of new ideas. At the time of the Peace Treaty of St-Germain in 1570, Montauban was known to be a safe refuge for Protestants. Henri of Navarre reinforced its fortifications, and it was on this site that the general meeting of all the reformed churches in France was held on three occasions. But the accession of Louis XIII heralded a "Catholic reconquest." In 1621, Montauban was besieged by an army of 20 000 men, under the command of the king himself and the royal favourite, De Luynes. The townspeople put up a magnificent resistance, repelling three assaults. After three months, on the king's order to abandon the fight, the Catholic army withdrew.

But success was to be short-lived, and when La Rochelle fell in 1628, Montauban, the last bastion of Protestantism, saw Louis XIII's army marching on it once again. This time, the town opened its gates without a fight and acclaimed the king and Cardinal Richelieu. The fortifications were destroyed, but the Huguenots were granted a taste of royal clemency.

Address Book

For coin categories, see the Legend.

EATING OUT

La Table de Virginie – *13 R. des Soubirous-Hauts* - ☎ *05 63 20 37 93*. Come enjoy the flavours of southwest France in this spanking new restaurant opposite the presbytery. A substantial fireplace completes the long, sunny dining room. The wine list gives pride of place to local vintages.

WHERE TO STAY

Chambre d'hôte Maison des Chevaliers – *Pl. de la Mairie - 82700 Escatalens – 14km/9mi W of Montauban on N 113* - ☎ *05 63 68 71 23 – claude.choux@wanadoo.fr* - *6 rooms – meals*. Irresistibly charming, this 18C manor restored with style and a touch of daring. The guest rooms, painted in meridional colours, feature handsome period pieces and superb antique bathtubs. A horse chestnut lords over the delightful shaded courtyard.

SHOPPING

Boucherie-Charcuterie Vernet – *14 R. Mary-Lafon - 17km/10.5mi NW of Montauban on D 927 - 82130 Lafrançaise* - ☎ *05 63 65 81 42 - Tue-Sat 7.30am-12.30pm, 3pm-7.30pm, Sun 8am-12.30pm – closed Christmas, 1 Jan, 1 May and holiday afternoons*. At the heart of the Lower Quercy region, the Vernet establishment prepares numerous regional specialities such as sausage, fritons, pâtés and their gold medal award-winning boudin with aplomb .

La Tome du Ramier – *Le Ramier* – ☎ *05 63 22 26 19 - terre.active@free.fr – daily, tour by appointment*. This family farm welcomes visitors year-round. You can make the acquaintance of their cows, watch a milking session, and visit the cheese dairy and maturing cellar where 4,000 tomes and raclettes are aged. The cheese may be sampled and purchased.

SIT BACK AND RELAX

Crumble Tea – *25 R. de la République, Passage du Vieux-Palais* - ☎ *05 63 20 39 43 - daily except Sun and Mon 10am-7pm*. Tucked away in a tiny passageway, this pleasant tearoom is hard to find. But worth the effort for the sweet and savoury snacks served before windows overlooking a charming courtyard.

ON THE TOWN

May we suggest - In Montauban, the best way to discover the Place Nationale is by stopping in for a drink at the Maracana or the Brasserie des Arts. This magnificent 12C square, built of red brick, is as old as the city itself. The next stop could be the Base de Loisirs de Lafrançaise for a swim, followed by the Charcuterie Vernet where one can stock up on local specialities. Evenings, Le Flamand is the livliest spot in town, a good choice for enjoying a concert while unwinding on the terrace.

GUIDED TOURS

Discovery tours *(1hr30min)* of Montauban, designated a City of Art and History, are offered by the tourist office in July and August. *Information:* ☎ *05 63 63 60 60 or at www.vpah.culture.fr.*

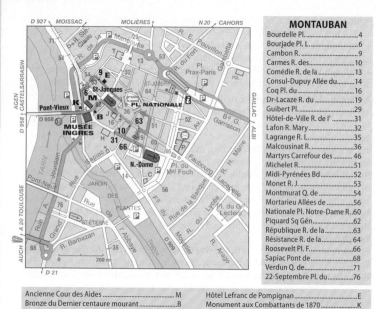

Famous Local Artists – Born in Montauban in 1780, the son of a minor painter and craftsman who gave him a solid grounding in music and painting until the age of 17, **Jean Auguste Dominique Ingres** attended the studio of the painter Roques in Toulouse before being drawn to Paris where he became the pupil of David. After winning second prize in the Prix de Rome at the age of 21, he spent nearly 20 years in Italy before moving to Paris where he opened a studio and founded a school. His greatest talent lay in draughtsmanship. He achieved a purity and precision of line which verges on technical perfection, while at the same time imbuing his works with extraordinary personality, often sensuality, in the composition of numerous portraits and studies frequently executed in pencil. Well before his death at the age of 87, Ingres had won considerable recognition and glory. He remained very attached to his home town and bequeathed it a major part of his work, now housed in the museum which bears his name.

Also born in Montauban, **Antoine Bourdelle** (1861-1929) owes much to his master, Rodin. In his compositions – busts or sculpted groups – he knew how to combine strong energetic poses, with simplicity of line and the evocation of noble sentiment. His **Héraklès Archer**, in the Musée Bourdelle in Paris, is one of his most impressive works.

Musée Ingres★

🕐 *Jul-Sep: daily 10am-6pm; rest of the year: daily except Mon 10am-noon, 2-6pm.* 🕐 *Closed Sun morning mid-Oct to mid-Apr, 1 Jan, 1 May, 14 Jul, 1 Nov, 25 Dec.* ♿ *6€ (4€ when no special exhibitions), no charge 1st Sunday in the month.* ☎ *05 63 22 12 91.*

The museum is housed in what used to be the bishops' palace, built in 1664 on the site of two castles. The first castle, called the "Château-bas," was built in the 12C by the Count of Toulouse. Demolished in 1229, it was replaced a century later by another fortress, built on the orders of the Black Prince, of which a few rooms still remain. The current palace was bought by the municipality when the diocese was suppressed at the time of the Revolution and converted to a museum in 1843. It is an imposing, sober pink-brick edifice consisting of a main building flanked by two pavilions.

1st floor – Devoted to the **work of Ingres**, this floor is the main attraction of the museum. French-style ceilings and marquetry floors provide a choice backdrop for the collection of the master's oeuvre.

After a room devoted to Ingres' work in the classical tradition, including his admirable canvas of *Jesus among the Doctors*, completed at the age of 82, a large room contains numerous sketches, academic studies, **portraits** – of Gilbert, Madame Gonse, Belvèze – and *Ossian's Dream*, a huge canvas executed in 1812 for Napoleon's bedchamber in Rome. Note also *Ruggiero freeing Angelica*, an oval copy of the original in the Louvre. Works by David, Chassériau, Géricault and Delacroix complete the exhibition. Carry on into the drawing rooms of the old bishops' palace to see a glass display case containing the master's personal mementoes – his paintbox and famous violin – as well as a selection of his 4 000 **drawings**, the highlight of the museum, displayed in rotation.

2nd floor – This contains excellent works by primitive schools and **paintings from the 14C to 18C**, mostly bequeathed by Ingres, Italian works from the 15C, beautiful paintings from the 17C Flemish (Jordaens, Van Dyck), Dutch and Spanish (José de Ribera) schools. Louis XV and Louis XVI style furniture complements the exhibition. From the windows there is a bird's-eye view of the Tarn and the Pont-Vieux.

Ground floor – A huge room is devoted to **Bourdelle**, tracing the evolution of this great sculptor's art. Works on display include a patinated plaster version of his *Héraklès Archer*, busts of Beethoven, Rodin, Léon Cladel and Ingres as well as bronzes such as *The Night* and *Rembrandt in Old Age*.
A gallery is devoted to the works of painter Armand Cambon (1819-85).

Basement – In the surviving part of the 14C castle, seven interestingly vaulted rooms on two floors are devoted to **regional archaeology, local history**, the **applied arts** and temporary exhibitions.

The former **guard-room**, known as the Black Prince's Room, contains medieval lapidary collections and has two beautiful 15C chimney-pieces adorned with the arms of Cahors. The Jean-Chandos room displays bronzes, antique terracotta pieces and a Gallo-Roman **mosaic** found at Labastide-du-Temple north-west of Montauban.

The main works of **Desnoyer** (1894-1972), a painter born in Montauban, are on display in one of the galleries.

Thanks to generous donations, a beautiful collection of **regional earthenware** has been put together (Montauban, Auvillar).

Opposite the Musée Ingres, on the edge of place du Général-Picquart, stands the admirable bronze **The Last of the Centaurs Dies**★, a powerful, compact sculpture by Bourdelle (1914) and, near the Pont-Vieux, on quai de Montmurat, the 1870 War Memorial, showing the artist's architectural capacities.

Old Town★

Restoration work has been going on for some years and it is now a pleasure to stroll through the town's historic centre.

Place Nationale★

It was to replace the wooden roofs or *couverts* above the galleries, destroyed by two fires in 1614 and 1649, that the arcades were rebuilt in brick in the 17C. There is now a double set of arcades around the square, vaulted with pointed or surbased arches. The fanciful detail and warm tones of the brick soften what would otherwise be a rather austere effect without destroying the stylistic homogeneity. The pink-brick houses surrounding this beautiful square have high façades divided into bays by pilasters, which are connected at each corner by a canted portico. On the corner of rue Malcousinat, there is a drapers' measure on the first pillar.

A. Thuillier/MICHELIN

Beneath the arcades on place Nationale

Every morning the square comes to life with a busy, colourful market.

▶ *Leave the square heading W towards Rue Cambon.*

Rue Cambon

Hôtel Lefranc de Pompignan boasts a handsome brick **doorway**★. In the courtyard at no 12 (*go right up to the railing to see*) there is an elegant wooden gallery supported by a stone colonnade.

▶ *Turn left at the end of the street, then left again.*

Place Léon-Bourjade

From the terrace of the brasserie there is a good view of the **Pont-Vieux** spanning the Tarn.

▶ *Continue to the River Tarn.*

Pont-Vieux

Built in brick in the 14C by the architects Étienne de Ferrières and Mathieu de Verdun, the Pont-Vieux is 205m/672ft long and spans the Tarn in seven arches resting on piers protected by cutwaters. Contemporary with the Pont Valentré in Cahors, it too was fortified.

Ancienne Cour des Aides

This beautiful 17C building, which once housed the Court of Excise Taxes, houses two museums (👃 *see Additional Sights*).

Église St-Jacques

Dominating the town, this fortified church, dedicated to St James, still bears traces on the tower façade of cannonballs fired during the 1621 siege. After the Catholic reconquest, in 1629, the church where Louis XIII was to be solemnly received in 1632 was raised to the rank of cathedral, a prerogative it was to keep until 1739. Resting on a machicolated square tower, the **belfry** dates from the late 13C. It is built of brick on an octagonal plan and has three rows of windows. The nave, flanked by side chapels, was renovated in the 15C and had rib vaulting added in the 18C.

▶ *Continue along Rue de la République alongside Église St-Jacques as far as Rue des Carmes and turn right.*

Rue des Carmes

At no 24, the **Hôtel Mila de Cabarieu** features a red-brick portico with surbased arcades which makes an interesting architectural composition.

▶ *Turn right onto rue de l'Hôtel-de-Ville.*

Rue de l'Hôtel de Ville

One of the interesting houses lining this street is the Hôtel Sermet-Deymie (late 18C), a typical example with its entrance doorway flanked by four Ionic columns.

▶ *Retrace your steps and follow Rue du Dr-Lacaze.*

Cathédrale Notre-Dame-de-l'Assomption

The cathedral is a classical building of vast proportions. The façade, framed by two square towers, has an imposing peristyle supporting colossal statues of the four Evangelists, copies of the originals which are to be found inside the cathedral (*by the entrance*).

In the north arm of the transept is a famous painting by Ingres, the **Vow of Louis XIII**. The king, in the foreground, clothed in a rich mantle decorated with fleur-de-lis, is turning towards the Virgin Mary, who is holding the Infant Jesus in her arms, and handing her his kingdom symbolised by a sceptre and crown (*painting can be illuminated; light switch to the right towards the middle of the church*).

Place Franklin-Roosevelt

Next to the building with caryatids, a partially vaulted alley (Passage du Vieux-Palais) linking two Renaissance courtyards leads to **Rue de la République**, emerging at no 25. At no 23 there is an attractive courtyard with multi-storey arcades on three sides.

▶ *Return to Place Nationale via Rue de la Résistance and Rue Michelet to the left.*

Additional Sights

Musée du Terroir

🕐 *Daily except Sun and Mon 10am-noon, 2-6pm.* 🕐 *Closed public holidays.* 🎫 *2.50€.* ☎ *05 63 66 46 34.*

On the ground floor of this regional folk museum, local society "Escolo Carsinol" presents a display on daily life in Bas Quercy. Most traditional crafts are represented by tools, instruments and model figures. One of the rooms is a reconstruction of the inside of a peasant home during the 19C, complete with inhabitants.

Musée d'Histoire Naturelle

🕐 *Daily except Mon 10am-noon, 2-6pm, Sun 2-6pm.* 🕐 *Closed public holidays.* 👝 *2.50€, no charge 1st Sunday in the month.* ☎ *05 63 22 13 85.*

Several rooms contain a variety of zoological exhibits and, in particular, a very large ornithological collection – 4 000 items, only some of which are displayed, including exotic birds such as parrots, humming birds and birds of Paradise.

Excursion

Château de Reyniès

🕐📷 *Jul-Sep: guided tours of the exterior (30min) daily except Wed 10am-6pm.* 👝 *2€.* ☎ *05 63 64 04 02. 11km/7mi. Leave Montauban travelling S on D 21 towards Villemur-sur-Tarn. Interior not open to the public.*

This is a brick building with three round towers, which create a triangle. A castle was built in 1289, then destroyed during the Wars of Religion (siege of 1622), as the Latour family had converted to the Protestant religion. The present château was rebuilt in 1650 and raised one storey in 1786 (the traces of the crenels are visible on the upper storey). The north-east façade is the most unusual: the two round towers flank two projecting parts of the building on either side of the entrance (triangular pediment above the gate). The southern façade, overlooking the River Tarn, is attractive; a room in the eastern tower is used for painting exhibits. On the western façade, a basket handle arch serves as an entrance to the vaulted cellars dating from the 13C.

MONT-LOUIS ★

POPULATION 270

MICHELIN LOCAL MAP 344: D-7

ALSO SEE LA CERDAGNE

Built 1 600m/5 200ft above sea level on a hillock commanding a view of the threshold of the Perche and the valleys of the Cerdagne to the west, the Capcir to the north and the Conflent to the east, Mont-Louis was originally a fortified town founded in 1679 by Vauban to defend the new borders laid down in the **Treaty of the Pyrenees**, which put an end to the hostilities between France and Spain.

Thus Mont-Louis, because of its geographical and strategic importance, became an excellent border stronghold,which was never needed.Now, a mobile defence and commando training centre has been set up in the citadel (1681), which lends itself perfectly to guerrilla warfare.

This austere fortress town pays tribute to General Dagobert (*in the church square*), a master in the art of mountain warfare who in 1793, during the dark hours of the invasion of Roussillon, drove the Spaniards out of the Cerdagne.

Visit

The fortified town

♿ ☞ *Jul and Aug: guided tours (30min) at 10am, 11am, 2.30pm, 3.30pm and 4.30pm.* ☜ *2€.* ☎ *04 68 04 21 97.*

This consists of a citadel and a lower town, built entirely within the ramparts. The citadel has a square layout, with cut-off corners extended by bastions. Three demilunes protect the curtain walls.
As the town, named after Louis XIV, the reigning monarch during its construction, was never besieged, the ramparts, the main gatehouse (Porte de France), the bastions and the watchtowers have remained intact.
Note the **Puits des Forçats**, an 18C well designed to supply the garrison with water in the event of a siege.

> **FOR HEARTY APPETITES**
>
> 🍽 **Lou Rouballou** – *r. des Écoles Laïques* – ☎ *04 68 04 23 26 - courivaudc@ aol.com – closed May, lunchtime and Wed, open Thu-Sun Oct-Nov – 19.50/30€.* Situated among the fortifications on the slopes above town, this old house with flower-bedecked balconies will delight those with a taste for authenticity. Generous portions are served in a small, elegant dining room with lace tablemats and straw-bottomed chairs.

Solar furnace (Four solaire)

♿ ☞ *Jul and Aug: guided tours (30min) 10-11.30am, 2-6pm; May, Jun, Sep and Oct: 10am, 11am, 2pm, 3pm, 4pm and 5pm; Nov-Apr: 10am, 11am, 2pm, 3pm and 4pm.* ◷ *Closed Sun (except school holidays). 5€ (8-17 year olds: 3.5€).* ☎ *04 68 04 14 89. www.four-solaire.com. Jul and Aug: guided tours (30min) 9.30am-12.30pm, 2-7pm; May, Jun, Sep and Oct: 10am, 11am, 2pm, 3pm, 4pm and 5pm; Nov-Apr: 10am, 11am, 2pm, 3pm and 4pm.* ◷ *Closed Sun (except school holidays).* ☜ *5€ (8-17 years: 3.50€).* ☎ *04 68 04 14 89.*

The solar furnace was installed in 1953. The concentrating panel, refurbished in 1980, consists of 860 parabolic mirrors and the heliostat of 546 flat mirrors. The structure focuses the sun's rays into its centre where temperatures can reach up to 3 000-3 500°C/5 400-6 300°F. Since July 1993 it has been put to commercial (rather than research) use.

Solar furnace

Excursions

Planès

6.5km/4mi S on the road to Cabanasse and St-Pierre-dels-Forçats. Leave the car in front of the Mairie-École in Planès and take the path on the right to the church. A small cemetery around the church offers a beautiful **view** of the Carlit massif. The tiny **church**★ has a curious ground plan in the shape of a sort of five-pointed star, the "rays" of which are formed by alternately pointed or blunted semicircular apsidal chapels. The central dome rests on three semi-domes.

The origins of this monument have given rise to intense speculation over the years, as its structure was extremely rare in the medieval western world. Local tradition attributes it to the Saracens, hence the church was known locally as *la mesquita* or mosque. It is probably a Romanesque building inspired by the symbol of the Holy Trinity.

Lac des Bouillouses★ – *See Le CAPCIR.*

Le Capcir★ – *From Mont-Louis to Puyvalador, see Le CAPCIR.*

MONTMAURIN

POPULATION 198

MICHELIN LOCAL MAP 343: B-5

Montmaurin sits in the region of the Gascony hills which is drained by the upper Save River, offering fine views of the Pyrenees; for tourists, however, the major attraction is archaeological: the remains of a Gallo-Roman villa lie just outside the village *(1km/0.6mi SE).*

Visit

Villa gallo-romaine

Unaccompanied tours: daily; guided tours for group visits by appointment only. ☎ *05 61 88 74 73.* The descendants of a certain Nepotius (from whose name the region of Nébouzan is derived) inherited a territory near Montmaurin extending over about 7 000ha/17 300 acres. The original *villa rustica* built on this land in the 1C AD concentrated the agricultural and rural dependencies around the big house, much like large farms do today. In the 4C, however, this residence was replaced by a marble mansion, which looked inwards and was separated from the agricultural buildings dispersed around the property. For the diversion of the host and amusement of his guests, this *villa urbana* was adorned with gardens, colonnades and statues of nymphs. Thermal baths and a system of hot air circulating beneath the tiled floors assured the inhabitants of comfort however inclement the weather. The regular consumption of quantities of oysters was further proof of the epicurean quality of this country life existence.

The mansion as a whole comprised 200 rooms arranged around a row of three separate courtyards graced with peristyles and pergolas. The chambers facing north-west on the left of the main courtyard could be heated, were near the kitchens and the gardens, and were doubtless dining halls. The complex was completed to the north-east by a series of summer apartments set on tiered terraces. The heated bathhouse stood near the outbuildings.

Museum

Unaccompanied tours: daily; guided tours for group visits by appointment only. ☎ *05 61 88 10 84.* Ground floor of the town hall (Mairie).

This local museum is divided into two sections: one is devoted to the prehistoric finds in the region and the archaeologists involved in their discovery; the other to the Gallo-Roman civilisation in the area. In the latter, a model of the villa can be seen, together with discoveries made on the site, including the contemporary bust of an adolescent.

Viewing Table

800m/880yd N of the village. From the viewing table here there is a very wide – but distant – **panorama**★★ extending from the Pyrenees in the Ariège département to Pic du Midi de Bigorre and Pic de Ger. Through the gap carved by the Garonne it is possible to see the Maladetta massif and the glaciated sections of the Luchon heights on the frontier.

Excursion

Gorges de la Save

▷ *Follow the Save Valley downstream for 1km/0.6mi, then cross the river.*

Château de Lespugue

The ruins crown a rocky spur above Save gorge. They can be reached on foot by descending through an oak grove and then climbing through the woods on the opposite slope of the valley.

▷ *Return to the car and continue down to the river. Just before the bridge, turn left on D 9.*

Gorges de la Save

The Save torrent, carving a deep channel here through the limestone folds of the Lesser Pyrenees, has hollowed out a number of caves or shelters beneath the rock. Several of these, excavated between 1912 and 1922 by the Comte and Comtesse de Saint-Périer, yielded finds dating back from the Magdalen-ian (late Palaeolithic) and Azilian (transitional Paleo-lithic-Neolithic) periods. Notable among the finds is the statuette known as the **Vénus de Lespugue** (the original is now in the Musée des Antiquités Nationales in St-Germain-en-Laye).

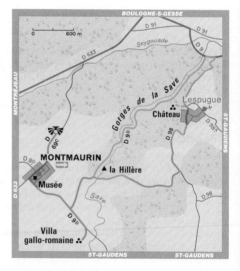

La Hillère

On the way out of the gorge, below the level of the road, archaeological digs have revealed a sanctuary includ-ing temples, baths, fountain and market, built during the 4C on the spot where the River Save resurfaces.

▷ *Return to Montmaurin.*

MONTPELLIER★★

POPULATION 287 981

MICHELIN LOCAL MAP 339: I-7

Bathed in uniquely Mediterranean light, Montpellier, the capital of Languedoc-Roussillon, owes much of its charm to its beautiful historical districts and superb gardens juxtaposed with modern buildings which bear witness to the dynamic character of this large administrative centre and university city. *30 allée De-Lattre-de-Tassigny (esplanade Comédie), 34000 Montpellier, ☎ 04 67 60 60 60. www.ot-montpellier.fr.*

▶ **Orient yourself:** The tourist office organises guided tours which include access to many areas usually closed to the public. *Reservation required.*

☺ **Don't Miss:** the Old Town.

A Bit of History

The Middle Ages – Unlike neighbouring Nîmes, Béziers and Narbonne, Montpellier did not enter the historical arena until about the 10C. Two villages formed the beginnings of the future major conurbation: Montpellieret, a dependency of the bishop of Maguelone, and Montpellier, owned by the lords of Guilhem.

In 1204, after the marriage of Marie de Guilhem to Peter of Aragon, Montpellier became a Spanish enclave and remained so until 1349 when John III of Majorca sold it to the king of France for 120 000 *écus*.

After that, the town developed quickly and played an important role in trade with the Levant. Its spice and dyestuff merchants were familiar with the therapeutic values of the products they sold; some of the more educated among them read translations of Hippocrates and were thus able to share their knowledge with scholars of medical science. This was how the first "schools" of medicine were created. These became a university in the early 13C and were later joined by law and art faculties. A bull issued by Pope Nicolas IV, recognising these establishments, was the basis for the founding charter of the **University of Montpellier**. A number of prestigious scholars were to be attracted to study here, among them **Rabelais**, who completed his studies in 1530, graduating as a doctor of medicine.

The end of the 14C was marked by several disasters (bubonic plague, famine etc). In the middle of the 15C, trade began to flourish once again and Montpellier became one of the centres of economic activity of **Jacques Cœur**, King Charles VII's financier. The union of Provence with France in 1481 struck Montpellier a harsh blow, since Marseille then became the main port for trade with the Levant.

Montpellier, capital city – In the 16C, the Reformation arrived in Montpellier, and Protestants and Catholics in turn became masters of the town. After becoming a Protestant fief, the town was the scene of violent confrontations; most of the churches and convents were destroyed. In 1622, the royal armies of Louis XIII laid siege to the fortifications of Montpellier, which capitulated after three months. Richelieu then had the citadel built to keep watch over the rebel city. Some of the Protestants left the town, selling up their affairs to the "good people of Montpellier."

Louis XIV made Montpellier the administrative capital of Bas Languedoc. The now prosperous town carried out extensive projects to embellish itself. Well-known architects, such as **d'Aviler** who had studied in Rome, and the **Giral** family vied with each other to display their talent. They built the Promenade du Peyrou, the Esplanade and fountains, while at the same time working for rich financiers and senior civil servants for whom they designed the superb town mansions which can be seen in the historic centre of Montpellier.

Place de la Comédie

384

y/MICHELIN

Address Book

TRANSPORTATION

Tramway – *Transports de l'Agglomération de Montpellier.* ☎ *04 67 22 87 87. www. tam-way.com*

A new Montpellier tram has joined local bus lines, allowing passengers to travel just about anywhere within the city and beyond in just a few minutes.

For coin categories, see the Legend at the back of the guide.

EATING OUT

Simple Simon – *1 r. des Trésoriers-de-France.* ☎ *04 67 66 03 43 - closed Sun May-Oct and in the evening – reservation recommended.* Simply British, Simple Simon serves a medley of British pastries, an Indian or sweet and savoury dish for lunch, salads in summer and soup in winter. Perfectly cosy setting, with tablemats and a thick carpet. Languedoc wines by the glass, lest we forget our French!

The Salmon Shop – *5 r. de la Petite-Loge.* ☎ *04 67 66 40 70 - closed Sun and Mon lunchtime - reservation recommended at weekends – 11.28€ lunch - 22.41/36.44€.* Steak-lovers, beware! Salmon rules supreme here, and it is served in every sauce imaginable with one accompanying vegetable: homemade French-fried potatoes. The singular decor represents the interior of a trapper's cabin: wood-panelled walls, old skis, a wooden kayak overhead, old rifles and a totem pole. Relaxed atmosphere.

C'an Jose – *8 bis r. du Petit-Saint-Jean.* ☎ *04 67 60 70 71 – closed 14 Jul-15 Aug, Sun and Mon.* This establishment in Old Montpellier houses all of Catalonia and the Baleares under its roof. Decorated in yellow and red, naturally, the dining room is covered in photographs of the island of Minorca. Tapas and Catalan, Spanish and Balearic cuisine are served here. *Buen provecho!*

Le Petit Jardin – *20 r. Jean-Jacques-Rousseau.* ☎ *04 67 60 78 78 - contact@ petit-jardin.com - closed Jan and Mon.* Located on a narrow street in the renovated Écusson quarter, this charming little house welcomes diners to its appealing terrace-garden whenever the weather obliges. Enjoy tasty regional fare as you admire the cathedral from your vantage point under the trees.

Les Bains de Montpellier – *6 r. Richelieu.* ☎ *04 67 60 70 87 - closed in Feb, Toussaint and Christmas holidays, Mon lunchtime and Sun – reservation recommended.* Whether seated in the shade of the courtyard palm trees, beneath the large glass roof or in one of the little drawing rooms, there's an ambience to suit every guest in the wonderfully well-restored old "Parisian baths". Cuisine made from fresh market produce.

WHERE TO STAY

Hôtel de la Comédie – *1 bis r. Baudin.* ☎ *04 67 58 43 64 – hoteldelacomedie@wanadoo.fr - 20 rms.* Located just off of La Place de la Comédie, this recently overhauled hotel with a 19C facade offers pleasingly modern bedrooms. Located in a lively Montpellier neighbourhood, it is an excellent starting point for discovering the city. Relaxed ambience.

Hôtel du Palais – *3 r. du Palais.* ☎ *04 67 60 47 38 - 26 rms.* This family hotel near the Peyrou gardens and the Place de la Canourgue has small rooms that are stylish and well kept.

Hôtel Maison Blanche – *1796 av. Pompignane.* ☎ *04 99 58 20 70 – hotelmaisonblanche@wanadoo.fr -* P *- 35 rms.* Tempted by a brief stay in Scarlett O'Hara country? This colonial-style wood house comes as something of a surprise in this part of the world. Jean-Edern Hallier sang a song about it; with its gangways and sculpted friezes it will no doubt captivate you as well. Spacious rooms.

Chambre d'hôte Domaine de Saint-Clément – *34980 St-Clément-de-Rivière. 10km/6mi N of Montpellier on D 17 then D112 -* ☎ *04 67 66 70 89 - calista. bernabe@wanadoo.fr - closed Dec-Feb -* 🖄 *- 5 rms.* Peace and quiet are guaranteed in this fine 18C farmhouse 10 minutes from the centre of Montpellier. The comfortable bedrooms, decorated with antique furniture and modern paintings, overlook the garden or the swimming pool. Do not miss the fine Portuguese azulejo tiles on the patio.

SIT BACK AND RELAX

Dorian's Kawa – *12 r. Four-des-Flammes.* ☎ *04 67 66 18 71 - Mon-Sat 8am-7pm – closed Aug and public holidays.* A tearoom to make a note of – the coffee is excellent and the owner very friendly. The shop sells coffeepots, tea services and English china. Ideal for a break or a tête-à-tête.

L'Heure Bleue – *1 r. de la Carbonnerie.* ☎ *04 67 66 41 05 - Tues-Sat noon-7pm.* This literary tearoom in an 18C mansion is also an art gallery and second-hand shop; as such its decor includes a lavish collection of sculptures and curios. Home-baked pastries and nearly 30 varieties of tea.

STOPPING FOR A DRINK

Café de la Mer – *5 pl. du Marché-aux-Fleurs.* ☎ *04 67 60 79 65 - end Jun-end Aug: Mon-Sat 8am-2am, Sun and holidays 3pm-2am; rest of the year: 8am-1am, Sun and holidays: 3pm-1am.* A large, popular café in the centre of town. Its decor of beautiful coloured mosaics and the large sunny terrace make this a fashionable meeting point for Montpellier residents of all ages.

Grand Café Riche – *Pl. de la Comédie - ☎ 04 67 54 71 44 - daily 8am-1am; summer: 6am-2am.* This century-old café is an institution in Montpellier. Its large terrace provides a front row seat for observing street entertainment on the Place de la Comédie. Art exhibitions are frequently held here.

La Pleine Lune – *28 r. du Fg-Figuerolles - ☎ 04 67 58 03 40 - daily 10.30am-1am.* This bar in the Plan Cabannes district is frequented by an inimitable clientele of artists, neighbours and original characters. Happenings, exhibitions by local artists and concerts are organized here regularly. An officially picturesque establishment!

ON THE TOWN

In Montpellier, a student's city, many bars and music cafés are partial to new trends in music and it is quite common to discover a rap concert being performed round the corner from a bourgeois manor. The city's cultural landscape is very diverse, with its jazz enthusiasts, accordion fans and lovers of salsa or classical music.

Rockstore – *20 r. de Verdun - ☎ 04 67 06 80 00 - www.rockstore.fr – bars: Mon-Sat 6pm-4am; disco: 11pm-4am.* This hotspot of Montpellier nightlife hosts numerous rock groups and organizes techno, rap and sound system evenings. With the huge red American car stuck above the entrance, the techno and rock bars and the disco, the decor mirrors the musical programming.

Centre dramatique national – *Domaine de Grammont, Avenue Albert-Einstein – ☎ 04 67 99 25 25 : reserv. by phone: 04 67 60 05 45.*

Opéra Comédie – *11 bd Victor-Hugo - ☎ 04 67 60 19 99 - tickets: Mon 2pm-6pm, Tue-Sat noon-6pm, Sundays of performances – closed Aug.*

Zénith – *Av. Albert-Einstein - ☎ 04 67 64 50 00 - www.zenith-montpellier.com – performance schedule variable - closed Aug.* Variety and rock shows.

SHOPPING

Aux Croquants de Montpellier – *7 r. du Faubourg-du-Courreau - ☎ 04 67 58 67 38 – Tue-Sun 7am-7pm, Mon 7am-1pm and 4-7pm ; closed Aug.* This tiny shop has been a mecca for biscuit lovers for over a century with an extensive array of confections available.

Aux Gourmets – *2 r. Clos-René - ☎ 04 67 58 57 04.* Run by the Fournier family for over 45 years, this shop close to Place de la Comedie offers a wide variety of sweets and cakes.

Librairie Sauramps – *Allée Jules-Milhau (Le Triangle) – Tramway Comédie – ☎ 04 67 06 78 78 - www.sauramps.com - Mon-Sat 10am-7pm – closed public holidays.* This vast, comprehensive bookstore carries a good choice of publications about the area.

Markets – Food markets are open every morning in centre city in the halles (covered markets) Castellane and Arceaux, on the Esplanade Charles-de-Gaulle, the halles Laissac, the new halles Jacques-Cœur in the Antigone district and on the Plan Cabannes. Organic produce is sold Tuesdays and Saturdays Place des Arceaux. On the 3rd Saturday of each month, used-book sellers gather on Rue des Étuves. Avenue Samuel-Champlain in the Antigone district holds a farmers' market Sunday mornings.

A flower market Tuesdays and a flea market Sundays are held in the west at La Paillade, Esplanade de la Mosson.

Maison régionale des vins et produits du terroir – *34 R. St-Guilhem - ☎ 04 67 60 40 41 – daily (except Sun in Dec) 9.30am-8pm.* All the finest produce of the region is represented here.

CALENDAR OF EVENTS

Montpellier and the surrounding area are rich in all manner of festivals

Festival international Montpellier danse – *☎ 04 67 60 83 60– www.montpellierdanse.com - late Jun-early Jul.* Traditional music and dance.

Festival de Radio France et Montpellier Languedoc-Roussillon – *☎ 04 67 02 02 01– www.festivalradiofrancemontpellier.com - first 3wks of Jul.* Concerts, chamber music, jazz, world music.

Festival international cinéma méditerranéen – *☎ 04 99 13 73 73 – www.cinemed.tm.fr - late Oct-early Nov.* Film festival.

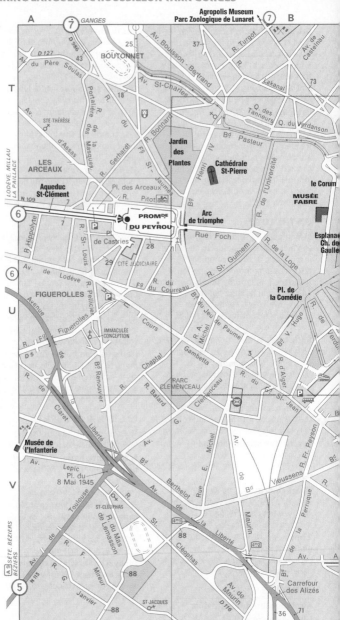

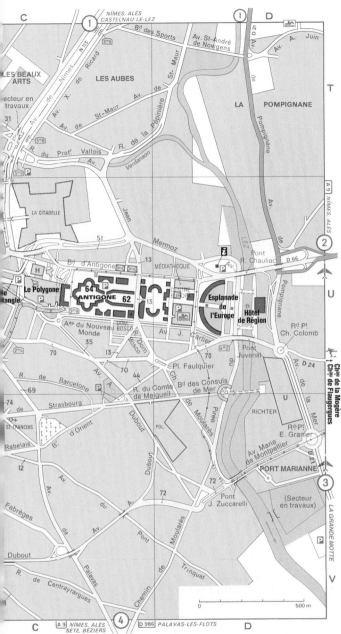

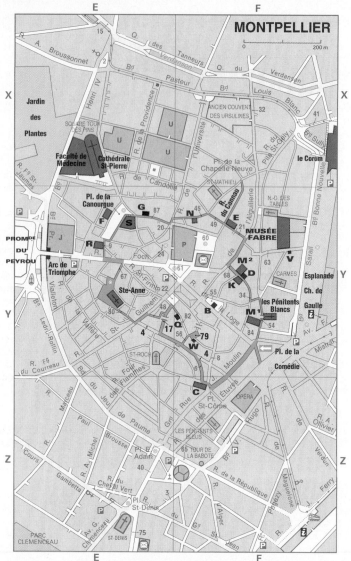

MONTPELLIER

Antigone	CU	Hôtel de Manse	FY K	Musée Fougau	FY	M²
Arc de Triomphe	EY	Hôtel de Région	DU	Musée Languedocien	FY	M¹
Cathédrale St-Pierre	EX	Hôtel de Solas et d'Uston	FY N	Musée Vieux Montpellier	FY	M²
Chapelle des		Hôtel de Varennes	FY M²	Musée d'Anatomie	EX M	
Pénitents Blancs	FY	Hôtel de la Vieille		Musée de l'Infanterie	AV	
Église Ste-Anne	EY	Intendance	EY G	Musée de l'histoire		
Faculté de Médecine	EX	Hôtel des Trésoriers		de Montpellier	FY B	
Hôtel Baschy du Cayla	FY D	de France	FY M¹	Polygone (Le)	CU	
Hôtel Baudon de Mauny	FY E	Hôtel des Trésoriers		Promenade du Peyrou	ABU	
Hôtel Cabrières-Sabatier		de la Bourse	FY Q	Salle St-Ravy	FY W	
d'Espeyran	FY V	Hôtel du Sarret	EY R	Triangle (le)	CU	
Hôtel Richer de Belleval	EY S	Jardin des Plantes	EX			
Hôtel St-Côme	FZ C	Musée Atger	EX M			
Hôtel de Cambacérès	EY F	Musée Fabre	FY			

Modern Montpellier – After the Revolution, the town had to forego its role as the capital of Languedoc to become the simple *préfecture* of the Hérault *département*. Only the university and the retail trade, especially that of wine, remained significant. With the return of the French from North Africa after 1962, the city found a renewed dynamism. To the west of the city a new residential suburb grew up, **La Paillade**. To expand the sphere of its economic activity and tourist industry, Montpellier has created various *pôles*: **Euromédecine**, with its numerous research laboratories and pharmaceutical companies; **Agropolis** to the north of the city, home to farm-produce industries; **Antenna**, with its various radio and television production centres; **Héliopolis**, which regroups businesses concerned with the tourist and leisure industries. A large number of the city's working inhabitants are employed in tertiary industries. The high speed (TGV) rail link means that Montpellier is now just over 4hr away from Paris.

Evidence of the dynamism of this city is provided more than anything else by the wealth of construction projects designed by contemporary architects that have been commissioned in recent years. To the north of the historic town centre is the **Corum**, a conference and concert centre; to the east, the **Antigone** district, linked to old Montpellier by the Triangle and Polygone shopping centres and, to the south, the **Odysseum** district, the latest addition to Montpellier's town-planning achievements.

Historic Montpellier★★

3hr. Since the courtyards of most of the hôtels are generally closed to the public, visitors are strongly recommended to go on one of the guided tours organised by the tourist office. For a change of pace, try a **cycling tour**. *(Hourly bicycle rental (1.50€), half-day (3€) or full day (6€) to avoid taking your car into the town centre which is full of one-way streets. Contact TaM Vélo, ☎ 04 67 92 92 67.0*

Between place de la Comédie and the Peyrou Arc de Triomphe, on either side of rue Foch, lie the historic districts of Montpellier, with their narrow, winding streets, the last vestiges of the original medieval town.

Lining the streets are superb 17C and 18C private mansions, or *hôtels*, with their main façades and remarkable staircases hidden from the public eye in inner courtyards.

Place de la Comédie

This lively square in the heart of Montpellier links the city's old districts with the new. The 19C façade of the theatre serves as a backdrop to a fountain of the Three Graces, by sculptor Étienne d'Antoine. The ovoid area of paving around the fountain is a reminder of the old egg-shaped terreplein (levelled-off earth embankment, often where guns were positioned) which earned place de la Comédie the nickname *l'œuf* ("the egg"). Place de la Comédie is continued to the north by the **Esplanade**, a beautiful promenade lined with plane trees where Montpellier residents come in summer to stroll among the outdoor cafés or listen to musicians playing in the bandstands. Closing off the view at the far end is the **Corum** (Guided tours (45min) by written request. Tours of the Corum and Berlioz Opera House are subject to bookings and schedule modifications. No charge. ☎ 04 67 61 67 61.), a vast concrete-and-red-granite complex designed by Claude Vasconi. It includes the Berlioz opera house with excellent acoustics and 2 000 seats. From the Corum terrace there is a fine view of the town's rooftops, St-Pierre Cathedral, the former Jesuit college and the white spire of Ste-Anne's Church.

To the east lie the **Triangle** and the **Polygone** complex (shopping centre, administrative buildings, including the town hall).

▶ *Take rue de la Loge.*

The name of this street is a reminder of the all powerful merchants' lodge in the 15C.

▶ *Turn right onto rue Jacques-Cœur.*

Hôtel des Trésoriers de France

No 7. This private mansion has been known by various names depending on who owned it at any particular time. It was called the Hôtel Jacques-Cœur when the king's treasurer was living there in the 15C – the vaulted cellars and polychrome coffered ceilings that adorn some of the rooms date from this period. In the 17C it became the Hôtel des Trésoriers de France, after the resident senior magistrates in charge of administering the royal estates in Languedoc. These dignitaries had the grand three-flight staircase built, along with the majestic façade overlooking the courtyard with its superimposed colonnades. Finally, the name Lunaret, by which it has also been known, is in memory of Henri de Lunaret who bequeathed it to the local archaeological society (Société Archéologique de Montpellier). The building houses the Musée Languedocien (& *see Museums below*).

To the right of the hôtel stands the **Chapelle des Pénitents Blancs**, once the church of Ste-Foy, which was rebuilt in the 17C and features a doorway with a triangular pediment.

▶ *Turn left onto rue Valedeau and right onto rue Embouque-d'Or.*

On the left stands the Hôtel de Manse, and opposite, **Hôtel Baschy du Cayla**, with its Louis XV façade, next to Hôtel de Varennes.

Hôtel de Manse

4 rue Embouque-d'Or. The count of Manse, who was treasurer to the king of France, had Italian artists design this interior façade with its double colonnade forming the bays of a beautiful staircase called the "Manse's Steps."

Hôtel de Varennes★

Information at the tourist office. ☎ 04 67 60 60 60. *2 place Pétrarque.*

An archway leads to several Gothic rooms with intersecting ribs. One of these rooms contains Romanesque columns and capitals from the original church of Notre-Dame-des-Tables; gemel windows and castle doors have been incorporated into the walls, forming a very harmonious whole. The 14C Salle Pétrarque, with its ribbed vaulting, is used by the city of Montpellier for receptions. The mansion houses two museums (& *see Museums below*).

▶ *Turn right onto rue de l'Aiguillerie.*

As this street's name ("needle factory") suggests, this was the town's street for arts and crafts in the Middle Ages. Some of the shops still have their beautiful 14C and 15C vaulted roofs.

▶ *Take rue Glaize on the right and continue along rue Montpellieret.*

Hôtel de Cabrières-Sabatier d'Espeyran

✎ *Possibility of guided tours by request at the musée Fabre. It is possible to visit this by applying to the Musée Fabre (& see Museums below).* This 19C private town house is an excellent example of a wealthy Second Empire mansion.

▶ *Return to rue de l'Aiguillerie going N around the Musée Fabre, then turn left onto rue de la Carbonnerie.*

Hôtel Baudon de Mauny

1 rue de la Carbonnerie. This house features an elegant Louis XVI façade decorated with garlands of flowers facing onto the street.

Rue du Cannau

This street is lined with classical town houses: at no 1, **Hôtel de Roquemaure** with a door studded with nail head stones and boasting fluted pilasters; at no 3, **Hôtel d'Avèze**; at no 6, **Hôtel de Beaulac**; at no 8, **Hôtel Deydé** featuring architectural innovations introduced by d'Avilar in the late 17C – a depressed arch and a triangular pediment.

▶ *Turn back and take rue de Girone on the right, then rue Fournarié.*

Hôtel de Solas

1 rue Fournarié. This 17C town house features a Louis XIII door. Note the plasterwork on the porch ceiling.

Hôtel d'Uston

3 rue Fournarié. This house dates from the first half of the 18C. The archway of the door is decorated with wreaths (with a female figure on the keystone) and the pediment with cherubs framing a vase of flowers.

▷ *Follow rue de la Vieille-Intendance.*

At no 9 is the **Hôtel de la Vieille Intendance**, which has been inhabited by many famous people including the philosopher Auguste Comte and the writer Paul Valéry.

Place de la Canourgue

In the 17C, this square was the centre of Montpellier, and numerous *hôtels* still remain around the garden with its Unicorn fountain, the last of three fountains designed to distribute water supplied by the St-Clément aqueduct.

From the square, there is a view down onto the cathedral of St-Pierre.

Hôtel Richer de Belleval – *Annexe of the law courts.* For a long time, this housed the town hall. The square courtyard is decorated with busts and balustrades typical of the late 18C.

Hôtel de Cambacérès – This house's façade, by Giral, shows the richness and elegance of 18C ornamentation – beautifully curved and shaped wrought-iron work, grotesque masks etc.

Hôtel du Sarret – This is known as the Maison de la Coquille ("shell house") because of its squinches, a real architectural feat in which part of the building itself is supported on part of the vault.

▷ *Take rue Astruc and cross rue Foch.*

This leads to the district known as **Ancien Courrier**, the oldest part of Montpellier, its narrow pedestrian streets lined with luxury boutiques.

▷ *From rue Foch, take rue du Petit-Scel.*

The 19C **church of Ste-Anne**, surmounted by a high bell-tower and now deconsecrated, houses temporary exhibitions.

Opposite the church porch stand the remains of a small building, which has been rebuilt here. Its early-17C decor is in Antique style.

▷ *Take rue St-Anne and rue St-Guilhem to rue de la Friperie, then turn left onto rue du Bras-de-Fer and right onto rue des Trésoriers-de-la-Bourse.*

Hôtel des Trésoriers de la Bourse★

4 rue des Trésoriers-de-la-Bourse. Also called Hôtel Rodez-Benavent, this town house by architect Jean Giral features an impressive open staircase in which sloping balustrades and rampant arches follow the line of the flights of steps, making an interesting contrast with the level balustrades and round arches framing the landings on either side. The façade overlooking the courtyard is decorated with delightful little cupids.

A second courtyard offers the peace and tranquillity of a large garden whose rear wall is decorated with flame ornaments.

▷ *Retrace your steps.*

The narrow **rue du Bras-de-Fer** is a medieval street spanned by a pointed archway. It leads down to **rue de l'Ancien-Courrier★**, once called rue des Relais-de-Poste and now lined with art galleries and elegant boutiques.

▷ *Turn left onto rue Joubert which leads to place St-Ravy.*

Place St-Ravy still boasts the remains (Gothic windows) of the Palace of the Kings of Majorca.

The **Salle St-Ravy**, in which temporary exhibitions are held, has beautiful vaulting decorated with keystones.

▷ *Return to rue de l'Ancien-Courrier and take rue Jacques-d'Aragon.*

Hôtel St-Côme

👐 *Free access to the inner courtyard. Guided tours of the anatomy amphitheatre as part of the theme guided tours organised by the tourist office.* ☎ *04 67 60 60 60.*

Now the Chamber of Commerce, this town house was built in the 18C by Jean-Antoine Giral thanks to a donation by François Gigot de Lapeyronie, surgeon to Louis XV, who bequeathed part of his fortune to the surgeons of Montpellier so that they could build an anatomical theatre similar to that in Paris.

The building facing the street is decorated with a double colonnade. The other building houses the famous polygonal anatomical theatre, under a superb dome with oculi and lanterns letting in a flood of light.

▷ *Return to place de la Comédie via the busy grand-rue Jean-Moulin.*

Château d'eau in the Peyrou

Promenade Du Peyrou★★ *1hr*

The promenade consists of two levels of terraces. The upper terrace, adorned with the equestrian statue of Louis XIV, affords a sweeping **view**★ of the Garrigues and Cévennes to the north, and the Mediterranean and, on a fine day, Mont Canigou in the distance to the south.

Monumental flights of steps lead to the lower terraces decorated with wrought-iron railings made after sketches by Giral. The most original feature of the Promenade du Peyrou is the ensemble of the *château d'eau* and St-Clément aqueduct, 880m/2 890ft long and 22m/72ft high. The aqueduct's two levels of arcades were inspired by the Roman Pont du Gard (*east of Nîmes*). It brings in water from Lez spring to the château d'eau, which in turn is connected to three fountains built in the town centre at the same time: the fountain of the Three Graces (*place de la Comédie*), the Cybele fountain (*place Chabaneau*) and the Unicorn fountain (*place de la Canourgue*). Promenade des Arceaux beneath the arches is transformed into a flea market on Saturdays.

The Arc de Triomphe

Built in the late 17C, the arch is decorated with low-relief sculptures depicting the victories of Louis XIV and major events from his reign. Towards the city: to the north, the linking of two seas by the Canal du Midi, and to the south, the revocation of the Edict of Nantes; towards the Promenade du Peyrou: to the north, Louis XIV as Hercules being crowned by Victory, and to the south, the capture of Namur in 1692 and the United Provinces of the Netherlands kneeling before Louis XIV.

The Rise and Fall of Louis XIV

In 1688, the town council decided to create a promenade in the highest-lying part of Montpellier to act as a framework for a monumental statue of Louis XIV. Cast in Paris in 1692, the statue did not reach its final location until 1718 after a long and arduous journey which took it from Le Havre to Bordeaux, then on to the Canal du Midi, and during which a number of misadventures befell it, not the least of which was falling into the Garonne. A channel was even cut through the Frontignan lagoons so that the statue could be transported from the Mediterranean to Montpellier. Having finally made it to its destination, the statue was destroyed during the Revolution. It was replaced by the present replica in 1838.

Antigone District★
45min

▶ *Starting from place de la Comédie (east side), walk to the Antigone district via the Polygone shopping centre.*

Behind the Polygone shopping centre and office complex, the new Antigone district is the boldly designed creation of Catalan architect, **Ricardo Bofill**.
Covering the 40ha/100 acres of the old polygonal army exercise ground, this vast neo-Classical housing project combines prefabrication technology (the prestressed concrete has been given the grain and colour of stone) with rigorously harmonious design on a gigantic scale. Behind a profusion of entablatures, pediments, pilasters and columns are low-income housing, public facilities and local shops, arranged around numerous squares and patios. The architect's quest for harmony has manifested itself in the smallest details, from the design of the paving to the street lighting.

Place du Nombre-d'Or, built to proportions based on an Antique architectural concept, is symmetrically composed of smooth curves and setback features around a vast area of ground planted with trees. The continuation of this square is formed by **place du Millénaire**, a long mall lined with cypresses, place de Thessalie then place du Péloponnèse. The almost 1km/0.5mi-long vista stretches from the "Échelles de la Ville" (*flights of steps backing onto the Polygone*), past **esplanade de l'Europe**, with its crescent-shaped buildings, to the **Hôtel de Région**, with its glass walls reflected in the Lez, which has been converted into a dock for Port Juvénal at this point.

Place du Nombre-d'Or

A. Thuillier/MICHELIN

Faculty of Medicine
Cathédrale St-Pierre
🕐 *Daily except Sun afternoon.*

The cathedral, towering up like a fortress, is made to seem even more massive than it is by the adjacent façade of the Faculty of Medicine that prolongs it. It is the only church in Montpellier that was not completely destroyed during the Wars of Religion. Although built in the Gothic style, the cathedral is reminiscent of the single-nave Romanesque churches along the coast. The porch consists of two 14C towers, in front of a vault resting on the façade. Inside, the chancel and transept, rebuilt in the 19C, contrast with the austere 14C nave. The altar and the ambo (pulpit) in the pre-chancel, as well as the altar and tabernacle door in the sacrament chapel, left of the chancel, are the work of sculptor Philippe Koeppelin. The 18C organ case was made by Jean-François Lépine.

Faculté de Médecine

The Montpellier Faculty of Medicine occupies a former Benedictine monastery, founded in the 14C by order of Pope Urban V. The building was renovated in the 18C; most notably the façade, which was reworked by Giral and crowned with machicolations. Two bronze statues, depicting the Montpellier doctors Barthez and Lapeyronie, stand guard at the entrance. The busts in the hall also depict famous doctors. From the courtyard, there is a view of the west side of the cathedral and the anatomical theatre built in the early 18C. The Faculty houses two museums (🔍 *see Museums below*).

Jardin des Plantes
🕐 *May-Sep: daily except Mon noon-8pm; Oct and Apr: daily except Mon noon-7pm; Nov-Mar: daily except Mon noon-6pm.* 🕐 *Closed 1 May. No charge* ☎ *04 67 63 43 22.*

Jardin des Plantes

The botanical gardens, the oldest in France, founded in 1593, initially stretched as far as the Peyrou. They were created for the Montpellier Faculty of Botany and for the study of medicinal plants. The gardens contain both temperate and tropical hothouses, and are home to various species of Mediterranean tree, such as the nettle tree, holm-oak and mock privet (phillyrea). A large ginkgo biloba (maidenhair tree), planted in 1795, is a graft from the first ginkgo plant introduced to France by Antoine Gouan.

The southern part is occupied by a botanical garden containing 3 000 species – set up following the principles of natural classification of plants based on their anatomy laid down by the botanist Augustin Pyrame de **Candolle** in the early 19C. An orangery occupies one end.

The busts of famous naturalists from the Montpellier faculty occupy the length of the garden.

Museums

Musée Fabre★★

⚲ *Closed for restoration. 37 boulevard Sarrail.*

The museum was founded in 1825 thanks to the generosity of the Montpellier painter **François-Xavier Fabre** (1766-1837), who studied under David and bequeathed several collections to the city of Montpellier.

The collections include a series of Greek and European ceramic ware (including 17C and 18C Montpellier apothecary's pots), as well as paintings from the Spanish (*The Angel Gabriel* by Zurbarán), Italian (Veronese, Allori, Il Guercino), Dutch and Flemish (Ruysdael, Rubens, Teniers the Younger) schools. The 17C and 18C French schools are represented by numerous masterpieces by S Bourdon, Poussin, Dughet, Vouet, David (*Hector*), a large collection of works by Greuze (*Le Petit Paresseux, Twelfth Night Cake*) as well as sculptures by Houdon (*Summer, Winter*).

Early-19C French painting is particularly well represented thanks to the Alfred Bruyas collection, as well as by works by the *luminophiles* (light-lovers), the nickname given to Languedoc painters who tried to capture on canvas the superb light of their region. Next to the Bruyas portraits are world-famous works by Delacroix (*Algerian women in their room, Fantasia*), Courbet (including La Rencontre, *Les Baigneuses*, which scandalised the public at the 1853 Salon with the "indecency" of the bathers, and *Ambrussum Roman Bridge*, which then had two arches), and Montpellier artist Frédéric Bazille (*View of the Village, The Ramparts at Aigues-Mortes* and *Black Woman with Peonies*).

Among sculptures by Bourdelle, Maillol and Richier (*The Bat*) are works by Van Dongen (*Portrait of Fernande Olivier*), De Staël, Marquet, Dufy, Soulages, Vieira da Silva, Viallat, Montpellier artist Vincent Bioulès (*Square in Aix-en-Provence, Homage to Auguste Chabaud*) and Jean Hugo (1894-1984 – *The Impostor*).

Musée languedocien★

🕐 *Daily except Sun 2-5pm.* 🕐 *Closed 1 Jan, Easter Monday, 1 May, Whit Monday, 14 Jul, 1 and 11 Nov, 25 Dec.* ⬡ *5€.* ☎ *04 67 52 93 03. Hôtel des Trésoriers de France, 7 rue Jacques-Cœur.*

The medieval room in this local museum houses a collection of Romanesque sculpture, including the Virgin Mary and the Three Wise Men from the abbey of Fontcaude (Aude), and capitals from the cloisters of St-Guilhem-le-Désert.

In the first-floor Gothic room, there is a Vias lead font (13C), wooden tableware and a collection of amusing painted panels. The main ceremonial hall, hung with 17C Flemish tapestries, houses a painting by the Fontainbleau School, two beautiful Languedoc cabinets, and a Coronelli celestial globe. The yellow room successfully evokes the spirit of the 18C with marquetry furniture and collections of Sèvres porcelain. The next room contains ceramic ware from various places (Moustiers-Ste-Marie, Marseille and Delft). Go through the apartments that once belonged to the Lunaret family to get to the second floor, devoted to archaeological collections and folk art and traditions.

Musée du Vieux Montpellier

🕒 *Daily except Sun and Mon 9.30am-noon, 1.30-5pm.* 🕒 *Closed public holidays. No charge.* ☎ *04 67 66 02 94. Hôtel de Varennes, 2 place Pétrarque, first floor.*

This museum of local history contains a selection of engravings, portraits of the town's leading citizens, old maps and religious objects, including the Virgin Mary reliquary from the church of Notre-Dame-des-Tables, penitents' staffs and documents from the Revolution.

Musée Fougau

🕒 *Wed and Thu 3-6pm.* 🕒 *Closed mid-Jul to mid-Aug. No charge. Hôtel de Varennes, 2 place Pétrarque, second floor.*

The museum derives its name from the Languedoc expression *lou fougau* (the hearth). Objects, furniture and decors give an idea of popular 19C local arts and traditions.

Crypte de Notre-Dame-des-Tables

🕒 *Daily except Sun and Mon 10.30am-12.30pm, 1.30-6pm (last admission 40min before closing).* 🕒 *Closed public holidays.* 👓 *1.50€.* ☎ *04 67 54 33 16. Place Jean-Jaurès (via rue de la Loge).*

The crypt of the original Église Notre-Dame-des-Tables, one of the oldest churches in Montpellier, is the venue of a multimedia presentation devoted to the history and destiny of this most gifted city (3D reconstructions, dioramas etc).

Musée Atger★

🕒 *Mon, Wed, Fri 1.30-5.45pm.* 🕒 *Closed Aug and public holidays. No charge.* ☎ *04 67 66 27 77. Faculté de Médecine, 2 rue de l'École-de-Médecine, first floor, access (signposted) via the Houdan staircase.*

This museum is devoted mainly to the collection of drawings bequeathed by Xavier Atger (1758-1833) who was at the Faculty of Medicine from 1813 to 1833, and includes works by artists from the south of France, representing the 17C and 18C French School (Bourdon, Puget, Mignard, Rigaud, Lebrun, Subleyras, Natoire, Vernet, Fragonard, J.-M. Vien), the 16C, 17C and 18C Italian School (Tiepolo) and the 17C and 18C Flemish School (Velvet Brueghel, Van Dyck, Rubens, Martin de Vos).

Musée d'Anatomie

🔒 *Closed for renovation work. Faculté de Médecine, 2 rue de l'École-de-Médecine, first floor, access signposted.*

The museum of anatomy is housed in an enormous room and comprises exhibits of normal and pathological anatomy.

▶▶ **Musée de l'Infanterie** – ♿🕒 *Daily except Tue 2-6pm.* 🕒 *Closed some public holidays.* 👓 *3€.* ☎ *04 67 16 50 43. Avenue Lepic.* Museum on the French Infantry.

Excursions

Parc zoologique de Lunaret★

🕒 *Mid-May to mid-Sep: 9am-7pm; Mid-Sep to mid-May: 9am-5pm, Mon 1-5pm. No charge.* ☎ *04 67 63 27 63. 6km/4mi N of the Hôpitaux-Facultés district. Leave town on rue Proudhon and take the road to Mende.*

Kids In this vast 80ha/200-acre park bequeathed to the town by Henri de Lunaret, the animals are kept relatively at liberty in a setting of garrigues and undergrowth. The zoo is a very pleasant place for a stroll, with the opportunity of watching zebras, bison, elk, alpacas, moufflons, wolves etc as well as exotic birds in aviaries.

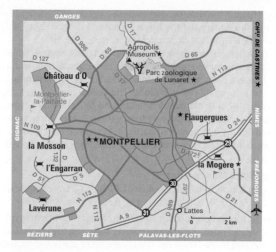

Agropolis Museum

🕐 *Daily except Tue 2-6pm. 5€ (children under 10: no charge).* 🕐 *Closed 1 Jan, 1 May, 25 Dec.* ☎ *04 67 04 75 00. www.agropolis.fr 500m/547yd from the Parc de Lunaret. Parking on the right-hand side of the road.*

This fascinating museum, run by the Agropolis scientific research complex, is devoted to agriculture and food throughout the world. A chronological presentation of the **three successive eras of man's feeding habits** (from fruit-gathering to Oxo!) leads to agriculture as it is today in different parts of the world: the comparison between a Moroccan shepherd from the Atlas mountains and a corn grower from Illinois is particularly striking! The various landscapes created by modern agriculture are shown on a giant screen. Next comes the **banquet of humankind**, with all the variety and inequality it entails. In addition, there are thematic exhibitions, a Cybermuseum and activities for children,

Pic St-Loup

23km/14mi N along D 986 then D 113 to Cazevieille. Park the car to the E of the village and follow the directions to Pic St-Loup.

🚶 *The wide stone path leads up to a Calvary. From there, take a little winding footpath which climbs up to the chapel and observatory. Allow 3hr there and back.*

St-Loup peak (alt 658m/2 158ft) marks the highest point of a long ridge above the Montpellier Garrigues. Its limestone strata rise almost vertically, making a dramatic break in the monotonous plains surrounding it.

From the summit, there is a magnificent **panorama**★★ of the surrounding coun-tryside. The north face drops straight down into a ravine, which separates St-Loup peak from the rocky ridge of the Hortus mountain; beyond, to the north-west and the north, the view embraces the Cévennes. To the east lie the ruins of Montferrand, the Nîmes plain and, beyond the Rhône Valley, Mont Ventoux, the Alpilles and the Luberon; to the south-east is the Camargue; to the south, the Montpellier plain and the Mediterranean with its string of coastal lagoons; to the south-west, Mont Canigou and the Corbières on the horizon.

Lattes

6km/4mi S of Montpellier. Leave by ④ on the town plan.

In 1963, the small town of Lattes rediscovered the archaeological site of Lattara, which, for eight centuries (from 6C BC to 3C AD) was a thriving port, handling Mediterranean trade. Situated at the delta of the Lez, it supplied the hinterland, particularly Sextantio, as Castelnau-le-Lez was known in Antiquity. The local people imported wine, oil, luxury ceramic ware and manufactured articles and exported the region's traditional resources in exchange – freshwater fish, wool and pelts, resin, mineral ore etc. However, although excellent for trade, the town's site surrounded by marshes led to problems and more particularly gradual subsidence. The numerous remains have shown that the port became a redistribution centre for Marseille trade until the Phocean city fell in 49 BC. Having served as a river port during Gallo-Roman times, the site was abandoned when an increase in rainfall caused the port to silt up and the water table to rise.

Musée archéologique Henri-Prades

&. ⏱ *Daily except Tue 10am-noon, 2-5.30pm.* ⏱ *Closed 1 Jan, 1 May, 14 Jul, 25 Dec.* ⊜ *2.30€, no charge 1st Sunday in the month.* ☎ *04 67 99 77 20. Leave Lattes SE on D 132 towards Pérols.*

This archaeological museum housed in the old farmhouse of the painter Bazille displays temporary exhibitions on the first floor (local archaeological collections) and, on the second floor and mezzanine, local discoveries. In this part of the museum, there is an exhibition on the conversion of the site into a town during the second Iron Age and the creation of the port, as well as daily life in Lattara (house, furniture, kitchen; large collections of ceramic and glass ware), funerary arrangements (steles and funerary furniture) and the port of Lattara itself.

Finally, part of the museum is devoted to the 3C and 4C necropolis of St-Michel in which 76 tombs were discovered.

Château de Castries★

12km/7mi NE of Montpellier. The present château, built on a hillock in the 16C by Pierre de Castries (pronounced Castres), is still owned by the Castries family. The Renaissance château includes a vast main courtyard decorated with a bust of Louis XIV by Puget. Sadly, one of the wings was destroyed during the Wars of Religion and its stones were used to make a series of terraces providing access to gardens designed by Le Nôtre.

Inside, the main staircase, lined with paintings from the Boucher School (1760), leads to the great hall of the États de Languedoc, which contains a painting evoking the huge assemblies held there in the past. It also has a remarkable Nuremberg earthenware stove and a Meissen porcelain table top (late 18C, early 19C) depicting the Judgement of Paris.

The library contains some handsome family portraits and fine bookbindings. In the dining room is a Louis XV Provençal olive-wood sideboard and a painting of Cardinal de Fleury by Rigaud. The kitchen contains a linen display.

After visiting the château, if you take D 26 to Guzargues, off N 110, there is a very interesting **view** of the **aqueduct** built by Riquet (creator of the Canal du Midi) to supply water to the château.

Palavas-les-Flots⬧⬧

12km/7mi S of Montpellier. Leave on ④ on the town plan.

Located at the mouth of the River Lez, now a canal, this fishing port has a charming, lively historical district. Palavas was transformed into a seaside resort highly popular with Montpellier families, who flocked here armed with their picnic lunches and shrimping nets every Sunday, by the opening of a railway line in 1872. For years, Palavas was the only beach on this stretch of the coast, until the Languedoc-Roussillon shoreline was developed for tourism and the neighbouring resorts of Grande-Motte and Carnon-Plage were built. Palavas has been nominated a "kid" resort for its activities and facilities specially intended for children. The *joutes nautiques* held in Palavas are very popular.

Musée Albert-Dubout

⏱ *Jul and Aug: 4-11pm; Feb-Jun, Sep-Nov and school holidays: daily except Mon 2-6pm.* ⏱ *Closed Mon and public holidays.* ⊜ *5€.* ☎ *04 67 68 56 41. Access on foot from the east bank along quai des Arènes or by boat.*

This museum in memory of the cartoonist Albert Dubout, who lived in Palavas for many years, occupies the Ballestras redoubt, a reconstruction of an 18C fortified tower built in the middle of Levant lagoon. Besides his boldly executed and amusing illustrations of Montpellier holidaymakers, Dubout also drew numerous scenes of bull-fighting, a sport of which he was a lifelong fan. From the terrace, there is a **panoramic view** from Mont St-Clair to the gulf of Aigues-Mortes.

Not far from Palavas is **Maguelone**★ with the remains of its interesting **cathedral** (⬧ *see MAGUELONE*).

Montpellier "Follies"

Dotted around the outskirts of Montpellier are a number of elegant "follies," built as summer residences in the 18C by aristocrats and wealthier bourgeois citizens of the city. Some have been swallowed up by suburbs as the city continues to expand, whereas others – about 30 or so – are still surrounded by acres of vineyards. Those outside the city suburbs provide particularly charming examples of old country mansions, set in pretty gardens, often with lakes and fountains.

East of Montpellier
Round tour of 9km/6mi.

▶ *From the city centre, follow the signs to the "Montpellier-Méditerranée" airport. After the bridge over the Lez, take the road to Mauguio (D 24). The Château de Flaugergues is situated about 2km/1mi down the road, on the right, in the Millénaire district.*

Château de Flaugergues★
🕐 ☀ *Jul and Aug: guided tours of the château (1hr30min) daily except Mon 2.30-6.30pm, park and gardens all year round daily except Sun and public holidays 9am-12.30pm, 2.30-7pm (Jul and Aug: Sun and public holidays 2.30-7pm); rest of the year, tours of the château by request.* ☞ *6.50€ (4€ park and gardens).* ☎ *04 99 52 66 37. www.flaugergues.com.*

This estate on a hillock overlooking the plain was purchased by Étienne de Flaugergues, Montpellier financier and advisor to the Parlement de Toulouse, in 1696. The château is the oldest of the Montpellier "follies" and is built in the style of an Italian villa. Inside the château, a monumental staircase, with a vaulted ceiling adorned with pendant keystones, is hung with a set of magnificent 17C Brussels tapestries depicting the life of Moses. The various rooms contain beautiful furniture as well as engravings and antique paintings. Flaugergues exudes the charm of a house that has been home to the same family for many years.

The tour of the château ends with an opportunity to taste some of the wine produced on the estate.

▶ *Return to the road to Mauguio, heading right, and drive past the Château de Flaugergues and under the motorway to get to the Château de la Mogère.*

Château de la Mogère★
♿ 🕐 ☀ *Gardens open to visitors, guided tours of the château (45min) 2.30-6.30pm.* ☞ *5€ (gardens only: 2.50€). By appointment for tours of the château.* ☎ *04 67 65 72 01. www.lamogere.com.*

Designed by Jean Giral, this elegant early-18C folly, renovated at the end of the 18C, has a harmonious façade surmounted by a pediment, which stands out against a backdrop of pine trees. In the park, a beautiful Italian-style Baroque fountain is decorated with shell motifs and surmounted by groups of cherubs. Inside the château are numerous family portraits, furniture and paintings from the 18C (A Brueghel, Hyacinthe Rigaud, Louis David, Jouvenet). The great hall is decorated with delicate plasterwork.

▶ *Return to the city centre on D 172E.*

West of Montpellier
Round tour of 22km/14mi.

▶ *From the city centre take the road to Ganges (D 986) for 6km/4mi, then turn left towards Celleneuve, and then right onto D 127. A little further on, two lion-topped pillars indicate the turn-off to Château d'O.*

Château d'O
🕐 *During exhibitions and cultural events.*

The 18C building is surrounded by a very beautiful park, decorated with statues from the Château de La Mosson. Owned by the Conseil Général de l'Hérault, the château is used as a theatre during the Printemps des Comédiens festival (despite its name, the festival is held in the summer months).

▶ *Carry onto Celleneuve. Follow signs to Juvignac, then turn left onto the road leading to the Château de La Mosson.*

Château de La Mosson
This was once the most sumptuous residence in the Montpellier area. It was built from 1723 to 1729 by a very rich banker, Joseph Bonnier, who was made Baron de La Mosson. The pediment on the garden façade was sculpted by the Lorraine artist, Adam. The park was decorated with beautiful statues that have now been dispersed. Only the Baroque fountain is a reminder of the originally lavish decoration of the park, which is now a public park.

▶ *Return to N 109 and take the first road on the left towards Lavérune.*

Before long, the road passes through vineyard country.

Château de l'Engarran
Beyond the superb wrought-iron entrance gate, which comes from the Château de La Mosson, stands a Louis XV style building.

▷ *Carry on towards Lavérune. The Château de Lavérune is on the far west side of the village.*

Château de Lavérune

🕐 *Sat-Sun 3-6pm.* 👓 *2€.* ☎ *04 99 51 20 00 (town hall) or 04 99 51 20 25 (museum).*

This imposing 17C-18C building in the middle of a park full of cypresses, plane trees, magnolias and sweet chestnut trees was once the residence of the bishops of Montpellier. The first floor houses the **Musée Hofer-Bury**, which displays a collection of paintings and sculptures by contemporary artists in temporary exhibitions. Artists whose work is featured here include Henri de Jordan, Gérard and Bernard Calvet, Roger Bonafé, Vincent Bioulès and Wang Wei-Xin. On the ground floor there is an Italian style music room decorated with a wrought-iron balustrade and ornate plasterwork.

To the east of the château is a 16C gateway, which looks as if it was part of some fortifications, despite the vermiculated bosses with which it is adorned (the side facing the church doorway).

▷ *Take D 5 back to the city centre.*

Chaos de
MONTPELLIER-LE-VIEUX★★★

MICHELIN LOCAL MAP 338: L-6

18KM/11MI NE OF MILLAU

ALSO SEE NANT

The chaos of Montpellier-le-Vieux is an extraordinary collection of rock formations, created by erosion and rainwater streaming over dolomite, which covers 120ha/300 acres of the Causse Noir. It was given its name by shepherds bringing their flocks from the Languedoc to summer pastures, who caught sight of this gigantic jumble of rocks, which looked for all the world as if it were a vast ruined city.

▶ **Orient Yourself:** Take the Petit Train Vert to go straight to the most interesting formations.

🅿 **Parking:** There is a car park at the entrance to the site.

🕓 **Organising Your Time:** Many visitors find themselves staying longer than they had planned. Make it a day trip if you can, but beware of getting lost; keep to the waymarked paths.

🕲 **Also See:** Massif de l'AIGOUAL, Gorges du TARN

A Bit of History

Until 1870, this mass of rocky outcrops overgrown with dense forest was considered by local inhabitants to be a cursed city and the haunt of the devil himself. Any adventurous sheep or goats that strayed there would vanish into the night, devoured by the numerous wolves that roamed the site. Eventually the area was cleared of these undesirable residents and of some of its trees, so that the tumbledown "city" of rocks could be seen.

Montpellier-le-Vieux was discovered in 1883 by J and L de Malafosse and De Barbeyrac-Saint-Maurice, who were amazed at the intricate maze of alleyways, arches and corbelled ledges. In 1885, E-A Martel mapped the site.

Visit

🕓 *Jul-Aug: 9.30am-7pm; Apr-Jun and Sep-mid Nov: 9.30am-6pm (5pm Nov).* 😅 *5€ (children: 4€)* ☎ *05 65 60 66 30. www.aven-armand-com.*

The entrance (ticket booth) to Montpellier-le-Vieux lies at the end of a private road leading from the hamlet of Maubert for 1.5km/1mi, past a viewing table and into a car park.

To get to Maubert:

▶ *from Millau, take D 110 (16km/10mi);*

▶ *from Rozier or from Peyreleau, take D 29 and then D 110 off to the right (10km/6mi);*

▶ *from Nant, take D 991 to La Roque-Ste-Marguerite, from which you take a very narrow road up past the church heading north of the village and then turn left onto D 110 (26km/16mi).*

The **Petit Train Vert**, a tourist train on tyres, takes visitors to the very centre of the site in order to admire the most picturesque rock formations: **Porte de Mycènes** *(1hr there and back)* including a short easy walk; **Circuit Jaune** *(1hr 30min there and back)* including a short walk *(😅 3.30€;* ☎ *05 65 60 66 30).*

🚶 There are several possibilities of **walks** along marked footpaths: Circuit du Belvédère *(30min, blue markings)*; Grand Tour *(1hr 30min, red markings)*; Camparolié *(30min starting from Porte de Mycènes, yellow markings)*; Circuit du Lac *(30min starting from the Cénotaphe, orange markings)*; Circuit du Château-Gaillard *(30min starting from Rond-Point de la Citerne, purple markings)*. A map is available at the entrance to the site. Bear in mind that it is easy to get lost if one wanders off the marked trails.

Porte de Mycènes

The Site

Montpellier-le-Vieux is such an unusual and captivating place, in a beautiful natural setting. The hours spent wandering among the rocks in this peaceful place, in the shade of pines and oak trees, past craggy columns and massive walls will leave any nature lover feeling refreshed, and it will be a day to remember.

Almost all the rock formations of Montpellier-le-Vieux have earned nicknames in keeping with their shape or outline: Skittle, Crocodile, Mycenae Gate, Sphinx, Bear's Head etc.

"Douminal"

From the top of this natural tower of rock overlooking four irregularly shaped cirques ("Le Lac," "Les Amats," "Les Rouquettes," "La Millière"), separated by tall rocky crests and surrounded by the cliffs of the Causse Noir, there is an extensive view. To the north lies the "Rocher de la Croix" (Cross) and, on the right, the Cirque du Lac thick with pine trees (in the distance, the sharply defined outline of the cliffs lining the Tarn gorge can be seen); to the south, lies the Dourbie Valley and the scenic ridge road of the Causse du Larzac; to the west, is the Cirque des Rouquettes; and to the east, the Chaos de Roquesaltes.

Having negotiated its way round the "Poterne" (Postern) footpath almost immediately reveals another spectacular view of the whole site from the "**Rempart**" (Rampart; alt 830m/2 723ft). Then the path leads down towards the Cirque des Amats and the "Porte de Mycènes" (Mycenae Gate).

"Porte de Mycènes"

To Martel, the Mycenae Gate evoked the celebrated Lion Gate of Ancient Greece. Its sheer size and the height of its natural arch (12m/39ft) make it one of the most original phenomena of Montpellier-le-Vieux.

After crossing a culvert, the path leads to the **"Baume Obscure"** cave where Martel discovered the bones of cave-bears. To the left of the mouth of the cave there is a glimpse of the **"Nez de Cyrano"** (Cyrano de Bergerac's famously large nose). Then the footpath leads up to the "Belvédère."

"Belvédère" (Viewpoint)

There is a view over the Cirque des Rouquettes, around which the path has just led, of the sunken Dourbie Valley to the south, and the Cirque de la Millière to the north. The path winds back towards the beginning of the various circuits, skirting along the Cirque de la Millière at mid height. On the right, about 200m/220yd on from the "Belvédère," is a yawning chasm – the **"Aven,"** which drops to a depth of 53m/174ft.

▶ *From here, the footpath leads straight back to the car park.*

MONTSÉGUR★★

MICHELIN LOCAL MAP 343: I-7

12KM/7.5MI S OF LAVELANET

The holocaust of the Cathar Church is vividly recalled by the Montségur crag – the setting for the final episode of the Albigensian Crusade which brought about the political downfall of Languedoc at the hands of the Capetian dynasty. High up on this rocky peak (alt 1 216m/3 989ft) stand the ruins of a castle. *09300 Montségur, ☎ 05 61 03 03 0. www.montsegur.org*

- 🅿 **Parking:** You'll find a parking lot along the D 9 from which to begin the climb.
- **Don't Miss:** The view from the fortress over the surrounding mountain ranges.
- 🕐 **Organising Your Time:** The hike up to the château and back takes about an hour and a half.
- **Also See:** FOIX

A Bit of History

In 1204 a second castle was built at Montségur to replace a fortress of unknown date. It was occupied by about 100 men under the command of Pierre-Roger de Mirepoix and beyond its ramparts by a community of Cathar refugees with their bishop, deacons and *parfaits*. The prestige of the place, and the pilgrimages it drew to it, found no favour with either the Roman Catholic Church or the French monarchy.

When, in 1242, Blanche de Castille and the clergy heard the news of the massacre of members of the Inquisition at Avignonet by a band of men from Montségur, the fate of the citadel was sealed.

> **IN THE VILLAGE**
>
> 🍽 **Hôtel Costes** – ☎ *05 61 01 10 24* – closed 12 Nov-31 Mar, Sun evening and Mon - 9 rooms - 🛏 *6.50€ – restaurant* 🍽🍽. To give you courage before tackling the climb up to the castle, stop at this little village house with an unassuming restaurant and friendly welcome. The dining room doubles as the local bar. Simple, traditional cooking.

The seneschal of Carcassonne and the archbishop of Narbonne were ordered to lay the fortress to siege, which they duly began in July 1243. It is thought that the Roman Catholic armies numbered about 10 000 men!

Under cover of the long winter nights, patrols of experienced mountain dwellers scaled the steep cliff (more easily than knights would have done) and, bypassing the fortress to the east, gained a foothold on the upper plateau. A huge ballista, taken up in separate pieces and then assembled on site, breached the castle walls with rock projectiles dug out from an open quarry on the mountainside.

Pierre-Roger de Mirepoix then surrendered on condition his garrison was spared. A truce was made lasting from 1 to 15 March 1244. The Cathars, who had not agreed to it, did not take advantage of this respite to try and escape their fate by recanting or taking flight. On the morning of 16 March, 207 of them came down the mountain and climbed onto a gigantic pyre. The self-assurance of the martyrs, and the mystery surrounding the safe hiding place of their "treasure," still fascinate scholars and all those who are true to the tradition of Occitania or who follow sects that promote Cathar philosophy.

In 1245, the new lord of Mirepoix, Guy de Lévis II, came to live there and swore allegiance to the king. A third castle was built towards the middle or end of the 13C; nothing is left of the castle that still stood in 1244.

Strategically placed, facing the Cerdagne, between France and Aragon, the late-13C castle made an ideal stronghold for observation and defence. It is the ruins of this castle that modern visitors explore.

Château★

🕐 *May-Aug: 9am-7.30pm; Apr, Sep and Oct: 9.30am-6pm; Mar: 10am-5pm; Feb: 10.30am-4pm (weather permitting); Nov: 10am-5.30pm; Dec: 10am-4.30pm (weather permitting). Guided tours (1hr) available Jul-Aug: 11am, 1pm, 3pm, 4.30pm; May-Jun and Sep: Sat-Sun and public holidays 2pm and 3pm.* 🕐 *Closed Jan, 25 Dec. Guided tour 3.70€, unaccompanied visit 3€, combined ticket with Musée Archéologique. ☎ 05 61 01 10 27 or 05 61 01 06 94.*

▶ *Leave the car in the car park along D 9. 1hr 30min there and back along a steep rocky footpath.*

🚶 Before climbing the sheer face of the crag itself, the path passes the stele erected in 1960 "to those martyred in the name of pure Christian love."

The castle occupies a **site**★★ on the top of towering cliffs more than 1 000ft high and offering a remarkable panorama over the ranges of the Plantaurel, the deep Aude Valley and the massif of St-Barthélemy.

The fortress, in the shape of a pentagon, follows the outline of the plateau on the summit. It is reached through a gate on the south side.

Around the inner courtyard, various buildings (living quarters, annexes) backed onto the ramparts.

In the past, access to the keep from the ramparts was through a doorway level with the first floor. Inside, a staircase led to the lower room, which was used for defence and as a storeroom. Nowadays, it is reached by walking round the curtain wall via the north gate and going through an opening overlooking the old water tank. In this room at the summer solstice, sunbeams shine in through two arrow slits and straight out through the arrow slits opposite.

North-west of the foot of the keep, the remains of the "Cathar village" are being excavated.

Village

This lies at the foot of the rock in the Lasset Valley. In the town hall (*mairie*) there is an **archaeological museum** (🕐 *Jun-Aug: 10am-12.30pm, 2-7.30pm; Sep: 10.30am-noon, 2-6pm; Feb and Dec: 2-4.30pm; Mar and Nov: 2-5pm; Apr and Oct: 2-6pm; May: 10.30am-12.30pm, 2-7pm;* 🕐 *closed in Jan, 25 Dec; combined ticket for chateau (prices above);* ☎ *05 61 01 10 27*), housing the discoveries of the excavations undertaken: a large amount of furniture from the 13C and tools have enabled experts to trace occupation of the Montségur crag back to Neolithic times.

The museum also contains information on Cathar philosophy.

Excursion

Intermittent fountain of Fontestorbes

11.5km/7mi NE along D 9 then D 5. Fontestorbes spring, which emerges from a rock cave in the Hers Valley, is the resurgence of water that has soaked into the chalky soil of part of Sault plateau. When water levels are low, the spring becomes intermittent (usually from mid-July to end of November); the flow then varies from 100-1 800l/22-396gal per second. When it is not in full flow, visitors can walk to the back of the cave (*ramp*).

Cirque de MOURÈZE★★

MICHELIN LOCAL MAP 339: F-7

8KM/5MI W OF CLERMONT-L'HÉRAULT

The Cirque de Mourèze lies concealed between the valleys of the Orb and the Hérault, on the south side of Liausson mountain. This vast jumble of dolomitic rocks forms a natural amphitheatre covering over 340ha/840 acres, with significant differences in height (varying from 170m/557ft to 526m/1 725ft). It is delimited by the green Petite Dourbie Valley to the south and crisscrossed by a network of footpaths.

Visit

The village

The picturesque old village of Mourèze, with its narrow streets, its little houses with outside staircases and its red-marble fountain, lies at the foot of a sheer rock face, the top of which is home to a castle.

The cirque★★

The cirque is surrounded by enormous boulders. A number of waymarked footpaths lead through fresh, green nooks and crannies in between rocks which have been eroded into the strangest shapes. These weird rocks resembling ruins are particularly eye-catching in the light at dawn and dusk.

From the viewpoint (*viewing table*), there is an **overall view** of the dolomitic cirque.

Parc des Courtinals

🕐 Apr-Aug: 9.30am-7pm; Sep to Oct: 10am-6pm; rest of the year: Sat-Sun 10am-6pm. ."4€ (children: 2€). ☎ 04 67 96 08 42. www.courtinals.com.

Situated east of the cirque and covering a surface of 40ha/98 acres, Courtinals park is an ancient Gallic settlement, which was inhabited as early as the Middle Neolithic Age until about 450 BC (end of the Bronze Age and early Iron Age). It is almost surrounded by a high barrier of rocks; at their foot there are natural cavities which once contained flints and pottery.

Along the archaeological and botanical trail, there are several sites of Iron Age huts, one of which has been reconstructed.

Cirque de Mourèze

MUR-DE-BARREZ

POPULATION 880

MICHELIN LOCAL MAP 338: H-1

This pretty little town occupying a volcanic ridge between the valleys of the Goul and the Bromme, is the ideal starting point for excursions in the surrounding countryside. 🛈 12 Grand-Rue, 12600 Mur-de-Barrez, ☎ 05 65 66 10 16.

Walking Tour

Old town

Once through the Porte de Monaco, visitors discover a network of narrow streets lined with fine Renaissance houses (particularly Grand-Rue) sometimes decorated with coats of arms, such as the Maison consulaire. Note also the Porte de l'Horloge, a gate that was once part of the town's fortified wall.

Château

From near the ruins of the castle there is a good view of the surrounding region: the Cantal mountains, the Bromme Valley, the Planèze and the Aubrac mountains. To the east, downhill, are the buildings of the convent of Ste-Claire, surrounded by houses typical of this area, with steeply pitched, four-sided roofs.

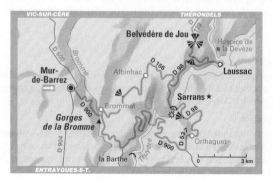

Église

The town's church is Gothic in style. It was demolished as far as the transept by Calvinists. Inside, there are some interesting capitals, a 17C altarpiece, representing the murder of Thomas Becket in Canterbury Cathedral, and keystones, one of which *(above the tribune)* is shaped like a recumbent figure.

Carladez Region

35km/22mi round tour – allow 2hr.

▶ *Leave Mur-de-Barrez on D 900 heading SE.*

Gorges de la Bromme

The road follows the course of the Bromme, a tributary of the Truyère, for a couple of miles or so, giving a good view of the stream flowing along a deep-set, rugged gorge.

Farther on, the River Truyère comes into view. The river flow is diverted by the **Barthe dam** at this point via a high-pressure pipeline 10.5km/6.5mi long. This forms part of the Sarrans-Brommat complex, one of the most important hydroelectric projects of its kind in France.

▶ *After negotiating several hairpin bends, turn left onto D 537, then D 98 towards the Sarrans dam; 1.5km/0.9mi before reaching the dam, there is a fine general view of the Sarrans installations.*

Sarrans dam★

This dam, one of the most important hydroelectric installations in the Massif Central, is 220m/722ft long, 105m/344ft high and 75m/246ft thick at its base. It is a "weight-dam," that is, it resists the force of the water it retains by its sheer mass, but a slight curve on the upstream side acts as a vault.

▶ *Having passed the crest of the dam, D 98 runs alongside the reservoir as far as the outskirts of the village of Laussac, which is reached along D 537.*

Laussac

The village is built on a promontory which, owing to the flooding of the valley, has become a peninsula.

▶ *Rejoin D 98 and turn right.*

Continue 1.5km/1mi on from the junction for a fine view of the reservoir.

▶ *Carry on along D 98 as far as a crossroads and turn right onto D 139.*

Sarrans dam

A. Thuillier/MICHELIN

Belvédère de Jou

Beyond the hamlet of Jou, there is a panorama of Laussac peninsula, Devèze hospice and Sarrans reservoir.

▶ *Return to Laussac along D 98 to the left, and then take D 166 towards Albinhac and Brommat.*

The road offers sweeping views of the Barrez countryside, and the Cantal and Aubrac hills. Note the pretty four-sided roofs, covered with limestone slabs arranged like fish scales, typical of the region.

▶ *Beyond Brommat, D 900 leads back to Mur-de-Barrez.*

NAJAC★

POPULATION 744

MICHELIN LOCAL MAP 338: D-5

Stretching along a promontory enclosed in a meander of the Aveyron, on the boundary of Rouergue and Quercy, the ancient village of Najac occupies a remarkable site★★. The ruins of the fortified castle tower above the slate rooftops of the village. Two large holiday villages (*villages de vacances*) in the vicinity contribute to the lively local atmosphere. 🛈 *Pl. du Faubourg, 12270 Najac, ☎ 05 65 29 72 05.*

🅿 **Parking:** In high season, traffic is barred from the centre of the village. Park the car in one of the parking areas situated at the western entrance to the village.

👁 **Don't Miss:** D 239, to the east, offers the best overall view of Najac.

Visit

The village

The village extends to the foot of the fortress. Place du Faubourg with its covered arcades was already the hub of activity in the 14C. Near the town hall, a fountain, carved from an enormous monolithic slab of granite dated 1344, bears the arms of Blanche de Castille, King Louis IX's (St Louis) mother.

Beyond the square, the village high street, rue du Bourguet, is lined with a few corbelled houses mainly built between the 13C and the 16C.

▶ *Turn right, leaving rue des Comtes-de-Toulouse to your left.*

Najac

Along rue Médiévale, near a former fortified gate, stands the **Château des Gouverneurs**, once a noble residence; a little farther up towards the fortress, on the left, note the equally elegant 13C-15C **Maison du Sénéchal**.

Fortress★

🕐 Jul and Aug: 10am-1pm, 3-7pm; Apr, May and Sep: 10am-12.30pm, 3-5.30pm; Jun: 10am-12.30pm, 3-6.30pm. 🕐 Closed Sep-Mar except on Sun in Oct. 3.75€. ☎ 05 65 29 71 65.

This masterpiece of 13C military architecture keeps watch over the Aveyron Valley. At the time, a large garrison lived in the village, which numbered more than 2 000 inhabitants.

Of the three original curtain walls there still remain considerable fortifications flanked by large round towers. The castle itself, built partly from pale-coloured sandstone, is protected by thick walls and is shaped like a trapezium. The most impregnable of the towers, on the south-east, was the keep.

Having passed the successive curtain walls through the postern gates, visitors reach the terrace of the keep. This gives a magnificent **view**★ over the fortress, the rows

Address Book

For coin categories, see the Legend at the back of the guide.

EATING OUT

L'Oustal del Barry – ☎ 05 65 29 74 32 - oustal@caramail.com - 1 Apr-15 Nov. Don't miss the chance to stop at this lovely spot, bordering the central square of one of France's finest medieval villages. The chef, who grew up in the region, creates excellent cuisine that pays homage to regional culinary traditions. "Rustic chic" dining room, and pretty terrace.

WHERE TO STAY

Hôtel Belle Rive – 3km/2mi NW of Najac on D 39 – ☎ 05 65 29 73 90 - hotel. bellerive.najac@wanadoo.fr - closed Nov-Mar, Sun evening and Mon lunchtime in Oct - ☐ - 29 rooms - ☐ 8€ – restaurant ☐☐. Overshadowed by the château, this hotel on the banks of the Aveyron is ideal for a peaceful stopover. Functional, well kept rooms. Dining room with a large shaded terrace. Traditional cuisine. Pool.

Chambre d'hôte Cambayrac – 82160 Cambayrac - 12km/7.5mi NW of Najac on D 39, D 84 then B-road - ☎ 05 63 24 02 03 - dvidal@wanadoo.fr – closed 15 Nov-1 Apr - ☐ - 4 rooms. A well-run guesthouse offering a warm welcome. Comfortable rooms with rustic-style furniture beneath the eaves of an old barn. Swimming pool. Good value for the euro.

FARM VISIT

Jacky Carles 'Ferme Carles' – Le Bourg - 9km/5.6mi N of Najac on D149 and D 47 – 12200 Monteils - ☎ 05 65 29 62 39 – daily from 9am. This ambassador of gourmet Aveyron raises and force-feeds his ducks according to tradition, then cooks them on a wood fire in copper cauldrons and preserves them according to time-honoured recipes. Visits of his kitchen and meals at the Table Paysanne, the Farmer's Table.

of village houses, the pretty Aveyron Valley and the church built between the castle and the river, in the heart of the original village.

▶ Walk down from the castle towards rue de l'Église.

The 13C **Porte de Pique** is the only one left of the 10 gates which once guarded the village.

Church

In spite of additions, this is an interesting Gothic building. The west front is adorned at the top with a rose window. Inside, the single nave ends with a flat chevet. On the left of the nave is an unusual 14C wrought-iron structure in which "the candle of Our Lady" (Easter candle) was kept. In the chancel note the original altar (14C) made from a vast slab of fine sandstone; a Crucifix by the 15C Spanish school; two 15C statues: the Virgin Mary and St John; and also a fine 16C polychrome wood statue of St Peter seated.

▶ Return via rue des Comtes-de-Toulouse, lined with medieval houses.

NANT

POPULATION 846

MICHELIN LOCAL MAP 338: L-6

This old market town stands on the banks of the Dourbie at the mouth of the river gorge. A monastic community founded in the 7C was largely responsible for converting the swampy region into a well-drained, fertile valley with vineyards and meadows. Pl. de l'Église, 12230 Nant, ☎ 05 65 62 25 12.

A Bit of History

A Catholic stronghold – The original monastery, destroyed by the Saracens in the 8C, was rebuilt two centuries later. The Benedictine community prospered and built vast monastery buildings and the church of St-Pierre in the valley. In 1135, the monastery was promoted to the status of abbey by Pope Innocent II and the church of St-Pierre was rebuilt. The town that grew up around the abbey was well fortified and became a bastion for the Roman Catholics during the Wars of Religion. In the 16C, the abbey was placed *in commendam* and became a mere source of income for the abbots, who were rarely seen in Nant. It prospered nonetheless until the Revolution. The college at Nant, founded in 1662, specialised in literature and philosophy and had the highest student intake in the Rouergue area.

Sights

Église abbatiale St-Pierre

The abbey church is very austere from the outside, dominated by a square keep that was topped by a spire (renovated in 1960) above the transept crossing, to replace the bell-tower demolished in 1794. The central arch leading into the narthex has a Gothic doorway and is surmounted by a trefoil arch moulding. Inside the church, which has several interesting features, note in particular the decoration on the **capitals**★.

Vieille halle

The old covered market was once part of the monastery – a squat, sturdy gallery with five arcades (14C).

Pont de la Prade

From the Chapelle du Claux (Wars of Religion memorial) there is a good view of the attractive span of the 14C bridge.

 For coin categories, see the Legend.

WHERE TO EAT AND WHERE TO STAY

 Gîtes et chambre d'hôte Catherine et Thierry Schreiber – R. Damade - ☎ 05 65 62 26 73 - ✉ - 3 rooms. Two houses in the old city snugged against the ramparts. Renovated rooms featuring exposed beams, original floor tiles and contemporary touches.

 Hôtel Midi-Papillon – 12230 St-Jean-du-Bruel - ☎ 05 65 62 26 04 - closed 12 Nov-2 Apr - 🅿 - 18 rooms - ✉ 4.60€ – restaurant . Run by the same family for four generations, this village hotel radiates hospitality and professionalism. The small bedrooms are well cared for, and the gourmet cooking is generous. Swimming pool in the pretty garden.

 Chambre d'hôte L'Hermitage St-Pierre – St-Pierre-de-Revens - 11km/6.8 NW of Nant toward Millau on D 991 - ☎ 05 65 62 27 99 - madeleine. macq@wanadoo.fr - ✉ - reservations required - 5 rooms - meals . This handsome house was a chapel in the 10C and 11C, then a Templars' inn, then a church. It has been renovated by a young retired couple and now contains guest rooms furnished with style. The pure waters of the Dourbie flowing nearby are an invitation to take a dip.

Gorges de la Dourbie★★ ①

From Nant to L'Espérou 35km/22mi – about 1hr.

 There are numerous sharp bends and road junctions that are, in many places, difficult to cross, especially between the village of Dourbies and the hamlet of Les Laupies.

▷ *Leave Nant SE on D 999.*

Between St-Jean and Nant, the Dourbie Valley is wide and cultivated. On the left are the four towers of Castelnau Castle, now a farm.

▷ *Leave the car at the "St-Michel" signpost to the left of the road and climb the narrow path to the chapel.*

St-Michel-de-Rouviac

This delightful Romanesque chapel, set against a background of trees and fields, blends in well with the graveyard and presbytery. In the 12C, this was a priory and a daughter-house of Nant Abbey and the decorative features are similar in both buildings, for example, capitals with knotwork and palmettes.

To the south are the ruins of the Château d'Algues; to the north, the scarp slopes of the Causse Bégon creating a spur of rock above Nant known as the Roc Nantais.

St-Jean-du-Bruel

This summer holiday resort, situated at the entrance to the Dourbie gorge, is the starting point for various hikes. An old 15C **humpback bridge** spans the Dourbie and, near the new bridge, there is an attractive 18C covered market.

Col de la Pierre Plantée

Alt 828m/2 691ft. There is an extensive view from the pass over the lower Dourbie Valley and beyond to the Lingas mountain range and the Causse du Larzac.

▷ *Turn left onto D 47.*

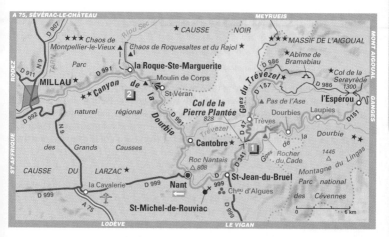

Gorges du Trévezel★

The River Trévezel flows between the Aigoual range and the Dourbie Valley, over a bed strewn with rocks and boulders. The valley gradually narrows to become a ravine between scarp slopes topped by tall cliffs 400m/1 300ft high of varying colours. The narrowest part, which is no more than 30m/97ft wide, is known in local dialect as the *Pas de l'Ase* ("Donkey's Step").

▷ *Return to Col de la Pierre Plantée and turn right onto D 151.*

As far as Dourbies, the road, which is narrow and winding in places, runs high above the **Gorges de la Dourbie**★★ (300m/975ft at the rock known as the Cade, or Juniper Bush, 5km/3mi from Dourbies).

This is a splendid drive along a cliff road that is impressive in many places, with breathtaking views over the wooded abyss bristling with granite and schist rocks. Far down on the valley floor is the river.

L'Espérou – *See Massif de l'AIGOUAL.*

Canyon de la Dourbie★★ ②

▷ *From Nant to Millau 32km/20mi – allow 1hr. Downstream from Nant, the valley narrows again between the limestone rocks of the Grands Causses.*

Cantobre★

This picturesque village at the confluence of the River Trévezel and River Dourbie stands on a rocky outcrop of the Causse Bégon. It is an extraordinary sight and the village fully deserves its name of *quant obra*, meaning "what a masterpiece."

Canyon de la Dourbie★★

The sides of the ravine bristle with limestone rocks that have been worn away into strange shapes by erosion.
Level with **St-Véran**, a hilltop village in a picturesque setting, the road provides a superb **view**★ of the village with its renovated houses and tower, all that remains of the old castle which was once the property of the **Marquis de Montcalm** (1712-59) who died in Quebec in Canada while defending the town during a siege laid by the English. Below the castle is the church of Treilles.

The road runs past **Moulin de Corps**, a watermill powered by a resurgent spring. The setting is delightful.

La Roque-Ste-Marguerite

This village, nestling at the foot of the machicolated tower of a 17C castle, is built in terraces at the entrance to the Riou Sec ravine. The Romanesque castle chapel, now used as the village church, stands at the end of narrow, winding streets. High above the village are the ruin-shaped rocks of Le Rajol and Montpellier-le-Vieux (*see Chaos de MONTPELLIER-LE-VIEUX and Causse NOIR*).
The road runs on along the banks of the Dourbie, through its magnificent canyon. On each side of the river upstream from Millau are the tall, vividly coloured cliffs of the Causse Noir and Causse du Larzac, topped by jagged rocks.

NARBONNE★★

POPULATION 45,510

MICHELIN LOCAL MAP 344: I-J 3

Narbonne, which has been in its time the ancient capital of Gallia Narbonensis, the residence of the Visigoth monarchy and an archiepiscopal seat, is now a lively Mediterranean city playing an important role as a wine-producing centre and a road and rail junction. Its municipal, military and religious architecture, the treasures in its museums, the charm of the river banks of the Robine, and its shaded boulevards all contribute to its appeal to visitors. ▮ *Pl. R.-Salengro, 11100 Narbonne, ☎ 04 68 65 15 60. www.mairie-narbonne.fr.*

▶ **Orient Yourself:** The N 9 surrounds Narbonne, offering direct access to the historic centre. The Canal de la Robine flows right through town. You'll find shops along the pedestrianised Rue Droite. See The Practical Canal for boat tours.

🅿 **Parking:** Seek out the lots along the canal, near the Quai Valière.

⊘ **Don't Miss:** The Archaeological Museum, with its fine collection of Roman paintings.

🕓 **Organizing Your Time:** Start out with a leisurely stroll of the town, then see the Archbishops' Palace and the Cathedral. See the museums of an afternoon, but save time for a refreshment break along the banks of the canal.

⚲ **Also See:** BÉZIERS, Abbaye de FONTEFROIDE, GRUISSAN, Oppidum d'ENSÉRUNE

A Bit of History

A sea port – Narbonne may well have served as a harbour and market for a 7C BC Gallic settlement on the Montlaurès hill to the north of the modern city. The town of "Colonia Narbo Martius," established in 118 BC by decree of the Roman Senate, became a strategic crossroads along the Via Domitia as well as a flourishing port. It exported oil, linen, wood, hemp, the cheeses and meat from the Cévennes so much appreciated by the Romans, and later on sigillated earthenware. Most of the river shipping business, however, was centred on the Italian, Iberian and then Gallic wine trade. During this period the city expanded dramatically and was embellished with magnificent buildings (Capitoline temple, forum).

A capital city – In 27 BC Narbonne gave its name to the Roman province created by Augustus. It was "the most beautiful," according to Martial, and, together with Lyon, the most densely populated city of Gaul. Cicero proclaimed Narbonensis to be "the boulevard of the Latin world."

The Roman Empire was then crushed by Barbarian invasions. After the sack of Rome in 410 by the Visigoths, Narbonne became their capital. Later, it fell to the Saracens; in 759 after a long siege Pépin the Short recaptured it.

Palais des Archevêques and Cathédrale St-Just

Address Book

 ♣ *For coin categories, see the Legend at the back of the guide.*

EATING OUT

☁ **L'Oléa** – *18 Bd. du Mar. -Joffre -* ☎ *04 68 41 74 55 – closed Mon – reservation recommended at weekends.* A holiday-by-the-sea atmosphere permeates this little restaurant serving imaginative Mediterranean cuisine. Between walls decorated with white boards, old stones and nautical canvases, the illusion is complete! Friendly welcome.

☁ **L'Estagnol** – *5 bis Cours Mirabeau -* ☎ *04 68 65 09 27 – lestagnol@net-up.com - closed 16-24 Nov, Mon evening and Sun - 16/20€.* This appealing brasserie near the covered market is well known by Narbonne natives. The modernized bistro setting, summer terrace on the small square, and regional cooking all contribute to l'Estagnol's success.

☁☁ **Table St-Crescent** – *Rte. de Perpignan, at the Palais du Vin -* ☎ *04 68 41 37 37 – saint-crescent@wanadoo.fr - closed 6-20 Sep, 21 Feb-7Mar, Sat lunchtime, Sun evening and Mon.* A restaurant housed in the Palais du Vin on the edge of town. It has a fine vaulted dining room, like a wine cellar, and a terrace with a small grapevine growing round it, a tribute to the noblest beverage of them all. The inventive cuisine complements the fine selection of regional wines.

☁☁☁ **L'Os à Table** – *Rte. de Salles-d'Aude - 11110 Coursan - 7km/4mi NE of Narbonne towards Béziers on N 9 -* ☎ *04 68 33 55 72 – osatable-coursan@wanadoo.fr - closed Feb holidays,1 wk after Toussaint, Sun evening and Mon.* Take a gourmet break in this popular restaurant tucked in a village house boasting a terrace, a small garden and an elegant interior. The owner attentively mans the ovens; his least expensive fixed-price menu is a good value.

WHERE TO STAY

☁ **Hôtel de France** – *6 R. Rossini -* ☎ *04 68 32 09 75 – hotelfrance@worldonline.fr - 15 rooms -* ☐ *6€.* A hotel in a late-19C building located on a quiet street downtown. The rooms are rather plain; those on the back promise a good night's sleep. Rooms on the top floor are very basic.

☁☁ **Résidence** – *6 R. du 1er-Mai -* ☎ *04 68 32 19 41 – closed 15 Jan-15 Feb - 25 rooms -* ☐ *7.50€.* A fine hotel in a renovated 19C building.

SHOPPING

Accent d'Oc – *56 R. Droite -* ☎ *04 68 32 24 13 - www.accentdoc.fr - Tue-Sun 10a-12.30pm, 2.30-7pm ; summer 10am-1pm, 3-7pm - closed 1 May.* For its young owners, the gastronomic delights of the Languedoc deserved a showcase of their own at this shop. Numerous products prepared according to recipes from long ago: fruit jams and vegetables preserved with spices; oils and vinegars infused with herbs, olive paste with lemon zest, etc.

Chocolaterie des Corbières – *42 R. du Pont-des-Marchands -* ☎ *04 68 32 06 93 - Tue-Fri 9am-noon, 2-7pm - closed 1 week in Feb and 4 weeks in Oct.* Nearly 80 different types of chocolates are made in-house at this renowned confectionary, including *les Galets du Languedoc* (dark chocolate covered with meringue), bonbons, pralines, ganaches, caramels and almond pastes.

Syndicat des producteurs de cartagène – *4 R. de l'Ancien-Port-des-Catalans -* ☎ *04 68 90 22 22. 9am-noon, 2-4pm - closed Sat.* Cartagène, a blend of grape must and brandy, is enjoyed as an aperitif or a dessert wine. This syndicat, or growers' union, is where you'll find growers' addresses.

The **Boutique du Palais** has taken over the superb Salle aux piliers; shop here for books about Narbonne and the area, copies of artwork and regional products.

SIT BACK AND RELAX

Chez Fred – *44 R. Jean-Jaurès – Mon-Sat 1pm-2am.* Go down a few steps to enter this pub boasting 8 draught beers and over 150 varieties of bottled beer. A popular place for ending the week with a concert of Celtic or Irish music.

RECREATION

Société Nautique – *12 R. Nauticards - La Nautique - 5km/3mi S of Narbonne -* ☎ *04 68 32 32 06.* A water sports centre on the Etang de Bages offering catamarans, optimists, dinghies, surfboards, funboards and swimming.

Cercle nautique des Corbières – *Base nautique de Port-Mahon - 11130 Sigean -* ☎ *04 68 48 44 52.* The fédération Française de Voile gives a seal of approval to sailing schools that guarantee a certain quality of training, equipment and security. Come to this one to learn how to handle an optimist, a catamaran, a surfboard, funboard, or canoe on the Étang de Bages or the Étang de Sigean.

The Via Domitia

The Via Domitia is the oldest of the Roman roads built in Gaul. It was named after the Consul of the Roman province of Gallia Narbonensis, Domitius Ahenobarbus, who had it built in 118-117 BC at the time the province was founded.

Following an ancient route once used by the Ligurians and Iberians, the Via Domitia ran from Beaucaire (Gard) to Le Perthus (Pyrénées-Orientales), forming a communications route between Rome and Spain. Beyond the Rhône, the Via Domitia led into the Via Aurelia. Spanned by bridges and punctuated along its length by milestones marking every Roman mile (1 481.5m) and staging posts, the Via Domitia linked Beaucaire (Ugernum), Nîmes (Nemausus), Béziers (Julia Baeterrae), Narbonne (Narbo Martius) and Perpignan (Ruscino).

Originally intended for military use, to enable Roman legions to reach the furthest outposts of the empire, Roman roads also aided the transportation of commercial goods and the spread of new ideas.

Charlemagne created the duchy of Gothie with Narbonne as the capital. It was divided into several seigneurial estates shared between the archbishop and the viscount: the city, with the cathedral and the archbishopric, on one side; the town, with the basilica of St-Paul-Serge, on the other; the city housed an important Jewish community. Municipal administration was carried out by Consuls.

In the 12C a troubadour, Bertrand de Bar, wrote a *chanson de geste* called "Aimeri de Narbonne," depicting the city, and the great ships made with iron nails, the richly laden galleys to which the city's inhabitants owed their wealth.

From the 14C, the change in course of the Aude, the havoc wrought by the Hundred Years War and plague, and the departure of the Jews caused Narbonne to decline.

Palais Des Archevêques★ *2hr*

The façade of the Archbishops' Palace overlooks the lively **place de l'Hôtel-de-Ville**, in the heart of the city, where a section of the Roman Via Domitia was recently discovered. It has three square towers: framing the Passage de l'Ancre, the Tour de la Madeleine (the oldest) and Tour St-Martial; and farther to the left the Donjon Gilles-Aycelin. Between the last two, Viollet-le-Duc built the present Hôtel de Ville (town hall) in a neo-Gothic style.

The Archbishops' Palace, originally a modest ecclesiastical residence, is now an example of religious, military and civil architecture bearing the imprint of centuries, from the 12C (Old Palace) to the 19C (Hôtel de Ville).

Donjon Gilles-Aycelin★

🕐 Jul to Sep: 10am-6pm; Oct-Jun: 9am-noon, 2-6pm. 🕐 Closed 1 Jan and 25 Dec. 🌐 2.20€ (under 10: no charge). ☎ 04 68 90 30 65. Entrance on the left inside the town hall.

This fortified tower with its rusticated walls stands on the remains of the Gallo-Roman rampart which once protected the heart of the old town. It represented the archbishops' power as opposed to that of the viscounts, who occupied a building on the other side of place de l'Hôtel-de-Ville. From the sentinel path on the platform (162 steps), the **panorama**★ stretches over Narbonne and the cathedral, the surrounding plain and away across La Clape summit, the Corbières and the coastal lagoons as far as the Pyrenees on the horizon.

▶ *Walk through the town hall to the main courtyard of the Palais Neuf.*

Palais Neuf (New Palace)

The New Palace complex surrounds the Cour d'Honneur (or Cour du Palais Neuf) and comprises the façade over the courtyard of the town hall, the Gilles-Aycelin keep, the St-Martial tower, the synods building and the north and south wings.

The **Salle des Synodes** is reached via a large staircase with balusters built in 1628 by Archbishop Louis de Vervins. This is where the States General of Languedoc met, and it contains four fine Aubusson tapestries.

Salle des Consuls

Enter via the Cour d'honneur. Located on the ground floor of the synods building, the room is supported on part of the old Roman fortified city wall. The room has a fine central row of pillars.

▶ *Leave the Palais Neuf via the door on the north side of the courtyard and enter the Palais Vieux via the door opposite, on the other side of passage de l'Ancre.*

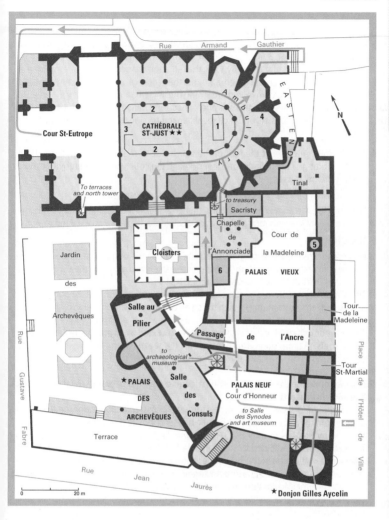

Palais Vieux (Old Palace)

The Old Palace consists of two main buildings flanking the Madeleine tower. To the east, a square staircase tower divides a Romanesque façade pierced by arcades (5). Note, to the south, a façade pierced with Romanesque, Gothic and Renaissance windows. Other monuments stand around Madeleine courtyard: the square Carolingian bell-tower of the church of St-Théodard (6), the apse of the Annonciade Chapel overlooked to the north by the imposing cathedral chevet, and the 14C **Tinal** (the canons' old storeroom) which has recently been restored.

▶ *Come out onto passage de l'Ancre and walk to the right.*

Passage de l'Ancre

This almost fortified street with its impressive walls separates the old and new palaces and leads from place de l'Hôtel-de-Ville (between the St-Martial and Madeleine towers) to the cathedral cloisters.

▶ *Enter the Salle au Pilier via a door to the left of the stairs leading to the cathedral cloisters.*

Salle au Pilier

🕐 *Jul-Sep: 10am-6pm; Oct-Jun: 9am-noon, 2-6pm.* 🕐 *Closed last 3 weeks in Jan, 1 May, 1 and 11 Nov, 25 Dec.* ☎ *04 68 90 30 65.*

This fine 14C room, with its vaulting supported by a huge central pillar, houses the Palais shop (books about Narbonne and its region, reproductions of works of art and regional products).

Cathédrale St-Just-et-St-Pasteur★★

It is possible to enter the cathedral via passage de l'Ancre and through the cloisters. The first stone was laid on 3 April 1272; it had been sent from Rome by Pope Clement IV, a former archbishop of the city. By 1332, the radiating chancel had been completed in the same style as the great cathedrals of northern France, but building the nave and the transept would have involved breaching the ancient rampart which still served in troubled medieval times, so this was postponed...and had just been begun by the 18C. Today, the edifice consists of the chancel flanked by cloisters on the south side.

Cloisters

The cloisters (14C) are at the foot of the south side of the cathedral; note the High Gothic vaulting of the galleries and, overlooking the courtyard, the gargoyles carved among the buttresses.

▶ *The west gallery gives access to the archbishops' gardens.*

From the 18C **Jardin des Archevêques**, there is a fine view of the flying buttresses, the south tower of the cathedral and the synods building, flanked by two round towers.

Interior

Inside, the strikingly well-proportioned chancel was the only part to be completed. The height of its vaulting (41m/134ft) is exceeded only by that in the cathedrals of Amiens (42m/137ft) and Beauvais (48m/157ft).

The supporting structure of the chancel exhibits great architectural purity: large arches beneath a triforium, in which the small columns are an extension of the lancets of the great windows.

The cathedral chancel comprises four bays, surrounded by an ambulatory and radiating chapels. In it are numerous works of art (👆 *see diagram*). The five chapels, the tall windows in the apse and the second tall window on the right still feature some fine 14C stained glass.

Located opposite the high altar with baldaquin (1) is the **organ case** (3) flanked by fine 18C **choir stalls** (2).

The chapel of the Annonciade (*access through the last radiating chapel on the right*), dating from the 15C, was the old chapter-house; opposite the entrance there is a fine painting by Nicolas Tournier (17C), *Tobias and the Angel*.

The Lady Chapel dedicated to Ste-Marie-de-Bethléem has regained its large Gothic **altarpiece**★ (4), discovered in 1981 under a coat of stucco and patiently restored (it took 10 years to put the altarpiece together again from the thousands of pieces buried in mortar). On either side of the statue of the Virgin and Child, are two sets of polychrome scenes, probably carved between 1354 and 1381: they represent episodes of Christ's life (*in the middle*) and the Last Judgement (*below*), surrounding the wide-open mouth of Leviathan. See how the damned scream on their way to hell in a cart! And, in striking contrast, note the chosen going up to heaven after a stay in Purgatory.

Treasury

🕐 *Jul–Sep: 11am–6pm, Sun 2–6pm; Oct–Jun: 2–6pm.* ☜ *2.20€.* ☎ *04 68 90 30 65.*

The treasury is in a room above the chapel of the Annonciade, in which the vaulting creates an unusual acoustic.

It includes illuminated manuscripts and, together with other church plate, a fine gilt chalice (1561). The most remarkable exhibit is a magnificent late-15C Flemish tapestry depicting the **Creation**★★, woven in silk and gold thread. It is the only one remaining from a set of 10 donated to the chapter by Archbishop François Fouquet.

Note also a fine late-10C carved ivory missal plaque and a marriage casket in rock crystal with antique intaglio decoration, which was used as a reliquary.

▶ *Leave the cathedral via a door located in the second radiating chapel from the left.*

Exterior

Note in particular the chevet with its High Gothic lancets, the great arches surmounted by merlons with arrow slits overlooking the terraces of the ambulatory, the flying buttresses with two arches, the turrets and the powerful defensive buttresses, and the lofty north and south towers. A visitor facing the wall bounding the choir will be impressed by the sturdiness of the 18C pillars on which the transept and the first two vaults of the nave would have rested, and which surround the **Cour St-Eutrope** (access via rue Gustave-Fabre). From this courtyard, the **terraces** (⚲ *Closed for renovation work.*) and the **north tower** can be reached, both of which give an interesting **view**★ over the flying buttresses of the cathedral, the archbishops' palace and the city.

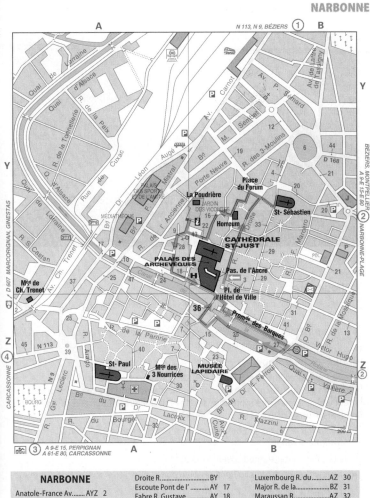

NARBONNE

Town Walk

▷ *Start from place de l'Hôtel-de-Ville and follow rue Droite, a pedestrianised shopping street.*

Place Bistan

Remnants of a 1C temple on the site of the Antique forum and Capitol.

▷ *Turn right onto Rue Girard then left onto Rue Michelet.*

Église St-Sébastien

This 15C church with 17C extensions, was built, according to legend, on the site of the saint's birthplace.

▷ *Return to Place Bistan and, from the SW corner, follow Rue Rouget-de-l'Isle.*

The itinerary takes you past the **Horreum**, a Roman warehouse (🕭 *see Additional Sights).*

▷ *Turn right onto Rue du Lieut.-Col.-Deymes and right again onto Rue Armand-Gauthier which leads to place Salengro.*

Pont des Marchands

La Poudrière

Situated behind the Jardin des Vicomtes, this 18C powder magazine houses temporary exhibitions.

▷ *Return to Place Salengro, turn right onto Rue Chennebier and left onto Rue du Lion-d'Or leading to the embankment; turn left.*

Banks of the Robine

The Robine canal links the Sallèles-d'Aude junction canal to Port-la-Nouvelle. The plane trees along its course, the Pont des Marchands and the colourful pedestrian street which spans it, the footbridge and the Promenade des Barques, all make it the ideal place for a leisurely stroll.

▷ *When you reach the end of Promenade des Barques, take Pont de la Liberté across the Robine canal.*

Note the fine metal-framed covered market.

▷ *Follow the south bank to Pont des Marchands and return to Place de l'Hôtel-de-Ville.*

Pont des Marchands★

This picturesque bridge, which is in fact a pedestrianised street lined with colourful shops overlooking the canal, follows the old Roman road known as Via Domitia.

Additional Sights

Archaeological Museum★★

🕐 *Apr–Sep: 9.30am–12.15pm, 2–6pm; Oct–Mar: daily except Mon 10am–noon, 2–5pm.* 🕐 *Closed 1 Jan, 1 May, 1 and 11 Nov, 25 Dec.* ⬡ *5.20€ (3.70€ for 1 museum only).* ☎ *04 68 90 30 54. Palais Neuf.*

Narbonne undoubtedly possesses one of the finest collections of **Roman paintings**★★ in France. Most come from the archaeological excavations at Clos de la Lombarde (north part of the ancient town) and the frescoes and floor coverings testify to the style in which the homes of the rich in Narbo Martius were decorated in the first two centuries AD. After an introduction to the architecture of a Gallo-Roman house and an explanation of the techniques of mural painting in the days of Antiquity, the museum visit leads into an area containing various examples of painted and mosaic decors. The style best represented in Narbonne is the Fourth Pompeian style (late 1C AD). The walls feature stylised motifs, hunting or pastoral scenes

Roman painting

and garlands, on a red or white background. The most famous decor of this type is the **painting of a Genie** which adorned the triclinium (dining room) of the villa: to the right, above the entablature of an aedicula, is a bust of Apollo wreathed in laurel; to the left is a Genie carrying a horn of plenty and a libations dish, accompanied by a winged Victory, damaged, brandishing a shield. Decorating a coffered section in a ceiling is a Maenad, or female follower of Bacchus, holding a beribboned thyrsus (wand tipped with a pine cone, an ancient fertility symbol). Most of the mosaics are in black and white and are inspired by works of this kind made in Pompeii. These are either marble inlaid on a black background (mid-1C), or geometrical motifs (strapwork, squares, lozenges etc).

In the upper chapel of La Madeleine is a display of artefacts discovered during excavations of the oppidum at Montlaurès. A large collection of stone fragments evokes the institutions, daily life, religious practices and commercial activities of Roman Narbonne: note a milestone, a 1C Drunken Silenus, a late-1C Roman Diana with a "bee-hive" hairstyle, the sarcophagus of the "Amours Vendangeurs" (grape-picking cupids) (3C), and a wooden and lead anchor discovered in Port-la-Nautique. In the lower room of La Madeleine, objects of note include a superb pagan mosaic, various sarcophagi decorated with narrative scenes or fluting and a 5C dedicatory lintel from the early cathedral built here by Bishop Rustique.

The **Tinal**, linked to the archaeological museum, houses prehistoric collections.

Museum of Art and History★

🕐 As for the Archaeological Museum. Palais Neuf, in the same building as the Salle des Synodes, on the second floor.

This museum occupies the old episcopal apartments where Louis XIII stayed during the siege of Perpignan in spring 1642.

Next to the **audience room**, where several portraits of archbishops hang, is the **King's bedchamber** which boasts a fine coffered ceiling depicting the nine Muses and, on the floor, a Roman mosaic with geometrical motifs in wonderfully preserved colours.

In the **great gallery**, there is a fine display of pharmacists' jars made of Montpellier faience; also on display are several 16C and 17C Flemish and Italian paintings.

The **faience room** contains an impressive collection of glazed earthenware pieces from some of the greatest French faience manufacturers (Montpellier, Narbonne, Marseille, Moustiers-Ste-Marie and Strasbourg).

In the **Grand Salon** hang Beauvais tapestries inspired by the Fables of La Fontaine and several interesting paintings, for example the *Adoration of the Shepherds* by Philippe de Champaigne.

Two rooms contain a remarkable collection of 19C and 20C works by **Orientalist painters** (Benjamin Constant, Lazerges, Bezombes etc).

Lapidary Museum★

♿🕐 As for the Archaeological Museum.

This is in the deconsecrated 13C church of Notre-Dame-de-la-Mourguié. The exterior looks magnificent with its projecting buttresses and crenellated chevet.

Crammed into four rows, a collection of almost 1 300 antique inscriptions, with steles, lintels, busts, sarcophagi and huge carved blocks of stone, most of them from the city ramparts, recalls the prestigious past of the ancient capital of Gallia Narbonensis.

Horreum

🕐 As for the Archaeological Museum.

It is only possible to visit two of the galleries of this public warehouse. Opening onto these underground galleries are small cells which made sorting out the goods easier. The warehouse was located near the forum, beneath the market to which it was linked by hoists. A few sculptures and low reliefs illustrate Roman civilisation.

Basilique St-Paul

🕐 Daily except Sun afternoon.

This basilica was built on the site of a 4C and 5C necropolis near the tomb of the city's first archbishop. Inside, near the south door, stands a font famed for the curious little sculpted frog which adorns it. The **chancel**★, which was begun in 1224, is notable for the height of its supporting structure (large arcades, double triforium, tall windows), its vaults in the style of Champagne and its overall elegance. The perspective of the nave is broken by three massive basket-handle arches. Beneath the great organ, two early Christian sarcophagi are embedded in the wall; a third is used as a lintel.

The **Paleo-Christian crypt** *(Visits by appointment with the keeper. No charge; entrance through the north door of the basilica)* formed part of the sizeable necropolis founded in the early 4C during the reign of Constantine. The remains of an edifice composed of a square room and an apse constitute a crypt which houses six sarcophagi. Of these the most interesting are one which is decorated with acroters, another with foliage in the Aquitaine style, and a third in white marble reminiscent of pagan sarcophagi.

Maison des Trois-Nourrices

In the street situated on the east side of the basilica.

This 16C house owes its unusual name ("House of the Three Wet-Nurses") to the generous curves of the caryatids supporting the lintel of a magnificent Renaissance window.

◐◑ **Maison natale de Charles Trenet** – ◐☜ *Apr-Sep: guided tours (1hr) daily except Tue 10am-noon, 2-6pm; Oct-Mar: daily except Tue 2-6pm.* ◐ *Closed 1 Jan, 1 May, 1 and 11 Nov, 25 Dec.* ☜ *5.20€ (children: 3.70€).* ☎ *04 68 90 30 66.* Birthplace of the popular composer/singer.

Excursions

Sigean African Safari Park★

17km/10.5mi S along N 9. ♿ *Description under Réserve africaine de SIGEAN.*

Fontfroide Abbey★★

14km/8.5mi SW along N 113, then left onto D 613. ♿ *See description under Abbaye de FONTFROIDE.*

Amphoralis-Musée des Potiers gallo-romains★

11km/6.5mi to Sallèdes-d'Aude. From there, take D 1626 NE and follow the signs to "Musée des Potiers." The road runs alongside the junction canal linking the Canal du Midi and Canal de La Robine. ◐☜ *Jul-Sep: 10am-noon, 3-7pm; Oct-Jun: daily except Mon 2-6pm, Sat-Sun and public holidays 10am-noon, 2-6pm. Guided tours available by request.* ◐ *Closed 1 Jan, 1 May, 25 Dec. 4€.* ☎ *04 68 46 89 48*

The central section of the modern museum building houses an exhibition on the craft of making amphorae, which was both varied and prolific, lasting from the 1C to the 4C AD. Open-sided structures here and there reveal the site of the excavations, comprising the workshop area around a dozen or so kilns (including one in working order), settling tanks, workshops with potter's wheels in which clay was made and various other utilitarian buildings. The open clay quarry is nearby. Besides the excavations,

---

Address Book

THE PRACTICAL CANALS

Autorail touristique du Minervois: Between Narbonne and Bize-Minervois; Jul-Sept: weekends and holidays, departure from quai de la rue Paul-Vieu in Narbonne at 2pm; return journey starts at 7pm; 9.50€, ☎ 04 68 27 05 94.

The timetable allows for a visit of Amphoralis and the L'Oulibo olive-oil cooperative in Bize-Minervois.

Petit train des Lagunes: From Narbonne to Port-la-Nouvelle; Jul-mid Sept: daily except Sunday, departure from Port-la-Nouvelle station at 3pm; 6€ (children 4€), ☎ 04 68 48 16 56 or 04 68 48 00 51 (Port-la-Nouvelle tourist office). Excursion and visit (3hr) of Ile Ste-Lucie, La Franqui and the Musée de la Baleine (Whale Museum).

Coche d'eau: From Narbonne to Port-la-Nouvelle; Jul-mid Sept: daily except Sunday, boats leave from Pont des Marchands at 9.30am and 6pm; duration: 2hr or all day; bookings essential; 6.10€ or

22.90€ depending on the trip chosen, ☎ 04 68 90 63 98.

CANAL BY HOUSEBOAT

Nichols – Port du Somail - Allée de la Glacière - 11120 Le Somail - ☎ 04 68 46 00 97. Rental of houseboats accommodating 2-12 people for cruising along the Canal du Midi and the Canal de la Robine. *Reservation centre: Rte. du Puy-St-Bonnet, 49300 Cholet,* ☎ *02 41 56 46 56.* www. nicols.com.

Connoisseur – Houseboat cruises on the Canal du Midi from Trèbes *(Port de plaisance, 11800 Trèbes,* ☎ *04 68 78 73 75)* and on the Canal de la Robine from Narbonne *(7 quai d'Alsace, 11100 Narbonne,* ☎ *04 68 65 14 55).* Reservation centre: Le Grand Bassin, BP 1201, 11492 Castelnaudary, ☎ 04 68 94 09 75, fax 04 68 94 52 73. E-mail: info@connoisseur.fr, www. connoisseurafloat.com.

the tour includes displays on the sorts of earthenware produced at Sallèles-d'Aude (domestic ceramic ware, tiles, wine amphorae), firing techniques (models of kilns), daily life and trade under the Roman Empire.

The reconstruction of a children's necropolis (the oldest bodies were of nine-month-old babies), discovered in part of the workshop area, sheds light on funerary rituals observed in the Gallo-Roman world in the 1C BC. To the north of the site are the remains of an aqueduct (early 2C) which brought water across the plain to Narbonne.

Canal de la Robine

Dug at the end of the 18C through the former riverbed of the Robine, it is supplied with water from the Lampy reservoir (*see MONTAGNE NOIRE*) and reaches the sea at Port-la-Nouvelle after flowing through the Bages, Sigean and Ayrolle lakes and skirting **Ste-Lucie island** famous for its varied fauna and flora.

Port-la-Nouvelle

28km/17.5mi S. Lying at the mouth of the Canal de la Robine, this is the only town on this part of the Mediterranean coast, apart from Sète and Port-Vendres, to have preserved some degree of economic activity outside the tourist season. The commercial port here handles the distribution of fuel oil for the whole of South-West France. The comings and goings of freighters and tankers make an exciting scene. The harbour at Port-la-Nouvelle also has yachting facilities. A beach of fine golden sand extends over 13km/8mi.

Montagne de la Clape

Round tour of 53km/33mi – allow 3hrs.

▶ *Leave town on 2 on the town plan, then take D 168 on the left towards Narbonne-Plage.*

The 214m/702ft-high limestone massif of La Clape towers above the sea, the coastal lagoons round Gruissan and the vine-covered lower Aude Valley. The steep and winding road offers splendid views over the cliffs and slopes of La Clape.

Narbonne-Plage ☺

This resort stretching along the coast is typical of the traditional Languedoc seaside resorts. There is sailing and water-skiing here.

Have fun with water at **Aquajet** park (🕐 *Early Jul to mid-Sep: 11am-7pm; May-Jun: noon-6pm.* 🎫 *8€.* ☎ *04 68 44 31 61.),* which offers three water chutes, a swimming pool and various aquatic games.

▶ *From Narbonne-Plage, carry on to St-Pierre-sur-Mer.*

St-Pierre-sur-Mer – Family seaside resort. The chasm of l'Oeil-Doux to the north is a curious natural phenomenon. It is 100m/328ft wide and contains a salt water lake 70m/229ft deep into which the sea surges.

Gruissan ☺ – 🍂 *See GRUISSAN.*

▶ *Leave Gruissan, turn right and immediately on the left take a little road signposted Notre-Dame des Auzils.*

Cimetière marin – 🍂 *See GRUISSAN: Excursion.*

▶ *Follow the little road across the lower slopes of La Clape. On reaching D 32, turn right towards Narbonne. At Ricardelle, take a steep, narrow little road on the right.*

Coffre de Pech Redon

This marks the summit of La Clape mountain. From it, there is a scenic view over the lagoons and Narbonne, with the cathedral of St-Just and the Archbishops' Palace rising above the city's skyline.

▶ *Turn back and return to Narbonne on D 32.*

Cirque de NAVACELLES★★★

MICHELIN LOCAL MAP 339: G-5

The Cirque de Navacelles is the most impressive natural feature of the Vis Valley, which cuts between the causses of Blandas to the north and Larzac to the south. The cirque is formed by an immense, magnificent meander, deeply embedded in almost vertical walls of rock. The meander, which once encircled a little promontory, was abandoned by the River Vis, which broke through the neck of a loop, just where the village of Navacelles had established itself. The flat valley floor has remained quite moist.

From Alzon to Ganges

57km/35mi – allow 2hr.

Downstream from Alzon, the road (D 814) drops to the floor of the valley, running through woods of oak and fir trees, then crosses the river which makes wider and wider meanders on the flat valley floor.

▶ *D 113 runs along the floor of the valley to Vissec and crosses a bridge over the river, which is frequently dried up at this point.*

Vissec

The aridity of the surrounding countryside, and the bleached white of the rocks lend this remote spot a slightly unsettling character. The village, squatting deep down inside the canyon, consists of two districts, each on an outcrop, one of which is almost completely encircled by the Vis.

Cirque de Vissec★

During the climb up to Blandas (*gradient 9%*), there is a view of the gorge with its bare cliff walls. The Vissec cirque, much less impressive than that of Navacelles, is nonetheless an attractive sight for anyone who loves wild and rugged landscapes.

▶ *The road reaches Blandas across the bleak limestone plateau. D 713 branching off D 158 reaches the edge of the Causse de Blandas.*

Belvédère Nord

Alt 613m/2 011ft. From this viewpoint on the north edge of the plateau there is an interesting view over the **cirque de Navacelles**★★★ and the Vis canyon. The long Séranne chain can be seen on the horizon.

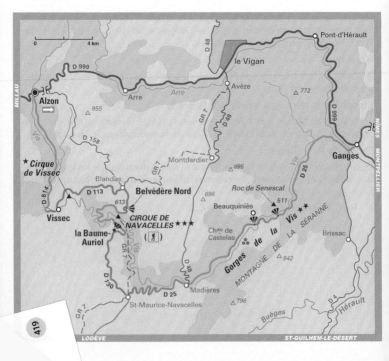

Cirque de Navacelles

The clearly marked road winds down one or two hairpin bends at the top of the cliff, then forms a large loop round the Combe du Four, before dropping steeply down to the floor of the cirque and onto the village of Navacelles perched on and around a rocky outcrop.

Navacelles

This little village 325m/1 066ft above sea level has a pretty single-arched bridge over the Vis.

🚶 A path starting from Navacelles leads to the resurgence of the River Vis and the River Virenque near three watermills.

▸ *D 130 climbs up the south face of the canyon.*

La Baume-Auriol

Alt 618m/2 037ft. From north of the farm, there is a magnificent view of the cirque. The canyon looks splendid as it cuts tight and meanders between narrow strips of land edged by steep cliffs on the upstream side.

▸ *Beyond La Baume-Auriol, the road continues to St-Maurice-Navacelles, where you should turn left towards Ganges.*

Farther along, the road plunges downhill in a series of hairpin bends, passing the Rau de Fontenilles, heading towards the Vis gorge. At the start of the downhill stretch to Madières, there is a good view of the gorge.

Gorges de la Vis★★

Beyond Madières, the road goes through nursery gardens thick with evergreen trees. It sticks closely to the bank of the Vis, which cuts a pretty course between the tall dolomitic cliffs of the Causse de Blandas, on the left, and the slopes of Séranne mountain, on the right. After Le Claux, note the ruins of the Château de Castelas, which can be seen clinging to a cliff at the mouth of a ravine.

After Gorniès, a bridge spans the Vis. Look out for a lovely view of **Beauquiniès**, a pretty terraced village, and then of the **Roc de Senescal**, which juts out like a ship's prow from the slope on the left. The valley becomes narrow and rugged, before running into the Hérault gorge. Carry on along the banks of the Hérault to Le Pont and Ganges.

Massif de NÉOUVIELLE★★★

This granite mountain mass attracts a great number of sightseers and hikers because of its hundred or so lakes and the clear air around it. The massif offers many examples of glacial relief, culminating in the 3 192m/10 465ft-high Pic Long.

Since 1850 tributaries of the Neste d'Aure (Aure Torrent) originating in the Néouvielle have helped regulate the flow of rivers from the hills of Gascony; these waters are used today in the production of hydroelectric power. 🛈 *37 R. Vincent-Mir, 65170 St-Lary-Soulan, ☎ 05 62 39 50 81. www.saintlary.com.*

▷ **Orient Yourself:** The best access to the massif is through the Bielsa tunnel; stop at the information centre in St-Lary-Soulon first, for maps and brochures. A nature reserve for the protection of the local fauna and flora was set up around Lake Aumar and Lake Aubert. The **lake road** is therefore ♿ closed to traffic in July and August *(9.30am-6.30pm; shuttle service operates from Lake Orédon Jul-mid Sep: departures every 30min 9.30am-6pm; 2.50€ one-way; ☎ 05 62 39 62 63).*

Ⓢ **Don't Miss:** The Cap-de-Long dam and its beautiful, fjord-like lake.

Ⓢ **Organising Your Time:** Take the driving tour in the early summer, as soon as the road *(normally closed from October to early summer)* and the path to Col d'Aubert are free of snow; the waterfalls and the lakes are at their best when water is most abundant.

Ⓢ **Also See:** Parc National des PYRÉNÉES

Hiking Tours

The Massif de Néouvielle is the ideal area for family hikes as well as for more demanding hikes in the mountains. There are numerous marked itineraries and appropriate topoguides are on sale in local shops or in the **Maison du Parc** in Saint-Lary-Soulan *(☎ 05 62 39 40 91)*; information is available from the **Bureau des Guides** in Saint-Lary-Soulan *(☎ 05 62 40 02 58 or 05 62 39 41 97).*

Col (or hourquette) d'Aubert★★

▷ *3hr on foot to the pass. From the Lac d'Aubert parking area, follow the marked path that skirts the lake by the NE. Alt 2 498m/8 196ft.*

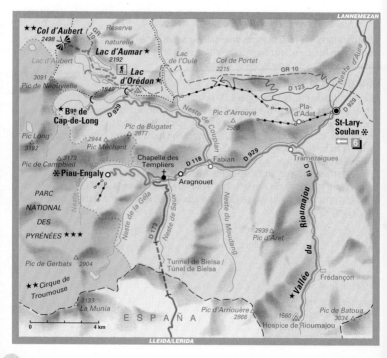

Lac d'Aubert and Lac d'Aumar

This pass links the depression cradling the Aubert and Aumar lakes with the desolate Escoubous coomb on the slopes towards Barèges. There is a remarkable **view**★★ of the tiered lakes, and the smaller stretch of water below them known as Les Laquettes, at the foot of Pic de Néouvielle. Far off to the south-east the glaciated ensemble of the Maladetta massif can be seen.

From St-Lary-Soulon to the Lakes
70km/43mi round tour – allow 5hr.

St-Lary-Soulan ✳

This small **winter sports resort** has developed since 1950 along the western slopes of the Vallée d'Aure. Its sunny location and liveliness make it very attractive.

Ski area

Access to the ski slopes above the town at Pla d'Adet and Espiaude (alt 830-2 450m/2 723-8 038ft; 48 ski lifts) is either via a gondola lift or via a longer, northern road route.
During the summer, the town is a useful base for mountaineers visiting the region – especially since it lies on the trans-Pyrenean highway, completed in 1976 by the opening of the Bielsa tunnel.

▸ *Leave St-Lary SW along D 929.*

Beyond St-Lary, the valley narrows to a gorge. Up on the left is the watchtower village of Tramezaïgues. In former times, its castle defended the whole valley against incursions by the Aragonese.

▸ *From Tramezaïgues take D 19, a road that is only partly surfaced. Beyond Fredançon, the last 4km/2mi of the road are so narrow that traffic is one-way only.*

Vallée du Rioumajou★

This is a densely wooded valley with numerous waterfalls. Not far from the Spanish frontier the former Rioumajou hospice (alt 1 560m/5 117ft), now a mountain refuge, stands in a fine amphitheatre with steep grassy or tree-covered slopes.

▸ *Return to Tramezaïgues and turn left on D 929.*

As the road follows the line of the Vallée de la Neste d'Aure, the silhouette of Pic de Campbieil comes gradually into view. The mountain, one of the highest points in the massif at 3 173m/10 407ft, is recognisable by its twin-peaked crest underlined by a *névé* (an area of snow not yet compressed into ice at the head of a glacier).

▸ *Beyond Fabian turn left on D 118.*

The road, climbing alongside the waters of the Neste de la Géla, passes through the scattered hamlets of **Aragnouet**. Below, on the right, the belfry-wall of the 12C **Chapelle des Templiers** (🕐 *Mid-Jul to end Aug: 4-7pm; low season: by request at the town hall, ☎ 05 62 39 62 63.)* appears; two ancient statues are housed in this restored sanctuary.

▷ *Leave the route leading to the Bielsa tunnel on the left.*

Piau ☀

At an altitude of 1 850m/6 000ft, the highest ski resort in the French Pyrenees is a stone's throw from the nature reserves of the Parc national des Pyrénées and the Parque Nacional de Ordesa y Monte Perdido in Spain. At the foot of the ski slopes (36 slopes, 21 ski lifts), modern apartment buildings, their sloping, snow-covered façades arranged in a half circle, discretely follow the lie of the land.

▷ *Return to Fabian and turn left on D 929 heading N.*

The old road, carved out by the French electricity authority to allow access to the Cap-de-Long site (👥 *see below*), climbs up through the valley of the Neste de Couplan, scaling an ancient glacial channel via a series of hairpin bends known as the Edelweiss.

▷ *Continue to Lake Cap-de-Long.*

Barrage de Cap-de-Long★

The dam (maximum height 100m/328ft) has created a volume of 67.5 million m3/89.7 million cu yd of water and is an important component of the Pragnères hydroelectric power station. The artificial lake with its inaccessible shores is frequently frozen over until the month of May, and resembles a fjord at the foot of the Néouvielle's rocky walls. It lies at an altitude of 2 160m/7 087ft.

▷ *Retrace your steps. The scenic Route des Lacs starts from the Orédon fork and the road stops at the Orédon Lake parking area. A path continues through the Néouvielle nature reserve, a conservation area for the local fauna and flora.*

Lac d'Orédon★

Alt 1 849m/6 066ft. The scree-covered slopes dipping down towards the lake are dotted with firs. The chalet-hotel makes this spot a good base camp for mountain expeditions. Upstream, the view is blocked by the wall of Cap-de-Long dam, which created this man-made lake.

▷ *Leave the car in the* **car park** *(1/2h: no charge; 3hr: 👥 2€; 8hr: 4€; over 8hr: 5€.).*

▷ *Continue on foot along the Sentier des Laquettes (1hr 30min) or take the shuttle to Lac d'Aubert.*

🔼 From here, continue the excursion on foot: walk back a short distance and take the trail marked GR 10 which skirts Lake Aumar.

Lac d'Aumar★

Alt 2 192m/7 192ft. This is a peaceful upland lake, surrounded by grassland and an occasional pine, draining into Lac d'Aubert.
At the northern end of the lake the summit of Pic de Néouvielle (alt 3 091m/10 142ft), bordered by a small glacier, comes into view.

Grotte de NIAUX★★

MICHELIN LOCAL MAP 343: H-8

This cave in the Vicdessos Valley is famous for its remarkably well-preserved prehistoric wall drawings.

▷ *Take a road uphill just after leaving the village of Niaux.*

Visit

Entrance porch

This houses a huge metal structure by Italian architect Fuksas. On entering the cave's vast entrance porch, 678m/2 224ft above sea level, the extent of the glacial erosion that occurred many thousands of years ago in the massif of the Cap de la Lesse, where the cave is situated, becomes immediately clear. Successive glaciers at times submerged the valley and completely covered the massif. The immense volume of water would then surge into crevices and wear down the rock, enlarging the cave and its entrance to their enormous size.

With time, the level of the valley floor became lower; the river now flows alongside D 8, about 100m/328ft below it. The valley has a cross-section characteristic of a glaciated valley, with a flat floor, enclosed by steep terraces and slopes.

The Cave★★

Tickets must be reserved (a week ahead in summer). Jul and Aug: 🕐☂️ *guided tours (every 45min) 9-11.30am, 12.30-5.45pm; Apr-Jun and Oct: 10.15am, 11am, 1.45pm, 2.30pm, 3.30pm, 4.15pm; rest of the year: daily except Mon (apart from school and public holidays) 11am, 2.30pm and 4.15pm.* 🕐 *Closed 1 Jan and 25 Dec.* 🎫 *9.40€ (children: 5.70€). The path to follow for the visit is long and over rough ground, wear sturdy shoes or boots in very rainy weather. Reservations strongly recommended.* ☎ *05 61 05 88 37 or 05 61 05 10 10.*

The cave consists of vast, high chambers and long passageways leading, 775m/850yd from the entrance, to a kind of natural rotunda known as the **"Salon Noir"** ("Black Chamber") with walls decorated with the outlines of bison, horses, deer and ibex seen in profile. These drawings executed during the Magdalenian period (11000 BC) using manganese oxides convey a vision of the world typical of the hunting populations of Western Europe at the end of the Paleolithic Age. Many are of an exceptionally high standard and testify to a well-developed technical skill in the art of animal drawing.

Causse NOIR★

MICHELIN LOCAL MAP 338: L-6 TO M-6

The smallest of the Grands Causses (200km²/77sq mi), is called "Noir" ("black" or "dark") because of the dense pine forests which once covered most of the plateau. It is bordered to the north by the Jonte river gorge and to the south by the Dourbie Valley. Dolomitic limestone predominates, with the result that the *causse* includes some of the finest "ruined cities" of rocks in the area. The Jonte gorge can be seen in all its splendour from the cliff road that runs along its edge.

Excursion

Round trip 75km/47mi – allow 4hr.

Peyreleau

Situated at the confluence of the River Jonte and River Tarn and built on the steep slopes of a hill, Peyreleau is an interesting place to stay for those who wish to explore the area. A modern church and an old crenellated square keep (all that is left on a feudal castle) tower above the village. From D 29 which climbs onto the Causse Noir, there are views of the 15C **Château de Triadou** where a treasure stolen by its owner from the Protestant army in the 17C was eventually found by peasants during the 1789 Revolution.

▸ *Reach the Causse Noir via D 29 S of Peyreleau. After 7km/4.3mi, turn right onto D 110.*

Chaos de Montpellier-le-Vieux★★★ – 👣 *See Chaos de MONTPELLIER-LE-VIEUX.*

The "tall rocks" of Roquesaltes

▷ *Return to D 29 and turn right. Beyond La Roujarie, turn right onto D 124 to St-André-de-Vézines. At the entrance of the village, take the street on the right and follow signposts to Roquesaltes. Leave the car at the intersection of the road with an unsurfaced path and walk along this path, signposted "Roquesaltes," to the right.*

Chaos de Roquesaltes et du Rajol★ – *See Hiking Tours below.* 2hr on foot.

▷ *Return to St-André-de-Vézines and turn right towards Veyreau. After 7km/4.3mi, turn left onto D 139.*

Grotte de Dargilan★★ – *See Grotte de DARGILAN.*

Meyrueis – *See MEYRUEIS.*

Gorges de la Jonte★★ – *See MEYRUEIS.*

Hiking Tours

Corniche du Causse Noir★★

Starting from Peyreleau - 6hr - beware of cliff passages.

▷ *Leave the car in the hamlet of Les Rouquets (east of Peyreleau – first road to the left coming from Le Rozier) and continue on foot along a road branching off to the left towards the River Jonte. Keep to the red markings.*

The wide path runs along the Jonte then climbs to the right through beech woods and pine woods before reaching St-Michel Hermitage.

▷ *It is possible to get close to the hermitage via three metal ladders (extreme caution is advisable). Rejoin the path waymarked in red.*

The path leads to "Point Sublime," a rocky promontory jutting out into the Jonte canyon. Exceptional **view**★★.

▷ *Keep following the red markings which lead you through woodland.*

Terraces make it possible to walk to the edge of the cliff and take in the view of the austere Jonte canyon and the peaceful village of Le Rozier. The path, which is now waymarked in red and yellow (GR de Pays or regional footpath) leads past a rock called "Champignon préhistorique."

▷ *Continue along the GR de Pays.*

The path leads to the television mast from which there is a great **view**★ of Peyreleau in its site at the confluence of the River Jonte and River Tarn.

▷ *Continue along the path to a clearing and turn right.*

The path runs down among box trees and rocks then skirts the Costalade ravine. It continues through forest pines and eventually joins up with a path running alongside vineyards near Les Rouquets.

Chaos de Roquesaltes et du Rajol★

2hr on foot. Medium difficulty. In St-André-de-Vézines, turn right onto the road to Roquesaltes. Leave the car at the intersection of the road with an unsurfaced path and walk along this path, signposted "Roquesaltes," to the right.

The path runs down through forest pines and junipers.

▶ *When you reach Roquesaltes farm, take GR 62 on the left towards Montméjean.*

Roquesaltes, meaning "tall rocks," looks for all the world like a natural fortress some 50m/162ft high overlooking the hamlet of Roquesaltes. From these rocky ramparts, the view extends over Montpellier-le-Vieux. Although the area of the rocky chaos is not very large, it constitutes a remarkable set of ruin-shaped rocks including a huge natural gateway.

By continuing south along GR 62, waymarked in red and white, you come to the **Chaos du Rajol**. Visitors are greeted by a "dromedary" with its chin nonchalantly resting on a rock. Other fantastically shaped rocks include an Egyptian Column, an Armless Statue and many more.

◉ *From a natural look-out platform, the view plunges down into the extraordinary Dourbie Valley.*

▶ *From the television mast, turn left onto a dirt track leading to the surfaced road which you had previously followed from St-André; turn left to return to the car.*

OLARGUES

POPULATION 571

MICHELIN LOCAL MAP 339: C-7

This village with its steep streets occupies a promontory encircled by the River Jaur. The village skyline is dominated by a tower, the vestige of an 11C feudal fortress that was converted into a bell-tower in the 15C. Cherry orchards brighten up the valley below. There is a fine overall view from the bridge, on the way in from St-Pons-de-Thomières. 🏢 *Ave. de la Gare, 34390 Olargues, ☎ 04 67 97 71 26. www.olargues.org.*

Old Town

▶ *Start from place de la Mairie.*

Enter the old town through the Porte Neuve (*to the left at the bottom of the square*). From the terrace beside the bell-tower, there is a pleasant **view** of the Jaur and the 13C humpback bridge which spans it, the Espinouse mountains, and Mont Caroux to the north-east.

From rue de la Place, take the covered stairway of the Commanderie on the right; it leads to another street just below the bell-tower. The Musée d'Olargues is located halfway.

Olargues

J. Malburet/MICHELIN

Museum

🕐 *Jun–Sep: daily except Mon 3.30-7pm; short school vacations: daily except Mon 3.30-6pm. No charge.* ☎ *04 67 97 71 26. www.olargues.org.*

This contains displays on traditional crafts and agricultural practices, most of which have now disappeared in the wake of modern technology.

Cebenna

♿🕐 *Jul and Aug: daily except Sun 9am-7pm; rest of the year: daily except Sat-Sun 9am-noon, 2-6pm.* 🕐 *Closed 25 Dec-1 Jan and public holidays. Kaleidoscope:* 🎟 *2.50€ (children under 7: no charge; 7-15 year olds: 1.50€).* ☎ *04 67 97 88 00. www.cebenna.org. On the way out of Olargues to the W.*

📶 This multimedia centre offers a reference library, lectures, and activities around nature, cultural heritage and the environment. A huge kaleidoscope adds colour and light to the scene.

Monts de l'Espinouse★

▶ *80km/50mi round tour – allow 6hr including the walk to the Caroux viewing table. Take D 908 out of Olargues and head W towards St-Pons then turn right onto D 14 to Fraisse-sur-Agout and La Salvetat. It is possible to do this tour taking Lamalou-les-Bains as a starting point.*

The pass road leading to the Col de Fontfroide along the western slopes of the Espinouse mountains starts in a Mediterranean setting of vines, olive trees, holm-oaks and chestnut trees. At higher altitudes, the Mediterranean vegetation gives way to moorland dotted with beech trees.

From the Col du Poirier, the view extends over the mountains in the Somail to the left beyond the Coustorgues gully. There is an even wider view to the south towards the Jaur Valley *(viewpoint)*.

Col de Fontfroide

Alt 971m/3 156ft. The Col de Fontfroide is a mountain pass set in an impressively wild spot. It marks the watershed between the Mediterranean and Atlantic sides of the range.

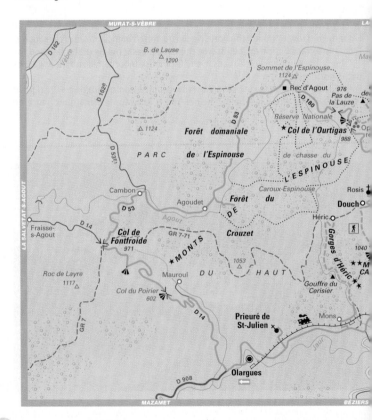

▷ *Turn right onto D 53 to Cambon.*

The road runs along the banks of the Agout, through the village of Cambon which gets quite lively in summer, and continues through rugged, lonely, mountainous scenery where the moorland is backed by the conifers in the Espinouse Forest.

Forêt domaniale de l'Espinouse

Tree planting began in the late 19C and has continued to the present day. Now, the forest of beech, pine, and spruce covers the entire Espinouse plateau. Much of the plateau has been designated as the Caroux-Espinouse hunting ground (*réserve de chasse*). Corsican mouflons (wild sheep), which have acclimatised to the local environment, are occasionally to be seen here. Only the western part of the forest around the forest ranger's house at Le Crouzet is easily accessible and then only on foot.

From the road near the Espinouse summit, the roof of the Espinouse farm or **Rec d'Agout** is visible farther down the hill to the right. It is here that the river rises. The road then reaches the foot of the bare dome-shaped crest of Espinouse (alt 1 124m/ 3 653ft) and runs on down through rugged countryside with ravines to each side, before crossing the **Pas de la Lauze**, a slender ridge linking the Espinouse and Caroux ranges.

Col de l'Ourtigas★

Alt 988m/3 211ft. An observation platform provides an interesting **view**★ of the rugged Espinouse range gashed by ravines. To the left is the Montagne d'Aret and to the right the two outcrops forming the Fourcat d'Héric.

▣ To the right is a path leading to the Plo des Brus *(45min on foot there and back).*

▷ *Continue to the road junction with D 180E branching off to Douch on the right.*

On the right side of the road, **Église de Rosis**, a rustic church with a stone bell-tower, stands out against particularly fine rural countryside.

Douch

The character of this village, which is typical of the Caroux region, is fairly well preserved. The narrow streets are flanked by stone houses roofed with stone slabs *(lauzes).*

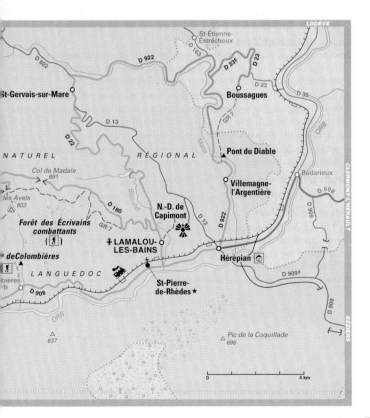

▷ *Leave the car in Douch and follow the path to the left up through the fields. Take the left fork 50m/55yd further on.*

Table d'orientation du Mont Caroux
2hr on foot there and back.

🚶 The path climbs up through clumps of broom, then a beech forest. To the left, at the top of the hill, is the highest point on Mont Caroux itself (alt 1 091m/3 546ft). The path then runs across a vast plateau where heather and broom tremble in the breeze. In the silence that envelops this isolated spot stands a viewing table *(table d'orientation)*, with the Plo de la Maurelle to the right. The rugged, bare Caroux peak towers above the Orb and Jaur valleys. The **panorama**★★ is a magnificent sight. From west to east are the rounded summits of the Montagne Noire with its highest peak, the Pic de Nore, the Pyrenees with the Carlit peak and Mont Canigou, then the plains around Narbonne and Béziers and on down to the Mediterranean. To the right of the plateau is the start of the Gorges de Colombières.

▷ *Return to D 180.*

Forêt des Écrivains Combattants
By car via chemin Paul-Prévost. 🚶 *On foot via a flight of steps 200m/220yd further on opposite an old inn.*

After the catastrophic floods in 1930, the slopes of the Caroux range had to be reafforested. The Association des Écrivains Combattants, the Touring Club de France and the villages of Combes and Rosis replanted the 78ha/193 acres of forest dedicated to writers who had laid down their lives for France. The steep flight of steps leads first to a plateau where there is a memorial commemorating the 560 writers who fell during the First World War (1914-18), then to the Rond-point Charles-Péguy with its gigantic Military Cross. From the roundabout radiate avenues, each named after a writer. The forest, crisscrossed by numerous footpaths includes some magnificent cedars, pines, chestnut trees and oaks. From it, there are several superb views of Mont Caroux and the eastern slopes of the Espinouse mountains.

▷ *The picturesque D 180 leads to Lamalou-les-Bains.*

Lamalou-les-Bains ✛ – 🕐 *See LAMALOU-LES-BAINS.*

▷ *Drive W out of Lamalou-les-Bains along D 908 to Colombières-sur-Orb; leave the car on the left, just beyond the bridge, and follow the path along the gorge.*

Gorges de Colombières
30min on foot there and back. 🚶 *The footpath is fitted in places with metal ladders and handrails to allow hikers to get past difficult passages. The more adventurous will follow a 13km/8mi loop (about 5hr 30min) waymarked with blue triangles.*

The path follows the stream which cascades down from one pool to the next. The section upstream from the gorge is renowned for the rock-climbing opportunities it offers. The short itinerary stops by a small dam. The loop carries on along the waymarked path past some strange troglodyte dwellings.

▷ *In Mons-la-Trivalle, travel NE along D 14E; leave the car at the entrance to the gorge. A footpath runs along the gorge to the hamlet of Héric.*

Gorges d'Héric★★ – 🕐 *See LAMALOU-LES-BAINS.*

▷ *Turn right off D 908 onto D 14E20 passing beneath the railway line.*

Prieuré de St-Julien

This 12C priory is surrounded by vineyards, wooded hills and cypresses, with the rugged summits of the Caroux and Espinouse ranges in the distance. Note the high square tower, the east end adorned with Lombard bands and the doorway inlaid with local black-stone motifs.

▷ *Return to D 908 and drive back to Olargues.*

PERPIGNAN★★

POPULATION 162,678

MICHELIN LOCAL MAP 344: I-6

Perpignan once the capital city of the counts of Roussillon and the kings of Majorca, is an outlying post of Catalan civilisation north of the Pyrenees and a lively commercial city, with shaded walks lined with pavement cafés. ▯ *Palais des Congrès, pl. A.-Lanoux, 66000 Perpignan,* ☎ *04 68 66 30 30. www.perpignantourisme.com. Guided tour of the town* ▲ *– Discovery tours (2hrs) Jun-Sep daily except Sun, 3pm; rest of the year Wed and Sat afternoons.* ☜ *4€. Inquire at the tourist office or at www.vpah.culture.fr.*

▸ **Orient Yourself:** The A 9 (exit 42) and the N 9 both lead to Perpignan; access to the downtown area by Boulevard Edmond Michelet (west), Avenue des Baléares *(south)* or Pont Arago *(north, over the Têt River)*. Shops may be found in the pedestrianised section of downtown *(Rue Mailly)*; also along Avenue du Général-de-Gaulle and Rue de l'Adjudant-Pilote-Paratilla (nicknamed Rue des Olives).

▯ **Parking:** Leave your car in the lots near the Promenade des Platanes.

◉ **Don't Miss:** Le Castillet, symbol of Perpignan.

◉ **Organising Your Time:** Take the town walk first, to get the lay of the land; save time for the Palace of the Kings of Majorca; visit the Additional Sights if your time allows. The Excursion to the Rousillon Plain will require a day.

▥ **Especially for Kids:** The Catalan folk museum in the Casa Pairal.

◔ **Also See:** PORT-BARCARÈS, TAUTAVEL

A Bit of History

Extending beyond the ramparts built by Vauban and demolished from 1904 onwards, the city developed at a safe distance from the Têt. Administration, business and the expanding university ensured the rapid growth of Perpignan.

In the 13C, the city profited from the great upsurge in trade between the south of France, the coast of North Africa and the Levant stimulated by the crusades. In 1276, Perpignan became the capital of Roussillon as part of the estates of the kingdom of Majorca. Its main activity at that time was the preparation and dyeing of cloth from the large cloth manufacturing cities of Europe.

The second Catalan city – After the kingdom of Majorca had ceased to be in 1344, Roussillon and Cerdagne were integrated into the princedom of Catalonia which, in the 14C and 15C, constituted a kind of autonomous federation in the heart of the State of Aragón. Catalan "Corts" sat at Barcelona, head of the federation, but delegated a "Deputation" to Perpignan. Between the two slopes of the Pyrenees, a commercial, cultural and linguistic community came into being.

French or Spanish? – In 1463, Louis XI put 700 men-at-arms at the disposal of King John II of Aragón to help him defeat the Catalans; with his usual great common sense, he rewarded himself by taking possession of Perpignan and Roussillon. However, the inhabitants fanned the flames of their nostalgia for Catalan autonomy, rebellious feeling ran high, hostilities with France broke out once more and French armies besieged the city. In spite of famine, the people of Perpignan put up fierce resistance (for many years afterwards, they were known as "rat eaters"). They surrendered only when ordered to do so by the king of Aragón, who gave the city the title of "Fidelissima" (most faithful).

In 1493, Charles VIII, who wished to have a free hand in Italy, sought to win the friendship of Spain, so he gave the province of Roussillon back to the Roman Catholic monarchs Ferdinand and Isabella. Perpignan represented to them the key to Spain, and they made it one of the most heavily fortified cities in Europe. In the 17C, Cardinal Richelieu, methodically implementing his policy of creating natural frontiers, seized the opportunity offered in 1640 by a Catalan rebellion against the government of Madrid and signed an alliance with them; the following year, Louis XIII became count of Barcelona.

Seal of the kings of Majorca

A Castor/Coll. Musée Puig

Address Book

For coin categories, see the Legend.

EATING OUT

Casa Bonet – *2 R. du Chevalet* – ☎ *04 68 34 19 45*. This Catalan *casa* in the pedestrian area of town houses a restaurant offering a buffet, tapas and a dozen different brochettes.

Les Casseroles en Folies – *72 Ave. L.-Torcatis* – ☎ *04 68 52 48 03 - closed Jul-Aug -* 🍴. Venture across the Têt to make the acquaintace of this impassioned chef and his Casseroles en Folies. Traditional cuisine with imaginative touches, accompanied by fine Roussillon wines.

Les Trois Sœurs – *2 R. Fontfroide -* ☎ *04 68 51 22 33 – closed Mon morning except summer and Sun*. When these three sisters went into business, they chose a restaurant on the cathedral square with three adjoining rooms. Contemporary decor with a fine archway made of cayrou (the local red stone) separating the restaurant from the tapas bar. Lovely terrace. Meridional cuisine.

Les Antiquaires – *Pl. Després* – ☎ *04 68 34 06 58 – closed 1-23 Jul, Sun evening and Mon*. This 1925 maisonette near the Place Rigaud has been run by the same proprietors for 30 years. In a setting featuring antique furnishings and embroidered tablecloths, their generous and spirited cuisine focuses on regional fare that is a good value for money.

Galinette – *23 R. Jean-Payra* – ☎ *04 68 35 00 90 - closed 26 Jul-16 Aug, 23 Dec-4 Jan, Sun and Mon*. Contemporary furnishings, beautifully set tables: a refined décor in which to sample southern-style dishes created with market-fresh ingredients. Good selection of regional wines.

WHERE TO STAY

Hôtel Alexander – *15 Bd. Clemenceau -* ☎ *04 68 35 41 41 - www.hotel-alexander.fr - 25 rooms -* 🛏 *6,50€ - repas 16€*. This little hotel, with its balconied guestrooms, is located right downtown. Air-conditioned rooms on three levels (there is an elevator) are perfectly maintained. Enthusiastic welcome.

Chambre d'hôte Domaine du Mas Boluix – *Chemin du Pou de les Colobres - 5km/3mi S of Perpignan towards Argelès -* ☎ *04 68 08 17 70 -* 🍴 *- 7 rooms*. Removed from the bustle of Perpignan, this nicely restored 18C *mas* is a peaceful place in the middle of Cabestany grapevines. Each guest room, beautifully decorated with yellow walls and Catalan fabrics, is named after a local artist.

New Christina – *51 cours Lassus -* ☎ *04 68 35 12 21 - info@hotel-newchristina.com – 25 rooms -* 🛏 *8.50€ - restaurant* 🍽. This small, modern hotel near the city centre has a rooftop swimming pool, a hammam and a jacuzzi (fee charged for the last two). This practical stopover enables its guests to mix relaxation with tourism or business while in Perpignan. Bright, practical rooms.

Chambre d'hôte Casa del Arte – *Mas Petit - 66300 Thuir - 17km/11mi W of Perpignan, towards Thuir and Ille-sur-Têt -* ☎ *04 68 53 44 78 - 6 rooms*. Your host, a painter by trade, has personalised every bedroom of this 11C and 14C *mas*; he uses the large salon to exhibit the work of local artists around the medieval fireplace. Outside, the swimming pool and park invite guests to relax and go with the flow.

SIT BACK AND RELAX

Espi – *43 bis quai Vauban* – ☎ *04 68 35 19 91 - winter: daily 7.30am-7.30pm; summer: 7.30am-12.30am*. Immense store where each type of product (candies, pastries, etc) features specialties original to the house, such as honey ice-cream or roasted pine-nuts. Don't miss the *gateau Roussillon à la crème catalane*. Tearoom with terrace; speedy service at lunchtime.

ON THE TOWN

May we suggest - After breakfast on the terrace at Petit Moka, it's time to visit the Byrrh caves at Thuir. This might be followed by a detour to the aero-club at Torreilles for a taste of motorized paragliding or an ultralight flight.

In the evening, there are numerous music bars to be discovered in Old Perpignan, such as the O'Shannon Irish pub, the Corto Maltese, Tio Pepe or Mediator on concert evenings.

Le Mediator – *Av. du Gén.-Leclerc* – ☎ *04 68 51 64 40 - www.elmediator.org - reception and ticket office open Tue-Sat 2.30-8pm - closed Jul-Aug*. This concert hall (1,000 seats) hosts some 60 shows yearly.

RECREATION

Centre équestre de loisirs du Barcarès – *Chemin de l'Hourtou - 66420 Le Barcarès -* ☎ *04 68 80 98 26 - daily 10am-noon, 2pm-8.30pm – 12€ per hour*. Tours on horseback, by the hour or the day, round Salses lake by the sea. 2-5 day excursions around the Cathar castles or along the Roussillon wine route are also organized. Snack bar on site.

SHOPPING

Markets – Fruit and vegetable markets are held daily except Mon on the Place de la République and every morning Place Cassanyes. Flea market Av. du Palais-des-Expositions Sun morning. Organic market Place Rigaud Wed and Sat morning.

Shopping streets – Centre city has a pedestrian district where one finds numerous clothing shops (beginning at the Rue Mailly). The Avenue du Gén.-de-Gaulle, in a lively part of town, is full of shops. The Rue de l'Adjudant-Pilote-Paratilla, also called la Rue des Olives by locals, is known for its two grocery shops and the delicatessen where roast meat is sold (*rôtisseur*), all three a century old.

Au Paradis des Desserts – *13 Ave. du Gén.-de-Gaulle - ☎ 04 68 34 89 69 - Tue-Sun 8am-12.10pm, 4-7.30pm - closed public holiday afternoons and 2 wks in Aug.* Make note of this address, where a talented patissier devotes himself to the creation of a wide range of truly individualised taste sensations.

Lor – *85 R. Pascal-Marie-Agasse - ☎ 0 68 85 65 05 - open daily except Sat-Sun 9am-noon, 2-6pm. No charge.* Come visit this big bon-bon factory where Catalan treats such as *touron* and *rousquilles* are made. Sweets samplings after the tour.

Maison Sala – *1 R. Adjudant-Pilote-Paratilla - ☎ 04 68 51 03 75 - Tues-Sat 8am-7pm - closed Jul and public holidays.* The Sala family has owned this gourmet grocery since 1913. Two house specialties: Collioure anchovies and wild cod of Islande. You'll also find spices, olives, dried fruits and vegetables.

Domaine Lacassagne – *Mas Balande, Route d'Elne - ☎ 04 68 50 25 32 - www.lacassagne.net - Mon-Fri 8.30-noon, 2-6pm.* Situated amid the vines, this *mas* welcomes devotees of the myriad specialties of the Rouissillon, such as oils pressed from local olives and wines from local vineyards. You'll also find local honey, vinegars and almond flours.

Jacques Creuzet-Romeu – *9 R. Fontfroide - ☎ 04 68 34 16 94 – Mon-Fri 9.30am-noon, 2pm-7pm – closed 1 week in Feb, 2 weeks in Aug and holidays.* Perpignan garnets. The studio may be visited (phone ahead).

Michel Gourgot – *13 R. Louis-Blanc - ☎ 04 68 34 67 79 - Mon 2.30pm-7pm, Tue-Sun 9.30am-noon, 2pm-7pm – closed holidays.* Jeweller's shop selling Perpignan garnets.

Centre d'artisanat d'art Sant-Vicens – *R. Sant Vicens - ☎ 04 68 50 02 18 - baudy@wanadoo.fr – Apr-Dec: 10am-noon, 2.30pm-7pm; Jan-Mar: 2.30pm-7pm – closed 1 Jan.* The ceramics presented here, called 'Sant Vicens,' are inspired by graphics by Jean Lurçat, Jean Picart le Doux, etc. Exhibition (and sales) of works by ceramists from the Roussillon.

The final siege of Perpignan – However, since a Spanish garrison was holding Perpignan, the city was laid to siege. Louis XIII arrived in person at the city walls with the elite of the French army (Cardinal Richelieu, who was ill, stayed in Narbonne) and Perpignan finally surrendered on 9 September 1642.

The Treaty of the Pyrenees ratified the reunification of Roussillon with the French crown, and Perpignan became French once and for all.

Town Walk

Le Castillet★

This monument, an emblem of Perpignan, which survived the demolition of the ramparts, dominates place de la Victoire. Its two towers are crowned with exceptionally tall crenellations and machicolations; note the windows with wrought-iron grilles.

During the reign of Louis XI, Le Castillet kept enemies from outside at bay and intimidated the townspeople, should they turn rebellious.

Le Castillet now houses the Casa Pairal devoted to Popular Arts and Traditions (⌖ *see Additional Sights*).

Promenade des Platanes

This wide avenue is lined with plane trees and adorned with fountains. Palm trees grow along the side avenues.

La Miranda

This is a small public park on the site of

Le Castillet, Perpignan

the old fortifications, behind the church of St-Jacques. It is principally given over to the plant life of the *garrigues* and shrubs which are either native or have been introduced to the region (pomegranates, olives, aloes etc).

PERPIGNAN

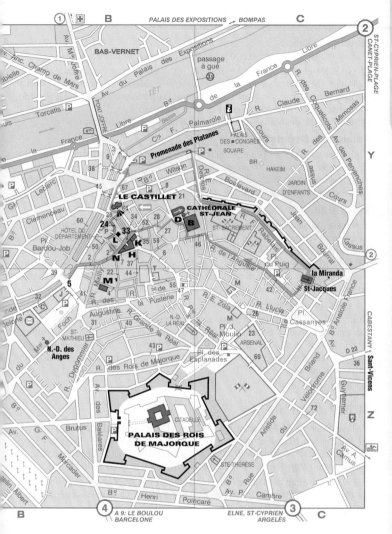

Église St-Jacques

🕐 *Daily except Mon: 11am–5pm.*

The church was built in the 14C in an old district on top of the ramparts inhabited by gardeners and weavers. Beneath the south porch there is a large cross with the instruments of the Passion.

The south apsidal chapel contains several works of art: a 14C Crucifix, a 15C statue of St James placed above a baptismal font which is still supplied by a spring, and a large Weavers' altarpiece (late 15C) depicting scenes from the life of the Virgin Mary.

At the west end of the nave, a vast chapel added in the 18C was reserved for the brotherhood of La Sanch ("of the precious Blood"). From 1416, this penitents' brotherhood, formed to give comfort to those condemned to death, performed a solemn procession on Maundy Thursday, carrying its *misteris* to the singing of hymns. This procession now takes place on Good Friday.

Place de la Loge

This square (with a statue by Maillol: Venus) and the pedestrianised rue de la Loge, paved in pink marble, form the lively centre of town life. Here, in summer, the *sardana* is danced several times a week.

Loge de Mer★

This fine Gothic building, dating from 1397 and refurbished and extended in the 16C, once housed a commercial tribunal in charge of ruling on claims relating to maritime trade.

The weather vane shaped like a galleon on one of the corners of the building symbolises the maritime activities of the Roussillon merchants.

Hôtel de Ville★

🕐 *Patio: daily except Sat-Sun and public holidays 8am-6pm, Fri 8am-5pm.*

The wrought-iron railings date from the 18C. In the arcaded courtyard stands a bronze by Maillol: *The Mediterranean*. On the façade of the building, three bronze arms, which are said to symbolise the "hands" or estates of the population required to elect the five consuls, were in fact originally designed to hold torches.

Inside, the Salle des Mariages (Marriage Hall) has a fine 15C coffered ceiling.

Palais de la Députation

During the reign of the kings of Aragón this 15C palace was the seat of the permanent commission or *députation* representing the Catalan "Corts." Note the huge, typically Aragonese voussoirs of the doorway, the fine masonry of the ashlar façade and the bays resting on very slender stone columns.

Place Arago

This lively, pleasant square adorned with palm trees and magnolias and bordered with cafés attracts crowds of people. In the centre stands the statue of the famous physician and astronomer François Arago (1786-1853). This extraordinary personality was fired not only with a love of research and a zeal for popularising scientific knowledge – he was admitted to the Académie des Sciences at the age of 23 – but also a passion for politics. He was a member of the provisional government of 1848.

▷ *Return to the Palais de la Députation.*

Opposite the Palais de la Députation, take a little detour down the small rue des Fabriques d'En Nabot, once in the heart of the **parayres** district (the cloth finishers who in the 13C and 14C formed the first guild of Perpignan). The **Maison Julia**★ at no 2 is one of the few well-preserved *hôtels* of Perpignan, possessing a patio with 14C Gothic arcades.

▷ *Return to Le Castillet.*

Additional Sights

Palais des rois de Majorque★ (Palace of the Kings of Majorca)

🕐 *Jun-Sep: 10am-6pm (last admission 30min before closing); Oct-May: 9am-5pm. Jun-Sep: possibility of a tour with a story of the site for children (ask for information).* 🕐 *Closed 1 Jan, 1 May, 1 Nov, 25 Dec.* ⬤ *4€ (children: 2€).* ☎ *04 68 34 48 29.*

📷 When the kings of Majorca came to the throne in 1276, Perpignan did not have a suitably grand residence to offer its new overlords, so a palace was built south of the town, on the hill of Puig del Rey.

Palais des rois de Majorque

B. Kaufmann/MICHELIN

A vaulted slope leads across the red-brick ramparts to a pleasant Mediterranean garden. Pass beneath a tower to the west, the **tour de l'Homage**, to get to the square-shaped main courtyard (*in summer this is the setting for the theatre festival "Estivales"*). This is open on the east and west sides with two storeys of arcades, in which the decoration fuses Romanesque and Gothic elements in a manner typical of the transitional style of southern France.

On the first floor of the south wing, the **great hall of Majorca** has a chimney-piece with three fireplaces. Beyond it, the Queen's suite has a superb ceiling painted with the Catalan colours (green and red).

The most splendid part of the building is the **chapel-keep** of Ste-Croix rising above the east wing. It comprises two sanctuaries built one above the other in the 14C by Jaime II of Majorca; their exterior architecture is in a French-inspired High Gothic style, whereas the interior is decorated in a manner typical of the Mediterranean.

The lower "Queen's" chapel, with its green ceramic flooring, contains a fine 15C Virgin and Child.

The upper chapel, taller and narrower, is entered through a **fine Romanesque doorway**★ decorated with stripes of alternate blue and pink marble around the doorway arch.

Cathédrale St-Jean★

The main church was begun in 1324 by Sancho, second king of Majorca, but was not consecrated until 1509.

A passage on the left leads to the old sanctuary of St-Jean-le-Vieux, where there is a remaining marble Romanesque doorway, on which the central pendentive is decorated with a Christ figure wearing a stern and powerful expression.

The oblong façade of the basilica is constructed from courses of pebbles alternating with bricks. It is flanked on the right by a square tower with a fine 18C wrought-iron campanile housing a 15C bell.

The impressive single nave rests on robust interior buttresses separating the chapels. One of the most interesting features of the cathedral of St-Jean is its sumptuous 16C and 17C altarpieces.

In the central alcove of the white-marble high altar stands a statue of St John the Baptist, patron saint of Perpignan: the effigy of the saint and the drapery of the royal arms of Aragón and Catalonia (gold and red) represent the city's coat of arms.

The 16C monumental organ has been restored; its painted shutters dating from 1504 depict the baptism of Christ and Herod's feast.

Beneath the organ case, a passage leads to the Romanesque chapel of Notre-Dame-dels-Correchs, in which there lies a recumbent effigy of King Sancho and, at the far end, a collection of antique reliquaries behind wrought-iron grilles.

By the exit to the cathedral through the doorway on the south side, there is a separate chapel which houses a poignant, even harrowing, early-14C carved wooden Crucifix known as the **Devout Christ**★, probably a Rhenish work.

Campo Santo

&. ⏰ *Apr-Sep: daily except Mon noon-7pm; Oct-Apr: daily except Mon 11am-5pm.* ⏰ *Closed Jul-Aug, 1 Jan, 25 Dec. No charge* ☎ *04 68 66 30 30. www.perpignantourisme.com.*

Situated south of the cathedral, the Campo Santo is a vast square graveyard dating from the early 14C, which exhibits great architectural unity with its pointed funeral alcoves and marble recesses, set into walls adorned with pebbles and courses of brick. It is one of the oldest surviving medieval churchyards in France.

Casa Pairal

⏰ *May-Sep: daily except Tue 10am-6pm (last admission 30min before closing); Oct-Apr: daily except Tue 11am-5.30pm.* ⏰ *Closed 1 Jan, 1 May, 1 Nov, 25 Dec.* ⊛ *4€ (children under 15 years: 2€).* ☎ *04 68 35 42 05.*

Kids Catalan folk museum: furniture, implements, ecclesiastical art, costumes, a fine cross with the instruments of the Passion ("Aux Outrages").

From the top of the turret *(142 steps)*, there is an attractive view over the city's monuments, Mont Canigou and the Albères mountains to the south, and the Corbières to the north.

Musée des Beaux-Arts Hyacinthe-Rigaud

&. ⏰ *May-Sep: daily except Tue noon-7pm; Oct-Apr: daily except Tue 11am-5.30pm.* ⏰ *Closed 1 Jan, 1 May, 14 Jul, 25 Dec.* ⊛ *4€.* ☎ *04 68 35 43 40.*

This museum is located in the Hôtel de Lazerme, a 17C mansion, and bears the name of the famous artist from Perpignan, **Hyacinthe Rigaud** (1659–1743). His portraits,

Christmas in Perpignan

Christmas celebrations are very much part of the Catalan tradition that holds sway in Perpignan. A number of Nativity crib scenes (*pessebres*) are set up in different parts of town, and various street entertainments (*nadals*) are organised, such as carol singing in Catalan. A Christmas market is held on place Gambetta. Caga Tio is a children's game that involves singing and dancing around a log and tapping it with a stick. When the little ones aren't looking, parents hide candy, fruit and gifts under the log for them to find.
Further details from the tourist office.

which were mainly ceremonial, earned him such a high reputation that to satisfy his patrons, Louis XIV and the royal court, he had to open a studio. His fame spread far and wide. The prized possession of the museum, the *Portrait of the Cardinal de Bouillon* was said by Voltaire to be "A masterpiece equal to the finest masterpieces by Rubens." Along with other works by the portraitist, Catalan Gothic paintings are displayed, among which is the famous 15C altarpiece of the Trinity.

Contemporary art is represented by such prestigious names as, among others, Maillol, Dufy, Picasso, Alechinsky and Appel. Hispanic art and the art of South America also hold an important place in the museum.

Musée numismatique Joseph-Puig★

🕐 *May-Sep: noon-6pm; Oct-Apr: 11am-5.30pm.* 🕐 *Closed Sun, Mon and public holidays.* 🎫 *4€.* ☎ *04 68 66 24 86. 42 Ave. de Grande-Bretagne.*

Part of the Villa "Les Tilleuls" (1907) has been converted into a museum, at the donor's request, to display the numismatic collection bequeathed by Joseph Puig to his native city of Perpignan. There are 1 500 permanent exhibits, out of a collection of 35 000. There is a room for temporary exhibitions.

With the aid of Fresnel lenses, visitors can see the mainly Catalan coins minted in Valence, Barcelona, Perpignan or Majorca, and also coins from Roussillon (after the Treaty of the Pyrenees) or from Mediterranean countries (Rome, Greece, Egypt). The collection of medals includes those of the Arago family, mother and son, struck by David d'Angers. Exceptional exhibits such as the double gold ducat depicting Ferdinand II of Aragón, or some Gallic gold staters copied from ancient Greece complete this well-presented collection tracing the history of numismatics.

Excursion

Cabestany

5km/3mi on D 22 to the SE. Inside the church of **Notre-Dame-des-Anges,** on the wall of the chapel on the right is a famous Romanesque **tympanum**★. This is the work of a 12C travelling sculptor, the master of Cabestany, depicting the resurrection of the Virgin Mary, her Ascension and her Glory between Christ and St Thomas to whom she had sent her girdle.

Roussillon Plain

Round tour of 128km/80mi – allow one day.

▶   *Leave Perpignan S, turn left onto N 114 then take a little road on the right towards Villeneuve-de-la-Raho.*

Mas Palégry

Situated among vineyards, Mas Palégry is the setting for an **Aviation museum** (♿🕐 *Apr-Oct: 10am-noon, 3-7pm; Sun and Mon 3-7pm; short school holidays: 2-6pm; rest of the year: by request.* 🎫 *3€.* ☎ *04 68 54 08 79).* Among the models on display are the Republic RF-84F "Thunderflash" and a De Havilland "Vampire."

Bages

A rough stone building, designed by François Carrère in 1954, houses the **Palais des Naïfs** (⟻ *Closed temporarily.).* The collection offers a good range of this type of art, which is largely associated with Le Douanier Rousseau (1844-1910). Visitors will discover other methods and media, including watercolour under glass, plaster, collage, tapestry, mosaic, sculpture and ceramics. Works are by artists from around the world, including some who have achieved renown (Javo, Toussaint, Mady de la Giraudière, Esteban-Ferreiro, Janus); all are characterised by what is commonly referred to as their naïveté, or a certain innocent quality.

▶ *Follow D 612 towards Thuir and turn right to Ponteilla.*

Jardin exotique de Ponteilla

&. ③ *Mid-Apr to mid-Oct: 2-6.30pm (open 10.30am Jul-Aug).* ∞ *4.50€.* ☎ *04 68 53 22 44.*

A signposted botanical trail running through this 3ha/7.4-acre park offers an interesting walk along footpaths named after famous botanists of the past. The trail is lined with magnolias, cacao trees, agaves, yuccas, araucarias (also known as monkey puzzle trees), rubber trees, several varieties of palm trees and all sorts of plants rarely seen in our part of the world. Thematic panels (vanilla, spices, rubb) complete this instructive visit.

▶ *Turn back, cross D 612 and drive on to Trouillas, turn right onto D 37 to Villemolaque and continue along D 40 towards Passa.*

Prieuré du Monastir del Camp

&. ③ ◌ *Apr-Jun and Sep-Oct: guided tours (45min) daily except Thu at 10am, 11am, 3pm, 4pm and 5pm (Jul and Aug: additional tour at 6pm); Sep-Mar: at 11am, 2pm, 3pm and 4pm.* ③ *Closed 1 Jan, Ascension and 25 Dec: call for information.* ∞ *4€.* ☎ *04 68 38 80 71.*

This imposing building with its elegant fortified front conceals a Gothic church with a fine white-marble doorway and capitals believed to be the work of the Master of Cabestany; in addition, there is a harmonious Gothic cloister with trefoil arcading which seems to invite meditation before a local-wine tasting session.

▶ *Drive along D 2 to Fourques then turn right onto D 615 to Thuir.*

Thuir

This is known mainly for its wine cellars, the **caves Byrrh** (&. ③ ◌ *Jul-Aug: guided tour (45min) 10am-11.45am, 2-6.45pm; Apr-Jun and Sep-Oct: 9-11.45am, 2.30-5.45pm; Nov-Mar: by request.* ③ *Closed Sun in Apr (except Easter), Sat-Sun Oct-May.* ∞ *1.60€ (-18 years : no charge).* ☎ *04 68 53 05 42).*
The "Cellier des Aspres" also contains information on the development of crafts in neighbouring villages.

▶ *Take D 48 W.*

The road climbs the slopes of the Aspre. Suddenly, at the end of a small valley, the medieval village of Castelnou comes into sight with Mont Canigou rising in the background, making a wonderful **view**★.

Castelnou

③ *Jun-Sep: 10am-7pm; Feb-May: 10.30am-6pm; Oct-Dec: 11am-5pm.* ③ *Closed Jan (except Sat-Sun 11am-5pm).* ∞ *4.50€.* ☎ *04 68 53 22 91.*

This fortified village was the seat of the military administration of the counts of Besalù in the north of the Pyrenees. Its tiny paved streets are clustered around the foot of the feudal **castle**, remodelled in the 19C. Artists and craftsmen vie with each other among the local population.

Castelnou

J. Malburet/MICHELIN

Église de Fontcouverte

The church lies off the beaten track, in a churchyard in the shade of a large oak tree. It is a beautiful isolated **site**★ overlooking the plain. Straight after the church, by the side of the road to Ille, there is a stopping place beneath the chestnut trees.

Ille-sur-Têt – See ILLE-SUR-TÊT.

▶ Follow D 21 N.

Bélesta

This remarkable village perched on a rocky outcrop rising up out of the surrounding vineyards used to be a border town between the kingdoms of Aragón and France. The town has been of interest for some time to archaeologists who have found numerous prehistoric remains in the galleries of the Caune de Bélesta, including a collective grave dating from roughly 6 000 years ago (Middle Neolithic) which contained a collection of 28 ceramic items, as well as the remains of 32 people.

Château-Musée – Mid-Jun to mid-Sep: 2-7pm; mid-Sep to mid-Jun: daily except Tue and Sat 2-5.30pm. Closed 1 Jan, 24-25 and 31 Dec. 4.50€. 04 68 84 55 55. Park the car near the wine cooperative or the post office. The medieval fortress that towers above the town houses archaeological collections. These are well presented in four main sections. First, visitors are introduced to techniques and materials used nowadays in archaeological excavation work (in particular, pollen analysis enabling specialists to make deductions about climate and vegetation). Then they are taken into an identical reconstruction of the Bélesta excavations, showing the square site of the dig, and the collective grave. The following room contains a display of the ceramic ware that was found with the bones: vases, bowls, cauldrons and basins all in perfect condition. Three dioramas depict daily life in the cave: milling, carving bones and metalwork.

▶ Take the pass road to the Col de la Bataille.

The Château de Caladroi soon comes into view in the middle of a park planted with tropical trees. A very pleasant stretch of road along the crest between the valleys of the Têt and the Agly leads to the Col and then to the hermitage of Força Réal.

Ermitage de Força Réal

The summit, 507m/1 663ft above sea level at its highest point, forms a bastion towering above the Roussillon. On it are a 17C chapel and a telecommunications station. There is an impressive **panorama**★★ over the plain, the coast from Cap Leucate to Cap Béar, the Albères mountains and Mont Canigou. To the north-west, the sharp peaks of Bugarach and the outcrop of rock on which the ruined castle of Quéribus stands loom up on the skyline from the ridge of the southern Corbières.

The contrast between the Têt Valley, with its chequerboard of market gardens outlined by straight rows of trees, and the Agly Valley, completely covered by vineyards, is striking.

Go back down to the pass, and from there on to **Estagel**, native village of François Arago who is commemorated by a bust – the work of David d'Angers – in the town hall.

Rivesaltes

This town on the south bank of the Agly is one of the wine-producing capitals of the Roussillon, famous in particular for its sweet aperitif wines.

It is the native town of **Maréchal Joffre** (1852-1931), Commander in Chief of the French forces on the western front during the First World War, the "Victor of the Marne" who won himself the reputation for keeping a cool head under pressure and being equal to any challenge. An equestrian statue of him stands on the avenue which bears his name, which is bordered with plane trees. Since 1987, there has been a **museum** (11 Rue du Maréchal Joffre; mid-Jun to mid-Sep: daily except Mon and Sat-Sun 10am-1pm, 3-7pm; 3€; 04 68 64 24 98) in the house where Joffre was born, devoted to his life and career.

▶ From Rivesaltes, drive SW on D 614.

Baixas

St Mary's Church houses several altarpieces illustrating Catalan Baroque Art; note in particular the gilt, high altar **retable**★ by Luis Generès, adorned with small columns, statues and low-relief scenes.

▶ Continue along D 614, turn left onto D 616 to Baho then take a road S over the River Têt and N 116. Turn right then left to reach Toulouges.

Toulouges

On the south side and at the east end of the church, two plaques and a stele commemorate the Synod of 1027 and the Council of 1064-66 which implemented the "Truce of God," one of a number of peace-keeping measures introduced in medieval Western Europe. Outside the apse stands a missionary Cross (1782) displaying the instruments of the Passion (⏲ *open by request;* ☎ *04 68 54 43 90*).

▷ *Return to Perpignan on N 9.*

Château de PEYREPERTUSE★★★

MICHELIN LOCAL MAP 344: G-5

ALSO SEE LES CORBIÈRES

The craggy outline of the ruined fortress of Peyrepertuse one of the "five sons of Carcassonne," on a crest in the Corbières, standing boldly atop its rocky base, only properly comes into view when seen from the outskirts of Rouffiac, to the north. Peyrepertuse is one of the finest examples of a medieval fortress in the Corbières.

▷ **Orient Yourself:** Visitors should have a good head for heights and take great care while exploring the castle, particularly if there is a strong wind (frequently the case on this exposed site). During the summer, be sure to bring drinking water, sunhats and sunscreen.

▣ **Parking:** Lot at the ticket office.

◉ **Don't Miss:** The view over the site and the surrounding valley from the outcrop just east of the castle.

◔ **Also See:** CARCASSONE, Abbaye de FONTFROIDE, Château de QUÉRIBUS

A Bit of History

In the 11C-12C, the castle was associated with the counts of Barcelona and Narbonne. During the Albigensian Crusade, the castle was apparently handed over without a battle by Guilhem de Peyrepertuse in 1240 to the Seneschal of Carcassonne, and thus joined the forces of France. The castle was fortified in 1242, for the purposes of defending against Spanish attacks. A second keep was built on the western side of the rocky outcrop.

Château de Peyrepertuse

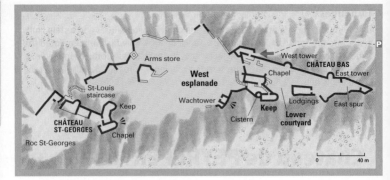

Visit *allow 2hr*

🕐 *Jun-Sep: 9am-8pm; Apr, May and Oct: 9am-7pm.* 🕐 *Closed Jan. No visits during stormy weather.* ✆ *4€.* ☎ *04 68 45 40 55. www.chateau-peyrepertuse.com.*

▶ *Get there from Duilhac: 3.5km/2mi up a steep, narrow road.*

🚶 *From the car park and ticket office, follow a path along the north face, which leads up to the entrance of the castle. About 30min on foot there and back.*

Peyrepertuse comprises two adjacent but separate castles, on the east (Peyrepertuse) and west (St-Georges) ends of the ridge, and measures 300m/984ft at its longest point. The higher, Château St-Georges, has never been accessible to horses, or even mules.

Château Bas

This lower castle is the actual feudal fortress. It stands on the tip of the promontory that tapers into the shape of a ship's prow.

Lower courtyard – The line of the enclosure adopts the triangular shape of the tapering end of the ridge. It is complete only on the north face, where it has a substantial curtain wall, with two round towers – the Tour Ouest and Tour Est – without a wall on the inside of the curtain wall, making them open facing the courtyard.

At the south end, it was only protected by a simple parapet, which has been reconstructed.

Going back towards the entrance to the castle, note the east side of the keep, which was completely redesigned in the 13C, with semicircular towers linked by a crenellated curtain wall.

Keep – *Enter through the tall door.* The old keep, the heart of the castle, is quadrilateral in shape. All that can be seen from the courtyard is the front flanked by a round tower (the cistern).

The finishing touches were added to the building in the 12C and 13C by attaching a fortified chapel (*left-hand wall*) to the original chapel with curtain walls that closed off the short walls of the courtyard.

West esplanade

The north wall runs close to the edge of the precipice. Note a polygonal building probably used as an armoury. To the south, near the keep of the lower castle, an isolated watchtower gives a view of Quéribus through a gaping hole.

Château St-Georges

▶ *Cross the west esplanade towards the Roc St-Georges.*

An impressive flight of steps cut into the rock, known as the "St-Louis" staircase, leads up to the castle ruins. This is dangerous in strong winds.

At an altitude of 796m/2 611ft, this royal fortress towers over the lower castle by about 60m/197ft. It was built in a single go on the highest point of the mountain, after Languedoc had been made part of the French royal estate. The high walls of large stones that are still standing are interesting more for their lofty site than their actual construction.

East of the castle (*head left from the top of "St-Louis" staircase*) is a prominent outcrop, the site of the old chapel, overlooking the lower castle. There are **views**★★ over the whole fortified complex and of its panoramic setting: the Verdouble Valley, the ruined castle of Quéribus, and the Mediterranean on the horizon.

PEYRUSSE-LE-ROC★

POPULATION 229

MICHELIN LOCAL MAP 338: E-4

Situated on the basalt plateaux separating the Aveyron and Lot valleys, Peyrusse-le-Roc offers visitors a journey back in time. The fortress had an eventful past, as can be seen from the remains of its old buildings.

A Bit of History

Conquered in 767 by Pépin the Short, united by Charlemagne with the kingdom of Aquitaine, handed over to England in 1152 after the divorce of Louis VII and Eleanor of Aquitaine, ancient Petrucia was the capital of the bailiwick until the 18C. During certain periods, it could number more than 3 000 inhabitants, and it prospered, largely due to its silver mines. These ceased to be mined, when silver arrived from America in the 18C. Having lost its raison d'être, the fortified lower town was abandoned and the present village of Peyrusse-le-Roc started to evolve on the plateau.

Medieval Ruins *1hr 30min*

🕐 ⏱ *May-Sep: guided tour (1hr30min) daily except Mon 10am-noon, 3-6pm; Oct-Apr: daily except Sun 10am-noon, 2-5pm, Saat 10am-noon.* 🕐 *Closed 1 Jan, 1 May. Fee information unavailable. Le Rempart meeting and reception point on Place des Treize Vents, open mornings all year. No charge (guide service: 3.50€).* ☎ *05 65 80 49 33.*

Walk across **place St-Georges**, noting the fine medieval 15C stone cross where a Virgin and Child can be seen beneath a canopy, then through **Porte du Château**, the castle gate forming part of the medieval curtain wall, to reach **place des Treize-Vents**. In the Middle Ages, this square was the site of the castle of the lords of Peyrusse. All that is now left of it is a room that was used as a prison, and a tower (the church bell-tower), which houses a small **archaeological museum** (⊶ *Currently closed; information ☎ 05 65 80 49 33.*).

Built in the 18C, the **church** is noted for its large single nave with five bays and its vaulting supported by square pillars. The 15C *Pietà*, sculptures and frescoes are by Henri Vernhes, a local artist.

▶ *Go through the Porte Neuve and the fortifications to the left of the church. The footpath on the left leads to the medieval site; beyond the graveyard, bear right (stairway).*

Metal steps (☺ *particular care needed on some sections*) lead to the **Roc del Thaluc**.

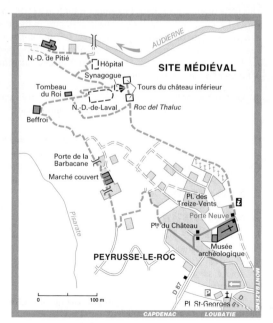

From this rock, crowned with the two square towers of the lower castle (*château inférieur*) and overlooking the Audierne Valley 150m/1 614ft below, it is easy to understand the role played by Peyrusse as an important strategic look-out post during troubled medieval times.

▷ *Follow the footpath to the bottom of the valley.*

A small chapel houses the Tombeau du Roi, a richly sculpted royal mausoleum probably dating from the 14C.

On the right stand the ruins of Notre-Dame-de-Laval, all that remains of the old parish church: directly beneath the two towers of the Roc del Thaluc, are the imposing Gothic arches of the collapsed nave, vestiges of the five south side chapels and of the three-sided chancel standing against a rock, and the remnants of a tomb, with recumbent figure, on the left.

The path leads to the synagogue, where Jews are supposed to have taken refuge in the 13C. However, this may possibly be the base of a tower that was part of the lower castle.

Turn back then right to the **Hôpital des Anglais** (13C). This "English Hospital" still features its fine round exterior chimney.

Farther on, the Chapelle **Notre-Dame-de-Pitié** was built in 1874 on the site of an old oratory.

On the way back to the village, stop by the **Beffroi** (belfry), a tall square tower, which, together with the **Porte de la Barbacane** (gateway with a fine Gothic relieving arch), protected the town to the north-west.

Farther on, on the left, are some vaulted cellars, known as the **marché couvert** (covered market).

> **EVERYTHING YOU NEED**
>
> ⊖ **Restaurant Savignac** – *Le Bourg* - ☎ *05 65 80 43 91*. This village grocer's/tobacconist's/restaurant has been run by the same family for four generations. The proprietor herself whips up local dishes, including a curious omelette with apples flambéed in plum brandy. Simple, country atmosphere. Exhibitions of regional artwork.

PÉZENAS ★★

POPULATION 7,443

MICHELIN LOCAL MAP 339: F-8

This little town, once called "Piscenae," is built in a fertile plain covered in vineyards. Pézenas prides itself on its past, reflected in its interesting little streets and its mansions unchanged since the 17C. ⓘ *Pl. Gambetta, 34120 Pézenas, ☎ 04 67 98 35 45. www.ville-pezenas.fr Guided tour of the town*  – *Discovery tours (1hr30min) Jul-Aug daily except weekends, 5pm. ⊜ 5€. Self-guided tour with brochure: 2€. Inquire at tourist office or at www.vpah.culture.fr*

▷ **Orient Yourself:** Place du 14-Juillet is the town's main square; the tourist office is a block away near Place Gambetta. Shops and artisans' studios dot the winding streets of Old Pézenas.

Ⓟ **Parking:** Try the large lot near Promenade du Pré-St-Jean if you're headed downtown; for sights south of Cours Jean-Jaurès, use the lot at Place Boby-Lapointe.

🕐 **Organising Your Time:** At a leisurely pace, the walking tour of Old Pézenas could take the better part of a day, including visiting the museum and meandering through the shops.

A Bit of History

A wool market – A fortified town at the time of the Romans, Pézenas was even then an important trading centre for woollen cloth. After it had become part of the royal estate in 1261, its trade fairs expanded. They took place three times a year. Everything possible was done to ensure their success: the merchandise was duty-free for 30 days; the merchants could not be arrested for debt; and by order of the king, local lords had to protect them on their travels. In exchange for these favours, the town paid the royal treasury a fee of 2 500 *livres*.

Address Book

For coin categories, see the Legend.

EATING OUT

La Pomme d'Amour – 2 bis R. Albert-Paul-Allies - ☎ 04 67 98 08 40 - closed Jan, Feb, Mon evening and Tues – reservation recommended Jul and Aug. This 18C house near the Office de Tourisme shelters a small, intimate dining room with beams overhead. In summer the street becomes a pedestrian zone and the terrace in the shade of neighbouring houses comes into its own. Sunny southern fare.

Après le Déluge – 5 Ave. du Mar.-Plantavit - ☎ 04 67 98 10 77 - closed 15 Nov-15 Dec. Will you dine at Noah's table, or in La Salle de Perrault? Choose among five different decors to sample the chef's recipes, many discovered in antique cookbooks. Fun setting and musical evenings. A unique opportunity to taste the Marquis of Sade's favourite cake!

WHERE TO STAY

Chambre d'hôte M. Gener – 34 Ave. Pierre-Sirven – 34530 Montagnac - 6.5km/4mi NW of Pézenas on N 9 then N 113 - ☎ 04 67 24 03 21 - ⚡ - 4 rooms. The rooms of this constabulary building dating from 1750 have been set up in the old stables. In the peace and quiet of a large shady courtyard, some of them have retained their loosebox separations. Breakfast is served on a terrace upstairs.

Le Molière – Pl. du 14-juillet - ☎ 04 67 98 14 00 - 🅿 - 23 rooms - ⏩ 7€. Sculpures ornament the façade of his ravishing hotel located in the centre of town. Comfortable, air-conditioned rooms renovated in the southern style. Frescoes evoking the works of Molière decorate the patio-salon.

SIT BACK AND RELAX

Confiserie Boudet – Chemin St-Christol - ☎ 04 67 98 16 32 - Jul-Aug: Mon-Fri 9am-11am; out of season: on request – no charge. A tour of the confectionery where berlingots de Pézenas are made. Sampling.

L'Aparté – 13 R. de la Foire - ☎ 04 67 98 03 04 - Sep-May: Tues-Sat 2.30pm-7pm, Sun 3pm-7pm; Jul-Sep: Mon 3-7pm, Tue-Sat 10.30-noon, 2.30-7pm, Sun 3pm-7pm – closed Jan and 25 Dec. Bookshop and tearoom where you can try homemade crumble or cake accompanied by an excellent cup of tea, while leafing through one of the old books on the shelves. The welcome is enthusiastic and the pleasures of the body and the mind are both catered to, making this a place to remember.

SHOPPING

Maison Alary – 9 R. des Chevaliers St-Jean - ☎ 04 67 98 13 12 - Tues-Sun 6am-8pm; daily in summer. Although the petits pâtés de Pézenas supposedly date from the British empire in India, folk here will swear that it was here at Maison Allary that a local pastrycook, Roucayrol, sold the very first of these delicacies made of sweetened meat.

Bouquinerie Car Enfin – 21 R. des Litanies - ☎ 04 67 98 18 49 - http://carenfin.free.fr - Jul-Aug: Tues-Sat 10.30am-12.30pm, 3pm-6.30pm; Sep-Jun: Wed-Sat 10.30am-12.30pm, 3pm-6.30pm – closed Sun-Mon. Car Enfin bookshop is installed in a 15C house backing onto the ramparts. With Edmond Charlot, who published Camus, as consultant, the bookshop offers a wide range of books old and new, covering all disciplines, including works dedicated to North Africa.

Maison des Métiers d'Art du Pays de Pézenas – 6 Pl. Gambetta - ☎ 04 67 98 16 12 – www.paysdepezenas.net – summer: daily 10am-noon, 2pm-6pm (8.30pm-11.30pm Wed and Fri); winter: 10am-noon, 2pm-6pm - closed 1 Jan, 1 May and 25 Dec. Information and exhibitions focusing on restoration work – wood, iron and stone – and the professions involved in theatre production.

Every Shrove Tuesday and first Sunday in July, the inhabitants of Pézenas commemorate the birth of a foal (poulain) to King Louis VIII's favourite mare here in their town in 1226. The celebrations take the form of a parade in which nine men dress up as the foal and prance through town to a musical accompaniment.

The "Versailles" of the Languedoc – For the first time, in 1456, the States General of Languedoc met at Pézenas. The town later became the residence of the governors of Languedoc: the Montmorencys, then the Contis. Armand de Bourbon, Prince de Conti, transformed Pézenas into the "Versailles," or royal court, of the Languedoc. Once settled on the estate of La Grange des Prés, where the beauty of the splendid gardens, flower beds and fountains was legendary, he surrounded himself with a court of aristocrats, artists and writers. Each session of the States General was celebrated with lavish entertainments.

Molière at Pézenas – During one of these celebrations, Molière, attracted by the town's reputation, came to Pézenas with his Illustrious Theatre in 1650. In 1653, having been permitted to put on a performance for Conti himself, he was such a success that the prince gave him the title of "Actor to His Supreme Highness the Prince of Conti."

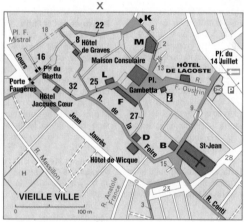

PÉZENAS

Molière also gave performances for the public, in the covered square. His repertoire comprised plays from the Italian *commedia dell'arte* and farces he had written himself.

A statue of Molière, by Injalbert (1845-1933) stands in a small garden situated on *place du 14 -Juillet*.

Old Pézenas★★

Old mansions, or *hôtels*, with elegant balconies and ornate doorways, and workshops, now occupied by craftsmen and artists, follow one after the other along streets with evocative names: rue de la Foire, rue Triperie-Vieille, rue Fromagerie-Vieille (Fair, Old Tripe Shop, Old Cheese Shop).

In summer, during the "Mirondela dels Arts," the town really comes to life, local crafts are displayed and folk festivals, theatre performances and concerts take place.

▶ *Leave from Place du 14-Juillet.*

Hôtel de Lacoste★

This early-16C mansion has a very fine staircase and galleries with Gothic arches.

Place Gambetta

This square , once known as "Place-au-bled" ("village square"), has retained its medieval structure.

On the left is Gély's old barbershop (*which now houses the tourist information office*) where Molière liked to go.

On the right, stands the **Consular House**; its 18C façade with pediment and wrought-iron work conceals the main building, which dates from 1552. The States General of Languedoc often met here; a particularly memorable session was held in 1632, at which the rebellion of Henry II of Montmorency against the king was hatched.

At the far end of the square, there is Rue **Triperie-Vieille**, once lined with market stalls. Farther down, at no 11, in a courtyard at the end of a vaulted passageway, is a fine early-17C stairwell.

At the corner of Place Gambetta and Rue Alfred Sabatier stands the **Hôtel Flottes de Sébasan** with a wide 16C façade; the right side was altered in the 18C (windows and ironwork), but retained its Renaissance (1511) corner niche which houses a 19C statue of St Roch. A plaque records that Queen Anne of Austria slept in the mansion in 1660.

▶ *Take Rue A.-P.-Alliès on the right.*

The **Hôtel de Saint-Germain** (*no 3*) is home to the Musée Vulliod-St-Germain (👁 *see Additional Sight*).

▶ *Take Rue Béranger on the left (17C house) which leads onto Rue de Montmorency.*

Rue de Montmorency

On the right stand the watchtowers of the **îlot des prisons**. On the way back up the street, note on the left a 17C faience **Pietà**, and on the right the gateway from the curtain walls of the old castle demolished on Cardinal Richelieu's orders, after the rebellion of Henry II of Montmorency. Just before Rue du Château is the **Rue des Litanies** which was one of the two main streets in the Ghetto.

Clive Pies

The little pies (*petits pâtés*) of Pézenas are a culinary speciality of Indo-British origin made with sweet and spicy minced meat. In 1768, Lord Clive, accompanied by his Indian cooks, stayed in the town and in the nearby Château du Larzac. Before returning to Market Drayton in England, the cooks gave the Pézenas bakers and confectioners the recipe for the spicy little pies shaped like spools for thread. It was forgotten during the 19C, but has been rediscovered today, thanks to the research of keen gastronomes. In England, the little pies known as "Clive Pies" are made with minced mutton, brown sugar, sultanas and curry; in Pézenas, glacé lemon zest is used instead of sultanas.

A. Thuillier/MICHELIN

Rue du Château

The beautiful ogee doorway of the **Hôtel de Graves** dates from the 16C.

Rue Alfred-Sabatier

At no 12 the **Maison des Pauvres** (almshouse) possesses a fine staircase and 18C wrought-iron work. No 3 on the right features a Renaissance Virgin Mary (1511) and the façade of no 1, decorated with grotesques, has fine basket-handle shaped windows.

Rue Émile-Zola

At no 7 the **Hôtel Jacques Cœur** features a façade adorned with culs-de-lampe in the shape of little figures. It is the only 15C mansion in Pézenas decorated in this way, and is probably the work of Franco-Flemish artists sent by the king's Superintendent of Finance.

At the end of this street the **Porte du Ghetto** opens onto **Rue de la Juiverie**, two names which indicate the past role of this district.

On the left, **Porte Faugères**, which leads onto cours Jean-Jaurès, was once part of the old 14C ramparts.

▶ *Walk across Cours Jean-Jaurès and take Rue Reboul opposite.*

Rue Henri-Reboul

The former Rue des Capucins was built in the 17C, when Pézenas started to expand beyond the medieval town walls.

On the left, coming from cours Jean-Jaurès, stands the façade of the 16C chapel of the Pénitents Noirs, converted into a theatre in 1804.

At no 13, the façade of the Hôtel de Montmorency, once the residence of the governor of Languedoc has a very fine 17C door with a pediment flanked with scrolls.

Farther down, the **Hôtel Paulhan de Guers** (now a hospital) also features an interesting 17C doorway.

▶ *Return to Cours Jean-Jaurès.*

Cours Jean-Jaurès

Cours Jean-Jaurès was constructed by Henry II of Montmorency who wished to extend the town beyond its fortified walls. At the time it was called Le Quay, and it supplanted rue de la Foire as the town's main centre of activity. Aristocratic mansions were built facing south, the back of the house opening onto rue de la Foire. These mansions can be entered through vaulted passageways leading into courtyards with attractive open staircases. The plain façades are sometimes decorated with masks. The most interesting buildings are at no 18, the **Hôtel de Landes de Saint-Palais** and, on the other side of the road, no 33, the **Hôtel de Latudes**.

▶ *Retrace your steps to Rue du Château and turn right onto Rue de la Foire.*

Rue de la Foire

Once known as Rue Droite (roughly meaning "main street"), this street was the setting for fairs and processions. At no 16, there is a carved lintel representing some charming child musicians.

Note the elegant Renaissance façade of the **Hôtel de Wicque** surmounting an art gallery. Opposite stands the **Hôtel de Carrion-Nizas** with a 17C doorway.

Collégiale St-Jean

This church, designed by Avignon architect Jean-Baptiste Franque, was built in the 18C on the site of an old Templars' church which collapsed under the weight of its bell-tower in 1733. Inside, the vaulting comes in a variety of styles: ribbed vaulting for the nave, domes on pendentives for the aisles and the crossing, oven vaulting for the chancel. A cornice runs all the way round the edifice.

Commanderie de St-Jean-de-Jérusalem

The commandery features two well-preserved early-17C façades with their mullioned windows. A corner turret is supported by a masonry buttress.

▶ *Follow Rue Kléber to Place de la République to the right of the collegiate church.*

This is where this tour leaves the old town centre to carry on into the faubourg ("suburb") which grew up in the 17C and 18C around rue Conti.

▶ *From the square, take Rue Barraterie (5th on the right at the end of the square) and turn left onto Rue du Commandant-Bassas.*

On the right, a porch leads through to the narrow Rue du Jeu-de-Paume. This is believed to be the site of the theatre where Molière performed. No 3 has a fine diamond-fret door.

▶ *Turn right onto Rue Victor-Hugo.*

At no 11 is the fine façade of the **Hôtel l'Epine** (18C).

Hôtel de Malibran★

This mansion's magnificent 18C façade is embellished with fine windows surmounted by masks representing smiling women, whereas the balconies are supported by garlands of leaves. The door leads straight to an interior 17C staircase supported by two tiers of superimposed columns.

▶ *At the end of Rue Alcide-Trinquat, walk down a flight of steps, cross Rue Victor-Hugo and follow Rue des Glacières opposite. Turn left onto Rue Conti.*

Rue Conti

Many private mansions were built along this street, which, in the 17C, was also full of inns and shops. Carry on past the **Hostellerie du Griffon d'Or** (no 36).

Hôtel d'Alfonce★ –*No 32 rue Conti.*
🕙 ♿ *Jun-Sep: daily except Sun 10am-noon, 2-6pm; rest of the year by request.* ⊚ *2€.* ☏ *04 67 98 10 38.* This fine 17C building, one of the best preserved in Pézenas, was used by Molière from November 1655 to February 1656. In the entrance courtyard is a pretty interior terrace adorned with balustrades. On the right, there is a fine 15C spiral staircase.

At no 30, the **Hôtel de Conti** features a façade, renovated in the 18C, with Louis XV balconies and wrought-iron window sills.

▶ *Return to St John's collegiate church via place de la République and turn right onto rue des Chevaliers-St-Jean, which leads back to place du 14-Juillet.*

Hôtel d'Alfonce (17C)

A. Thuillier/MICHELIN

Additional Sight

Musée Vulliod-St-Germain

🕙 *May to Oct: daily except Mon 10am-noon, 2-6pm; Nov-Apr: daily except Mon and Sun monring 10am-noon, 2-5pm (last admission 30min before closing)* 🕙 *Closed 1 and 2 Jan, Shrove Tuesday, 14 Jul (if Mon), 25 Dec.* ⊚ *2€ (children under 10 years: 1€).* ☏ *04 67 98 90 59.*

The collections of this museum are displayed in the Hôtel de Saint-Germain, a fine 16C building, the exterior of which was renovated in the 18C, and the interior in the 19C.

On the ground floor, next to the entrance hall, which contains tombstones and some sculptures from different buildings in the town, there is a reconstruction of a rustic Pézenas interior.

On the first floor, a group of 17C Aubusson tapestries depict the Triumph of Alexander. Among the 16C, 17C and 18C furniture is a fine Louis XIII wardrobe with carved panels representing the four horsemen of the Apocalypse. A neighbouring room has been given over to Molière memorabilia.

The upper floor contains a collection of earthenware and pharmacist's jars.

There is an audio-visual presentation on the history of Pézenas and the time Molière stayed here.

Excursion

Abbaye de Valmagne★

🚹🕐🍴 *Mid-Jun to end-Sep: guided tours (1hr) 10am-noon, 2.30pm-6pm; early Oct to mid-Dec and mid-Feb to mid-Jun: 2-5.40pm; mid-Dec to mid-Feb: daily except Tue 2-5.40pm.* 🕐 *Closed 1 Jan and 25 Dec.* 🎫 *6.50€ (children: 5.30€).* ☎ *04 67 78 06 09. 14km/9mi NE along N 9, N 113 to Montagnac then left on D 5.*

The great rose-coloured abbey of Valmagne, set in splendid isolation amid a clump of pine trees, rises serenely above the surrounding sea of Languedoc vineyards.

This Cistercian abbey was begun in the mid-13C and completed in the 14C. The abbey church, with its architecture and soaring nave, is an example of a classic Gothic style, as far removed from the traditions of Languedoc as it is from those of the Cistercians. Its dimensions recall those of the cathedrals of northern France (23m/75ft high and 83m/272ft long), as do the façade flanked by towers, the nave supported by flying buttresses, the size and number of the windows in its walls (unfortunately the clerestory windows were blocked up in the 17C) and the semicircular chancel with its great three-pointed arches and ambulatory with radiating chapels.

Since the Revolution, the church has been used as a storehouse for the ageing of wine, which has enabled it to be kept in good repair.

The **monastic buildings** date in part from the founding of the abbey in the 12C, but they have been extensively restored since the 13C. The **cloisters**, rebuilt in the 14C, are charming with their golden-coloured stonework. There is a minimum of decoration in the galleries and openings onto the cloister garth. The 12C **chapter-house** is slightly more ornate, however, containing a variety of decoration on the colonnettes and capitals, and the **fountain**★★ is delightful, surmounted by an elegant 18C structure consisting of eight ribs linked by a pendant keystone.

The vast **refectory** (*open only for concerts*) features a remarkable Renaissance chimney-piece.

The traditional Cistercian herb garden has been recreated.

Le PONT-DE-MONTVERT

POPULATION 272

MICHELIN LOCAL MAP 330: K-8 – ALSO SEE MONT LOZÈRE

The tall grey houses of Le Pont-de-Montvert stand on either bank of the Tarn, which is spanned by a 17C humpback bridge surmounted by a toll tower. Local produce and craftwork are sold at the market which takes place every Wednesday morning in season. 🛈 *48220 Le Pont-De-Montvert,* ☎ *04 66 45 81 94.*

A Bit of History

The death of the Abbot of Chayla – This abbot, in charge of Roman Catholic operations in the Cévennes, was staying in Le Pont-de-Montvert and holding prisoner there some Protestants he had managed to capture. On 24 July 1702, two members of the Protestant movement, Abraham Mazel and Esprit Séguier, decided to secure the release of their fellows. The expedition they mounted to this effect resulted in the death of the abbot of Chayla, who was caught whilst trying to make good his escape through the village (his body was thrown into the river from the old humpback bridge over the Tarn), and sparked off the Camisard uprising.

Le Parc National des Cévennes

The Cévennes National Park covers an area of 91 500ha/226 101 acres, surrounded by a peripheral zone of 237 000ha/585 639 acres. It was founded in September 1970 and is the largest of the seven French national parks.

The region displays great variety. Depending which face of the mountain you are on, the climate may be Mediterranean or more typical of northern France. Landscape ranges from snowy summits (the Lozère and Aigoual peaks, the Bougès range) to low-lying valleys in which mimosa flour-

Parc national des Cévennes

ishes. The park can boast forest cover over almost two thirds of its surface area, including the peripheral zone. One of the most characteristic, although not at all well known, landscapes is that of Mont Lozère, a mountain ridge with flattened contours which stretches for nearly 30km/18mi, more than 1 500m/4 921ft above sea level, a vast windswept fell bereft of trees.

One of the aims of classifying the central zone as a national park is the preservation of the landscape, the flora and the fauna, which includes some magnificent birds of prey. Various deer, including roe deer, as well as beavers, wood grouse and wild vultures have been reintroduced into the region. However, the

main objectives are to sustain local agriculture and stem the gradual deterioration of the local environment, in which hamlets were falling into rack and ruin as the local inhabitants left the area to seek a living somewhere less punishing. It is now the only French national park with a resident population in its central zone.

Tourist facilities for activities well-suited to large expanses, such as all forms of hiking, with accommodation in renovated rural dwellings, are contributing to demographic and economic revival.

Since 1984, the Cévennes National Park has been twinned with the Saguenay National Park (Quebec, Canada – 👆 *see The Green Guide Quebec),* and as part of a programme of scientific cooperation the Cévennes park (made a biosphere reserve by UNESCO in 1985) was twinned with the Montseny Reserve in Catalonia in Spain in 1987.

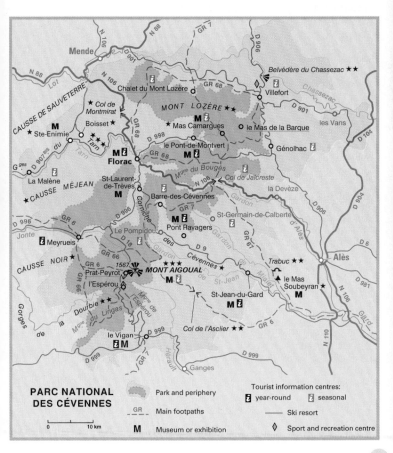

PARC NATIONAL DES CÉVENNES

0   10 km

Park and periphery

GR   Main footpaths

M   Museum or exhibition

Tourist information centres:
year-round   seasonal

Ski resort

Sport and recreation centre

Maison du Mont Lozère

&. ① *Apr-Sep: daily 10.30am-12.30pm, 2.30-6.30pm.* ① *Closed 1st 3 weeks in Oct, and from early Nov-early Apr.* ⊕ *3.50€.* ☏ *04 66 45 80 73.*

This centre is the headquarters of the Écomusée du Mont Lozère, an open-air museum set up by the Parc national des Cévennes. A large polygonal building houses an exhibition on the natural and human history of Mont Lozère, and an overnight shelter (*gîte*) for hikers.

Sentier de l'Hermet

6km/4mi from the Tour de l'Horloge, the clock tower in the centre of Le Pont-de-Montvert; allow 3hr there and back.

This footpath, which includes 12 observation points, reveals the landscapes, flora and fauna of the Tarn gorge, the traditional architecture of L'Hermet hamlet, various types of shepherds' huts and a panorama of the south face of Mont Lozère.

Écomusée de la Cévenne

Created to safeguard and develop the natural and cultural heritage of the Cévennes region, this open-air museum offers visitors a tour of various sites spread throughout the Parc national des Cévennes, such as the prehistoric site in St-Laurent-de-Trèves, the discovery trail in Barre-des-Cévennes (& *see FLORAC*), or the Musée des Vallées Cévenoles (& *see SAINT-JEAN-DU-GARD*).

Excursion

Cascade de Rûnes

11km/7mi W. From Le Pont-de-Montvert take the road to Florac, then turn right onto D 35 towards Fraissinet-de-Lozère. This road, lined with ash trees, gives some pretty views of the Tarn Valley.

South of Rûnes, a footpath (*45min on foot there and back*) leads to a lovely waterfall in the Mirals hills, which drops 58m/190ft.

Mont Lozère★★ – & *See MONT-LOZÈRE.*

PORT-BARCARÈS ⚓

POPULATION 3,514

MICHELIN LOCAL MAP 344: J-6

The urban planners of this resort developed this site to satisfy tourists, providing for easy access to swimming and other outdoor activities and building self-catering accommodation, family camps and conventional hotel facilities. Residential areas have been grouped together, saving the seafront from overbearing blocks of buildings that would stifle the horizon. ▮ *Pl. de la République, 66420 Port-Barcarès,* ☎ *04 68 86 16 56. www.barcares.com.*

Sunsets along this part of the coast can be spectacular. Most likely they looked the same to Greek traders who occupied the site in Antiquity: the Corbières range is an iridescent purple mass behind the dark, shiny surface of Leucate lagoon.

Visit

The Lydia

This ship, which was deliberately run aground in 1967, is the main attraction of the new Roussillon shoreline (disco and casino). Just by the *Lydia*, along an esplanade by the sea, the **Allée des Arts** (*signposted*) hosts a small display of contemporary sculpture including the "Soleillonautes," totem poles sculpted from the trunks of trees from Gabon. The resort's park is a lovely place for a walk. A modern sea-water cure (*thalassothérapie*) centre treats patients suffering from ailments such as overwork, depression and rheumatism.

L. Campion/MICHELIN

The Lydia

Aqualand

In Port-Leucate. ⏱ *Open daily 18 Jun to late Aug: 10am-6pm.* ⟳ *19€ (children: 14€)* ☎ *04068 40 99 98.*

Kids This seaside leisure park (water chutes, swimming pool) is particularly suitable for young children.

The marina

The new harbour complex of **Port-Leucate** and **Port-Barcarès** constitutes the largest marina on the French Mediterranean coast. It is a major centre for yachting and water-skiing. A part of the Étang de Salses-Leucate (the lagoon is known by both names) is hemmed in by a spit of land that creates a calm stretch of water about 10km/6mi long. Canals lead off this "main boulevard" to individual marina areas, providing quiet berths on the "side streets."

Hiking Tour

Cap Leucate★

2hr via a footpath running along the cliffs. Start from the Sémaphore du cap, at Leucate-Plage (10km/6mi N of Port-Barcarès along D 627).

▮ From the look-out point by the signal station on the cape, there is a **view**★ along the coast, from Languedoc to the Albères mountains.

As you walk along the cliff path, you can see the cliffs closing off the north end of the Leucate or Salses lagoon. They offer fine views over the whole of the Golfe du Lion. The path leads to **La Franqui**, a small seaside resort where the writer Henry de Monfreid (1879-1974), born in Leucate, used to enjoy staying.

PRADES

POPULATION 5,800

MICHELIN LOCAL MAP 344: F-7

ALSO SEE LE CANIGOU

Lying at the foot of Mont Canigou, in the midst of orchards, Prades became home to the cellist Pablo Casals (1876-1973) from 1950. The great concerts of the **Pablo Casals Festival** take place in the abbey of St-Michel-de-Cuxa and other fine churches in the area. In the old district around the church, the kerbstones, the gutters and the doorsteps are frequently made of pink marble from the Conflent. Prades is the starting point of hikes and excursions in the beautiful surrounding area.
🛈 *4 R. Victor-Hugo, 66500 Prades, ☎ 04 68 05 41 02. www.prades-tourisme.com.*

Visit

Église St-Pierre

The church, rebuilt in the 17C, has nonetheless conserved its typical southern French Romanesque bell-tower. An unexpected wealth of furnishings adorns the interior. In the chancel, the Baroque **altarpiece** (1696-99) by the Catalan sculptor Joseph Sunyer includes over 100 carved figures and narrates in six sculpted scenes the life of the Apostle Peter, whose statue occupies the centre of the composition. Other Baroque works are on view in side chapels: St-Gaudérique altarpiece (1714), probably from Sunyer's workshop; Trinity altarpiece sculpted by Louis Generès (1655); St-Benoît altarpiece in carved and gilded wood and decorated with paintings on canvas dating from the 16C. In the north transept, note a 16C figure of Christ in black wood and an 18C processional Virgin Mary with a typical Catalan feature – a carved and gilded canopy, known as a *cadireta*, over the statue.
The **treasury** *(Kids ⏱ ♿ July-Aug: guided tours available daily except weekends 10.30am-12.30pm, 3.30-5.30; Sept: Mon, Wed, Thu, Fri 9am-noon, 3.30-5.30pm; rest of the year by reservation only; ♿ 2.40€ (under 12: no charge); inquire about combined visit to church and treasury ☎04 68 05 23 58)* contains many reliquaries from the abbey of St-Michel-de-Cuxa (note in particular St Valentine's shrine), liturgical gold plate and the splendid 14C carved wooden statue of Notre-Dame de la Volta.

Musée Pablo Casals

4 rue Victor-Hugo. ⏱ Jul-Aug: Tue-Fri 9am-1pm, 2-5pm, Sat 9am-1pm; Sept-Jun: Tue 10am-noon, 3-7pm, Wed 10am-7pm, Fri 3-7pm, Sat 10am-1pm. ⏱ Closed Christmas school holidays. No charge (museum currently being reconstructed). ☎ 04 68 05 41 02 or 04 68 96 52 37.

Address Book

ௗ *For coin categories, see the Legend.*

EATING OUT

⊖⊖ **Le Jardin d'Aymeric** – *3 Ave. du Gén.-de-Gaulle - ☎ 04 68 96 53 38 - jardin. aymeric@wanadoo.fr - closed Feb holidays, 25 Jun-8 Jul, Wed evening 15 Oct-15 Apr, Sun evening and Mon.* What a great find this little restaurant is. The young chef takes great care over his preparation of dishes clearly inspired by the flavours of the region. The decor features pleasant colours, art exhibitions and pretty floral compositions.

WHERE TO STAY

⊖⊖ **Hôtel Les Glycines** – *129 Ave. du Gén.-de-Gaulle - ☎ 04 68 96 51 65 - les-glycines2@wanadoo.fr - closed 6 Oct-16 Nov - 🅿 – 19 rooms - ⊡ 5.30€ - restaurant* ⊖⊖. This hotel at the heart of Prades

offering simple, spick and span rooms, is ideal for those on a tight budget. The restaurant has a sunny decor, relaxed service and traditional cuisine without airs.

⊖⊖ **Hexagone** – *Molitg roundabout on the bypass - ☎ 04 68 05 31 31 – hh6604@ inter-hotel.com – 🅿 - 30 rooms - ⊡ 6.60€.* Basic rooms with standard hotel fittings and furnishings, breakfasts served with homemade preserves: this is a handy address for stopping over when the city is busy with its music festival.

PABLO CASALS FESTIVAL

During the Pablo Casals Festival (*mid-Jul to mid-Aug*), 30 or so concerts are given in St-Michel-de-Cuxa and St-Pierre de Prades as well as in the region's most attractive churches (from mid-Jul to mid-Aug)
🛈 *Reservations and information: ☎ 04 68 96 33 07.*

A Cellist's Happy Whim

In 1939, **Pablo Casals** fled the Franco regime in his native country, choosing to live in exile in Prades and thus not abandoning his beloved Catalonia altogether. For 10 years this world-famous cellist, a committed pacifist, refused to play in public as a sign of protest. He relented at last in 1950, founding a festival which he dedicated to Bach, firmly stipulating, however, that the festival should take place in his adopted home town. Since then, Prades has become a major venue for chamber music. Every year, between 25 July and 15 August, some of the world's leading chamber musicians convene here to teach 150 outstandingly talented music students. Twenty-five concerts are given at the abbey of St-Michel-de-Cuxa, the church of St-Pierre in Prades and some of the other particularly beautiful churches in the region.

This museum is dedicated to the world-famous Spanish violoncellist by his adopted city: recordings, concert clothes, letters, photographs, instruments all help to evoke the personality of the artist and illustrate his outstanding career.

Excursions

Abbaye de Saint-Michel de Cuxa★★

3km/2mi S. ♿🕐🍴 May-Sep guided tour (45min) 9.30-11.50am, 2-6pm, Sun and public holidays 2-6pm; Oct-Apr: 9.30-11.50am, 2-5pm, Sun and public holidays 2-5pm. 🎧 4€ (12-18 years: 2.50€). ☎ 04 68 96 15 35.

The elegant crenellated tower of the abbey, founded under the protection of the counts of Cerdagne-Conflent, rises from one of the valleys at the foot of Mont Canigou.

There have been four successive churches in Cuxa. The present church, was consecrated in 974.

In the 11C, Abbot Oliba developed the great Catalan monasteries: Montserrat, Ripoll and St-Michel. He enlarged the chancel of the abbey church by adding a square ambulatory to it and chapels opening off it, built two bell-towers in the Lombard style and hollowed out the underground chapel of La Crèche.

After a long period of decline, the abbey of St-Michel was abandoned, then sold during the Revolution. Its works of art disappeared and the cloister galleries were dismantled. In 1907, the American sculptor George Grey Barnard found and bought over half of the original capitals. They were bought in 1925 by the New York Metropolitan Museum, which undertook the restoration of the cloisters by adding new elements carved in the same Pyrenean marble. Since 1938, the cloisters of St-Michel-de-Cuxa have stood in the midst of a park, on the hillside overlooking the Hudson Valley.

From 1952, considerable work has been undertaken in Cuxa: the abbey church has been restored and some of the cloister galleries have been put back in place. Since 1965, the abbey has been occupied by Benedictine monks subordinate to Montserrat.

First walk round the outside of the buildings to see the abbey church's fine Romanesque **bell-tower**★, with four tiers of twinned bays, surmounted by round windows and crenellations.

Cloisters★

These consist of arches and capitals found in Prades or in private ownership and recovered. The arches of the gallery adjacent to the church and those of most of the west gallery and the front of the east gallery have all been used to reconstruct almost half of the cloisters. The sculpture on the capitals (12C) is distinguished by the absence of any religious theme in the motifs; only the decoration itself seemed to matter to the artist. The pink cloisters form a harmonious whole over which towers the lofty massive church.

Abbey church

The church has retained very little of its original appearance. It is entered through a doorway reconstructed from a single archway, the remains of a gallery put up in the 12C at the far end of the nave. The nave is one of the very rare surviving examples of pre-Romanesque art in France, exemplified here by the horseshoe or "Visigothic" arch which can be seen in part of the transept standing out against later construction. Covered once more by a timber-framed roof, the central nave ends in a rectangular apse.

Crypt of the Vierge de la Crèche

Located at the centre of an underground sanctuary, which has managed to escape destruction or alterations since the 11C, this circular chapel has a vaulted ceiling supported by a single central pillar. Despite its lack of ornamentation, it exudes elegance.

Mosset

12km/7.5mi NW along D 619 and D 14.

Kids The **Tour des Parfums** (🕐 *Mid-Jul to end Aug: 10am-noon, 3-7pm; Sep, early May to mid-Jul and school holidays: daily except Mon 3-6pm; rest of the year: Sat-Sun 3-6pm.* 🕐 *Closed Jan.* ⊕ *3€.* ☎ *04 68 05 38 32.*) houses an interactive exhibition about fragrances and organises themed walks, visits and workshops connected with the sense of smell.

PRATS-DE-MOLLO ★

POPULATION 1,080

MICHELIN LOCAL MAP 344: F-8

Prats-de-Mollo lies in the broad upper Tech Valley overlooked by the close-cropped slopes of the Costabonne massif and Mont Canigou. It combines the character of a walled fortress town designed by Vauban with the charm of a lively Catalan mountain town. A picturesque Fête de l'Ours (bear festival) takes place in February. ⏹ *Pl. du Foiral, 66230 Prats-de-Mollo-la-Preste,* ☎ *04 68 39 70 83. www.pratsdemollolapreste.com.*

Town Walk

▶ *Enter the town through Porte de France and follow the shopping street of the same name.*

Opposite place d'Armes, climb the steps up rue de la Croix-de-Mission, overlooked by a Cross and Instruments of the Passion.

Church

A Romanesque church, of which only the crenellated bell-tower remains, predated the present building which has a Gothic structure, despite dating from the 17C. The 13C portal has scrolled hinges. A curious votive offering has been stuck in the wall to the right – a whale rib more than 2m/6ft long. In the chapel facing the door stands the statue of Notre-Dame-du-Coral, a copy of the 13C statue worshipped in the old shepherds' sanctuary of the same name situated near the Col d'Ares. The Baroque **altarpiece**★ on the high altar, nearly 10m/32ft tall and which was covered in gold leaf in 1745, depicts the life and the martyrdom of St Justa and St Rufina of Andalusia, patron saints of the town.

▶ *Go along the south side of the church and take a fortified rampart walk round the chevet. Leave the precinct and walk uphill for about 100m/110yd towards Fort Lagarde.*

Turn round for a good view of the roof and upper sections of the church.

L. Campion/MICHELIN

Church of Ste-Juste-et-Ste-Rufine

Address Book

Fort Lagarde

🕓 ☜ *Apr-Oct and school holidays: 2-5pm. Possibility of guided tours and tours with a story of the site (inquire for information).* ⊜ *4€ (children under 12: no charge).* ☎ *04 68 39 70 83.*

🄺🄸🄳🅂 The fortress was built in 1692 on a rocky spur overlooking the town, and at the centre of the site there are now the remains of the old castle. A redoubt, halfway between the fort and the town, stood guard over the path that linked the two. Take the steps up the side of the curtain wall to get to the fort.

▷ *Return to the church and take the street to the right.*

In sight of the almshouse, go down the steps on the left and follow the street as it runs along below the almshouse gardens. Cross the torrent over the fortified bridge, just downstream of the old humpback bridge of La Guilhème, to get to the upper town.

Upper Town (Ville haute or Ville d'Amoun)★

Place del Rey, where an old house once belonging to the military Engineers stands, used to be the site of one of the residences of the counts of Besalù, who, in the 12C, reigned over one of the pieces of land which formed part of the patchwork of Catalan territory. Where rue des Marchands leads off to the left, take a carved stairway up to the right. From the top of the steps, there is a fine view of the church towering above the lower town.

▷ *Continue along the curtain wall. Leave the town through a modern gateway, and return to it through the next one round (a gatehouse), the "Porte du Verger."*

The street leads to a crossroads, overlooked by a house in the shape of a ship's prow; some people think this was once a palace of the kings of Aragón, and others think that it once housed the trade union of the weavers' guild. High quality cloth and linen were once produced in the Haut-Vallespir region. An alleyway leads downhill to the exit from the upper town.

Go through Porte d'Espagne onto the footbridge over the Tech, from where there is a good view of the south side of the town.

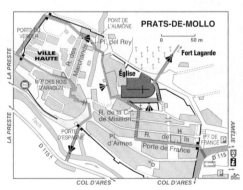

Excursion

La Preste

8km/5mi NW along D 115A. The spa town of La Preste (alt 1 130m/3 707ft) has five springs (temperature 44°C/111°F) which are recommended for the cure of infections of the colon. Napoléon III had this road up to the spa built. As he was unwell, he had intended to follow a course of hydrotherapy at the spa, but the war of 1870 intervened and he was forced to abandon the idea.

Parc national des PYRÉNÉES★★★

MICHELIN LOCAL MAPS 342: K-5

The Pyrénées National Park was created in 1967 with the aim of preserving the beauty of the natural environment. The park varies in width from 1km/0.6mi to 15km/9mi, at an altitude between 1 000m/3 250ft and 3 298m/10 820ft (at the summit of the Vignemale). Including the Néouvielle Nature Reserve, the park covers an area of 45 700ha/176sq mi.

The Pyrenean Bear

In France, the only place to find the European brown bear (Ursus arctos) is the central Pyrenees mountains, in particular on rocky slopes and in beech and fir forests which overlook the Aspe and Ossau valleys at an altitude of 1 500-1 700m/4 921-5 577ft. This once carnivorous plantigrade animal now varies its diet according to the season, eating tubers, fruit, insects, acorns but also small mammals and sometimes sheep.

Unfortunately, the extension of the road network as well as of forestry work and tourism combined with the bear's slow reproduction cycle (females have a cub every two years), have led to the regression of the species. Its numbers have dwindled from 40 twenty years ago to a mere six or seven.

In order to save this endangered species, a five-year charter was signed in 1994; its aim is to include the safeguard of bears in a wider nature-protection programme. Thus, hunting is banned in an area of 7 000ha/17 300 acres during the autumn period when bears stock up for their long hibernation period.

In addition, a programme of reintroduction of bears in the area was launched: in June 1996, two females from Slovenia, Melba and Ziva were released in the central Pyrenees followed in 1997 by a male called Pyros, also from Slovenia.

Melba had three cubs in 1997. Unfortunately she was shot by a hunter in early 1998. It is believed that one of the three cubs survived and is somewhere between France and Spain. Ziva, on the other hand, is bringing up two cubs. The total bear population of the Pyrenees mountains is therefore estimated to be around 10.

PARC NATIONAL DES PYRÉNÉES

0   5 km

🅿 Information centre

⚠ Guarded refuge

● Winter sports area

🚴 Cross-country skiing area

🏇 Riding centre

🧗 Climbing site with facilities

The park itself is surrounded by a peripheral area of 206 000ha/795sq mi, including 86 municipalities in the Hautes-Pyrénées and Pyrénées-Atlantiques départe-ments. The development programme in this area has concentrated on revitalising the pastoral economy of the mountain villages and improving tourist facilities.

▶ **Orient Yourself:** The park extends for more than 100km/60mi along the French border region from Vallée d'Aspe in the west to Vallée d'Aure in the east. Seven Maisons du Parc and several other seasonal outposts offer maps, brochures and tourist information (👌 *see Address Book*).

👌 **Also See:** La BIGORRE, CAUTERETS, GAVARNIE, Massif de NÉOUVIELLE

The park provides shelter for 4 000 izards, a local species of chamois, particularly in the valleys of Ossau and Cauterets, where they can be easily spotted, as well as more than 200 colonies of marmots. It is now very rare to catch sight of one of the few remaining brown bears, but it is not unusual to see vultures, royal eagles or huge bearded vultures in flight in a region still frequented by wood grouse, ptarmigan and Pyrenean muskrats.

Excursions

The Parc national des Pyrénées and its peripheral area attract thousands of tourists every year. In winter, the mountains are a kingdom where skiers reign – children and adults, beginners and experts alike. In summer, both experienced and occasional hik-ers take to the mountain trails. Although the park can be toured by car, the countryside is better appreciated on foot or by bicycle.

😊 *Various tours (by car and on foot) are suggested in this guide.*

Within the Park

Vallées de Cauterets★★ – This consists of four short itineraries through the park itself (👌 *see CAUTERETS*).

Vallée de Gavarnie★★ – The valley can be visited in three separate stages: the **Valley★★**, **Cirque de Gavarnie★★★** and **Pic de Tentes★★** (👌 *see GAVARNIE*).

Massif de Néouvielle★★★ – This excursion includes the Néouvielle wildlife reserve (cars prohibited; 👌 *see Massif de NÉOUVIELLE*).

Haut Ossau★★ – This area offers three itineraries: **Vallée du gave de Bious★**, **Vallée du Soussouéou★**, and **Vallée du gave de Brousset** (👌 *see The Green Guide Atlantic Coast*).

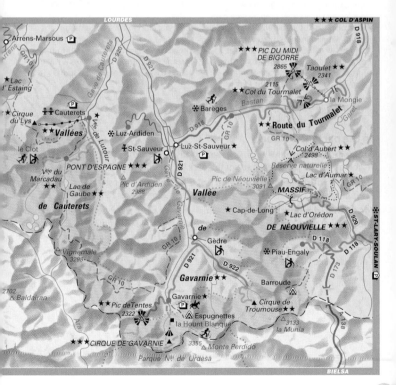

Address Book

USEFUL ADDRESSES

Parc national des Pyrénées – *59 Rte de Pau - 65000 Tarbes -* ☎ *05 62 44 36 60 - www.parc-pyrenees.com.*

Maisons du Parc – These visitor centres provide information on the flora and fauna in the park, hiking in the mountains and present exhibits on topics such as the Pyrenean bear and the history of mountain exploration. **Maison du Parc** (Vallée d'Aure) - *65170 St-Lary-Soulan -* ☎ *05 62 39 40 91;* **Maison du Parc et de la vallée** (Vallée de Luz-Gavarnie) - *65120 Luz-St-Sauveur -* ☎ *05 62 92 38 38;* **Maison du Parc** (Vallée de Luz-Gavarnie) - *65120 Gavarnie -* ☎ *05 62 92 42 48;* **Maison du Parc** (Vallée de Cauterets), *65110 Cauterets -* ☎ *05 62 92 52 56;* **Maison du Parc et de la vallée** (Vallée d'Azun) - *65400 Arrens-Marsous -* ☎ *05 62 97 43 13;* **Maison du Parc** (Vallée d'Ossau) - *64440 Laruns -* ☎ *05 59 05 41 59;* **Maison du Parc** (Vallée d'Aspe) - *64880 Etsaut -* ☎ *05 59 34 88 30.* Information points in summer: **Réserve Naturelle du Néouvielle** (Vallée d'Aure) and **Pont d'Espagne** (Vallée du Cauterets).

WHERE TO STAY

Refuges du parc – In the park, there are refuge huts, some of which have wardens present (these are open only from mid-June to September) and others which are classified as *"non gardés,"* (usually there is room for about 10 people). Hikers passing through may use them. In the *refuges gardés,* you may either prepare your own food or eat meals prepared by the warden. In the summer months, places in these refuges (usually 30 to 40) are in great demand. Advance reservations are thus imperative. The list with telephone numbers is available from the Parc

national des Pyrénées. There are five refuges managed by the Park: **Refuge de Barroude** (2 370m/7 773ft), in the Aure Valley, accommodates 35, ☎ *05 62 39 61 10;* **Refuge des Espuguettes** (2 077m/6 812ft), in the Luz Valley, accommodates 60, ☎ *05 62 92 40 63;* **Refuge de Migouélou** (2 290m/7 511ft), in the Azun Valley, accommodates 35, ☎ *05 62 97 44 92;* **Refuge d'Ayous** (1 960m/6 429ft), in the Ossau Valley, accommodates 50, ☎ *05 59 05 37 00;* **Refuge d'Arlet** (1 990m/6 527ft), in the Aspe Valley, accommodates 40, ☎ *05 59 36 00 99.*

Refuges managed by the Club Alpin – Most of the refuges that are not part of the park services are managed by the Club Alpin Français - Service du Patrimoine bâti - *23 R. Renan, 69007 Lyon,* ☎ *04 37 27 10 47.*

Camping – Camping is prohibited in the national park, but bivouacking is tolerated (overnight or in case of bad weather, it is permissible to set up a tent, on the condition that you are more than a 1hr walk from a road used by motor vehicles). Tourist offices and syndicats d'initiative can provide you with a list of camp sites near the park.

LEISURE AND RECREATION

Activities in the Parc national des Pyrénées – There are more than 350km/210mi of marked footpaths in the park. The GR 10, sentier de grande randonnée, crosses the park in several places.

Hunting, picking flowers, lighting campfires, and bringing in dogs are all prohibited. However, fishing in the rapid streams and the park's 250 lakes is subject to ordinary regulations on the sport.

In the peripheral area

Route de l'Aubisque★★★ – This itinerary runs through the Béarn region and winds in and out of the peripheral area of the park (👓 *see The Green Guide Atlantic Coast*).

Route du Tourmalet and **Route du Col d'Aspin★★★** – These tours through the peripheral area of the park explore the Bigorre region (👓 *see La BIGORRE*).

Pic du Midi de Bigorre★★★ – This familiar landmark of the Pyrenees is located in the peripheral area of the national park (👓 *see Pic du MIDI DE BIGORRE*).

Skiing is available at the following resorts situated in the peripheral zone or in the heart of the park: Cauterets (👓 *see CAUTERETS*), Gavarnie (👓 *see GAVARNIE*), Piau-Engaly (👓 *see Massif de NÉOUVIELLE*).

Château de QUÉRIBUS★★

MICHELIN LOCAL MAP 344: G-5

ALSO SEE LES CORBIÈRES

The castle occupies a spectacular site★★, perched 729m/2 391ft above sea level on top of a rocky outcrop, looking for all the world like a "thimble on a thumb."

Access – *These castle ruins are reached by taking D 123 S from the village of Cucugnan and then, from Grau de Maury (& see Les CORBIÈRES), up a very steep road.*

From the car park and ticket office a footpath leads up to the castle (20min there and back). When visiting this and other fortified sites, take extra care on windy days. Hold on to the handrail to get through the small east doorway leading into the castle compound (steps). In the summer, carry drinking water and use sun protection (hat and lotion).

A Bit of History

As late as 1241, the castle of Quéribus was providing refuge for Cathar deacons. When it was besieged in 1255, eleven years after the fall of Montségur, in what was to be the last military operation of the Albigensian Crusade, the castle appears not to have been taken by a full-scale assault. Quéribus was then made a royal fortress. It stood on the frontier between France and Aragón, with the role of observing and defending the plain of Roussillon.

The castle atop its rock "like a thimble on a thumb"

B. Kaufmann/MICHELIN

Visit

Choice of unaccompanied visit or audioguide tour. ◷ *Jul and Aug: 9am-8pm; Apr-Jun and Sep: 9.30am-7pm; Apr and Oct: 10am-6.30pm; Nov-Jan: 10am-5pm; Feb: 10am-5.30pm; Mar: 10am-6pm.* ◷ *Closed 3 wks in Jan, 1 Jan, 25 Dec.* ⊛ *5€.* ☏ *04 68 45 03 69.*

From the castle terraces, which are unsafe in strong winds, there is a splendid all-round **view**★ of the Roussillon plain, the Mediterranean, the Albères mountains and Mont Canigou, the Puigmal and Carlit massifs. To the north-west, in clear weather, the ruins of Peyrepertuse Castle can be seen on the other side of the valley.

Three successive lines of fortifications protect the two-storey polygonal keep which stands at the summit of the rocky spur.

The castle is a fascinating place to visit, as inside it has an intriguing maze of winding passages, doorways and flights of steps to be explored. Here and there, arrow slits give glimpses of the outside world. The most impressive part of the interior is the keep's high **Gothic hall**★ with vaulting resting on a central pillar. Its unusual layout and lighting have given rise, as at Montségur, to interpretations linked to solar symbolism. These are, however, unfounded since almost nothing remains of the original castle, which was completely transformed to meet the changing needs of the artillery. On the lower level, on the north side of the keep, a vaulted room leads to an underground gallery and a casemate.

QUILLAN

POPULATION 3,542

MICHELIN LOCAL MAP 344: E-5

This town is a major tourist centre for the upper Aude Valley and one of the best points of departure for forays into the forests of the Pyrenean foothills. Rugby has enjoyed a passionate following locally since the period between the two World Wars, the hat-making industry's swansong. Modern local industry includes laminates (Formica), luxury and garden furniture, trousers and shoes.

Visit

On the esplanade in front of the station there is a quaint little monument to Abbot Armand (see Défilé de Pierre-Lys below).
On the east bank of the Aude stand the ruins, sadly being left to fall into disrepair, of a 13C fortress with a square ground plan – most unusual in this region.

Excursion

Sault plateau and river gorges★★

144km/90mi round tour – allow one day.

This trip includes a large stretch of the **Route du Sapin de l'Aude**, a drive through woodland where there are conifers over 50m/160ft tall.

▶ *Leave Quillan W along D 117 and turn left onto D 613 which runs across the Sault plateau. Beyond Espèze, watch out for a crossroads marked with a cross and turn right onto D 29 towards Bélesta.*

▶ *Take the left turn past the forest lodge, drive along the forest road to a left bend and park the car by the Langarail drinking troughs.*

Langarail pastures★
45min on foot there and back.

As its name suggests, this is a rural site. Follow the stony track until the bumpy stretch from which there is a **view** to the north, beyond the Bélesta Forest as far as the foothills of the chain towards the Lauragais.

▶ *Get back onto the forest road and continue W.*

Pas de l'Ours★
The road runs along a rocky cliff above the Gorges de la Frau.

▶ *At Col de la Gargante, take the steep road to the left which is signposted "belvédère à 600m."*

Belvédère du Pas de l'Ours★★

15min on foot there and back.

⚐ From the look-out point, there is a magnificent view of the Gorges de la Frau; 700m/2 296ft lower down are the Montségur outcrop and the Tabe mountain; beyond these, and much higher up, the white patches of the Trimouns quarry can be seen.

▷ *Beyond Col de la Gargante, follow the road to Comus and turn right.*

Gorges de la Frau★

1hr 30min on foot there and back.

⚐ Park the car at the entrance to a wide forest track climbing a tributary valley. The path runs along the base of yellow-tinged limestone cliffs. After a 45min walk, turn back at the point where the valley makes a sharp bend.

▷ *Return to Comus and take the road to the right towards Camurac.*

Camurac ski area

Alt 1 400-1 800m/4 593-5 906ft. Camurac is a family resort equipped with 16 Alpine ski runs suitable for all levels of proficiency, a country-skiing loop and a marked track for snowshoeing.

▷ *The road climbs up to Col des Sept Frères. Turn left onto D 613 then right onto D 20 to Niort de Sault; turn left.*

Drive down the **Rebenty gorge**, passing beneath the impressive overhangs of the **Défilé d'Able** and through the **Défilé de Joucou**, where the road follows a series of tunnels and overhangs, to reach **Joucou**, a sheltered village gathered around an old abbey.

▷ *Turn back. After driving through a couple of tunnels, turn left onto D 29 which runs through Rodome, Aunat and Bessède-de-Sault before joining D 118. Turn left towards Axat.*

This pretty stretch of road runs along the edge of the Sault plateau.

Grottes de l'Aguzou

Potholing outings by appointment (3 days in advance); departure at 9am. ✆ 1 day (7hrs): 50€ (10-13 years: 40€); ½ day (2hrs): 30€. Take plimsolls, light walking boots or shoes and a cold meal. ☎ 04 68 20 45 38. www.grotte-aguzou.com.

This complex network of caves was discovered in 1965. On the tour, visitors can see a large number of crystals and some wonderful examples of aragonite.

Gorges de St-Georges★

This river gorge, cutting straight down through bare rock, is the narrowest in the upper Aude Valley.

In the **Aude gorge**, a reach of some 10km/6mi, the river surges along between high cliffs thickly covered with plant life.

▷ *Drive on to **Axat**, a popular white-water sports resort, then turn left onto D 177 towards Quillan.*

Défilé de Pierre-Lys★

This is an impressive stretch of road between the ravine's sheer cliff walls, to which the odd bush clings tenaciously. The final tunnel is known as the **Trou du Curé** ("priest's hole") in memory of Abbot Félix Armand (1742-1823), parish priest of St-Martin-Lys, who had the passage cut through the rock with pickaxes.

Défilé de Pierre-Lys

A. Thuillier/MICHELIN

RODEZ★

POPULATION 23,707

MICHELIN LOCAL MAP 338: H-4

Once the capital of the Rouergue, Rodez is situated on the borders of two very different regions, the dry Causses plateaux and the well-watered Ségala hills. The old town stands on a hill some 120m/393ft above the Aveyron river bed.
🛈 Pl. Foch, 12005 Rodez, ☎ 05 65 75 76 77. www.ot-rodez.fr.

A Bit of History

Divided loyalties – In the Middle Ages, the town was shared between two masters. The bishops, who for a long time were the more powerful, occupied the Cité; the counts ruled the Bourg.

These two adjacent areas were separated by tall fortifications, and for many centuries, the rivalry between the two prompted endless fighting between the inhabitants. The two main squares, place de la Cité and place du Bourg, reflect the town's former duality.

When Henri IV became king, the Comté de Rodez was united with the French crown; the bishops promptly took advantage of this, styling themselves bishops and counts of Rodez and adding a count's coronet to their coat of arms.

Address Book

For coin categories, see the Legend.

EATING OUT

◎◎ **La Taverne** – 23 R. de l'Embergue - ☎ 05 65 42 14 51 - closed 1 week in May, 2 weeks in Sep, Sat noon in low season, Sun and holidays. The owner calls his restaurant "a country inn in town." The cuisine is distinctly regional, including such specialities as picaùcel, and of course l'aligot. Choose between the large room downstairs with a vaulted ceiling or the terrace on a pedestrian square.

◎◎ **Les Jardins de l'Acropolis** – R. Athènes, in Bourran - ☎ 05 65 68 40 07 - acropolys@wanadoo.fr. This restaurant offers two contemporary dining rooms with rosewood accoutrements. Sophisticated modern cuisine.

WHERE TO STAY

◎ **Hôtel du Midi** – 1 R. Béteille - ☎ 05 65 68 02 07 - hotel.du.midi@wanadoo.fr - closed 20 Dec-6 Jan - 🄿 - 34 rooms - ▨ 7€ - restaurant ◎◎. Facing the cathedral, this hotel has simple, well-kept and well-lit rooms. The rooms in the back are quieter. Two dining rooms. Classic regional cuisine.

◎◎ **Biney** – R. Victoire-Massol - ☎ 05 65 68 01 24 - hotel.biney@wanadoo.fr - 29 rooms - ▨ 13€. This modern hotel near the centre of town is part of a building complex surrounding a quiet green park. The salon is cute and the rooms are furnished simply.

SIT BACK AND RELAX

Le Petit Moka – Pl. des Maçons - ☎ 05 65 75 63 34 – Mon-Sat 8am-7pm. This is a nice place to stop for a quick bite to eat. Choose a salad or a toasted sandwich at noon; in the morning or at tea time, have a fresh waffle or home-made pastry. 20 kinds of coffee and 23 varieties of tea on the menu.

Le Broussy – 1 Ave. Victor-Hugo - ☎ 05 65 68 66 01 - Jul-Aug: Mon-Wed 7am-1am; Thur-Sat 7am-2am; Sept-Jun: Mon-Thur 7am-1am, Fri-Sat 7am-2am. Built in 1920, this old Art Deco café has kept some of its old-fashioned decor. Although it had become quite run-down, the new Italian owner has brightened it up again. This café specialises in…coffee! Try the Jamaican Blue Mountain, a fine aroma at the price of an ordinary expresso.

SHOPPING

Market – Weekly markets: Saturday morning at Place e la Cité and Place du Bourg; Friday afternoon at Place du Sacré-Cœur

Domaine du Vieux Porche - Jean-Luc Matha – Lieu-dit Bruéjouls - 12330 Marcillac-Vallon – ☎ 05 65 72 63 29 - Mon-Fri (daily Jul-Aug) 9am-noon, 2-6pm, Sat by appointment - closed public holidays. Boutique showcasing local products, installed in a vaulted wine cellar. Here you'll find Marcillac wines (red and rosé, as well as three types of housemade apéritifs: Lo Grabel, Lo Rascalou and Lo Ratafia.

SPORT

École de parapente Azimut – Michel Savy - rue des Lauriers - Carbassas - 12520 Paulhe - ☎ 05 65 59 43 78 or 06 81 26 55 02. Paragliding instruction and practice.

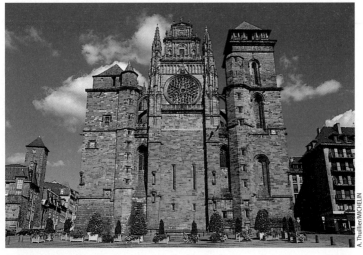

Cathedral of Notre-Dame

Cathédrale Notre-Dame★★ *1hr*

The red-sandstone cathedral was begun in 1277 after the collapse, a year earlier, of the choir and bell-tower of the previous building. Half a century later, the apse and two bays of the chancel had been completed, by the 14C a transept and two bays of the nave, and by the 15C the whole building was finished.

Exterior – The west front overlooking place d'Armes has a forbidding, fortress-like appearance. The lower half of the wall is quite bare, with no porch and only the occasional arrow slit. It has massive buttresses, turrets with windows cut at an angle and two plain, unadorned towers. This austere façade, built outside the city wall, acted as an advance bastion to defend the city. Only the upper part between the two towers, which was completed in the 17C, is decorated in the Renaissance style with a Classical pediment.

▶ *Go round the church to the left.*

The late-15C north door, known as the Portail de l'Évêché (bishops' doorway), opens beneath three rows of archivolts and a pointed arch. Sculptures, sadly damaged, depict, on the lintel, the Nativity, the Adoration of the Shepherds and the Magi, and the Presentation in the Temple and, on the tympanum, the Coronation of the Virgin.

The magnificent **bell-tower**★★★, which interestingly stands apart from the cathedral, was built on top of a solid 14C tower; it is 87m/285ft high and comprises six tiers *(tower open ⏰ Jul-Aug: daily except Sun 3-5pm, by request at the tourist office. ☞ 4€. ☎ 05 65 68 02 27)*. The third tier, built in the 16C, is decorated with large window openings with distinctive tracery; the fourth, octagonal in shape, has statues of the Apostles adorning the niches in between the window openings; the fifth is elaborately decorated with turrets, Flamboyant arcades and pinnacles. On the top tier, which has a terrace with a balustrade, a dome and a lantern light, stands a statue of the Virgin Mary.

The interest of the east end lies in the way the terrace roofs of its chapels and ambulatory support double-span flying buttresses, which in turn receive the thrust from the upper walls of the chancel level with the springing line of the vaulting.

On the south door, the work of Jacques Maurel (late 15C), note the elegant windows adorning the tympanum.

Interior – *1hr.* The elegance of the Gothic style is apparent in the soaring elevation of the chancel with its delicate lancet windows, in the finesse of the pillars in the nave, barely perceptibly moulded at the level of the capitals, and in the height of the great arches surmounted by a triforium which reproduces the same pattern as that of the upper windows. The beauty of the great nave and its vast side aisles, flanked with well-lit side chapels, is best appreciated standing behind the parish altar, at the far west end of the nave.

The **choir stalls**★ are by André Sulpice (15C), and the furnishing of the choir was modelled on that of St-Aphrodise in Béziers. There are 62 tall stalls beneath Gothic oak canopies, as well as a remarkable stall for the bishop surmounted by a little

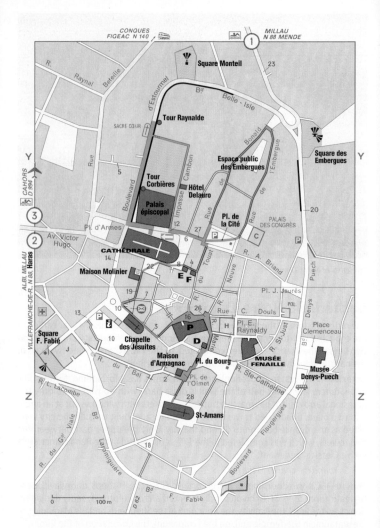

RODEZ

pyramid and an angel (restored in the 19C) displaying the coat of arms of Bertrand de Chalençon, Bishop of Rodez. The skilfully crafted, amusing scenes on the misericords are well worth a closer look.

The third side chapel off the south side aisle is closed off by a fine 16C **stone screen**★, unfortunately with badly damaged carved decoration. The pillars were decorated with 12 statues of sibyls, the prophetesses of Antiquity who, according to Christian tradition, foretold the coming of the Messiah. Only four of these statues are left, together with an Ecce Homo on the inside of the screen. This chapel also contains a Renaissance altar (1523), surmounted by a large altarpiece depicting an Entombment, three little Resurrection scenes, and Christ leaving the Tomb; sadly, the faces were very crudely repainted at the end of the 19C.

In the next chapel along, there is a fine 15C altarpiece: "Christ in the Garden of Olives." The large and richly decorated **rood screen**★ (1470) was moved into the south arm of the transept, because it blocked the view of the nave. The **organ case**★, in the north arm of the transept, is a superb piece of 17C carved woodwork (height 20.5m/67ft). On the high altar stands a fine statue of the Virgin and Child (late 14C). The choir (*choir stalls described above*) is surrounded by an ambulatory with chapels leading off it. In the first bay of the side aisles of the choir are two beautiful marble sarcophagi and an early-15C Entombment. The chapels contain the tombs of several bishops of Rodez, including, in the axial chapel, the particularly interesting tomb of Bishop Gilbert de Cantobre (d 1349), surmounted by a Romanesque marble altar-table with scalloped decoration. The Renaissance chapel at the entrance to the sacristy is also of interest.

Old Rodez

The old town, which formed part of the bishops' estate, lies around the cathedral. Several interesting houses and mansions still remain.

▸ *Start from the north side of the cathedral. Cross Rue Frayssinous and enter the courtyard of the bishops' palace.*

Palais épiscopal

The courtyard of the bishops' palace offers the best **view** of the bell-tower of Notre-Dame. There is an interesting double staircase, which dates from the late 17C and was partially restored in the 19C.

Tour Corbières and Tour Raynalde

These two 15C towers are the vestiges of the walls and the 30 towers that once fortified the town.

▸ *Opposite the portal of the church of Sacré-Cœur, take the stairway leading to impasse Cambon.*

Hôtel Delauro

This 16C and 17C mansion, once a canon's residence, now belongs to an association – the Compagnons du Devoir – who restored it.

▸ *Return to Rue Frayssinous and carry on to Place de la Cité.*

Place de la Cité

At the east end stands the bronze statue of an illustrious local hero, Monseigneur Affre, Archbishop of Paris, who was killed on the barricades of Faubourg St-Antoine on 25 June 1848 whilst attempting to make peace.

Take rue de Bonald then rue de l'Embergue past beautiful old houses, antique shops and craft workshops. Between these two streets lies the **Espace public des Embergues**, an Italian-style square or piazza full of cafés and restaurants in summer.

▸ *Cross place de la Cité diagonally and follow Rue du Touat, until it intersects with Rue Bosc.*

Maison de Guitard dite Tour des Anglais

This 14C house (also known as the Tower of the English) features a massive fortified tower and fine gemel windows. The Guitards were rich bankers in the 14C.

Maison de Benoît

Place d'Estaing. A Gothic gallery runs along two sides of the courtyard (*private*) of this Renaissance house.

Maison Molinier

2 Rue Penavayre. This old 15C canon's house stands behind an enclosing wall surmounted by a gallery and two Gothic loggias (15C).

▶ *Carry on along Rue Penavayre and turn right.*

Chapelle des Jésuites

🕐 *Early Jul to mid-Sep: 10am-1pm, 2-7pm.*

This 17C Baroque chapel is now used as a conference and exhibition centre. Known as the "Chapelle Foch," because the future Maréchal Foch went to school at the *lycée* next to it, it contains a massive altarpiece and some fine **wooden galleries**★ decorated with frescoes of a more naturalistic style than would normally be expected in a Jesuit chapel.

▶ *Walk along Rue Louis-Blanc and round the handsome 18C mansion that now houses the Préfecture.*

Place du Bourg

This square, once the centre of the old town known as the Bourg, frequented by counts and merchants alike, is still a busy shopping area surrounded by pedestrian precincts lined with shops. There are some old houses on the square.

Maison de l'Annonciation

This 16C house is named after the low relief of the Annunciation on the corner turret.

Maison dite d'Armagnac

4 Place de l'Olmet. The façade of this fine 16C mansion is adorned with charming medallions depicting the counts and countesses of Rodez.

From place de l'Olmet, a 16C house that now houses a chemist's can be seen in rue d'Armagnac.

Église St-Amans

🕐 *Daily except Sun 8.30am-noon, 2-7pm.*

This church was built in the 12C, but the exterior was completely restored in the 18C. Inside, it has some of the original fine Romanesque capitals. The choir and the ambulatory are hung with 16C tapestries. In the baptismal chapel there is an unusual statue of the Trinity in polychrome stone.

The Town

From its site on a hill, Rodez offers numerous points of view of the surrounding countryside. The boulevards built on the line of the old ramparts render it possible to make a round tour of the town by car (*outside peak times*).

▶ *Leave from Place d'Armes and take Boulevard Estourmel.*

To the right, the remains of the ramparts (16C) and terraces of the bishops' palace lead to Corbières tower (14C).

Square Monteil

View of the Causse de Comtal and the Aubrac and Cantal mountains.

Square des Embergues

Views to the north and west of town (*viewing table*).

Square François-Fabié

Memorial to the local poet of this name. View of the Ségala region.

Additional Sights

Musée Fenaille★★

14 place Raynaldy. 🕐 ♿ *10am-noon, 2-6pm, Wed and Sat 1-7pm, Sun 2-6pm.* 🕐 *Closed Mon, 1 Jan, 1 May, 1 Nov, 25 Dec.* ⊛ *3€, no charge 1st Sun in month.* ☎ *05 65 73 84 30.*

The museum is housed partly in the oldest mansion in Rodez (the 13C façade was remodelled until the 18C) and partly in an adjacent modern building which blends harmoniously with its neighbour. Inside are the most extensive collections concerning the Rouergue region, each section displaying a time scale for easy reference.

In order to follow the exhibition's chronological order, start on the 3rd floor, in the modern building devoted to **prehistory**. Note in particular the **menhir-statues**★ from the south of the Aveyron (3 300-2 200 BC), the most famous being that of the "St Sernin Lady," a very fine 16C Virgin of the Annunciation.

The 2nd floor displays archaeological finds from the Gallo-Roman period; of particular interest is the glass case containing samples of Gaulish cursive writing (very rare in France). There is also a collection of ceramic ware from the Graufesenque pottery. A model shows the Gallo-Roman settlement on the Rodez spur, another one the city forum.

The visit continues in the old **mansion** ★★whose interior is enhanced by the collections and a glass roof. The Middle Ages are illustrated through daily life (fabrics, ceramics, weapons), religious life (pietas) and the cathedral (white-marble Romanesque crucifix).

The first floor, devoted to the Renaissance, houses a fine collection of statues (polychrome wooden Christ from Bonnecombe, oratory cross) and stone fragments (16C rood screen originally in the cathedral).

Musée Denys-Puech

&🕑👣 *Guided tours available (1hr30min) daily except Mon 10am-noon, 2-6pm, Sun and public holidays 2-6pm.* 🕑 *Closed 1 Jan, 1 May, 1 Nov, 25 Dec.* ⊙ *2.50€, no charge Fri and 1st Sunday in the month.* ☎ *05 65 77 89 60. Boulevard Denys-Puech.*

Founded in 1910 by the sculptor **Denys Puech** (1854-1942), born in the Aveyron, this museum contains both permanent collections of 19C and 20C art (works by Denys Puech and other artists from the Aveyron) and temporary exhibitions on contemporary art.

Since its renovation in 1989, the museum has displayed a monumental work by François Morellet entitled "Integration" on the two gable walls of the building.

◐◖ **Haras** – &🕑👣 *Jun- Aug: guided tour (1hr15min) Tue and Thur 10am.* 🕑 *Closed public holidays.* ⊙ *4€ (children under 10: no charge).* ☎ *05 65 75 76 77. Rue Eugène-Loup, via avenue Victor-Hugo.*

Kids Stud farm in a former 16C-17C Carthusian monastery.

◐◖ **Lacs du Lévézou**★ – *Office du tourisme de Pareloup-Lévézou, 34 Ave. de Rodez, 12290 Pont-De-Salars,* ☎ *05 65 46 89 90. 24km/15mi SE along N 88 and D 911 to Pont-de-Salars.* Three lakes set in open undulating countryside offer swimming and many water sports facilities as well as boat trips on **Lake Pareloup**★, the largest of the three lakes.

ROQUEFORT-SUR-SOULZON ★

POPULATION 679

MICHELIN LOCAL MAP 338: J-K7

The name of this market town, situated in the heart of the Parc naturel regional des Grands Causses, has become synonymous with one of the most famous and widely appreciated of French cheeses, succulent blue Roquefort. However, not a sign of Roquefort's main economic activity is to be seen in the town itself, for production of the cheese takes place underground. ⓘ *Ave. de Lauras, 12250 Roquefort-sur-Soulzon,* ☎ *05 65 58 56 00. www.roquefort.com.*

Roquefort-sur-Soulzon

P. Blot/MICHELIN

A Bit of History

A romantic legend – Legend has it that, one day, a shepherd and his sweetheart met in one of the Combalou caves; when they left, the shepherd forgot his bag containing a piece of rye bread and some ewe's cheese. A few days later he met his sweetheart in the same cave and found his bag with the bread and cheese still inside; however, the cheese was covered with greenish blue mould, its smell and taste were different but the two lovers found it delicious!

Roquefort cheese – Strict boundaries define the area of production of ewe's milk and the region of caves in which Roquefort cheese is matured. French law decrees that only ewe's milk cheese produced within these boundaries may be labelled "Roquefort." As an official label of origin (*appellation d'origine*), "Roquefort" is probably one of the oldest in France – since Roquefort is known to have been appreciated in Rome by Pliny and in Aix-la-Chapelle (Aachen) by Charlemagne. The cheese's official status was confirmed by decree on 22 October 1979.

The region of production of ewe's milk has progressively expanded north up to the Lot Valley, west to the Montagne Noire, and south and south-east beyond the Grands Causses into the mountains of the Hérault region and the foothills of the Cévennes. Roquefort cheese is made exclusively from full-fat, untreated ewe's milk, neither homogenised nor pasteurised, in dairies located where the milk is drawn.

In the dairies, the milk is first made into a cheese in which the curd has been mixed with a natural mould, *Penicillium roqueforti*, which comes from the caves at Combalou. The rounds of cheese are transported to Roquefort for maturation.

Sights

The Roquefort caves

Note: be sure to wear warm clothing, as the caves are maintained at a cool temperature.

Roquefort Société

🕐 Jul- Aug: 9.30am-6.30pm; Apr-Jun and Sep: 9am-noon, 1-6pm; mid-Apr to end Jun: 9.30am-noon, 1.30-5.30pm; Mid-Sep to early Nov: 9.30am-noon, 1.30-5.30pm (4.30pm early Nov to mid-Apr); Oct: 8.30-noon, 1.30-5pm. 🕐 Closed 1 Jan and 25 Dec. 🎫 3€ (under 16 years: no charge). ☎ 05 65 59 93 30.

Roquefort Papillon

🕐 Jul-Aug: 9.30am-7.30pm; Ap-Jun and Sep: 9.30am-12.30pm, 1.30-6.30pm; Oct-Mar: 9.30am-12.30pm, 1.30-5.30pm (last entrance 1 hr before closing). 🕐 Closed 1 Jan, 25 Dec. No charge. ☎ 05 65 58 50 08. www.roquefort-papillon.com.

Above the town of Roquefort, which lies at the foot of the cliff, is a little limestone plateau known as "Combalou," the north-east side of which collapsed when it slipped on its clay substratum. These special conditions gave rise to natural caves between the displaced rocks, in which temperature and humidity are constant and ideal for curing cheese, hence their attraction for the very first makers of Roquefort.

After the cheese has been made in the dairy, the rounds are set out in long rows on oak shelves in the specially adapted natural cellars. A gradual maturing process gets under way, carefully monitored by experts. Aided by the cold, damp air circulating from the *fleurines*, narrow natural chimneys at ground level, the *Penicillium roqueforti* mould grows, and the cheese takes on its characteristic blue-green veining. A minimum maturation of three months is necessary for a good Roquefort.

Farm Visits

See how ewes are milked, how and where the cheese is made before being taken to mature in the Roquefort cellars. Five sheep farmers offer farm visits followed by tastings, *(by reservation, Jun to mid-Sep, daily from 4pm).*

Martine Fabrèges, ☎ 05 65 62 76 19; **Alice Ricard**, ☎ 05 65 99 06 46; **Anne-Marie Gineste**, ☎ 05 65 62 53 22; **Isabelle Anglars**, ☎ 05 65 47 69 40; **Annie Bernat**, ☎ 05 65 99 51 53.

Musée archéologique

⚲ Closed temporarily. ☎ 05 65 59 91 95.

This museum displays objects found in excavations (pottery, bronze and copper utensils etc) which show that there were periods when the Roquefort and Causses regions were quite densely populated between the beginning of the Neolithic period and the Gallo-Roman era.

Rocher St-Pierre

Access via some steps from the Caves Société car park.

This rock (alt 650m/2 132ft) against the Combalou cliff offers a **view**★ (*viewing table*) as far as the Lévézou mountains to the left, over the Soulzon Valley and Tournemire cirque to the right, opposite to the tabular cliffs of the Causse du Larzac, and to the town of Roquefort at the foot of the cliff.

Sentier des Echelles

Allow 2hr 30min; some difficult sections (narrow passages, slippery ladders in rainy weather).

On the way out of the village (alt 630m/2 067ft), this path leads to the Combalou plateau (alt 791m/2 595ft), from which there is a **panoramic view**.

There are two more hiking trails around Roquefort: Sentier du Menhir *(3.5km/2.2mi)* and Sentier de Trompette (4km/2.5mi). For information, apply to the tourist office.

ST-ANTONIN-NOBLE-VAL★

POPULATION 1,887

MICHELIN LOCAL MAP 337: G-7

The town's houses, with virtually flat roofs covered in half-cylindrical tiles faded by the sun, are built in gentle tiers on the north bank of the river. ⓘ *Place de la Mairie, 82140 St-Antonin-Noble-Val, ☎ 05 63 30 63 47. www.saint-antonin-noble-val.com.*

A Bit of History

So delightful was the setting of the Gallo-Roman settlement, forerunner of the present town, that it was given the name "glorious valley" *(noble val)*. An oratory founded by St Antonin, who came to convert this part of the Rouergue, was replaced in the 8C by an abbey. The viscount of St-Antonin, Ramon Jordan, born in 1150, ranks among the most gifted troubadours of his age.

Town Walk

The town developed rapidly during the Middle Ages, due to trade in cloth, fur and leather, as can be seen by the 13C, 14C and 15C houses which were once the residences of wealthy merchants.

Ancien hôtel de ville★

This mansion was built in 1125 for a rich, newly ennobled townsman, Pons de Granholet, and is one of the oldest examples of civil architecture in France. In the 14C, it was the consuls' residence. Viollet-le-Duc restored it in the 19C, adding a square belfry crowned by a machicolated loggia in the Tuscan style, based on a project he presented in 1845.

The façade is composed of two storeys. The gallery of colonnettes on the first storey is decorated with two pillars bearing statues of King Solomon and **Adam and Eve**. The building now houses a museum accessed through the arcaded ground floor.

Museum

🕐 *Jul and Aug: daily except Tue 10am-1pm, 3-6pm; rest of the year: by request* ⊙ *2,29€.* ☎ *05 63 68 23 52.*

The museum contains prehistoric collections and is particularly rich in material from the Magdalenian Period. One room covers local traditions and folklore.

Rue Guilhem Peyre

This street leads off from beneath the belfry of the old town hall. It used to be the grand route taken by all processions. On the right there is what used to be the Royal Barracks, known as the "English Barracks," and in a bend in the road a splendid 13C-16C mansion.

▸   *Walk down the street towards Place de Payrols then turn right.*

Rue des Grandes Boucheries

The Maison du Roy, now a restaurant, situated on the corner of rue de l'Église, has five large pointed arches looking in at ground-floor level, and the same number of twin windows on the first floor, with youthful faces adorning the capitals.

▸   *Walk up Rue de l'Église towards the new town hall.*

Ancien Couvent des Génovéfains

Built in 1751, this convent of the Order of St Genevieve is now home to the town hall and the tourist office.

St-Antonin-Noble-Val

J. Boyer/MICHELIN

Address Book

For coin categories, see the Legend.

EATING OUT

Les Gorges de l'Aveyron – *Le Bugarel - 82800 Montricoux -* ☎ *05 63 24 50 50 - closed 3 Jan-3 Feb, 1-29 Mar, 2 Nov-2 Dec, Tue and Wed except id-Jul to mid-Sep.* Classic cuisine in a fine villa overlooking the Aveyron.

La Corniche – *82140 Brousses - 9 km SW of St-Antonin by D 115 -* ☎ *05 63 68 26 95 - closed early Nov-15 Apr, Sun evenings off-season and Wed.- - reservations suggested.* Situated near the gorges, this charming village house serves up tasty, authentic cishes. Lovely terrace overlooking the valley.

WHERE TO STAY

Chambre d'hôte La Résidence – *37 R. Droite -* ☎ *05 63 67 37 56 - info@ laresidence-france.com - - 6 rooms - meals .* British charm blends happily with the colors of the South of France in this lovely guesthouse run by a British couple.

SHOPPING

Les Conserves d'Autrefois – *Las Couchos - 12km N of St-Antonin by D 19 - 82160 Caylus –* ☎ *05 63 67 06 14 - www.ramond-fils.fr - lMon-Sat 9am-12.30pm, 2-7pm, Sun (Jul-Aug) 10am-12.30pm.* Fine preserved meats take centre stage at this establishment owned and operated by the Ramond family for four generations. Recipes of yesteryear are used in the fabrication of duck, poultry, and other meats. Tastefully decorated boutique and workshops (visit and tastings).

SPORT AND RECREATION

Planète grimpe – *Le Cayronnet - 82140 Servazac -* ☎ *05 63 30 66 66.* International climbing centre.

Festive events – Fête des Moissons (harvest festival) in July. Fête des Battages (threshing festival) in August.

▷ *Walk to Place de la Halle via Rue Saint-Angel and Place du Buoc.*

Croix de la Halle

In front of the solid pillars of the covered market, there is a strange lollipop-shaped 14C **Cross**, carved on both sides. This rare piece of work would once have stood at the entrance to or in the middle of the town graveyard.

Rue de la Pélisserie

There are 13C-14C houses redolent of the former wealth of master tanners and furriers all along this street.

▷ *Turn left onto Rue des Banhs.*

Rue Rive-Valat

A little canal spanned by bridges flows along this street; it is one of many tributaries of the River Bonnière which were dug during the Middle Ages to provide a main drainage system and water for the tanneries. These have open top floors, which are used to store and dry skins.

▷ *Rue Rive-Valat leads back to Place de la Halle via Rue Droite.*

Rue Droite

Two houses stand out because of their interesting carved keystones: the late-15C **Maison de l'Amour** (House of Love) where a man and woman are depicted chastely touching lips, and the Maison du Repentir (House of Repentance) where, in contrast, two faces are shown turned away from one another. About halfway along the street, there is a beautiful double-corbelled façade, decorated with half-timbering interspersed with slightly golden porous limestone and wooden mullions.

▷ *Walk left to Place des Capucins then along Rue du Pont-des-Vierges.*

Rue du Pont-des-Vierges

Close to place du Bessarel, an old walnut-oil press can be visited (*apply to the museum*).

Gorges de l'Aveyron★

Round trip of 49km/30mi – allow 3hrs.

▷ *Leave St-Antonin S, crossing the bridge over the Aveyron and turning right onto D 115 which runs alongside the river.*

After 2.5km/1.5mi turn left onto a steeply climbing, narrow road up to the top of the cliffs (*signposted "corniche"*). This picturesque **scenic route**★★ leads through the hamlet of Viel-Four with its pantiled roofs. Shortly after going through a tunnel

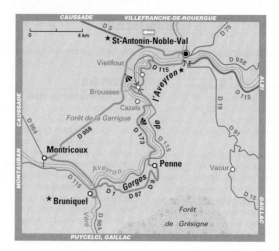

there is a viewpoint by the edge of the road, above a sheer drop, from which there is a marvellous view of the Aveyron cutting between tall rocky cliffs. As the road drops back towards the river, the picturesque hamlet of **Brousses** comes into sight.

▸ *At Cazals, cross the river and turn left.*

The road (D 173) begins to climb again immediately, heading through farming country, giving good views of the Aveyron's meanders and the valley floor covered with peach and apple orchards and fields divided by rows of poplar trees.

▸ *Cross back to the south bank of the Aveyron.*

Penne

This old village, overlooked by its castle ruins, occupies the most remarkable **site**★, perched on the tip of a bulbous rocky outcrop rising sheer from the south bank of the Aveyron and somewhat precariously overhanging the river on one of the prettiest reaches of its course. There are good views of the village from the roads approaching it from the north (D 33) and south (D 133). The intricate outline of the powerful medieval fortress with its jagged walls, in some cases poised on the very edge of the rock seemingly defying the laws of gravity, rises above the flat roofs of the village houses.

▸ *Park the car by the side of the road (D 9), at the entrance to the village.*

A narrow street leads to the church, where the belfry spanning a pointed arched gateway marks the entrance to the fortified village.

From the belfry, a pretty little street lined with old houses leads up to the castle, then down to Peyrière gate on the opposite side of the village. The 17C plague cross, harking back to a scourge that hit Penne on several occasions, marks the beginning of the steep footpath that leads up the rockface to the **castle** ruins.

The castle's site ensured it a leading role throughout the history of Quercy. At the time of the Albigensian Crusade, it became the stake in the bloody wars fought between the lord of Penne, rallying to the cause of the Cathar "heretics," and the followers of Simon de Montfort. Later, during the Hundred Years War, it passed back and forth several times between the hands of English and local troops. It finally fell into ruins in the 19C.

From the tip of the promontory, there is a good **view**★ of the towers and jagged walls of the castle, the village of Penne and the Aveyron Valley.

▸ *Leave Penne S on D 9.*

There are some excellent **views**★ of the village. The road scales the edge of the plateau before crossing a region of sparse vegetation in which stunted bushes are interspersed with a few vines.

Then it drops into the valley once more heading through a landscape of lofty wooded hillsides on which bare rock is frequently in evidence.

▸ *D 1E on the left leads to Bruniquel.*

Bruniquel★ – ◔ *See BRUNIQUEL.*

▸ *Cross the Aveyron and follow the road along the north bank to Montricoux.*

Montricoux

Montricoux is built on terraces above the north bank of the River Aveyron where it broadens out into a wide plain. The town's old curtain walls are still standing. Place Marcel-Lenoir and some of the streets contain picturesque medieval half-timbered houses with over-hanging upper floors (13C-16C).

Musée Marcel-Lenoir★ – ♿⏱ *Jul and Aug: 10am-12.30pm, 2.30-7pm; Apr-Jun 10am-12.30pm, 2.30-6pm.* ⊙ *5€.* ☎ *05 63 67 26 48. www.marcel-lenoir.fr.st.* Inside the château at Montricoux is an exhibition of most of the work of painter Marcel Lenoir, born in 1872 in Montauban. This local artist became one of the leading lights of the Montparnasse art scene in Paris after the First World War, admired by Giacometti, Braque and Matisse. However, he chose to marginalise his talent, alienating critics and refusing to adhere to any one style. As a result he failed to achieve the same degree of fame as his erstwhile admirers and ended his days in obscurity at Montricoux. His original and powerful work deserves to be rediscovered.

▶ *Take D 958 back to St-Antonin.*

This road runs through the forest of La Garrigue, giving glimpses of the Aveyron below and to the right. The final stretch before St-Antonin is once again a spectacular cliff road overlooking the river.

ST-BERTRAND-DE-COMMINGES★★

POPULATION 237

MICHELIN LOCAL MAP 343: B-6

ALSO SEE LE COMMINGES

St-Bertrand is one of the most picturesque villages in the foothills of the Pyrenees, perched on an isolated hilltop at the entrance to the upper valley of the River Garonne. It is encircled by ancient ramparts and dominated by an imposing cathedral; the belfry-porch of this sanctuary, crowned by a defensive wooden gallery, is a landmark visible for miles around.

Apart from its remarkable **site★★**, St-Bertrand is noted for the artistic and architectural treasure it contains, and for the charm of its steep, narrow streets crowded with medieval houses and artisans' workshops. In summer, in conjunction with nearby Valcabrère and St-Gaudens, the village holds a music festival.

Today St-Bertrand-de-Comminges, formerly a stopping place on the pilgrims' route to Santiago de Compostela, remains one of the most impressive sights on any journey through the Pyrenees.

A Bit of History

Memories of Herod – The town that preceded St-Bertrand enjoyed a distinguished Roman past as **Lugdunum Convenarum**, capital of the tribe of Convenae in the 1C BC; it is thought to have had between 5 and 10 000 inhabitants. The Jewish historian Flavius Josephus asserts that it was the place of exile of Herod, the Tetrarch of Galilee, and his wife Herodias, responsible for the decapitation of John the Baptist, four years after the death of Christ.

Ongoing **excavations** have unearthed two Roman bathhouses, the remains of a theatre, a temple probably consecrated to Rome and to Augustus, a 5C Christian basilica and a market place on one side of a large square flanked by porticoes.

Two Bertrands – The Roman colonial capital was eventually sacked by the Barbarians. Subsequently rebuilt on the hill only and enclosed within a wall, it was totally destroyed for a second time by the Burgundians in the 6C. For nearly 500 years after that the town stood empty and fell into decay.

Around 1120 the Bishop of Comminges, Bertrand de L'Îsle-Jourdain, appreciating the site of the old acropolis, had the ruins cleared and built a cathedral. To serve it he appointed a chapter of canons. The effects of the future St Bertrand's actions were felt almost immediately; the faithful flocked to the town that grew up around the church, and pilgrims broke their journey here. The town adopted the name of the man who had brought it back to life.

By the end of the 13C the cathedral founded by St Bertrand was no longer large enough for its congregation. A namesake, Bertrand de Got, who was himself destined to become Clement V, the first Avignon Pope, continued the bishop's work; the enlargement of the church was completed by his successors in 1352.

Cathédrale Ste-Marie★ *2hr*

🕐 *May-Sep: 9am-7pm; Feb to Apr and Oct: 10am-noon, 2-6pm; Jan, Nov and Dec: 10am-noon, 2-5pm. No visits Sun morning and public holidays (services). Guided tours available by appointment (cloisters, terraces and treasury).* ☎ *05 61 89 04 91.*

The Romanesque part of the cathedral comprises the west front crowned with an 18C belfry, the porch and the three western bays; the rest is Gothic. The tympanum (west door) is carved with an effigy of Bishop St Bertrand and an Adoration of the Magi.

Cloisters★★

The pervading sense of spiritual peace and retreat from the world distilled by the architectural setting is enhanced by the temporal poetry of the splendid mountain landscape visible through the arcades of the south gallery, open to the outside world.

One gallery is Romanesque (12C), the other three are Gothic; the gallery adjoining the church was altered in the 15C and 16C – it houses several sarcophagi. The capitals in the cloisters are exceptional for their carvings showing biblical scenes, foliage and scrolls. Note the celebrated pillar portraying the Evangelists Matthew, Mark, Luke and John (1), with its capital representing the signs of the zodiac for each of the seasons.

St-Bertrand-de-Commingues – Cathedral cloisters

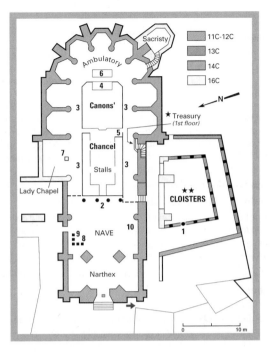

Trésor★

The treasury is located above the northern gallery (*access from inside the church*). The upper level chapel and the former chapter rooms contain 16C Tournai tapestries, episcopal ornaments, a mitre, two liturgical copes (the needlework on these vestments represents the Virgin Mary and the Passion), and the shaft of St Bertrand's crook, fashioned from the tusk of a narwhal whale. The copes, exquisitely embroidered in *broderie anglaise*, were the gift of Bertrand de Got on the occasion of the translation of Bishop St Bertrand's relics (1309).

Canons' Chancel

The chancel boasts the superb **woodwork**★★ commissioned from sculptors in Toulouse by Bishop Jean de Mauléon and inaugurated by him in 1535. The carvings include the rood screen (**2**), the choir screen (**3**), the high altar reredos (**4**) – unfortunately disfigured by painting – a bishop's throne (**5**) surmounted by a three-tiered pyramidal dome, and 66 **stalls**, 38 of them with tall backs and canopies. Piety, wit, satire – even lechery – are given free reign in the little world created by the craftsmen, the general theme of which is the Redemption.

St Bertrand's Tomb (**6**)

The tomb is a 15C stone-built tabernacle in the form of a shrine, covered in paintings depicting the miracles of St Bertrand; it supports an altar.

Lady Chapel

The chapel, a 16C addition on the northern side of the church, contains the marble tomb of Hugues de Chatillon (**7**), who completed the building in the 14C. The lierne and tierceron vaulting signify the end of the Gothic period.

Nave and narthex

Space for the congregation on the outer side of the rood screen is somewhat limited but this is compensated for in the richness of the furnishings: a 16C **organ**★ (recitals are given in season) (**8**); a 16C pulpit (**9**); the former parish altar (**10**), which dates from 1621. The altar frontispiece is made of Cordoba leather.

Excursions

Valcabrère★

2km/1mi N. The 11C-12C **Basilique St-Just**★ (◷ *Jul-Sep: 9am-9pm; May-Jun: 9am-noon, 2-7pm; Apr-Oct: 9am-noon, 2-6pm; rest of the year: weekends and school holidays 2-5pm.* ☎ *05 61 95 49 06 or 05 61 88 31 31)* stands isolated in the middle of fields, surrounded by its cypress-filled cemetery. The Romanesque basilica is one of the concert venues of the Comminges Music Festival. Note in particular the four column-statues decorating the north doorway. Most remarkable, however, is the **apse**★ with its "carved-out" decoration of triangular recesses. Inside, opposite the entrance, is Valeria Severa's 4C tombstone, all that remains of an important necropolis that once occupied the site. Fragments of sarcophagi incorporated in the walls, antique friezes (shields, helmets), all testify to the proximity of the Roman city.

Gouffre de Saoule (caves)

▷   *11km/6.6mi S via D 26A towards Luchon, then D 925 towards Sarp.*

The Vallée de l'Ourse contains a multitude of tiny villages scattered over the hillsides. From Sarp to Mauléon the road runs pleasantly alongside the river.

▷   *Cross the bridge in Mauléon, follow the road running parallel to the Ourse de Ferrère and leave the car near the beginning of the footpath leading to the cave.*

There is a natural bridge over the stream in a shady setting (*panoramic viewpoint*).

St-Gaudens

17km/10mi NE via D 26, D 33 and D 8.

The **Musée de St-Gaudens et du Comminges** (◷☀☛ *May-Aug: daily 9am-noon, 2-6pm; guided tour (30min) available;* ◷ *closed Sun, Mon, 8 and 21 May.* ⊗ *2.70€.* ☎ *05 61 89 05 42)* focuses on local history, folklore and customs, porcelain, religious art, and has an important mineral collection.

ST-FÉLIX-LAURAGAIS

POPULATION 1,301

MICHELIN LOCAL MAP 343: J-4

St-Félix in a pretty site★ **overlooking the Lauragais plain, passed into history (or legend, as some see it) when the Cathars held a council here to set up their church.** ▯ *Pl. Guillaume-de-Nogaret, 31540 St-Félix-Lauragais,* ☎ *05 62 18 96 99. www. revel-lauragais.com.*

A Bit of History

Déodat de Séverac – St-Félix prides itself on being the birthplace of this composer (1873-1921) of melodies evoking the beauty of nature and the countryside. Debussy said of De Séverac's music that "it smelt good." A pupil of Vincent d'Indy and Magnard at the Schola Cantorum in Paris, Déodat de Séverac was also profoundly influenced by Debussy's work. There are few composers who were able to draw so much inspiration from their native soil: *Song of the Earth, In the Languedoc* and *On Holiday (Le Chant de la Terre, En Languedoc, En Vacances)* are ranked by many as among the finest pieces of music written for the piano in the 20C.

Dyer's Woad – Known for its medicinal properties since ancient times, and still used today for fodder and as a source of nectar for honey bees, dyer's woad or Isatis tinctoria (*pastel* in French) is the plant traditionally used by dyers to obtain varying shades of blue dye.

Shades of blue

S. Sauvignier/MICHELIN

Mainly grown around the Mediterranean, dyer's wood was cultivated particularly intensively in the triangle formed by Albi, Toulouse and Carcassonne. The 14C marked the beginning of an astonishing boom in woad production and trade in the Albi area. Results were so successful that the cultivation of dyer's woad gradually spread farther south until it reached the Lauragais region.

In the 15C, a few wealthy inhabitants of Toulouse began growing dyer's woad more intensively on their estates. They built woad mills that ground up the leaves to obtain an almost homogeneous pulp. This was then divided into piles and left to ferment for two weeks, giving rise to the *cocagnes*, or rounded heaps of blue dye material. Four months' further treatment produced the finished dye ready for export.

> ⚖ *For coin categories, see the Legend.*
>
> **EATING OUT AND WHERE TO STAY**
>
> ⊖⊖ **Auberge des Remparts** –*31540 St-Julia* – ☎ *05 61 83 04 79 - closed Sun evening, Tue evening and Mon.* Two pleasant dining rooms, one done in shades of blue, the other more rustic. Menu changes daily depending on what's fresh at the market.
>
> ⊖⊖ **Auberge du Poids Public** – *R. St-Roch* - ☎ *05 62 18 85 00 - poisdpublic@wanadoo.fr – closed Jan, 25 Oct-1 Nov, Sun evening, Tue evening and Mon - 10 rooms -* ☷ *11€ - restaurant* ⊖⊖*.* Goods used to be weighed on the public scales in front of this house. Several rooms have a sweeping view of the countryside, as does the restaurant's panoramic terrace. The delicious food is also served in a rustic dining room.

Toulouse, which was a financial capital, became aware of the importance of its geographical location between the dyer's woad-growing areas and the Atlantic ports. The town's leading merchants first took control of local dye production, then of regional and European trade. This was the golden age of dyer's woad in the "Pays du Cocagne" which, despite a large number of cultural and economic initiatives, was only to last about 60 years. Decline was rapid, due to the Wars of Religion and the arrival on the scene of indigo (or dye from the "Indies").

Dyer's woad makes a comeback – There has been a revival of interest in dyer's woad in recent years as a result of various initiatives, mainly of a scientific nature, due to research conducted by the École nationale de Chimie (National College of Chemistry) in Toulouse, but also agricultural, with 60ha/148 acres given over to the cultivation once more of dyer's woad in the Lauragais area.

The cosmetics industry is being envisaged as a potential outlet, while the possibility of using woad as a blue dye for tapestry thread is under investigation.

Sights

Castle

There is a pleasant walkway round this castle, built in the 13C and later extended and remodelled, which affords fine views to the east over the Montagne Noire with Revel at its foot. To the north, the belfry of St-Julia and, high up, the castle of Montgey can be seen. Not without reason did the Revolutionaries rename St-Félix "Bellevue."

Church

This collegiate church dates from the 14C and was rebuilt at the beginning of the 17C. To the right of the church stands the sober façade of the chapter-house. Note the 18C painted-wood vaulting over the nave. The third chapel on the south side contains a fine 14C Virgin and Child in polychrome wood.

To the left of the church doorway, a well has been hollowed out of the wall. Legend has it that it is as deep as the bell-tower is high (42m/137ft). The bell-tower is in the Toulouse style: octagonal, with two tiers of openings with mitre arches.

Walk

Not far from the church a vaulted passageway leads to an area where there is a view to the west over peaceful countryside with hills and cypresses.

Dyer's Woad Country

80km/50mi – about 2hr.

This little area of Languedoc grew wealthy in the 16C from the cultivation of dyer's woad. Nowadays, the plain is given over to the cultivation of wheat, barley and rape seed, and stock raising (cattle, sheep and poultry). An offshoot of poultry rearing has been the installation of factories for food processing.

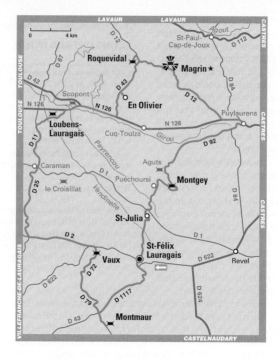

▶ *From St-Félix-Lauragais head N on D 67.*

St-Julia

An old fortified "free" town, with some ramparts and a church with an unusual bel-fry-wall.

▶ *Drive N to the intersection with D 1, turn left towards Montégut-Lauragais, then immediately left again towards Puéchoursi; go through the village and turn right.*

Montgey

High on a hill, this village has a big **castle** (⏰ *Park and terraces: 10am-6pm.* ☎ *05 63 75 75 81)*, an old medieval fortress that was captured by Simon de Montfort in 1211, then renovated in the 15C and 17C. From the terrace, there is a view over the Lauragais hills.

▶ *Drive W to Aguts along D 45 then N along D 92 to Puylaurens and turn left onto D 12 to Magrin.*

Magrin

This little village in the Tarn Valley is famous for its castle (12C-16C), which has housed the only museum on dyer's woad in France since 1982.
Perched on top of a hill, the Château de Magrin offers a splendid **panorama**★ of the Montagne Noire and the Pyrenees.

Château-musée du Pastel★ – ⏰💬 *Mid-Jul-Sep: guided tours (1hr30min) 3-6pm; Sun and public holidays 3-5.30pm; mid Jan-mid-Jul and Oct-mid-Nov: Sun and holidays 3-5.30pm, by appointment during the week.* ⮫ *6€ (children: 4,57€).* ☎ *05 63 70 63 82.*
The dyer's woad museum in the Château de Magrin contains a woad mill and drying rack and presents the various stages involved in making blue dye from dyer's woad, including the history of the *Isatis tinctoria* plant, traditional objects and documents and samples of woad at various stages during the manufacturing process. An audio-visual presentation completes the tour.
The **woad mill**, which comes from an old farm in the village of Algans, has been completely restored. It comprises an enormous, 2t granite millstone (1.40m×0.40m/ 4ft 6inx1ft 3in), a solid oak crossbeam resting on iron axles and two wooden drive shafts.
Do not miss the **woad-dryer**, of which only four of the original eight racks remain. On them the heaps of dried, fermented woad were piled, separated by wickerwork. Each rack can be used to store nearly 2t of woad.

▶ *Leave the Château de Magrin heading NW on D 12.*

Château de Roquevidal

🕐 ☕ *Mid-Jul to mid-Sep: guided tours (45min) Sun and public holidays 4-7pm.* 📧 *3.50€ (children: no charge).* ☎ *05 63 41 32 32.*

The body of the castle is flanked by four corner towers, one storey of each of which was removed during the years following the Edict of Nantes. The main façade shows the influence of the Renaissance.

▶ *On leaving the castle, take two right turnings to join D 43.*

En Olivier

This little hamlet is home to the **Musée Nostra Terra Occitana** (🔒 *currently closed; for information:* ☎ *05 63 75 72 95.),* devoted to agricultural tools and machinery. Various objects and family souvenirs adorn this reconstruction of the interior of a rural dwelling at the beginning of the 20C.

▶ *Go back to N 126 and head in the direction of Toulouse.*

Loubens-Lauragais

This charming village, bright with flowers in season, is tucked up against a **château** (🕐 *Jul: 1st and last Sunday 2.30-6.30pm; Aug: Thu, Sun and public holidays 2.30-8.30pm; early May to end Jun and early Sep to 11 Nov: Sun and public holidays 2.30-6.30pm.* 📧 *5€.* ☎ *05 61 83 12 08).* A tour round this follows the story of the Loubens family, which gave the French State a number of fine civil servants. In the 16C, Hugues de Loubens was a cardinal, prince, and sovereign of the Order of Malta. His brother Jacques rebuilt the castle at the end of the 16C.

The façade, with its two large protruding towers, looks out onto a peaceful park. Inside, there is a lovely Gothic library and a series of nine Flemish tapestries (16C).

▶ *Drive S along D 11 to Caraman, then follow D 25 towards Villefranche-de-Lauragais; 8km/5mi farther on, turn left on D 2.*

Vaux

This hilltop village has a Gothic church, which has retained its turreted belfry-wall (1551). The **château** (🕐 *May to end Oct: Sat-Sun 2.30-6pm;* 🕐 *closed public holidays (unless weekends);* 📧 *4€ (under 12 years: no charge);* ☎ *05 62 18 94 00)* is a Renaissance work (1550-60), as illustrated by the many mullion windows, some of them sculpted (southern façade), and the door surmounted by a triangular pediment and surrounded by vermiculated voussoirs (marked with fine, wavy lines said to resemble something "worm-eaten," thus "vermiculated").

▶ *Leave Vaux S on D 72 to Mourvilles-hautes then turn left onto D 79 to Montmaur.*

Château de Montmaur

Outside only open to the public. This castle was taken time and again by Simon de Montfort, in 1211 and 1212; pillaged by Protestants in 1577; and rebuilt and renovated in the 16C-17C. The main building is square, flanked by four round towers; the keep is in the middle. The main curtain wall has a door surmounted by a defensive oriel on the machicolations. Loopholes are visible on the towers and curtain walls; mullion windows were installed in the 16C.

▶ *Return to St-Félix-Lauragais.*

SAINT-GIRONS

POPULATION 6,254

MICHELIN LOCAL MAP 343: E-7

Situated at the confluence of three rivers, St-Girons soon became an important market town and the main administrative centre of the Couserans region, known locally as "18 valleys" country. Today, St-Girons is the ideal starting point for those who wish to explore an area of picturesque green valleys, mountain streams, waterfalls and lakes. 🛈 *Pl. Alphonse-Sentein, 09200 St-Girons,* ☎ *05 61 96 26 60. www.ville-st-girons.fr.*

"18 valleys" country – This region, just north of the "axial zone" or backbone of the Pyrenees was closely linked with the neighbouring district of Le Comminges in medieval times, even though it was independent enough to have its own bishop in

St-Lizier. "Couserans of the 18 valleys" corresponds geographically to the basin of the Upper Salat River, with St-Girons as the administrative seat. The relatively soft sedimentary rocks in this area, particularly schist, have been gashed by tributaries of the River Salat to form heavily indented mountain massifs separated by wide valleys. Luminous skies above a cool green landscape and abundant vegetation characterise this upland country, but life in the mountains is precarious and in the absence of industry, the region is being gradually depopulated.

The mountains along the border, marked by the pyramid-like silhouette of Mont Valier (alt 2 838m/9 314ft), visible from as far away as Toulouse, remain a favourite haunt for the sturdier and more determined hill-walkers and mountaineers (most of the recommended walks require at least 10hr).

The prehistoric painted caves of Vallée du Volp are closed to the public.

Le Couserans

Biros and Bethmale Valleys ①

Round trip from St-Girons. 78km/48mi – about 4hr.

▷ *Leave St-Girons SW along D 618 towards Luchon.*

The picturesque road follows the River Lez through a wide sunny valley dotted with attractive villages.

Audressein

This is a pleasant little village at the junction of the River Bouigane and River Lez. The pilgrims' **church** (mainly 14C), dedicated to Notre-Dame-de-Tramezaygues, is crowned by an openwork belfry. The central porch is decorated with 15C murals.

▷ *The route follows the Lez Valley upstream.*

Castillon-en-Couserans

This little village on the east bank of the Lez is built at the foot of a wooded hill. The 12C **Chapelle-St-Pierre**, in Parc du Calvaire, was fortified in the 16C.

Les Bordes

At the entrance to the village, next to a roadside cross, there is a scenic view of the oldest bridge in the Couserans area and the Romanesque church in Ourjout.

▷ *This marks the beginning of the Biros Valley.*

Vallée de Biros

Climbing up the valley of the River Lez, the road passes a number of tributary valleys on the south side, at the far end of which are glimpses of the mountains along the border: Mont Valier, at the top of Riberot Valley, and Mail de Bulard in the Vallée d'Orle.

Sentein

This village makes a good base camp for mountain climbing. The church with its fine three-storey belfry crowned with a spire is flanked by two square towers, all that remains of a curtain wall with a circumference of 200m/220yd.

⚡ Hiking enthusiasts and nature lovers could continue to the end of the valley, the road ending at Eylie.

▷ *Turn around and go back down the valley to Les Bordes. Turn right on D 17.*

Vallée de Bethmale★

The valley is wide open, its hilly slopes dappled with barns and, along the roadside, tightly clustered villages.

The village of Bethmale (which in 1990 had only 96 inhabitants) used to be known for the imposing bearing of its population and their distinctive dress – the traditional men's jackets, for example, were made of raw wool with multicoloured facings – a fact which continues to intrigue ethnologists and experts in folklore, for similar garments are a part of ceremonial peasant costume in the Balkans.

Clog-maker in the Bethmale Valley

A. Thuillier/MICHELIN

Address Book

For coin categories, see the Legend.

EATING OUT

Auberge du Gypaète Barbu – *09320 Biert - 15km/9mi E of Vic on D 3 and D 618 towards Tarascon - ☎ 05 61 04 89 92 – gypaete.barbu@free.fr – closed 20-30 Jun, 20-30 Sep, Dec, Sun evening and Mon except Jul -Aug.* The bearded vulture, an imposing bird from the loftiest mountain regions, has lent its name to this little inn near the village church. The bar, which opens onto the country-style dining room, is usually peopled by a handful of locals. Traditional and regional cooking.

L'Auberge d'Audressein – *09800 Audressein - 1km/0.6mi from Castillon-en-Couserans towards Luchon - ☎ 05 61 96 11 80 – aubergeaudressein@club-internet.fr - closed 10 Jan-4 Feb, Sun evening and Mon from 15 Sep-5 May except school vacations.* A refreshing stream flows at the foot of this stone house, an old 19C forge whose rustic dining room sports a veranda. Well-prepared, reasonably priced fare. Some pleasant rooms available.

Ferme-auberge Le Moulin Gourmand – *09800 Engomer - 8.5km/5mi SW of St-Girons on D 618 – ☎ 05 61 96 83 38 - closed 2 Sep-10 Jul , Mon and Tues – reservations required.* Learn how to make Brousse cheese during a morning visit to this family-run dairy farm on the banks of the Lez - it is used in the *ravioles au confit de canard* that you can order here. Sale of products from the farm.

WHERE TO STAY

Hôtel Eychenne – *8 Ave. Paul-Laffont – ☎ 05 61 04 04 50 - eychen@club-internet.fr - closed Dec-Jan, Sun evening and Mon Nov-Mar - P - 36 rooms - 8.50€ - restaurant* . A former coaching inn, this hotel has been run by the same family for several generations and is a veritable local institution. The bedrooms and dining room contribute to the pleasant, prosperous atmosphere. Inviting summer terrace facing the flower garden and pool.

Camping Le Coulédous – *09140 Aulus-les-Bains – ☎ 05 61 96 02 26 – couledous.matt@couledous.com – closed Jan and 17-30 Nov - 70 sites – food service.* Not far from town, this campsite is popular with spa guests who camp here during most of the year. The lush, green setting is its main attraction. Chalets for hire.

Camping La Bellongue – *09800 Augirein - 12km/7.5mi W of Castillon-en-Couserans on D 4 as far as Cescau then D 618 – ☎ 05 61 96 82 66 – earl@lavieenvert.com - open 15 May-15 Oct - - reservation recommended - 15 sites.* Situated along a burbling brook, this fairly basic yet appealing campsite is bright with flowers. The general decoration scheme and plantings give the site much charm. There are also two guest rooms in an old stone barn.

Maison de La Grande Ourse – *09800 Salsein - 3km/2mi W of Castillon-en-Couserans – ☎ 05 61 96 16 51 – open weekends in winter - - 3 rooms - meals* . Do a bit of stargazing before you fall asleep in this charming mountain house at the heart of a typical little village. Breakfasts and meals are served in the fine kitchen featuring a stone floor and furniture discovered in second-hand shops. We love it!

SIT BACK AND RELAX

Croustades Martine Crespo – *38 Rue Pierre Mazaud – ☎ 05 61 66 67 11 - www.croustade.com – Mon-Fri 9am-12.30pm, 3pm-7pm, Sat 8am-7.30pm, Sun 8am-1pm.* *La croustade du Couserans*, a dessert traditionally made for Gascon holiday meals, is the speciality of this old-fashioned boutique. Several flavours are available; they can also be made to order. You'll find quiches, tartes and preserves as well.

SHOPPING

Pascal Jusot – *Aret – 09800 Bethmale - ☎ 05 61 96 74 39 – daily from 9am (visit by appointment).* Traditional village clogs, gardening clogs and decorative objects are made by this artisan whose woodworking atelier is open year 'round. He is happy to share the secrets of his trade with interested visitors.

Le Moulin Gourmand – *3.5km/2.2mi NE of St-Girons - 09800 Engomer - ☎ 05 61 96 83 38 - open Mon-Sat 9am-noon, 2pm-6pm; daily in Jul-Aug.* Housed in a mill on the banks of the Eze, this cheese maker is one of the last of his kind to use only valley milk for his cheeses. Enjoyable visit of the maturing cellar. In July and August, Le Moulin becomes a restaurant.

RECREATION

Horizon Vertical – *Former SNCF station - ☎ 05 61 96 08 22 - www.horizonvertical.net – summer: 10am-12.30pm, 4-7pm - reservation required.* Cave exploring, canyoning, mountain biking, climbing, rambling, snowshoeing, adventure trails and sports-adventure holidays.

Aéro-club de l'Ariège – *Aérodrome de St-Girons-Antichan - ☎ 05 61 66 11 00*

Pyren'Aventure – *Moulis – ☎ 05 61 04 84 84 or 06 84 08 01 34.* Paragliding school.

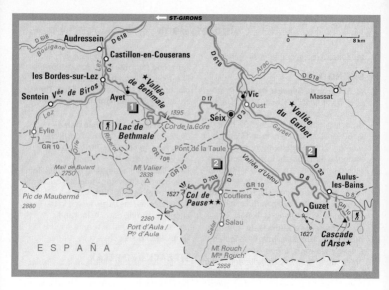

Ayet

The church, built on a raised site, contains examples of 18C "primitive" woodwork – note especially the Rococo openwork carving (*in poor condition*) in the baptistery chapel.

▷ *About 5km/3mi farther on, park by the roadside near a sharp bend to the left and walk into Bethmale Forest.*

Lac de Bethmale

15min on foot round trip. The lake sits in an attractive setting surrounded by beech trees.

🚶 The road climbs through a cirque of pastureland to Col de la Core (alt 1 395m/ 4 577ft) which looks back down over Bethmale Valley.

East of the pass is Esbints Valley, where the landscape is wooded and wilder. The secondary chain of Mont Valier massif can be seen to the south-west. The road goes back down past orchards and barns to the junction of the River Salat and River Garbet near Oust, the geographic centre of the Upper Salat region.

Seix

The village is overlooked by a 16C château.

Vic

The **church** here is typical of those in the Ariège *département*, with a wall-belfry and Romanesque triple apse. Inside, the 16C coffered and painted ceiling of the nave and aisles is echoed in the murals covering the vaulting above the chancel.

In the small square by the entrance, a wrought-iron cross, testimony to the skill of the Ariège blacksmiths, commemorates the fallen in the First and Second World Wars.

▷ *To return to St-Girons, turn left onto D 3 towards the Gorges de Ribaouto. Alternatively, you could continue your journey through the Upper Salat and Garbet valleys.*

Upper Salat and Garbet Valleys★

Round tour from Seix ②

78km/48mi – allow 1 day.

▷ *From Seix, drive S along D 3 which follows the Upper Salat upstream as far as Salau, quite close to the Spanish border. For 10km/6mi beyond Seix, the road runs alongside the river in a narrow, steep-sided valley; at the entrance to Couflens, branch off towards Col de Pause and Port d'Aula. The surface of this very steep, narrow road is poor and badly rutted over the final 3km/1.8mi (generally obstructed by snow from October to May).*

The little road climbs above the impressive, forested Vallée d'Angouls. Off to the south, through the gap carved out by the Salat, the summits of the valley's last cirque can be seen above Salau; the highest is Mont Rouch (alt 2 858m/9 377ft). The route continues beyond the strikingly situated village of Faup, perched on a rocky ledge, to the pass.

Col de Pause★★

Alt 1 527m/5 010ft. The road above the pass, on the right-hand slope beneath Pic de Fonta, offers a different **view** of Mont Valier on the far side of the Vallée d'Estours breach. The chasms gashing the east face of the summit and the ridges of its northern foothills are clearly visible.

▶ *Beyond Col de Pause, the steep and narrow road to Port d'Aula is in very poor condition. Return to Pont de la Taule and turn right on D 8.*

The road follows **Vallée d'Ustou**, climbs for a few miles, and then drops down again in a series of sharp bends to Aulus-les-Bains. There are fine views during the descent.

Guzet

This peaceful winter resort, with its chalets dotted among fir trees, stands in very picturesque surroundings in the Upper Ustou Valley.

Guzet-Neige ski area

Alt 1 100-2 100m/3 609-6 890ft. 28 Alpine ski runs of mixed difficulty, 4km/2.5mi of cross-country skiing tracks running through the forest, and a children's ski area with three specially adapted ski lifts.

Aulus-les-Bains

The sulphur, calcium and magnesium-containing mineral waters which rumble through Aulus are used to treat metabolic disorders and are particularly effective in the treatment of high cholesterol and urological disorders. The spa also has special health and physical fitness weeks. Aulus is a convenient starting point for excursions into the three upper valleys of the Garbet (the Fouillet, the Arse and the Upper Garbet), all of which abound in waterfalls and small lakes.

🔝 *Continue SE up Vallée du Garbet. After 1km/0.6mi, park the car and take the signposted GR 10 path, on the right (5km/3mi on foot).*

Cascade d'Arse★

After crossing the river and winding south, GR 10 leads to the foot of these superb falls which plunge 110m/360ft in three separate stages.

▶ *Return to Aulus and take D 32 N down the Garbet Valley.*

Vallée du Garbet★

This is one of those most regularly formed and best exposed valleys in the Upper Couserans. It is sunny and dotted with pretty hamlets often boasting thatched cottages with stepped gables. It was once known locally as *Terra Santa* (The Holy Land) on account of the large number of chapels and wayside shrines.

▶ *At the far end of the valley, the road goes through the village of Oust then on to Seix.*

Cascade d'Arse

A. Thuillier/MICHELIN

ST-GUILHEM-LE-DÉSERT★★

POPULATION 245

MICHELIN LOCAL MAP 339: G-6

ALSO SEE GANGES

This pretty little village is built around an old abbey, in a delightful site, at the mouth of untamed river gorges, where the Verdus flows into the Hérault. It owes much of the story of its origins to legend, related in the 12C chanson de geste by Guillaume d'Orange. ⓘ *2 R. de la Font-du-Portal, 34150 St-Guilhem-le-Désert,* ☎ *04 67 57 44 33.*

A Bit of History

Childhood friends – Guilhem, the maternal grandson of Charles Martel (famous for his successful intervention in the Saracen advance in the early 8C), was born in about 755. He was brought up with Pépin the Short's sons and was soon noted for his skilful handling of weapons, his intelligence and his piety. The young princes were very attached to him; his friendship with one of them, Charles, the future Charlemagne, was to last until his death.

In 768 Charlemagne came to the throne. Guilhem was one of his most valiant officers; he conquered Aquitaine and became its governor. Attempted Saracen invasions gave him the opportunity of winning further victories at Nîmes, Orange and Narbonne, and earned him the title of Prince of Orange. His final victory was in Barcelona. On his return to France, he was 48, and his wife, whom he had loved dearly, was dead. From this point on, the great warrior decided to dedicate himself to a quest for solitude. He delegated the government of Orange to his son and went to Paris to inform the king of his decision.

On one occasion, Guilhem, who was inspecting his estate in the Lodève region, discovered the Gellone Valley. This remote place struck him as ideal for a holy retreat. He had a monastery built there, in which he settled with some monks. After being recalled once more by Charlemagne, Guilhem finally took leave of his sovereign lord; Charles gave him the relic of the Cross, which was placed in the abbey church. Guilhem returned to his monastery. For another year, he busied himself with further work on the abbey, laying out gardens, building a water supply and improving access. Then turning his back on worldly things for good, the war hero retreated to his cell and spent the rest of his life in fasting and prayer until he died in 812. He is buried in the abbey church.

The abbey of St-Guilhem – After Guilhem's death, the monastery of Gellone became an important place of pilgrimage. Pilgrims came in great numbers to pray before the relic of the Cross and the tomb of St Guilhem. The abbey was also a recommended stopping place on the pilgrimage route to Santiago de Compostela. By the 12C and 13C, the monastery was home to more than 100 monks and the village of Gellone was renamed St-Guilhem-le-Désert.

...n-le-Désert

L. Campion/MICHELIN

Abbey Church★

All that remains of the abbey founded in 804 by Guilhem is the abbey church, which was built in the 11C and deconsecrated during the Revolution, when the monastic buildings were demolished and the sculptures in the cloisters dispersed throughout the region.

The large church doorway adorned with archivolts, which leads off a square shaded by a magnificent plane tree is surmounted by a 15C bell-tower. The colonnettes on the engaged doorposts and the inlaid medallions are Gallo-Roman fragments. This doorway leads into the narthex *(lo gimel),* in which the intersecting rib vaulting dates from the end of the 12C.

Chevet★

To see this, walk round the church to the left. From the alley lined with old houses, the rich decoration of the chevet can really be appreciated. Flanked by two apsidal chapels, it features three windows and a series of tiny arched openings separated by slender columns with curious capitals. The whole is embellished by a frieze of cog-tooth indentations echoing that of the doorway.

Interior

The 11C nave is austere in design. The oven-vaulted apse is decorated with seven great arches. On either side are niches in the walls, displaying on the left the reliquary of St Guilhem, complete with his bones, and on the right the fragment of the True Cross given by Charlemagne. This relic is carried in procession to the village square every year in May.

Beneath the sanctuary lies the **crypt**, which originally contained St Guilhem's tomb. It is a remnant of the original church.

The organ is the work of JP Cavaillé and was played for the first time in 1789. It is decorated with angel musicians.

Cloisters

Entrance through the door in the south arm of the transept. Only the north and west galleries on the ground floor remain of the two-storey cloisters. They are decorated with gemel windows in which the arches are supported on very crudely executed capitals.

Some of the sculptures and columns from the upper cloisters, which were bought by the collector George Grey Barnard in 1906, have made it possible to reconstruct an approximation of the cloisters in the famous Cloisters Museum in New York (& *see The Green Guide New York City).*

Museum – Mid-Jul to Aug: daily except Tue 11am-noon, 2.30-5.30pm, Thurs 3.30-5.30, Sun 2.30-5.30pm; Sep-mid-Jul: daily except Tue 2-5pm, Sun 2.30-5pm. 2€. 04 67 57 75 80. This contains sculpture work from the abbey and a photographic archive on the history of the abbey.

Note the early Christian (6C) grey-marble sarcophagus, said to have housed the remains of St Guilhem's sisters. The front shows Christ with the Apostles, the sides Adam and Eve being tempted by the serpent and the three young Hebrews in the fiery furnace, and the lid Daniel in the lions' den.

Another sarcophagus in white marble (4C) is said to be that of St Guilhem.

Village★

Narrow winding streets lead through St-Guilhem to place de la Liberté, the square onto which the abbey's west doorway opens. There are one or two fine medieval façades with twin or Gothic arched windows lining the square. More such residences are to be seen in the streets leading off from the west and north of the square (rue du Bout-du-Monde and rue du Font-du-Portal).

Viewpoint

At the foot of the village across D 4. At the bottom of a stairway immediately after the Hôtel Fonzes, there is a very unusual view of the Hérault flowing in a sunken channel between steep limestone banks pockmarked with numerous large rounded hollows.

Hiking Tour

Castle ruins

1hr there and back. From the church, take rue du Bout-du-Monde and follow the red and white markings of the long-distance footpath (GR).

▣ This footpath passes under one of the gates of the old curtain wall, then offers good views over the Cirque de l'Infernet.

▶ *After reaching the top of the ridge, leave the GR to follow the steep path to the right leading to the castle (great care is needed).*

From the ruins of this castle perched high up, there is a good **view**★ over St-Guilhem and the Verdus gorge.

Excursion

Grotte de Clamouse★★★

🕐☞☏ *Jul and Aug: guided tours (1hr) 10am-7pm; Jun and Sep: 10am-6pm; Feb-May and Oct: 10am-5pm; Nov-Jan: daily except Sat noon-5pm. ☞ 7.50€. ☏ 04 67 57 71 05; 1hr; temperature: 17°C/62.5°F.*

The Clamouse cave is hollowed out of the Causse du Sud Larzac, near where the gorge of the River Hérault opens onto the Aniane plain. It was explored in 1945, during an exceptional summer drought, and opened to tourists in 1964.

The cave takes its name from the resurgent spring which bubbles out below the road, cascading noisily into the Hérault after very heavy rain, amply justifying its dialect name of Clamouse ("howler"). However, there is a poignant popular legend according to which the origin of the name is a mother's cry of grief. The story goes that there was once a peasant family living in the Hérault gorge. The parents sent their eldest son up onto the causse to work as a shepherd. One day when the youth was visiting his family, he recognised to his surprise a carved stick he had thrown into a swallow-hole out on the causse. His mother had found it in the hole from which she regularly came to collect water, and they deduced it must have been carried along by an underground river. After this, the shepherd boy regularly sent things to his parents using this route. But one day, he was pulled into the swallow-hole by a more than usually vigorous sheep, and his poor mother saw the body of her son come floating down on the peaceful waters of the stream.

The guided tour leads through various natural galleries to the Gabriel Vila chamber, also called the sand chamber because of the layers of sand the river deposits on it each time it floods. At first the route leads through various caverns, following the old river bed, along which water still runs when the river is in spate. These initial galleries, in which the chiselled, jagged rock forms a ghostly backdrop, are a good illustration of the effects of the slow corrosive action of water on the easily dissolved dolomitic limestone of which the cave is made.

The next galleries contain two types of formation: the classic calcite stalagmites, stalactites, columns, discs and draperies, in some cases coloured by mineral deposits; and **delicate crystallisations**, relatively young formations (several thousand years old), sparkling white and much more rarely found in caves than the former: **crystalline "flowers"** of aragonite arranged in "bouquets"; showers of **tube-like formations** which sway in the slightest draught; weird and wonderful **eccentrics**; **crystalline dams** transforming subterranean lakes into beautiful jewellery caskets containing "**cave pearls**" (pisolites). The Couloir Blanc (White Corridor) and Cimetière (Graveyard) feature a particularly impressive number and variety of formations. At the exit of the Cimetière is a huge translucent white concretion made of several discs run together, known as the "Méduse" (jellyfish).

A man-made exit tunnel leads back to the open. There is a picturesque view of the Hérault Valley and an exhibition on life in prehistoric times at Clamouse.

Delicate Crystallisations

The Grotte de Clamouse is renowned for the great number and variety of delicate crystalline formations it features. Unlike the calcite formations usually found in caves, those at Clamouse are made of aragonite, calcite or a mixture of these two different forms of calcium carbonate crystallisation. Their clear white colour, another particularity, indicates that they contain hardly any impurities or mineral deposits.

The underground network at Clamouse provides a set of conditions well-suited to the development of such crystallisations: dolomitic rocks which lend themselves to the formation of aragonite; porous rock walls; plentiful supply of water; above average temperatures; and a permanent slight draught.

ST-JEAN-DU-GARD

POPULATION 2,563

MICHELIN LOCAL MAP 339: I-4

The narrow high street of this ancient town, lying on the banks of the Gardon, is lined with austere houses. An old humpback cutwater bridge spanning the river, which was partially destroyed by flooding in 1958, adds a picturesque note to the scenery. The clock tower dominates the old town. ▯ *Pl. Rabaut-St-Étienne, 30270 St-Jean-du-Gard, ☎ 04 66 85 32 11.*

Visit

Musée des Vallées cévenoles★

🕐 *Jul and Aug: 10am-7pm; Apr-Jun, Sep and Oct: 10am-12.30pm, 2-7pm; Nov-Mar: Tue and Thu 9am-noon, 2-6pm, Sun 2-6pm.* 🕐 *Closed 1 Jan and 25 Dec.* ☜ *4€. ☎ 04 66 85 10 48. www.museedescevennes.com.*

Housed in a 17C former inn, this museum illustrates local daily life and traditions through collections of objects, tools, documents, photographs…gathered by the town's inhabitants. There are agricultural tools used for tending cereals, vines, chestnut trees, for sheep and goat farming, for bee-keeping; traditional ways of carrying heavy burdens are also illustrated and the two main local activities (chestnut trees and silk worms) are particularly well represented.

Atlantide Parc

♿🕐🚻 *Jul and Aug: 10am-7pm (last admission 1hr before closing); Jun: 10am-noon, 2-6pm; Apr-May and Sep-Nov: daily except Mon 10am-noon, 2-6pm. Guided tours by request (1hr).* ☜ *5.50€ (children 4.50€). ☎ 04 66 85 40 53. Avenue de la Résistance, on the right bank of the Gardon.*

Kids Several aquariums present a variety of colourful tropical fauna. A foaming waterfall feeding the artificial river enhances the exotic atmosphere.

Excursions

Corniche des Cévennes★

58km/36mi from St-Jean-du-Gard to Florac – allow 2hr

▶ *Leave St-Jean NW along D 983 towards Moissac-Vallée-Française.* 👣 *This itinerary is described in the opposite direction under FLORAC.*

Route du col de l'Asclier★★

44km/27mi from St-Jean-du-Gard to Pont-d'Hérault – allow 1hr 30min.

▶ *Take extra care along the twisting narrow road, particularly between l'Estréchure and Col de l'Asclier; the pass is usually blocked by snow from December to March.*

This itinerary leads from the Gardon Valley to the Hérault Valley across a typical Cévennes ridge.

D 907 meanders up the Gardon Valley from St-Jean, following the river closely.

▶ *Just before l'Estréchure, turn left onto D 152 towards Col de l'Asclier.*

Beyond Milliérines, the landscape becomes wild; the road overlooks the valleys of several tributaries of St-Jean-Gardon, then runs round the Hierle ravine.

▶ *Turn left towards Col de l'Asclier.*

Col de l'Asclier★★

Alt 905m/2 969ft. The road runs beneath a bridge, part of the Margeride track (*draille*) used by flocks of sheep on their way to high pastures. From the pass there is a magnificent panoramic view to the west: in the forefront one can distinctly see the deep ravine of Notre-Dame-de-la-Rouvière; in the distance, the Pic d'Anjeau and Rochers de la Tude rise proudly to the left; beyond the Pic d'Anjeau, the limestone ridge of the Séranne mountain appears on the horizon; the Causse de Blandas extends to the right, towering over the Arre Valley; and more to the right still stands the imposing Massif de l'Aigoual.

Col de la Triballe

Alt 612m/2008ft. From the pass there is an extensive view of the Cévennes range; the village of St-Martial can be seen in the valley below.

The picturesque D 420 leads down into the Hérault Valley, with a few hamlets hanging onto the slopes on both sides.

▶ *Cross the River Hérault in Peyregrosse then turn left onto D 986 to Pont-d'Hérault.*

Abbaye de
ST-MARTIN-DU-CANIGOU★★

MICHELIN LOCAL MAP 344: F-7

ALSO SEE LE CANIGOU

2.5KM/1.5MI SOUTH OF VERNET-LES-BAINS

This abbey perched in its eagle's eyrie 1 055m/3 460ft above sea level is one of the prime sights to be seen in the area around Vernet-les-Bains. Guifred, Count of Cerdagne, great-grandson of Wilfred le Velu, founder of the Catalonian dynasty, chose Mont Canigou, a solitary place venerated by his people, to found a Benedictine monastery in 1001.

Access – *The abbey can be reached by Jeep from Vernet-les-Bains. Alternatively, park the car in Casteil and continue on foot.*
🚶 *Follow a steep road uphill – a little over 1hr there and back.*

Visit

Kids ⏱ 🔆 *Jun-Sep: guided tours (1hr) at 10am, 11am, noon, 2pm, 3pm, 4pm, 5pm, Sun and public holidays 10am, 12.30pm, 2pm, 3pm, 4pm, 5pm; Oct-May: daily except Tues 10am, 11am, 2pm, 3pm, 4pm, Sun and public holidays 10am, 12.30pm, 2pm, 3pm, 4pm.* 🕐 *Closed Jan.* 🎫 *4€ (children: 3€).* ☎ *04 68 05 50 03.*

Cloisters

At the beginning of the 20C, all that remained of the cloisters were three galleries with somewhat crude semicircular arcades. Restoration work included rebuilding a south gallery, overlooking the ravine using the marble capitals from an upper storey which was no longer extant.

Churches

The lower church (10C), dedicated to "Notre-Dame-sous-Terre" in accordance with an old Christian tradition, forms the crypt of the upper church (11C). The latter, consisting of three successive naves with parallel barrel vaults, conveys an impression of great age with

Abbaye St-Martin-du-Canigou

M. Buffard/MICHELIN

its rugged, simply carved capitals. A statue of St Gaudérique is a reminder that the abbey was long an important meeting place for Catalan peasants. A capital from the old cloisters has been used as the base for the high altar. Depicted on it are two scenes from the life of St Martin. On the north side of the choir stands a bell-tower crowned with a crenellated platform.

Near the church, two tombs have been hollowed out of the rock: the tomb of the founder, Count Guifred de Cerdagne, which he dug out with his own hands, and that of one of his wives.

Viewpoint

This walk will enable you to appreciate the originality of St-Martin's site.
🚶 *After reaching the abbey, take a stairway to the left (itinerary no 9) which climbs into the woods. Just past the water outlet turn right (30min on foot there and back).*
From here, there is an impressive view of the abbey, which lies in the shadow of Mont Canigou until late in the morning. Its **site**★★ dominating the Casteil and Vernet valleys is most striking.

Abbaye de ST-MICHEL-DE-CUXA★

MICHELIN LOCAL MAP 344: F-7

ALSO SEE LE CANIGOU

The elegant crenellated tower of the abbey of St-Michel-de-Cuxa rises from one of the valleys at the foot of Mont Canigou. After a series of misfortunes, the abbey is once again the seat of Catalan culture north of the Pyrenees. Every summer, it is the venue for the "Journées Romanes" and for the concerts of the Prades festival.

A Bit of History

There have been four successive churches in Cuxa. The last, which is the present church, was consecrated in 974. Founded under the protection of the counts of Cerdagne-Conflent, with St Michael as its patron saint, the abbey won renown largely due to Abbot Garin, a great traveller and man of action.

In the 11C, Abbot Oliba developed the great Catalan monasteries: Montserrat, Ripoli and St-Michel. He enlarged the chancel of the abbey church by adding a square ambulatory to it and chapels opening off it, built two bell-towers in the Lombard style and hollowed out the underground chapel of La Crèche.

After a long period of decline, the abbey of St-Michel was abandoned, then sold during the Revolution. Its works of art disappeared and the cloister galleries were dismantled. In 1907, the American sculptor George Grey Barnard found and bought over half of the original capitals. They were bought in 1925 by the New York Metropolitan Museum, which undertook the restoration of the cloisters by adding new elements carved in the same Pyrenean marble. Since 1938, the cloisters of St-Michel-de-Cuxa have stood in the midst of a park, on the hillside overlooking the Hudson Valley.

From 1952, considerable work has been undertaken in Cuxa: the abbey church has been restored and some of the cloister galleries have been put back in place. Since 1965, the abbey has been occupied by Benedictine monks subordinate to Montserrat.

Visit

Allow 45min. ○ ⌖ *May-Sep: guided tours (45 min) 9.30am-11.50am, 2-5pm, Sun and public holidays 2-5pm; Oct-Apr: 9.30am-11.50am, 2-6pm, Sun and public holidays 2-6pm.* ☜ *3.80€.* ☎ *04 68 96 15 35.*

First walk round the outside of the buildings to see the abbey church's fine Romanesque **bell-tower**★, with four tiers of twinned bays, surmounted by round windows and crenellations.

St-Michel-de-Cuxa

A. Cassaigne/MICHELIN

Crypt of the Vierge de la Crèche

Located at the centre of an underground sanctuary, which has managed to escape destruction or alterations since the 11C, this circular chapel has a vaulted ceiling supported by a single central pillar. Despite its lack of ornamentation, it exudes elegance.

Abbey church

The church has retained very little of its original appearance. It is entered through a doorway reconstructed from a single archway, the remains of a gallery put up in the 12C at the far end of the nave. The nave is one of the very rare surviving examples of pre-Romanesque art in France, exemplified here by the horseshoe or "Visigothic" arch which can be seen in part of the transept standing out against later construction. Covered once more by a timber-framed roof, the central nave ends in a rectangular apse. The pointed vaulting in the chancel dates from the 14C.

Cloisters★

These consist of arches and capitals found in Prades or in private ownership and recovered. The arches of the gallery adjacent to the church and those of most of the west gallery and the front of the east gallery have all been used to reconstruct almost half of the cloisters. The sculpture on the capitals (12C) is distinguished by the absence of any religious theme in the motifs; only the decoration itself seemed to matter to the artist.

In the west building (10C), the history of the abbey is retraced in an exhibition of documents, photographs and a model.

SAINT-PONS-DE-THOMIÈRES

POPULATION 2,287

MICHELIN LOCAL MAP 339: B-8

This pretty mountain town in the upper Jaur Valley, near the river's source, grew up around a Benedictine abbey founded in 936 by Count Raymond Pons of Toulouse.

Parc naturel régional du Haut-Languedoc

Maison du tourisme du Parc - Pl. du Foirail - 34220 Saint-Pons-de-Thomières - ☎ 04 67 97 06 65. www.saint-pons-tourisme.com. Tourist information, works on local plant life, accommodation, park discovery trails, practical guides to the park.

St-Pons is now the administrative centre for the Haut Languedoc Regional Nature Park; founded in 1973 to preserve the natural wealth of the region, the park comprises the Caroux-Espinouse massif, the Sidobre, part of the Montagne Noire and the Lacaune mountains. It injected new life into these breathtakingly beautiful, but isolated regions, which are too remote for any economically stimulating industrial development to be viable.

Parc naturel régional du Haut-Languedoc

Depending on the time of year, numerous sporting activities can be undertaken, such as canoeing on the Orb and the Agout, sailing on the lakes (Lac des Saints-Peyres, Lac de la Ravièje, Lac de Lauzas), rock climbing on the Caroux massif, speleology, hiking throughout the park, cross-country cycling, cross-country skiing etc.

Particularly interesting natural features include the Caroux, inhabited by wild sheep, the Mediterranean garden at Roquebrun and Devèze cave.

The tourist offices and "Maisons du Parc" have many suggestions for tours, walks and excursions.

> **HEAD FOR THE HILLS**
>
> 🍽 **Auberge du Cabaretou** – *34220 St-Pons - 10km/6mi N of St-Pons on D 907 - ☎ 04 67 97 02 31 - closed lunchtime 15 Jun-15 Sep, Sun evening, Tue evening and Wed 15 Sep-15 Jun - 29/36€.* While this former stagecoach inn at the top of a pass is fairly basic, the food served here is cooked in the traditional manner. The service is friendly and efficient and the alpine dining room with a wood-frame ceiling is comfortable. A few rooms are available.

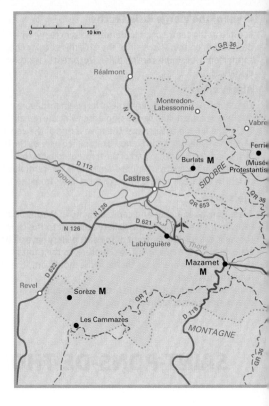

Source of the River Jaur

Access via the right bank of the river. The crenellated tower of the Comte de Pons, which formed part of the fortifications of the former bishopric, can be seen from the bridge over the Jaur. The Jaur springs up at the foot of a rock then flows peacefully on.

Ancienne cathédrale

🕐 ⚑ *Guided tours available, ask at the tourist office.* ☎ *04 67 97 06 65. Allow 30min.*

The old cathedral dates from the 12C, with modifications in the 15C, 16C and 18C. The north side retains some fortified features: two of the original four crenellated corner towers and a row of arrow slits above the windows. The richly sculpted doorway presents something of a puzzle in the shape of seven niches and four unidentified figures above the archivolt. The west front, where the main entrance used to be, has two sculpted tympana (unfortunately rather difficult to see) depicting the Last Supper and the Washing of Feet to the left, and the Crucifixion to the right (note the unusually tortuous position of the two thieves). The strikingly spacious interior has undergone numerous modifications. The choir stalls date from the 17C, whereas the cathedra is 19C. The chancel is closed off by a railing and contains numerous sculpted marble decorations. The organ dates from the 18C.

Musée de Préhistoire régionale

🕐 *Late Mar-mid Jun: Wed, Sat and Sun 10am-noon, 2.30-6pm; mid Jun-mid-Sep: daily except weekends 10am-noon, 2.30-5.30.* ⚐ *3.05€.* ☎ *04 67 97 12 56.*

The museum contains objects discovered on archaeological digs in caves in the region (particularly that at Camprafaud).

Excursions

Grotte de la Devèze★

🕐 ⚑ *Jul-Aug: guided tour (1hr) 10am-6pm; Apr-Jun and Sep: 2-5pm; Oct-Mar: Sun 2-5pm.* 🕐 *Closed Jan.* ⚐ *6€ (children: 3€; under 7: no charge); ticket combined with the museum.* ☎ *04 67 97 03 24. 5km/3mi W along N 112, beneath Courniou station.*

This cave was discovered in 1886 when a tunnel was being drilled through Devèze mountain to carry the Bédarieux-Castres railway line and explored in 1893 by a team including Louis Armand, Martel's faithful assistant. From 1928 to 1930, it was explored

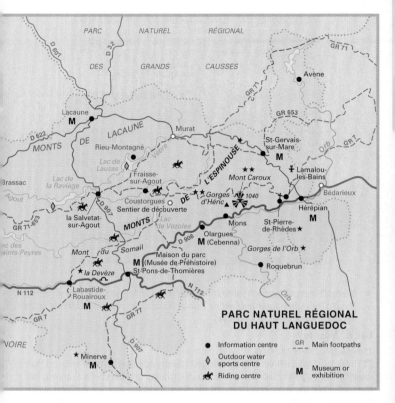

in more detail by Georges-Milhaud and his team and, in 1932, part of the cave was opened to visitors. It lies beneath the railway station at Courniou and is a trace of the old course of the Salesse, a tributary of the Jaur.

🚶 A waymarked path (*yellow markings*) starting near the entrance to the cave leads (*1hr 15min*) to seven capitelles, drystone shepherd huts.

Tour of the cave – *allow 1hr; temperature: 12°C/54°F.*
The tour begins on the middle level, from where there is a view of some fine mineral draperies of various shapes and colours. All along the cave walls are slender, white concretions forming delightful bouquets of aragonite flowers. At the end of the chamber is a large petrified fall dropping down onto the lower level.

In the middle of a pile of boulders resulting from a rockfall are a number of rocks of varying shapes and forms, the most impressive of which is a huge stalagmite known as the "Cenotaph" or "Bridal Cake," an architectural structure on a pedestal beneath a roof covered with tubular shapes and draperies.

The upper chamber, 60m/195ft above (*access via a flight of steps*), is full of eccentrics, draperies and discs.

The tour ends in the Georges-Milhaud chamber, which is dotted with dazzling white crystallisations.

Musée français de la Spéléologie – This museum houses collections of documents and items related to cave exploration and famous French speleologists: Édouard-Alfred Martel, Robert de Joly, Norbert Casteret, Guy de Lavaur de la Boisse etc. Displays also concern paleontology, the protection of the underground environment and cave fauna.

Le Somail

76km/47mi round tour – allow 2hr.

The Somail is the most fertile part of the Espinouse uplands. It is an area of rolling hills covered with chestnut or beech groves and carpeted with heather that takes on russet tones in the autumn.

▶ Leave St-Pons via D 907, the Salvetat-sur-Agout road.

The road winds picturesquely uphill, providing some fine views of St-Pons and the Jaur Valley before reaching the Col de Cabaretou.

▷ *Beyond the pass, turn right onto D 169 that crosses the Somail plateau. A narrow road to the right signposted Saut de Vésoles leads to the shores of a lake set in the middle of woodland (parking area).*

Lac de Vésoles

15min on foot there and back.

🔲 The Bureau, which flows through rugged countryside, used to form an impressive waterfall with a 200m/650ft drop over gigantic granite boulders before running into the Jaur. Since the building of the hydroelectric dam that supplies the Riols power station, the waterfall has lost some of its vigour but the beauty spot has remained as impressive as ever.

▷ *Return to D 169 and head back to Fraisse-sur-Agout.*

The road crosses some superb heather-clad moorland and the Col de la Bane (alt 1 003m/3 260ft).

Prat d'Alaric

🕐➴ *Jul and Aug: guided tour (2hr) Thu 10am. Departs from tourist office of Monts de l'Espinouse in Fraisse-sur-Agout.* ☎ *04 67 97 38 22.*

This typical Espinouse farmstead has been renovated by the Haut-Languedoc regional park authority and is now used as a visitor centre (*maison du pays*). Near the farmhouse stands the long, low barn that is so characteristic of local architectural style. Its steeply sloping roof runs down onto side walls that are less than 2m/6ft 7in in height. The building is unusual in that the rafters do not include any crossbeams. The house is roofed with broom laid across rafters that cut across each other at the ridge and are supported by the side walls.

The peaceful village of **Fraisse-sur-Agout** is famous for its angling. It gets its name from its tall ash trees.

▷ *From the village, either head for the Col de Fontfroide and the tour through the Espinouse uplands or continue to La Salvetat.*

On the outskirts of the village *(heading towards La Salvetat)*, there is another house with a broom roof, at the junction of the road to Le Cambaissy.

La Salvetat-sur-Agout

This is a summer holiday resort perched on a rocky promontory high above the confluence of the River Vèbre and River Agout. Its name is a reminder of the days (11C and 12C) when prelates, abbots, and commanders of the Knights Templar founded "new towns" on their lands to increase their value. The "guests" arriving in these new towns (or *sauvetés*) were given a house and a plot of land. Later, for economic and military reasons, the ecclesiastical authorities and noblemen set up hilltop villages known as bastides.

HIKING

Les Randonnées des Signoles – *34330 Fraisse-sur-Agout* - ☎ *04 67 97 63 61* – *www.signoles.com* - *42€ per day*. Hire a donkey and set off on an expedition along the Somail.

The **water-bottling factory** (&.☉ Mid-Jun to mid-Sep: guided tour appointment Tue, Wed and Fri 2pm and 3pm. ☉ Closed public holidays. No charge. ☎ 04 67 97 64 44.) at La Salvetat is open for visits.

▷ *From La Salvetat, there is a road running right round the Lac de la Raviège.*

Lac de la Raviège

Not far from La Salvetat on the shores of this vast reservoir covering an area of 450ha/1 112 acres, there is a beach named Les Bouldouïres (swimming, water sports, water-skiing, sailing etc). The road crosses the dam and runs along the right bank of the reservoir, returning via the left bank. The shores are wooded and there are very few views of the lake.

▷ *From La Salvetat, return to St-Pons via D 907.*

Fort de SALSES★★

MICHELIN LOCAL MAP 344: I-5

ALSO SEE LES CORBIÈRES

16KM/10MI N OF PERPIGNAN

Rising above the surrounding vineyards, this half-buried fortress is surprisingly big. The colour of the brickwork, bronzed by the sun, blends harmoniously with the golden sheen of the stonework, mainly of pink sandstone.

Salses fortress was built in the 15C, on the Roman road from Narbonne to Spain, known as the Via Domitia, at the strategic point where the waters of coastal lagoons are almost lapping at the foot of the Corbières mountains. It is a unique example in France of Spanish medieval military architecture adapted by Vauban in the 17C to meet the demands of modern artillery.

A Bit of History

Hannibal's passage – In 218 BC, Hannibal made plans to cross Gaul and invade Italy. Legend has it that after following the same route as Hercules, he had to cross the Perthus Pass, then the threshold of Salses which links Roussillon to the plains of Bas Languedoc. Rome immediately sent five venerable senators, as emissaries, to ask the Gauls to resist the Carthaginians' advance. There was uproar among the Gauls, who were incensed that they should be expected to wage war on their own soil in order to prevent fighting in Italy. Therefore, Hannibal was allowed through as "a guest." The Romans remembered this episode with bitterness. When they occupied Gaul, they built a camp at Salses and linked it by the Via Domitia to the Perthus Pass.

A Spanish fortress – After Roussillon had been restored to Spain in 1493, Ferdinand of Aragón gathered his troops in the province and in 1497 had this fortress built in record time by his gunner-engineer Ramirez. The stronghold was designed to house a garrison of 1 500 men and to withstand attack by newly evolving artillery.

When Richelieu undertook to reconquer Roussillon, Salses became the focus of a bitter struggle. The French seized the fort in July 1639, but lost it again in January 1640.

Finally, it was decided to attack from land and sea simultaneously; Maillé-Brézé was at the head of the fleet. The governor of Salses, learning of the fall of Perpignan, resigned himself to surrendering with full battle honours.

At the end of September 1642, the garrison returned to Spain.

In 1691, Vauban made some improvements and ordered the demolition of superstructures that were decorative rather than useful as a defence. However the line of fortifications between France and Spain was determined from then on by the new "natural" frontier of the Pyrenees, bringing the military role of the Fort de Salses to an end.

👛 *For coin categories, see the Legend.*

VINEYARD DINING

🍽🍷 **Auberge de Vespeille** – *Au Mas Vespeille - 66600 Salses-le-Château - 11km/7mi W of Salses, towards Opoul then Rivesaltes and B-road - ☎ 04 68 64 19 51 - closed weekdays except in summer - reservation recommended.* The wine-growers at this mas abandon their grapes to prepare a hearty local meal of meat grilled over vine stock and the delicious parillade catalane. Food, served in the castle's old sheepfold, is accompanied by home-produced Côtes-du-Roussillon.

Fort de Salses

Visit *1hr*

Jun-Sep: 9.30am-7pm (last departure 1hr before closing); Oct-May: 10am-12.15pm, 2-5pm. Guided tours available for large groups upon request (45min). Closed 1 Jan, 1 May, 1 and 11 Nov, 25 Dec. *6.10€ (under 18s: no charge), no charge 1st Sunday in the month (Oct-Mar).* 04 68 38 60 13.

Kids The fortress has an oblong ground plan and is laid out around a central courtyard – the old parade ground. This is reached through a redoubt, a demilune outwork and three drawbridges.

The visit starts on the upper parts of the **curtain wall**. Various cunning devices are in evidence, such as the rounded top of the curtain walls, an unusual feature added in the 15C and designed to make cannon-balls ricochet off and to discourage climbers, and the polygonal layout of the counterscarp (wall on the outside of the moat), which enabled those being besieged to make their shots ricochet into the corners. The scarp (wall on the inside of the moat) averages 9m/29ft in thickness.

The buildings inside the curtain wall were used as a barracks and a blockhouse. The vaulted basement around the central courtyard housed the stables (about 300 horses), above which ran large vaulted galleries to protect against fire and missiles; one of these, in the east wing, was used as a chapel.

The **redoubt** in the keep is then reached; it is separated from the central courtyard by an interior moat and a high wall with a spur. In it were located the cowshed, the bakery and, adjacent to it, a building where water could be stored.

The **keep** itself is divided into five storeys alternately with ceilings or vaulting. Originally designed as the governor's residence, it was used as a powder magazine in the 19C. Zigzag passages, designed so as to be protected by the gunfire of the look-outs, and drawbridges for foot soldiers only were its ultimate defences.

Causse de SAUVETERRE

MICHELIN LOCAL MAP 330: H-8 TO I-8

Bordered to the north by the River Lot, this is the most northerly and least arid of the Grands Causses. Its western section (SW of D 998) has vast stretches of woodland and fairly steep hills.

Local people have taken advantage of even the slightest hollow; there is not a single plot of arable land that has not been carefully cultivated, with the result that the countryside is dotted with bright patches of red or green depending on the season.

This causse owes it name to the picturesque village of Sauveterre situated on its eastern edge, which has retained its drystone houses roofed with limestone slabs known locally as tioulassés, as well as some fine examples of roofs with dormer windows, old shepherds' huts with vaulted roofs, and an old village oven in perfect working order.

Excursion

Round trip of 66km/41mi – allow 5hr.

La Canourgue

Leave the car in the parking area located on the other side of D 998.

Narrow canals carry water from the River Urugne through this ancient city overlooked by an imposing clock tower. The former collegiate church built in Provençal style between the 12C and the 14C is surrounded by old corbelled houses straddling canals.

▷ *Leave La Canourgue along D 998 towards Ste-Énimie and, after 2km/1.2mi, turn right onto D 46; 1.8km/1.1mi further on, leave the car on the left near the Sabot de Malepeyre.*

Sabot de Malepeyre★

This enormous clog-shaped (*sabot*) rock, 30m/98ft tall, also known as the *pont naturel* (natural bridge) *de Malepeyre* was formed by the erosive action of the water which once flowed on the surface of the *causse*. There is a huge opening right the way through it beneath a basket-handle arch. You can go through the arch, which is 3m/10ft high and 10m/33ft wide. From the terrace on which the heel of the "clog" rests there is a lovely view of the Urugne Valley with the Aubrac mountains in the distance.

▷ *Continue and turn left onto D 43 which joins up with D 32; turn left again, drive on to D 998 and turn right. 6km/3.7mi further on, turn left towards Roussac and Sauveterre.*

Champerboux

Picturesque hamlet with typical causses houses.

▷ *Follow D 44 left.*

The road to Chanac is lined with drystone shepherds' huts.

Chanac

The old keep is proudly camped at the top of the village (*from the tourist office, follow the signpost to "La Tour"*). Note the clock tower in place du Plö (*market on Thursdays*). The Église St-Jean-Baptiste in the lower part of the village houses a 17C gilt-wood altarpiece surmounted by a baldaquin.

▷ *Cross the River Lot and turn left onto N 88.*

Le Villard

This charming village overlooking the Lot Valley was once guarded by a fortress built in the 14C to protect the inhabit-

Le Villard

A. Thuillier/MICHELIN

ants from roaming bands of robbers. All that remains today are the **guard-house**, which houses an exhibition on prehistory in the Lozère region, and the turreted Renaissance building facing the church. From the esplanade, there is a fine view of the valley.

Domaine médieval des Champs – ⏰ *Mid-Jul to end Aug: 11am-7pm; mid-Apr to mid-Jul and Sep to Oct: by request 7€. Workshops and meals on request. Vehicles prohibited: car park 200m below (not many places)* ☎ *04 66 48 25 00.* This group of fine traditional buildings has been brought back to life by volunteers dressed in period costumes. Workshops illustrate traditional activities and crafts, thus helping to recreate daily life between the 5C and the 15C.

▶ *The road follows the River Lot southwards. Cross over to reach Banassac.*

Banassac

Housed in the town hall, the **Musée archéologique** (♿⏰ *Daily except Sat-Sun and public holidays 8am-noon, 2-6pm, Wed 8am-noon. No charge.* ☎ *04 66 32 82 10.)* displays sigillated pottery, sought after all over Europe between the 1C and 3C AD. Later on, between the 5C and the 9C, four workshops, supplied by local silver mines, minted one tenth of all the coins used throughout the kingdom.

Prieuré de SERRABONE★★

MICHELIN LOCAL MAP 344: G-7

The steep, winding road up to Serrabone in the rather bleak part of Roussillon known as Les Aspres, does not at any stage give so much as a glimpse of the splendid Romanesque priory which lies at the end of it.

Visit *allow 30min*

⏰ *10am-6pm (last admission 30min before closing).* ⏰ *Closed 1 Jan, 1 May, 1 Nov, 25 Dec.* 🎟 *3€ (children: 2€).* ☎ *04 68 84 09 30. www.cg66.fr.*

🧒 The exterior of the priory has an impressive, if somewhat forbidding, appearance with its rugged architectural style and dark schist stonework. The building is modest, with no frivolity – probably to blend in better with the severity of its surroundings, so it is all the more surprising therefore to discover that the interior features a wealth of sculpted ornamentation.

Tribune

B. Kaufmann/MICHELIN

▶ *Entrance to the church is through the south gallery.*

South gallery★

12C. Overlooking the ravine, the gallery was used as a covered walkway by Augustinian canons. The carved capitals show traces of oriental influence, as is usual with Romanesque sculpture in Roussillon. There is a significant difference, artistically, between the interior capitals, which do not differ much from those of the tribune, and the exterior capitals in low relief, which are indisputably the work of less accomplished craftsmen.

Church

The nave dates from the 11C, the chancel, transept and the north side aisle are 12C. The church contains a pink-marble **tribune**★★ with impressively rich ornamentation. The 10 columns and two oblong pillars supporting the six intersecting ribs are adorned with capitals representing, in a stylised manner, rampant animals: eagles, griffons, floral motifs, angels and above all lions – which feature in every carving, since the role played by these beasts in the Bible, mythology and fables was so great. The most remarkable decoration is to be found in the delicate ornamentation of the three archivolts, incised in the marble, and the corner stones adorned with flowers, as if they were embroidered onto the stone.

SÈTE ★

POPULATION 66,177

MICHELIN LOCAL MAP 339: H-8

Sète was built on the slopes and at the foot of Mont St-Clair, a limestone outcrop 175m/541ft high, on the edge of the Thau lagoon. Once an island, it is linked to the mainland by two narrow sand spits. The new town, east and north-east of Mont St-Clair, runs right up to the sea itself and is divided up by several canals. A fine sandy **beach** stretches over 15km/9mi west from Sète as far as Cap d'Agde.

🛈 *60 Grand'Rue Mario-Roustan, 34200 Sète, ☎ 04 67 74 71 71. www.ville-sete.fr. Guided tours of the town organised by the Sète tourist office cover the themes of "Façades and canals," "Old Sète" and "The auction fish market." ☎ 04 67 74 71 71. www.ot-sete.fr.*

Sète is the scene of the famous *joutes nautiques*, joust tournaments particularly well attended on the day of St-Louis in August.

- ▶ **Orient Yourself:** The main strolling and shopping streets are found on the east side of the "island," beaches to the west.
- 🅿 **Parking:** You'll find lots near the canal fringing Sete on the east.
- 👁 **Don't Miss:** The trip up Mont St-Clair, for memorable views of the surrounding area.
- 🕐 **Organising Your Time:** Stroll about the town before heading up to Mont St-Clair. If your time allows, head for the beach or take a cruise of the lagoon or the harbor area.
- 👣 **Also See:** Sète is one of the principal bases for excursions to the Thau lagoon.

A Bit of History

Birthplace of poets – **Paul Valéry** (1871-1945) wrote to Sète town council, which had congratulated him on his election to the Académie Française, "It seems to me that all my work reflects my roots." In *Charmes*, published in 1922, the poet celebrated the marine cemetery where he was to be buried in July 1945. At the foot of this peaceful setting, the sea can be seen spreading away to the horizon like a vast flat roof. This is the first stanza of the poem, in the Cecil Day Lewis translation:

> *This quiet roof, where dove-sails saunter by*
> *Between the pines, the tombs, throbs visibly.*
> *Impartial noon patterns the sea in flame -*
> *That sea for ever starting and re-starting -*
> *When thought has had its hour, oh how rewarding*
> *Are the long vistas of celestial calm!*

Another famous native of Sète, the singer-songwriter **Georges Brassens** (1921-81) sang about his place of birth in his *Supplique pour être enterré à la plage de Sète (Request to be buried on Sète beach)*.

canal

D. Pazery/MICHELIN

Address Book

🜚 *For coin categories, see the Legend.*

EATING OUT

🍴🍴 **La Huchette** – *82 Grand'Rue Mario-Roustan - ☎ 04 67 74 40 24 - closed lunchtime and Sun except Jul-Aug.* Night-owls and theatregoers are partial to this little bistro open from 9pm to 1am where you can nibble on a few tapas or try the bourride, a house speciality. Friendly atmosphere within a wine cellar decor.

🍴🍴 **The Marcel** – *5 R. Lazare-Carnot – ☎ 04 67 74 20 89 - closed Christmas week, Sat lunchtime and Sun.* Much appreciated by local residents, this restaurant in a quiet street in the old part of Sète is a pleasant place to meet. The eclectic decor happily blends Art Deco with velvet armchairs, bistro furniture etc,; it is also used as an art gallery by local painters. Regional dishes, among others.

🍴🍴 **Le Jas d'Or** – *2 Bd. Victor-Hugo - 34110 Frontignan - ☎ 04 67 43 07 57 - closed Tue evening and Wed off-season, Monday lunchtime Jul-Aug.* Exaggeration is the order of the day here: colorfully-designed plates, high-sounding names and elaborate cuisine. This former *chai* welcomes a devoted slate of regular clients to its intimate dining room decorated with rustic stonework.

🍴 **Palangrotte** – *Rampe Paul-Valéry, quai Marine - ☎ 04 67 74 80 35 - kiefferbern@wanadoo.fr - closed Sun evening and Mon Jul-Aug.* This Marine restaurant offers seafood specialties in its softly-colored dining room.

WHERE TO STAY

🛏️🛏️ **Grand Hôtel** – *17 quai du Mar.-de-Lattre-de-Tassigny - ☎ 04 67 74 71 77 - info@sete-hotel.com - closed 18 Dec-2 Jan - 43 rooms - 🍴 8.50€.* This fine 1882 edifice on the quays is a local institution. Visitors will be charmed by the vast patio topped by a Belle Époque-style glass roof, cosy bedrooms, period furniture and chic bar.

🛏️ **Hôtel Port Marine** – *Môle St-Louis - ☎ 04 67 74 92 34 - contact@hotel-port-marine.com - 🅿 - 46 rooms - 🍴 9€ - restaurant 🍴🍴.* A modern hotel located near the marina and pier. The functional rooms are reminiscent of a boat's cabin; six suites overlook the sea. Regional food is served in the Bleu Marine restaurant.

🛏️ **Camping Les Tamaris** – *34110 Frontignan - 1km/0.6mi S of Frontignan on D 60 - ☎ 04 67 43 44 77 - les-tamaris@wanadoo.fr - ⏰ open Apr-20 Sep - reservation required - 250 sites - food service.* Take full advantage of the beach by pitching your tent on this campground right by the water! You'll need walk only a few steps to lay down your beach blanket and dive into the waves! Nice pool, bar, restaurant and shop.

SHOPPING

Marché aux Puces – *Pl. de la République - Sun 6am-1pm.* Flea market.

Chez David – *67 R. Paul-Bousquet - ☎ 04 67 53 14 30 - daily except Tues 7am-12.30pm, 4pm-8pm - closed Feb.* If you fancy *tielles sétoises*, a sort of small pasty filled with fresh octopus, it is worth going out of your way to find this shop beyond the town centre. David, an excellent artisan-chef, is very tuned in to life in Sète and is happy to chat about all nature of things, especially about *tielles*, a local speciality.

Biscuits Catagnia – *35 Grand'Rue Mario-Roustan - ☎ 04 67 74 49 11 - Mon-Fri 6am-7pm - closed 3 weeks in Jan–* A wonderful aroma of baking sweets pervades this tiny factory in the centre of town. *Navettes* and *mantecaos* in a variety of flavors, *Antillais au rhum* and *au citron, Cyrano aux prumeaux* and *à l'armagnac, rocher coco* and *croquets aux amandes* list among the 26 different types of biscuits here.

Cave coopérative du Muscat de Frontignan – *14 Ave. du Muscat - 34110 Frontignan - ☎ 04 67 48 12 26/04 67 48 93 20 - www.frontignan-coopérative.fr -* Jun-Sep: **guided tour** *(20min):* 10m, 11am, 3.30pm, 4.30pm; **shop**: *Jun-Sep: 9.30am-12.30pm, 3-7.30pm; Oct-May: 9.30am-12.30pm, 2.30-6.30pm - closed Christmas and New Year.*

ON THE TOWN

Bar du Passage – *1 quai Mistral - ☎ 04 67 74 21 25 - Jul-Aug: daily 7am-2am; Sep and Jun: daily 7am-8pm.* Located in the Pointe Courte fishing district, where Varda's film Bar du Passage was shot, its namesake is a magical place. Come and savour the beauty and poetry of this place. or simply savour a kebab in summer. Photography exhibitions.

CinéGarage – *29 Grande Rue Haute - ☎ 04 67 46 12 18 - Sep-Jun: Mon-Fri 9am-noon, 2pm-5pm; Jul-Aug: Mon-Fri 2pm-6pm.* A new, multi-purpose cultural locale proposing exhibitions of paintings, film production, creative workshops, a short films festival (July). This rather counter-cultural venue promises enriching encounters with numerous artists and other prominent figures from Sète's artistic sets.

Théâtre de la Mer – *Rte. de la Corniche - ☎ 04 67 74 70 55 - culture@ville-sete.fr - open mid-Jun to mid-Aug - closed Sep-May.* Also called the 'Théâtre Jean-Vilar', this 2,000-seat outdoors theatre at the foot of the maritime cemetery is set in a fort built by Vauban. Several festivals take place here in summer, including a theatre, music and dance festival and a jazz festival.

The town developed in the 17C when Colbert decided to have a port constructed, making Sète the outlet on the Mediterranean for the Canal des Deux-Mers. The foundation stone was laid in 1666 by **Pierre-Paul Riquet,** architect of the Canal du Midi. To stimulate expansion, in 1673 Louis XIV gave permission for "everyone to build houses, sell and produce any goods with exemption from tax duty." Before very long the town had become a thriving commercial and industrial centre. Meanwhile, Riquet supervised the building of the two jetties protecting the outer harbour, and of the Sète canal linking Thau lagoon to the sea.

Nevertheless, it was not until the 19C that Sète embarked upon its golden age. The harbour and the maritime canal were developed, while the railway companies linked Sète to the PLM network and to the Midi network. By about 1840 Sète was the fifth most important French port. After the conquest of Algeria, Sète, which specialised in the wine trade, found its main outlets in North Africa.

Today, the three main areas of its activity are the handling of bulk goods (mineral ores, coal, raw materials, animal foodstuffs, exotic timbers, raw paper), passenger and container traffic to North and West Africa, South America, the French Caribbean and Australia, and storage.

Sea Front

Vieux port★

The old harbour, with its picturesque fishing boats and yachts, is the most interesting part of Sète port.

Quai de la Marine is lined with fish and seafood restaurants, with terraces overlooking the Sète canal. It is the departure point for various **boat trips** (👜 *see Address Book*) around the coastline and harbour.

A little farther down, fishermen and bystanders are summoned by the **"criée électronique"** (electronic auction) when the boats come in at around 3.30pm.

It is worth taking a stroll round the other basins and the canals as well.

Sailing is practised at high level near the St-Louis pier.

Promenade de la Corniche

This busy road, leading to the Plage de la Corniche, situated 2km/1mi from the centre of town, cuts around the foot of Mont St-Clair with its slopes covered by villas.

Plage de la Corniche

This 12km/7.5mi-long sandy beach stretches across a conservation area.

Mont St-Clair★ *allow half a day.*

▶ *From promenade Maréchal-Leclerc, carry on along avenue du Tennis and take the right fork onto montée des Pierres Blanches.*

A trip to Mont St-Clair will leave visitors with one of the best of their memories of Sète. This hill, once covered by pine forests and oaks, rises 175m/574ft above sea level and forms an ideal viewpoint from which to appreciate the surrounding area.

Parc panoramique des Pierres Blanches

This park is well covered by waymarked footpaths and makes a pleasant place for a stroll exploring the area. From the viewing table, there is a wide **view★** over the west end of the Thau lagoon, the lower Hérault plains, the open sea, the Promenade de la Corniche and the beach.

Chapelle Notre-Dame-de-la-Salette

Mont St-Clair is named after a saint who was venerated here as early as the Middle Ages. In the 17C, a hermitage still existed near the small fort of "La Montmorencette" built by the Duke of Montmorency as a defence against Barbary pirates. But when the duke rebelled, the king had the fort dismantled and a former blockhouse transformed into an expiatory chapel. In 1864, it was dedicated to Notre-Dame-de-la-Salette. It is a centre of pilgrimage all year round, but especially on 19 September.

Viewpoints

From the esplanade opposite the chapel, where a large cross is lit up every night, there is a splendid **view**★ of Sète, the east end of the Thau lagoon, the Garrigues, the Cévennes, St-Loup peak, the Gardiole mountain and the coast itself with its necklace of lagoons and small towns.

A viewing tower on the presbytery terrace gives a marvellous **panorama**★★. Whereas the foreground reflects light and colour, shapes in the distance blend into hazy tints. On a clear day, the view extends over the lagoons and the sea as far as the Pyrenees, to the south-west, and the Alpilles, to the east.

▶ *Carry on along chemin de St-Clair which drops steeply downhill.*

On the right lies the cliff-top **cemetery**★ celebrated by Paul Valéry and the museum dedicated to him.

▶ *Return to Sète along Grande-Rue-Haute.*

Additional Sights

Espace Brassens

67 boulevard Camille-Blanc. ♿ ⏰ *Jul and Aug: 10am–noon, 2–7pm; Jun and Sep: 10am–noon, 2–6pm; Oct–May: daily except Mon 10am–noon, 2–6pm.* ⏰ *Closed 1 Jan, Easter, 1 and 8 May, 11 Nov, 25 Dec.* ⊛ *5€ (10-18 years: 2€).* ☎ *04 67 53 48 28. www.ville-sete.fr/brassens.*

This museum traces the life and work of the singer-songwriter from Sète, Georges Brassens (1921-81) in an interesting and original exhibition combining audio-visual input *(visitors wear headphones)* with visual displays (posters, photographs, newspaper articles etc).

Brassens wrote simple, often irreverent lyrics and melodies, which he sang to a guitar accompaniment, evoking eternal themes such as friendship *(Chanson pour l'Auvergnat)*, love *(Je me suis fait tout petit)* or death *(Pauvre Martin)*.

The display retraces Brassens' childhood in Sète, his arrival in Paris and his early successes, as well as the work of writers who inspired him *(Ballade des Dames au temps jadis by Villon, Il n'y a pas d'amour heureux by Aragon)*. There is a short video

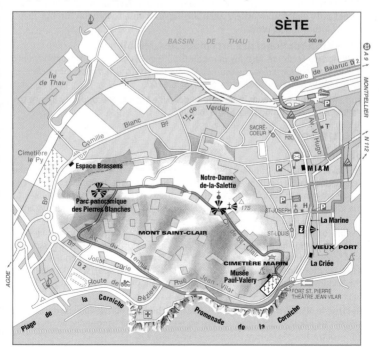

Oyster beds on Thau lagoon

of a selection of songs he recorded at the Bobino music hall, including many of his best-known numbers, which may get quite a few feet tapping.

Georges Brassens is buried in the Le Py cemetery, which is to be found opposite the museum.

Musée Paul-Valéry

Jul and Aug: 10am-noon, 2-6pm; Sep-Jun: daily except Tue and public holidays 10am-noon, 2-6pm. 3€ (12-18 yesars: 1.50€), no charge 1st Sunday in the month. 04 67 46 20 98.

Facing the sea and very close to the **cimetière marin** where Paul Valéry *(in the upper part)* and Jean Vilar *(in the lower part)* are buried, the museum contains many documents on the history of Sète. The various rooms are separated by movable panels to enable variation in the layout of the exhibitions.

On the ground floor are archaeological remains from excavations in Le Barrou and literature on the nautical jousts. These lively, colourful games have been a source of inspiration to painters and, over the centuries, have made use of a variety of costumes, of which the history can be traced from 1666 to 1891.

On the first floor, a room is devoted to Paul Valéry, from his childhood in Sète onwards. A poet and a philosopher, Valéry could also express himself admirably through drawing, sculpture and painting.

Musée international des Arts modestes (MIAM)

Quai Mar.-de-Lattre-de-Tassigny, along the Grand Canal. Daily except Tue and public holidays (except Jul and Aug) 10am-noon, 2-6pm. 5€ (children under 10: no charge), no charge 1st Sunday in the month. 04 67 18 64 00.

This entertaining museum is devoted to daily-life objects and publicity (hence the name *"modestes"*) going back to the mid-20C.

Excursion

Bassin de Thau

The Bassin de Thau covers an area of 8 000ha/19 768 acres and is the largest lagoon on the Languedoc coast. It is separated from the sea by the isthmus of Onglous (Sète beach). Its shores are home to a whole range of activities: to the east is a busy industrial complex; to the south, the offshore sand bar is a beach; whereas on the north shore several villages, such as Bouzigues and Mèze, specialise in oyster and mussel farming. Boat trips enable visitors to take a closer look at the oyster and mussel farming concerns in the lagoon.

Built on flat land on the shores of the Bassin de Thau, **Balaruc-les-Bains** *(5km/3mi N of Sète),* the third most popular spa resort in France, has many amenities to offer, especially for those keen on outdoor activities and water sports. In the evenings, the floodlit shoreline around Sète and Mont St-Clair provides a sparkling backdrop to the resort's night-life.

Balaruc-le-Vieux, the old village of Balaruc, perched on a hill overlooking the lagoon, still has its original, defensive circular layout and typical Languedoc atmosphere. Some of the houses feature striking arched doorways.

Réserve africaine de SIGEAN ★

MICHELIN LOCAL MAP 344: I-4

ALSO SEE LES CORBIÈRES

This **safari park** (nearly 300ha/740 acres) owes much of its unique character to the wild landscape of coastal Languedoc, with its *garrigues* dotted with lagoons, and to the fact that for each species large areas have been set aside, which resemble their original native environment as closely as possible.

Tour of the Park

Visit by Car

1hr. Please observe the safety instructions displayed at the entrance. ♿🕐 *Apr-Sep: 9am-6.30pm; rest of the year: 9am-4pm.* 👓 *21€ (children: 17€).* ☎ *04 68 48 20 20.*

Kids The route for visitors in cars goes through four areas, reserved for free ranging animals: **African bush** (ostriches, giraffes, impalas, **Tibetan bear park** (these bears are recognisable by the white V on their chests), **lion park** and **African savannah** (white rhinoceros, zebras, ostriches and a species of antelope with spiral horns).

Visit on Foot

3hr. Start from the central car parks, inside the safari park.

Walking round the safari park, visitors will come across the fauna of various continents – elephants, dromedaries, antelopes, zebras, cheetahs, alligators – and, near the lagoon of L'Oeil de Ca, bird life such as pink flamingoes, cranes, ducks, white storks, sacred ibis, macaws, swans and pelicans.

Three observation posts enable those visitors who are quiet and patient enough to observe various types of antelope from the African plains (oryx, springboks, gnus, impalas, white-faced damaliscus, water buck, South African eland) and to watch the behaviour of a group of chimpanzees on their own island.

One of the safari park's lions

A. Thuillier/MICHELIN

TARASCON-SUR-ARIÈGE

POPULATION 3,446

MICHELIN LOCAL MAP 343: H-7

Tarascon lies in an accessible, sheltered site in the centre of the Ariège Valley floor. The surrounding chalk cliffs carved out by the river's passage, and the tributary River Vicdessos add to the charm of the site. The town is a major centre in the Pyrenees for speleological experts (mainly engaged in studies of the Neolithic period). It is also of interest to amateur enthusiasts, seeking to unravel the mysteries contained in the many caves that pepper the slopes at this confluence of river valleys, called Sabarthès in the Middle Ages. *Ave. des Pyrénées, 09400 Tarascon-Sur-Ariège,* ☎ *05 61 05 94 94.*

Prehistory in the Ariège Region

With its 12 decorated caves and its splendid park devoted to prehistoric art, the Ariège *département* can rightly claim to be one of the main centres of Prehistory in France.

Parc de la Préhistoire★★

1km/0.6mi N. Drive along N 20 towards Foix then follow the signposts (parking area). ⏰ *Jul and Aug: 10am-8pm; Apr-Jun: 10am-6pm, Sat-Sun and public holidays 10am-7pm; Sep to Oct: daily except Mon, 10am-6pm, Sat-Sun and public holidays 10am-7pm.* ⚟ *9€ (children: 5.50€).* ☎ *05 61 05 10 10.*

Kids This museum of prehistoric art, located in a beautiful mountain setting at Lacombe on the road to Banat *(NW of Tarascon)*, is devoted to cave wall paintings.

A resolutely contemporary building beside a lake houses the **Grand Atelier**, where visitors wearing infrared helmets go round an initiatory exhibition in semi-darkness.

In the entrance corridor, drops of water falling on steel cylinders evoke the passage of time, while the history of art since its origins unfolds on screens on the walls. A reconstruction of the Dune des Pas gallery from the Clastres network at Niaux *(⚟ a section not open to the public)* shows the poignant imprint of children's feet in the ground made thousands of years ago. From the same part of the subterranean network, the skilfully executed sketches of a weasel and a horse have been reproduced on a neighbouring wall. The next part of the visit is a short film on methods of excavation and dating used by archaeologists with an overview of cave wall art from all over the world. It illustrates the path taken by prehistoric artists as they searched for the right place to adorn with their images of animals.

The exhibition also covers themes such as painted symbols, carved weapons and jewellery, other carvings and techniques used by artists of the Magdalenian period. At the end of the exhibition there is a life-size reproduction of the Salon Noir at Niaux, its walls decorated with paintings of horses, ibex and bison and carved symbols. This is the work of Renaud Sanson, the artist responsible for Lascaux II at Montignac in the Dordogne, and in fact shows the images more complete than they are in reality. Using photographic evidence revealed in ultraviolet light, the artist has reconstituted the drawings as they were before deposits of calcite built up and obscured parts of them.

Address Book

👜 *For coin categries, see the Legend.*

PARK HOTEL

🍽️🍽️ **Parc** – *09400 Ussat - 2km/1mi SE of Tarascon-sur-Ariège on D 123* – ☎ *05 61 02 20 20* – thermes.ussatwanadoo.fr – *closed 3 Jan-6 Feb and 1 Nov-18 Dec* – 🅿 *- 49 rooms* - 💤 *6.30€ - restaurant 13€.* This recently built hotel stands opposite a lovely wooded park. Rooms are sober and functional. There are thermal baths on the first floor, a covered pool and terrace solarium on the roof. Family-style meals are served in a contemporary-style dining room.

SPICE OF LIFE

Hypocras – *1 R. Croix-de-Quié* - ☎ *05 61 05 14 80* - www.hypocras.com – *Tue-Sat 3pm-7pm – closed holidays.* Hypocras is a spiced medieval aperitif. The original recipe has just been rediscovered and is a well-kept secret. Gaston Fébus, the 14C Sun Prince, is said to have been particularly fond of this beverage – have a glass and find out why!

The visit can be continued outside in a specially landscaped setting focusing on water and rock features such as the "Torrent of tracks," "Panorama of the hunt" with its sculpted bison, "Labyrinth of sounds" and "Pyrenean meadow" giving an idea of the plant life that would have existed in the Magdalenian period.

During the high season, various activities are organized: introduction to prehistoric hunting methods, flint cutting, cave wall painting, archaeological excavations. There are restaurant facilities and a souvenir shop and bookshop.

Grotte de Niaux★★ – 5km/3mi S. Turn right off N 20 onto D 8. ⤵ See Grotte de NIAUX.

Grotte de la Vache

8km/5mi S. Carry on along D 8 and turn right towards Alliat. ⏰⤵ *Jul and Aug: guided tours 10am-5.30pm; Apr-Jun, Sep and school holidays: afternoons.* ⤵ *7€ (children: 4€).* ☎ *05 61 05 95 06. www.grotte-de-la-vache.org.*

This cave was occupied at the end of the Magdalenian period and consists of two galleries, one of which is called Monique, explored up until 1967. There is a display of weapons, tools and, most interestingly, carved or sculpted artefacts (on bone or animal horn) which reveal something of life 13 000 years ago.

Grotte de Bédeilhac

6km/3.7mi NW along D 618. ⏰⤵ *Jul and Aug: guided tours (1hr45min) 10am-5.30pm; Apr-Jun, Sep and school holidays: afternoons.* ⤵ *8€ (children: 4€).* ☎ *05 61 05 95 06. www.grotte-de-bedeilhac.org.*

This cave has a huge entrance (36m/118ft wide by 25m/82ft high, large enough to allow a plane to take off and land during a film that was shot here once). From the entrance, go past an enormous stalagmite (120m/394ft circumference) to the end gallery. The prehistoric drawings inside the cave, dating from the Magdalenian period, were discovered in 1906. Over the last 15 000 years the cave roof has remained water-tight, ensuring that the paintings of animals and the rock carvings (some of which even adorn the floor of the cave) are well preserved. The artists used the texture of the rock itself to give added expression to their work (large bison, beautiful deer, horses).

Grotte de Lombrives★ – 3km/1.9mi S. ⤵ See below.

Upper Ariège Valley★

▶ *From Tarascon-sur-Ariège towards the Col de Puymorens – 54km/33.6mi – allow half a day.*

The Ariège rises on the Andorra border, in the Font-Nègre cirque, and flows into the Garonne just south of Toulouse, having covered 170km/106mi.

In its upper reaches, the river flows along a glacial channel which widens out and changes direction at Ax. The traces of the old glacier are much in evidence around Tarascon. The Ariège then flows through the Labarre ravine, cutting across the limestone Plantaurel range to reach the Pamiers plain, laid down by the river's own alluvial deposits, where it finally leaves the Pyrenees.

▶ *Leave Tarascon along N 20 towards Ax-les-Thermes.*

Grotte de Lombrives★

⏰⤵ *Jul and Aug: guided tours (1hr30min) on a tourist train 10am-7pm; Jun, Sep and Easter school holidays: 10am, 2pm, 3.30pm and 5pm; May: 2pm, 3.30pm and 5pm, Sat-Sun and public holidays 10am, 2pm, 3.30pm, 5pm; mid-Mar to end Apr and early Oct to mid-Nov: Sat-Sun and public holidays 10am, 2pm, 3.30pm and 5pm. Rest of the year by request.* ⤵ *6.60€ (children: 3.70€).* ☎ *06 61 05 98 40 or 05 70 74 32 80.*

These vast caves, south of Tarascon and just north of Ussat-les-Bains, have certainly been used as a shelter for many centuries. While the first people to enter the cave may have been seeking protection from wild animals or bad weather, later the cave become a hideout for bandits, or a place of refuge for those fleeing religious persecution. Today, visitors can take the short tour *(1hr 30min)* of the upper and lower galleries, and admire some of the spectacular formations, or one of the longer tours *(3hr or 5hr)* which are more adventurous and include views of an underground lake and many remarkable formations.

Beyond the dip in which the village of Les Cabannes lies, where the River Aston flows into the Ariège, the road enters the Sabarthès region. The steep valley sides, riddled with caves, make up the Val d'Ariège at this point – once a glacial valley, as its deep, symmetrical cross-section suggests.

A Mineralogical Museum

Thanks to its wide range of geological deposits and mineral seams, the département of Ariège has been over the years a mining region with resources that have been worked or left abandoned depending on demand in world markets. Quantities of iron, bauxite, zinc, manganese and, more recently, tungsten (in Salau) have been mined here. At present only the talc (French chalk) mined at **Luzenac** is a mineral resource of any national significance (10% of world production).

▷ *From Les Cabannes, the narrow D 522 on the right leads to the Plateau de Beille.*

Plateau de Beille ski area

Alt 1 800-2 000m/5 905-6 561ft. This is one of the loveliest places for cross-country skiing in the Pyrenees, with beautiful views over the mountain range and the peaks of Andorra. The high altitude guarantees snow cover from December to May, on 65km/40mi of groomed trails. There is also a dog sled run and a snowshoe trail.

▷ *Continue along N 20.*

The contrast between the slope facing the sun, covered with fields of crops and farmhouses, and the slope in the shade, clad in forests, is particularly striking along the next stretch of road. On the closer outcrops to the right of the road the ruins of first the Château de Lordat and then the Ermitage de St-Pierre can be seen, against the towering backdrop of the Pic de St-Barthélemy (alt 2 438m/7 999ft).

– 🎧 *See AX-LES-THERMES: Excursions.*

On the way to Ax-les-Thermes, the road crosses the River Ariège to run along the south-west bank. On the other side of the river, the lovely Romanesque bell-tower of the church at Unac can be seen.

Ax-les-Thermes⚓ – 🎧 *See AX-LES-THERMES.*

▷ *Continue along N 20 towards Puymorens and Andorra.*

The road runs alongside some of the bridges – remarkable engineering feats – of the trans-Pyrenean railway line, one of the highest in Europe.

Mérens-les-Vals

The village was rebuilt along the roadside after the fire that destroyed Mérens-d'en-Haut in 1811 in an arson attack by the "Miquelets" (Spanish mercenaries feared since the 16C), during the Franco-Spanish Napoleonic War.
Beyond Mérens and the Mérens gorge, the road runs upstream along the upper valley of the Ariège in between magnificent forests. On the left is the peak called "Dent d'Orlu."

Centrale de Mérens

Alt 1 100m/3 575ft. This automated power plant is the middle stage of the hydroelectric project of the same name, made possible by the raising of the level of Lake Lanoux. This reservoir, fed by redirecting the tributary waters of the River Segre (and so also the River Ebro) in Spain into the Garonne Valley, is the object of an agreement between the French and Spanish governments, to compensate Spain for the loss of water.
There is a viewing table to help you identify the mountain peaks at the far end of the valley.

L'Hospitalet

Alt 1 436m/4 667ft. This is the first village in the Ariège Valley. As the road climbs towards it, the landscape becomes bleaker and more rugged; keep careful watch for the troops of wild horses that frequently follow this route.

The Puymorens Tunnel

Since 20 October 1994, a tunnel has enabled traffic to avoid the trip across the Puymorens Pass itself, which tends to be a difficult journey in the winter. The building of the Puymorens tunnel, 4 820m/almost 3mi in length, was welcomed by local residents, although it was less well received by ecologists. The tunnel was a physical realisation of the economic and cultural opening up of the Ariège region to Catalonia. The improved communications between France and Spain are expected to be greatly helped by a road which is planned to link Toulouse and Barcelona. This highway between Toulouse and the Spanish border will not be completed, however, until 2010.

Drystone Huts

The countryside around Auzat and Vicdessos is dotted with numerous drystone shepherd's huts – known as orris – with corbelled roof vaults covered with tufts of a particular species of local grass which keeps the water out. These huts were used by shepherds during the summer grazing season. Two footpaths have recently been marked out to enable visitors to explore the area and its huts, some of which date from the 13C. The first path leaves from Pradières and for much of its length follows the GR 10 long-distance footpath, going past the huts at La Caudière and Journosque and running above Lake Izourt and the Arties Valley. The second leaves from the Carla huts, which have just been restored, and leads past several more huts and the lakes of Roumazet and Soucarrane.

Further details are available from the local tourist office (rue des Pyrénées, Auzat, ☎ 05 61 64 87 53).

Beyond L'Hospitalet, one can either continue up to the **Col de Puymorens** (alt 1 920m/6 300ft) and drive through the Cerdagne region into Spanish Catalonia or follow N 22 towards Pas de la Casa and Andorra (👁 *see Principat d'ANDORRA*).

Route du Port de Lers

87km/54mi round trip – allow 3hr.

The Port de Lers road reveals the marked contrast between the wooded, coppiced landscape of the Atlantic watershed and the harsher, more rugged countryside towards the Mediterranean.

▷ *Leave Tarascon-sur-Ariège towards Ax-les-Thermes and turn immediately right onto D 8 towards Alliat.*

Grotte de Niaux★★ – 👁 *See Grotte de NIAUX.*

Niaux

On the edge of the village, the **musée pyrénéen de Niaux** (🕐 *Jul and Aug: 9am-8pm; Sep-Jun: 10am-noon, 2-6pm.* 🎟 *6€ (children: 4€).* ☎ *05 61 05 88 36*) is devoted to traditional popular crafts of the region. Many objects are related to shepherding (cheese moulds, bells), wool carding and weaving, linen making, horn combs, forges etc.

High on a rocky promontory, stand the ruins of the 14C Château de Miglos. The route continues to Junac, where the monument to the dead of the First World War was sculpted by Bourdelle.

At Laramade the valley opens out to the left as it is joined by the Siguer Valley. The Port de Siguer (alt 2 396m/7 860ft) is a pass that was frequently involved in the exchanges between France, Andorra and Spain. During the Second World War it was used by many French fleeing the country.

The road follows the deep, rugged **vallée du Vicdessos** where the extended pasturelands play host to flocks of sheep and herds of cattle, with little sign of human habitation. To the right the villages of Orus and Illier perch on the steep mountainside.

Vicdessos

This mountain village is built on a site carved out by glacial action below the hanging Suc Valley.

▷ *Take D 18 to the right up to Port de Lers.*

Port de Lers

Alt 1 517m/4 980ft. As you climb, look back for a good view of the Goulier Valley. The road runs alongside a rushing stream, past several waterfalls. It is here that the difference between the Atlantic and the Mediterranean vegetation can most clearly be seen.

Lers-Trois Seigneurs ski area

Alt 1 275-1 600m/4 183-5 250ft. Some 35km/21mi of cross-country trails go around the lake, at the foot of the Pic de Montbéas.

Étang de Lers★

This superb, solitary lake at the foot of the Pic de Montbéas is set in mountain scenery carved out long ago by glacier action. In the early autumn, it is brilliant with the flowering gorse and furze on the surrounding slopes.

The road carries on round the Cirque de Lers, where horses, sheep and herds of cattle, complete with tinkling cowbells, share the pastures.

Peyre Auselère

This is the first hamlet in the sparsely inhabited Courtignou Valley. Leave the car in the village for a short break at the side of the pleasant waterfalls of the Courtignou. A bridge gives access to the opposite (west) bank of the river.

After Mouréou the landscape becomes less austere, then the road runs across narrow valleys cut through schist.

Massat – *See FOIX: Excursions.*

▶ *Drive E along D 618.*

Col de Port – *See FOIX: Excursions.*

▶ *D 618 leads back to Tarascon-sur-Ariège.*

TARBES

POPULATION 77,414

MICHELIN LOCAL MAP 342: M-3

Tarbes, the capital of Bigorre since the 9C, is the most important town in the central Pyrenees. Traditionally a hussar garrison town, it has the largest museum in France devoted to these valiant and illustrious horsemen. Tarbes is also an important trading centre and the traditional home of fairs and markets, as well as the second largest university centre in the Midi-Pyrénées region after Toulouse. In addition, Tarbes is in close proximity to a number of ski resorts.
🛈 *3 cours Gambetta, 65000 Tarbes, ☎ 05 62 51 30 31. www.ville-tarbes.fr.*

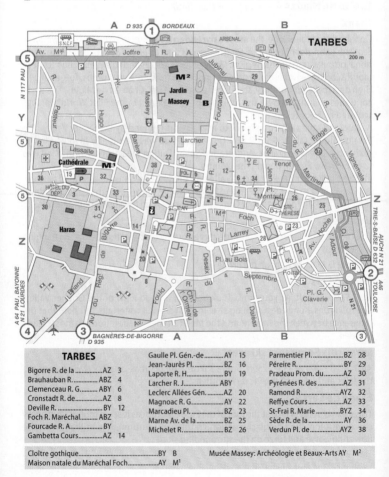

TARBES								
Bigorre R. de la	AZ	3	Gaulle Pl. Gén.-de	AY	15	Parmentier Pl.	BZ	28
Brauhauban R.	ABZ	4	Jean-Jaurès Pl.	BZ	16	Péreire R.	BY	29
Clemenceau R. G.	ABY	6	Laporte R. H.	BY	19	Pradeau Prom. du	AZ	30
Cronstadt R. de	AZ	8	Larcher R. J.	ABY		Pyrénées R. des	AZ	31
Deville R.	BY	12	Leclerc Allées Gén.	AZ	20	Ramond R.	AYZ	32
Foch R. Maréchal	ABZ		Magnoac R. G.	AY	22	Reffye Cours	AZ	33
Fourcade R. A.	BY		Marcadieu Pl.	BZ	23	St-Frai R. Marie	BYZ	34
Gambetta Cours	AZ	14	Marne Av. de la	BZ	25	Sède R. de la	AY	36
			Michelet R.	BZ	26	Verdun Pl. de	AYZ	38

Cloître gothique	BY	B	Musée Massey: Archéologie et Beaux-Arts	AY	M²
Maison natale du Maréchal Foch	AY	M¹			

Sights

Musée Massey: Archaeology and Fine Arts

☞ *Currently closed for renovation. Call for information.* ☎ *05 62 51 30 31.*

One of the rooms in the museum displays knives and fibulae from the early Iron Age and a bronze mask (1C or 2C) probably depicting the Pyrenean god, Ergé. Other rooms contain paintings from the 15C-19C French, Flemish, Italian and Spanish schools. Note the 15C triptych by Cock, *Madonna, Child, St John and St Jerome*, a 16C Holy Family (Italian school) with their blissful faces, a 17C *Wild Boar Hunt* (Flemish school) and *Bigorre Market* (regional work by Henri Borde, 1888-1958).

Musée International des Hussards, Tarbes

Le Comte de Bercheny, chef de corps du Premier Régiment de Hussards (1669-1778)

Address Book

🪙 *For coin categories, see the Legend.*

EATING OUT

🍽️🍽️ **Le Fil à la Patte** – *30 R. Georges-Lassalle -* ☎ *05 62 93 39 23 – closed 11-18 Jan, 8-31 Aug, Sat lunchtime, Sun and Mon.* This restaurant in a downtown house is pleasant indeed. The small, spruce dining room sports a mahogany floor and yellow walls where posters and slate menus are hung. The owner mans the ovens; he uses market-fresh ingredients to prepare appetizing meals with a distinctly regional accent.

🍽️🍽️ **Le Petit Gourmand** – *62Ave. Bertrand-Barère -* ☎ *05 62 34 26 86 – closed 25 Aug-7 Sep, Sat lunchtime, Sun evening and Mon.* This is a brasserie and bistro in one. The pleasant decor is appealingly retro with red velvet chairs and old advertising posters. Contemporary cuisine and a good selection of area wines at affordable prices.

🍽️🍽️ **La Vieille Auberge** – *Côte de Ger - 65420 Ibos - 12km/7.5mi W of Tarbes on RN 117, towards Pau -* ☎ *05 62 31 51 54 – closed Sun evening and Mon and 2nd fortnight in Aug.* This handsome stone inn along the main road has been impeccably renovated. Both dining rooms are pleasant: wood tables and chairs, white tablecloths, salmon-coloured walls and curtains. The food is carefully prepared from fresh ingredients.

🍽️ **Ferme-auberge La Métairie** – *R. du Bois - 65380 Ossun - 9.5km/6mi SW of Tarbes on N 21 then D 936 and B-road -* ☎ *05 62 32 81 89 - closed mid Aug-end Aug -* 🍴 *- reserv. essential 48hrs in advance.* You can count on a friendly welcome in this pretty poultry farm with a smart yellow facade. Enjoy dishes of guinea fowl, duck or chicken raised on the farm and served on large wooden tables.

WHERE TO STAY

🛏️ **Chambre d'hôte Relais du Barboutou** – *15 Cami Deth Barboutou - 65190 Oueilloux – 13 km E by N 117, Rte. de Toulouse, then right by D 5 -* ☎ *05 62 35 07 66 -* 🍴 *- 3 rooms and 1 self-catering room -meals 12€.* Guestrooms outfitted in a restored farmhouse adjacent to the owners' property; simple but beautifully decorated (woods, white walls) Meals served in a pleasant dining room with fireplace and antique furniture.

🛏️🛏️ **Hôtel Henri IV** – *7 Ave. Bertrand-Barère -* ☎ *05 62 34 01 68 -* 🅿️ *- 22 rooms -* 🍽️ *8€.* A venerable old building located right in the centre of town. The rooms in this family-run hotel are bright and pleasant. If weather permits, breakfast can be taken in the little flower-filled courtyard.

🛏️🛏️ **Hôtel La Chaumière du Bois** – *65420 Ibos - 6km/4mi W of Tarbes on N 117 -* ☎ *05 62 90 03 51 - hotel@chaumieredubois. com -* 🅿️ *– 22 rooms -* 🍽️ *6€ - restaurant* 🍴. Pretty, modern thatched cottages in a shady landscaped park surrounded by meadows. This peaceful motel's pleasant rooms overlook the swimming pool. Round dining room with exposed ceiling frame. Terrace beneath the trees.

ON THE TOWN

Le Monocle – *1 Ave. Bertrand-Barère -* ☎ *05 62 34 29 29 - traiteur.monocle@free.fr - Mon-Thu 8.30am-2am, Fri, Sat 8.30am-3am.* A wide range of beers, whiskies and ice cream sundaes are served in this elegant bar-restaurant. The dynamic owner has been organizing Trivial Pursuit parties here every Wednesday for years. The monthly "Cause café" (causer: to chat) evenings, where the most diverse of issues are tackled head-on in heated debates, are a legend in Tarbes.

SIT BACK AND RELAX

Nectar – *19 Pl. Marcadieu -* ☎ *05 62 44 19 44 - Tue-Fri 9am-7pm, Thu 8am-7pm, Sat 9am-noon, 2pm-7pm.* This tearoom opposite the Marcadieu market offers coffee roasted on the premises, a choice of fifty varieties of tea and some delicious drinking chocolates. The lady in charge is a most hospitable hostess.

SHOPPING

Grand marché – *Halle Marcadieu –* *Thu 7am-12.30pm.* The largest market for regional specialities for miles around.

Shopping streets – The main shopping streets run perpendicular to the Place de Verdun: Mar.-Foch, Brauhauban, Gonès and Gambetta. This is where you will find a cinema, clothing shops, pastry shops, bookshops and other stores of every sort, including Nouvelles Galeries, Tarbes' major department store.

Christian Laporte – *65500 Nouilhan -* ☎ *05 62 96 75 80 – daily 8am-7pm.* Laporte grows renowned Tarbes beans and sells them dried in bags of 500g/1.1lbs, 2.5kg/5.5lbs or 5kg/11lbs, or cooked according to his own recipes: Tarbes beans with gizzards or duck *aiguillettes.* Scrumptious!

Le Pic Bigourdan – *12 R. du Moulin - 65360 Momères -* ☎ *05 62 45 31 28 - daily 8am-6pm - 5.30€.* Established in a renovated farm, this family bakery shows visitors how the local cake called *Le Rocher des Pyrénées* is made and cooked on a wood-burning fire. Tastings on-site for those who think to call ahead.

HORSE OF ANOTHER COLOUR

Equestria, festival du Cheval et de l'Art – The Massey Garden is the setting for this major equestrian event, which is very popular in Tarbes. In the evening, various shows are put on, and in the day time there are circus events, acrobatics, initiation to pony riding, exhibitions of stallions, harnesses, traps and farriery, all with the participation of the National Stud Farm and regional clubs. Some events incorporate music, dance, painting and sculpture. There are booths selling regional foods, crafts and saddlery. The fair lasts 5 days (end of July-beginning of August, 10am-10pm). Further information is available from the tourist office.

Journée nationale du cheval – The third weekend in September is devoted to horses here in Tarbes, known as the *ville du cheval.*

Horse-drawn carriage rides – There are two tours offered from late June to early September: a trip around the Massey Garden, (10min) and a tour of Tarbes (30min). Both trips start at the refreshment stand in the Massey Garden (2.30pm-7pm).

Maison natale du Maréchal Foch

2 Rue Victoire. ◷━ *Late May-late Sep: guided tours daily 9am-noon, 2-6.30pm; rest of the year: 9am-noon, 2-5pm.* ◷ *Closed Tue and certain Wed (enquire), 2nd and 4th Sun in the month, 1 Jan, 1 May, 1 Nov, 25 Dec.* ◌ *4€ (under 18: no charge).* ☎ *05 63 93 19 02.*

Ferdinand Foch (1851-1929), future Marshal of France (and honorifically, of Britain and Poland after the victorious conclusion of the First World War), was born in this house on 2 October 1851. The building is now a museum exhibiting souvenirs and biographical items relating to the Marshal.

Cathédrale Notre-Dame-de-la-Sède

Place Charles-de-Gaulle. Of Romanesque origin, the cathedral was repeatedly refurbished in the 13C, 14C, 18C and 19C, making it difficult to imagine the original medieval church. The most interesting part is the east end with its stone and brick bonding (either coursed work or chequerboard); rows of stones and pebbles alternate in the upper part.

Haras (Stud Farm), Maison du cheval

70 Ave. du Régiment-de-Bigorre. 🄺🄸🄳🄸 ⟨♿⟩◷━ *Jul and Aug: guided tours daily except Sat-Sun 10am, 11am, 11.30am, 2pm, 3pm, 4pm.* ◷*Closed Sat-Sun and public holidays.* ◌ *5.50€ (children: 2.30€).* ☎ *05 62 56 30 80. www.haras-nationaux.fr.*

This 9ha/22-acre park with its low, pale pavilions, shaded by cedars and magnolias, retains the distinguished atmosphere of the First Empire.

In the 19C, the stud farm produced the best cavalry chargers in Europe, developed from a cross between local strains and Arabs imported soon after the farm was founded in 1806. Tarbes, which was then a garrison town, soon became famous among Hussars, Dragoons, Lancers and the men of other select cavalry brigades.

Today the horses here are mostly bred for competition – especially steeplechases – and for show-jumping, dressage, and riding for pleasure.

After a tour of the stables, the forge and the saddlery, walk round the Maison du Cheval which has replaced the former arena.

Gorges du TARN★★★

MICHELIN LOCAL MAP 330: H-9 TO J-9 AND 338: L-5 TO N-5

The Tarn gorges are one of the most spectacular sights in the Causses region. Stretching over more than 50km/30mi, the gorges offer a seemingly endless succession of admirable landscapes and sites.

▶ **Orient Yourself:** There are three possibilities open to tourists for exploring the Tarn gorges, which might also be combined: driving along the scenic road; taking boat trips along the most spectacular stretch of the valley (see Boat Trips); or striding out along the footpaths on the high cliffs of the Causse Méjean or alongside the river.

◉ **Don't Miss:** Glorious views of the gorges abound, but perhaps the finest is from Point Sublime.

Especially for Kids: The gorges are a wonderland for kids, with hiking paths, rocy outcrops, lone castles and Cliffside villages.

◔ **Also See:** Grotte de DARGILAN, Chaos de MONTPELLIER-LE-VIEUX, ROQUEFORT-SUR-SOULZON, MEYRUEIS

Geographical Notes

The course of the Tarn – The Tarn rises in the uplands of Mont Lozère, at an altitude of 1 575m/5 167ft, and gushes turbulently down the Cévennes slopes. On its way, it picks up many tributaries, notably the Tarnon near Florac.

The Tarn then reaches the Causses region. Its course is now determined by a series of rifts which it has deepened into canyons. In this limestone region, it is fed solely by 40 resurgent springs from the Causse Méjean or Causse de Sauveterre, of which only three form small rivers over a distance of a few hundred yards. Most of them flow into the Tarn as waterfalls.

Address Book

◔ *For coin categories, see the Legend.*

EATING OUT

◌ **La Calquière** – *12720 Mostuéjouls -* ☎ *05 65 62 64 17 –* ◕ *closed Oct-Mar – reservations required.* Situated along a well-travelled road through the gorges, this inn has a terrace with a pretty view overlooking a small 10C church and graveyard on the banks of the Tarn. The simple family-style cuisine prepared from fresh farm produce is served in an enjoyable vaulted dining room.

WHERE TO STAY

◌ **Gorges du Tarn** – *48400 Florac -* ☎ *04 66 45 00 63 – gorges-du-tarn.adonis@wanadoo.fr –* ◕ *closed 1 Nov-Easter and Wed evening except Jul-Aug –* 🅿 *– 23 rooms -* 🛏 *6.50€.* This hotel is at the entrance (or exit) of the Tarn gorges. Rooms in the main building have been renovated; those in the annex are less fresh but more spacious. The small restaurant decorated in cheerful Mediterranean colours serves Cévennes specialities.

◌ **Hôtel-restaurant Malaval** – *Au village - 48500 St-Georges-de-Lévéjac - 12 km N of Vignes by D 995 toward Massegros and D 46 -* ☎ *04 66 48 81 07 - closed 5-20 Oct and from Christmas to New Year -* 🍴 🅿 *-*

10 rooms - 🛏 6€ - restaurant ◌. This hotel-reataurant also serves as the tabac for the local village located near Point Sublime. Copious family meals at reasonable prices, all with a warm welcome from the hosts.

◌ **Chambre d'hôte Jean Meljac** – *Quartier des Salles - 12640 Rivière-sur-Tarn - At Millau, drive toward les Gorges-du-Tarn ; at the Rivière-sur-Tarn exit, take a left toward « Chambres d'hôtes Vin-de-Côtes de Millau » -* ☎ *05 65 59 85 78 - closed Jan -* 🍴 *- 5 rooms - meals 15€.* This guesthouse operated by some wonderfully kind winegrowers, is located in the village just minutes from the gorges. Rooms are simple but very well maintained, and the garden offers great views. Wine tastings available.

◌◌◌ **Manoir de Montesquiou** – *48210 La Malène -* ☎ *04 66 48 51 12 - montesquiou@demeures-de-lozere.com - closed end Oct-end Mar -* 🅿 *- 12 rooms - 🛏 12.50€ - restaurant ◌◌.* Immerse yourself in the history of La Malène, a surprising village in the bosom of the Tarn gorges by staying in this enticing 15C residence. You can admire the wild beauty of the natural surroundings before savouring their flavoursome local cuisine and making the most of the inviting, comfortable rooms.

Human presence – Deep in the gorges, where the sun beats down in summer, towns or villages risk flash floods when the river is in spate and are therefore few and far between. Villages are more usually found at the mouth of dried-up river valleys or ravines, or in places where the Tarn Valley widens. The slopes surrounding such settlements are thick with orchards and vines.

The density of human habitation in certain areas contrasts with the lack of habitation on the Causses. This may come as a surprise to visitors who have travelled for miles on the plateaux, without encountering so much as a single hamlet. In many places, on the banks of the Tarn or perched high up on the valley sides, stand ruined castles which, in the Middle Ages, mostly harboured bands of robbers.

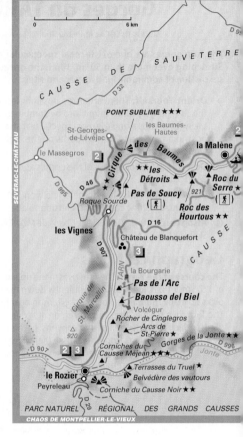

Touring Options

D 907bis, which runs along the entire stretch of the gorges, offers a magnificent landscape of castles, look-out points and picturesque villages.

Travelling by boat or canoe gives a close-up view of the cliffs and beautiful scenery views otherwise invisible from the road.

However, the most breathtaking landscapes and the closest contact with the rocky cliffs are reserved for those who take up the challenge of an exploration on foot. The natural grandeur of the site is all the more stunning when you can stop and soak it all in.

Tarn Gorges Road

The scenic road, D 907bis, runs along the floor of the gorges, on the right bank of the Tarn. The journey is never monotonous owing to the constantly changing appearance of the gorges, tinted with different hues depending on the time of day. Late afternoon, when the sun's slanting rays shed a golden light upon the cliffs, shows the canyon at the height of its splendour.

From Florac to Ste-Énimie ①

30km/18mi – about 1hr 30min.

All along this road, there are one or two houses that are still roofed with the heavy schist slabs known as lauzes; the roof ridge is made of slabs laid out like the sails of a windmill, which is evidence of the proximity of the Cévennes.

Florac – 👁 *See FLORAC.*

N 106 heads N along the Tarn Valley bordered to the east by the Cévennes and to the west by the cliffs of the Causse Méjean which tower above the river bed by 500m/1 640ft.

▶ *Within sight of the village of Biesset, on the opposite bank of the Tarn, leave the road to Mende via Montmirat Pass to the right and take D 907bis to the left, which runs along the north bank of the river.*

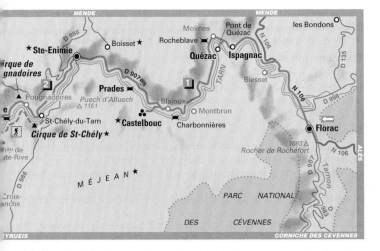

Level with Ispagnac, the Tarn makes a sharp meander; this is where the canyon really begins, as a gigantic defile 400-600m/1 300-2 000ft deep separating the Causse Méjean and the Causse de Sauveterre.

Ispagnac

At the mouth of the Tarn canyon, the little dip in which Ispagnac lies, sheltered from the north and north-west winds and basking in a mild climate which has always been renowned, is planted with orchards and vineyards. The cultivation of strawberries is also developing here. This "garden of Lozère," which once attracted the nobility of Lozère, is now a summer holiday resort.

Ispagnac church, dating from the 11C and 12C, is entered through a Romanesque doorway beneath a fine rose window. The interior, with three naves, is notable mainly for its chancel and capitals. Above the transept crossing, an octagonal bell-tower rises from a dome. The other bell-tower was built recently *(a button to the right of the entrance switches on a 15min recorded guided tour with music)*. The building is adjacent to a priory that still bears traces of fortifications. Note also the gate of the old castle and several 14C Gothic houses with their fine casement windows.

▶ *Continue 1km/0.6mi after Ispagnac then bear left.*

Quézac

At Quézac a Gothic **bridge** spans the Tarn. Pope Urban V, born in Grizac in the Lozère, thought of building it to enable pilgrims to reach the sanctuary he had founded in Quézac; his successor carried out the project. The bridge, demolished during the Wars of Religion, was rebuilt in the early 17C by the bishop of Mende, following the original plan.

A narrow street, lined with old houses, leads to **Quézac Church,** built on the same site where a statue of the Virgin Mary, which attracts numerous pilgrims, was discovered in 1050. A 16C porch leads into the church. Inside, the keystones and some of the capitals are embellished with the arms of Pope Urban V. A major pilgrimage takes place in September.

▶ *Return to D 907bis.*

Between Molines and Blajoux stand two castles.

First, on the north bank, is the **Château de Rocheblave** (16C) – with its distinctive machicolations – overlooked by the ruins of a 12C manor and by a curious limestone needle. Farther down, on the south bank, stands the **Château de Charbonnières** (16C), situated downstream of Montbrun village.

Castelbouc★

On the south bank of the Tarn. The strange site of Castelbouc ("Goat's Castle") can be seen from the road. The name is said to date from the Crusades. A lord, who stayed at home with the womenfolk, died of his complacency. The story goes that when his soul left his body, an enormous billy-goat was seen in the sky above the castle, which after that became known as Castelbouc.

The ruins of Castelbouc Castle stand on a steep rock, 60m/196ft high, which over-hangs a little village, nestling in a hollow of the rock, with the backs of its houses against the cliff.

A very powerful resurgent spring gushes out of three apertures, two in a cave, and one in the village.

▶ *Shortly afterwards, to the left of the road, Prades Castle comes into view.*

Château de Prades

Perched on a rocky spur overhanging the Tarn, this castle was built in the early 13C to protect Ste-Énimie Abbey and to defend access to the gorges. At the outset, it belonged to the bishops of Mende then, from 1280 to the Revolution, to the priors of Ste-Énimie Abbey.

Ste-Énimie★

Ste-Énimie lies in terraced rows below the steep cliffs bordering a loop of the Tarn, where the canyon is at its narrowest. The village is named after a Merovingian princess who chose to live in a grotto in order to dedicate her life to God, and founded a convent.

A leisurely stroll through the pretty little streets of Ste-Énimie is a good way to discover the village's charm.

All that remains of the **convent** is a Romanesque chapter-house. Around the site are the ruins of some old fortifications. **Place au Beurre,** the main square of the old village, features an attractive old house and the **corn market**, which contains an old wheat measure. **Le Vieux Logis,** *(combined visit with the church; call for information;* ☎ *04 66 31 60 20)* a museum of local traditions located in a room with an alcove, hearth, table and various utensils, gives an idea of the local way of life in bygone days. The **church,** *(*🕐 *by appointment at the tourist office.* ☎ *04 66 48 50 45)* dating from the 12C, has a fine oven-vaulted apse and contains an interesting 14C stone statue of St Anne. Modern ceramic panels, by Henri Constans, depict the legend of St Énimie, daughter of Clotaire II and sister of King Dagobert (known to all French school children as "the good king who put his pants on backwards").

According to legend, Énimie's father opposed the girl's project to devote her life to religious worship and ordered her to marry instead. She was struck with leprosy, and the putative husband quickly changed his mind. Disfigured but not dishonoured, Énimie made her way to the spring waters of the **Source de Burle**, where she was cured and subsequently established the convent.

It is only a short walk to the **cave-hermitage**, where St Énimie retired from the world and eventually passed away c 628. At the entrance to the cave, two rocks hollowed out into the shape of armchairs are said to have been used by the saint. *(45min on foot there and back from Ste-Énimie along a footpath located behind the Gîtes St-Vincent; or 3km/2mi along D 986 towards Mende, then 30min on foot there and back).*

From Ste-Énimie to Le Rozier ②

60km/37mi – allow 2hr 30min.

▶ *Leave Ste-Énimie on D 907bis to the S.*

Cirque de St-Chély★

The pretty village of St-Chély stands on the south bank of the Tarn at the threshold of the huge desolate cirque of St-Chély with its superb cliffs, at the foot of the Causse Méjean.

Cross to the other bank of the Tarn to see the Romanesque church with its pretty square belfry, the communal bread oven on the square, the old houses (Renaissance doors and chimneys) still full of character, and the fine orchards.

Two resurgent springs tumble into the Tarn as waterfalls. The source of one is in Cénaret cave at the mouth of which stands a chapel (12C).

D 986 on the opposite bank of the Tarn also affords fine **views**★★ of the cirques of St-Chély and Pougnadoires.

Cirque de Pougnadoires★

The houses in Pougnadoires village are embedded in the rock. The village is built against the colossal cliffs of the Pougnadoires cirque, pocked with caves. The reddish hue of the rocks indicates the presence of dolomite.

Château de la Caze★

This 15C château *(hôtel-restaurant)* stands in a romantic setting on the banks of the Tarn.

It was built during the reign of Charles VIII, by François Alamand, a former prior of Ste-Énimie. He gave it to his niece, Soubeyrane Alamand, on her marriage to the baron of Montclar.

The château is still remembered for the eight young girls who inhabited it, known as the "Nymphs of the Tarn," who were so beautiful that all the squires in the neighbourhood were in love with them.

The backdrop of leafy trees, ancient stones and overhanging rocks looks like something out of a fairy tale.

On the far bank, farther to the south, the ruins of Haute-Rive Castle appear above a village with fine traditional houses of grey and golden stone, which have been well restored.

La Malène

Located at the junction of the roads which wind through the Causse de Sauveterre and Causse Méjean, La Malène has always been a thoroughfare. In the spring and autumn, huge flocks of sheep on their way to new pastures used to cross the Tarn here and drink from the river's waters. Throughout the region of the Tarn gorges, the Revolution spread fire and bloodshed in its wake. In 1793, a detachment of revolutionary troops shot 21 inhabitants and set fire to La Malène. This incident left an indelible black mark on the Falaise de la Barre, a cliff overlooking the village, said to be caused by the oil-filled smoke from a house full of walnuts.

Tourists should visit the 12C Romanesque **church**, the little street lined with historical houses beneath Barre rock, and the 16C castle which is now a hotel.

▷ *Cross the bridge over the Tarn out of La Malène and take D 43.*

Just off the road to the right stand a cave chapel and a statue of the Virgin Mary from where there is a fine view of the village and its surroundings. The climb up the south bank of the Tarn is spectacular – 10 hairpin bends offer a splendid view of La Malène tucked in its hollow.

▷ *At Croix-Blanche, take D 16 to the right; 5km/3mi further on, turn right again. After passing through the village of Rieisse, take the road signposted "Roc des Hourtous-Roc du Serre" near a café.*

Roc des Hourtous★★

Follow the signs along the surfaced track off to the left. Car park. This cliff overlooks La Momie cave, just upstream from the Détroits gully, which is the narrowest section of the Tarn canyon. From here there is a superb **view★★** of the Tarn gorges, from the hamlet of L'Angle to the Cirque des Baumes and the Point Sublime.

▷ *Go back to the fork in the road; leave the car and take the track on the right to the Roc du Serre.*

Roc du Serre★★

30min on foot there and back. 🚶 This is the only place that gives this marvellous **view★★** of the narrow river gorge as it squeezes between the Causse de Sauveterre and Causse Méjean, with, farther off, Mont Lozère, the Aigoual range, the village of La Malène and the hairpin bends of D 16 as it wends its way up the causse.

Take D 16 on the right across the causse and down to Les Vignes via an impressive cliff-face road that runs past the ruins of the **Château de Blanquefort.**

▷ *Return to La Malène.*

On leaving La Malène, the road runs through some narrow straits known as the **Détroits★★** (👁 *see boat trips below*). A **viewpoint**, on the left, offers a good view over this, the narrowest part of the gorges.

Farther down, the road passes round the foot of the **Cirque des Baumes★★** (👁 *see boat trips below*).

Pas de Soucy

At this point, the Tarn disappears beneath a chaotic heap of enormous boulders – the result of two rock slides (*soussitch* in dialect), the more recent being due to an earthquake in 580.

A more poetic legend ascribes the origin of this pile of boulders to the following: the devil fled over the rocks along the cliff above the Tarn, with St Énimie in hot pursuit. When the saint realised she would never catch up with the devil, she called to the rocks for help. In answer to her prayer, a colossal rock slide occurred. One particularly huge rock, Roque Sourde, hurled itself onto Satan with full force. However, the Evil One, though badly bruised, slipped into a crevice in the river bed and returned to Hell.

⚡ Climb down to the edge of the river bank *(15min there and back, rocky path quite steep and overgrown)* for a view of the massive Roque Sourde which fell without shattering. Some 150m/492ft higher up, the 80m/262ft-tall needle, Roche Aiguille, leans towards the abyss. Take care if crossing the Tarn by stepping from one rock to the other, as the slippery surface of the rocks and the strength of the rushing torrent can make this dangerous.

⚡ A climb *(steps; 15min there and back)* to the **viewpoint** (🕐 *Easter to All Saints: 8am-7pm.* 🚌 *0.40€.* ☎ *04 66 48 82 00.0)* on **Roque Sourde** will give a bird's-eye view of the Pas de Soucy.

▷ *At Les Vignes turn right onto D 995, a cliff road with tight hairpin bends. After 5km/3mi, take D 46 to the right which runs across the Causse de Sauveterre and, at St-Georges-de-Lévéjac, turn right once more.*

Point Sublime★★★

From the Point Sublime, there is a splendid view over the Tarn gorges, from the Détroits to the Pas de Soucy and the Roche Aiguille. At the foot of the little plateau, which overlooks the Tarn from a height of more than 400m/1 312ft, lies the magnificent, deep-set Cirque des Baumes, with its colossal limestone cliffs.

▷ *Return to Les Vignes and the Tarn gorges road.*

Soon, flanking the Causse Méjean, the last remaining ruins of **Château de Blanquefort** can be seen clinging tenaciously to a large rock.

Farther along, the huge Cinglegros (🕐 *see Causse MÉJEAN*) rock looms into sight, jutting up starkly detached from the Causse Méjean. On the right bank, cliffs at the edge of the Causse de Sauveterre slope away from the Tarn, forming the cirque of St-Marcellin.

Then, on the left, appears Capluc rock, recognisable by the cross surmounting it. Like the prow of a ship at the end of the Causse Méjean, it overlooks the confluence of the River Tarn and River Jonte.

Finally, having crossed a bridge over the river adorned with a monument in honour of Édouard-Alfred Martel, the road comes to Le Rozier.

Le Rozier

This little village on the confluence of the River Jonte and River Tarn, dwarfed by the cliffs of the Causse Sauveterre, Causse Noir and Causse Méjean, is inevitably the threshold for those visiting the Tarn gorges. It is an excellent point of departure for exploring the gorges on foot or by car. In autumn, Le Rozier is gripped by gourmet fever at the start of the game season. Although the species of thrush indigenous to the *causses* is no longer found here, there are wild boar, woodcock and other game in abundance. Local truffles are also a highly sought-after delicacy.

Boat Trips

From La Malène to the Cirque des Baumes

It is advisable to make this trip in the morning, since this section of the canyon is at its best in the morning light. 🕐🚤 *Apr-Oct: guided tours with commentary (1hr) by a local boatman. In Jul and Aug, departure before 9.30am and after 5pm (morning departure recommended).* 🚌 *72€ per boat of 4 persons. Bateliers des Gorges du Tarn, 48210 La Malène,* ☎ *04 66 48 51 10, fax 04 66 48 52 07, www.gorgesdutarn.com.*

The waters of the Tarn, which gush along turbulently in some places while flowing almost imperceptibly in others, are quite clear; even in the deepest stretches of the river, it is still possible to see the pebbles of the river bed.

Les Détroits★★

This is the most spectacular, and the narrowest, section of the Tarn gorges. The boat passes in front of an opening known as the Grotte de la Momie ("mummy's cave"), then carries on into a magnificent ravine between two tall, sheer cliffs which plunge abruptly into the river. The higher cliff towers in tiers to over 400m/1 312ft above the Tarn. The impressive effect of the limestone walls hemming in the river is heightened by their colour.

Cirque des Baumes★★

Downriver from Les Détroits, the gorge widens, flowing into the splendid Cirque des Baumes (*baume* means cave). The surrounding rock faces are resplendent with colour: predominantly red, but also tinges of white, black, blue grey, and yellow. Clusters of trees and brushwood blend in green and dark tones.

The boats stop at Les Baumes-Hautes.

Canoe Trips

These can be undertaken by any canoeist with some experience of fast-flowing rivers.

During the summer months, the water level between Florac and Ste-Énimie may be too low for trips to be possible. Apart from a few passages of rapids, the journey from Ste-Énimie to the Pas de Soucy is easy. The short stretch of river from here to the Pont des Vignes is very dangerous, so canoes will have to be carried overland. The stretch from Pont des Vignes to Le Rozier is quite turbulent; care should be taken negotiating some of the rapids.

Keen explorers of gorges, leaving from La Malène in the morning, could take a picnic, linger on a beach at Les Détroits, have a swim, lunch by the river and explore the gorges further during the afternoon, on foot or by canoe.

Canyon Location – *48210 Ste-Énimie -* ☎ *04 66 48 50 52 - www.canoecanyon. com or www.canoe-france.com. Canoe/ kayak hire.*

Hiking Tours

Corniche du Tarn 3

Round tour from Le Rozier – 21km/13mi by car, then 3hr 30min on foot.

▶ *From Le Rozier, take the road along the Tarn gorges (D 907) as far as Les Vignes. Turn right towards Florac. The steep road climbs in a series of hairpin bends above the gorges. Turn towards La Bourgarie and park the car there.*

At the end of the hamlet, follow the path waymarked in red. It passes in front of the Bout du Monde ("End of the World") spring. Soon after, at a fork, the right-hand path leads down to the Pas de l'Arc.

Pas de l'Arc – This is a natural pointed arch, formed by erosion of the rock.

▶ *Turn back to the fork and then continue to Baousso del Biel.*

Baousso del Biel

This opening, measuring 40m/131ft up to the arch roof, is the largest natural arch in the region.

The path reaches the point where the arch merges with the plateau. Several hundred yards after this bridge, follow the path up to the left to reach the abandoned farm of Volcégure.

▶ *From here, a forest footpath (GR 6A) leads back to La Bourgarie.*

Tarn Gorge

A. Thuillier/MICHELIN

Tarn Valley footpath 4

From La Malène to St-Chély-du-Tarn – 3hr one way.

▶ *In La Malène, cross the bridge and follow a footpath on the left, waymarked in yellow and green, which leads to another path running along the river bank towards Hauterives (crowded in summer).*

This footpath which follows the River Tarn offers hikers the freedom of discovering the gorges and the cliffs at their own pace.

The path first runs through a wooded area where weeping-willows lean over the river dipping their branches into the water. On the opposite bank stand the Causse de Sauveterre limestone cliffs eroded by the river.

The path then climbs some steps hewn out of the rock, affording a totally different landscape: the luxuriant vegetation growing close to the river has given way to Mediterranean-type scrubland with stunted oaks and sparse wild grasses. Follow the path across a scree *(take particular care here)* to the ghost hamlet of Hauterives (abandoned ruins) then through a forest of pines and oaks; further on, the Château de la Caze and the Cirque de Pouqnadoires come into view just before St-Chély.

TAUTAVEL

MICHELIN LOCAL MAP 344: H-6

Located 28km/17mi NW of Perpignan, this little village in the Corbières, on the banks of the Verdouble, has become a major centre of prehistory due to the discovery in the area of objects which have proved to be of vital significance in the study of the origins of human life. The significant archaeological finds recorded on the various strata of habitation (which are still being excavated) have provided evidence that the area was occupied alternately by prehistoric men and animals between 700 000 and 100 000 BC.

A Bit of History

In the **Caune de l'Arago**, a karst cavity 40m/131ft long by 10-15m/32-49ft wide *(off D 9 to Vingrau)*, fragments of human skull, some of the oldest ever to be found in Europe, were excavated in 1971 and later in 1979. With the aid of these, the appearance of **Tautavel Man** was conjectured. This prehistoric hunter lived in the Roussillon plain about 450 000 years ago (🔥 *see Introduction*). Beyond Vingrau, D 9 reaches **Pas de l'Escale**, a rocky gap in the crest of the eastern Corbières through which the **view**★ extends all the way to Mont Canigou and Puigmal.

Visit

Centre européen de Préhistoire★★

Route de Vingrau. 🐾🕐 *Jul and Aug: 10am-8pm; Apr-Jun and Sep: 10am-12.30pm, 1.30-7pm; Oct, Nov and Jan-Mar: 1.30-5.30pm.* 🎟 *7€ (children: 3.50€; combined ticket with the Musée Préhistoire Européenne).* ☎ *04 68 29 07 76.*

The **European Centre of Prehistory** is devoted to the evolution of man and his environment (based on the significant discoveries made in the Caune de l'Arago and surrounding area). This vast museum makes use of the latest technology and state-of-the-art scenography to take visitors on a journey far back in time, in search of their earliest origins. The rooms are equipped with interactive control panels and video screens which give information on several themes: man's place in the universe, the first tools found on the terraces of the rivers along the Roussillon coastline, the geological formation of the cave and its contents, climatic variations and the corresponding types of fauna, and the tools used by Tautavel Man.

> ### NECTAR FROM THE VINE
>
> 🍷🍷 **Le Grill du Château de Jau** – *66600 Cases-de-Pène – 12km/7.5mi S of Tautavel on D 59 then B-road -* ☎ *04 68 38 91 38 - daurewanadoo.fr - closed 30 Sep-14 Jun and evenings - reservation recommended – 28€.* Have a seat in the shade of a 300 year-old mulberry tree to sample the wines from this winery along with hearty regional dishes. This former Cistercian abbey also houses an art gallery.

A whole floor is devoted to the visual and auditory evocation of life in the Lower Paleolithic Age. Besides several very realistic dioramas showing hunting scenes and wall mounted graphics tracing the evolution of the landscape in the Roussillon plain,

Prehistoric hunting scene

the main attraction is the **life-size reproduction** of the Caune de l'Arago, made with castings of the ceiling and walls of the original cave. Standing at the back of the cave, visitors can watch film extracts of scenes depicting various stages of the cave's occupation: first there are prehistoric men returning from the hunt, hacking up and eating the game they have just caught; then a bear is seen going into hibernation in its lair; finally the progressive transformation of the cave to its present form is shown. A room with a large picture window and a viewing table overlooks the plateaux of Devèze and the Caune d'Arague.

The **reconstituted skeleton of Tautavel Man** and fragments of his skull give an idea of the stature of one of the oldest human species known to date outside Africa: upright and about 1.65m/5ft tall. He was related to Homo Erectus and preceded Neanderthal man by about 300 000 years.

Musée de la Préhistoire européenne - Préhistorama

Inside the Palais des Congrès, rue Anatole-France. 🕐🖐️ *Jul and Aug: guided tours (1hr30min) 11am-9pm; Apr-Jun and Sep: 11am-1.30pm, 2.30-8pm; Jan-Mar and Oct-Dec: 11am-1.30pm, 2.30-6pm.* 🎫 *3.20€ (7-14 years: 1.60€). No charge "Printemps des musées."* ☎ *04 68 29 07 76.*

Five "virtual theatres" offer visitors 3D illustrations of the daily life of Europe's first inhabitants, the tools they used, their hunting methods, their dwellings. This exhibition is a must after a visit to the Centre européen de Préhistoire.

TOULOUSE★★★

POPULATION 398 423

MICHELIN LOCAL MAP 343: G-3

Bathed in Mediterranean light, Toulouse can take on a variety of hues depending on the time of day, ranging from scorching red to dusky pink or even violet. Once the capital of all the regions united by the Occitanian dialects *(langues d'oc)*, Toulouse is now a famous centre of the French aeronautical construction industry, to which numerous high-tech industries have appended themselves, as well as a lively university town. The many and varied cultural opportunities – concert halls, theatres, museums – and leisure facilities the city has to offer play a great part in making it the worthy capital of the Midi-Pyrénées region. 🛈 *Donjon du Capitole, 31000 Toulouse,* ☎ *05 61 11 02 22. www.toulouse-tourisme-office.com.*

▸ **Orient yourself:** From St-Michel bridge, a prestressed concrete construction with great simplicity of line, there is an interesting view. On a clear day, from a position between the centre of the bridge and the west bank, the outline of the Pyrenees can be seen far to the south. From the opposite bank, the view embraces much of the city, from the Jacobins to La Dalbade, and most buildings are easily identifiable. The view of the city is at its best when the warm red tones of the brickwork are set aglow by the rays of the setting sun.

🖐️ *Guided tour of the town. Discovery tours (2hr) 7.70€ to 10€. "Passport" tickets are available which are valid for 2 to 5 tours during your stay. Information available at the tourist office or on www.vpah.culture.fr*

😊 **Don't Miss:** The Old Town, Basilique St-Sernin

A Bit of History

From Celtic to "Capitoul" rule – The ancient settlement of the Volcae, a branch of Celtic invaders, was probably situated in Vieille-Toulouse *(9km/5mi S)*, but moved site and expanded into a large city which Rome made the intellectual centre of Gallia

A "Red-Brick" City

Brick, the only construction material available in any sufficient quantity in the alluvial plain of the Garonne, has long predominated in the buildings of Toulouse, lending the city its unique style and beauty. As brick is so light and mortar adheres to it easily, the master masons of Toulouse were able to construct extravagantly wide vaults spanning a single nave.

Violets

The violet, originally from Parma in Italy, is thought to have been introduced to Toulouse during the 19C by French soldiers who had fought in Napoleon's Italian campaign. It was enthusiastically received by the people of Toulouse, and became the most sought-after item at florists', perfume-makers' and confectioners' (the famous sugared violets). At the beginning of the century, some 600 000 bouquets a year were being sent to the capital, Northern Europe and even Canada. Sadly, disease and mildew soon got the better of this delicate winter plant with its tiny purple flowers. However, from 1985, scientists began research into ways of saving the plant. Ten years later, they succeeded in cultivating it under glass. Nowadays, the greenhouses of Lalande, north of Toulouse, are once again fragrant with the scent of this pretty flower and Toulouse has had its emblem restored to it.

Every year, the *fête de la violette*, a festival in honour of this lovely bloom, is held in late February-early March.

R. Corbel/MICHELIN

Narbonensis. In the 3C, it was converted to Christianity and became the third most important city in Gaul. Visigothic capital in the 5C, it then passed into the hands of the Franks.

After Charlemagne, Toulouse was ruled by counts, but it was far enough removed from the seat of Frankish power to keep a large degree of autonomy. From the 9C to the 13C, under the dynasty of the counts Raimond, the court of Toulouse was one of the most gracious and magnificent in Europe. The city was administered by consuls or *capitouls*, whom the count would systematically consult concerning the defence of the city or any negotiation with neighbouring feudal lords. The administration of the *capitouls* meant that the merchants of Toulouse had the possibility of becoming members of the aristocracy (to mark their rise in station, the new-fledged noblemen would adorn their mansion with a turret). By the time the city passed under the rule of the French crown in 1271, only 12 *capitouls* remained. A Parliament, established in 1420 and reinstated in 1443, supervised law and finance.

The oldest academy in France – After the turmoil of the Albigensian conflict, Toulouse once more became a centre of artistic and literary creativity. In 1324, seven eminent citizens desiring to preserve the *langue d'Oc* founded the "Compagnie du Gai-Savoir," one of the oldest literary societies in Europe. Every year on 3 May, the best poets were awarded the prize of a golden flower. Ronsard and Victor Hugo were honoured in this way, as was poet, playwright and revolutionary journalist Philippe-Nazaire-François Fabre (1755-94), author of the Republican calendar and the ballad *"Il pleut, il pleut, bergère,"* who immortalised his prize by changing his pen-name to **Fabre d'Églantine** (wild rose). In 1694, Louis XIV raised the society to the status of **Académie des Jeux floraux.**

The dyer's woad boom – In the 15C, the trade in **dyer's woad** launched the merchants of Toulouse onto the scene of international commerce, with London and Antwerp among the main outlets. Clever speculation enabled families like the Bernuys and the Assézats to lead the life of princes. Sumptuous palatial mansions were built during this period, symbolising the tremendous wealth and power of these "dyer's woad tycoons." The thriving city of Toulouse, which had been largely medieval in appearance, under-

Public transport – Toulouse has an extensive public transport network: 65 bus routes and, since 1993, a metro line. Six bus routes and the metro operate at night from 10pm; the last buses on each route leave from "Matabiau SNCF" at 5 minutes past midnight; the metro runs from 5.15am to midnight from Sun to Mon; 42 min past midnight Fri and Sat departure from the terminus. Cars can be parked free of charge in the "transit car parks" and you can then take the bus or metro. A red ticket (1.30€ each) allows you to travel anywhere on the network for 1hr. Day round-trip tickets (2.30€), day (5€) and season tickets are also available. For further information contact: Espace Transport - 7 pl. Esquirol - or Allô Semvat - ☎ 05 61 41 70 70, *www.semvat.com.*

Museum pass – Combined tickets are available for the Jacobins church and the following museums: St-Raymond, Paul-Dupuy, Georges-Labit and Augustins. One at 5€ gives access three times; another at 8€ gives access six times. Moreover, entrance to the museums is free on the 1st Sunday of each month.

Address Book

For coin categories, see the Legend.

EATING OUT

A QUICK BITE

La Faim des Haricots – *3 r. du Puits Vert - ☎ 05 61 22 49 25 - schongfrance@yahoo. com - closed Sun -* . A mere stone's throw from the Capitole, this vegetarian restaurant gives diners a choice of varied, plentiful fixed-price menus at painless prices. The warm decor blends brick and yellow shades; the mezzanine is also very appealing.

Jean Chiche – *3 r. St-Pantaléon - ☎ 05 61 21 80 80 - closed evenings.* This pleasant patisserie and tearoom is close to the Capitole. The menu offers a choice of around a dozen light meals, plus cakes and ice creams.

L'Autre Salon de Thé – *45 r. des Tourneurs - lautresalondethe@yahoo.fr - closed lunch, Mon, Tue.* Delicious pastries and nouvelle cuisine are on offer in this restaurant-tearoom right in the city centre. Tea is taken in a small sitting room in the comfort of armchairs set beneath an impressive chandelier. Popular with the locals.

Le Petit Bacchus – *16 r. Pharaon - ☎ 05 62 26 54 87 - closed Aug, Sat and Sun – reservation recommended.* The walls of this charming wine bistro are covered with a great array of miscellany. Interesting selection of regional vintages, enormous salads and 'Croustons', a worthy house speciality using toast made of famous Poilâne bread.

A LEISURELY MEAL

La Madeleine de Proust – *11 r. Riquet - ☎ 05 61 63 80 88 -* . Childhood memories inspire the original, carefully designed decor of this restaurant featuring yellow walls, waxed tables, antique toys, an old school desk, a time-worn cupboard. The cuisine gives the starring role to vegetables that have fallen out of common use.

La Cave des Blanchers – *29 r. des Blanchers - ☎ 05 61 22 47 47 - closed Tues.* An attractive spot, situated among other restaurants on a street which is very popular in the evenings. Vaulted ceiling and pink brick inside, while in summer diners can eat on the pavement terrace. Regional cuisine blending characteristic sweet and sour flavours.

La Régalade – *16 r. Gambetta - ☎ 05 61 23 20 11 – closed Sat lunch, Sun and 2 weeks in Aug.* Located between the Capitole and the Garonne, this small restaurant's pink brick facade leads to a pleasant interior of exposed beams, modern art, wood furniture and bistro chairs. Bountiful traditional fare.

Bon Vivre – *15 bis pl. Wilson - ☎ 05 61 23 07 17 -* . With its terrace giving onto Place Wilson and an attractive interior decorated with photos of Gers (where the proprietor was born), this is an appealing spot with a solid traditional menu.

Le Mangevins – *46 r. Pharaon - ☎ 05 61 52 79 16 – closed Aug and Sun.* In this local tavern where salted foie gras and beef are sold by weight, the bawdy, fun atmosphere is enhanced by ribald songs. There is no menu, but a set meal for hearty appetites. Anyone in search of peace and quiet should look elsewhere!

Colombier – *14 r. Bayard - ☎ 05 61 62 40 05 - colombier@wanadoo.fr - closed Aug, 1 Sep. 25 Dec, Sat lunch, Sun - reservation recommended.* Opened in 1874, this is an essential stopping point for culinary pilgrims in search of authentic cassoulet. Delightful dining room with pink bricks and wall paintings. Friendly and efficient service.

Le Châteaubriand – *42 r. Pargaminières - ☎ 05 61 21 50 58 – closed end Jul-21 Aug .* The atmosphere in this little restaurant in old Toulouse is particularly pleasant. Cosy interior with a parquet floor, red brick walls, a huge mirror and houseplants. Southwestern cooking on the menu.

L'Envers du Décor – *22 r. des Blanchers - ☎ 05 61 23 85 33 – closed Sun and Mon -* . Cuisine of the southwest with some exotic touches is served in this restaurant in a small, busy street not far from the Garonne. Dice, cards, and theatre contribute to the playful ambience; perhaps you will win yourself a second meal. Good luck!

7 Place St-Sernin – *7 pl. St-Sernin - ☎ 05 62 30 05 30 – closed Sat lunch, Sun.* This pretty 19C house typical of Toulouse stands opposite the basilica. Bright red and yellow Catalan colours, contemporary furniture and a display of paintings from a local art gallery garnish the dining room. Contemporary cuisine.

Brasserie de l'Opéra – *1 pl. du Capitole - ☎ 05 61 21 37 03 - closed Sun.* The brasserie of the Grand Hôtel de l'Opéra is the essential place to go and see and be seen. The inviting decor, leather wall seats and autographed photos of the many artists who have spent time here create a special atmosphere. Cuisine of southwest France.

Le Bellevue – *1 av. des Pyrénées - 31120 Lacroix-Falgarde - 13 km au S de Toulouse par D 4 - ☎ 05 61 76 94 97 - closed 20 Oct-20 Nov, Tue and Wed.* A cosy traditional ambience with windows overlooking the Ariège; in summer the large riverside terrace gets busy so reservation is advised.

○○🍴 **Au Gré du Vin** – *10 r. Pléau - ☎ 05 61 25 03 51 – closed Aug, Christmas-New Year, Sat, Sun and public holidays – reservations required.* A casual restaurant opposite the Musée Paul-Dupuy. The rustic setting, pink brick walls, convivial ambience, good selection of wines by the glass and simple, toothsome fare make this a popular address.

○○🍴 **Brasserie "Beaux Arts"** – *1 quai Daurade - ☎ 05 61 21 12 12.* The atmosphere of a 1930s brasserie is recreated here with bistro-style chairs, wall seats, retro lighting, wood panelling and mirrors. The cuisine, in keeping with the decor, features seafood, sauerkraut and a few regional specialities.

○○🍴 **Toulousy-Les Jardins de l'Opéra** – *1 pl. du Capitole - ☎ 05 61 23 07 76 - toulousy@wanadoo.fr - closed 1-7 Jan, 29 Jul-28 Aug, Mon lunch and Sun.* The excellent restaurant of the Grand Hôtel de l'Opéra. Sophisticated cuisine in luxurious surroundings.

WHERE TO STAY

○○ **Hôtel de France** – *5 r. d'Austerlitz - ☎ 05 61 21 88 24 - contact@hotel-france-toulouse.com - 64 rms.* In business since 1910, this attractive hotel is situated a few steps from the Place Wilson. The rooms are of various sizes; though not luxurious, they are shipshape and affordable. Some of the largest come with a balcony.

○○ **Hôtel le Capitole** – *10 r. Rivals - ☎ 05 61 23 21 28 - hotelcapitole@wanadoo.fr - 33 rms: 42/75€ - ⊡ 8€.* Situated very near to the Place du Capitole, this old mansion has a brick facade that has just been redone. Some of the spacious bedrooms are sparkling new, and half are air-conditioned. A bonus: breakfasts are served 'til noon.

○○ **Hôtel St-Sernin** – *Pl. St-Senin - ☎ 05 61 21 73 08 - 🅿 - book in advance – 18 rms.* Some rooms at this family hotel have fine views of the famous basilique St-Sernin; all are simply decorated with yellow or pale pink walls and well presented. Open fireplace in the breakfast room.

○○ **Ours Blanc** – *25 pl. Victor-Hugo - ☎ 05 61 23 14 55 - victorhugo@hotel-oursblanc.com - 38 rms.* Situated opposite the marché Victor-Hugo, this hotel has simple yet comfortable rooms (recently renovated) which are air conditioned and sound proofed; bright breakfast room with some attractive pictures embellishing its walls.

○○ **Hôtel Castellane** – *17 r. Castellane - ☎ 05 61 62 18 82- castellanehotel@wanadoo.fr 49 rms.* This small hotel close to the Capitole is slightly set back from the main thoroughfare. The simple, practical rooms are housed in three different buildings; some rooms are particularly well suited to families. Breakfast is served on the veranda.

○○🍴 **Park Hôtel** – *2 r. Porte-Sardane - ☎ 05 61 21 25 97 - contact@au-park-hotel. com - 44 rms.* An excellent location within a stone's throw of the city's most prominent sights. Renovated, functional rooms (most of which are air-conditioned), effective double glazing, mini-gym… What more could one need?

○○🍴 **Hôtel des Beaux Arts** – *1 pl. du Pont-Neuf - ☎ 05 34 45 42 42 - contact@ hoteldesbeauxarts.com – 19 rms.* A handsome 18C building on the raised banks of the Garonne. The rooms are rather compact but pleasant: a select decor, silky fabrics, nice furniture and a cosy atmosphere prevail. Some rooms overlook the river.

○○🍴 **Hôtel Mermoz** – *50 r. Matabiau - ☎ 05 61 63 04 04 - reservation@hotel. mermoz.com - 🅿 – 52 rms.* The inner flower garden of this hotel near the city centre provides a haven of calm. Many decorative touches, notably portraits of pilots, bring aviation's early years to mind. Spacious rooms furnished in 1930s style.

○○🍴 **Chambre d'hôte Château des Varennes** – *31450 Varennes - 18km/11.2mi E of Toulouse on D 2, Revel road - ☎ 05 61 81 69 24 - j.mericq@wanadoo.fr - ✉ - 5 rms.* This 16C pink brick château and its main courtyard are very impressive. The guest rooms, reached via a stately double stairwell, are elegant indeed; the 'Bedouin' room is particularly colourful. Marvellous vaulted cellars and a park with splendid old trees.

SIT BACK AND RELAX

Maison Octave – *11 allée Franklin-Roosevelt - ☎ 05 62 27 05 21 - octave.fm@ wanadoo.fr - daily noon-midnight.* Come to this famous ice cream parlour for a overwhelming choice of sherbets, ice cream, *vacherins.* Over thirty different flavours to enjoy in the parlour or take home.

ON THE TOWN

Bar La Loupiote – *39 r. Réclusane - ☎ 05 61 42 76 76 - 🕐Mon-Fri 5.30pm-1.30am, Sat 7pm-2.30am – closed Aug, 5 Jan, 1 May, 20 Dec.* Café-theatre, concerts, board games, art and photography exhibitions: the local music and theatre crowd flocks to this bar where conviviality and good humour prevail.

Le Bibent – *5 pl. du Capitole - ☎ 05 61 23 89 03 - daily 7am-1am.* Classified as an historic monument because of its Belle Époque decor, this roomy café has a superb terrace giving onto the Place du Capitole.

Le Père Louis – *45 r. des Tourneurs - ☎ 05 61 21 33 45 – Mon-Sat 8.30am-2.30pm, 5-10.30pm – closed 1 week in Spring, 3 weeks in Aug, Christmas-1 Jan and public holidays.* First opened in 1889 and now a registered historical building, this wine bar is a local institution. The portrait of Père Louis, the founding father, conspicuously observes goings-on from above; his debonair visage also adorns wine bottle labels. Wine is sipped around fat-bellied barrels; an appetizing choice of open-faced sandwiches is available evenings.

Place du Capitole – The famous central square of the city is a pedestrians-only meeting place where numerous markets are held. It is surrounded by alluring terraces, notably those belonging to the Brasserie Le Bibent (magnificent panelling), Le Café des Arcades and the Brasserie de l'Opéra, all facing the Capitole. To the right, Mon Caf is a typical establishment.

SHOWTIME

The magazine *Toulouse Cultures* (monthly and its *Agenda Cultures* (every 2 months) list all current and upcoming events. Don't forget the tourist office Web site: *www.ot-toulouse.fr* and the mairie's Web site: *www.mairie-toulouse.fr*

Cinémathèque de Toulouse – *69 r. du Taur, BP 824 - ☎ 05 62 30 30 10 / 11 - contact@lacinemathequedetoulouse.com - Tue-Sat 2pm-10pm, Sun 2pm-7pm.* This cinematic citadel, founded in 1950 by Raymond Borde, was overseen by Daniel Toscan du Plantier between 1996 and 2003. Numerous theme cycles and film festivals. Exhibition hall, library and bar.

SHOPPING

Markets – The Sunday morning country market held round the Eglise St-Aubin is where farmers come sell their fruit, vegetables and poultry, live or butchered. Wednesday and Friday from November to March, geese, ducks and foie gras are sold Place du Salin. Saturday mornings an organic farmers' market is held Place du Capitole. Sunday mornings L'Inquet, a renowned flea market, takes place around the Basilique St-Sernin. Used-book sellers gather around Place St-Étienne Saturdays and Place Arnaud-Bernard Thursdays (many are present at L'Inquet as well). Another flea market is held in Allée Jules Guesde the first weekend of each month.

Shopping streets – The main shopping streets are Rue d'Alsace-Lorraine, Rue Croix-Baragnon, Rue St-Antoine-du-T., Rue Boulbonne, Rue des Arts and the pedestrian sections of Rue St-Rome, Rue des Filatiers, Rue Baronie and Rue de la Pomme. There is also a shopping mall, St-Georges, in the centre of the city.

Busquets – *10 r. Rémusat - ☎ 05 61 21 22 16 – www.extrawine.com – Mon afternoon-Sat, 9.45am-12.45pm, 2.15-7.15pm – closed Sun and public holidays.* Connoisseurs of wines from the southwest, *foie gras, cassoulet, confit,* and other regional specialities will be in seventh heaven in this shop founded in 1919.

La Maison de la Violette – *Bd de Bonrepas - Canal du Midi - ☎ 05 61 99 01 30 – Tue-Sat 10am-12.30pm, 2pm-6.30pm.*

The celebrated Toulouse violet is the star of this shop housed on a pastel-coloured barge. The very hospitable owner's enthusiasm for this noble flower is contagious – let her guide you through an array of violet-scented perfumes, liqueurs, sweets and cosmetics.

Librairie des Arcades – *16 pl. du Capitole - ☎ 05 61 23 19 49.* This shop specialises in comic books.

Ombres Blanches – *50 r. Gambetta – ☎ 05 34 45 53 33 - info@ombres-blanches.fr – Mon-Sat 10am-7pm.* Toulouse's biggest bookshop.

Privat – *14 r. des Arts - ☎ 05 61 12 64 20.* This publisher and bookshop is a local institution.

Atelier du Chocolat de Bayonne – *1 r. du Rempart-Villeneuve - ☎ 05 61 22 97 67 - Mon-Sat 9.30am-7.30pm – closed early-mid Aug, Christmas, New Year.* All the chocolates in this shop are guaranteed 100 % pure cocoa with no added fat. Faced with such abundance, it is difficult to make a choice: chocolate flavoured with cinnamon, orange or ginger, or rather chocolate from Madagascar, Java or Ecuador??

Olivier Confiseur-Chocolatier – *20 r. Lafayette - ☎ 05 61 23 21 87 - Mon-Sat 9.30am-12.30pm, 1.45pm-7.15pm.* Olivier, a master chocolate maker, produces irresistible specialities, including the famous candied violets, capitouls (almonds covered in dark chocolate), *Clémence Isaure* (Armagnac-soaked grapes covered in dark chocolate), *brindilles* (nougatine covered in chocolate praline) and *Péché du Diable*, The Devil's Sin, (dark chocolate ganache with orange peel and ginger). Heaven help us!

RECREATION

Le Capitole – *Quai de la Daurade - ☎ 05 61 25 72 57 – Apr and Oct daily at 10.30am, 3pm and 4.30pm; May-Sep daily at 10.30am, 3pm, 4.30pm and 6pm - 8€ (children: 5€); Jul-Aug: night cruises, 9pm, 10pm - 5€ (children: 3.50€).* Embark upon the pleasure steamer Le Capitole for a cruise along the Garonne. You'll discover the Pont Neuf, the Saint-Michel lock, the untamed banks of the Île du Grand Ramier… A sightseeing tour full of sights worth seeing!

Parc toulousain – Set on an island in the river Garonne, the Parc toulousain offers four swimming pools, three outdoors and one covered; the Stadium, where the Stade Toulousain rugby team plays; the Parc des Expositions and the Palais des Congrès.

Péniche Baladine – *☎ 05 61 80 22 26 or 06 74 64 52 36 – www.bateaux-toulousains. com - departs quai de la Daurade.* Oct-May: open Wed, Sat, Sun and public holidays; Jun-Sep and school holidays: open every day, Canal du Midi cruises *(1hr 15mins)* depart at 10.50am and 4pm, Garonne cruises *(1hr 15mins)* depart at 2.30pm, 5.30pm and 7pm. 7€. Details of night cruises on request.

Golf club de Toulouse – *31320 Vieille-Toulouse* – ☎ *05 61 73 45 48.* 18 holes.

Golf club de Toulouse Palmola – *Rte d'Albi - A 68 sortie N° 4 - 31660 Buzet-sur-Tarn* – ☎ *05 61 84 20 50 - www.golfdepalmola.com - 9am-6.30pm - closed Mar.* 18-hole golf course. Clubhouse with restaurant, tennis court and swimming pool.

Golf Seilh – *R. de Grenade - 31840 Seilh* – ☎ *05 62 13 14 14 - www.maeva-latitudes-toulouse.co - Mon-Fri 8am-6.30pm, Sat and Sun 8am-7pm - closed 1 Dec, 25 Dec.* Golf Latitudes Toulouse Seilh; two 18-hole golf courses.

CALENDAR OF EVENTS

Fête de la violette – *First or second weekend in Feb* – ☎ *05 62 16 31 31.* Growing, selling, exhibiting… the ideal opportunity to learn all about the flower that is the city's emblem.

Printemps du rire – *Late Mar* - ☎ *05 62 21 23 24, www.printemps-du-rire.com.* Spring comedy festival.

Garonne le Festival – *Late Jun* - ☎ *05 61 32 77 28, www.garonne-rioloco.org.* Visitors from all over the world congregate for concerts and other events.

Piano aux Jacobins – *Sep* - ☎ *05 61 22 40 05, www.pianojacobins.com*

Le Printemps de Septembre – *Late Sep* - ☎ *01 43 38 00 11, www.printempsdeseptembre.com.* Festival of photography and visual arts.

Festival Occitania – *Oct* - ☎ *05 61 11 24 87, www.ieotolosa.free.fr.* Regional culture celebrated through various media (cinema, poetry, song etc…).

Jazz sur son 31 – *Oct* - ☎ *05 34 45 05 92, www.jazz31.com.* Large jazz festival established 18 years ago.

Cinespaña – *Octobre* - ☎ *05 61 12 12 20, www.cinespagnol.com.* Spanish cinema.

RECREATION

Le Capitole – *Quai de la Daurade* - ☎ *05 61 25 72 57* – *Apr and Oct daily at 10.30am, 3pm and 4.30pm; May-Sep daily at 10.30am, 3pm, 4.30pm and 6pm - 8€ (children: 5€); Jul-Aug: night cruises, 9pm, 10pm - 5€ (children: 3.50€).* Embark upon the pleasure steamer Le Capitole for a cruise along the Garonne. You'll discover the Pont Neuf, the Saint-Michel lock, the untamed banks of the Île du Grand Ramier.

went harmonious changes influenced by Italian architectural style, in particular that of the Florentine revival. However, with the introduction of indigo into Europe and the outbreak of the Wars of Religion, the boom collapsed after 1560 and recession set in.

No head is too great – Henri de Montmorency, governor of Languedoc, "first Christian baron" and member of the most illustrious family of France, was renowned for his courage, good looks and generosity and soon became well loved in his adopted province. In 1632, he was persuaded by Gaston d'Orléans, brother of Louis XIII, to take up arms in the rebellion of the nobility against Cardinal Richelieu, a decision that was to cost him dear. Both Orléans and Montmorency were defeated at Castelnaudary, where Montmorency fought valiantly, sustaining more than a dozen wounds, before being taken prisoner. He was condemned to death by the Parliament at Toulouse. Nobody could believe that such a popular and high ranking figure would be executed, but the king, who had come in person to Toulouse with Cardinal Richelieu, turned a deaf ear to the pleas of the family, the court and the people, claiming that as king he could not afford to show favour to any particular individual. He did however graciously concede that the condemned man could be beheaded inside the Capitole, instead of in the market place. On the specially constructed scaffold in the interior courtyard, at the foot of the statue of Henri IV, the 37-year-old duke met his death with all the dignity befitting a noble lord. When his head was shown to the crowd in front of the Capitole, there were howls of vengeance levelled at the cardinal.

Born in Toulouse – Toulouse is the birthplace of several famous French figures, including Jean-Pierre Rives, champion of the Toulouse rugby team, and Claude Nougaro, a late-20C troubadour. Those familiar with the little round tins of Lajaunie sweets (in aniseed and other flavours) will be interested to know that Lajaunie, a chemist, was also a native of Toulouse.

Old Town★★★

From St-Sernin to the Capitole 1

Basilique St-Sernin★★★

This is the most famous and most magnificent of the great Romanesque pilgrimage churches in the south of France, and one which can also boast the largest collection of holy relics. The site was home, in the late 4C, to a basilica containing the body of St

Sernin (or Saturninus). This Apostle from the Languedoc, the first bishop of Toulouse, was martyred in 250 by being tied to the legs of a bull he had refused to sacrifice to pagan gods, which dragged him down a flight of stone steps.

With the donation of numerous relics by Charlemagne, the church became a focus for pilgrims from all over Europe, and also a stopping place for pilgrims on their way to Santiago de Compostela. The present building was constructed to meet these growing needs. It was begun in c 1080 and completed in the mid-14C. General restoration was undertaken in 1860 by Viollet-le-Duc. The current programme of repair work is intended to restore the roof to its appearance prior to the work carried out in 1860. The transept arms and the nave are now covered once again by ample overhanging roofs with open galleries (mirandes) just beneath the eaves.

Exterior – St-Sernin is constructed from red brick and white stone. On the chevet, begun in the late 11C, stone is much in evidence, whereas the nave is built almost all of brick, which in turn is the only material used in the belfry.

The 11C **chevet** is the oldest part of the building. It forms a magnificent ensemble of five apsidal chapels and four transept chapels combining with the tiered roofs of the chancel and transept, and the elegant bell-tower rising out of the whole.

The five-tier octagonal **bell-tower** stands majestically above the transept crossing. The three lower tiers are embellished with early-12C Romanesque round arches. The two upper storeys were added 150 years later; the openings, shaped like mitres, are surmounted by little decorative pediments. The spire was added in the 15C.

The doorway known as the **Porte des Comtes**, originally dedicated to St Sernin, opens into the south transept. The capitals on their colonnettes, relatively crudely executed, depict the parable of Lazarus and the Rich Man (right portal), concentrating on the punishments meted out to the latter for his sins of avarice (left portal, first capital on the left) and lechery (left portal, first capital on the right and second capital on the left). On either side of the central pillar, the Rich Man asking if he might return to earth to warn his brother is depicted being kept imprisoned in Hell (the repetition of the same motif stresses the eternal duration of the punishment).

To the left of the doorway, in an alcove protected by a metal grille, are four sarcophagi, the coffins of the counts of Toulouse, hence the name of the doorway. Farther to the left is a Renaissance arcade, all that remains of the fortified wall which, until the early 19C, surrounded the church, the buildings of the chapter of canons and the adjacent cemeteries.

The Romanesque sculpture on the **Porte Miégeville** (leading into the south side of the nave) set a fashion throughout the south of France. Dating from the early 12C, it conveys expression and movement more vividly than any work of the previous century.

Interior – St-Sernin is the epitome of a major pilgrimage church. It was designed to accommodate large congregations, with room for a choir of canons and consists of a nave flanked by double side aisles, a broad transept and a chancel with an ambulatory from which five radiating chapels open off.

For a Romanesque church, St-Sernin is particularly vast, measuring 115m/377ft in length, 64m/210ft in width at the transept and 21m/68ft in height to the roof vault.

Imagine a cross-section of the church to appreciate the perfection of its height and proportions. The barrel-vaulted nave is supported by a first set of side aisles, with ribbed vaulting and surmounted by pretty half-barrel vaulted galleries. The first side aisles themselves rest on a second, slightly lower set of side aisles, again with ribbed vaulting but supported by buttresses. In this way, all of the elements that make up this enormous building combine to ensure its solidity.

Chancel – Beneath the dome of the transept crossing, there is a fine table of Pyrenean marble from the old Romanesque altar signed by Bernard Gilduin and consecrated in 1096 by Pope Urban II.

Transept – The vast transept is laid out as three aisles with east-facing chapels. The capitals of the tribune gallery and the Romanesque mural paintings are worthy of attention. In the north transept, two groups of Romanesque mural paintings have been uncovered (the Resurrection and the Lamb of God presented by angels).

One of the south transept chapels is dedicated to the Virgin Mary (note the 14C statue of "Notre-Dame-la-Belle"); on the chapel's oven-vault are frescoes one above the other mingling the theme of the Virgin seated "in Majesty" (13C) with the Coronation of the Virgin.

TOULOUSE

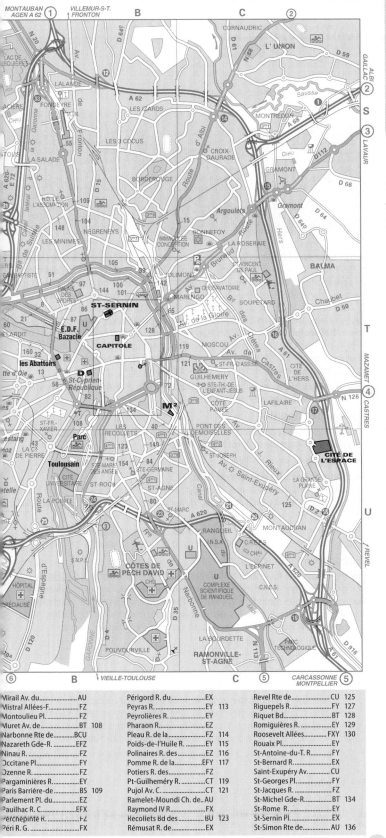

Ambulatory and crypt – ⏲ *Jul-Sep: 8.30am-6.15pm, Sun 8.30am-9.30pm; Oct-Jun: 8.30-11.45am, 2-5.45pm, Sun 8.30am-12.30pm, 2-7.30pm.* ⊚ *2€.* Numerous altarpieces and reliquaries on display in the ambulatory have led to its being known as the Corps Saints, or Holy Relics, since the 17C. Carved, gilded and painted wooden caskets contain the remains of St Asciscle, St Victoria, St Hilary and St Papoul, among others. On the wall curving round the outside of the crypt are seven impressive late-11C **low-relief sculptures**★★ in St-Béat marble from the studio of Bernard Gilduin: Christ in Majesty, with the symbols of the Evangelists, surrounded by angels and Apostles. The upper crypt contains the reliquary of St Saturninus (13C); the lower crypt contains various reliquary chests and statues of the Apostles (14C).

▷ *Follow rue du Taur, one of the favourite haunts of students, lined with many bookshops selling new and second-hand books.*

Collège de l'Esquila

This opens off no 69 rue du Taur through a doorway decorated with bosses, a Renaissance work by Toulouse sculptor N Bachelier.

▷ *Turn left onto rue du Périgord.*

Ancienne chapelle des Carmelites

♿⏲ *May-Sep: daily except Mon 9.30am-1pm, 2-6pm; Oct-May: daily except Mon 10am-1pm, 2-5pm.* ⏲ *Closed 1 Jan, 1 May, 1 and 11 Nov, 25 Dec. Price information not provided.* ☎ *05 61 21 27 60.*

The decoration of this chapel – woodwork and paintings commemorating the Carmelite order (by the Toulouse painter Despax) – is a fine example of 18C art.

Bibliothèque municipale

The city library was founded in 1866, combining the libraries of the local clergy and of the Collège Royal, which itself had benefited from the confiscation of a dozen or so conventual libraries during the Revolution. The building is the work of Montariol and is a handsome example of 1930s architecture – note in particular the reading room, with its large windows and dome and striking ceiling of coloured glass tiles.

▷ *Return to rue du Taur and turn left.*

Église Notre-Dame-du-Taur

This church, known as St-Sernin-du-Taur until the 16C, replaced the sanctuary erected where the martyr saint was buried. The gable wall of the façade, flanked by octagonal towers and decorated with mitre arches, is characteristic of the region, where it served as a model for numerous country churches. The bell-tower is crenellated and topped by a triangular gable. The church is a catalogue of the various decorative devices to which brick lends itself, such as diamond-shaped windows and dog-tooth friezes.

▷ *On reaching place du Capitole, turn right onto rue Romiguières then left onto rue Lakanal.*

Les Jacobins★★

In 1215, **St Dominic**, alarmed by the spread of the Albigensian heresy, founded the Order of Preachers (Dominican Order). The first Dominican monastery was founded in Toulouse in 1216; the friars reached Paris a year later and set up a community in

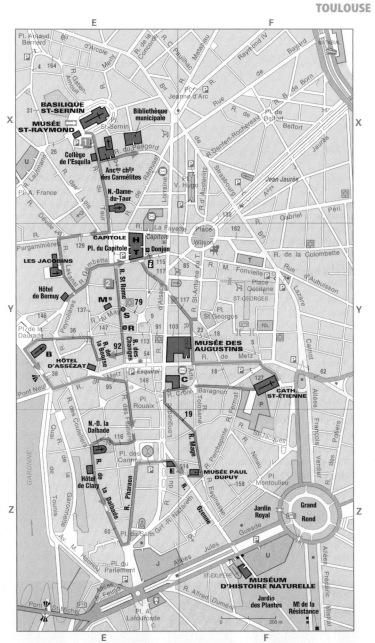

a chapel dedicated to St James the Great (St Jacques in French), from which they acquired the name of "Jacobins." The construction of the church and the monastery – the first university in Toulouse – was begun in 1230, and continued throughout the 13C and 14C. The buildings suffered badly when they were converted into barracks to house an artillery regiment during the First Empire (Napoleon I), with the church pressed into service as stables.

Extensive restoration work resulted in the church, cloisters and surviving conventual buildings, including the great sacristy (⚷ closed to the public), being restored to their former glory by 1974.

The red-brick church is a masterpiece of the southern French Gothic, marking a milestone in the evolution of this style. In 1369, the body of St Thomas Aquinas was placed in the "mother-church" of the Order of Preachers, which had been completed around 1340. The church has a striking exterior, featuring huge relieving arches surmounted by oculi between massive buttresses, and an ornate octagonal bell-tower adorned with mitre arches, which served as a model for the bell-towers of numerous prosperous churches throughout the region. On its completion in 1298, the tower was fitted with the only bell of the Dominican university (👁 the interior is described under Additional Sights).

Hôtel de Bernuy (Lycée Pierre-de-Fermat)

🕐 Mon-Fri 8am-5pm. 🕐 Closed public holidays.

This mansion was built in two stages in the early 16C. The beautiful main doorway (1 rue Gambetta) blends curves and counter-curves, in typically Gothic style, with medallions. The first courtyard provides an architectural interlude in stone. On the reverse side of the doorway is a sumptuous Renaissance portico complete with loggia, to the right of which is a heavily depressed arch. A passage with ribbed vaulting leads into a second courtyard, in which all the charm of the "red-brick city" is once again in evidence. An octagonal corbelled **staircase turret**★, one of the tallest in old Toulouse, is lit through windows that neatly follow the angle where two walls meet.

▸ Rue Gambetta leads to place du Capitole.

Place du Capitole

Along the east side of this vast square, the main meeting point for local residents, stretches the majestic façade of the Capitole building. At the centre of the square, inlaid into the paving, is an enormous bronze Occitan cross, surrounded by the signs of the zodiac, by Raymong Moretti who is also the author of 29 colourful pictures displayed under the arcades, depicting episodes and characters from the town's history.

Capitole★

♿🕐 8.30am-5pm, Sat 9am-noon, Sun and public holidays 10am-7pm. No charge. ☎ 05 61 22 34 12.

This is the city hall of Toulouse, named after the "capitouls," or consuls, who used to run the city. The façade overlooking place du Capitole dates from the mid-18C.

Café in the arcades, place du Capitole

Quai de la Daurade

Measuring 128m/420ft in length, it is a fine and colourful example of architectural composition, with the skilful alternating use of brick and stone and the decorative Ionic pilasters. The right wing houses the theatre of Toulouse, refurbished in 1995-96. The courtyard was the scene of the execution of the duke of Montmorency in 1632 (👁 *see above*), for which there is a commemorative plaque on the flagstones.

▷ *Enter the courtyard.*

The staircase, hall and various rooms, most notably the **Salle des Illustres** dedicated to the most glorious representatives of Toulouse, were decorated with appropriate grandiosity at the time of the Third Republic, by specially commissioned officially approved painters.

Cross the courtyard and walk diagonally through the gardens to get to the keep *(donjon)*, a remnant of the 16C Capitole, restored by Viollet-le-Duc. It now houses the tourist office.

Around the Capitole ②

▷ *Leave place du Capitole heading S along rue Saint-Rome.*

Rue St-Rome

Pedestrian street. This busy shopping street is part of the old *cardo maximus* (Roman road through town from north to south). At the beginning of the street (no 39) stands the interesting house of Catherine de' Medici's physician (Augier Ferrier). Pierre Séguy's fine Gothic turret is tucked inside the courtyard of no 4 **rue Jules-Chalande.** At no 3 rue St-Rome is an elegant early-17C town house, the Hôtel de Gomère.

Rue des Changes

The square known as "Quatre Coins des Changes" is overlooked by the Sarta turret. Nos 20, 19 and 17 boast some interesting decorative features (timbering, window frames etc), whereas no 16, the 16C Hôtel d'Astorg et St-Germain, has a façade with a gallery just beneath the eaves – a local feature known as *mirandes* – and a pretty courtyard with timber galleries and diagonally opposed spiral staircases with wooden handrails.

▷ *Turn right before reaching the place Esquirol crossroads.*

Rue Malcousinat

At no 11, the 16C Hôtel de Cheverny, the attractive main building, which is Gothic-Renaissance, is flanked by an austere 15C keep.

▷ *Turn right onto rue de la Bourse.*

Rue de la Bourse

Note at no 15 the Hôtel de Nupces (18C). No 20, the late-15C Hôtel Delfau, is the house of Pierre Del Fau, who hoped to become a *capitoul* – hence the turret – but who never fulfilled his ambition.

The 24m/78m-high turret, pierced with five large windows, is quite remarkable. The windows on the second and fifth floors feature an elegant ogee-arch-shaped lintel.

▶ *Turn left onto rue Cujas and follow it to place de la Daurade.*

Basilique Notre-Dame-de-la-Daurade

The present church, which dates from the 18C, occupies the site of a pagan temple that was converted into a church dedicated to the Virgin Mary in the 5C, and a Benedictine monastery. The inhabitants of Toulouse are very attached to this church (pilgrimages to Notre-Dame-la-Noire, a Black Madonna, prayers for the welfare of expectant mothers and ceremonies for the blessing of the flowers awarded to the winners of the Jeux Floraux). It has an interesting façade with a heavy peristyle overlooking the Garonne.

Take a short stroll along **quai de la Daurade,** downstream of the Pont Neuf (16C-17C), past the fine arts academy (École des Beaux-Arts); there is a good view of the St-Cyprien district (west bank) with its two hospitals, the Hôtel-Dieu and the domed Hospice de la Grave.

▶ *Take rue de Metz to the left, and bear left again.*

Hôtel d'Assézat★★

&. © *Daily except Mon 10am-12.30pm, 1.30-6pm, Thu 10am-12.30pm, 1.30-9pm.* © *Closed 1 Jan and 25 Dec.* ☞ *4.60€.* ☎ *05 61 12 06 89. www.fondation-bemberg.fr.*

This, the finest private mansion in Toulouse, was built in 1555-57 according to the plans of Nicolas Bachelier, the greatest Renaissance architect of Toulouse, for the Capitoul d'Assézat, who had made a fortune from trading in dyer's woad.

The façades of the buildings to the left of and opposite the entrance are the earliest example of the use of the Classical style in Toulouse, characterised by the three decorative orders – Doric, Ionic, Corinthian – used one above the other, creating a marvellously elegant effect. To add a bit of variety to these façades, the architect introduced rectangular windows beneath relieving arches on the ground and first floors. On the second floor, the lines are reversed, with round-arched windows beneath straight horizontal entablatures.

The sophistication of this design is matched by the elaborate decoration on the two doorways, one with twisted columns and the other adorned with scrolls and garlands. Sculpture underwent a revival in Toulouse at the time of the Renaissance, when stone began to be used again, in conjunction with brick.

On the inside of the façade facing the street, there is an elegant portico with four arcades, surmounted by a gallery. The fourth side was never completed, as Assézat, having converted to the Protestant faith, was driven into exile, a ruined man. The wall is adorned only by a covered gallery resting on graceful consoles.

Hôtel d'Assézat

B. Kaufmann/MICHELIN

The mansion houses the **Bemberg Foundation** (& *see Additional Sights*).

▶ *Take rue des Marchands to the right and turn right onto rue des Filatiers, then right again onto rue des Polinaires and rue H.-de-Gorsse, in which there are some attractive 16C houses. Turn left onto rue de la Dalbade.*

Église Notre-Dame-la-Dalbade

The present church was built in the 16C, on the site of an earlier building, which had white walls. In 1926 the bell-tower fell in, damaging the church, which was subsequently restored, with particular attention paid to its beautiful brickwork. The Renaissance doorway has a ceramic tympanum dating from the 19C.

Rue de la Dalbade

© *Closed Sun afternoons.*

This street is lined with the elegant mansions of former local dignitaries. Nos 7, 11, 18 and 20 have fine 18C façades. Note no 22, the Hôtel Molinier, which boasts an extravagantly ornate, sculpted doorway (16C) of quite profane inspiration. The **Hôtel de Clary,** at no 25, has a beautiful Renaissance courtyard. Its façade, fairly groaning with pillars, festoons and cherubs among other things, caused a sensation when it was put up in the 17C, as it was made of stone, considered the ultimate symbol of the owner's wealth in a city of predominantly brick buildings (hence the other name by which the building is known – the Hôtel de Pierre).

The Hôtel des Chevaliers de St-Jean-de-Jérusalem (no 30), a grand 17C mansion, was the headquarters of the great priory of the Order of Malta (1668).

Rue Pharaon

This really pretty street has a number of interesting features: the Hôtel du Capitoul Marvejol at no 47 (charming courtyard); 18C façades at no 29; turret dating from 1478 at no 21.

▶ *Walk along rue Pharaon to place des Carmes then turn right onto rue Ozenne.*

Hôtel Béringuier-Maynier also known as Hôtel du Vieux-Raisin

The main building at the back of the courtyard marks the first manifestation of the Italian Renaissance in Toulouse, in the style of the châteaux of the Loire Valley (stone as well as brick work). The ornamentation of the wings is much more turbulent in style, verging on the Baroque – windows adorned with caryatids, for example.

▶ *Behind the mansion, take rue Ozenne.*

Rue Ozenne

At no 9 the Hôtel Dahus and Tournoër turret make a handsome 15C architectural group.

▶ *Take rue de la Pleau to the left.*

The Hôtel Pierre-Besson houses the Musée Paul-Dupuy (see Additional Sights).

Rue Mage

This is one of the best-preserved streets in Toulouse, with period houses at nos 20 and 16 (Louis XIV) and no 11 (Louis XIII); the Hôtel d'Espie (no 3) is an example of French Rococo (Louis XV or Regency style).

Rue Bouquières – Note the splendid architecture of the Hôtel de Puivert (18C).

Hôtel de Fumel (Palais Consulaire)

This mansion houses the Chamber of Commerce. It features a fine 18C façade, at right angles, overlooking the garden.

From the corner of rue Tolosane, the façade and tower of the cathedral can be seen, whereas to the left the tower of Les Augustins rises from among trees. No 24 **rue Croix-Baragnon** is home to the city's Cultural Centre. No 15, "the oldest house in Toulouse," dating from the 13C, is distinguished by its gemel windows.

Place St-Étienne

In the middle of the square stands a 16C fountain – the oldest in Toulouse – known as "Le Griffoul."

Cathédrale St-Étienne★

Compared to St-Sernin, the cathedral appears curiously unharmonious in style. It was built over several centuries, from the 11C to the 17C, and combines the Gothic styles of both southern and northern France. As funds ran out, the nave and the upper level of the chancel were left uncompleted. In the 13C, the bishops and the chapter had a rose window inserted into the façade of the original church, which was begun in 1078. Then, in the 15C, a doorway was added. Finally, in the 16C, a rectangular belfry-keep was built, quite unlike the polygonal openwork bell-towers found throughout the region.

▶ *Enter through the doorway on the west front.*

The nave and the chancel are not quite in line with each other and do not give the impression of having been designed as a unit. This is because reconstruction of the church (after Toulouse passed under the rule of the French crown) began with the chancel, without taking the nave, built in 1209, into consideration as it was planned to demolish it. It was eventually decided to adopt a makeshift solution and link the two, thereby necessitating considerable architectural feats in what should have been the north arm of the transept (note the arrangement of the vault ribs fanning out from the supporting pillar).

The vast single nave, as wide as it is high, is the first manifestation of the southern French Gothic style and gives a good idea of the progress made in architectural techniques: St-Étienne's single vault spans 19m/62ft, and St-Sernin's Romanesque vault a mere 9m/29ft.

The austerity of its walls is alleviated by a fine collection of 16C and 17C tapestries made in Toulouse, tracing the life of St Stephen. On the keystone of the third span of the vault, note the "cross with 12 pearls," the coat of arms of the counts of Toulouse, and later of the province of Languedoc.

The construction of the choir, begun in 1272, came to a halt 45 years later and the building was covered with a timber-frame roof. In 1609, the roof was destroyed by fire and replaced by the present vault, which is only 28m/91ft high, instead of the 37m/121ft anticipated in the original design.

The altarpiece adorning the high altar, the choir stalls, the organ case, and the stained glass in the five large windows in the apse date from the 17C. In the ambulatory, there are some very old stained-glass windows, notably a 15C window in the chapel immediately to the right of the axial chapel, portraying King Charles VII (wearing a crown and a blue cape with gold fleur-de-lis) and the dauphin Louis, the future Louis XI (depicted kneeling, dressed as a knight).

Leave by the south door and walk round the church to appreciate the robust solidity of the buttresses supporting the chancel, evidence that they were intended to support greater things...

▶ *Turn left onto rue de Metz then right onto rue des Arts and left again onto rue de la Pomme, which leads back to place du Capitole.*

Additional Sights

Église des Jacobins★★
Rue Lakanal. Exterior described under ① *above.* ♿ ⓘ *9am-7pm.* ⚊ *2.20€, no charge 1st Sun in the month.* ☎ *05 61 22 39 52.*

The awesome **main body**★★ of the church, which has two naves, is the result of successive enlargements and additions of further storeys. It reflects the Dominican Order's prestige, its prosperity and its two main aims: the service of God and the preaching of God's word.

On the floor of the church, the ground plan of the original rectangular sanctuary (1234) which was covered by a timber-frame roof is indicated by five black-marble slabs (the bases of the old pillars) and by a line of black tiles (the old walls). The church's roof vault, which reaches a height of 28m/91ft up to the keystones, is supported on seven columns. The **column**★★ at the far east end supports the entire fan vaulting of the apse; its 22 ribs, alternately wide and narrow, resemble the branches of a palm tree. As much of the original polychrome painted wall decoration remained, those in charge of the restoration work were able successfully to recreate the atmosphere of the church. Up as far as the sills of the clerestory windows, the walls are decorated with painted imitation brickwork in ochre and pink. Other stripes of contrasting colours are used to emphasise the upward thrust of the engaged colonnettes and the graceful sweep of the ribs on the roof vault.

The stained-glass windows were inserted from 1923: *"grisaille"* (monotonal) windows round the apse, and brighter-coloured windows in the nave. The rose windows on the façade date from the 14C.

Since the ceremony for the seventh centenary of the death of St Thomas Aquinas in 1974, the relics of the "saintly doctor" have once more been on display beneath a high altar of grey marble, from Prouille.

Cloisters – The north door opens into cloisters adorned with twin colonnettes, typical of Languedoc Gothic (other examples may be found in St-Hilaire in the Corbières and Arles-sur-Tech). It was possible to reconstitute the south and

Jacobins' cloisters

B. Kaufmann/MICHELIN

east galleries, which were destroyed in c 1830, by using fragments of work in the same style, which had been found scattered throughout the region.

Chapelle St-Antonin – This chapel, on the left of the chapter-house, was built from 1337 to 1341 as a funeral chapel by friar Dominique Grima, who became bishop of Pamiers (keystone of the arch above the head of Christ of the Apocalypse).

The bones were transferred from tombs in the floor of the nave into an ossuary beneath the raised altar. The chapel is a delicate example of the Gothic style. It was decorated, in 1341, with predominantly blue mural paintings.

The medallions inscribed in the segments of the vault depict the second vision of the Apocalypse. On the walls, beneath angel musicians, are two tiers depicting scenes from the fantastic legend of St Antonin of Pamiers which reaches its conclusion on the keystone of the arch of the apse: the martyr's relics are shown being escorted by two white eagles.

Chapter house – This was built in c 1300. Two very slim facetted columns support the roof vault. The graceful apsidal chapel once more boasts colourful mural decoration.

Grand Réfectoire – The great refectory (north-east corner of the cloisters) is a vast room, built in 1303, with a timber-frame roof supported on six transverse arches separating the bays. It is open during temporary exhibitions of modern art.

Musée St-Raymond★★

Place St-Sernin. ♿🕐 *Jun-Aug: 10am-7pm; Sep-May: 10am-6pm.* 🕐 *Closed 1 Jan, 1 May, 25 Dec.* 🎟 *2.20€.* ☎ *05 61 22 31 44.*

This museum, housed in one of the buildings of the old Collège St-Raymond (13C), rebuilt in 1523 and restored by Viollet-le-Duc, was recently refurbished and now displays its collections of archaeology and antique art (remarkable collection of Roman emperors' heads) on three levels.

The top floor presents artefacts from Tolosa and the Ancient province of Narbonne; the first floor is devoted to mosaics (some of them are exceptionally fine) and to sculpture from the Roman villa of Chiragan in Martres-Tolosane. As for the basement, it has been specially reorganised to display various finds uncovered during the renovation of the building (in particular a lime kiln) as well as a collection of early-Christian sarcophagi found in the St-Sernin necropolis.

The Salle du Tinel on the ground floor presents thematic exhibitions that enable the museum to display its stock on a rota system.

Fondation Bemberg★★

The Hôtel d'Assézat now houses the donation of private art collector **Georges Bemberg**. This impressive collection comprises painting, sculpture and objets d'art from the Renaissance to the 20C.

Old Masters (16C-18C) are displayed as they would be in a private home. There are paintings by the 18C Venetian School (*vedute* by Canaletto and Guardi), 15C Flemish works such as *Virgin and Child* from the studio of Rogier Van der Weyden and 17C Dutch painting, with *Musicians* by Pieter de Hooch. Displayed with the paintings are 16C objets d'art such as a nautilus and a *grisaille* Limoges enamel plaque depicting Saturn. The **gallery of Renaissance portraits** includes paintings (*Charles IX* by François Clouet, *Portrait of a Young Woman with a Ring* by Ambrosius Benson and *Portrait of Antoine de Bourbon* by Franz Pourbus) and 16C sculpture groups. The small room adjoining this contains bronzes from Italy, such as a superb figure of Mars attributed to Giovanni Bologna, alongside Limoges enamels, leather-bound books and paintings by Veronese, Tintoretto and Bassano.

One wing illustrates 18C art through painting, furniture and decorative arts (in particular porcelain).

An open gallery overlooking the courtyard leads to the staircase up to the second floor, which is devoted to Modern Masters (19C-20C). The collection, in which a high point is the series of paintings by Bonnard, executed in a vibrant palette (*Woman with a Red Cape, Le Cannet, Still Life with Lemons*), includes works by almost all the great names of the Modern French School, offering an overview of the main movements in paintings from the late 19C to the early 20C: Impressionism, Pointillism, Fauvism. Artists featured include Louis Valtat (*La Lecture*), Paul Gauguin (*Face of a Young Peasant*), Matisse (*View of Antibes*), HE Cross (*Canal in Venice*), Eugène Boudin (*Crinolines on the Beach*), Claude Monet (*Boats on the Beach in Étretat*) and Raoul Dufy (*Kessler Family on Horseback*).

The vaulted rooms in the basement house temporary exhibitions.

From May to October, a tearoom takes over the gallery in the information area.

Musée des Augustins★★

Rue de Metz. 🚻🕐 *Daily except Tue 10am-6pm, Wed 10am-9pm.* 🕐 *Closed 1 Jan, 1 May, 25 Dec.* 💶 *2.20€, no charge 1st Sunday in the month.* ☎ *05 61 22 21 82. www.augustins. org.*

This museum is housed in the former Augustinian monastery designed in the southern French Gothic style (14C and 15C), specifically the chapter-house and the great and small cloisters. The building facing rue d'Alsace-Lorraine was constructed by Darcy in the 19C, following plans by Viollet-le-Duc, on the site of the former refectory.

Gothic sculptures (13C-15C) – The graceful galleries of the great cloisters (14C) shelter an interesting collection of early-Christian stonework, and a series of Gothic gargoyles from the Cordeliers Church (south gallery). The eastern wing includes the sacristy (14C sculpted consoles), Notre-Dame-de-Pitié Chapel (14C) and the chapter-house. Notre-Dame-de-Pitié Chapel is devoted to the *Cycle de Rieux* sculpture collection, from a 14C funeral chapel found in Rieux-Volvestre. The chapter-house (late 15C) has original works from that period, including the *Pietà des Récollets* and the famous Virgin and Child known as *Notre-Dame de Grasse*; the drapery of her gown is rendered with great silkiness, and her attitude is striking.

Religious painting (14C-18C) – The church is characteristic of the southern Gothic style; the chevet has three chapels opening directly on a large nave, without a transept. The paintings are from the 15C, 16C and 17C (Perugino, Rubens, Murillo, Guercino, Simon Vouet, Nicolas Tournier, Murillo), and the sculptures from the 16C-17C.

Romanesque sculptures★★★ (12C) – In the western wing, built on plans by Viollet-le-Duc and punctuated by great arches, the admirable historiated or foliated capitals were mostly taken from the cloisters of St-Sernin Basilica, the monastery of Notre-Dame de la Daurade and buildings from the chapter-house of St-Étienne Cathedral. Among the especially beautiful capitals are the story of Job (La Daurade Monastery), the Wise and Foolish Virgins (St-Étienne), and **Death of Saint John the Baptist** (St-Étienne), attributed to Gilabertus, one of the great masters of Romanesque sculpture.

French painting (17C-19C) – Upstairs, the *salon rouge*, which is evocative of 19C museums in its presentation (there are many paintings on the wall, some of them quite high up), is largely devoted to 19C French painting. There are a good number of works by artists from Toulouse: Jean-Paul Laurens (1838-1921), Henri Martin (1860-1943), and also works by Corot, Gros, Courbet, Isabey, Benjamin-Constant and Delacroix. There are also works from the late 19C: Toulouse-Lautrec, Vuillard, Manguin.

The salon brun is devoted to works created in Toulouse in the 17C-18C.

The salon vert displays 17C-18C French paintings: Philippe de Champaigne *(Réception d'Henri d'Orléans)*, Largillière, Oudry etc.

After visiting the museum, return to the **cloisters**, where different gardens have been recreated as they would have existed in medieval monasteries and abbeys. From the gardens, there is a view over the bell-tower and the nave of the old church belonging to the Augustins.

Muséum d'Histoire Naturelle★★

Located in the Jardin des Plantes (botanical gardens). ⊶ *Closed for renovation work.*

The natural history museum has extensive collections, most notably of ornithological, prehistoric and ethnographical exhibits.

Take this opportunity to discover the **Jardin des Plantes,** the **Jardin Royal** and the **Grand Rond**, well laid out gardens that make a very pleasant place for a stroll. At the southern end of allée Fréderic-Mistral, in the botanical gardens, stands the **Musée départemental de la Résistance et de la Déportation**. (🚻🕐 *Daily except Sun 9.30am-noon, 2-6pm, Sat 2-5m.* 🕐 *Closed public holidays. No charge.* ☎ *05 61 14 80 40.)* An arrangement of lenses ensures that sunlight enters the crypt only on 19 August, the anniversary of the liberation of Toulouse.

Musée Paul-Dupuy★

13 rue de la Pleau. 🕐 *Jun-Sep: 10am-6pm; Oct-May: daily except Tue 10am-5pm.* 🕐 *Closed public holidays.* 💶 *2.20€, no charge 1st Sunday in the month.* ☎ *05 61 14 65 50.*

This museum is devoted to the applied arts from the Middle Ages to the present: metal and wood work, clock-making, weights and measures, coins, musical instruments, enamel work, gold plate, costumes and weapons, as well as a reconstruction of the Jesuit college dispensary (17C). The print room contains some interesting works by local artists.

Musée Georges-Labit★

Along the Canal du Midi, near rue du Japon. &.🕐 *Jun-Sep: daily except Tue 10am-6pm; Oct-May: daily except Tue 10am-5pm.* 🕐 *Closed public holidays.* 🎫 *2.20€, no charge 1st Sunday in the month.* ☎ *05 61 14 65 50.*

This museum is located in the Moorish villa in which Georges Labit (1862-99), a citizen of Toulouse and enthusiastic collector of anything to do with the Orient, from India to the Far East, assembled the artefacts he had brought back from his travels. After numerous additions, the museum now displays remarkable collections of sculpture, paintings, textiles, ceramic ware and various other items reflecting the great Oriental civilisations (China, Japan, Cambodia, India, Tibet, Nepal, Thailand), as well as Egyptian antiquity and Coptic art.

Les Abattoirs★

76 allées Charles-de-Fitte (west bank of the Garonne). &.🕐 *Summer: daily except Mon noon-8pm; winter: 11am-7pm.* 🕐 *Closed 1 Jan, 1 May, 25 Dec.* 🎫 *6.10€, no charge 1st Sunday in the month.* ☎ *05 62 48 58 00.*

The brick buildings of the former slaughter houses have been turned into a museum of modern and contemporary art illustrating various post-war trends: Abstract Expressionism, Informal Art, Arte Povera, supporting surfaces, figurative narrative etc, represented by artists such as Antoni Tàpies, Pierre Soulages, Simon Hantaï, Lucio Fontana, Jean Dubuffet, Robert Morris and Richard Braquié, to quote but a few.

Musée du Vieux Toulouse

7 rue du May. 🕐 *Mid-May to mid-Oct: daily except Sun 2-6pm.* 🕐 *Closed public holidays.* 🎫 *2.20€.* ☎ *05 62 27 11 50.*

This museum in the Hôtel du May (16C-17C) displays collections tracing the history of the city, and local traditional arts and crafts, including ceramic ware.

Galerie municipale du Château d'eau

1 place Laganne. 🕐 *Daily except Mon 1-7pm.* 🕐 *Closed 1 Jan and 1 May.* 🎫 *2.30€.* ☎ *05 61 77 09 40.*

The red-brick tower (1823) at the head of the Pont Neuf on the west bank of the Garonne marks the site of the pumping station which supplied Toulouse's 90 public fountains until about 1855. It was abandoned after 1870, but since 1974 the old water tower has housed a photographic gallery which runs temporary exhibitions and an information centre on the history of photography up to the present. Inside the tower, the old machinery for operating the hydraulic pump is still to be seen.

EDF Bazacle

Near the Pont Neuf. Call for information. ☎ *05 62 30 16 00.* This site was occupied from the 12C onwards by watermills, tanneries, spinning-mills etc until a hydroelectric power station was built in 1890 to supply the town with electricity. The plant is still operating and one of the original turbines has been reconstructed. Migrating fish on their way to the ocean between May and July are now allowed through via a special channel.

There is a plan to open the site to the public and visitors will be able to watch the fish swim by through a window inside the plant. Exhibitions may also be held here.

Aerospace Industrial Heritage

"La Ligne" – During the inter-war period, Toulouse became the departure point for France's first ever scheduled airline, thanks to the efforts of industrialists such as P Latécoère, administrators such as D Daurat, and pilots such as Mermoz, Saint-Exupéry and Guillaumet.

25 December 1918: first trial flight from Toulouse to Barcelona.

1 September 1919: official inauguration of the first airmail service between France and Morocco. Military aircraft, with hardly any modification, linked Toulouse-Montaudran with Rabat, stopping at Barcelona, Alicante, Malaga and Tangiers.

1 June 1925: aircraft reach Dakar. Pioneering pilots operate routes to and in South America.

12 May 1930: first commercial South Atlantic crossing by a crew comprising Mermoz, Dabry and Gimié, making an air link between France and South America a reality.

The post-war period – After the Second World War and the maiden flight of the Leduc 010, prototype of high-speed aircraft on 21 April 1949, four important projects helped to boost the French aeronautical industry. Two military aircraft (Transall,

Breguet Atlantic) and two civil aircraft (Caravelle, Concorde) enabled French engineers and research consultants to hone their talents as aircraft designers and to develop teamwork with their British and German counterparts.

1 May 1959: maiden flight of the Caravelle on the Paris-Athens-Istanbul route.

2 March 1969: first test flight of "Concorde 001," the first supersonic airliner, piloted by André Turcat.

Despite their technological sophistication, the two civil aircraft projects did not attract the expected industrial interest. The commercial and financial problems of Concorde were to serve as lessons for the Airbus project.

1 January 1970: founding of Aérospatiale, amalgamation of Nord-Aviation, Sud-Aviation and Sereb.

Ariane rocket

Ph. Gajic/MICHELIN

The success of Airbus – A product of European ambition (initially Anglo-French, then Franco-German from 1969, and Franco-Spanish after 1987), Airbus Industrie has in 20 years become the second most important civil aviation manufacturer in the world, enabling the old world to develop a complete range of aeroplanes seating 150 to 300, starting with one successful model, the A 300. The project was realised largely due to the tenacity of three men, Roger Béteille, project co-ordinator of the Airbus project, Henri Ziegler, managing director of Airbus Industrie, and Franz-Joseph Strauss, president of the supervisory council, who transformed it from a seemingly foolhardy venture to a world class enterprise, with a presence on every continent.

The success of Airbus Industrie is due mainly to a willingness to produce airliners that always meet the airlines' needs. It is also the result of an impressive series of technological innovations, such as electronic flight control, advanced aerodynamics, and design for a two-man cockpit with innovative flight management systems.

The future A 380 Airbus will, like its predecessors, be assembled in the Toulouse factory.

Concurrently with the development of Airbus, Franco-American collaboration between Snecma and General Electric resulted, in 1981, in the production of the CFM-56 engine, one of the most popular aircraft engines in the world.

Aérospatiale Matra-Airbus

Colomiers, in the western suburbs of Toulouse. ⏰📷 *Mar-Oct: guided tours (1hr30min) 8.30am-6pm; Nov-Feb: daily except Sun and Mon 9am-noon, 2-5pm. By appointment (3 days in advance), visitors must have identification papers with them.* ⏰ *Closed public holidays and 2 weeks in Jan.* 🎫 *9€ (children 7.50€).* ☎ *05 61 18 06 01. www.taxiway.fr.*

This plant is the assembly site for A 330/A 340 long-distance carriers. After a bus tour, a short film, various models and explanatory panels help visitors to get a clearer idea of the Airbus programme. This plant was designed with visitors in mind, and so there is a walkway that affords a panoramic view over the assembly work in progress.

Cité de l'espace★

Parc de la Plaine, along the eastern side of the ringroad. ♿⏰ *Daily except Mon (other than during school holidays) 9am-6pm, Sat-Sun and public holidays 9am-7pm.* ⏰ *Closed 2 weeks in Jan.* 🎫 *12€ (children: 9€).* ☎ *05 62 71 48 71. www.cite-espace.com.*

Kids Visible from quite a distance thanks to the rocket standing there and to a surprising contemporary sculpture which serves as the Exposition Pavilion (the work of Henri-Georges Adam – 1904-67), the Cité de l'Espace is a place for discovering, experimenting and learning about the universe. Three main areas structure the site: the park, the planetarium and the exhibit area.

The **park** features a life-size model of an Ariane 5 rocket, with its launching pad, identical to the one in Kourou, Guyana. You can also see the various motors that make up the launching device.

Nearby, the Terrdome is a hemisphere with a 25m/82ft diameter, which uses special effects and pictures to illustrate 5 billion years of the life of our planet.

Farther on, a model of the Mir space station invites visitors to experience the living conditions of astronauts in space.

The **planetarium** has several 3-D programmes scheduled. One room is now entirely devoted to the planet Mars.

Eight interactive **exhibitions** with different themes give visitors an insight into our universe, from the Earth to the most remote planets. For instance, visitors can watch important space launches live; the different means of communication by satellite are explained, and a wide choice of satellite pictures of the Earth is available; living in space and weightlessness are demonstrated.

"Prévoir le Temps" (weather forecast) gives weather conditions in all the countries of the world, even on the day you were born if you wish.

"Explorer l'Univers" enables visitors to observe the movement of planets through space telescopes.

You can plan your visit in advance by checking out the Cité's Web site: www.cite-espace.com (English option). Audio guides in English are available for the exhibits. A restaurant serves regional dishes at reasonable prices; there is a picnic area and a museum shop.

Touch and go, backstage at Toulouse airport

Kids *Leaving from Toulouse – Discovery of the region by plane, with a cultural and gastronomic stopover. Flights last approximately 30min.* ☎ 05 61 71 62 11.

The daily life of an airport is illustrated here through the various jobs that make it function from the firemen chasing birds off the runways to the mechanics and the weather forecasters.

Excursions

Château de Merville

20km/12mi. Leave Toulouse, travelling towards Grenade (D 902). 6km/3.6mi beyond Seilh, turn left on D 87A. ⚓◑✎ *Jul and Aug: guided tours (1hr) daily except Mon 2.30-6.30pm; Easter to All Saints: Sat-Sun and public holidays 2-6.30pm.* ✇ *5€ (children: 2€).* ☎ 05 61 85 67 46. *The château is on the right at the entrance to the village.*

This "country house" was built between 1750 and 1759 on the site of two fortified houses by the Marquis de Chalvet-Rochemonteix, the *grand sénéchal* of Toulouse.

The two brick façades have many windows, as was common at the time. The ground floor opens onto a hall leading to a series of rooms: the summer salon, with **18 painted panels** based on chinoiseries by Boucher; the winter salon; the office, hung with late-16C tapestries illustrating the Trojan War; the bed chamber with a canopy bed; and the dining room. Each room is furnished and decorated in 16C style, and each overlooks a lovely terrace that crowns the landscaped park.

The **boxwood garden** with its 6km/3.6mi of walkways, leads the visitor into a labyrinth. To the east, the lawns roll away, punctuated by a pool in the centre.

Château de Larra

From Merville (5km/3mi), take D 87A NW. Cross D 17 and turn right on D 87. A road to the left leads to Larra. ◑✎ *Mid-Mar to mid-Nov: guided tours (30min) Thu-Sun 3-6pm (last admission 1hr before closing).* ✇ *5€ (children: no charge).* ☎ 05 61 82 62 51.

This grand brick mansion is laid out on a square plan, and was built by Guillaume Cammas (who also designed the façade of the Capitole in Toulouse), for a Member of Parliament in the 18C. The main façade opens up onto a vast hall and a stairway with a wrought-iron railing embellished with family portraits. All of the rooms are decorated with attractive plaster work, some painted. The salon opens onto the garden, where the boxwood forms the shape of a fleur-de-lis.

Plaisance-du-Touch

14km/9mi SW along D 632.

Kids How about an **African Safari**? (◷ *Apr-Sep: 9.30am-8pm; Oct-Mar: 10am-6pm.* ✇ *9€ (children under 10: 6€).* ☎ 05 61 86 45 03.) The visit starts with a round tour by car among lions, zebras and other large animals. The rest of the zoo can be seen on foot. Animals on the premises include wolves, apes, kangaroos, otters, each group in its own enclosure of course.

Le VALLESPIR★

MICHELIN LOCAL MAP 344: F-8 TO H-8

The Vallespir is the region in the eastern Pyrenees occupied by the Tech Valley. Lying upstream of Amélie-les-Bains, this area with its pastoral, highland charm has a most varied attractive appearance. It is, moreover, an area of geographical interest in that it comprises the most southern communities on French territory. Here, orchards and crops are found only on the floor of the valleys. Instead, there are forests of chestnut trees and beech, and vast expanses of pastureland.

Living traditions contribute to the region's unique character. Local festivities provide the best opportunity for getting a glimpse of the region's Catalan traditions. Anyone fortunate enough to see the *sardana* being danced, or rather celebrated, is unlikely ever to forget the experience.

Vallée du Tech

Starting in Amélie-les-Bains – 120km/75mi – allow 6hr.

Arles-sur-Tech

Arles grew up around an abbey built on the banks of the Tech in around 900, of which the church and cloisters have survived. The village has been the focal point of religious and folk traditions in the Haut-Vallespir region and is now a centre of production of traditional Catalan fabrics.

Abbey church

Access from the main square (S of D 115) via a flight of stairs. ◔⟶ *Jul-Aug: 9am-7pm; Sep-Oct: 9am-noon, 2-6pm, Sun 2-5pm; Nov-Mar: daily except Sun 9am-noon, 2-6pm. Guided tour available.* ◉ *3.50€ (under 12: no charge).* ☎ *04 68 39 11 99.*

Arles-sur-Tech

J. Malburet/MICHELIN

The tympanum depicts Christ in Majesty, set in a Greek cross with medallions on the arms bearing the symbols of the four Evangelists (dating from the first half of the 11C, as does the whole of the west front). To the left of the main door, just before entering the church, note a 4C white-marble sarcophagus behind a wrought-iron grille. This is the **Sainte Tombe** ("holy tomb") from which several hundred litres of pure clear water seep every year. To date, no scientific explanation has been found for this phenomenon. Above it there is a fine, early-13C funerary statue of Guillaume Gaucelme de Taillet.

In the first chapel on the south side is a great Baroque altarpiece dedicated to Saint Abdon and Saint Sennen, once venerated throughout Roussillon as protectors in time of disaster. In a series of 13 panels it depicts the martyrdom of these young Kurdish princes and the transporting of their relics, first by boat, then in barrels loaded on the backs of mules. The second chapel contains three images of Christ known as *misteris*, carried by Penitents in the night-time procession on Good Friday.

A door at the far end of the north aisle leads to the Gothic **cloisters** (13C).

▶ *Leave Arles S along D 115. The road crosses the river. Park the car near the footpath off to the right which leads to the pretty gorge of the River Fou.*

Gorges de la Fou★★

◔ *Apr-Nov: 10am-6pm.* ◔ *Closed if heavy rain.* ◉ *5€ children under 12: 2.50€).* ☎ *04 68 39 16 21 or 04 68 39 11 99 (tourist office). 1hr 30min there and back on foot (just under a mile, along well-maintained footbridges).*

▨ The crevice cut by the river is less than 1m/3ft wide in some places, despite being over 200m/656ft deep. Stretches where cataracts can be seen thundering down from one deep pool to the next alternate with calmer, more open reaches. There are a number of large boulders that have tumbled down and got wedged below.

Address Book

HOLIDAY VILLAGE

Les Glycines – 🔲 - R. du Jeu-de-Paume - 66150 Arles-sur-Tech - ☎ 04 68 39 10 09 - hotelelesglycines@wanadoo.fr - Closed 15 Nov to 15 Feb - 🅿 - 15 rooms - 7€ - restaurant ⌣. A pretty ochre facade leads to a pleasant hotel-restaurant. Functional guestrooms, contemporary dining room and terrace shaded by a century-old wisteria vine.

Domaine de Falgos – 66260 St-Laurent-de-Cerdans - 6.5km/4mi SW of St-Laurent on D 3 and B-road - ☎ 04 68 39 51 42 - contact@falgs.com - ⏲ closed 29 Nov-27 Feb - 🅿 - 20 rooms - 15€ - restaurant ⌣⌣⌣. If you fancy a holiday in the middle of nature, come discover this attractive, nicely decorated modern hotel. At 1,100m/3,608ft above sea level, it is set in a magnificent estate in the heart of the Pyrénées Orientales. Golf course and fitness training centre. Some apartments have a kitchen.

▶ *Return to D 115 and, after 3km/1.9mi, turn left onto D 3.*

The road is well laid out on the "shady" slopes of the Vallespir, covered in luxuriant vegetation (maples, chestnuts) and watered by numerous streams.

St-Laurent-de-Cerdans

This is the most populated village of the southern Vallespir region, which specialises in the production of espadrilles and the weaving of traditional Catalan fabrics. A **museum** (⏲ Jun- Aug: 10am-noon, 3-6pm; Sep-May: daily except Sat-Sun 3-6pm; short school holidays: 10am-noon, 3-6pm. 2€. ☎ 04 68 39 55 75) is devoted to this activity.

Coustouges

This small mountain village stands close to the Franco-Spanish border, on the site of an Ancient Roman sentry post (reflected in its name). It is home to an interesting 12C fortified **church** which has weathered well over the years. A decorative crenellated moulding runs under the eaves, beneath which there is a dainty scalloped motif around the east end of the church. The same pattern adorns the tower, below the parapet. Inside the south porch is a Romanesque door carved – most unusually for Roussillon – in soft stone (rather than marble) and decorated with numerous sculptures. The chancel is closed off by a beautiful wrought-iron grille, featuring the scroll motifs so often found in Vallespir on the hinges of old doors.

Can Damoun

Panoramic **site**★ sweeping across wild remote valleys. From Notre-Dame-du-Pardon oratory there is a fine view of Rosas Bay on the end of the Costa Brava.

▶ *Turn back to La Forge-del-Mitg and bear left onto D 64 then turn left to Serralongue.*

Serralongue

Walk up to the church. A nettle tree grows on the esplanade; the wood of this tree was once used for making the famous whips known as perpignans.

At the top of the hill stands a ruined conjurador, a small building with four apertures above which were alcoves housing the four Evangelists. When the harvest was threatened by storms, the parish priest would come and recite the appropriate prayers to ward off *(conjurer)* the danger, turning towards the storm clouds darkening the horizon as he did so.

▶ *Turn back and take the scenic road, D 64, to the left then D 115 left to Le Tech.*

Baillanouse ravine

The original road, swept away by the catastrophic floods of October 1940, was rebuilt higher up. On the left, a cavity in the side of Puig Cabrès is still visible, from which a huge landslide (6-7 million m³/212-247 million cu ft) broke away, blocking the valley to a height of 40m/131ft.

Prats-de-Mollo★ – ⌣ *See PRATS-DE-MOLLO.*

On the way up to the Cop d'Ares, **Mir tower,** one of the highest watchtowers in Roussillon, can be seen immediately to the south. Farther on, **Cabrens towers** come into view rising above the wooded valleys converging towards Serralongue. Soon afterwards, the chapel of Notre-Dame-de-Coral appears on the left.

Col d'Ares★

Alt 1 513m/4 964ft. Situated on the border, this pass is the gateway to Spain (Ripoll, Vich, Barcelona).

▶ *Turn back and drive to Le Tech then turn left onto D 44.*

On the left stands a strange pyramid-shaped mountain topped by Cos tower (alt 1 116m/3 661ft).

Montferrer

There's a church with a delightful bell-tower; to the left are the ruins of a castle.

▶ *Carry on along D 44.*

In a bend to the left, at the highest point along the road (899m/2 922ft), the panorama sweeps across the Canigou peak, the Albères mountains, Roussillon and the Mediterranean. The road soon runs across the River Fou (good view), past the former **Corsavy** watchtower then through the village of the same name (ruins of the old parish church).

D 43 runs down into the pleasant Riuferrer Valley.

IN STEVENSON'S FOOTSTEPS

Âniers en Vallespir – *Hameau de Leca - 66150 Corsavy - ☎ 04 68 83 93 28.* Hire a donkey to accompany your hikes and carry your bags.

VERNET-LES-BAINS★

POPULATION 1,440

MICHELIN LOCAL MAP 344: F-7

ALSO SEE LE CANIGOU

Vernet's **setting**★, at the foot of the wooded lower slopes of Mont Canigou, on which the bell-tower of St-Martin can be seen, is one of the most refreshing in the eastern Pyrenees. The roar of the Cady torrent in the background lends an unexpectedly mountainous note to this otherwise Mediterranean setting, of which Rudyard Kipling was fond. The spa clinic doubles as a rehabilitation centre. The narrow sloping streets of Old Vernet, on the east bank of the Cady, are a pleasant place for a stroll. ▯ *Pl. de l'Ancienne-Mairie, 66820 Vernet-Les-Bains, ☎ 04 68 05 55 35. www.ot-vernet-les-bains.fr.*

Visit

Old town centre

From place de la République, take Rue J.-Mercader, lined with colourful little houses bright with flowers, up to the top of the hill on which the church stands.

Église St-Saturnin

🕐 *During religious services; call for information ☎ 04 68 05 55 35.*

The church's main interest lies in its picturesque site, in full view of the upper Cady cirque and the tower of St-Martin.

The 12C chapel of Notre-Dame-del-Puig, backed onto a fortified castle (reconstructed), is worth a visit for the furniture and various other objects of interest it contains: a font (opposite the entrance), a predella of the Crucifixion which used to be part of an altarpiece painted in the 15C, a Romanesque altar table and an impressive 16C Crucifix hanging in the apse.

Musée de géologie

🕐 *May-Oct: 10am-noon, 2-6pm, weekends and public holidays 2-6pm.* 3€ *(under 12: no charge). ☎ 04 68 05 77 97.*

FIT FOR ROYALTY

▭▭ **Princess** – *R. des Lavandières - ☎ 04 68 05 56 22 - info@hotel.princess. com - closed 1 Dec-14 Mar -* ▯ *- 40 rooms -* ▭ *8€ - restaurant* ▭. Modern building with rustic guestrooms outfitted with loggias. Patio-terrace: folk performances and videos on the lower level. Several types of menu available in the large, functional dining room.

A. Thuillier/MICHELIN

Vernet-les-Bains

This interesting museum will not only appeal to those who are keen on fossils and minerals, but to everyone, for the exhibits are presented by a dedicated collector: ammonites and marine fossils, including a fossilised fish, with its scales and fins still intact, going back 120 million years!

Excursions

Abbaye de St-Martin-du-Canigou★★ – *3km/2mi S as far as Casteil.*   *See ST-MARTIN-DU-CANIGOU.*

Col de Mantet★
20km/12.5mi SW – allow 1hr. The cliff road is very steep and narrow (overtaking very difficult) upstream of Py.

After leaving Vernet to the west, the road (D 27) climbs, from Sahorre on, the Rotja Valley first amid apple trees then along a gorge sunk into the granite rock.

Above **Py**, a pretty little village 1 023m/3 356ft above sea level, the road scales steep slopes with granite outcrops bristling here and there. After 3.5km/2mi, in a wide bend in the road, a **look-out point**★ gives a good view of the village with its red roofs and Mont Canigou.

The Mantet Pass opens up at an altitude of 1 761m/5 777ft, near the evergreen forest of La Ville. On the opposite slope, the strikingly austere site of **Mantet**, an almost deserted village *(population 12)*, can be seen huddled in a dip.

VILLEFRANCHE-DE-CONFLENT★

POPULATION 225

MICHELIN LOCAL MAP 344: F-7

Villefranche-de-Conflent, which was founded in 1090 by Guillaume Raymond, Count of Cerdagne, occupies a remarkable site, on the confluence of the Cady and the Têt, closely surrounded by rock cliffs. Villefranche was a fortified town from the start. Its fortifications were improved over the centuries and finally completed in the 17C by Vauban.

The quarries in the area provided the pink marble enhancing numerous monuments both in the village and throughout Roussillon.

The fair of St-Luc, first held in 1303, is evidence of the town's economic importance, particularly in the Middle Ages, derived from the dyeing and selling of cloth. *Pl. de l'Église (saison), 66500 Villefranche-De-Conflent, ☎ 04 68 96 22 96. www.conflent. com. Guided tour of the town – Tours are conducted by a guide-lecturer from the Rendez-Vous du Patrimoine association ☎ 04 68 96 25 64. By appointment.*

The Fortified Town★ *2hr*

Park the car outside the ramparts, in the car park situated by the confluence of the Têt and the Cady.

Go through the fortified wall at the Porte de France, built in Louis XVI's reign, to the left of the old gateway used by the counts.

Ramparts★

Entrance at no 32 bis, Rue St-Jacques. ◷ Jul and Aug: 10am-8pm; Jun and Sep: 10am-7pm; Oct-May: 10.30am-12.30pm, 2-5.30pm. ◷ Closed Jan and 25 Dec. ⊙ 3.50€ (children under 10: no charge). ☎ 04 68 96 22 96.

The tour of the ramparts takes in two storeys of galleries one above the other: the lower watch-path, dating from the construction of the fortress in the 11C; and the upper gallery, dating from the 17C.

In the 13C and 14C, round towers were built adjoining the curtain walls (late 11C-early 12C). Then in the 17C, six bastions were added, which, starting clockwise from the Porte de France, have the following names: Corneilla, Montagne (Mountain), Reine (Queen), Roi (King), Boucherie (Butcher's) and Dauphin. The watch-path between the Boucherie and Dauphin bastions is in the open air, and provides a view of the north face, along the River Têt.

B. Kaufmann/MICHELIN

Watchtower with Fort Liberia in the background

Rue St-Jean

After returning to the Porte de France, walk through the village along rue St-Jean (note the 14C wooden statue of St John the Evangelist) with its 13C and 14C houses, many of which still feature their original porches with rounded or pointed arches.

There are some fine wrought-iron shop signs.

Église St-Jacques

The church, which dates from the 12C and 13C, comprises two parallel naves. Enter the church through the doorway with four columns and a cabled archivolt; the capitals are by the St-Michel-de-Cuxa School.

In the left nave, the pink-marble font is quite deep, as baptism by total immersion was practised in Catalonia until the 14C.

A 14C marble Virgin and Child, Notre-Dame-de-Bon-Succès, is invoked against epidemics. Above the altar in the small nave is an altarpiece (1715) dedicated to Notre-Dame-de-Vie by Sunyer.

In the right nave, the central side chapel houses a large 14C Christ on the Cross, crafted in the realistic Catalan tradition. The other side chapels contain some interesting Baroque altarpieces.

At the back of the church, as in many Spanish churches, is the west choir, known as the choir of the stalls; these date from the 15C (Flamboyant rosettes on the cheek pieces); on the podium lies a recumbent figure of Christ, a poignant example of 14C popular art.

Porte d'Espagne

This gateway, like the Porte de France, was refurbished as a monumental entrance in 1791.

The machinery for operating the old drawbridge is still in evidence.

Fort Liberia★

Access via the staircase of a "thousand steps," via a footpath of by means of a 4-wheel-drive vehicle. Departure from within the ramparts, to the right of Porte de France. ⏰ *Jun-Sep: 9am-8pm; Oct-May: 10am-6pm.* 🎟 *5.50€.* ☎ *04 68 96 34 01 and 04 68 05 74 29.*

Overlooked as it is by Mont Belloc, the town was rather too exposed to attack from any enemy encamped above it. Therefore, from 1679 when he was in charge of the project to fortify the town, Vauban planned to protect it by building a fort.

This fort, equipped with a cistern and powder magazines, clearly illustrates some of Vauban's strategic defensive designs. It was modified during the 19C (the entrance was moved). Most notably, the "stairway of a thousand steps" (there are in fact 734) was built from pink Conflent marble to link the fort to the town by the little fortified St-Pierre bridge over the Têt.

In order to follow the line of the steeply sloping ground, the fortress consists of three sections one above the other. The highest of these, towards the mountain, is shaped like the prow of a ship and protected by a moat. A gallery pierced in the counterscarp reinforces the defences. The pavilion, with a covered balcony, contains a bread oven on the ground floor.

From the fort, there are **wonderful views**★★ of the valleys below and Mont Canigou.

😊 We recommend taking the "stairway of a thousand steps" back down into the village.

The Caves

Cova Bastera

⏰ *Apr-Aug: 11am-6pm.* 🎟 *7€, ticket combined with the Grandes Canalettes caves: 15€ (children: 3€ and 7€).* ☎ *04 68 96 23 11.*

This cave, situated on the Andorra road opposite the ramparts, is at the far end of the Canalettes network. It reveals Vauban's underground fortification system and the various phases of occupation of the site, portrayed in life-size tableaux.

Grotte des Canalettes

Car park 700m/770yd S, below the Vernet road. ⏰ *Jul and Aug: Guided tours 11am-6pm.* 🎟 *7€, ticket combined with the Grandes Canalettes caves: 15€.* ☎ *04 68 05 20 76.*

The concretions in this cave take on an amazing variety of shapes: petrified calcite torrents and eccentrics. Some of the finest include the Table, a natural hollow *(gour)* which gradually filled up with calcite, and some dazzling white draperies.

Grotte des Grandes Canalettes

Mid-Jun to mid-Sep: 10am-6pm; early Apr to mid-Jun and mid-Sep to end Oct: 10am-5.30pm; short school vacations and public holidays: 10am-5pm; rest of the year: Sun 2-5pm. Closed 1 Jan and 25 Dec. 8€ (children: 4€, ticket combined with the Grandes Canalettes caves. 10€. 04 68 96 23 11. www.grottes-grandes-canalettes.com.

This cave forms part of the same network as the Canalettes cave. The exhibition hall (display of geodes) opens into a man-made gallery (Couloir des Cupules) leading to the Salle Blanche with its stalactites, stalagmites, lakes... The Balcony of Shadows precedes the "Lac aux Atolls," with its underground corals, and the superb "Temple d'Angkor," a vast chamber covered with stalactites and draperies, which has been turned into an auditorium for the purpose of a permanent *son et lumière* show.

VILLEFRANCHE-DE-ROUERGUE★

POPULATION 11,919

MICHELIN LOCAL MAP 338: E-4

On the border of the Rouergue and Quercy regions, the ancient bastide of Villefranche-de-Rouergue, with its rooftops clustered round the foot of the massive tower of the church of Notre-Dame, lies in the bottom of a valley surrounded by green hills, at the confluence of the Aveyron and the Alzou. *Prom. du Guiraudet, 12200 Villefranche-De-Rouergue, 05 65 45 13 18. www.villefranche.com. Guided tour of the town – The tourist office organises a commented tour of the town (1hr) in Jul and Aug, Mon-Fri at 11am and 3pm. 3.50€.*

A Bit of History

Trade and prosperity – Villefranche was founded in 1099 by Raymond IV de Saint-Gilles, Count of Toulouse, on the south bank of the Aveyron. The town enjoyed a new phase of expansion when, in 1252, Alphonse de Poitiers, brother of St Louis, decided to build a new town on the north bank of the river. This was built with the geometric layout typical of a bastide and completed in 1256. Despite the disagreement between the founder and the bishop of Rodez, who went so far as to excommunicate any newcomers, the town's population soon grew. Its situation near the Causses and the Ségala region, at the crossroads of major routes used since the days of Antiquity,

Address Book

For coin categories, see the Legend.

EATING OUT

L'Assiette Gourmande – *Pl. A.-Lescure - 05 65 45 25 95 - closed spring holidays, 30 Aug-5 Sep, Nov school holidays, Tues evening and Wed evening off-season and Sun.* This rustic little inn in a 13C house near the church of Notre-Dame and the bastide has an open fireplace for grilling meat and fish. The regional fare served here will not break the budget.

WHERE TO STAY

L'Univers – *Pl. de la Républqiue – 05 65 45 15 63 - 30 rooms - 6.50€.* This hotel is situated in front of the bridge over the Aveyron. Simple rooms in two buildings in process of renovation; for a quieter stay, choose one in the annex. Salon, restaurant and bar.

Francotel – *Centre comm. Hyper U – 05 65 81 17 22 - - 28 rooms - 7€.* Near a commercial centre, this functional hotel features adjoining rooms, making it attractive to families. Pool and sauna.

SHOPPING

Pavillon du Causse – *Allée Aristide-Briand - 05 65 81 25 11 – Mon-Fri 8.30am-12.30pm, 2.30-7.30pm, Sat 8am-12.30pm, 2.30-7.30pm - closed Sun and holidays.* The place to go and stock up on local products, such as the renowned Causse hams hanging above the entrance. Very nice selection of meats, delicatessen, dairy, cheeses, preserves (mushrooms, duck) and area wines.

La Bastide Gourmande – *Montbressous - 05 65 29 91 59 – daily from 9am.* Local tradition has pride of place in this farm where ducks and hogs are raised according to age-old methods. Their meat is transformed into *confit*, foie gras, delicatessen. The canning factory may be visited and products purchased for future enjoyment.

made Villefranche an important trade centre during the Middle Ages. It was also a stopping place for pilgrims on their way to Santiago de Compostela. In the 15C, Charles V granted the town the right to mint money, and silver and copper mines added to the town's wealth, as it prospered in its function as seat of the Rouergue seneschalsy and capital of Haute Guyenne. The Wars of Religion halted the town's expansion. Villefranche is now a centre of the farm-produce and metallurgy (bolts) industries.

The Bastide★

With the destruction of its moats, its ramparts and its fortified gates, Villefranche has now lost some of its medieval appearance, although it has kept many of the features of a bastide with its main square and its grid street plan. *Guided tours of the town are organised by the tourist office, Jul-Aug daily except Sat-Sun 11am and 3pm; 3.50€.*

Place Notre-Dame★

This fine square, in the heart of the town and always buzzing with life on market days *(Thursdays)*, is framed by houses with covered arcades, some of which have retained their mullioned windows and stone turrets. On one side of the square the tall, solid shape of the old collegiate church can be seen.

Go round the arcades *(avoiding the cars)* to take a closer look at the arches and old sculpted doorways. In front of the terrace overlooking the square to the north stands a large ironwork figure of Christ. The whole scene is reminiscent of Spain, which inspired André Malraux to shoot some scenes from his film *L'Espoir (Hope)* here.

At the corner of rue Marcellin-Fabre and the square, there is a lovely 15C half-timbered house facing the street; the central section, which is seven storeys high, houses a staircase lit through mullioned

Market day on place Notre-Dame

windows. This staircase can be entered through a fine **stone door** on which the lower part of the canopy is adorned with sculpted scrolls and foliage.

On rue du Sergent-Boriès, south of the square, the first **house** on the right features another fine staircase tower (late 15C), with pilasters and a carved tympanum.

Maison du Président Raynal

This has a fine 15C façade with adjoining windows, on three storeys, in the Romanesque tradition.

Maison Dardennes

Next to the Maison du Président Raynal. At the far end of the courtyard, a Renaissance staircase tower features two galleries adorned with sculpted portraits, in vogue at the time of its construction.

Église Notre-Dame★

The construction of this church, which began with the apse in 1260, lasted for over three centuries, with varying degrees of luck. The belfry-porch, 59m/193ft high, bears witness to the rivalry between Villefranche-de-Rouergue and Rodez, with each town intending their cathedral spire to be the highest. As far as can be judged from the massive foundations of its tower, Villefranche must have harboured pretty fierce ambitions; war and lack of money however prevented further efforts, and in 1585 the bell-tower was covered by the present roof. With its powerful corner buttresses adorned with pinnacles, this **belfry-porch**, beneath which a road passes resembles a fortress. On the second storey, a balustraded gallery runs all around the sides of the tower, whether set back or protruding, also successfully negotiating the buttresses.

A doorway surmounted by a gable ornamented with openwork leads into the spacious single nave lined with chapels tucked in between the interior buttresses, as was customary in medieval southern French Gothic architecture. In the north arm of the transept, the altar features a marble medallion attributed to the Pierre Puget School,

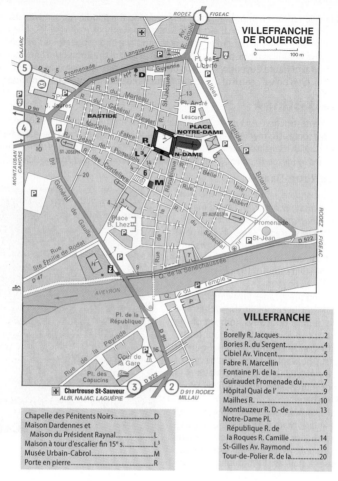

representing the Visitation. The chancel, into which light is shed through tall narrow windows including two 15C stained-glass windows donated by Charles VII, contains 36 oak stalls from the workshop of André Sulpice (1473-87), which unfortunately were damaged during the Wars of Religion. Note the carving on the panels (the Virgin Mary, the prophets) and on the misericords (mythical animals, figures etc). To the left of the entrance, the font is surrounded by an interesting ironwork railing.

Chapelle des Pénitents Noirs

🕐 Jul-Sep: 10am-noon, 2-6pm; by request at the tourist office. ☎ 05 65 45 13 18.

This chapel, which is surmounted by a curious double turret, was built during the 17C to serve as an oratory for the Black Penitent brotherhood. This brotherhood was founded, in 1609, at a time of renewed religious fervour following the Wars of Religion. It attracted up to 200 members and flourished until 1789; it ceased to exist in 1904. The chapel, in the shape of a Greek cross, is decorated with a painted ceiling, the work of a local artist. It contains an 18C altarpiece, in gold leaf, depicting scenes from the Passion. The sacristy contains 18C priestly ornaments, the brotherhood's first register, the great processional cross, together with cowls and staffs decorated with religious scenes that were carried by the Penitents.

Musée Urbain-Cabrol

🕐 Jul and Aug: Tue-Sat 10am-noon, 3-6.30pm; Jun and Sep: 3-6pm; Apr-May: Thu, Fri, Sat 3-6pm. 🚫 Closed Sun, Mon and public holidays. No charge. ☎ 05 65 45 44 37.

The collections of Urbain Cabrol on archaeology, history, and the popular traditions of Villefranche and the region are on display in an elegant Louis XV mansion.
In front of the museum stands a fine 14C fountain, after which the square has been named.

Ancienne Chartreuse St-Sauveur★

Take D 922 towards Najac and Laguépie. ◐☙ Jul-Sep: 10am-noon, 2-6pm. Guided tour available (1hr). 3.50€. ☎ 05 65 45 13 18.

This charter house, founded in 1451 by Vézian-Valette, a wealthy local merchant, was built in eight years of continuous effort, which resulted in an almost perfectly consistent Gothic style. At the Revolution, it became public property and would have been demolished, had not the municipality of Villefranche bought it for use as a hospital.

Chapelle des Étrangers – This chapel used to stand outside the charter house wall. It housed pilgrims on their way to Santiago de Compostela and was also used for celebrating mass with the local churchgoers. It has fine stellar vaulting.

Great Cloisters – These are some of the largest cloisters in France (66x44m/216x144ft). They have strikingly harmonious perspectives. The 13 houses of the Carthusian friars opened out from them. Each comprised four rooms, two on the ground floor, used for storing wood and as a workshop, and two on the upper floor, used as an oratory (known as "Ave Maria") and bedroom. The house was framed by a small garden.

Small Cloisters – These are the only authentic "cloisters," in the strictly monastic sense (gallery with communal buildings opening onto it). They are a masterpiece of Flamboyant Gothic, with intersecting rib vaulting adorned with highly ornate keystones, window openings decorated with elegant tracery and culs-de-lampe embellishing the points from which the arches spring. At the entrance to the refectory, a fountain depicting the "Washing of the Feet" is evidence of the influence of the Burgundian School.

Refectory – In accordance with the rule of the order, this was used by the Carthusian friars only on Sundays and for special feast days; it was a vast rectangular room with three bays with intersecting rib vaulting. The stone **pulpit**★ with its balustrade decorated in the Flamboyant Gothic style was set into the thickness of the wall. Carthusians never speak in the refectory; every year, they listen to nearly the whole of the Bible, either in church, or during communal meals.

Chapter house – This is lit through 16C stained-glass windows depicting, in the centre, the Shepherds being told of the Birth of Christ, and the founders on either side.

Chapel – A large porch leads into a nave with three bays and a chancel with a polygonal apse. The leaves of the chapel door depict two Carthusian friars bearing the arms of the founders. Other interesting decorative features are the late-15C stalls by the master cabinetmaker André Sulpice, a Louis XV style altar in gilded wood, and a Flamboyant Gothic alcove at the foot of which lie the tombs of the founder and his wife.

Excursions

Abbaye de Loc-Dieu★

10km/6mi W along D 926 then right onto D 115. The abbey is on the right-hand side of the road. ♿◐☙ Jul-Sep: guided tours (1hr) daily except Tue 10am-noon, 2-6.30pm. Park open to the public daily except Tue. ☙ 4.50€ (park: 2€). ☎ 05 65 29 51 17.

The 12C Cistercian abbey is built in sandstone of various colours (mainly yellow and ochre). Being a haven of peace and meditation, it was given the name *Locus Dei*, the place of God.

Church★ – Built between 1159 and 1189, the church is a splendid example of Cistercian harmony and simplicity. The nave, rising to a height of more than 20m/66ft, is flanked by narrow aisles. Note the five-sided apse closing off the chancel, instead of the usual flat east end found in most Cistercian churches. The transept has four oriented chapels; the first one on the south side contains a carved and painted wooden triptych (15C), framing a Virgin and Child. The Early Gothic influence is apparent in the quadripartite vaulting.

Cloister and chapter-house – Destroyed during the Hundred Years War, they were rebuilt in the 15C. The cloister, surrounding a garden, has retained only three of its four galleries, restored in the 19C. The chapter-house, dating from the same period, rests on two delicately fluted central columns.

◖◗ **Grottes de Foissac** – *22km/13.7mi N along D 922. ◐☙ Jul and Aug: guided tours (1hr, last admission 1hr before closing time) 10am-7pm; Jun and Sep: 10am-12.30pm, 2-7pm; Apr, May and Oct: daily except Sat 2-7pm; Nov-Mar: by request; ◐ Closed 1 Jan, 1 and 11 Nov, 25 Dec. ☙ 6.60€ (children: 5€). ☎ 05 65 64 77 04.* Evidence of human occupation of the caves going back 4 000 years includes a child's footprint! Several chambers contain beautiful concretions of various shapes and colours.

INDEX

MAPS AND PLANS

COMPANION PUBLICATIONS

Motorists who plan ahead will always have the appropriate maps at hand. Michelin products are complementary: for each of the sights listed in The Green Guide, map references are indicated which help you find your location on our maps. To travel the roads in this region, you may use any of the following:

- the series of Local maps at a scale of 1:150 000 include useful symbols for identifying tourist attractions, town plans and an index. The diagram below indicates which maps you need to travel in Languedoc-Roussillon-Tarn Gorges.

- the Regional maps at a scale of 1:200 000 nos 526, and 527 cover the main roads and secondary roads and show castles, churches and other religious edifices, scenic view points, megalithic monuments, swimming beaches on lakes and rivers, swimming pools, golf courses, race tracks, air fields, and more.

And remember to travel with the latest edition of the map of France 721, which gives an overall view of the region, and the main access roads that connect it to the rest of France. Also available in atlas and mini-atlas formats.

Michelin is pleased to offer a route-planning service on the Internet: www.ViaMichelin.com. Choose the shortest route, a route without tolls, or the Michelin recommended route to your destination; you can also access information about hotels and restaurants from the Michelin Guide, and tourist sites from The Green Guide.

Bon voyage!

Legend

Selected monuments and sights

◉ ⇨ Tour - Departure point

⌂ ✝ Catholic church

⌂ ✝ Protestant church, other temple

▦ ▣ ⛩ Synagogue - Mosque

▰▰ Building

■ Statue, small building

✝ Calvary, wayside cross

◎ Fountain

●━■ Rampart - Tower - Gate

⤬ Château, castle, historic house

∴ Ruins

⏝ Dam

☼ Factory, power plant

☆ Fort

∩ Cave

▱ Troglodyte dwelling

⛟ Prehistoric site

▼ Viewing table

\⩔/ Viewpoint

▲ Other place of interest

Special symbol

⠿ Fortified town (bastide): in southwest France, a new town built in the 13-14C and typified by a geometrical layout.

Sports and recreation

🏇 Racecourse

⛸ Skating rink

≋ ≋ Outdoor, indoor swimming pool

🎥 Multiplex Cinema

⟁ Marina, sailing centre

⛺ Trail refuge hut

▫■▪■▫ Cable cars, gondolas

▫+++++▫ Funicular, rack railway

🚂 Tourist train

◆ Recreation area, park

🐎 Theme, amusement park

Ψ Wildlife park, zoo

❀ Gardens, park, arboretum

🐦 Bird sanctuary, aviary

🚶 Walking tour, footpath

☺ Of special interest to children

Abbreviations

A Agricultural office (Chambre d'agriculture)

C Chamber of Commerce (Chambre de commerce)

H Town hall (Hôtel de ville)

J Law courts (Palais de justice)

M Museum (Musée)

P Local authority offices (Préfecture, sous-préfecture)

POL. Police station (Police)

🛡 Police station (Gendarmerie)

T Theatre (Théâtre)

U University (Université)

	Sight	**Seaside resort**	**Winter sports resort**	**Spa**
Highly recommended ★★★		��☐	❄ ❄ ❄	♯♯♯
Recommended	★★	☐☐	❄ ❄	♯♯
Interesting	★	☐	❄	♯

Additional symbols

🄳	Tourist information
═══ ═══	Motorway or other primary route
❶ ❶	Junction: complete, limited
⇉ ⇉	Pedestrian street
⊏====ェ	Unsuitable for traffic, street subject to restrictions
⊥⊥⊥⊥ ----	Steps – Footpath
🚆 🚆	Train station – Auto-train station
🚌 S.N.C.F.	Coach (bus) station
•——•—	Tram
⌾	Metro, underground
🅿️	Park-and-Ride
&.	Access for the disabled
✉	Post office
☏	Telephone
⊠	Covered market
•⁺×⁺•	Barracks
△	Drawbridge
ᴜ	Quarry
✕	Mine
B F	Car ferry (river or lake)
⚓	Ferry service: cars and passengers
⟶	Foot passengers only
③	Access route number common to Michelin maps and town plans
Bert (R.)...	Main shopping street
AZ B	Map co-ordinates

Hotels and restaurants

Hotels- price categories:

	Provinces	Large cities
⊖	<40 €	<60 €
⊖⊖	40 to 65 €	60 to 90 €
⊖⊖⊖	65 to 100 €	90 to 130 €
⊖⊖⊖⊖	>100 €	>130 €

Restaurants- price categories:

	Provinces	Large cities
⊖	<14€	<16€
⊖⊖	14 to 25 €	16 to 30 €
⊖⊖⊖	25 to 40 €	30 to 50 €
⊖⊖⊖⊖	>40 €	>50 €

20 rooms: 38/60 €	Number of rooms: price for one person/ double room
⊐ *7.50 €*	Price of breakfast; when not given, it is included in the price of the room (i.e., for bed-and-breakfast)
120 sites: 13 €	Number of camp sites and cost for 2 people with a car
13 € lunch-16.50/39 €	Restaurant: fixed-price menus served at lunch only – mini/maxi price fixed menu (lunch and dinner) or à la carte
rest. 16.50/39 €	Lodging where meals are served mini/maxi price fixed menu or à la carte
meal 15 €	"Family style" meal
reserv	Reservation recommended
⊘	No credit cards accepted
🅿	Reserved parking for hotel patrons
≋	Swimming Pool
▤	Air conditioning
⊘×	Hotel: non-smoking rooms Restaurant: non-smoking section
&.	Rooms accessible to persons of reduced mobility

The prices correspond to the higher rates of the tourist season

MICHELIN

Manufacture française des pneumatiques Michelin

Société en commandite par actions au capital de 304 000 000 EUR
Place des Carmes-Déchaux – 63000 Clermont-Ferrand (France)
R.C.S. Clermont-Fd B 855 200 507

No part of this publication may be reproduced in any form
without the prior permission of the publisher.

© Michelin et Cie, Propriétaires-éditeurs
Dépot légal mars 2006 – ISSN 0763-1383

Pre-Press : Nord Compo à Villeneuve-d'Ascq
Printing and Binding: IME
Printed in France, janvier 2006

Made in France